MW01132970

AN INTRODUCTION TO CLASSICAL NAHUATL

Now available to an English-speaking audience, this book is a comprehensive grammar of classical Nahuatl, the literary language of the Aztecs. It offers students of Nahuatl a complete and clear treatment of the language's structure, grammar and vocabulary. It is divided into thirty-six lessons, beginning with basic syntax and progressing gradually to more complex structures. Each grammatical concept is illustrated clearly with examples, exercises and passages for translation. A key is provided to allow students to check their answers. By far the most approachable textbook of Nahuatl available, this book will be an excellent teaching tool both for classroom use and for readers pursuing independent study of the language. It will be an invaluable resource to anthropologists, ethnographers, historians, archaeologists and linguists alike.

Michel Launey, now retired, was a professor at the Université Denis Diderot, Paris, and the Institut de Recherches pour le Développement, Cayenne. He was a visiting professor at the Universidad de Guadalajara, Universidad Nacional Autónoma de México and Yale University, among others. His other books include *Introduction à la langue et à la littérature aztèques* (the French edition of this book, published in 1979), *Une grammaire omniprédicative* (1994) and *Awna Parikwaki: Introduction à la langue palikur de Guyane et de l'Amapa* (2003).

AN INTRODUCTION TO CLASSICAL NAHUATL

MICHEL LAUNEY

Université Denis Diderot, Paris

Translated and Adapted by

CHRISTOPHER MACKAY

University of Alberta

CAMBRIDGE
UNIVERSITY PRESS

32 Avenue of the Americas, New York NY 10013-2473, USA

Cambridge University Press is part of the University of Cambridge.

It furthers the University's mission by disseminating knowledge in the pursuit of education, learning and research at the highest international levels of excellence.

www.cambridge.org
Information on this title: www.cambridge.org/9780521732291

© Michel Launey and Christopher Mackay 2011

First published as *Introduction à la langue et à la littérature aztèques* by L'Hartmattan, 1979
First published as *Introductión a la lenguay a la literatura Nàhuatl* by UNAM, Mèxico, 1992
First published in English 2011

A catalogue record for this publication is available from the British Library

Library of Congress Cataloguing in Publication data

Launey, Michel.
[Introduction à la langue et à la littérature aztèques. English]
An introduction to classical Nahuatl / Michel Launey; translated and adapted by Christopher Mackay.
    p.   cm.
Translation from French to English.
Includes bibliographical references and index.
ISBN 978-0-521-51840-6 (hardback) – ISBN 978-0-521-73229-1 (pbk)
1. Nahuatl language.   2. Nahuatl literature.   I. Mackay, Christopher S., 1962–   II. Title.
PM4061.L3813   2010
497'.45282421–dc22   2010015176

ISBN 978-0-521-51840-6 Hardback
ISBN 978-0-521-73229-1 Paperback

CONTENTS

PREFACE

he people generally known as the Aztecs called themselves "Mexica" (*méxìcâ*). "Aztec" means 'from Aztlān', the mythical starting point of the Mexica's migration to the south. Their language was called *nāhuatl* or *nāhuatlàtōlli* 'clear speech' or even *méxìcatlàtōlli* 'Mexica speech'.

The century that followed the Spanish conquest saw the death of a great part of the native population, the dismantling of their social system and the irrevocable alteration of their culture. This historic catastrophe – one of the greatest in human history – was partially attenuated thanks to the efforts of some enlightened friars and certain native notabilities, who gathered or composed all sorts of texts in Nahuatl: legends, discourses, historical chronicles, compilations of traditional knowledge.

This textbook is an introduction to this language. It aims to satisfy the interest in Nahuatl that has arisen in recent years. In various universities and institutions, historians, ethnographers and linguists have offered students and investigators of very diverse origins courses and seminars relating to the Aztec sphere. I hope that this work will be of some utility to them and that it will receive a favorable welcome.

I imagine that it will be of equal interest to linguists, who may not particularly deepen the study of indigenous Mexican history and culture, but who seek to expand the field of available linguistic data and so are looking for reliable descriptions of as many languages as possible.

Let us specify again that the language described here is Classical Nahuatl, the literary language of the century following the Conquest. Nearly five centuries on, there is clearly no region in which this variety of Nahuatl is still spoken. It is thus a dead language, or rather, a dead variant of the language, in the same way as the English of, say, Christopher Marlowe is a dead form of the English language. No one nowadays speaks exactly like that, but many hundreds of thousands of people speak present-day variants of Nahuatl, some of them fairly close to the classical one, so that travelers to Mexico today may be pleasantly surprised when recognizing words and expressions, thereby gaining more inside knowledge of the country and its people.

The original version of this book was published in 1979 in French, and a Spanish translation by Cristina Kraft appeared in 1992. Several English-speaking friends and colleagues suggested that an English version be made available to scholars and students. So when Christopher Mackay volunteered to take on the task of translation, I readily and thankfully accepted. It quickly appeared that the original version needed some modifications, both in view of a few grammatical points which did not seem totally clear to me thirty years ago and of the specific referential background of English-speaking potential readers. After many e-mail exchanges and a personal encounter at the University of Alberta, which gave rise to intensive discussions and fruitful adjustments, the final result is indeed impressive. Christopher Mackay did a painstaking, marvellous job of it, and I am deeply indebted to him.

My gratitude also extends to all the colleagues and friends, *nahuatlatos* and/or linguists, who helped me enlarge my field of knowledge and deepen my interest in this wonderful language and culture. A special mention is due to the organizers of Nahuatl or Uto-Aztecan sessions: Fernando Leal and José-Luis Iturrioz in Guadalajara, Jonathan Amith at Yale and most of all to Una Canger and Karen Dakin, who kindly took a last decisive look at the final version.

Michel Launey

HOW TO USE THIS BOOK

he thirty-six lessons are divided into two parts. The sixteen that comprise the first part cover the most basic elements of the language, and at the end of this section, there is an extensive set of review exercises to help make sure that you are in full command of the fundamental elements of the language before proceeding to the finer points dealt with in the second part. Each lesson also has a large number of exercises. These are very thorough in the earlier lessons, with a particular emphasis on acquiring an active knowledge of the forms. Experience shows that students have an aversion to translating from English into the language being learned. Naturally, it is more difficult to produce the forms rather than simply converting the Nahuatl sentences into English, but it is the very act of manipulating the language through active composition that allows you to understand the forms and their uses. A key to the exercises is provided in Appendix Four, but you are strongly advised to avoid using it until you have finished all the exercises and have done your best to find the solution to something you are having trouble with in the lesson (many fine points in the exercises can be figured out this way). Each lesson comes with a list of vocabulary items at the end, and these should be memorized. Those who have learned all these words should have a very good basic vocabulary at their fingertips when they go on to reading texts. The English-Nahuatl vocabulary at the end of the book is a full listing of all the words in the vocabularies of the individual lessons, but the Nahuatl-English is limited to words useful for completing the English-Nahuatl exercises.

Those who have fully internalized the material of the thirty-six lessons should be in a good position to make the transition to attempting to read Nahuatl texts as they are spelled in the traditional orthography. Appendix One is intended to help you with this by explaining the aspects of the traditional (Spanish-based) method of spelling Nahuatl, which is both an inherently unsatisfactory method of representing the phonology of the language and has the additional disadvantage of being irregularly applied. An additional aid in Appendix Two lays out in a summary fashion the methods of producing a number of derivational forms. Finally, Appendix Three contains a synopsis of the two Aztec calendars because a number of texts provide information about these somewhat complicated systems of telling time.

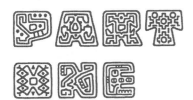

PART
ONE

Phonetics and Writing

ince the time of the conquest, Nahuatl has been written by means of the Latin alphabet. There is, therefore, a long tradition to which it is preferable to conform for the most part. Nonetheless, for the following reasons, some words in this book are written in an orthography that differs from the traditional one.

▶ The orthography is, of course, "hispanicized." To represent the phonetic elements of Nahuatl, the letters or combinations of letters that represent identical or similar sounds in Spanish are used. Hence, there is no problem with the sounds that exist in both languages, not to mention those that are lacking in Nahuatl (**b**, **d**, **g**, **r** etc.). On the other hand, those that exist in Nahuatl but not in Spanish are found in alternate spellings, or are even altogether ignored. In particular, this is the case with vowel length and (even worse) with the glottal stop (see Table 1.1), which are systematically marked only by two grammarians, Horacio Carochi and Aldama y Guevara, and in a text named *Bancroft Dialogues*.[1]

▶ This defective character is heightened by a certain fluctuation because the orthography of Nahuatl has never really been fixed. Hence, certain texts represent the vowel /i/ indifferently with **i** or **j**, others always represent it with **i** but extend this spelling to consonantal /y/, that is, to a different phoneme. Most texts represent with **-ia**, **-oa** the sequence of sounds that in phonetic terms can be either /-ia/, /-oa/ (two vowels in hiatus) or /-iya/, /-owa/ (vowel, consonant, vowel) etc. Therefore, it is necessary to regularize such writings in the form of an unequivocal notation.

---

[1] Horacio Carochi, *Arte de la lengua mexicana* 1645; Aldama y Guevara, *Arte de la lengua mexicana* 1754; F. Karttunen and J. Lockhart, eds., *The Art of Nahuatl Speech: The Bancroft Dialogues* (Los Angeles: University of California Press, 1987).

TABLE 1.1

Vowels

/a/	**a**	[a]	
/e/	**e**	[ɛ] or [e]	free variation between the e of 'b**e**t' and the sound represented by a in 'b**a**te', though without the **y**-glide after the vowel
/i/	**i**	[i]	the sound of 'f**ee**t', but pronounced shorter; not as in 'p**i**n'
/o/	**o**	[ɔ], [o] or [u]	varies between an open and closed **o** sound, may approach the **u** of gl**u**e
/a:/	**ā**	[a:]	long [**a**], as in f**a**ther
/e:/	**ē**	[e:]	long [**e**], as in ag**ai**n, without the **y**-glide after the vowel
/i:/	**ī**	[i:]	long [**i**], as in f**ee**t
/o:/	**ō**	[o:]	varies between the close **o** of h**o**ve and the **u** sound of pr**o**ve

Consonants

/p/	**p**	[p]	in initial position, it never is followed by a puff of air, as the corresponding English sound would
/t/	**t**	[t]	"
/k/	**qu** (before **i, e**) **c** (elsewhere)	[k]	"
/c/	**tz**	[ts]	like **ts** in **ts**etse; counts as one consonant
/č/	**ch**	[tʃ]	like **ch** in **ch**air, but with no puff of air; counts as one consonant
/λ/	**tl**	[tl]	counts as one consonant
/kʷ/	**cu** (before vowel) **uc** (elsewhere)	[kw]	like **qu** in **qu**iet, but with no puff of air; counts as one consonant
/m/	**m**	[m]	
/n/	**n**	[n]	
/s/	**s** (before **i, e**) **z** (elsewhere)	[s]	always voiceless as in 'cat**s**', never voiced as in 'dog**s**'
/š/	**x**	[ʃ]	as in '**sh**ip'
/y/	**y**	[j]	as in '**y**ard'
/w/	**hu** (before vowels) **uh** (elsewhere)	[w]	as in '**w**ar'; cf. the Spanish loanword 'chi**huahua**'
/l/	**l**	[l]	always with the "light" sound of 'be**ll**' and never the "dark" sound of 'ba**ll**'
/'/	` (on non-final vowels) ^ (on final vowels)		glottal stop; as in the non-standard between the words 'a apple'

TABLE 1.2

c	before **e, i** represents [s].
	before **a, o** and consonants and at the end of words represents [k].
cu	(prevocalic)/**uc** (preconsonantal and word final) are the equivalent of English **qu** [kw]. Note. **chua** (and **chue, chui**) represent **c+hu+a(e/i)** and hence are read /kwa/ (/kwe/, /kwi/). The spelling used to represent /čwa/ is **chhua** (**ch+hu+a**).
h	appears only in association with other letters: **ch** represents /č/. **hu-** (prevocalic)/**-uh** (preconsonantal and word final) represents /w/
ō	is often pronounced [u] (as in 'b**oo**t').
q	appears only in the combinations **que, qui, quē** and **quī**, which represent /ke/, /ki/, /kē/ and /kī/.
u	appears only in association with other letters: **cu-, -uc** representing /kw/ (see earlier discussion). **hu-, -uh** representing /w/ (see earlier discussion).
x	represents /š/ as in '**sh**ip' and is never pronounced like '**ex**tra' or '**ex**act'.
z	represents /s/ before **a, o,** consonants or in word final position and is never pronounced like English voiced **z** as in '**z**oom'.

The notation proposed here has the advantage of representing the phonetic reality of Nahuatl while remaining close to the traditional system (both the precise usage of Carochi's grammar and the regular practice of actual documents). It is better to start out using a precise orthography and then turn to texts in which the orthography is less exact rather than to begin via a defective orthography that will necessitate later corrections because it is always more difficult to shift to proper usage once bad habits have become ingrained.

Tables 1.1 and 1.2 should be useful both for people familiar with the problems of phonetics and for those who are not.

Table 1.1 starts with phonetic elements and then gives the spelling for them. From left to right are found the phonetic element between slashes (those who are not students of phonetics will not worry about this); its written notation, in boldface; its realization (pronunciation) between square brackets in the International Phonetic Alphabet (IPA), with notes on any problems that arise (in the absence of notes, the reader is to consider that the writing in square brackets is equivalent to English spelling).

Table 1.2 starts with letters and gives their phonetic representation. Here we restrict ourselves to the letters or groups of letters that present certain difficulties from the point of view of English.

The macron (ˉ) above a vowel indicates that it is long (e.g., ō).

A grave accent (ˋ) above a non-final vowel and a circumflex accent (ˆ) over a final vowel indicate that that vowel is followed by the glottal stop (often referred to with the Spanish word "saltillo," see note 3).

COMPLEMENTARY NOTES

1 Accent

The accent in Nahuatl is both tonic and melodic, so that one syllable of each word is pronounced more emphatically and in a higher pitch than the others.

The accented syllable is the next-to-last (penultimate) syllable of the word. The only exception (apart from monosyllables, which are obviously accented on their only syllable) is the vocative (forms by which people are addressed or summoned). Vocatives are accented on the last syllable, and this exceptional accent is indicated here with an acute accent (ˊ) on that vowel. Examples:

nopiltzin	'my dear child' (accented on **-pil-**)
nopiltzé	'O my dear child!' (accented on **-tzé**)

2 -ll-

This spelling represents a double l (and not a palatalized Spanish l like the sound in English million). Thus, **calli** is pronounced **cal-li**, with both l's fully articulated.

3 /ˋ/

This phoneme, which the old grammars call the "saltillo," is written with a grave accent (in the middle of a word) or a circumflex (at the end of a word) on the preceding vowel (the sound only appears after a vowel). These orthographic conventions go back to the Jesuit grammarian Horacio Carochi. Thanks to his work (as well as the modern dialects), the existence of this consonant is known for Classical Nahuatl (the majority of old texts fail to mark it).

The saltillo can be realized as a glottal occlusion. This sound exists in German at the front of words whose spelling begins with a vowel. It does not appear in standard English words but appears in the middle of the interjections 'uh-oh' and the non-standard pronunciation 'a apple'. The glottal stop also is used in the Cockney pronunciation of words like 'bottle'. It can be heard as an interruption of the flow of air caused by closing the glottis (the opening between the vocals chords). Thus, to pronounce the Nahuatl **èecatl** 'wind', you can momentarily cut off the flow of your breath between the two e's.

However, the saltillo can also be realized as /h/, as in the English 'horse'. This is how it generally appears in modern dialects, and we advise the reader to adopt this pronunciation. This sound is very weak in word-final position (e.g., **cochî** 'they sleep', **tlacuâ** 'they eat') and in front of the nasal consonants **m** and **n** (e.g., **àmo** 'not'). It is clearly stronger in front of other consonants as well as intervocalically (e.g., **èecatl** 'wind', **tlàtoa** 'he speaks', **tlàcuiloa** 'he writes', **àci** 'he arrives', **yèhuātl** 'he'; in some modern dialects, its pronunciation in the last word approaches that of the Spanish 'jota' or the velar spirant of the German 'nach', the Scottish 'loch').

▶ **Note.** It sometimes happens that in analyzing a word it is necessary to separate the saltillo from the preceding vowel, and in this case, it will be represented with an apostrophe. For example, the word **ticochî** 'we sleep' is analyzed as follows: **ti-** third person plural subject prefix; **-cochi-** stem of the verb for 'sleep'; **-'** (saltillo) marker of the plural. This analysis is spelled **ti-cochi-'**.

4 tz, ch, tl, cu (uc)

These sounds, though phonologically complex, are considered single consonants and not consonantal clusters. That is, each is a single "sound" consisting of two methods of articulation that in English are considered separate and distinct sounds.

At the end of the word, be careful to pronounce **-tl** as a single consonant. The Nahuatl words **ātl** 'water', **mītl** 'arrow' and **etl** 'bean' are monosyllabic: there is no vocalic effect on [l], which is just a part of the complex consonant /λ/, in contrast with English words like 'cattle', 'beetle', 'kettle', in which there is a syllable break after the **-t** and the word-final /l/ (**-le** in English orthography).

Similarly, the two-consonant spellings **qu** and **hu** (**uh**) represent phonetically simple consonants (respectively /k/ and /w/).

5 /k^w/

This consonant presents no problems of pronunciation in the prevocalic position (written **cu**): **tlacua** 'he eats'. However, it can also be found in preconsonantal and word-final position (written **uc**), which seems odd to an English speaker. A word like **tēuctli** 'lord' (phonologically /te:k^{w}λi/) has two syllables, with the accent on the **ē**. You have to try to pronounce the [k] and the [w] elements at the same time. If you find this difficult, you can, as a last resort, pronounce the [w] in front of the [k] ([te:^{w}ktli]), but you have to make sure that the [w] doesn't become a vowel. The word must not be pronounced 'tē-uc-tli' (with three syllables), much less 'tē-cut-li'.

6 Word-final and syllable-final consonants

In word-final position, a weakening of certain consonants takes place. In particular:

▶ The nasal consonants /m/ and /n/ are articulated very weakly and with an imprecise point of articulation that makes them easy to be confused (see, e.g., 8.4[2]). We always represent this sound with **n** (traditional orthography represents it this way or frequently doesn't represent it at all).

▶ /l/ is devoiced to [ḻ], that is, a voiceless **l** (without the vibration of the vocal chords). You have to get used to making this sound after a vowel, for example, in **nocal** 'my house', **nopil** 'my son', **īcēl** 'he alone',

▶ /w/ is similarly devoiced as [w̥]. This sound does not exist in English. It is merely a puff of air that is emitted from the mouth with rounded lips: **ōquichīuh** 'he did it', **ōmocāuh** 'he remained'.

▶ /y/ is also devoiced, and it is then confused with /š/. The result is usually written **x** (see, e.g., 8.4), but in a few cases **z** (see, e.g., 29.1).

In syllable-final position (i.e., in the middle of a word before a consonant, see 1.3), the same phenomena take place, apart from the treatment of nasal consonants, whose point of articulation depends on that of the following consonant (see 1.3).

7 Words of Spanish origin

Some are modified in accordance with Nahuatl phonology: **cahuayo** 'horse' (Sp. 'caballo'), **Caxtillān** 'Spain' (Sp. 'Castilla'); in **Caxtillān** the double **l** is pronounced in the Nahuatl manner and the **-n** is analogous with Nahuatl place names in **-tlān**, **-lān**, see 30.6); see 23.2 for further details. The majority, however, remain in their original form and are to be pronounced in the Spanish manner: **padre** 'father' (i.e., Catholic priest), **marqués** 'marquis', **diablo** 'devil', **Dios** 'god' (i.e., the Christian God, the Nahuatl **teōtl** being reserved for the pagan gods). The same goes for proper names, though again some are adapted: **Petolo** (more frequently **Pedro**) 'Peter'.

8 Difficult consonantal clusters

Certain consonantal clusters like **-tzch-**, **-chtz-**, **-tztz-** and **-chch-** can be articulated in a simplified way, with the first consonant having a tendency to be dropped. Thus, **mitzchiya** 'he's waiting for you' and **nēchchiya** 'he's waiting for me' can be pronounced as merely **michiya**, **nēchiya**.

---

[2] In citations like this, the number before the period signifies the lesson and the one after it the subsection, with a comma separating the numbers of different subsections within the same lesson.

EXERCISE 1

Read the following words in a loud voice (pay attention to the accent):

āmatl	*paper*	citlālin	*star*
quicaqui	*he hears him*	xihuitl	*year*
nocamac	*in my mouth*	xōchitl	*flower*
etl	*beans*	yacatl	*nose*
tetl	*stone*	mōyōtl	*mosquito*
tēntli	*lip*	mināya	*he hides*
calli	*house*	huāqui	*it dries up*
ōme	*two*	huāllāuh	*he comes*
tōtōtl	*bird*	noconēuh	*my child*
piltōntli	*child*	cualāni	*he gets angry*
quipiya	*he keeps it*	nomīl	*my field*
quicelia³	*he receives it*	calê	*he has a house*
quitlālia	*he places it*	cochî	*they're sleeping*
quipoloa	*he loses it, he destroys it*	èecatl	*wind*
		tōptli	*coffer, chest*
yāōtl	*enemy*	tōpco	*in the coffer*
teōtl	*god*	cactli	*shoe*
pāqui	*he's happy*	tōchtli	*rabbit*
tēmictia	*he kills (someone)*	tlatzcan	*cypress*
quilitl	*quelite (an edible grass)*	tecpatl	*flint*
		itztli	*obsidian, razor*
quimaca	*he gives it to him*	itzmōlini	*it sprouts*
tzontli	*hair*	tēuctli	*lord*
chapōlin	*grasshopper*	neuctli	*honey*
chichi	*dog*	cencâ	*very*
tletl	*fire*	tēnyô	*famous*
cualli	*good, beautiful*	ēyi	*three*
yèhuātl	*he, she, it (third person independent pronoun)*	cāmpa	*where*
		tepoztli	*metal, copper, iron*
		icxitl	*foot*
tēcuāni	*wild animal*	tlaxcalli	*tortilla*
ōquitzauc	*he closed it*	āmoxtli	*book*
zoquitl	*mud*	yēcyōtl	*honesty, goodness*
cēcēc	*cold*	totēucyo	*our lord*

³ In words ending -ia, -oa, the accent is on the i or o because two vowels separated by hiatus make two syllables.

teuhyô	*dusty*	tilmàtli	*cape, coat*
niccua	*I eat it*	àci	*he arrives*
nictlazòtla	*I love her*	àcualli	*bad*
tlàtoāni	*ruler, king*	tzàtzi	*he shouts*
Mēxìco	*Mexico (City)*[4]	àmo	*not*

EXERCISE 2

Pronunciation of certain difficult consonants.

(1) The glottal stop (see Complementary Note 3)

▶ pronounced weakly: àmo *not*; mìmati *he's clever, dextrous*; quìnecui *he smells it*; ōmicquê *they died*; tlacuāzquê *they'll eat*; cihuâ *women*; miquî *they die*; tēteô *gods*.

▶ pronounced strongly: tlàtòquê *rulers, kings*; tlàtlacoāni *sinner*; àco *upward*; àci *he arrives*; nèhuātl *I, me*; òtli *road*; mìtoa *it is said*; nictlàpaloa *I greet him*; tzàtzi *he's shouting*; chìcha *he spits*; ìiyōtl *breath*.

(2) /w/ (written **uh**) in word- or syllable-final position (see Complementary Note 6). The word written **iuh** is phonologically /iw/, that is, the only vowel is **i**, and any pronunciation like 'you' is to be avoided. Similarly:

ōnicchīuh *I did it*; ōniccāuh *I left it*; ōpoliuh *he's disappeared*; ōniccōuh *I bought it*; ōmēuh *he got up*; ōticchīuhquê *we did it*; ōticcāuhquê *we left it*; ōticcōuhquê *we bought it*; ōmēuhquê *they got up*; cuauhtlâ *woods, forest*; noconēuh *my child*; nocihuāuh *my wife*; nomīuh *my arrow*; cuauhtzintli *little tree*; cuāuhtin *eagles*; cuāuhyōtl *the nature of eagles*.

(3) /kʷ/ (written **uc**) in word- or syllable-final position (see Complementary Note 5, with attention to the pronunction of **tēuctli**):

iucci *it cooks* (pronounce it [ikʷsi] and not 'ee-ouksi'); neuctli *honey*; tzauctli *glue*; ōquitzauc *he's closed him in*; ōniquìneuc *I've smelled it*; chiucnāhui *nine*; notēucyo *my lord*.

EXERCISE 3

Now read this text in a loud voice:

Nopiltzé, nocōzqué, noquetzalé, ōtiyōl, ōtitlācat, ōtimotlālticpacquīxtīco; in ītlālticpac in totēucyo ōmitzyōcox, ōmitzpīc, ōmitztlācatilî in īpalnemōhuani in Dios. Auh mīxco mocpac ōtitlachixquê in timonānhuān, in timotàhuān, īhuān in māhuìhuān, in motlàhuān, in mohuānyōlquê ō mīxco ō mocpac

---

[4] In this book, *Mexico* will be used to refer to the pre-Columbian and colonial city that is now known in English as Mexico City.

tlachixquê, ōchōcaquê, ōtlaōcoxquê mopampatzinco in ic ōtiyōl, in ic ōtitlācat in tlālticpac.

Translation: "My dear child, my jewel, my beautiful feather, you were conceived, you were born, you came upon the earth. It's Our Lord, it's God, our creator, who formed and created you and placed you on the earth. We considered you, we who are your mother and father; your aunts and uncles, your relatives also considered you, and they groaned and were touched when you were born and came to the world."

EXERCISE 4

If you have studied phonetics, transcribe exercises 1 and 3 in phonetic notation. If you have not studied phonetics but wish to give this a try, consult the first column of Table 1.2 for the phonetic symbols.

Intransitive Verbs, Word Order, Absolutive Suffix

1.1 Present Tense of Intransitive Verbs

As in all languages, the sentence in Nahuatl is constructed around a *predicate*. The predicate is the essential element of the sentence, representing what is being said about someone or something, or about various persons or things.

Intransitive verbs are the first type of predicate that we will examine. As in English, they are verbs that have a subject but not an object.

In Nahuatl, an intransitive verb is preceded by a subject prefix that indicates the grammatical person. Here, for example, is how the verb **ēhua** 'to get up, to depart' is conjugated:

nēhua	*I depart*	tēhuâ	*we depart*
tēhua	*you (s.) depart*	amēhuâ	*you (pl.) depart*
ēhua	*she/he/it departs*	ēhuâ	*they depart*

(Note that for convenience's sake, from now on we will only indicate the English version of the third person verb with "he," and it is to be understood that this is short for "she, he, it.")

The prefixes, therefore, are:

Singular		Plural	
1st person	**n-**	1st person	**t-**
2nd person	**t-**	2nd person	**am-**
3rd person	**ø-**	3rd person	**ø-**

These prefixes are used with all tenses (with a single exception pertaining to the second person, which we will see in Lesson 9).

Nahuatl does not have grammatical gender. The "zero" prefix ø- (i.e., 'ø' indicates the lack of any marker when such a lack is grammatically significant) can therefore refer to a male or female being or to an inanimate entity and can be translated with 'he', 'she', 'it' (as appropriate to the context).[1]

Although English does not normally make a distinction between singular and plural in the second person, Nahuatl rigorously distinguishes these forms (in English translations in this book a parenthentical "s." or "pl." will always appear after 'you' to make it clear which is meant).

In addition, if the subject is plural, the predicate will always take a plural *suffix*. In the present, this suffix is -' (i.e., the glottal stop), but we will see that there are other suffixes that mark the plural.

The following forms, then, need to be clearly distinguished:

tēhua	*you (s.) depart*	tēhuâ	*we depart*
ēhua	*he departs*	ēhuâ	*they depart*

The present is the basic form of the verb. It is from this that all the other forms are derived. It is therefore considered the *stem* of the verb, and this is the form that one looks for in the dictionary. For 'to depart', a dictionary gives **ēhua**.

Note that Nahuatl does not distinguish between simple present and present progressive: so **nēhua** can be translated in English as 'I depart' or 'I am departing'.

The majority of verb stems (and hence present forms) end in **-a** or **-i**. There are some that end in **-o** and a very small number of irregular verbs (Lesson 5).

1.2 Form of the Prefixes in Front of a Vowel

Ēhua begins with a vowel. In front of a consonant, the prefixes are slightly different: **n-** and **t-** become **ni-** and **ti-**.

nimiqui	*I die*	timiquî	*we die*
timiqui	*you (s.) die*	ammiquî	*you (pl.) die*
miqui	*he dies*	miquî	*they die*

Here we see an important phonetic rule that we will have occasion to come across in other uses:

> RULE: A syllable in Nahuatl takes the shape /(C)V(C)/

(C = any consonant; V = any vowel; the parentheses indicates an optional element.)

---

[1] It is certainly possible to speak of a man or woman and of a male or female animal, but it is the noun used and not a grammatical marker that indicates this distinction.

In other words, the syllable consists of a vowel that is sometimes preceded and sometimes followed by a single consonant. Whenever there is a risk of this rule being violated, a "helping vowel" (most commonly /i/) appears. For example:

ēhua 'he departs' two syllables, **ē–hua** (/e:–wa/, in phonetic terms)
tēhua 'you depart' is divided in terms of syllabification **tē–hua**, even if the components are **t-** and **-ēhua** 'depart'.
miqui 'he dies' is divided **mi-qui** (/mi-ki/)
****tmiqui**[2] 'you die' is impossible because the first syllable begins with two consonants (/tmi–ki/). The helping vowel restores an acceptable syllable form: **ti-mi-qui** (/ti–mi–ki/).

▶ *Important notes*

(1) The consequence of this rule is that Nahuatl does not allow
   ▶ more than one consonant at the start of a word
   ▶ more than one consonant at the end of a word
   ▶ more than two consecutive consonants in the middle of a word
(2) Let us repeat once more:
   ▶ the glottal stop (`) is a consonant
   ▶ certain groups of two letters are used to represent a consonant (**hu, uh** for /w/, **qu** for /k/)
   ▶ finally, despite being articulated in a complex manner, **tz, ch, tl** and **cu** (**uc**) each count as a single consonant. Thus, **tzàtzi** 'he shouts', and **tōchtli** 'rabbit' are allowed, the syllabification being **tzà-tzi** (/ca'–ci/, i.e., /CVC–CV/) and **tōch-tli** (/tōč–λi/, /CVC–CV/)

1.3 Assimilation of Nasals

The second person plural also varies slightly:

nimiqui	*I die*	nitzàtzi	*I shout*
ammiquî	*you (pl.) die*	antzàtzî	*you (pl.) shout*
nichōca	*I cry*	nicochi	*I sleep*
anchōcâ	*you (pl.) cry*	ancochî	*you (pl.) sleep*
niyōli	*I live*		
anyōlî	*you (pl.) live*		

In front of a consonant, **m** tends to be articulated in the way that the other consonant is. In front of **m** and **p**, it remains **m**. In front of all other consonants,

---

[2] The appearance of two asterisks in front of a form is a linguistic convention for indicating that this is a hypothetical form that does not exist in fact in the language (i.e., is ungrammatical). A single asterisk signifies a (reconstructed) historical form that is posited as having existed but is not attested in surviving evidence.

however, **n** is written, and this represents the sound [n] (in front of **t**, **tz**, **ch**, **tl**, **n**) or [ŋ], as in English 'si**ng**' (in front of **c**, **qu**, **cu**, **hu**) or [ɲ], as in 'ca**ny**on' (in front of **y**).

Let us note at this point that an **n** is treated in exactly the same way, that is, in particular, that in front of **p** or **m**, it becomes **m**.

The technical expression for these changes is that the nasal consonants **n** and **m** *assimilate* to the following consonant in terms of their point of articulation.

1.4 Word Order

When the subject is stated in the form of a noun, the word order may be VERB–SUBJECT or SUBJECT–VERB. Thus:

Cochi in cihuātl *or* in cihuātl cochi *the woman is sleeping* (**cihuātl** signifies 'woman'; **in**, which is probably the most common word in the language, has many uses, one of which corresponds broadly to the definite article of English).

The word order VERB–SUBJECT (and in a general way PREDICATE–SUBJECT) is the most common one, and it is stylistically neutral. The opposite order constitutes a method of drawing attention that is often called *topicalization*. (The term *topic* signifies the element in the sentence that is already known from the previous discourse, while the thing that is said about it is called the *focus*.) **In cihuātl cochi** could be somewhat clumsily translated as "As for the woman, she's sleeping." In practical terms, both versions (VERB–SUBJECT and SUBJECT–VERB) are most frequently translated without differentiation ('the woman is sleeping'), but it is necessary to consider these nuances, which at times are significant.

1.5 Number in Nouns and the Absolute Suffix

The predicate agrees with the subject in number:

Cuīca in cihuātl	*The woman is singing*
Cuīcâ in cihuâ	*The women are singing*
Miqui in tlācatl	*The man is dying*
Miquî in tlācâ	*The men are dying*
Ēhua in mēxìcatl	*The Mexica[3] (person) is departing*
Ēhuâ in mēxìcâ	*The Mexica are departing*

[3] In this book, following the majority of specialists in Aztec civilization and the dominant use for the names of indigenous people, the Nahuatl word **mēxìcatl**, pl. **mēxìcâ**, will be translated as 'Mexica', in both singular and plural. For the same reason, 'Otomi' (the name of inhabitants of Central Mexico, neighbors of the Aztecs) will be used in both singular and plural.

In the nouns **cihuātl** 'woman', **tlācatl** 'person' and **mēxìcatl** 'Mexica (person)', the final -**tl** is a suffix called the *absolute suffix*. The great majority of nouns in Nahuatl take this ending, and it appears in the dictionary entries. For instance, the form **tlācatl** is found for 'person' (and not **tlāca**, even though this is the stem). We will return to this suffix in Lesson 2.

With these three nouns, the ending disappears in the plural and is replaced with the glottal stop.

Note that the plural of **cihuātl** is **cihuâ** and not **cihuā'** (i.e., a long vowel followed by a glottal stop) because the glottal stop has the effect of shortening a preceding vowel.

> RULE: A long vowel becomes short when a glottal stop is placed directly after it.

The determiner **in** does not vary in number.

VOCABULARY

Verbs

chōca	*to cry*	miqui	*to die*
cochi	*to sleep*	tzàtzi	*to shout*
cuīca	*to sing*	yōli	*to live*
ēhua	*to depart, to stand up*		

Nouns

cihuātl	*woman (pl. cihuâ)*
mēxìcatl	*Mexica (person) (pl. mēxìcâ)*
tlācatl	*human being, person (pl. tlācâ)*

Determiner

in

EXERCISES

(a) Conjugate the verbs in the vocabulary in all persons.
(b) Translate into English.
   1. Nicuīca.
   2. Miquî.
   3. Titzàtzî.
   4. Ticochi.
   5. Chōca in cihuātl.

  6. Miquî in mēxìcâ.

  7. Ēhuâ in cihuâ.

  8. Antzàtzî.

  9. Yōlî.

(c) Translate into Nahuatl.

  1. He dies.

  2. We live.

  3. The Mexica are sleeping.

  4. I am shouting.

  5. The women are crying.

  6. You (pl.) are sleeping.

  7. You (s.) are singing.

  8. We are singing.

Nouns and Nominal Predicates, the Plural of Nouns, Questions and Negation

2.1 Nominal Predicates

In English, we have sentences like 'Peter is a Mexica' or 'Mary is a woman'. In such sentences, adjectives or nouns like 'Mexica' and 'woman' function as *predicates*. In Nahuatl, there is no verb "to be" in such sentences, and the noun itself serves as the predicate, receiving the subject prefixes exactly as a verb does. Thus:

Nimēxìcatl	*I am a Mexica*
Timēxìcatl	*You (s.) are a Mexica*
Mēxìcatl	*He is a Mexica, it is a Mexica*
Timēxìcâ	*We are Mexica*
Ammēxìcâ	*You (pl.) are Mexica*
Mēxìcâ	*They are Mexica*

As can be seen, when the noun acts as the predicate, the same prefixes are used (in the singular and plural) as when the noun is the subject (see 1.5). In fact, to understand what a Nahuatl noun really signifies, we should consider that **mēxìcatl** does not mean simply '(a) Mexica' but 'to be a Mexica'. Similarly, **cihuātl** is not just '(a) woman' but 'to be a woman', and so on.

If the noun begins with a vowel, for example, **otomitl** 'Otomi' (name of an indigenous people), the prefixes have the form **n-**, **t-** (just as they do with verbs):

Notomitl	*I am an Otomi*
Totomî	*We are Otomi*

In front of a consonant other than **p** or **m**, the form **an-** is likewise used in place of **am-** (1.3):

Antlācâ	*You (pl.) are persons*

2.2 Forms of the Absolute Suffix

The absolute suffix (1.5) takes the form **-tl** after a vowel, as in the nouns **mēxìcatl**, **cihuātl**, **tlācatl** and **otomitl**. If the stem ends in a consonant, the helping vowel (see 1.2) intervenes and the suffix becomes **-tli**:

oquichtli	*man,*[1] *male, husband* (stem **oquich-**)
tōchtli	*rabbit* (stem **tōch-**)

with the syllable rule (1.2) prohibiting forms like ****oquichtl** or ****tochtl**.

When the final consonant of the stem is **l**, the suffix takes the form **-li**. This change of **tl** to **l** after **l** is an absolute rule:

RULE: /l/ + /λ/ > /ll/ (i.e., **l** + **tl** becomes **ll**)

Thus:

pilli	*child* or *nobleman* (stem **pil-**)
calli	*house* (stem **cal-**)

2.3 Nouns without the Absolute Suffix

The majority of nouns (perhaps more than ninety percent) have the absolute ending **-tl**, **-tli**, **-li** in the singular. There are two other types of nouns, however:

(1) Nouns with the suffix **-in**. The majority are nouns for animals or plants (although many nouns for animals or plants take the absolute suffix, and some, such as the ones following, have none). Thus:

michin	*fish* (stem **mich-**)

(2) Nouns without suffix. We will take up this type of noun again later (23.1). For the most part, these are nouns with an affective or expressive meaning. For example:

chichi	*dog* (stem **chichi**, which is also the dictionary form)

2.4 Plural of Nouns

It is not possible to predict the plural of a noun from its singular form. This constitutes the only real difficulty in the morphology of Nahuatl grammar. One can merely state the following principles:

---

[1] In the sense of 'male' (i.e., not 'human' in the general sense, which is **tlācatl**).

PRINCIPLE 1

The absolutive suffix and **-in** disappear and are replaced with one of the suffixes **-'**, **-tin** or **-mê**.

PRINCIPLE 2

-' is used only after a vowel, **-tin** is used only after a consonant and **-mê** can appear after either.

PRINCIPLE 3

With **-'** or **-tin** (but not **-mê**), the procedure known as *reduplication* can also be used. An important element in Nahuatl grammar, this procedure involves prefixing to the stem a syllable that consists of the first consonant of the stem (if it begins with a consonant) and its first vowel, which is lengthened if it is short in the stem. The following examples illustrate the reduplication procedure.

If we put these three principles into practice, we see that there can be five formations for the plural of nouns:

(a) type /–'/   **cihuātl** *woman, pl.* **cihuâ** *(so too* **tlācatl, mēxìcatl,**
    ("–" = stem)   **otomitl***)*
(b) type /R–'/   **teōtl** *god, pl.* **tēteô**
    (R = reduplication)   **cōhuātl** *snake, pl.* **cōcōhuâ**
                         coyōtl *coyote, pl.* **cōcoyô**[2]
                         conētl (*little*) *child, pl.* **cōconê**
(c) type /–tin/   **oquichtli** *man, male, pl.* **oquichtin**
(d) type /R–tin/   **tōchtli** *rabbit, pl.* **tōtōchtin**
                         pilli *child, son, daughter (also: noble person),*
                             pl. **pīpiltin**[3]
(e) type /–mê/   **michin** *fish, pl.* **michmê**
                         chichi *dog, pl.* **chichimê**

2.5 Details about the Plural

Because the plural form cannot be predicted, it is necessary to learn it at the same time as the singular, and the dictionary gives both forms. For example,

---

[2] Remember that a long vowel is shortened in front of a saltillo.

[3] There are two words for 'child'. Their use may overlap, but **conētl** is rather a small child and mostly in relation with the mother; **pilli**, on the other hand, is not necessarily young and is in relation with the parents in general: it is often translated with 'son' (or 'daughter'), and just like the Spanish word 'hidalgo' (etymologically *hijo de algo*, 'son of something', i.e., 'of high lineage'), is often used to mean 'lord', 'noble'.

in the list of words in this book you will find:

tōchtli   (*pl. /R–tin/*) *rabbit*

and from this, you understand that the plural is **tōtōchtin.**

The plural in Nahuatl was never very fixed, and there are many doublets. Thus, alongside the forms indicated in 2.4, which are the usual ones, the forms **cihuāmê** 'women', **cōhuāmê** 'snakes', **oquichmê** 'men' and **mīmichtin** 'fishes' can be found. In doubtful cases, adding -**mê** after vowels and -**tin** after consonants is an acceptable strategy. One would then have every chance of hitting upon a possible form, if not the normal one.

A restriction on the pluralization of nouns seems strange at first to English speakers. *Only the names of animate beings (people and animals) can be put in the plural.* Nouns for things and plants *cannot* be put in the plural. It is, therefore, possible to translate

Calli   as *(It is) a house,* or *(They are) houses*
Tetl   as *(It is) a stone,* or *(They are) stones*

This practice is surprising for someone who is familiar only with Indo-European languages, but it is widespread elsewhere (particularly in eastern languages like Chinese, Japanese and Malay). It may be helpful to think of this convention as similar to collective nouns in English (i.e., ones that can be measured but not counted). Thus, Nahuatl says **Ātl**, and this is translated into English as 'It is water', in both instances regardless of how much water there is. Nahuatl extends this usage to aggregate nouns (i.e., ones that can be counted), and so **Calli** signifies 'It is house' regardless of the number of houses in question.

This procedure can be extended to nouns for animate beings. For instance, one can say

Michin   *It's fish*

in reference to several fish.

The singular (often called "generic") can also be used when one is speaking of an entire class of beings. For example, 'The coyote is a fierce animal', 'The Mexica is a brave warrior' etc.

2.6 Pluralizable Inanimate Objects

A very small number of nouns for inanimate "things" have a plural form, probably as a result of mythological personification. Only two such nouns are common:

tepētl   *mountain pl. /R–'/* (**tētepê**)
citlālin   *star pl. /R–tin/* (**cīcitlāltin**)

Also, if a noun for a thing is used as the predicate with a subject marker in the plural, the noun has to agree with the subject in number. Let us assume that you wish to say, for example, 'We are stone(s)'. You would say, **titemê**. In such cases, which are naturally uncommon, an inanimate noun forms a plural in -**mê** (after a vowel) or -**tin** (after a consonant) (see 2.4 and 2.5).

2.7 The Particle *Ca*

One-word sentences in which that word acts as a nominal predicate, such as **Nimēxìcatl** 'I am (a) Mexica', **cihuātl** 'it is a woman' or **calli** 'it is a house', are not impossible. However, they have something of the stiffness of a dictionary entry (like "coyote: a wild animal of North America" or "Disraeli: British novelist and politician"), and this is the sort of situation in which they are found. Most frequently, a nominal predicate (especially one in the third person) is preceded by the particle **ca**.

Ca is the mark of an assertion whose sense is pretty much 'it is a fact that', 'certainly', 'in fact', but the use of it is so frequent that one can dispense with it in the translation. Instead, we say:

Ca mēxìcatl	*It is a Mexica, he is a Mexica*
Ca cōcoyô	*They are coyotes*
Ca tetl	*It's a stone, they're stones, it's stone*

Ca can also precede verbal predicates:

Ca tzàtzi in pilli	*The child is shouting*

But in that case, it is less necessary (**tzàtzi in pilli** is perfectly acceptable) and retains more of its proper sense. It would be somewhat but not entirely exaggerated to translate a sentence that contains **ca** with 'as for shouting, the child shouts' or 'it is the case that the child is shouting'.

2.8 Word Order and Focalization

If the subject of a nominal predicate is expressed, then, the word order can be PREDICATE–SUBJECT or SUBJECT–PREDICATE (as is the case with a verb, 1.4):

Ca mēxìcatl in Pedro[4]	*Peter is a Mexica*
In Pedro ca mēxìcatl	*Peter is a Mexica, Peter (as opposed to other people being discussed) is a Mexica*

[4] Note the possibility of using **in** with a proper name.

A very frequent turn of phrase is: (**Ca**)–noun–**in**–verb. This corresponds to the grammatical figure known as *focalization*, that is: 'It is noun that verbs' (the focus is the part of the sentence that provides new information).

Ca cihuātl in tzàtzi	*It is a woman who is shouting (i.e., not a man)*
In tzàtzi ca cihuātl	*The one who is shouting is a woman*

In analyzing such sentences, we must conclude that **cihuātl** is the predicate and **in tzàtzi** is the subject! In fact, by putting the determiner **in** in front of the verb (as in the English 'he/she who verbs', 'those who verb', 'that which verbs'), we have a phrase that functions as a noun. In particular, this means that it can function as the subject (or the object) of the predicate. If we consider that in Nahuatl nouns can function as predicates, we will see that the translation of **(ca) tzàtzi in cihuātl** as 'the woman is shouting' somewhat conceals the true nature of the Nahuatl expression. A better approximation would be: 'the one who is a woman is shouting'. In practice, of course, such belabored and unnatural (from the point of view of English) translations are to be avoided, but it is always a good idea to be aware of what underlies the Nahuatl sentence structure.

2.9 Questions and Negation

If instead of making a statement, one is asking a question, one can say, for example:

Cuix coyōtl?	*Is it a coyote?*
Cuix timēxìcatl?	*Are you (s.) a Mexica?*
Cuix cochi in Pedro?	*Is Peter sleeping?*
Cuix mēxìcatl in cochi?	*Is it a Mexica who is sleeping? (The person who is sleeping, is he a Mexica?)*

Just a rising tone of voice is sufficient to mark a question, but the use of **cuix** is most frequent.

The reply to these questions can be:

Quēmâ (*or* Ca quēmâ)	*Yes*
Àmo (*or* Ca àmo)	*No*

Àmo also negates a statement:

Àmo nicochi	*I am not sleeping*
Àmo mēxìcatl in cochi	*It is not a Mexica who is sleeping (the one who is sleeping is not a Mexica)*

In this case, **àmo** can be preceded by **ca** (to negate a statement is still making a statement), but **ca** and **cuix** are incompatible. Also, one can have a negated question:

Cuix àmo timēxìcatl?   *Aren't you a Mexica?*

▶ *Note.* In front of a nominal or verbal predicate, the negation is sometimes found in the form **à**. The whole unit is generally written as a single word: **ànichochi, àmēxìcatl.**

VOCABULARY

Particles

àmo	*not, no*	cuix	(interrogative marker)
ca	(statement marker)	quēmâ	*yes*

Nouns

ātl	*water*	oquichtli	(*pl.* /–tin/) *man, husband*
calli	*house*	otomitl	(*pl.* /–'/) *Otomi*
chichi	(*pl.* /–mê/) *dog*	pilli	(*pl.* /R–tin/) *child, nobleman*
citlālin	(*pl.* /R–tin/) *star*	teōtl	(*pl.* /R–'/) *god*
conētl	(*pl.* /R–'/) *(little) child*	tepētl	(*pl.* /R–'/) *mountain*
coyōtl	(*pl.* /R–'/) *coyote*	tetl	*rock, stone*
cōhuātl	(*pl.* /R–'/) *snake*	tōchtli	(*pl.* /R–tin/) *rabbit*
michin	(*pl.* /R–tin/ or /–mê/) *fish*		

EXERCISES

(a) Put the following forms into the plural and translate.
1. Ca tichichi.
2. Àmo nicōhuātl.
3. Cuix coyōtl in tzàtzi?
4. Miqui in tōchtli.
5. Cuix tepētl?
6. Àmo citlālin.
7. Ca michin in ēhua.
8. Ca oquichtli in cuīca.
9. Àmo titeōtl.
10. Ca nipilli.
11. Cuix totomitl?

(b) Apply focalization (2.8) to the following phrases and translate. (Ex.: Chōca in cihuātl > Ca cihuātl in chōca *it's a woman who's crying*)
1. Cochi in chichi.
2. Cuīcâ in cōconê.
3. Tzàtzî in otomî.
4. Miqui in oquichtli.

(c) Translate into English.
1. Ca mēxìcatl in cihuātl.
2. Cuix mēxìcâ in cōconê?
3. Àmo, ca àmo mēxìcâ, ca otomî.
4. Cuix àmo ancochî?
5. Ca àmo cuīcâ in mīmichtin.
6. Yōlî in tlācâ.
7. Àmo chōcâ in mēxìcâ.
8. Cochî in chichimê.
9. Ca àmo tetl, ca tētepê.
10. Chōcâ in tēteô.
11. Àmo cōconê in chōcâ, ca cihuâ.
12. Cuix cīcitlāltin? – Quēmâ, ca cīcitlāltin.

(d) Translate into Nahuatl.
1. The snakes are sleeping.
2. The Otomi are departing.
3. Is the woman singing?
4. Is the Mexica sleeping? – Yes, he is sleeping.
5. The woman is not a Mexica.
6. Are you (pl.) Mexica? – No, we are Otomi.
7. Are the stars alive?
8. Don't the gods die?
9. The coyotes are departing.
10. The children are singing.
11. Those are not houses.
12. Is it dogs? – No, it is coyotes.
13. The Otomi are not dogs, they are people.

Transitive Verbs

3.1 Object Prefixes

Until now we have seen two types of predicates: intransitive verbs and nouns. They share the characteristic of having a subject but not an object. *Transitive verbs*, which we are now going to examine, are (as in English) verbs that have both a subject and an object. The object refers to the entity (thing, person or concept) that the function of activity indicated by the verb operates on or affects.

In Nahuatl, the object is indicated with a prefix that is placed directly *after* the subject prefix. For example, with the verb **itta** 'to see':

nimitzitta	*I see you (s.)*	mitzitta	*he sees you (s.)*
niquitta	*I see him*	quitta	*he sees him*
tinēchitta	*you (s.) see me*	namēchitta	*I see you (pl.)*
tiquitta	*you (s.) see him*	niquimitta	*I see them*
nēchitta	*he sees me*	titēchitta	*you (s.) see us*

There prefixes are:

Singular		Plural	
1st person	**-nēch-**	1st person	**-tēch-**
2nd person	**-mitz-**	2nd person	**-amēch-**
3rd person	**-c-/-qu-**	3rd person	**-quim-**

▶ *Note.* For the variants in the spelling of the third person forms, see 3.2 and 3.3.

In front of the vowel **a** of **-amēch-**, one naturally has the **i**-less form of the subject prefix (**namēchitta** 'I see you (pl.)', **tamēchittâ** 'we see you (pl.)'). Otherwise, the form with **i** is used because the other prefixes begin with a consonant (1.2).

Contrary to what happens with the subject, a plural object does not result in a plural suffix; the verb agrees in number only with the subject and not with the object. Thus, one has:

quitta	*he sees him*	quimitta	*he sees them*
quittâ	*they see him*	quimittâ	*they see them*

▶ **Note.** The reflexive forms use special prefixes (6.5). Hence, it would be wrong to translate "I see myself" as ****ninēchitta**.

3.2 Writing of /k/

In the third person, -**qu**- is only a graph for the phoneme /k/ (see Preliminary Lesson). In front of a consonant or any vowel other than **i** or **e**, one writes -**c**-:

nimitzāna	*I seize you, take you captive* (**āna** 'to seize')?
nicāna	*I seize him, take him prisoner*
nimitztlazòtla	*I love you (s.)* (**tlazòtla** 'to love')
nictlazòtla	*I love him/her*

3.3 The Helping Vowel /i/ with the Third Person Object

Just like the subject prefixes **n**- and **t**-, the sound /k/ (written **c** or **qu**) of the third person object obeys the syllable rule (1.2). A helping vowel appears (and the prefix is written -**qui**-) under two circumstances:

(1) The verb stem begins with a consonant, and the subject is in the third person singular or plural ('he/she…him/her' or 'they…him/her'), which is marked by the the lack of a subject marker (ø). Through the appearance of the helping vowel, two initial consonants are avoided. Thus, one has:

cāna	*he seizes him*, but
quitlazòtla	*he loves her* (and not ****ctlazòtla**)

(2) The verb stem begins with a consonant, and the subject is in the second person plural ('you (pl.)…him/her'), which has the form **an**-. In this way, three internal consonants are avoided. Thus, one has:

ancānâ	*you (pl.) seize him/her*, but
anquitlazòtlâ	*you (pl.) love him/her* (and not ****anctlazòtlâ**)

3.4 Third Person Plural Object

Just like the final **m** in **am**-, the one in -**quim**- assimilates to a following consonant (1.3). For example, one has:

niquimāna	*I seize them*, but
niquintlazòtla	*I love them*

3.5 Combination with a Noun Object

When the object is expressed with a noun, this noun does not change its form (in Nahuatl, there is no "accusative" form as in Latin, Greek, German etc.). However, *the verb must have the object prefix*:

tiquittâ in cōhuātl	*we see the snake*
nictlazòtla in cihuātl	*I love the woman*
nicāna in otomitl	*I take the Otomi person prisoner*
anquicuâ in nacatl	*you (pl.) eat the meat* (**cua** 'to eat')
quî in ātl	*they drink the water* (**i** 'to drink')

In effect, Nahuatl always says 'We see it, the snake', 'I love her, the woman' etc. It is impossible to say ****tittâ in cōhuātl**, ****nitlazòtla in cihuātl** etc.

If the object is plural, so is the prefix:

niquimitta in tlācâ	*I see the people*
niquintlazòtla in pīpiltin	*I love the children*

By "plural" we understand the plural marked as such in the Nahuatl, because if the noun has the "plural meaning" but is marked as singular (inanimate entities, 2.5), then the prefix agrees with the noun in being singular:

cāna in tetl	*he seizes the stone* or *stones*
niquitta in calli	*I see the house* or *houses*

But one does say:

niquimitta in cīcitlāltin	*I see the stars*

because here one has a true plural form.

3.6 Indefinite Prefixes

In English, it is sometimes possible to omit an object if one cannot say anything about it or does not wish to do so, for example 'I love' (someone that I am not specifying) or 'I eat' (something about which I am not saying anything). In this instance, too, it is impossible in Nahuatl to say ****nitlazòtla**, ****nicua** (with no object prefix). Instead, the following forms are used:

nitētlazòtla	*I love (someone, people)*
nitlacua	*I eat (something, things)*

Nahuatl has two indefinite prefixes:

-tē-	for humans (indefinite people)
-tla-	for non-humans (indefinite things or animals)

These prefixes say nothing in terms of number, and are therefore translated according to the context:

| **-tē-** | *someone* or *people* or *others* or *everybody* |
| **-tla-** | *something* or *things* or *everything* |

(though of course English idiom often dictates that the prefix will have no overt reflection in the translation). The indefinite object prefix appears (like the definite one) after the subject prefix.

Other examples:

nitēāna	*I take a prisoner* or *prisoners*
nitlacaqui	*I hear (something* or *things)* (**caqui** 'to hear')
nitēitta	*I see people* etc.

3.7 Variation in the Stem after *-tla-*

The prefix -**tla**- has a morphological peculiarity. If the verb stem begins /iCC-/ (i.e., **i** followed by two consonants), the **i** disappears. Thus:

nimitzitta	*I see you*
nitlatta	*I see things, I see* (and not ****nitlaitta**)
niquìtoa	*I say it, I mention it, I speak of it* (remember that the glottal stop is a consonant)
nitlàtoa	*I speak, I say things*
niquìcuiloa	*I paint it, I write it*
nitlàcuiloa	*I paint, I write*

This does not happen with -**tē**-:

| nitēitta | *I see people* (and not ****nitētta**) |
| nitēìtoa | *I speak of people, I speak of others* |

3.8 Word Order in Transitive Constructions

(1) When the subject is expressed with a noun in addition to the subject prefix, we have seen (1.4) that the order can be V–S (VERB–SUBJECT) or S–V (SUBJECT–VERB),[1] the first order being more "neutral," and the second being more "marked" in the sense of a topicalization of the subject ('as for the woman, she is sleeping'). The same remarks also apply to the object.

---

[1] Or more generally, PREDICATE–SUBJECT or SUBJECT–PREDICATE; see 2.8.

Here again, the preferred order is V–O (VERB–OBJECT):

niquitta in calli   *I see the house*[2]

but topicalization of the object is also found, though this is much rarer than that of the subject:

in calli niquitta   *as for the house, I see it* (O–V order)

(2) What then happens if one has both a subject and an object in the form of nouns (or noun phrases)? The most frequent and neutral order is V–S–O:

quitta in cihuātl in calli   *the woman sees the house*

but here too the subject can be topicalized (hence S–V–O)

in cihuātl quitta in calli   *(as for) the woman, (she) sees the house*

Topicalization of the object and the order O–V–S (**in calli quitta in cihuātl** 'as for the house, the woman sees it') is not impossible, though it is rare. The same goes for double topicalization, with the order S–O–V (**in cihuātl in calli quitta** 'as for the woman and the house, she sees it'). The order O–S–V is virtually unknown.

The order V–O–S is restricted to a single case. Let us suppose that the object is simply **calli** instead of **in calli**. The absence of **in** is most often the equivalent of either the indefinite singular without the article in English or the indefinite plural: **niquitta ātl** *I drink water*, **niquitta calli** *I see houses* (for *I see a house*, see 7.2). If the object is indeterminate, it must directly follow the verb. One therefore says, with the order V–O–S:

Quicua nacatl in cihuātl   *The woman eats meat*
Quichīhua calli in Pedro   *Peter builds houses* (**chīhua** *to make, to build*)
Quimitta cōcōhuâ in pilli   *The child sees snakes*

or with the order S–V–O:

In cihuātl quicua nacatl   *(As for) the woman (she) is eating meat*

(3) Let us return to sentences in which there is a transitive verb with a single noun. We understand that in, for example:

niquitta in pilli   *I see the child*

in pilli is the object because there is a first person subject and a third person object. Similarly, in

nēchitta in pilli   *the child sees me*

---

[2] Or *the houses*. This possibility will no longer be cited systematically.

the subject is in the third person and the object in the first. Therefore, **in pilli** is the subject. But if both prefixes are in the third person, there can be ambiguities. For example:

> quitlazòtla in pilli

can signify either *he loves the child* or *the child loves him* because **in pilli** can correspond either to the zero-marker third person subject (ø-) or the third person object prefix **qui-**. In practice, it is very rare for the context or the sense[3] not to resolve this ambiguity.

Number agreement prevents ambiguity in the following examples:

quitlazòtlâ in pilli	*they love the child (**pilli** s., pl. subj.)*
quintlazòtla in pilli	*the child loves them (**pilli** s., pl. obj.)*
quitlazòtlâ in pīpiltin	*the children love him (pl. subj., s. obj.)*
quintlazòtla in pīpiltin	*he loves the children (pl. obj., s. subj.)*

Once again, we have ambiguity in:

quintlazòtlâ in pīpiltin	*they love the children* or *the children love them*

because both the subject and the object are in the plural.

When ambiguities are possible, the order O–V–S is avoided. A sentence like **in cihuātl quitta in pilli** almost certainly signifies 'the woman sees the child' (and not 'as for the woman, the child sees her').

3.9 Focalization of the Object

We have already spoken (see 2.8) of the method of drawing attention to a particular element that we call focalization ('it is…who…'). In Nahuatl, as in English, the object of a verb can be focalized. The procedure is the same as with the subject. The focalized noun is placed at the head of the sentence, without article but sometimes preceded by **ca**,[4] and it is followed by **in**, after which the rest of the sentence is placed:

(Ca) nacatl in niccua	*it's meat that I'm eating, what I'm eating is meat*
(Ca) cihuâ in niquimitta	*they're women that I see*
(Ca) ātl in niqui	*it's water that I'm drinking*
(Ca) ātl in qui (in) pilli	*it's water that the child is drinking*
(Ca) àmo calli in quichīhua (in) Pedro	*they aren't houses that Pedro is building*

---

[3] **Quicua in nacatl** is theoretically ambiguous, but for obvious reasons, the translation has to be 'he eats the meat' and not 'the meat eats him'.

[4] In all the examples given until now, the focalized noun is indefinite ('it is a woman who…', 'it is meat that…'). For the way to focalize a definite noun ('it is the woman who…', 'it is the meat that…'), see 4.2.

In these examples, it is necessary to understand 'what I see is women', 'what I drink is water' etc.: such sentences could constitute a response to questions like 'What do you see?', 'What are you drinking?' and not 'What is this?'[5]

Note that in such sentences, the **in** of the subject can be dropped without the lack of **in** signifying an indefinite expression in the strict sense. Instead, the effect is to unite the verb and subject in a single idea. The nuance is slight, and it is generally untranslatable. In **(ca) ātl in qui in pilli**, we have something like "the child being given, what he is drinking is water." In **(ca) ātl in qui pilli**, on the other hand, "child" and "drink" are grouped together: "as for what the child drinks, this is water."

To conclude this chapter, let us repeat the most common constructions:

Quicua in pilli in nacatl	*The child is eating the meat*
Quicua nacatl in pilli	*The child is eating meat*
In pilli quicua in nacatl	*(As for) the child, (he) is eating the meat*
In pilli quicua nacatl	*(As for) the child, (he) is eating meat*
(Ca) pilli in quicua in nacatl	*It's a child that is eating the meat*
(Ca) pilli in quicua nacatl	*It's a child that is eating meat*
(Ca) nacatl in quicua (in) pilli	*It's meat that the child is eating*

and if topicalization and focalization are combined:

In pilli (ca) nacatl in quicua	*As for the child, it's meat that he is eating*
In nacatl (ca) pilli in quicua	*As for the meat, it's a child who is eating it*

VOCABULARY

Transitive verbs

āna	*to take, to seize, to take prisoner*	itta	*to see*
caqui	*to hear, to listen*	ìcuiloa	*to paint, to draw, to write*
chīhua	*to make, to build, to do*	ìtoa	*to say, to speak of, to*
cua	*to eat*		*mention*
i	*to drink*	tlazòtla	*to love*

Nouns

nacatl	*meat*

---

[5] Also note that English idiom can indicate focalization by using regular word order and putting an emphatic stress on the focalized element: 'I'm eating *meat*' (as opposed to something else). The more elaborate forms in the text make the focalization clearer, though focalization through stress would often give the more natural translation.

EXERCISES

(a) Translate into Nahuatl.
  1. I love you (s.).
  2. I love her.
  3. I love you (pl.).
  4. We love you (pl.).
  5. We hear you (pl.).
  6. He hears you (pl.).
  7. They hear you (pl.).
  8. They hear us.
  9. They see us.
 10. They see me.
 11. They see you (s.).
 12. We see you (s.).
 13. We are seizing you (s.).
 14. He is seizing you (s.).
 15. He is seizing them.
 16. He loves them.
 17. He loves us.
 18. You (pl.) love us.
 19. You (s.) love us.
 20. You (s.) love them.
 21. You (s.) love (people).
 22. You (s.) are speaking of people.
 23. You (s.) are speaking of us.
 24. He is speaking of us.
 25. He is speaking of you (s.).
 26. He is speaking.
 27. He is writing.
 28. He is listening.
 29. You (pl.) are listening.
 30. You (pl.) are eating.
 31. You (pl.) eat it.
 32. You (pl.) are doing it.
 33. You (s.) are doing it.
 34. You (s.) drink it.
 35. You (pl.) drink it.

(b) Translate into English.
  1. Quitlazòtla in Pedro.
  2. Quicaqui in oquichtli in cihuātl.

   3. Quichīhua in calli.
   4. Qui in ātl.
   5. Qui in Pedro.
   6. Niquitta in calli.
   7. Tēāna in Pedro.
   8. Quincaqui in Pedro.
   9. Quicaquî in cihuâ.
  10. Quimittâ cōcoyô in chichimê.
  11. Quimitta in cōcoyô.
  12. Quimitta in coyōtl.
  13. Ca calli in quichīhua Pedro.
  14. Cuix titlàcuiloa?

(c) Translate into Nahuatl.
   1. The woman is eating.
   2. Peter sees (things).
   3. The rabbit is drinking water.
   4. It is water that the rabbit is drinking.
   5. The woman loves the Mexica (person).
   6. The woman is hearing Mexica (people).
   7. The Mexica are hearing the woman.
   8. He sees the stars.
   9. I'm not eating the stones.
  10. Peter builds houses.
  11. Peter is drawing mountains.
  12. Aren't you (s.) speaking of Peter?
  13. No, I'm speaking of the women.
  14. They are coyotes that you (s.) are hearing

Emphatic, Interrogative, Demonstrative and Negative Pronouns

4.1 Emphatic Pronouns

In addition to the pronominal subject and object prefixes (1.1 and 3.1), Nahuatl has independent pronouns called *emphatic* pronouns. These pronouns have two forms, one short and one long. In terms of meaning, the short and long forms are equivalent. The most that can be said is that long forms are more common.

Singular	Short forms	Long forms
1st person	**nê**	**nèhuātl**
2nd person	**tê**	**tèhuātl**
3rd person	**yê**	**yèhuātl**
Plural		
1st person	**tèhuān**	**nèhuāntin**
2nd person	**amèhuān**	**amèhuāntin**
3rd person	**yèhuān**	**yèhuāntin**

4.2 Predication and Focalization with the Emphatic Pronouns

(1) Basically, the emphatic pronouns serve to identify some element within the sentence. Like nouns (in fact, these pronouns are somewhat peculiar nouns), they have a predicative use that signifies 'it is me, it is you...'

Cuix tèhuātl? – Quēmâ, ca nèhuātl   *Is it you (s.)? – Yes, it's me.*

They are therefore frequently found in expressions to mark out and emphasize one element (2.8):

(Ca) nèhuātl in nitzàtzi	*It's me who is shouting* (note the agreement in person: Nahuatl says 'it is I who am shouting')
Cuix tèhuātl in tiPedro?[1]	*Are you (s.) Peter?*
(Ca) yèhuātl in cochi	*It is he/she that is sleeping*
(Ca) yèhuāntin in mēxìcâ	*It's the Mexica (pl.). These are the Mexica*

Note that in such sentences, it is possible to omit the determiner **in**. That is, one could also say **Ca nèhuātl nitzàtzi** or **Ca yèhuātl cochi** to give the same sense.

Yèhuātl can stand for something inanimate ('it is this').

(Ca) yèhuātl in nicnequi	*This is what I want* (**nequi** 'to want')

(2) These pronouns have to be used if one wishes to focalize a noun modified by **in**. We have seen that 'it is a child that is crying' is expressed as: **(ca) conētl in chōca**. The sentence 'it is the child that is crying,' however, cannot be translated with ****ca in conētl in chōca**.

Rather, it must be rendered as

(Ca) yèhuātl chōca in conētl

that is, 'it is he, the child, that is sleeping.' We also find (more rarely): **(ca) yèhuātl in conētl in chōca**, or **in chōca (ca) yèhuātl in conētl**.

(3) Generally speaking, the predicate in Nahuatl should not bear any mark of determination. In a case where in English you would have a substantive modified by the definite article, the emphatic pronoun is used in Nahuatl. Thus, "Peter is a lord" is expressed as **ca tēuctli in Pedro** or **in Pedro ca tēuctli**. But "Peter is the lord" cannot be expressed as ****(ca) in tēuctli in Pedro** or ****in tēuctli ca in Pedro**.

This has to be expressed as:

In Pedro (ca) yèhuātl in tēuctli	*or*
In tēuctli (ca) yèhuātl in Pedro	*or*
Ca yèhuātl in Pedro in tēuctli	

that is, 'Peter is him, (that is) the lord', or 'the lord is him, (that is) Peter'.

4.3 Topicalized Pronouns

The emphatic pronouns can also be used as the subject or object of a predicate, but in this case, they are always topicalized. This means that they become the "topic" of the statement. Remember that the topic is the person or thing that is under discussion (as indicated by the previous discourse), and the focus (predicate) is what is said about this topic. In the focalization in 4.2, the

---

[1] Note the subject marker on **tiPedro**. This usage is explained in 26.2.

predicate activity is known, and the point is to identify who is carrying it out (with the focalized pronoun providing the answer). In topicalization, on the other hand, the pronoun is what we know, and the sentence is meant to provide new information about this pronoun. As with focalization, this effect is generally indicated in English merely through the intonation of the sentence. The topicalized pronoun has a steady, comparatively low accent, and the predicate is emphasized: 'I'm *eating* (in response to the question 'what are you doing?') as opposed to the emphasis on the pronoun in focalization: '*I'm* eating' (in response to the question 'who's eating'?). Sometimes the topicalized element can be introduced with the phrase 'as for …': 'as for me, I'm eating'.[2]

In Nahuatl, the emphatic pronoun appears most frequently at the head of the sentence, optionally preceded by **in**.

(In) nèhuātl, (ca) nicochi	*(As for me), I'm sleeping*
(In) tèhuātl, (ca) nimitzitta	*(As for you), I see you*
(In) yèhuātl, (ca) mēxìcatl	*(As for him), he's a Mexica*
(In) tèhuāntin, (ca) titlācâ	*(As for us), we're people*

Note. As with focalization (4.2), the **in** is not obligatory. In a written sentence like **nèhuātl nicochi**, whether we have focalization or topicalization is ambiguous. In fact, this ambiguity exists only on paper, as Classical Nahuatl certainly availed itself to use intonation to distinguish between the two sorts of sentences in the same way that modern Nahuatl and English do (as noted earlier).

4.4 'Who?'

In Nahuatl, the interrogative for "who?" is **āc**:

Āc tèhuātl? – Nèhuātl niPedro.	*Who are you? – I'm Peter*
Āc amèhuāntin? – Tèhuāntin timēxîcâ.	*Who are you (pl.)? – We're Mexica*

But many interrogative words have a long form, which is obtained by adding **in** to the simple form. For **āc**, the simple form is especially used with the emphatic pronoun, as in earlier examples, and in that case, it is invariable in number. In the majority of other cases, the long form, written **āquin**, is used:

Āquin chōca? – Ca nèhuātl.	*Who's crying? – I am (lit., It's me).*
Āquin tzàtzi? – Ca yèhuātl in conētl.	*Who's shouting? – (It's) the child.*

In instances where a response in the plural is expected, **āquin** has the plural form **āquìquê** (cf. Spanish 'quienes').

Āquìquê cuicâ?	*Who (which people) are singing?*

---

[2] French regularly uses a similar construction for thematizing the pronoun in a formal way: 'moi, je mange'.

4.5 Demonstratives

There are two demonstrative pronouns: **in**, which refers to someone or something close by, and **on**, which refers to someone or something far off.

Ca tetl in	*This is a stone (or stones)*
Ca calli on	*That is a house (or houses)*
Āquin in? Ca conētl in.	*Who is this? This is a child.*

The demonstrative pronouns have two peculiarities:

(1) They cannot be predicates. You can't say ****ca in** or ****ca on**. If you wish to say, 'This is it', you have to use a phrase like:

Ca yèhuātl in	*This is it*
Ca àmo tetl in, ca tetl on	*This isn't a stone, that's a stone.*

(2) They are not specific in terms of number. You can say for example:

Āquìquê on?	*Who are those people?*
Ca cōconê in	*These are children*

4.6 Demonstratives Combined with *in*

The demonstratives combine with the determiner **in** to give the forms **inin** and **inon**. These forms are used as:

(1) topicalized demonstrative pronouns:

Inin, ca niccua	*This I eat*
Inon, ca àmo niccua	*That I don't eat*

(2) demonstrative adjectives modifying a noun:

Cuix ticmati inin tlācatl?	*Do you know this person?*
Àmo nicnequi inon michin	*I don't want that fish*

In both cases, there is a plural form, **inìquê in** and **inìquê on**:

Inìquê in ca cuīcâ	*These ones are singing*
Cuix tiquimmati inìquê on cihuâ?	*Do you (s.) know those women?*

4.7 *In* and *On* after a Noun

In and **on** can also appear as demonstrative adjectives after a noun (itself preceded by the determiner **in**). In this case, there is no plural form.

Niccui in tetl in	*I'm taking this stone*
Niquinnōtza in cōconê on	*I'm calling those children*

Similarly, **in** and **on** can follow the emphatic third person pronouns.

Āc yèhuātl in?	*Who is this (person)?*
Ca yèhuātl on nicnequi	*That's what I want*

▶ *Note.* In certain uncommon cases, **in** can appear in its capacity as determiner after the demonstratives **in** and **on**. It's not easy to say **ca yèhuātl in in nicnequi**, and for this reason, a sentence like **ca yèhuātl in nicnequi** can signify either 'that's what I want' (with **in** introducing **nicnequi**, see 2.8) or 'what I want is this' (a contraction of **ca yèhuātl in in nicnequi**, with the first **in** acting as the demonstrative).

The vowel of demonstratives can be optionally lengthened: **ca tetl īn, ca calli ōn, inōn piltōntli** etc.[3]

4.8 'What?'

The interrogative for "what?" is **tlê**, which appears most often in the long form (see 4.4) **tlein** (note the loss of the glottal stop).

Tlein in? – Ca calli	*What's this? – A house*
Tlein on? – Ca tetl on	*What's that? – Those are stones.*
Tlein ticnequi?	*What do you (s.) want?*

There is a plural form **tleìquê** for questions like "what is this?" when applied to animate beings:

Tleìquê in?	*What are these people (or animals)?*

4.9 'No One', 'Nothing'

Two negative pronoun/adjectives correspond to the two interrogatives: **ayāc** 'no one' and **àtle** 'nothing'. Here we recognize the negative **à-** (2.9), slightly modified in the case of **ayāc**, and the short form of the interrogatives (without glottal stop in **àtle**).

Like the interrogatives, these forms necessarily precede the verb:

Āquin cochi? Ca ayāc.	*Who is sleeping? No one.*
Ayāc niquitta.	*I don't see anyone. (I see no one.)*
Tlein ticchīhua? – Ca àtle nicchīhua.	*What are you (s.) doing? – I'm not doing anything.*

---

[3] The vowels of **in** and **on** are listed as long in F. Karttunen, *An Analytical Dictionary of Nahuatl*, and one can see such forms frequently in regularized transcriptions of old texts that are based on this usage. Carochi marks the forms as long when he discusses them directly, but the view is taken here that while these vowels may have been pronounced long in careful speech, they were normally shortened (both Carochi and the *Bancroft Dialogues*, which are the main sources for the vowel lengths of Classical Nahuatl, do not mark them as long in the great majority of instances).

We also find with the same meaning the "expanded" forms **àmo āc** and **àmo tlê**. Generally speaking, if there is a compound negation, only the first of the elements takes the negative, and the rest remain in the interrogative form:

Ayāc tlê quichīhua	*No one is doing anything*
	Ayāc and **àtle** often express non-existence and are used adjectivally, being translated as 'there is no ...'[4]
Ayāc pilli	*There is no child*
Àtle ātl	*There is no water*

or 'no':

Ayāc tēuctli miqui	*No lord is dying*
Àtle calli niquitta	*I see no house*

Though this is rare, one can have predicative uses, in the following forms:

for **àtle**: **ànitlein**, pl. **àtitleìquê** 'I am nothing', 'we are nothing(s)' (in the sense 'we are insignificant'; for the plural, see 2.5). Here, the long form of the interrogative reappears. Still, **(ca) àtlein** 'he's nothing' can be contrasted with **(ca) àtle** 'it's nothing'. One can also say: **(ca) àmo nitlein** etc.

for **ayāc**: **àmo nāc** 'I am nothing' (lit., 'no one') and especially in the plural **àmo tāquê** 'we are nothing' (in the sense 'we aren't very numerous'). As can be seen, the short form of **āc** is maintained, with the suffix **-ê** in the plural.

4.10 Interrogatives Preceded by *In*

There is another important use of the interrogatives. We have seen (2.8) that one of the possible translations for 'he who ...' 'the one who ...' etc. is simply **in** placed in front of a verb form. For example:

nicnōtza in cochi	*I'm calling the one who's asleep*

Instead of **in**, however, one can have **in āquin** (pl. **āquìquê**) or **in tlein**. There is a difference. When used by itself in front of the verb, **in** refers to a specific person or thing, while **in āquin** and **in tlein** give a general meaning similar to 'whoever' or 'whatever'. For example:

nicnōtza in āquin cochi	*I'm calling (any/some) one who is asleep (whoever that may be), I'm calling whoever is asleep*

---

[4] For 'there is', see 5.1 and 6.2.

Nictlazòtla in āquin nēchtlazòtla	*I love whoever loves me* (the same phrase without **āquin** alludes to someone specific)
Quichīhua in tlein quinequi	*He does whatever he wants* (the same phrase without **tlein** would mean *he is doing the specific thing that he wants to*)
Chōca in āquin conētl	*Whoever is a child cries (every child cries)*
Niccua in tlein nacatl	*I eat anything that is meat (of whatever sort)*

In addition, this expression corresponds to the indirect question of English:

Àmo nicmati in tlein ticnequi	*I don't know what you want*
Àmo nicmati in āquin nēchnōtza	*I don't know who is calling me*

In this case, **in** can be omitted (**Àmo nicmati tlein ticnequi** etc.).

VOCABULARY

Emphatic pronouns

nè(huātl)	*I*	tèhuān(tin)	*we*
tè(huātl)	*you (s.)*	amèhuān(tin)	*you (pl.)*
yè(huātl)	*he, she, it*	yèhuān(tin)	*they*

Demonstratives

in	*this*	inin	*(pl.* inìquê in*)*
on	*that*	inon	*(pl.* inìquê on*)*

Interrogatives

āc, āquin	*who?*	tlê, tlein	*what?*
	(pl. āquìquê*)*		*(pl.* tleìquê*)*

Negatives

ayāc	*no one*	àtle	*nothing*

Transitive verbs

cui	*take*[5]	nequi	*want*
mati	*perceive, know, understand*[6]	nōtza	*call, speak to*

Nouns

tēuctli	*(pl.* /R–tin/*) lord*[7]

---

[5] **Cui** and **āna** are both translated as 'take', but they differ in sense. **Āna** is "stronger", indicating either that the taking is done by violence or that what is being taken is active or resisting. **Cui**, on the other hand, indicates that what is being taken is inert or passive.

[6] The original (basic) sense of **mati** is to 'feel' or 'perceive' (by a sensory, emotional or intellectual operation). The more frequent sense is to 'know'.

[7] For the pronunciation of **tēuctli**, see Preliminary Lesson, Complementary Note 5.

EXERCISES

(a) Convert the following phrases by focalizing the subject and then the object
    (if there is one). Example: **Nimitznōtza** *I am calling you (s.)* > **Ca nèhuātl
    in nimitznōtza** *it's me who's calling you (s.)* or *I'm the one who's calling you
    (s.).* **Ca tèhuātl in nimitznōtza** *it is you (s.) that I am calling.*
    1. Tamēchnōtzâ
    2. Nitzàtzi
    3. Cochi in Pedro
    4. Titlacuâ
    5. Niquimitta in cīcitlāltin
    6. Mitzcaquî in tētēuctin
    7. Nēchtlazòtla in Pedro.
    8. Nicmati in
    9. Anquicuî in tetl

(b) Translate into English.
    1. Tleìquê in? Ca cōcoyô in.
    2. Tlein tiquitta? – Ca yèhuātl in calli.
    3. Āquìquê tiquimitta? – Ca yèhuāntin in otomî.
    4. Ca àmo cōcoyô in niquimitta, ca chichimê.
    5. Nacatl in quicua Pedro.
    6. Ca yèhuātl quicua nacatl in Pedro.
    7. Ca yèhuātl in nacatl in quicua Pedro.
    8. In nèhuātl ca nimēxìcatl, in amèhuāntin ca amotomî.
    9. Miqui in āquin tlācatl.
    10. Àmo nicmati in āquin ticnōtza.
    11. Àmo niccaqui in tlein tiquìtoa.

(c) Translate into Nahuatl.
    1. What do you (s.) want? – Water.
    2. What are you (pl.) eating? – It's the meat.
    3. Who are those (people)? – They aren't Mexica. They're Otomi.
    4. Who is singing? – It's a child who is singing. – No, it's Peter.
    5. You're not a Mexica. (As for you, you're not ...)
    6. Those men don't eat fish.
    7. I don't know who is eating.
    8. I don't know what he is eating.
    9. I don't see who is eating meat.
    10. Whoever's a Mexica knows this.

Irregular Verbs, Introduction to Locatives

5.1 *Câ* 'To Be'

We have said (2.1) that there is no verb 'to be'. This is true with reference to constructions with a nominal predicate. If, however, what one wishes to say is not 'to be someone or something' but 'to be somewhere', then a verb is needed. This verb is irregular. In the present, the singular is **câ** and the plural is **catê**. Thus:

Singular		Plural	
1st person	**nicâ**	1st person	**ticatê**
2nd person	**ticâ**	2nd person	**ancatê**
3rd person	**câ**	3rd person	**catê**

This verb is used with locatives (5.4), for example:

Nicān nicâ	*I'm here (**nicān** 'here')*
Mēxìco ticatê	*We're in Mexico*
Tlaxcallān catê in cihuâ	*The women are in Tlaxcala*

If the subject is indefinite, it is better translated with 'there is/are':

| Nicān câ calli | *There are houses here* |
| Nicān catê tētepê | *There are mountains here* |

The subject prefixes cannot be used with locatives, so ****ninicān** or ****nimēxìco** are impossible.

▶ *Note.* The present tense, at any rate, of **câ** can be considered regular, for two reasons:

(1) A word-final **t** is generally confused with the glottal stop.[1] The real stem is **cat**, and it is only to follow the textual tradition that we write **câ**.

(2) The glottal stop has the peculiarity of not appearing at the start of a syllable. This amounts to saying that it cannot appear either at the start of a syllable or as the second element in a consonantal cluster. Hence, the plural suffix -' does not obey the usual rule about the helping vowel (which would give ****cat'i**). The helping vowel, which in this case has the quality **e** instead of **i**, appears between the preceding consonant and the glottal stop.[2]

5.2 *Yauh* 'To Go'

The verb for 'to go' is clearly irregular:

Singular		Plural	
1st person	**niyauh**	1st person	**tihuî**
2nd person	**tiyauh**	2nd person	**anhuî**
3rd person	**yauh**	3rd person	**huî**

Mēxìco niyauh	*I'm going to Mexico*
Tlaxcallān huî in cihuâ	*The women are going to Tlaxcala*

5.3 *Huītz* 'To Come'

In the present, the verb 'to come' has the form **huītz** in the singular and **huītzê** in the plural (plural -**ê** after a consonant, as with **catê**). This verb is built on **huī**, which we have seen in the plural of **yauh** (5.2), and a suffix -**tz**, which indicates approach. Hence, we conjugate:

Singular		Plural	
1st person	**nihuītz**	1st person	**tihuītzê**
2nd person	**tihuītz**	2nd person	**anhuītzê**
3rd person	**huītz**	3rd person	**huītzê**

Cuix anhuītzê?	*Are you (pl.) coming?*
Àmo huītz in Pedro	*Peter isn't coming*

Câ, **yauh** and **huītz** are the only irregular verbs in Nahuatl.

---

[1] The final consonant of English words like 'don't' and 'can't' is often pronounced in a similar way, with a glottal stop in place of a fully articulated **t**.

[2] We have already seen this kind of plural in **āquê** (4.9).

5.4 Locatives

Alongside nouns and verbs, *locatives* constitute an important class of words in Nahuatl. These include:

(1) Interrogatives. The most common is **cān** 'where?', which, like **āc** and **tlê** (4.4 and 4.8), has a long form of the same meaning (**cānin**) and a negative (**àcān** 'nowhere').

> Cān/cānin tiyauh? – Mēxico niyauh   *Where are you going? – I'm going to Mexico*
> Àcān niyauh   *I'm not going anywhere*
> Cān câ in tēuctli? – Nicān câ   *Where's the lord? – He's here*

In cānin is used to signify the relative 'where' in an indefinite sense (cf. **in āquin** and **in tlein**, 4.10).[3]

> Niyauh in cānin yauh Pedro   *I go where(ver) Peter goes*

(2) Various adverbs, including other demonstratives. Most frequent are (in order of increasing distance): **nicān** 'here', **oncān** 'there', **ōmpa** 'over there'.

> Nicān cochi in Pedro   *Peter sleeps here*
> Oncān câ ātl   *There's water there*
> Ōmpa quichīhua calli   *He builds houses (over) there*
> Niyauh in ōmpa yauh Pedro   *I'm going (to the place) where Pedro is going (i.e., to a specific, known location)*
> Huītz in nicān ticatê   *He's coming (here) where we are*

(3) Place names (of towns and regions):

> Mēxìco ninemi   *I live in Mexico*
> Tlaxcallān yauh in Pedro   *Peter is going to Tlaxcala*
> Cuauhnāhuac tlacua   *He eats at Cuernavaca*
> Xōchimīlco câ xōchitl   *There are flowers at Xochimilco*

(4) Denominative locatives, that is, ones derived from nouns, signifying, for example, 'at home', 'near the tree', 'on the mountain' etc. (see Lesson 13).

(5) Deverbal locatives, that is, ones derived from verbs, signifying 'place where such-and-such thing happens' (see 24.8, 24.9).

We will see later how locatives are formed from nouns or verbs, and for the time being, we will deal with only the general syntactic characteristics of locatives.

First let us note that the most common place in the sentence for a locative phrase is directly in front of the verb, as is shown by the majority of examples

---

[3] For the definite relative 'where', see Subsection 2.

seen so far. The order is LOCATIVE–VERB–SUBJECT (e.g., **nicān cochi in Pedro**) or SUBJECT–LOCATIVE–VERB (**in Pedro nicān cochi**). The locative can follow the verb, but in that case, it is most often preceded by **in**. The order is then SUBJECT–VERB–**in**–LOCATIVE or (more rarely) VERB–SUBJECT–**in**–LOCATIVE:

In Pedro cochi in nicān	*Peter sleeps here*
Cochi in Pedro in nicān	*Peter sleeps here*

Let us now look at the characteristics of the locatives themselves.

5.5 Syntax of Locatives

The first characteristic is that in terms of function a locative can be:

(1) Subject or predicate in conjunction with another locative (i.e., one locative is described by or equated with another):

Cān(in) Mēxìco?	*Where is Mexico?*
Ōmpa Cuauhnāhuac	*There's Cuernavaca, Cuernavaca's there*

It is impossible to say ****Cān câ Mēxìco?** or ****Ōmpa câ Cuauhnāhuac**. Because a locative is by nature localized, **câ**, being the verb for localizing, cannot be used, whereas it is necessarily used when the subject is a noun.

(2) Adverbial modifier (complement) or predicate of the entire sentence. These two sorts of function are often hard to distinguish. A regular adverbial complement is what we find in:

Nicān nitlacua	*I eat here*
Mēxìco nemi	*He lives in Mexico*

but one also finds:

(Ca) nicān in nitlacua	*It's here that I eat*
(Ca) Mēxìco in nemi	*It's in Mexico that he lives*

In the second type of sentence, we clearly have a sort of focalizing, which could be clumsily translated as '(the place) where I eat is here' or '(the place) where he lives is Mexico', that is, with a locative acting in some way as the predicate to the whole sentence. Such an interpretation is not excluded for the preceding variety, though the effect would be more "neutral" and the locative apparently acts more like a simple adverbial complement.

(3) On the other hand, a locative cannot be either the subject or the predicate in conjunction with a noun. One can say for example:

(Ca) cualli in calli	*The house is beautiful*

but not **Ca cualli in nicān, **Ca cualli in Mēxìco. To say something like *it's beautiful here* (i.e., *this place is beautiful*) or *Mexico is beautiful*, it is necessary to make use of a locative form derived from **cualli** 'beautiful, good', in this case **cualcān** 'beautiful place'. So you can say:

(Ca) cualcān in nicān	*This is a beautiful place*
(Ca) cualcān in Mēxìco	*Mexico is beautiful (lit., Mexico is a beautiful place)*

In the second case, one can also use the expedient of saying:

(Ca) cualli in āltepētl Mēxìco	*The town (altepētl) of Mexico is beautiful (or rather the town at Mexico is beautiful)*

(4) A locative cannot be a direct object.[4] If you wish to say, for example, 'I see Mexico', you do not say **niquitta in Mēxìco, but:

Mēxìco nitlatta lit.	*I see things in Mexico*

It is also possible to say:

Niquitta in āltepētl Mēxìco / *see the town of Mexico* (lit. *I see the town at Mexico*)

5.6 No Indication of Direction with Locatives

The second characteristic of the locative is that unlike most languages, Nahuatl does not indicate in a locative form whether it concerns the place in which the person or thing is or to which he or it is going or from which he or it is coming. It is the verb that carries out this function. Thus:

Ōmpa câ	*He is there*
Ōmpa yauh	*He's going there*
Ōmpa huītz	*He's coming from there*
Cuauhnāhuac àci	*He arrives at Cuernavaca*
Xōchimīlco nìcihui	*I'm hurrying to Xochimilco*
Tlaxcallān niquīza	*I'm passing by Tlaxcala*

5.7 *Nicān* and *Ōmpa* with Another Locative

We see that a problem arises under these circumstances. **Ōmpa huītz** can only mean 'he is coming from there' and **nicān huītz** only 'he is coming here'.

---

[4] One can sometimes find deviations from this principle, as well as certain examples of a verb having a locative subject.

Mēxìco huītz, however, could theoretically be ambiguous. Hence, we regularly find:

Nicān Mēxìco huītz	*He's coming (here) to Mexico*
Ōmpa Mēxìco huītz	*He's coming from (there) Mexico*

Generally speaking, it is a very common practice to use place names (i.e., the locatives in sections 3, 4 and 5 of 5.4) with **nicān** or **ōmpa**, depending on whether or not the person is in the place being spoken of. The following word orders are possible:

(SUBJECT)–**nicān/ōmpa**–PLACE NAME–VERB–(SUBJECT)[5]
(SUBJECT)–**nicān/ōmpa**–VERB–PLACE NAME –(SUBJECT)
(SUBJECT)–VERB–(SUBJECT)–**in nicān/ōmpa**–PLACE NAME

Thus, for 'Peter is going to Mexico', in addition to **Mēxìco yauh in Pedro** (and the other possible word orders, see 5.4), one can say:

Ōmpa Mēxìco yauh in Pedro
In Pedro ōmpa Mēxìco yauh
Ōmpa yauh Mēxìco in Pedro
In Pedro yauh in ōmpa Mēxìco

and more rarely:

In Pedro ōmpa yauh Mēxìco
Yauh in Pedro in ōmpa Mēxìco

5.8 The Suffix *-pa*

If we add the suffix **-pa** to a locative, we have a form that can indicate two things:

(1) A vague localization, a place that is not reached:

Cāmpa tiyauh?	*Where (the devil) are you going?*
Tlaxcallāmpa yauh	*He's going toward Tlaxcala*
Mēxìcopa huî	*They're going in the direction of Mexico*

(2) An elative (a form indicating motion from the inside toward the outside):

Mēxìcopa quīza	*He is coming out of Mexico (**Mēxìco quīza** would mean he is passing by Mexico)*
Cāmpa tihuītz?	*Where are you coming from?*

---

[5] The appearance of SUBJECT twice in parentheses is meant to indicate that the subject is found in one or the other place.

▶ **Note.** -**pa** cannot be added to demonstratives (you cannot say ****nicāmpa**, ****oncāmpa**, ****ōmpapa**). Also, **cāmpa** cannot be used emphatically (you cannot say ****cāmpa in** ...).

VOCABULARY

Intransitive verbs

àci	*to arrive*	nemi	*to live*[6]
câ	*to be (located)*	quīza	*to emerge,*
huītz	*to come*		*to pass by*
ìcihui	*to hasten, to hurry*	yauh	*to go*

Nouns

āltepētl	*town*	tlaōlli	*corn*
cualli	*(pl. –tin)*	xōchitl	*flower*
	good,		
	beautiful		

Locatives

Interrogative

cān(in)	*where?*

Negative

àcān	*nowhere*

Demonstrative

nicān	*here*	oncān	*there*
ōmpa	*over there*		

Place names

cualcān	*nice place*	Tlaxcallān	*(at) Tlaxcala*
Cuauhnāhuac	*(at) Cuernavaca*	Xōchimīlco	*(at) Xochimilco*
Mēxìco	*(at) Mexico*		

EXERCISES

(a) Translate into English.
   1. In Pedro oncān câ, cuix àmo huītz?
   2. Cuix Mēxìco in anhuî? – Àmo, ca Xōchimīlco.
   3. Cuix Tlaxcallān câ in Pedro? – Àmō, ca nicān Mexìco.
   4. Oncān catê tlācâ, tlein quichīhuâ?

---

[6] **Yōli** and **nemi** both are translate 'to live' but **yōli** means 'to be alive', while **nemi** originally meant 'to be in motion' (a meaning that it still has in compounds), and from this it developed the meaning 'live, reside in a place'.

    5. Nicān àcî in otomî.

    6. Oncān quīzâ cōcōhuâ.

    7. Cuix huītzê in cihuâ? – Quēmâ, cuix àmo anquimittâ?

    8. In nèhuātl nicān nitlacua. – In tèhuāntin ca ōmpa.

    9. Ōmpa Mēxìco nemî inìquê in tētēuctin.

    10. Cualcāmpa tiquīzâ; àmo cualcān in ōmpa tihuî.

    11. Cānin nicān? Cuix Mēxìco? – Àmō, ca Tlaxcallān.

(b) Translate into Nahuatl.

    1. We are hurrying to Mexico.

    2. Are we arriving at Xochimilco?

    3. The Mexica are going (there) to Tlaxcala.

    4. Those women are coming from (there) Cuernavaca.

    5. Do you (s.) like Mexico?

    6. Are you (s.) going where Peter is going? – No, it is he who is coming where we are.

    7. It is beautiful where you (pl.) live.

    8. I'm hastening to go to where it is beautiful. ('I'm hurrying toward anywhere that is a beautiful place.')

    9. It is at Cuernavaca that those people live.

    10. Whoever goes in the direction of Tlaxcala sees that mountain.

Directional and Reflexive Prefixes

6.1 Directional Prefixes

The Nahuatl verb can take one of two *directional prefixes*, which indicate motion in terms of a reference point. This reference point can be specifically the location where the speaker is, but it can sometimes (in a narrative, for instance) be any place to which attention is being directed for one reason or another. In terms of this reference point:

-on-	indicates motion away
-huāl-	indicates motion toward

The use of these prefixes is especially clear in the case of verbs of motion:

onēhua	*he departs* (going away from here)
huālēhua	*he departs* (from there in order to come here)
onìcihui	*he's going away rapidly* (hastening to depart)
huālìcihui	*he's hurrying to come* (hastening in this direction)
ōmpa onquīza	*he's going out for there* ('emerging there from here')
ōmpa huālquīza	*he's coming out from there* ('emerging there in this direction')
nonyauh, tonhuî	*I'm, we're going away*
nihuāllauh, tihuālhuî	*I'm, we're coming*

The compound **huāllauh** is synonymous with **huītz** (5.3). Note the assimilation of the **y** of **yauh** to the **l** of **huāl**. This is regular, just like the similar assimilation of **y** after **tl** (2.2):

RULE: $/l/ + /y/ > /ll/$

6.2 Metaphorical Uses of the Directional Prefixes

-**On**- and **huāl**- are never found at the front of a noun. They can be found at the front of virtually any verb, not merely verbs of motion. They may retain their proper sense:

conitta	*he's going to see it* (lit. *he's seeing it toward there*)[1]
quihuālitta	*he's coming to see it* (lit. *he's seeing it toward here*)

More often, however, they have a very attenuated or a figurative sense, which is sometimes untranslatable. **On**- indicates real or metaphorical movement toward other people or a process that is continuing or ongoing. **Huāl**- indicates a real or metaphorical movement that is focused on the subject. With each, this nuance of motion can mean that the subject has to move before carrying out the action of the verb. One might compare an English phrase like 'come have dinner at our house', where the real point is an invitation to dinner, and the motion that necessarily precedes the dinner is not the main focus of the action (cf. the directional conjugations in 22.4 and 22.5 and the compound verbs in Lesson 27, all of which coordinate an actual verb of motion with the main verb). For example:

quitlātia	*he's hiding it*
contlātia	*he's hiding it* (at a distance), *he's going to hide it*
quihuāllātia[2]	*he's hiding it on himself*
conchīhua	*he's going to do it* or *he's continuing to do it*
concua, coni	*he's eating it (food and drink) up* (Here the use of -**on**- is contrary to what one might image. The point is not that the movement of the food in terms of the eater but that its disappearance from the situation.)

The "reference point" of the motion is often understood as the human world, as opposed to the (unknown, dangerous or supernatural) outside world, for example, the forest, desert, ocean, fire. Thus:

huetzi	*he falls* (e.g., on the ground)
onhuetzi	*he falls* (into the fire, the water, a gorge)

---

[1] In the translations of the prefix **on**- as 'going to VERB', be sure to understand 'going' only in its literal sense as a verb of motion and do not confuse this with the use of 'going to' as a sort of future tense.

[2] Remember that **l** + **tl** gives **ll**.

It can also be understood as 'us' (i.e., the Mexica) as opposed to 'them' (i.e., for-eigners). Thus, given that we know a Mexica is speaking, there in no ambiguity in sentences like:

Quimommīnâ in Mēxìcâ	*The Mexica shoot arrows (mīna) at them*
Quinhuālmīnâ in Mēxìcâ	*They shoot arrows at the Mexica*

Another way of understanding the reference point is "good" as opposed to "bad", or the social norm as opposed to disagreeable or immoral actions.[3] Thus:

Huāltotōni in ātl	*The water is getting warm (which is what I wanted)*
Ontotōni in ātl	*The water is becoming too hot*
Oncochi	*He sleeps too late*
Tlein conchīhua?	*What (bad thing) is he doing?*

Oncâ indicates existence and corresponds to the English 'there is', especially if the sentence doesn't include a locative:

Cuix oncatê tēteô?	*Are there gods? Do the gods exist?*
Nicān àmo oncâ ātl	*There's no water here* (one could also simply use **câ** or also say: **nicān àtle ātl**, 4.9)

6.3 The Helping Vowel in Front of -*c-on*-

There is a morphological peculiarity involving –**on**-. In the combinations **nic**- and **tic**- ('I...it', 'you...it', 'we...it') followed by -**on**-, the helping vowel takes on the quality **o**. For example, we have:

noconitta	*I'm going to see it*
toconitta	*you're going to see it*
toconittâ	*we're going to see it*

in place of ****niconitta, **ticonitta** and ****ticonittâ**. But we have as usual:

nimitzonitta	*I'm going to see you*
tiquimonitta	*you're going to see them*

---

[3] For the negative sense of the "away" prefix, one might compare the English idiom 'go and VERB', as in 'we were planning a nice picnic, but it went and rained all day', where no actual motion is involved at all and the phrase signifies an obstructive action that takes place contrary to the affected person's wish or expectation.

6.4 Order of Prefixes

In terms of the order of prefixes, -**on**- and -**huāl**- appear, as we have seen, *after* the subject and definite object prefixes. However, they are placed *in front of* the indefinite object prefixes (including the reflexives, see below 6.5). Thus, we have:

noconitta	*I'm going to see it*
nontēitta	*I'm going to see people*
nichuālitta	*I'm coming to see it*
nihuāltēitta	*I'm coming to see people*
noconcua	*I'm eating it up*
nontlacua	*I'm eating things up*
nichuāllātia (ni-c-huāl-tlātia)	*I'm hiding it on myself*
nihuāllatlātia (ni-huāl-tla-tlātia)	*I'm hiding things on myself*

6.5 Reflexive Prefixes

To complete the inventory of prefixes, let us look at the reflexive prefixes. These have the following forms:

Singular		Plural	
1st person	**-no-**	1st person	**-to-**
2nd person	**-mo-**	2nd person	**-mo-**
3rd person	**-mo-**	3rd person	**-mo-**

and are placed after the subject prefix. For example, we conjugate:

ninotlātia	*I hide myself*	titotlātiâ	*we hide ourselves*
timotlātia	*you hide yourself*	ammotlātiâ	*you hide yourselves*
motlātia	*he hides himself*	motlātiâ	*they hide themselves*

If there is a directional prefix, however, it is placed between the subject prefix and the reflexive:

nonnotlātia	*I'm going to hide myself*
tihuālmotlātia	*you are going to hide yourself*

We can now give the definitive order of the prefixes:

SUBJECT + DEFINITE OBJECT + DIRECTIONAL (**on** , **huāl**) + REFLEXIVE + **tē** + **tla**

The combination of a reflexive plus an indefinite or that of both indefinites (-**tē**-, -**tla**-) can appear in bitransitive verbs (18.1, 4).

6.6 Meaning of the Reflexive

In terms of meaning, the Nahuatl reflexive corresponds to the reflexive pronoun in English ('myself,' 'yourself/-selves', 'himself' etc.), which is used when the subject of the verb acts upon itself.[4] In addition, the Nahuatl reflexive has a number of other uses that have little or no correspondence in English. Thus:

(1) action of the subject upon itself:

ninotlātia	*I hide myself*
ninopāca	*I wash myself* (**nicpāca** *I wash him*)
ninoxima	*I shave myself* (**nicxima** *I shave him*)

Note that English often uses an intransitive version of a transitive verb in a reflexive sense (i.e., 'I wash' and 'I shave' in place of 'I wash myself' or 'I shave myself').

(2) reciprocal action (i.e., several people performing the action upon each other; as one would expect, this usage is restricted to the plural). Here English normally uses 'each other' or 'one another':

titotlazòtlâ	*we love each other* or *one another*

(3) with verbs of motion and placement:

ninocāhua	*I stop (myself), I rest* (**niccāhua** *I stop it, leave it*)
ninoquetza	*I raise myself, I stand* (**nicquetza** *I erect it*)
ninotlāza	*I throw myself headlong* (**nictlāza** *I throw it*)
ninotlālia	*I sit (myself) down* (**nictlālia** *I place it*)
ninotēca	*I lie (lay myself down)* (**nictēca** *I lay it down, extend it*)

(4) with verbs of emotion or physical state:

ninozōma	*I lose my temper, I am (or become) angry* (**niczōma** *I annoy him*)
ninotolīnia	*I grieve, am distressed* (**nēchtolīnia** *he harasses me*)
ninococoa	*I'm sick, ill, I suffer* (**nēchcocoa** *it makes me sick, he/it hurts me*)

Note carefully that the sense of the reflexive verb here is normally not the same as that of the corresponding non-reflexive verb. Whereas in **nēchzōma** 'he annoys me' the subject does something annoying that leads to this emotion in the object, the reflexive form **ninozōma** does not

---

[4] Note that there is some ambiguity in English because the same form is used for the reflexive pronoun and the intensive modifier: in 'he killed himself' the form is reflexive, but in 'he killed the lion himself (i.e., without assistance)' it is intensive. Only the former use is relevant here.

mean that I do something annoying to provoke this reaction in myself but in reaction to something *external* that annoys me, I put myself in this emotional state. That is, the reflexive here means that I adopt this frame of mind without 'causing' it in myself through some action on my part. Similarly, while we say of a disease **nēchcocoa** 'it makes me ill', the reflexive does not signify that I physically make myself ill (though it could mean that, for instance, if I mistakenly eat bad food), but simply that I 'take on' this condition (i.e., 'I become ill') without actually causing it through some action on my part.

(5) quasi-passive (a widespread usage, see 15.9):

mochīhua	*it happens, it is being done* (lit., *it does itself*)
mochīhua in calli	*the house is being built*

This usage is unknown in English, but it is common in Romance languages and German.

(6) with certain verbs that appear only in the reflexive:

ninotlaloa	*I run*

(7) with certain verbs that use the reflexive form with a meaning quite far removed from their original sense:

ninomati	*I feel well, I have the feeling (that …)* (lit., *I feel myself*)
ninocaqui	*I'm satisfied, I agree* (lit., *I hear myself*)

6.7 Morphology of the Reflexive in Front of a Vowel

In front of a vowel:

(1) in general, the **o** of the reflexive prefix is omitted:

mi	*it gets drunk*
māna	*it is extended* (lit., *it takes itself*)
ninēhua	*I get up* (lit., *I raise myself*)
titēhuâ	*we get up*
timēhua	*you (s.) get up*

However, if the stem begins with /iCC/ (cf. 3.7), the procedure is determined by the first consonant of the consonantal cluster:

(2) If the the first consonant is the glottal stop, the **-o** of the reflexive is dropped as already mentioned:

mìtoa	*it is said, one says*
mìcuiloa	*it is written, painted*

(3) If the first consonant is not the glottal stop, the initial -i of the verb stem is dropped and the -o of the prefix is kept:

ninotta	*I see myself*
motta	*he sees himself* or *he* or *it is seen*
titottâ	*we see ourselves* or *each other*
ninolpia	*I bind, attach myself* (niquilpia *I bind him* or *it*)

In summary, what happens in (3) is similar to what happens with –tla- (3.7). Recall, however, that the elision of i- after –tla- applies to all instances of initial /iCC-/. Compare:

| tlatta | *he sees* | | motta | *he is seen, it is visible* |
| tlalpia | *he binds things* | | molpia | *he is bound, it is attached* |

but

| tlàtoa | *he speaks* | | mìtoa | *it is said* |
| tlàcuiloa | *he writes* | | mìcuiloa | *it is written* |

Also recall that **tla-** is never elided: **tlaāna** 'he binds things', **tlaēhua** 'he raises things' etc.

VOCABULARY

Intransitive verbs

| huetzi | *to fall* | totōni | *to become heated up* |

Transitive verbs

cāhua	*stop, leave* (mo-: *stay, remain*)[5]	tlaloa	(mo-: *run*)[7]
		tlālia	*set, place*
cocoa	*make ill, injure* (mo-: *be sick*)	tlātia	*hide*
		tlāza	*throw, hurl*
ēhua	*raise, lift*[6]	tolīnia	*torment* (mo-: *be wretched, unfortunte*)
ilpia	*bind, tie*		
pāca	*wash*	xima	*shave*
quetza	*raise*	zōma	*irritate, annoy*
tēca	*lay down, spread out*		

---

[5] In the vocabulary, we will use parenthetical explanations when the sense of the reflexive is not self-evident.

[6] The verb **ēhua** can be used both transitively and intransitively. The transitive version means 'to pick up'. The intransitive one properly means 'to get up to leave' and then simply 'to leave'.

[7] This is how a verb that appears in the reflexive is listed.

EXERCISES

(a) Add -on- and then -huāl- to the following forms.
1. ninotlālia
2. nictlālia
3. nitētlālia
4. timopāca
5. titlacāhua
6. titēchcāhua
7. tiquincāhua
8. ticcāhua
9. quicāhua

(b) Translate into English.
1. Ōmpa nonnotēca.
2. In yèhuāntin on àmo motlazòtlâ.
3. Cuix nicān tichuāllālia in xōchitl on?
4. Nicān huālmotlātia in tōchtli.
5. Cuix amonhuî? – Àmo, ca nicān titocahuā.
6. Cuix timoxima? Ca àmo, ca ninopāca.
7. Cuix mococoa in Pedro? Mìtoa in.
8. Ommotlaloâ in cōcoyô.
9. Cāmpa tonyauh? Cuix nicān àmo timomati?
10. Ōmpa tocontlāzâ in tetl in.

(c) Translate into Nahuatl.
1. Where are the children going to hide (themselves)?
2. You (pl.) are hurrying away. Is it to Tlaxcala that you are going?
3. This is not done ("doesn't do itself").
4. Here the city can't be seen ("doesn't see itself").
5. Does one eat snakes ("Do the snakes eat themselves")?
6. One doesn't drink this water ("This water doesn't drink itself"). It makes people sick.
7. I'm devouring ("eating away") the meat. I'm drinking up ("away") the water.
8. You (s.) get up ("raise yourself"), wash ("yourself"), run to Mexico.
9. We get up, wash, run to Mexico.
10. What are you going to do? – I'm going to pick up the stone.

Quantifiers, *Zan, Ye, Oc*

7.1 Number Nouns

The interrogative for 'how many?' is **quēzqui**. It does not have a long form.

The system by which Nahuatl counts is not based on multiples of ten like the decimal system but on multiples of twenty (the name for this is a *vigesimal* system). Here are the numbers from 1 to 20:

1 **cē**	6 **chicuacē**	11 **màtlāctli oncē**	16 **caxtōlli oncē**
2 **ōme**	7 **chicōme**	12 **màtlāctli omōme**	17 **caxtōlli omōme**
3 **ēyi**	8 **chicuēyi**	13 **màtlāctli omēyi**	18 **caxtōlli omēyi**
4 **nāhui**	9 **chiucnāhui**	14 **màtlāctli onnāhui**	19 **caxtōlli onnāhui**
5 **mācuīlli**	10 **màtlāctli**	15 **caxtōlli**	20 **cempōhualli**

There are four units (1 to 4) and three sub-bases (5, 10, 15). The other numbers are formed by adding units to a sub-base. From 11 to 14 and 16 to 19, counting is done with the sub-bases 10 and 15 followed by a second element consisting of the particle **om** ('and') and the appropriate unit.

From 6 to 9, use is not made of the sub-base **mācuīlli** '5' but of the prefix **chiuc** (/čik^w/). However, **chicuacē** is said in place of **chiuccē** and **chicōme** in place of **chicuōme**. The form **chicōme** is phonetically regular. Nahuatl doesn't permit the sequence **cu + o** and reduces it to **co**. Similarly, the sequence **hu + o** is reduced to **o**. In other words, any **w** element is dropped in front of **o**.

RULE: $/k^w/ + /o/ > /ko/$
$/w/ + /o/ > /o/$

7.2 Place for Numbers

When numbers modify a noun, they are put in front of it:

Niquitta ēyi cuahuitl   *I see three trees*

However, the two elements of the compound numbers (11 to 14 and 16 to 19) can be placed on either side of the noun:

Niquitta màtlactli omōme cuahuitl   *I see twelve trees*
Niquitta màtlactli cuahuitl omōme   *I see twelve trees*

Quēzqui is likewise placed in front of the noun, but like all interrogatives it has to be placed at the front of the clause:

Quēzqui cuahuitl tiquitta?   *How many trees do you see?*

A numerical expression can be made definite with **in**:

Niquitta in ēyi cuahuitl   *I see the three trees*

It is a quite frequent practice to separate the number from its noun by placing it in front of the verb. The noun, which follows the verb, is generally precede by **in**:

Ēyi niquitta in cuahuitl   *I see three trees* (the nuance being something like *I see the trees numbering three* or *I see the trees and there are three of them*)

The number **cē** 'one' can act as the indefinite article (**niquitta cē cuahuitl** 'I see a tree'). The situations in which the determiner is not used correspond roughly to what happens in English. In both languages, we can have no determiner with animate nouns in the plural (e.g. **niquimitta cihuâ** 'I see women') and with collective (uncountable) inanimate nouns (e.g., **niquitta ātl** 'I see water'). Recall that the indefinite plural is not marked as such (**niquitta cuahuitl** 'I see trees').

7.3 Plural of Numbers

Strange as it may seem, the numbers in Nahuatl have both singular and plural forms. This is simply because they agree with their noun. If a noun that can be put into the plural (2.4–6) appears in the plural, so does the number.

The numbers from 2 to 4 as well as **quēzqui** have a plural form in **-n** or **-ntin** (the latter is more frequent).

The base 20 and the sub-bases 5, 10 and 15, which take the absolute ending, have a plural of the type **-tin**.

Cē has the plural form **cēmê** (see later discussion)

Compound numbers take the plural in both elements.

Quēzquin(tin) tlācâ tiquimitta? Ēyin(tin).	*How many people do you (s.) see? Three.*
Ōmentin nēcî in tētepê.	*The mountains appear, two in number*
Niquimitta caxtōltin cihuâ oncēmê	*I see sixteen women*
Niquimitta caxtōltin oncēmê cihuâ	*I see sixteen women*

▶ *Note.* The plural of **chicuacē** is generally **chicuacēntin** rather than **chicuacēmê**, by analogy with the numbers from 2 to 10.

Pluralization is an option. Even with animate nouns, the entire numerical expression can be put in the singular:

Quēzqui tlācatl tiquitta? Ēyi tlācatl niquitta.	*How many people do you (s.) see? I see three people.*

Either way, the agreement must be uniform (noun, number, prefix). You can't say ****ēyi tlācatl niquimitta** or ****ēyi tlācâ niquimitta**.

7.4 Plural of *cē*

Taken to its logical conclusion, the principle of agreement means that **cē** 'one' can certainly appear in the plural (**cēmê**) if, for example, there is a group of people represented by a noun in the plural and the sentence concerns one of these people. This usage is quite different from the English (*partitive*) construction whereby the 'one' becomes the subject and the group to which the one belongs appears after the preposition 'of'. Thus:

Niquimitta cēmê cihuâ	*I see one of the women*

In effect, the Nahuatl says 'one women' instead of 'one of the women', and so the number agreement with the verb prefix is in the plural.

So too with 'one of us', 'one of you (pl.)':

Cēmê amèhuāntin ancochî	*One of you (pl.) is sleeping*
Cēmê tèhuāntin tēhuâ	*One of us is departing*

If the noun cannot be put into the plural, this "partitive" nuance cannot be expressed: **cē calli** can signify either either 'one house' or 'one of the houses' without formal distinction (only the context can decide which is meant).

7.5 Numbers as Predicates

All the words that we have seen can have predicative uses, and in particular, they can take subject prefixes:

Quēzqui inon cuahuitl? – Ca caxtōlli.   *How many of those trees are there? (lit., How*
                                        many are those trees?) – Fifteen.
Anquēzquintin? – Ca timācuīltin.   *How many of you are there? – (We are) five.*

If the number is compound, the subject prefix is put in front of both elements:

Ca timàtlāctin tomōmen   *There are twelve of us (We are twelve)*

7.6 Other Quantifiers

The numbers and the interrogative **quēzqui** belong to a family of words called *quantifiers*. These somewhat peculiar nouns indicate an amount or quantity. In terms of morphology, quantifiers (except for the bases and sub-bases) don't take the absolute suffix and have a plural in **-n** or **-ntin** after a vowel and **-in**, **-tin** or **-intin** after a consonant.

7.6.1 *Miyac*

Miyac (pl. **miyaquin, miyactin, miyaquintin**) is a quantifier signifying 'many, much'. It has the same syntactical characteristics as the numbers:

Àmo timiyaquintin   *We aren't many*
Huĩtz miyac tlācatl   *Many people are coming*
Huĩtzê miyaquintin tlācâ   *Many people are coming*
Miyaquintin huĩtzê in tlācâ *The people are coming in large numbers*
Nictequi miyac xōchitl   *I'm cutting many flowers*
Miyac in ticnequi   *You (s.) want a lot of it (lit., what you want is*
                            much)

7.6.2 *Moch*

Moch or **mochi** 'all' (pl. **mochin, mochtin, mochintin**) has the same characteristics, but it is rarely used predicatively. It appears most often at the head of its clause. English idiom sometimes dictates translation with expressions like 'every', 'everyone', 'everything'.

Moch tlācatl huĩtz   *Everyone is coming*

Mochintin (mochtin) tlācâ huītzê	*Everyone is coming (lit., all are coming)*
Tlacuâ in mochintin pitzōmê	*All the pigs are eating*
Mochintin tlacuâ in pitzōmê	*The pigs are all eating*
Moch quicuâ in pitzōmê	*The pigs are eating everything*
Niccua in mochi nōchtli	*I'm eating the whole prickly pear* or *all the prickly pears*
Moch niccua in nōchtli	(Same translation as previous, with emphasis on the totality, entirety)

Note the agreement in number and person:

Timochintin ticmatî	*We all know it*
Ticmatî in timochtin	*We all know it*

7.7 Counting Nouns

Certain nouns that can be used by themselves also appear in compounds with quantifiers indicating their number. These compounds are generally written as one word, and the number takes a slightly modified form: 1 becomes **cem-**, 2 **ōm-**, 3 **ēy-** or **ē-** (respectively, the prevocalic and the preconsonantal form), 4 **nāuh-**, and the absolute suffixes of the other numbers disappear. Thus:

(1) The nouns **ilhuitl** 'day', **mētztli** 'month',[1] **xihuitl** 'year'

cemilhuitl *one day*	cemmētztli *one month*	cenxihuitl[2] *one year*
ōmilhuitl *two days*	ōmmētztli *two months*	ōnxihuitl *two years*
ēyilhuitl *three days*	ēmētztli *three months*	ēxihuitl *three years*
nāhuilhuitl *four days*	nāuhmētztli[3] *four months*	nāuhxihuitl *four years*
mācuīlilhuitl *five days*	mācuīlmētztli *five months*	mācuīlxihuitl *five years*

If the number is a compound, the counting noun can appear on both elements or only on the second one:

màtlāctli omōmilhuitl/màtlāquilhuitl omōmilhuitl   *twelve days*

Quēzquilhuitl 'how many days' is also written as a single word. The other compounds are generally written as two words: **quēzqui xihuitl** 'how many days', **miyac ilhuitl** 'many days' etc.

---

[1] The word literally means 'moon'.

[2] Also, **cē xihuitl**.

[3] Also, **nāmmētztli**. /w/ frequently assimilates to a following bilabial, that is, **uh** + **m** gives **mm**, **uh** + **p** gives **pp**. This rule is optional.

All these words are temporal phrases indicating a period of time:

Ōmilhuitl ninocāhua   *I'm staying for two days*
Caxtōlxihuitl yōli in chichi   *A dog lives fifteen years*[4]

(2) **Tlamantli** 'thing' is generally used with a quantifier to modify a noun with the meaning 'so many kinds/varieties of. ...' If the noun is animate, there is a plural in **-tin**:

Nicān câ ētlamantli cuahuitl   *There are three sorts of trees here*
Nicān nemî ōntlamantin tlācâ   *Two sorts of people live here*

(3) **Tetl** 'stone' was originally used to count items that are more or less round, for example, **centetl tomātl** 'one tomato', **ōntetl nōchtli** 'two prickly pears', but by the Classical period, its use had spread to any sort of material object: **ētetl calli** 'three houses', **nāuhtetl cuahuitl** 'four trees' etc. Sometimes this noun is also used (with a plural in **-mê**) to count animals: **mācuīltemê tōtoltin** 'five turkeys' (**tōtolin** 'turkey'). This usage is quite widespread, but at the same time it is always optional. One can also say **ēyi calli**, **nāhui cuahuitl** etc.

7.8 *Zan, Ye, Oc*

Along with **ca** (2.7), the most commonly used particles are **zan** 'only, just', **ye** 'already, now' and **oc** 'again, still, now'. **Zan** is very similar to the English 'just' in its range of meaning. While **ye** and **oc** can often be translated respectively with the English words 'already' and 'still', their basic meanings do not correspond exactly to a single English word. **Ye** resembles the Spanish 'ya', which, in addition to being the equivalent of 'already', can signify that a new action/process is taking place as a result of some change. This meaning is often rendered in English with 'now' (e.g., 'now it's time to go', which was previously not the case). The basic sense of **oc** is to signify that the action/process continues to be the same, undergoing no change or variation over the period of time in question. This sense can be represented in English in a number of ways depending on the specific situation: 'now' (the present time without reference to other times), 'still' (continuation of previous action), and 'in the meanwhile' (the

---

[4] Note that as in many languages, Nahuatl uses the determiner to indicate that a singular noun is representative of the category as whole, whereas English regularly uses the plural without the definite article to express this idea (here 'dogs live fifteen years').

current situation as correlated with other events going on at the same time).
Thus:

Àmo nāhuin, zan ēyin	*There aren't four of them, there are only three (lit., they aren't four, they are only three)*
Cuix ye tonyauh?	*Are you (s.) already leaving (going away)?*
Cuix oc ticochi?	*Are you (s.) still sleeping?*

They can be used in nominal clauses (2.7):

Zan ancōconê	*You (pl.) are only children, just children*
Oc niconētl	*I'm still a child*
Ye oquichtli	*He's already a man*

These particles can be combined, in the order **ca/cuix + zan + ye/oc**. Strings
of particles, like **ca zan ye**, are very frequent, and often untranslatable. In a
conversation like

Tlein ticchīhua? – Ca zan oc nitlacua.	*What are you doing? – I'm just eating.*

the response is not translated with 'In truth (**ca**) the only (**zan**) thing I'm doing
at the moment (**oc**) is eating', but such is the sense. In particular, **zan** in some
way "tones down" statements (like 'just'), and turns up especially in polished
style.

Let's look at some noteworthy usages of these particles:

(1) **Ye** in front of a verb is often translated with 'look, here's X VERBing ...':

(Ca) ye huītz in Pedro	*Look, here comes Peter*

(2) **Ca ye** + PERIOD OF TIME (7.7) + **in** + SENTENCE signifies 'it's been so long
that ...':

Ca ye ōmilhuitl in nicmati	*It's been two days that I have known ...*
Ca ye nāuhxihuitl in nicān ninemi	*It's been four years that I have lived here*

> ▶ **Note.** Like many other languages, Nahuatl uses a present tense to
> indicate a process that started in the past and is still going on, but
> English uses the so-called present perfect ('I have VERBed') under such
> circumstances: 'I've lived here for five years (and still do so)'.

(3) **Ca ye cualli** means 'okay', 'fine'.

(4) **Oc** in front of a verb often means 'meanwhile', 'during this time':

Yèhuātl quichīhua tlaxcalli, in nèhuātl oc ninopāca	*She's making tortillas, (as for me) I'm washing*

(5) **Oc** in front of a number is often translated with 'more' or 'other', with **occē** and its compounds generally written as one word:

Nicān câ cē tepētl: cān câ in occē?	*One mountain's here. – Where's the other?*
Quichīhua oc ēyi tlaxcalli	*She's making three other (or three more) tortillas*
Occemilhuitl mocāhua	*He's staying one more day*
Occentlamantli nicmati	*I know one more thing, something else*
Oncatê occentlamantin tlācâ	*There are other sorts of people*

(6) **In zan cē** means 'the same':

Ca yèhuātl in zan cē tlācatl	*He's the same person*

(7) **Zan quēzqui** means 'few':

Nicān câ zan quēzqui calli	*There are only a few houses here*
Zan quēzquintin tlācâ huītzê	*Few people are coming*

7.9 *Ayamo* and *Aoc*

The negation of **ye** is **ayamo** (less commonly **aya**) 'not yet', and that of **oc** is **aoc** or **aocmo** 'no longer':

Cuix ye tēhua? – Ca ayamo, zan oc ninopāca	*Are you leaving already? – Not yet, I'm still washing.*
Cuix oc ticochi? – Ca aoc nicochi, zan ye nìcihui	*Are you still sleeping? – I'm no longer sleeping, I'm in a hurry.*

'No one/nothing any more' (4.9) is translated respectively with **aoc āc**, **aoc tlê**, and 'no one/nothing yet' with **ayamo āc**, **ayamo tlê** (or **ayayāc**, **ayàtlê**).

Aoc tlê niquitta	*I don't see anything any more*
Ayamo āc huītz	*No one is coming yet*

'Nowhere any more' and 'nowhere yet' are translated with **aoccān**, **ayàcān**.

Also note the following expressions with a predicative use of **āc**:

Aoc nāc	*I'm no longer anyone (i.e., am no longer anyone of consequence)*
Aoc tāquê	*We don't exist any more*
Aoc āquê in mēxìcâ	*There are no more Mexica*

VOCABULARY

Quantifiers

cē	*one*	mācuīlli	*five*	quēzqui	*how many?*
ōme	*two*	màtlāctli	*ten*	miyac	*much, many*
ēyi	*three*	caxtōlli	*fifteen*	moch(i)	*all, every*
nāhui	*four*	cempōhualli	*twenty*		

Particles

oc	*still*	ye	*already, now*
aoc(mo)	*no longer*	zan	*only*
aya(mo)	*not yet*		

Nouns

cuahuitl	*tree, wood,*[5] *stick*	tlamantli	*thing*
ilhuitl	*day*	tlaxcalli	*tortilla*
mētztli	*moon, month*	tomātl	*tomato*
nōchtli	*prickly pear*	tōtolin	*(pl. /–tin/ or /-mê/) turkey*
pitzōtl	*(pl. /-mê/) pig*	xihuitl	*year*

Intransitive verb

nēci	*to appear, to be visible*

Transitive verb

tequi	*to cut*

EXERCISES

(a) Translate into Nahuatl.
1. three dogs
2. six rabbits
3. nine fish
4. sixteen snakes
5. fifteen coyotes
6. eight gods
7. eleven women
8. nineteen turkeys
9. seven mountains
10. twelve prickly pears

[5] 'Wood' as material.

   11. eighteen flowers
   12. thirteen tortillas
   13. many pigs
   14. all the Mexica
   15. How many stars?
(b) Translate into English.
   1. Nicān ye huītzê ēyin otomî.
   2. Nicān ye ēyin huītzê in otomî.
   3. In chicuacē tlaxcalli quicuâ ōmentin chichimê.
   4. In cihuātl ca caxtōlli conchīhua in tlaxcalli.
   5. Cuix antēchnōtzâ in timochintin?
   6. Zan quēzquintin niquimitta in cīcitlāltin.
   7. Oncān catê oc ōmentin pitzōmê.
   8. Inìquê on pitzōmê moch quicuâ in tlaōlli.
   9. Ca ye cempōhualilhuitl in mococoa.
   10. In pīpiltin ca nāhuintin in aoc mococoâ, zan oc cēmê mococoâ.
   11. Mēxìco yauh in Pedro, in nèhuātl oc nicān ninocāhua.
   12. Ayamo nēci, ayamo motta in mētztli.
(c) Translate into Nahuatl.
   1. I know many other people.
   2. One of the Otomi is sleeping.
   3. One of us wants fish.
   4. Do you all want tortillas?
   5. It's eight years now that he's been here.
   6. This star is visible (during) six months.
   7. You are not fifteen, you are only fourteen.
   8. The two children are not yet sleeping.
   9. The turkeys are all here.
   10. There are many kinds of tomato ('of many sorts are the tomatoes').
   11. Look, here come four children. Where are the other two?
   12. I'm going to take three more sticks there. The ones that are here are
       few.

Preterite Tense

8.1 Introduction to the Tenses

In Nahuatl, the principal difference between nouns and verbs is the ability of the latter to express tense and mood and the impossibility of this with the former.[1]

Nahuatl verbs have nine tense and mood forms plus two derived conjugations called directional (22.4, 5). Thanks to its morphological regularity, this system, which we will look at one piece at a time, is actually quite simple.

Each of the nine forms is built upon one of the four verb *bases*. In this sense, the term "base" signifies a variant of the verb stem.

We have seen (1.1) that all the forms can be derived from the present tense and that the present form is also the dictionary listing. This dictionary form is called *base 1* (*long base*).

We are now going to study the *preterite* tense. This form pretty much corresponds to the simple past (and occasionally the pluperfect) of English,[2] and is built on base 2.

8.2 Principles for Forming the Preterite

The preterite consists of the following elements:

(1) optionally, the augment ō- (8.8)
(2) the regular verb prefixes
(3) *base 2* (the *short base*) of the verb (8.3–7)
(4) the participial suffix (see later discussion)
(5) in the plural, the suffix -ê.

---

[1] Here we retain the traditional terms "tense" and "mood," although they do not apply in a completely satisfactory manner to Nahuatl.

[2] We will see later that it can also correspond to the future perfect.

Base 2 is in principle a *reduced stem* formed through omission of the final vowel.

The *participial suffix*, which we will frequently encounter, in principle has the form /-k/, but it causes problems by often disappearing. It appears in the form of four variants – /-k/ (written **-c**), ø (i.e., no ending), /-ki/ (**-qui**) and /-kā/ (**-cā**) – whose distribution we will examine at the appropriate time.

Let us now look at the application of these principles in the formation of the preterite.

8.3 Formation of Base 2 by Dropping the Final Vowel

This is the most common method. It is the way to form the short base for verbs that end in **-a** or **-i** *preceded by a single consonant* (except for verbs ending in **-ca**, **-tla** and, in certain cases, **-hua**, **-ya**, **-na**; also, this rule does not apply to monosyllables, see 8.6, 7).

In the preterite singular of these verbs, the participial suffix has the form ø, and thus the preterite is equated with base 2. For example (with the stem/base 1 cited in parentheses):

coch	*he slept* (**cochi**)
ticān	*you (s.) caught it* (**āna**)
nicnōtz	*I called him* (**nōtza**)
niquīz	*I emerged* (**quīza**)
quitlāz	*he threw it* (**tlāza**)

▶ *Note.* The reason the participial suffix cannot appear here in the form /-k/ (**-c**) is because two final consonants are prohibited. But according to what we have seen in other circumstances (in particular with the absolute suffix), we might have expected /-ki/ (**-qui**) with the helping vowel. Forms like **cochqui** do in fact exist, but they do not have the temporal significance of the preterite (see 16.5).

In the plural, which takes the ending **-ê**, the participial suffix appears in the form /-k/ (written **qu-**) because in that case, the cluster of two consonants appears in the interior of the word, where this is permitted:

cochquê	*they slept*
ancānquê	*you (pl.) caught him*
ticnōtzquê	*we called him*
tiquīzquê	*we emerged*
quitlāzquê	*they threw it*

Once you have gotten used to the conventions of writing, there will not be anything surprising in the changes that the stem-final consonant undergoes in the preterite, such as:

quitzauc 'he closed it',   *pl.* quitzaucquê[3] *from* tzacua
(/k^w/ is written **cu-** in front of a vowel, and **-uc** after one)
quicāuh 'he left it',   *pl.* quicāuhquê *from* cāhua
(/w/ is written **hu-** in front of a vowel, and **-uh** after one)
mic 'he died',   *pl.* micquê *from* miqui
(/k/ is written **qu** in front of **i** and **e**, and **c** elsewhere)
nēz 'he appeared'   *pl.* nēzquê *from* nēci
(/s/ is written **c** in front of **i** and **e**, and **z** elsewhere)

and similarly with verbs ending in **-cua, -cui, -hua, -hui, -qui, -ci.**

8.4 Modification of the Final Consonant

Certain changes are more than simply a matter of spelling. Refer to Preliminary Lesson, Complementary Note 6, for the first two changes and to 5.1 (Note) for the third.

(1) Verbs ending in **-ma, -mi**. In word-final position, there is only one nasal, which is written **n**. Thus we have:

ninoxin   *I shaved (myself)* (**xima**)
tlan   *it ended, is finished* (**tlami**)
titoxinquê   *we shaved (ourselves)*

(2) Verbs ending in **-ya, -yi**. In word- or syllable-final position, **-y** is not maintained as such. Instead, it is devoiced in the form **-x**, or sometimes **-z**. Thus we have:

nicpix   *I guarded it* (**piya**)
nitlachix   *I looked* (**chiya**)[4]
celiz   *it blossomed* (**celiya**)
ticpixquê   *we watched it*

(3) Verbs ending in **-ti**.[5] Final **-t** often interchanges with the glottal stop (see 5.1 Note). Traditionally, this is marked only in the preterite of **mati**:

quimâ   'he understood it'

---

[3] Or **quitzacquê** (by simplification of the sequence /k^{w}k/ to /kk/).
[4] With a definite object, **chiya** means 'await' and also 'take care of'. With **tla-**, it means 'look', with the thing that corresponds to the object of the English 'look at' appearing as a locative in Nahuatl (see, e.g., 24.5).
[5] There are no verbs ending in **-ta** apart from **itta** (see 8.7).

and even here only in the singular, the plural being **quimatquê**. The other verb endings in **ti** have a preterite written with -**t**:

tlācat	*he was born, pl.* **tlācatquê (tlācati)**

8.5 Base 2 Formed by Dropping the Final Vowel and Adding a Glottal Stop

This procedure is used with verbs ending in two vowels (always -**ia** and -**oa**). Because the glottal stop is a consonant, the participial ending appears in this case only in the plural (8.3):

quìtô	*he said it, pl.* **quìtòquê (ìtoa)**
mococô	*he fell ill, pl.* **mococòquê (cocoa)**
quilpî	*he bound it, pl.* **quilpìquê (ilpia)**
motlālî	*he sat down, pl.* **motlālìquê (tlālia)**

Verbs following this pattern are very common.

8.6 Base 2 Formed with the Glottal Stop without Dropping the Final Vowel

This procedure is used with monosyllables ending in -**a** (and not those ending in -**i**).[6] There are only three of these, the most usual being **cua** 'to eat'; it is also used with three disyllabic verbs ending in -a, the most common being **zōma** 'to annoy'.[7]

tlacuâ	*he ate, pl.* **tlacuàquê (cua)**
mozōmâ	*he got angry, pl.* **mozōmàquê (zōma)**

8.7 Base 2 without Modification

In certain phonetic contexts, the reduction of the final vowel does not take place, in which case base 2 is identical to base 1. For lack of a better term, we will refer to these as "verbs with vowel-retaining preterites." With base 2 ending in a vowel, the participial suffix is now able to appear in the perfect singular in the form -**c**. This procedure is used with:

(1) verbs ending in -**o**. This -**o** is always lengthened:

panōc	*he passes pl.* **panōquê (pano)**
temōc	*he comes down pl.* **temōquê (temo)**

---

[6] It may be that historically the present of these verbs is actually a contraction of -**aa**, in which case their preterite is completely analogous to that of verbs in -**ia** and -**oa**. See 23.6 for a few non-monosyllables that follow this pattern.

[7] Also see 23.6.

(2) monosyllables ending in **-i** (there are three of these in total). This **-i** is likewise lengthened.

quīc	*he drank it pl.* **quīquê (i)**
quicuīc	*he took it pl.* **quicuīquê (cui)**

(3) verbs ending in **-a** or **-i** that have two consonants in front of the final vowel:

quittac	*he saw it, pl.* **quittaquê (itta)**
àcic	*he arrived, pl.* **àciquê (àci)**

(4) verbs ending in **-tla** and **-ca**:

quimōtlac	*he stoned him, pl.* **quimōtlaquê (mōtla)**
chōcac	*he cried, pl.* **chōcaquê (chōca)**
motēcac	*he lay (himself) down, pl.* **motēcaquê (tēca)**

One exception: **pāca** 'to wash' can also have a preterite **quipāc** 'she washed
him' *pl.* **quipācquê**.

(5) verbs ending in **-hua** *but only if they are intransitive*:

ēhuac	*he departed, pl.* **ēhuaquê (ēhua)**

Transitive verbs ending in **-hua** have the reduced form of base 2:

mēuh	*he got up, pl.* **mēuhquê** (*trans.* **ēhua**)

(6) the impersonal verb **tōna** 'to be warm, sunny':[8]

tōnac	*it was warm*

(7) optionally, intransitive verbs ending in **-ya**:

huēyiyac/huēyix	*he became big pl.* **huēyiyaquê/huēyixquê (huēyiya)**

With the verbs in sections 3–7, the final vowel is not lengthened.

8.8 The Augment

The "augment" **ō-** is not properly speaking a prefix, although it is traditionally
written as a single word with a verb that it directly precedes. In fact:

(1) Certain words can intervene between the augment and the verb (see 13.4
sec. 2),

(2) The helping vowel is not dropped from the subject prefix: **ōnicoch** 'I have
slept' (and not ****ōncoch**), **ōquinōtz** 'he called him' (not ****ōcnotz**). That
is, the augment is ignored in determining whether or not the helping vowel
is needed.

---

[8] The original sense is 'to prosper'. In this meaning, it can take a human subject and conjugates
normally, with the plural **tōnaquê** 'they prospered'.

All forms of the preterite can be preceded by ō-, but its use is not random. The augment indicates that a completed event can have consequences at a later time – in particular, at the moment of speaking. This notion of "consequence" is taken in a very broad sense, and the mere fact that this event can be spoken of can ultimately be considered a consequence of it. The result of this is that in conversation the preterite almost always appears with the augment, and the preterite without augment is reserved for historical narrative and myth (in such texts, the preterite with augment can be found indicating that one event took place before another). The upshot is that even though the Nahuatl preterites with and without the augment correspond broadly to the English present perfect ('has VERBed') and simple past ('VERBed') tenses respectively, the distribution of the two forms is not the same. The unaugmented forms are usually translated with the simple past, but the augmented ones can be translated with either the present perfect or preterite as dictated by English idiom.[9]

> ▶ *Note.* In front of the directional prefix **on-** (6.1), the augment may or may not be written:
>
> onquīz *or* ōonquīz   *he has emerged*

8.9 The Tense with *Ayamo*

The Nahuatl preterite differs in some details of usage from the past tenses of English. One of these differences concerns the translation of 'not yet' (**ayamo**, 7.10). In situations where English says 'I haven't eaten yet', Nahuatl uses the present tense: **ayamo nitlacua.**

Nahuatl indicates in this way that the action of 'eating' has not yet been put into operation. The use of the preterite with **ayamo** (**ayamo ōnitlacuâ**) indicates that the operation has not yet been brought to completion, which is translated as 'I have not *finished* eating yet'. In effect, one might think of this idiom as saying 'it cannot yet be said that I have eaten' (because I am still eating).

Naturally, **ayamo** is used with the present in the great majority of instances.

8.10 Preterite of Irregular Verbs

(1) **Yauh** has (ō)yâ 'he went', *pl.* (ō)yàquê as its preterite.
(2) **Huītz** has (ō)huītza 'he came', *pl.* (ō)huītzâ as its preterite.

---

[9] For those who know French, it can be said as a rule of thumb that the Nahuatl preterite appears without the augment in the sorts of contexts where the French *passé simple* is used, while the preterite with the augment corresponds to the *passé composé* (or sometimes the pluperfect).

As can be seen, this is not a regular preterite, as there is no participial suffix.

(Ō)huītza does not have the same sense as the preterite (ō)huāllâ from huāllauh 'to come' (6.1). If you say that someone ōhuāllâ 'he has come', this indicates that he is still there. If you say ōhuītza, this signifies that he came but has already gone away again. We will see (22.1) that such a nuance is characteristic of the pluperfect. Huītz has no other forms. The corresponding forms of huāllauh (see 6.1) are used for all the other tenses.

(3) Câ has (ō)catca pl. (ō)catcâ as its preterite. Once again, this is not a true preterite, and catca also has the sense of the imperfect (see 9.10). The form catca (as well as the other tenses of câ) serves in addition to conjugate nominal predicates in the past. The subject prefix appears on both the nominal predicate and on catca, for example:

| nitēuctli nicatca | *I was a lord* |
| ticualli ōticatca | *you (s.) were good* |

VOCABULARY

Intransitive verbs

celiya	*to sprout, to blossom*	tlami	*to end, to finish*
huēyiya	*to grow big*	tlācati	*to be born*
pano	*to pass*	tōna	*to prosper* (impersonal:
temo	*to come down, to descend*		*it is warm*)

Transitive verbs

chiya	*to await, to watch*	piya	*to guard, to save*[10]
	(tlachiya: *to look*)	tzacua	*to close, to shut*
mōtla	*to stone*[11]		

EXERCISES

(a) Put the following verbs in the first person singular and plural of the preterite with augment (for transitive verbs, add the object prefix of the third person singular). Example: itta – ōniquittac – ōtiquittaquê.

1. caqui
2. chīhua

[10] Also 'to have' (see 11.5).

[11] The object of **mōtla** represents the person (more rarely, thing) at which something is being thrown (properly, stones). Thus, **nicmōtla** signifies 'I throw stones at him'. If you simply wish to say 'I throw stones', you must say **nitlamōtla**, lit. 'I throw stones at something' or use a different verb (**nictlāza tetl**).

    3. cua

    4. cuīca

    5. ìcihui

    6. i

    7. ìcuiloa

    8. ìtoa

    9. nemi

   10. nequi

   11. tequi

   12. tlazòtla

   13. tlātia

   14. tolīnia

   15. tzàtzi

   16. yōli

(b) Put the sentences from Lesson 6, Exercise b, into the preterite.

(c) Translate into English.

    1. Cuix ye Tlaxcallān ōticatca?

    2. Ōmpa Cuauhnāhuac ōniquimittac.

    3. Ayamo oncān nitlachiya.

    4. Ōmpa ōnitlachix, àmo ōniquittac.

    5. Tlein ōticchīuh? – Ca àtle, zan ōnicoch.

    6. Zan ōnicnōtz, ye huītz.

    7. Tlein ōanquichīuhquê? – Zan ōtictecquê xōchitl.

    8. Ye ōmic in Pedro.

    9. Ca zan xōchitl in ōniquilpî.

   10. Cuix ōmpa ōammomatquê in Mēxìco?

   11. Àmo ōmpa ōtiyàquê, zan nicān ōtitocāuhquê.

   12. Inin cihuātl ōquitlazòtlac cē otomitl.

(d) Translate into Nahuatl.

    1. The Otomi appeared there, they threw stones at us ("they stoned us").

    2. Who shouted?

    3. I looked after ("guarded") the children. They didn't cry, they only sang.

    4. The men cut (pret.) stones.

    5. The children haven't gotten up ("raised themselves") yet.

    6. Have you (pl.) heard this? – Yes, Peter called us.

    7. We have already eaten the tortillas, we have already drunk the water.

    8. Everyone has already left. They have gone down to Cuernavaca.

9. Peter has already lain down. I think (**ninomati**, 6.6, 7), he is not yet sleeping.
10. Few people have written.
11. Peter came, we spoke, he left for Mexico.
12. Peter has come, he hasn't left yet.
13. It is here that we were born and that we grew up ("became big").

Imperative/Optative, Vocative, Future, Imperfect

9.1 Imperative/Optative

With the verb forms that we have so far studied, the speaker makes factual statements (whether true or not) about the world. In the optative, the speaker is making a statement about how he/she *would like the world to be*. Basically, the speaker views the action of a verb in the optative as being in some way contingent, and a main verb in the optative expresses a *wish* or *command* (later we will see that it is also used to express hypothetical conditions, see Lesson 34).

Let us first look at the second person, where this form mostly corresponds to the English imperative (i.e., a direct command). (Occasionally, the second person optative is more of a wish, along the lines of 'may you live in interesting times'; see 9.5 for more on this usage.) This form is composed of:

(1) a subject prefix **x-** or **xi-** (9.2) followed by any other prefixes as appropriate (definite object, directional, reflexive, indefinite object)
(2) *base 3* (the *middle base*) of the verb (see later discussion)
(3) in the plural, the special suffix -**cān** (9.3).

Base 3 is much simpler to form than base 2:

(1) In verbs ending in two vowels (-**ia**, -**oa**), base 3 is made by dropping the final vowel (without adding the glottal stop, unlike base 2, cf. 8.5). This gives, for example, the following imperatives:

ximotlāli	*sit down* (**tlālia**)
xinēchpalēhui	*help me* (**palēhuia**)
xitlàto	*speak* (**itoa**)
xictēmo	*look for it* (**tēmoa**)[1]

[1] Do not confuse **tēmoa**, a transitive verb 'search/look for', with **temo**, the intransitive verb 'come down, descend'.

(2) In all other regular verbs, it is identical to base 1:

xitlapōhua	*read, count* (**pōhua**)
xicnōtza	*call him* (**nōtza**)
xitlachiya	*watch, look* (**chiya**)
xēhua	*leave* (**ēhua**)
ximocuepa	*come back* (**cuepa** return)
xitlacua	*eat* (**cua**)
xicochi	*sleep* (**cochi**)
xiqui	*drink it* (**i**)
xinēci	*show yourself* (**nēci**)
xipano	*pass* (**pano**)

9.2 Variants of *x*-

The variants **x**- and **xi**- appear in the same circumstances as **n**- and **ni**- and **t**- and **ti**-, that is, **x**- in front of a vowel (e.g., **xēhua**), **xi**- in front of a consonant (e.g., **xicochi**).

Also, there is the same variation with **o** in front of -**c**-**on**- (6.3):

xoconcua	*eat it up*

9.3 Lengthening of the Stem Vowel

The vowel preceding the plural suffix -**cān** is lenghtened:[2]

(1) in verbs in -**o**:

xipanōcān	*pass (pl.)*
xitemōcān	*come down (pl.)*

(2) in monosyllabic stems:

xiquīcān	*drink it (pl.)*
xiccuācān	*eat it (pl.)*

(3) in verbs in -**ia**, -**oa**:

ximotlālīcān	*sit down (pl.)*
xitlàtōcān	*speak (pl.)*

---

[2] In fact, the underlying vowel is long in these stems, but every long vowel is shortened in word-final position (except in monosyllables). Hence, the suffix allows the original length to be retained.

Otherwise, it remains short:

xicochicān	*sleep (pl.)*
xitlapōhuacān	*read, count (pl.)*
xēhuacān	*leave (pl.)*
xitlachiyacān	*watch (pl.)*

9.4 Imperative/Optative in Irregular Verbs

(1) **Yauh** is irregular: **xiyauh** 'go (s.)', **xihuiyān** 'go (pl.)':

> As we have seen (8.10), **huītz** has no optative; that of **huāllauh** is used instead: **xihuāllauh** 'come (s.)', **xihuālhuiyān** 'come (pl.)'.

(2) **Câ**: base 3 is built upon a different stem, **ye-**: **xiye** 'be, stay (s.)', **xiyecān** 'be, stay (pl.)'.

9.5 The Optative in Other Persons

In the first and third person, the usual subject prefixes are used. However, the verb must be preceded by a particle, either **mā** or **tlā**. **Mā** is most common and generally expresses a wish. **Tlā**, however, expresses a hypothesis, although like the English 'if only', it can be taken as a wish. These forms are translated in English with 'may I, we, he, they' + VERB or with "let me, us, him, them' + VERB, depending on the extent to which the phrase is taken to be respectively a wish or a command. The Nahuatl optative covers both these senses:

Mā ōmpa tihuiyān	*Let's go there*
Mā ticcuācān in etl	*Let's eat the beans*
Mā niquitta in	*May I see this, Let me see this*
Mā quitta in	*Let him/may he see this*
Mā tlàtōcān	*Let them/may they speak*

As a rhetorical figure, the optative can be used to indicate resigned acquiescence in a situation that is not in fact desired (English has a similar usage with 'let'). For instance, a peasant faced with dying crop may say:

Mā ontlami in tlaōlli	*Let the corn be done with, Never mind if the corn runs out (lit., finishes)*

The point is not that he does want the crop to die but that he cannot do anything to prevent this and is expressing his acquiescence in the inevitable.

Mā can also appear with the second person, giving the nuance of an eager or polite request:

Mā xitlàtōcān	*Do speak (pl.), please speak*

In all these instances, **mā** can be replaced with **tlā**, which gives a nuance of heightened politeness:

Tlā niquitta in	*Could I see this?*
Tlā xitlatōcān	*Would you (pl.) like to speak?*
Tlā tlàto	*If only he would speak*

Mā and **tlā** belong to the same series of particles as **ca** and **cuix**, and they take the same position in relation to the other particles (7.8):

Mā zan oc xitlacua	*Go (s.) on eating*

9.6 Negation of the Optative

The imperative/optative has a special negation. For all persons this is **mācamo**:

Mācamo xicchīhua in	*Don't (s.) do this*
Mācamo quicōhua etl	*Let him not buy beans*

9.7 Vocative of Nouns

If, in talking to someone, you address that person with a noun, the noun/name assumes a special form called the vocative.

There are two ways to form the vocative, one used by men and one by women. That is, the method to be used is determined by the gender of the speaker and not that of the addressee.

(1) Men add the suffix **-é**. The acute accent reflects the fact that contrary to regular practice this ending bears the word accent:

Cihuātlé!	*Woman!*
Pedroé!	*Peter!*
Mēxìcàé!	*Mexica!*
Tētēuctiné!	*Lords!*

As can be seen, the vocative **-é** is added to the complete noun form (including the absolute or plural suffix as appropriate) and not to its stem. The helping vowel **-i** of the absolute suffix is dropped in front of **-é**:

Pillé!	*Child!*
Tēuctlé!	*Lord!*

(2) Women simply shift the accent from the next-to-last to the last syllable:

Cihuátl!	*Woman!*
Pedró!	*Peter!*
Tētēuctín!	*Lords!*
Pillí!	*Child!*

The vocatives are the only words to be accented on the last syllable (Preliminary Lesson, Complementary Note 1).

9.8 Morphology of the Future

The future is composed of:

(1) regular prefixes
(2) base 3 (the middle base) of the verb
(3) the suffix /-s/ (written -z)
(4) the participial suffix (see 8.2)

We have seen in connection with the preterite (8.3–7) that the participial suffix appears in the singular only after a vowel. Because the future always has a consonant (-z) in front of it, this suffix appears only in the plural:

nicochiz *I will sleep*	ticochizquê *we will sleep*
timocāhuaz *you (s.) will stay*	ammocāhuazquê *you (pl.) will stay*
quinōtzaz *he will call her*	quinōtzazquê *they will call her*

The vowel lengths are determined in the same way as in the optative plural (9.3):

panōz *he will pass*	motlālīz *he will sit down*
tlàtōz *he will speak*	tlacuāz *he will eat*
quīz *he will drink it*	

The future of **yauh** is **yāz**.

The future of **câ** is **yez**. **Yez** makes it possible to conjugate a nominal predicate in the future (with the subject prefix on both the verb and the predicate noun):

Titēuctli tiyez	*You (s.) will be a lord*

9.9 Meaning of the Future

The future in Nahuatl covers the uses of the future in English, but it also includes many uses of the English infinitive (we will look at these later).

In the second person, it can have the sense of a weakened imperative:

| Ticcōhuaz octli | *You (s.) are to buy pulque* |
| Tictequiz in metl | *You (s.) are to cut the maguey* |

The future is obligatory with adverbs referring to the future. Nahuatl says:

Mōztla niyāz Mēxìco   *I'll go to Mexico tomorrow*

and does not use the present tense in conjunction in such contexts the way English does (e.g., 'I leave for Mexico tomorrow').

It is often not accurate to translate the Nahuatl future with the simple future in English. For instance, one text recounts that when the Lord of the Dead saw Quetzalcoatl arrive, he asked him with some disquiet:

Tlein ticchīhuaz, Quetzalcōhuātlé?

Clearly, this cannot be translated with 'What will you do?'. 'What are you going to do?' is a bit better. In fact, the sense is, 'What are you preparing to do?', and it borders on 'What do you want to do?' Hence, it is sometimes appropriate to translate the Nahuatl future with 'want to VERB' or 'have to VERB'.

9.10 The Imperfect

The Nahuatl imperfect is generally similar to the imperfect of the Romance languages. That is, it signifies a repeated or continuing process in the past and is translated with the English 'used to do', 'would do' or 'was doing' (these translations can be too heavy handed, as English sometimes marks this imperfect meaning with an appropriate adverb used with the simple past tense).

The imperfect is composed of:

(1) the regular prefixes
(2) base 1
(3) the suffix -**ya**
(4) in the plural, the suffix -' (i.e., the glottal stop):

| nicochiya | *I was sleeping* | tlachiyayâ | *they used to look* |

Lengthening of the vowel in front of -**ya** takes place under the same conditions as with base 3 (9.3). With verbs in -**ia** and -**oa**, the final -**a** is retained (because we are using base 1), and it is this vowel that is lengthened.

| tlàtoāya | *he would speak* | quilpiāya | *he used to bind it* |
| tlacuāya | *he ate* | panōya | *he would pass* |

Yauh has two imperfects: **huiya** and **yāya**, the second of which was considered "not very elegant" by the old grammarians.

We have seen that **câ** has the imperfect **catca** (8.10).

VOCABULARY

Nouns

etl	*beans*[3]	octli	*pulque*[4]
metl	*maguey*[5]	Quetzalcōhuātl	(divine name)

Transitive verbs

cōhua	*to buy*	pōhua	*to count, to read*
cuepa	*to turn, to return*		(mo-: *to be arrogant,*
	(mo-: *return*)		*to be presumptuous*)
palēhuia	*to help*	tēmoa	*to look for, to search for*

Adverbs[6]

āxcān	*today, now*	mōtzla	*tomorrow*
yālhua	*yesterday*		

Particles

mā	(optative marker)	tlā	*if*

EXERCISES

(a) Put the following verbs in the second person singular and plural for the
imperative/optative, future and imperfect (if the verb is transitive, give it
the third person singular object prefix).

1. āna
2. caqui
3. chīhua
4. cocoa
5. cui
6. cuīca
7. ìcihui
8. ilpia
9. ìcuiloa
10. piya
11. temo

---

[3] These are the black beans called 'frijol' in Spanish.

[4] "Aztec wine" obtained by fermenting maguey juice.

[5] A sort of agave whose fibers were used for clothing and whose core produces a drinkable
liquid (see note 4).

[6] Temporal adverbs are actually just a variety of the locative (5.4).

12. tēmoa
13. tlātia
14. tzàtzi
15. zōma

(b) Convert the following vocatives in the female idiom to the corresponding male version.
   1. Chichí!
   2. Chichimê!
   3. Cihuâ´!
   4. Oquichtlí!
   5. Pīpiltín!
   6. Tōchtlí!
   7. Teōtl!
   8. Otomítl!

(c) Translate into English.
   1. Mōztla Xōchimīlco tiyāzquê: ōmpa tlaxcalli ticcuāzquê, octli tiquīzquê.
   2. Àmo quipōhuaz in Pedro in etl, zan quitlāzaz.
   3. Nicān câ tomātl, cuix ticcōhuaz centetl?
   4. Cān amàcizquê mōztla? Cuix zan Tlaxcallān?
   5. Āxcān niccāhua inin nacatl, zan mōztla niccuāz.
   6. Oc huēyiyazquê inìquê in cōconê.
   7. Mācamo xiquintolīni in pīpiltin: ca chōcazquê.
   8. Mācamo xonyauh, zan ximotlāli: titlàtōzquê.
   9. Xiccōhuacān inon nōchtli, ca cualli.
   10. Yālhua mococoāya in Pedro; in nèhuātl ōnoconittac.
   11. Tlein ticchīhuaya? – Zan ninopācaya.
   12. Pīpiltiné, mācamo xiquimmōtlacān in pitzomê.
   13. Nicān câ nacatl, etl, tlaxcalli, tomātl: mā zan titlacuācān.
   14. Xiquittacān inon oquichtli, cuix àmo yèhuātl in Pedro?
   15. Àmo nicmatiya in āc amèhuāntin.

(d) Translate into Nahuatl.
   1. Peter, are you going to Mexico tomorrow? – No, I'll just stay here and I'll read.
   2. I've bought tomatoes, meat: we'll eat them tomorrow, the women will make tortillas.
   3. They're still children, they shouldn't (won't) drink pulque.
   4. Are you (s.) going to write? – I already wrote yesterday.
   5. These children aren't going to sing. – They're going to cry.
   6. Yesterday I wasn't here. – I was making purchases in Mexico.
   7. Stay (s.) there, don't come. – Peter is sick.

8. Don't (pl.) eat this meat, it isn't good.
9. I'd like to (let me) sit here. – Then do sit down.
10. Hide (pl.) this! – Here comes Peter, he's going to get mad.
11. This child was throwing stones at the dogs – That's not good.
12. Come down (pl.), don't go away, we'll help you.
13. Please look for Peter. – Yes, I'll run there. Peter was there yesterday.
14. I'm not going to speak to you any more. – May you die wherever you go.
15. Don't (s.) get mad. – I didn't know what you were doing.

Possessed Forms of the Noun

10.1 Morphology of the Possessed Form

Nouns in Nahuatl can be put in the possessed form, which corresponds to phrases in English with a noun and a possessive adjective (e.g., 'my', 'your', 'his' etc.). The possessed form consists of:

(1) a possessive prefix (10.3)
(2) a noun stem (without absolutive suffix)
(3) in general, the possessive suffix (10.2)
(4) a special plural as appropriate (10.4)

10.2 Forms of the Possessive Suffix

The possessive suffix in principle has the form /-w/ (written **-uh**), but it has the same peculiarity as the participial suffix (8.2), namely that it is often dropped, especially after a consonant. The variants of the possessive suffix number four and are reminiscent of those of the participial suffix: /-w/ (**-uh**), **-ø** (no ending), /-wi/ (**-hui**), /-wā/ (**-huā**).

Most frequently, /-w/ appears after a vowel and **-ø** after a consonant, but this principle is subject to qualification (particularly if the stem ends with a short vowel, see 10.7–9).

10.3 Possessive Prefixes

The possessive prefixes have the following forms:

Singular		Plural	
1st person	**no-**	1st person	**to-**
2nd person	**mo-**	2nd person	**amo-**
3rd person	**ī-**	3rd person	**īm-**

Note that **īm-** naturally becomes **īn-** in front of a consonant other than **p** or **m**.

Thus, with stems ending in a consonant (the absolute form is given in parentheses):

nocal	*my house(s)* (**calli**)
mopil	*your (s.) child* (**pilli**)
īmich	*his/her fish* (**michin**)
totōtol	*our turkey* (**tōtolin**)
amotlaxcal	*your (pl.) tortilla(s)* (**tlaxcalli**)
īnnōch	*their prickly pears* (**nōchtli**)

and with stems ending in a vowel in which the possessive suffix appears:

noteuh	*my stone(s)* (**tetl**)
mochichiuh	*your (s.) dog* (**chichi**)
īcihuāuh	*his woman (wife)* (**cihuātl**)
toteōuh	*our god* (**teōtl**) etc.

If the stem of the noun begins with a vowel, the **-o** of the prefixes disappears:

nāuh	*my water* (**ātl**)
moquich	*your (s.) man (husband)* (**oquichtli**)
tāltepēuh	*our town* (**āltepētl**)
ameuh	*your (pl.) beans* (**etl**)

but the **ī-** of the third person is retained:

īāuh	*his water*
īoquich	*her husband*

However, in front of an **i** (long or short), whatever number of consonants follow, the **ī-** of the third person can be freely kept or dropped:[1]

icpal *or* īicpal	*his seat* (**icpalli**)
īx *or* īīx	*his eyes* (**ixtli** 'eyes, face')

However, noun stems beginning with /iCC/ (short **i** followed by two consonants) manifest phenomena similar to those of verbs (3.7 and 6.7). In this case, there is a choice between eliding either the **o-** of the first or second person possessive prefix or the **i-** of the stem:

nocpal	*my seat*
nicpal	*my seat*

---

[1] See 8.8 for a similar phenomenon with the augment **ō-**.

10.4 Plural of the Possessed Forms

The plural[2] has the suffix -**huān** (actually, the -**huā** variant of the possessive suffix plus the plural marker -**n**). On account of its phonological shape, this suffix is permissible after consonants as well as vowels. It is used with all possessed forms, whatever the formation of their absolute plural (2.4–6) may be. In particular, there is never any reduplication of the possessed plural:

nopilhuān	*my children*	tocihuāhuān	*our wives*
momichhuān	*your (s.) fishes*	amochichihuān	*your (pl.) dogs*
ītōtolhuān	*his turkeys*	īmoquichhuān	*their husbands*
ītōchhuān	*his rabbits*	īnteōhuān	*their gods*

Naturally, nouns that do not take a plural in the absolute form do not take one in the possessed form either.

10.5 Syntax of Possessed Nouns

Possessed nouns have the same syntactical characteristics as other nouns. They can be predicates:

Ca nocal	*It's my house*
(Ca) tinocihuāuh	*You (s.) are my wife*
(Ca) antopilhuān	*You (pl.) are our children*
(Ca) tīpilhuān	*We are his children*

When they act as subject or object, they take the same constructions regarding determiners and quantifiers that other nouns do:

Niquintlazòtla in nopilhuān	*I love my children*
Ye ōmpa huītz cē nochichiuh	*Look, one of my dogs is coming from there*
Xiccui ōntetl nonōch	*Take two of my prickly pears*

10.6 Constructions Indicating Possession

(1) If you want to express the possessor in English, it appears as the object of the preposition 'of' after the possessed noun or the possessor noun is put in the genitive case (normally marked in the singular with the addition of **s**). In Nahuatl, the possessor is not marked, and it is the "possessed" that appears in the possessed form. Whereas in English we say 'the house of

---

[2] That is, the plural of the "possessed" and not of the "possessor," which, as we have seen, is marked only by the prefix.

the woman' or 'the woman's house', the Nahuatl equivalent literally means 'the woman her house'.

Niquitta in īcal cihuātl	*I see the woman's house*
Niquitta in cihuātl īcal	*I see the woman's house*

One can also say: **in īcal in cihuātl** or **in cihuātl in īcal.**
Such expressions can appear in a "chain":

In īntlaxcal (in) īchichihuān noquich	*The tortillas of my husband's dogs*
In ītōtolhuān in īcihuāuh Pedro	*The turkeys of Peter's wife*

(2) The two elements of the possessive construction (the possessor and the possessed) are commonly separated by being placed on either side of the predicate. This is a matter of topicalizing the possessor. This nuance can be rendered with a translation like:

In cihuātl niquitta in īcal	*As for the woman, I see her house*
In Pedro (ca) mococoa in īcihuāuh	*As for Peter, his wife is sick*
Inon cihuātl (ca) yālhua ōmic in īoquich	*As for that woman, her husband died yesterday* or *That woman has a husband who died yesterday*

(3) A nominal predicate statement that includes an adjective or quantifier can be the equivalent of an English sentence with the verb 'to have'. The possessor of the Nahuatl noun becomes the subject of the English verb, which takes the noun (plus the modifier) as its direct object.

Ca cualli in īcal Pedro[3]	*Peter's house is beautiful* or *Peter has a beautiful house*
In Pedro ca cualli in īcal	*As for Peter, his house is beautiful* or *Peter has a beautiful house*
In nèhuātl zan ōmen in notōtolhuān	*As for me, I've got only two turkeys (my turkeys number only two)*

(4) The possessor can appear in the form of an emphatic pronoun, in any person. This is a way to assert possession:

Ca nèhuātl notlaxcal	*This is my tortilla*
Cuix amèhuāntin amocal?	*Is the house yours?*

---

[3] Or **in Pedro īcal** or **in īcal in Pedro** or **in Pedro in īcal** and so on with all the other examples; see the earlier discussion.

(5) A locative cannot be the possessor of a noun. Instead, the locative simply appears as a modifier of that noun:

in Cuauhnāhuac cihuâ	*the women of Cuernavaca*
in Mēxìco tētēuctin	*the lords of Mexico*
in nicān tlācâ	*the people here, the local residents, the natives*

That is, something like 'the women in Cuernavaca' etc., and it is not possible to say **in Cuauhnāhuac īcihuāhuān etc.

10.7 Dropping of Short Vowels in the Possessed Form

There are some morphological difficulties associated with the possessed form of nouns ending in -**atl** or -**itl** (i.e., nouns with stems ending in a short vowel). The rule, which has exceptions that we will look at in 10.8, is to drop the final -**atl** or -**itl** in the possessed form. Note that for practical purposes, we can speak of dropping -**atl** or -**itl**, it is, strictly speaking, only the stem-final -**a** or -**i** that is dropped (because the absolutive ending -**tl** never appears with possessed nouns anyway). Thus:

nonac	*my meat* (**nacatl**)
nocuauh	*my tree, stick* (**cuahuitl**)
nopetl	*my mat* (**petlatl**)
nocax	*my bowl* (**caxitl**)
nocuīc	*my song* (**cuīcatl**)
nocōn	*my jar* (**cōmitl**) (note how the final -**m** becomes -**n**)

If dropping the vowel in this way leaves two consonants in word-final position, the helping vowel -**i** is normally added:

nocōzqui	*my necklace* (**cōzcatl**)
notlatqui	*my goods* (**tlatquitl**)

Some words end in -**āitl** or -**ēitl** in the absolute form. These words follow the rule laid out in the earlier discussion, and in that case the long vowel is retained, which is unusual in word-final position:[4]

nocuē	*my skirt* (**cuēitl**)
nomā	*my hand* (**māitl**)
nāxcā	*my property* (**āxcāitl**)

▶ *Note.* The word **āxcāitl** is used in expressions like **inin ca nāxcā** 'it's mine', lit., 'this is my possession'. If one wishes to say 'this house is mine',

---

[4] In principle, only short vowels appear in word-final position (9.3 n.2).

one can either similarly say **inin calli ca nāxcā** or repeat the noun: **inin calli ca nocal**, lit. 'this house is my house'.

10.8 Retention of Short Vowels in Nouns Ending in *-atl*, *-itl*

The rule in 10.7 is violated in three specific instances in which it is not applied and the possessive suffix appears without loss of the vowel:

(1) the possessed noun is animate:

> notlācauh   *my person, slave* (**tlācatl**)
> notīciuh   *my doctor* (**tīcitl**)

Needless to say, these forms have a plural: **notlācahuān, notīcihuān.**[5]

(2) the noun ends in **-quitl, -titl, -chitl** preceded by a vowel:[6]

> notequiuh   *my task, job* (**tequitl**)
> īpatiuh   *its price* (**patitl**)[7]
> noxōchiuh   *my flower* (**xōchitl**)

(3) after the dropping of the final vowel, the word would be monosyllabic, whereas its absolute form is disyllabic. Here we have a manifestation of what we will call the "constraint against short words," which could be characterized as a general tendency to lengthen any form that is considered too short.

> This includes words like **āmatl** 'paper', **omitl** 'bone' and in a general way all nouns whose stem has the structure /VCV/.[8] If these words obeyed the rule laid out in 10.7, then given that the **-o** of the prefix disappears (10.3), we would have ****nān**, ****non**. Such a reduction in the number of syllables is what Nahuatl seeks to avoid when it restores:

> nāmauh   *my paper*
> nomiuh   *my bone*

> Also note that the noun undergoes the same treatment with the third person prefix: **īāmauh** 'his paper' and not ****īān**, even though the latter would be disyllabic.

---

[5] The same goes for **chichi: nochichiuh** 'my dog' (and not ****nochich**).

[6] This explains why the form **notlatqui** is used and not ****notlatquiuh** (10.7).

[7] This word appears only in the possessed form. It is also the only noun stem that ends in **-ti** preceded by a vowel.

[8] Remember that V signifies any vowel and C any consonant.

(4) stems in /VCCV/ are also treated in this way:

nilhuiuh	*my day, my feast*
nolhuiuh	*my day, my feast*

and not ****nilhui**, ****nolhui**, even though these forms would be disyllabic as the absolutive ones.

10.9 Possessed Form of Monosyllables

Recall the rule of 10.8 sec. 3:

> RULE: The possessed form cannot be monosyllabic if the absolutive form is disyllabic.

This rule also affects another type of words, namely those whose stem has the form /VC/, which have an absolutive ending **-tli**, and so are disyllabic. Words like **òtli** 'path', **ichtli** 'thread', **itztli** 'obsidian, razor' would have the possessed forms ****nô**, ****nich**, ****nitz**, and to avoid these forms, the possessive suffix appears in its variant form **-hui**, that is, with the additional of the helping vowel:

nòhui	*my path*
nichhui[9]	*my thread*
nitzhui	*my obsidian, razor*

▶ *Note.* It is also the case with these words that the third person is treated in the same way as the other persons: **īòhui** 'his path' (and not ****īô**, even though this form wouldn't violate the principle prohibiting a reduction in the number of syllables).

Here the rule is less absolute. Certain early grammars give **nich** as a correct form for 'my thread'. Also, the rule is not applied if the stem vowel is long. We have seen that **nīx** is the form for 'my eyes' and not ****nīxhui**.

Optionally, the same procedure can be used to maintain as a trisyllabic word a noun whose stem has the shape /VCVC/. Thus, for **oquichtli** 'man, husband' we find:

noquich/noquichhui	*my husband*

Of course, there are no problems with nouns whose stem has the form /V/. Here the absolutive and the possessed forms are both monosyllabic:

nāuh	*my water* (**ātl**)
neuh	*my beans* (**etl**)

---

[9] The form **nochhui** is also found.

10.10 Vocative of Possessed Forms

The vocative of possessed forms is formed in the same way as those of the absolutive forms (9.7):

nocihuāhué!   *my wife!*
nopilhuāné!   *my children!*

The helping -**i** is dropped before -**é**:

nocōzqué!   *my jewel!* (said to a child)

The addition of the vocative ending -**é** to a consonant stem does not cause -**uh** to be used (i.e., the regular possessed form is determined first and the vowel of the vocative is then added to this form):

nopilé!   *my child!* (and not ****nopilhué!**)

VOCABULARY

Nouns

āmatl	*paper, amate*[10]	īxtli	*eye, face*[11]
āxcāitl	*property*	māitl	*hand*
caxitl	*bowl*	omitl	*bone*
cōmitl	*jar*	òtli	*path, road, way*
cōzcatl	*necklace, jewel*	patitl	*price*
cuēitl	*skirt*	petlatl	*mat, petate*[12]
cuīcatl	*song*	tequitl	*job*[13]
ichtli	*thread*[14]	tīcitl	*(pl. /R–'/) doctor, midwife*
icpalli	*seat*	tlatquitl	*property*
itztli	*obsidian, razor*		

EXERCISES

(a) Put the following nouns into the possessed form (with third person singular possessed form).

   1. cōhuātl
   2. cōcōhuâ

[10] Traditional paper is a sort of parchment made from the fiber of the maguey plant. Today sketches made on this paper are designated with the term 'amate'.

[11] **Īxtli** signifies the 'eyes, look' and hence the 'face (facial) expression'.

[12] Petates of various sizes still are important as coverings used as protection against the sun and as places to sit, kneel or lie down on.

[13] Originally, 'tribute' or 'physical labor' (corvée) owed to a lord. In the colonial period, this word took on the general sense of 'work'.

[14] Traditional thread made out of maguey fiber.

3. pitzōtl
4. pitzōmê
5. tōchtli
6. tōtōchtin
7. tīcitl
8. tītīcî
9. cuahuitl
10. metl
11. tetl
12. tlaōlli

(b) Translate into English.

1. Miyac in quicuâ notōchhuān.
2. Cuix àmo ticcuāz in meuh?
3. Cuix ye ticmati in tāltepēuh?
4. Ca miyac in moxōchiuh, cuix ye moch ōticpōuh?
5. Ōticcuàquê in mocihuāuh cualli ītlaxcal.
6. Ye huītzê in Tlaxcallān tētēuctin.
7. Ca cualli in mocuīc.
8. Àmo quimati in īòhui.
9. In Mexìco cihuâ ca cualli in īncuē.
10. Mācamo xiccui inin petlatl: ca nèhuātl nopetl.
11. Inin tlaōlli ca moch nāxcā, àmo Pedro iāxcā.

(c) Translate into Nahuatl.

1. As for Peter, all his turkeys have died
2. The son of the doctor of Xochimilco has beautiful eyes.
3. Do you know the road (to) Tlaxcala?
4. The woman is looking for her thread.
5. Have you (pl.) already eaten all your meat?
6. Yes, we've left only our bones.
7. As for my wife's jewels, I bought them.
8. I have only a few magueys.
9. Tomorrow I'll start working ("seize my work").
10. We are your (pl.) children, don't abandon us!
11. Gods, hear our songs!
12. Are these your (pl.) pigs? – No, these are the pigs of our doctor's son.
13. What is the price of your (s.) jar?

Inherent Possession, the Suffix -yō, 'To Have', Possessive Nouns

11.1 Nouns for Family Relationships

It is theoretically possible to encounter in a Nahuatl text absolute forms like **tàtli** 'father' or **nāntli** 'mother'. Such forms are exceptional, however, and you should avoid using them in the exercises. In fact, in Nahuatl usage, it is considered that there can be no 'father' without him being the father of someone. Hence, nouns indicating a family relationship almost always appear in the possessed form (**notâ** 'my father', **nonān** 'my mother' etc.). Therefore, if you wish to say, for example, 'he is a father', you have to use the possessed form with **tē** indicating an indefinite possessor:

Ca tētâ in Pedro	*Peter is a (someone's) father*
Chōcâ in tēnānhuān	*The mothers are crying*

▶ *Note.* This constraint does not apply to words like **cihuātl**, **oquichtli** and **pilli**. In their possessed form, these words can express a family relationship ('wife', 'husband', 'child'), but their basic sense is independent of any conceptions of family ('female/male/young person').

The indefinite possessive can also be used in front of any noun. Most often, it signifies 'someone else's', 'other people's':

Àmo ticcuīz in tētlatqui	*You are not to take anyone else's property*

11.2 Nouns for Parts of the Body

The same phenomenon is encountered in nouns for parts of the body. Sentences can exceptionally be encountered in which absolute forms like **īxtli** 'eyes' and **māitl** 'hands' are found, but most of the time if you wish to speak of eyes or hands in general, you say:

| tīx | *eyes*, lit. *our eyes* |
| tomā | *hands*, lit. *our hands* |

with the first person plural possessor referring to mankind as a whole. Similarly:

tonacaz	*(our) ears* (**nacaztli**)
totlan	*(our) teeth* (**tlantli**)
totēn	*(our) lips* (**tēntli**)
tocxi *or* ticxi	*(our) feet* (**icxitl**)
tòti *or* tìti	*(our) stomach* (**ititl**)
tomàpil	*(our) fingers* (**màpilli**)
tozti or tizti	*(our) fingernails* (**iztitl**)
toyac	*(our) nose* (**yacatl**)
toyōllô	*(our) heart* (**yōllòtli**)
tocuā	*(our) head* (**cuāitl**)

▶ *Note.* Two hypotheses are available to explain the forms **tocxi, tòti, tozti** (or **ticxi** etc., and not ****tocxiuh**, ****tòtiuh**, ****toztiuh** …). The first is that these nouns follow the rule laid out in 10.7 (dropping of -**itl** and adding of the helping vowel). However, we have seen (10.8) that stems with the structure /VCCV/ take the possessive suffix (**nolhuiuh** 'my day', 'my feast'). Therefore, it is probably necessary to fall back on the second hypothesis, that nouns for parts of the body do not take the possessive suffix. We will in fact see (11.5) that the possessive suffix in a way indicates the "external possessor" and is not applied to the fundamental and inherent relationship of the whole to its parts. Unfortunately, apart from these three nouns, all the nouns for parts of the body end in a consonant or short vowel, so that the absence of the possessive suffix is not altogether conclusive.

11.3 The Suffix *-yō*

One of the important suffixes in Nahuatl is **-yō**. Its meaning is quite close to that of the suffixes '-ity' or '-ness' in English. It is added to a noun stem to form a new noun signifying:

(1) an abstract quality (like 'beauty' or 'goodness') or
(2) a group or collection (collective nouns like 'humanity') or
(3) the material manifestation of the abstract notion (like 'a beauty' meaning a 'beautiful person or thing')

Thus:

in mēxìcayōtl	*Mexica civilization* or *the Mexica people*
in tlācayōtl	*humanity* (the quality of being a human or the human race)
in cuallōtl[1]	*beauty, goodness*
in pillōtl	*infancy, children, childishness*
in cihuāyōtl	*femininity, womanhood, female sexual organs*
in tàyōtl,	*paternity/fatherhood, maternity/motherhood*
in nānyōtl	

In some cases, the meaning can be relatively far removed from that of the noun stem:

in tēnyōtl	*renown, fame* (**in tēntli** 'the lips')
in yāōyōtl	*war* (**in yāōtl** 'the enemy')
in teōyōtl	*doctrine, ritual* (**in teōtl** 'God')

11.4 -yō in the Possessed Form

Nouns in -**yōtl** are particularly common in the possessed form. This form does not take the suffix -**uh**. That suffix actually indicates a relationship with something external, whereas -**yōtl** is used precisely in the case of constituent elements (see 11.2 Note). The -**ō** becomes short in word-final position (9.3 n. 2).

in motlācayo	*your humanity, your human qualities*
in īcuallo	*her goodness, beauty*
in īntēnyo	*their fame*
in amopillo	*your (pl.) childishness*

The possessed form of nouns in -**yōtl** is sometimes equivalent to a noun of politeness. Thus, 'my, our lord' is more frequently expressed as **notēucyo, totēucyo** than as **notēuc, totēuc** (cf. English 'your lordship').[2] Forms of this type can then have a plural: **totēucyōhuān** 'our lords'.

11.5 -yō of Inalienable Possession

A special use of the possessed form of nouns with the ending -**yō** is peculiar from the point of view of English. For certain nouns, Nahuatl makes a distinction between the situation in which the noun means something separate

---

[1] Note the regular assimilation of -**y**- to -**l**- after -**l** (6.1).

[2] Note that 'our lord' frequently appears in the form **totēcuiyo** with an **i**-glide inserted between the ending and final consonant of the stem, which thus remains as regular /k^w/ (**cu**) insteading of being unvoiced (**uc**).

from the entity in which it is formed and the one in which it means something attached to that entity. In the former case, we have the simple noun, but in the latter case, the noun has the suffix -**yō** added to it and must by definition be possessed. The circumstance described with this usage is traditionally referred to as *inalienable possession*. An example of this distinction is provided by the word for 'bone': **omitl** refers to a bone that exists outside of the body that created it (for instance, one that a dog is gnawing on), while -**omiyo** (which necessarily has the appropriate possessive prefix) signifies the same bone in its previous state as part of the animal from which it was eventually taken. In other words, this opposition reflects the contrast between an external (incidental) possession by someone else and its inalienable possession by its original "owner" as part of the inherent make-up of that owner. Other examples:

in nonac	*my meat* (which I have bought and am eating)
in nonacayo[3]	*my body* (the structure of flesh that constitutes my person)
in momiuh	*your bone* (e.g., which you have on your plate)
in momiyo	*your bone* (which is part of your body), your bones
in īezhui (10.9)	*its blood* (speaking of the meal of a blood-drinking beast)
in īezzo[4]	*his blood* (flowing through a person's veins)
in īāuh	*his water* (which he drinks or carries)
in īāyo	*its water* (e.g., of a sauce), *its juice* (of a plant)
in īquetzal	*his feather* (ornament of a person)
in īquetzallo	*its plumage* (the feathers attached to a bird)
in īxōchiuh	*his flower* (belonging to the owner of a garden)
in īxōchiyo	*its flower* (of a plant)

▶ *Note.* Some nouns for parts of the body take -**yō** and others do not. This is because Nahuatl considers that some things are in a certain way naturally inherent to a body and others are not necessarily so. If, for example, Nahuatl says **nòti** 'my stomach' and not ****nòtiyo**, the reason for this is that the language basically conceives of the 'stomach' as the stomach of a living creature, that is, as something that cannot be imagined as having an independent existence. If, on the other hand, it says **nonacayo, nomiyo** and **nezzo** for 'my body, bone, blood' (and not **nonac, nomiuh** or **nezhui**), the reason is that the body, bone and blood are conceived of as things which can appear independently in nature and for which an external possessor can be imagined outside of any inherent relationship. In the same way, 'feather' and 'flower' are conceived of from the start as isolated objects,

---

[3] Note that the stem of **nacatl** is **naca-**, even though the final vowel is dropped in the possessed form (e.g., **nonac**).

[4] -**y**- generally assimilates to a preceding -**z**, just as it does with -**l**-. The form **īezyo** can also be found. This optional assimilation also takes place after **x, tz, ch.**

separate from a bird or plant. Of course, the dividing line between these two types of conception cannot be guessed in advance.

11.6 'To Have': *Piya* and Possessed Forms

Nahuatl does not have a word for 'to have' any more than it has one for 'to be'. It is true that **piya** 'to guard' can sometimes be translated with 'to have'[5], but this involves the sense 'to have in a chance manner', 'to have on one', for example:

Cuix ticpiya ichtli?	*Do you (s.) have a thread (on you)?*
Nicān nicpiya ōntetl tomātl	*I have two tomatoes here*

As we have seen (10.6, 3), 'to have' followed by a qualified or quantified object ('Peter has a pretty house', 'I have ten fingers') is expressed with the possessive construction ('Peter's house is pretty', 'My fingers are ten'), for example:

Ca cualli in mocal	*Your (s.) house is pretty, you have a pretty house*
Inon cihuātl ca miyac in īcōzqui	*That woman has many necklaces*
Ca màtlāctli in tomàpil	*We have ten fingers*

11.7 Possessive Nouns

To say just 'I have a house', 'I have children' (i.e., when no adjective or quantifier is present), the expressions in 11.6 are no longer available. One possibility consists of using **oncâ** (6.2) with a possessed noun:

Oncatê nopilhuān	*I have children (my children exist)*

Frequently, Nahuatl avails itself of a *possessive noun*, which pretty much signifies 'furnished with a house' or 'furnished with children' (for the earlier examples).[6] English has a similar procedure with adjectives in '-ed' derived from NOUN + ADJECTIVE phrases, as in 'this river is wide-mouthed' (it has a wide mouth). Nahuatl simply generalizes this procedure by saying 'I am house-ed', 'I am husband-ed', that is, 'I am one with a house', 'I am one with a husband'.

Possessive nouns have the following structure:

(1) stem of the possessed noun
(2) in some cases, the possessive suffix /-wā-/ (11.8)
(3) glottal stop /'/ (after a vowel) or /-e'/ (after a consonant)

---

[5] In modern dialects, under the influence of Spanish with 'tener', **piya** has been generalized and the possessive nouns have become rare.

[6] Be sure not to confuse the terms *possessive noun* and *possessed noun*. A *possessed noun* is simply a noun that has one of the possessive prefixes on it. A *possessive noun* is a derivative noun signifying someone that *possesses* the original noun from which the possessive form is derived.

(4) participial suffix (8.2)

(5) in the plural, /-e'/.

Because there is always a glottal stop, that is, a consonant, at the end of the suffix, the participial suffix does not appear in the singular. The combination of (2) and (3) means that in the singular the suffix is either **-huâ** (the possessive suffix **-huā** shortened by the glottal stop) or **-ê** (glottal stop preceded by its helping vowel). In the plural, **-quê** (participial suffix in /k/ **-qu-** plus the plural marker **-ê**, cf. 8.3) is added to this suffix. Thus:

nicalê	*I have a house (*lit., *I am one with a house)*
ticalèquê	*we have a house (or houses)*
ticihuāhuâ	*you (s.) have a wife, you are married (*lit., *you are one with a wife)*
ancihuāhuàquê	*you (pl.) are married*
(Ca) oquichhuâ	*she has a husband, she is married (*lit., *she is one with a husband)*
(Ca) oquichhuàquê	*they have husbands, are married*

These possessive nouns have the same syntax as other nouns. They can be predicates, subjects, objects, possessors:

Àmo tiquincocōzquê in pilhuàquê	*we won't harm the parents (those with children)*
in īncal pilhuàquê	*the houses of people who have children*

▶ *Note.* The stem of the "thing posssessed" says nothing of its number. **Nipilhuâ** signifies 'I have a child' or 'I have children' (i.e., I have offspring). If you want to specify, you can say, for example, **zan cē in nopil** 'I have only one child' ('my child is unique'), **miyactin in nopilhuān** 'I have many children' ('my children are many), see 11.1.

11.8 *-huâ* or *-ê*?

There remains the question of potential differences between **-huâ** and **-ê**. To tell the truth, the distribution is somewhat variable. In principle, **-huâ** is used when the stem ends in a vowel – even if this vowel is dropped in the possessed form (10.7) – unless the noun in question is a part of the body (see later discussion):

āhuâ tepēhuâ	*citizen (possessor of water and mountain,* which is the literal meaning of **āltepētl** *'city')*
petlahuâ	*one who has mats, maker or seller of mats*
tlatquihuâ	*one who has property, rich person*

The suffix **-huâ** is likewise used with animate nouns, whether they end in a consonant or a vowel:

cihuāhuâ	*a person with a wife, married man*
chichihuâ	*one who has a dog/dogs, dog owner*
pitzōhuâ	*one who has a pig/pigs, pig owner*
tōtolhuâ	*one who has a turkey/turkeys, turkey owner*
oquichhuâ	*a person with a husband, married woman*
pilhuâ	*a person with a child/children, parent*
michhuâ	*a person with fish, fisherman*

with the exception of:

nānê	*person with a mother*
tatê	*person with a father (**tatê** and not ****tàê** because in **tàtli** the glottal stop derives from a **t**, cf. 5.1 Note, but reverts to its full articulation in the possessive noun).*

The suffix **-ê** is used on inanimate noun stems that end in a consonant, as well as on nouns for parts of the body that end in a vowel (which is always lost):

calê	*a person who has a house, homeowner*
tlaōlê	*a person with corn*
īxê	*a person who has eyes, prudent, clever*
nacacê	*a person who has (big) ears, perceptive*
tēnê	*a person who has (big) lips*
yaquê (and not **yacahuâ)	*a person with a (big) nose*
iztê	*a person with (long) fingernails*
icxê	*a person with (big) feet*
ìtê	*a person with a (big) belly, fat*

There is inconsistency with nouns in **-āitl** and **-ēitl**. While the forms **māyê** 'a person with hands' and **cuēyê** 'someone in a skirt' take **-ê**, **āxcāhuâ** 'someone with property, rich person' takes **-huâ**. (Note how **māyê** and **cuēyê** are based on the stems **māi-** and **cuēi-**, with the /i/ realized consonantally as a **y**-glide in intervocalic position.)

11.9 Possessive Nouns in -*yô*

Possessive nouns in **-yô** are derived from nouns in **-yōtl**. The structure of this formation is based on the steps laid out in 11.7, without step 2 (i.e., /-wān/ is not added). In effect, the singular is formed by adding a glottal stop (which shortens the **-yō**).

These forms are most commonly translatable with adjectives or expressions like 'full of …', 'is made of …'.

āyô	*full of water, watery*
teyô	*rocky*
tēnyô	*famous*
nacayô	*made of flesh, fleshy*
omiyô	*a person with bones (in him)*
ezzô	*a person with blood, bloody*
patiyô	*pricey, expensive*

11.10 The Possessed and Derivative Forms of Possessive Nouns

Possessive nouns can themselves have a possessed form. This is formed like the possessed forms of regular nouns (10.1), that is, the possessive suffix -**uh** is added to the stem (as constituted by the first four elements of 11.7), but the participial suffix then takes the form -**cā**-:

nocalècāuh	*my homeowner*
totēnyòcāuh	*our famous person*
totēnyòcāhuān	*our famous people*

Bear in mind from now on that *this form* -**cā**- *of the participial suffix appears when the participial suffix is followed by another suffix.* In other words, if you take a possessive noun with the variant -**cā**- of the participial suffix (**calècā**-, **tēnyòcā**-), you have a base to which you can add the suffixes that are added to a regular noun stem.

There are three exceptions to the use of the -**cā**- form before suffixes.

(1) Possessive nouns do not take the absolute suffix (the form is not ****calècātl** but just **calè**).

(2) They do not take the regular plural suffix (not ****calècâ** or ****calècāmê** but **calèquê**).

(3) The vocative suffix -**é** (9.7) is simply added to the singular (not **calècāé** but **calèé**).

Among the suffixes that can be added to a noun stem in -**cā**- are the possessive suffix (see earlier discussion) and the suffix -**yō** (11.3). It is perfectly possible to form nouns like:

in calècāyōtl	*homeownership*
in ìtècāyōtl	*obesity*
in pilhuàcāyōtl	*having children, parenthood*
in oquichhuàcāyōtl	*being married, the status of being a wife*

VOCABULARY[7]

Nouns

cuāitl	*head*	quetzalli	*feather*
eztli	*blood*	tàtli	(*pl. /–tin/*) *father*
icxitl	*foot*	tēntli	*lip* (-yōtl: *fame, glory*)
iztitl	*fingernail, claw*	tlantli	*tooth*
ìtitl	*stomach*	tōtōtl	(*pl. /–mê/*) *bird*
màpilli	*finger*	yacatl	*nose*
nacaztli	*ear*	yāōtl	(*pl. /–'/*) *enemy* (-yōtl: *war*)
nāntli	(*pl. /–tin/*) *mother*	yōllòtli	*heart*

Intransitive verbs

huetzca	*to laugh*	pāqui	*to rejoice, to be happy*
polihui	*to become lost,*		
	to disappear		

EXERCISES

(a) Translate into English.
1. Ca teyô inin òtli.
2. Àmo tehuàquê, àmo titlaōlèquê.
3. Nicān câ cē chichi: āquin īchichihuàcāuh?
4. Inon cihuātl àmo oquichhuâ.
5. Inìquê in pīpiltin aoc tatèquê.
6. Ca iztèquê in tōtōmê.
7. Mā miquicān in mochintin toyāōhuān.
8. Ayamo titētàhuān.
9. Ca ōme in tomā, màtlāctli in tomàpil.
10. Ca zan titlācâ: ca miquiz, polihuiz in tonacayo.
11. Zan pillōtl in ticchīhua.
12. Mācamo chōca in moyōllô: mā zan xipāqui, xihuetzca.
13. Mācamo xictēmo in tēnyōtl, zan yèhuātl xictēmo in cuallōtl.
14. Quēmâ, nimitzcaqui, cuix àmo ninacacê?
15. Ye ontlami in tlatquihuàcāyōtl.
16. Àmo niquīz in īezzo in pitzōtl.

(b) Translate into Nahuatl.
1. Who will speak of divine things (divinity)?
2. My lord, I know your goodness.

[7] For derivative nouns, only those forms are listed in the vocabulary that are not readily deducible from their component parts. This applies to **-yōtl** in the present list and to every derivational process that will be examined later.

3. I haven't bought fish today. The fisherman hasn't come.
4. The lord has slaves (is a master of people).
5. (The) turkeys don't have teeth.
6. You (s.) will be prudent (will have eyes, will have ears).
7. (The) pigs don't have hands.
8. We are made of flesh, bone, blood.
9. We will not make war.
10. Mexica civilization won't die, it won't disappear.
11. Fatherhood, motherhood is good.
12. My body makes me ill.
13. These tomatoes are full of water.
14. Those lords are famous.
15. This city has a large population (is full of people).
16. This bird has beautiful feathers.
17. The lord has beautiful feathers.
18. Do you have children? – Yes, I have two (my children are two).

Nominal Suffixes, "Adjectives"

12.1 Honorific, Deprecatory, Diminutive and Augmentative Suffixes

Nahuatl has suffixes that are placed at the end of noun stems to add a nuance of size or attitude. Romance languages have a regular series of such suffixes. English does not and instead uses suitable adjectives. These suffixes are covered in the following sections.

12.1.1 -tzin

This is by far the most common. It was originally a diminutive suffix (see 12.1.2), but by the Classical period, it essentially indicated respect or affection. It is followed by the absolute suffix if the noun that it is added to normally takes the absolutive:

in cihuātzintli	*the dear woman* or *the honorable woman*
in piltzintli	*the dear child*
ca cualtzintli	*he is nice (good and charming)*

but

in chichitzin	*the dear dog*
in Pedrotzin	*dear (or honorable) Peter*

The plural is made through reduplication of the suffix (with a short vowel: **-tzitzin**) followed by **-tin** if the singular takes **-tli**. Any initial reduplication of the noun is retained:

in cihuātzitzintin	*the honorable women*
in pīpiltzitzintin	*the dear children*
in chichitzitzin	*the dear dogs*

In front of -**tzin**, the participial suffix has the form -**cā**- (11.9), and -**tli** is generally added:

in calēcātzintli   *the honorable homeowner*

The possessed form is regular. In the plural, the reduplicated -**tzitzin** is retained, and -**huān** can turn up in front or in back of it (any initial reduplication of the noun is as usual dropped):

nopiltzin   *my dear child*
nopiltzitzinhuān *or* nopilhuāntzitzin   *my dear children*

The vocative of this possessed form is -**tzé** rather than -**tziné**:

nopiltzé   *o my dear child!*

It's a principle of *honorific forms* (that is, signs of respect) that they are never used in speaking of oneself, however grand the status of the speaker may be. Thus, one can have exchanges like this:

Cuix tinonāntzin? – Quēmâ, ca nimonān.   *Are you (s.) my mother? – Yes, I'm your mother.*

A child talking to or about his parents always says **nonāntzin, notàtzin**. Similarly, in speaking to a person about his parents, you say to him **monāntzin, motàtzin**. Note that the -**tzin** of the possessed form indicates respect for either the possessed noun (in **nonāntzin** it's the mother to whom respect is being given) or its possessor. If you say **mopetlatzin** or **īpetlatzin** to or about someone, it is obviously the possessor of the mat that you are showing respect to and not the mat itself. In this regard, it can be seen that while such respect does not refer to the first person, it can refer not only to the second but also to the third person.

The pronouns of the second and third person also have an honorific form in -**tzin**:

Singular		Plural	
2nd person	tèhuātzin	2nd person	amèhuāntzitzin
3rd person	yèhuātzin	3rd person	yèhuāntzitzin

12.1.2 -*tōn*

This is a diminutive suffix. A diminutive formation signifies a smaller version of the thing described by the base noun. A somewhat comparable ending in

English is the formative '-ette' (e.g., a 'kitchenette' is a small 'kitchen'). The suffix **-tōn** has the same morphological characteristics as **-tzin**:

piltōntli *little child*	*pl.* pīpiltotōntin
cihuātōntli *little woman*	*pl.* cihuātotōntin
chichitōn *little dog*	*pl.* chichitotōn
nopiltōn *my little child*	*pl.* nopilhuāntotōn *or* nopiltotōnhuān

12.1.3 *-pōl*

This is an augmentative suffix. An augmentative formation signifies a larger version of the thing described by the base noun. Note that if such a noun is not given the absolute ending in an instance where it could take it, the noun acquires a deprecatory sense (i.e., it is being disparaged by the speaker; a similar effect is achieved in English with the conjoined adjectives 'big fat'):

cihuāpōlli *big woman*	*pl.* cihuāpopōltin
cihuāpōl *(miserable) big woman*	*pl.* cihuāpopōl

12.1.4 *-pil*

This is a diminutive suffix, with the nuance of tenderness or pity. It has no absolutive suffix:

tōtōpil *(poor) little bird*	*pl.* tōtōpipil

12.1.5 *-zol*

This is a deprecatory suffix that is used of inanimate objects. It always takes the absolutive suffix:

calzolli	*broken-down house* or *lousy house*
petlazolli	*worthless old mat*

In front of the suffixes that we have just looked at, it is regular practice for a short final **-i** to be dropped. We will encounter this phenomenon again when a noun is part of a compound noun:

momātzin	*your arm* (of you whom I respect)
cuauhtōntli	*little tree*
cōntōntli	*little jar* (**cōmitl** 'jar')
caxzolli	*old bowl*
otompōl	*lousy Otomi*

12.2 The Problem of Adjectives

Take the words **cualli** 'good, beautiful', **ìtê** 'with stomach, fat' and **teyô** 'rocky'. These are translated in English with adjectives, but in Nahuatl nothing distinguishes **cualli** from ordinary nouns (in particular, it has the absolute suffix) or **ìtê** or **teyô** from other possessive nouns (11.6–8). They have not only the morphology of nouns but also their syntax. They can be predicates (predicate adjectives with the verb 'to be' in English) as well as subjects or objects. **In cualli** signifies the 'good or beautiful person or thing' (but not 'beauty', which is **cuallōtl**, 11.3), **in ìtê** is 'the fat person' and **in teyô** is 'the rocky thing(s)'. The three words under consideration can certainly act as *attributive adjectives*; that is, they can modify another noun, as in English:

in cualli tlācatl	*the good person*
in ìtê tlācatl	*the fat person*
in teyô òtli	*the rocky path*

(Note that the word order given in the previous examples is not the only one available. It is also possible to say **in tlācatl ìtê** or **in tlācatl in ìtê**, the second of which is clumsy, like the phrase 'the person who is fat'.)

Virtually any noun can act as the attributive of another, for example:

in mēxìcatl cihuātl	*the Mexica woman*
in pàtli xihuitl	*the medicinal plant*, lit., *the medicine* **(pàtli)** *plant* **(xihuitl)**

In fact, there is no class of words in Nahuatl that consists specifically of adjectives. The most that can be said is that there are nouns that tend to be translated as adjectives in a language like English.

Nouns indicating materials can appear as predicates indicating what the subject is made of. In such circumstances, English can use a construction in which the predicate noun appears with no determiner (i.e., by itself without 'a'). English can also say 'to be (made) of ...' or use an adjective corresponding to the material.

Ca cuahuitl in notlapech	*My bed is wood/made of wood/wooden*
Ca tetl in metlatl	*The metate is stone/made of stone*
Ca teōcuitlatl inin cōzcatl	*This necklace is gold/made of gold/golden*

12.3 'Large' and 'Small'

Let's now look at the categories of nouns that correspond to adjectives in English. Some are quantifiers (7.5), such as those that mean 'large' and 'small':

huēyi 'large, big' (pl. **huēyin, huēyintin**); **tepi-** 'small'. The latter form does not appear as such in the Classical period. It is always followed by either **-tōn** (**tepitōn** 'small in size', pl. **tepitotōn**) or **-tzin** (**tepitzin** 'small in amount', 'a little'; **zan tepitzin** 'little' in reference to an collective noun that cannot be counted, like water):

Inin tōtōtl zan tepitōn	*This bird is quite small*
Tepitzin ātl ōniquīc	*I drank a little water*
Zan tepitzin ātl ōniquīc	*I've drunk little water*

12.4 "Adjectives" in -*qui*

Among the words that tend to be translated as adjectives, there are several series of words that end in the participial suffix. A major series of such "adjectives" is derived from intransitive verbs.[1] The verb stem is in base 2, and the participial suffix after a consonant has the form **-qui** in the singular, the plural of course being **-quê** (it can seen that what we actually have here is a variant of the preterite used adjectivally). A form derived in this way characterizes something or someone as being affected by the action/activity of the verb. Thus:

micqui	*dead*
cochqui	*asleep*
cualānqui	*irritated, angry* (**cualāni** 'boil', hence 'get mad')

There are some isolated forms derived from verbs that are seldom if ever used in the Classical period. For instance, **totōnqui** 'hot' and **cocoxqui** 'sick, ill' are much more common than the intransitive verbs **totōni**[2] 'become hot' and **cocoya** 'become ill'.

12.5 "Adjectives" in -*huac* and Verbs in -*hua*

A specific instance of the forms discussed in the previous section consists of the extensive series of "adjectives" in **-huac**, such as:

canāhuac	*thin*	melāhuac	*right, just*
catzāhuac	*dirty, impure*	patlāhuac	*broad*
chicāhuac	*strong*	pitzāhuac	*narrow*
chipāhuac	*clean, pure*	tomāhuac	*fat*

The plural is obviously **chipāhuaquê** etc. Here again, we have an adjectival use of the preterite of intransitive verbs in **-hua** (which always end in **-āhua**

---

[1] For the same formation based on transitive verbs, see 16.1.

[2] At any rate, such a form is implied by **totōniya** 'become hot" (with inchoative **-ya**; cf. 29.1.1) and the semi-causative **totōnia** 'make hot' (see 19.8).

or -**ēhua**). These verbs have the peculiarity that they all have a corresponding transitive homonym. The intransitive form generally indicates a change in state ('become' + ADJECTIVE), while the transitive form indicates the action that causes such a change in state ('make...' + ADJECTIVE),[3] such as:

chipāhua	*it becomes clean, is purified*
chicāhua	*it is strengthened*
nicchipāhua	*I clean, purify it*
nicchicāhua	*I strengthen it*

Base 2 of the transitive version is formed by dropping the final vowel (8.3), while the final vowel is retained in the intransitive version (8.7), so that the respective preterites are:

ōnicchipāuh	*I have cleaned, purified it*
ōchipāhuac	*it has been purified, it has become clean*[4]

▶ *Note.* The transitive verb used reflexively, for instance **mochipāhua** 'he cleans himself', indicates that the subject undertakes an action that results in making itself clean, while the intransitive **chipāhua** indicates in general that the subject becomes clean naturally without any active or voluntary effort.

12.6 "Adjectives" in *-tic*

A large number of "adjectives" are derived from noun stems to which the compound suffix -**tic** (the final -c is the participial suffix) has been added.[5] These signify 'one that has the manner/characteristics of...', such as:

tetic	*petrified, hard as a rock* (**tetl**)
cuauhtic	*tall* (like a 'tree' **cuahuitl**)
tlīltic	*black* (like 'ink' **tlīlli**)

Sometimes, there is reduplication with a short vowel in front of the noun stem:

chichīltic	*red* (like 'chili pepper' **chīlli**)

The noun from which the form is derived may not be in use:

coztic	*yellow* (what **coztli** means is not known for sure)

In the plural, the form is naturally **cuauhtiquê** etc.

---

[3] We have already seen **ēhua** 'get up, depart' and its transitive homonym 'raise up, make rise'.

[4] Note that **chipāhuac** does not imply that it has been dirty before, but simply indicates that it *is* clean.

[5] Here again, we have the preterite of verbs in -**ti** derived from nouns (see 29.3).

12.7 "Adjectives" in -c

About twenty common adjectives seem to be formed by adding the participial suffix directly to a noun stem. Apart from two or three, however, these noun stems are not used in the Classical period to form actual nouns.[6] For instance:

iztāc	*white* (**iztatl** 'salt')
cecēc	*cold, icy* (**cetl** 'ice')
cocōc	*spicy* (also *painful*)
tzopelīc	*sweet-tasting, sugary*
poyēc	*salty*
xocōc	*sour* (like the **xocotl** fruit)
chichīc	*bitter*

Plural: **iztāquê** etc.

12.8 Derivation of Adjectives

When used substantivally (as nouns), all these adjectives may, if the sense is suitable, be put in the possessed form, with the participial suffix becoming -**cā**-:

tomiccāuh	*our dead person* (the one that we have at home, e.g.)
nococoxcāhuān	*my sick people*

The honorific -**tzin** (along with the other suffixes discussed in 12.1) can also be used. It most often takes the absolute suffix:

in miccātzintli	*the venerable dead man*
in mococoxcātzin	*your (honorable) sick person*

Naturally, there are also abstract nouns in -**cā-yō-tl**:

tlīlticāyōtl	*blackness*
iztācāyōtl	*whiteness*
chipāhuacāyōtl	*cleanliness, purity*

The possessed form of the abstraction is rarely expressed with -**cā-yō**-, however. We most often find just -**ca** (shortened, as usual, in word-final position):

īchipāhuaca in Dios	*the purity of God*
ītlīltica in yohualli	*the blackness of the night*
īpoyēca in iztatl	*the saltiness of salt*
īcocōca in chīlli	*the strength/spiciness of chili pepper*

---

[6] Note that the adjective has a long final vowel, whereas the corresponding vowel in the noun is short.

12.9 'Very'

To indicate a high level in the realization of the notion contained in an adjective or adverb (this is expressed with 'a lot', 'much', 'very' in English), there are three possibilities in Nahuatl:

(1) **cencâ** 'very, much':

Ca cencâ cualli in	*It's very good*
Cencâ nimitztlazòtla	*I love you a lot*

(2) **huel**, whose proper meaning is 'well', but which can often be translated as 'very':

Huel ammiyaquintin	*You (pl.) are very numerous*
Huel huēyi inin calli	*This house is very big*

Note that in front of a verb, **huel** can be translated with 'to be able to', 'can' + INFINITIVE.[7] In fact, there is no verb 'to be able' in Nahuatl. The negation is **àhuel** or **àmo huel**.

Āquin huel quitequiz inin cuahuitl?	*Who will be able to cut this tree?*
Huel mococoa, àmo huel mēhua	*He is very sick, he can't get up*
Aoc huel niquilnāmiqui in tlein ōquìtô	*I can't remember what he said any more*

(3) **achi**, whose proper meaning is 'quite', 'rather', but which can take on the same meaning as **cencâ** or **huel**:

Achi mococoa	*He's quite (or very) sick*
Achi miyac tlamantli ōniquittac	*I have seen very many things*

VOCABULARY

Intransitive verb

cualāni	*to boil, to become angry*

Transitive and intransitive verbs[8]

canāhua	*to make thin, to become thin*	melāhua	*to straighten (melāhuac straight, just, righteous)*
catzāhua	*to dirty, to become dirty*		
chicāhua	*to strengthen*	patlāhua	*to broaden, to become wide*

---

[7] One might compare the English expression 'he doesn't really do X', which is virtually equivalent to 'he can't do X'.

[8] See 12.5. For all these verbs, there is a corresponding adjective in -c whose meaning is for the most part immediately deducible.

chipāhua	to clean, to become clean	pitzāhua	to narrow, to become narrow
		tomāhua	to fatten, to become fat

Transitive verb

zaca   to carry, to transport

Nouns

cetl	ice	teōcuitlatl	precious metal [9]
chīlli	chili pepper	tlapechtli	bed
iztatl	salt	tlīlli	black ink
metlatl	metate, grinding stone [10]	xihuitl	plants [11]
pàtli	medicine		

Quantifiers

huēyi	(pl. /–n/, /–ntin/) large, big	tepitōn	(pl. /–totōn/) small

Adjectives [12]

cecēc	cold, frigid	iztāc	white
chichic	bitter	poyēc	salty
chichīltic	red	totōnqui	hot
cocōc	strong, spicy, harsh, painful	tzopelīc	sweet, sugary
		xocōc	tart, sour
cocoxqui	ill, sick	coztic	yellow

Adverbs

achi	rather, very	cencâ	much, very
huel	very (also = be able to)	cenquīzcā-	totally

EXERCISES

(a) Translate into English.

1. Cuix ye ōcatzāhuac inin petlatl? – Ca ayamo, oc chipāhuac.
2. Ye cencâ ōchicāhuac inin piltōntli.
3. Ca huel tomāhuaquê inìquê on oquichtin.
4. Cuix oc pitzāhuac in òtli? – Ca aoc, ye ōpatlāhuac.

[9] I.e., 'silver' or 'gold' without distinction. One can specify **iztāc teōcuitlatl** for 'silver' and **coztic teōcuitlatl** for 'gold'.

[10] A 'metate' is a stone plate, about twenty by twelve inches, that is slightly inclined and generally equipped with three feet carved from the same block. It is used for grinding or kneading.

[11] A homonym of **xihuitl** 'year' (perhaps the two words were originally the same).

[12] Despite what has been said about the absense of a morphological class of adjectives, the rubric "adjective" is retained in the vocabulary lists for formations whose connection with a noun or verb is not clear or not immediately predictable in terms of meaning.

5. Yālhua ōniquimittac ōmentin tlīltiquê tlācâ.
6. Āxcān aoc ampīpiltotōntin, ye ōanchicāhuaquê, ye ōanhuēyiyaquê, ye amoquichtin.
7. Zan tlaxcalzolli in: àmo niccuāz.
8. Àmo cualli inin chichipōl.
9. Àmo huel niczacaz in tetl in.
10. Ca achi miyaquintin: àmo huel niquimpōhuaz in mochintin.
11. Xicchiya inon oquichtli īcuauhtica.
12. In Pedro huel ìtê catca, in āxcān huel ōpitzāhuac.
13. Ayāc huel quìtōz in īchipāhuaca in Dios.
14. Ca huel melāhuac in tiquìtoa.

(b) Translate into Nahuatl.
1. This path is very narrow. – Those people are going to widen it.
2. Those pigs are very dirty. – They have dirtied the house.
3. As for my wife, she has cleaned all the mats.
4. It is we who have fattened up the pigs. – Yes, I see (it), they are very fat.
5. Your (s.) beans are still hot, eat them. – No, they're already cold.
6. These small rabbits are white.
7. My dog is not male (a "man"), it is female (a "woman").
8. You (pl.) are just disgusting ("miserable dirty ones").
9. Leave (s.) these wretched feathers there.
10. Peter has bought very beautiful, very expensive necklaces.
11. The (honorable) Mexica (pl.) came yesterday (and are gone).
12. Those little Otomi children are very nice.
13. Who'll be able to do this? – It's Peter, he's very strong.
14. Who'll go to Xochimilco? – I will be able to go there.
15. I'm very sick. – I can't get up.
16. The doctor is going (in order) to see the (dear) sick people.
17. The heat of this tortilla has made me sick.

The Principal Locative Suffixes

13.1 The Suffix -c(o)

We have already spoken of the morphological and syntactic characteristics of locatives (Lesson 5). Now we will look at how locatives are formed on the basis of noun stems. Here we will deal with the most common forms.

Properly speaking, there is only one locative suffix (the others are locative noun suffixes). This suffix is -**c** (after a vowel) or -**co** (after a consonant), which is added directly to a noun stem:

tepēc	*on the mountain*	ilhuicac	*in the sky, in heaven*
cōmic	*in the jar*	calco	*in the house*

Monosyllables take -**co** and not -**c**:[1]

tleco	*in the fire* (and not ****tlec**)

The suffix -**c(o)** cannot be added to an animate noun stem: ****cihuāc**, ****oquichco** and ****cōhuāc** are not permitted forms.

This is the suffix that is found in a number of toponyms (place names) such as **Xōchimīlco** 'in the field (**mīlli**) of flowers (**xōchitl**)', **Chapōltepēc** (Chapultepec) 'on grasshopper (**chapōlin**) mountain (**tepētl**)', **Ācapōlco** (Acapulco) 'in the big (-**pōlli**, see 12.1.3) reeds (**ācatl**)', **Tlāchco** (Taxco) 'in the ball court (**tlāchtli**)', and naturally **Mēxìco** (though the exact meaning of **Mēxì-** continues to be a subject of controversy).

Like all locatives, forms in -**c(o)** do not indicate a specific direction of movement or the absence of movement, such indications being made by the verb (5.6):

Ilhuicac catê in cīcitlāltin	*The stars are in the sky*
Tlapechco mocāhua	*He's staying in bed*

---

[1] This is another example of the "constraint against short words".

116

Xictlāli etl in cōmic	*Put beans in the jar*
Tleco ōmotlāz	*He threw himself into the fire*
Calco huālquīza	*He's coming out of the house*[2]

Also, -**pa** can be added to this suffix (5.8). The compound form most often remains -**copa** even after a vowel, though -**cpa** (and even -**ccopa**) are attested:

Ilhuicacopa ēhua in nocuīc	*My song rises up toward the sky*

This compound suffix -**copa** can also mean 'in the manner of'. In this case, it can be found on animate stems:

Cuix mēxìcacopa (*or* mācēhualcopa) titlàtoa?	*Do you speak Nahuatl?* (i.e., in the manner of Mexica or of **mācēhualtin** 'commoners')

13.2 Placement of Locatives

Locatives in -**c(o)** often appear at the head of a phrase. Variations in word order produce effects that are most often untranslatable but would be perceptible to a Nahuatl speaker:

Ilhuicac catê in cīcitlāltin	*The stars are in the sky*
In cīcitlāltin ilhuicac catê	*As for the stars, they're are in the sky*

Such locatives can be combined with **nicān, oncān, ōmpa** (5.7):

Ōmpa ilhuicac catê in cīcitlāltin	*The stars are (up there) in the sky*
In cīcitlāltin ōmpa ilhuicac catê	*The stars are (up there) in the sky*
Ōmpa catê ilhuicac in cīcitlāltin	*The stars are (up there) in the sky*
In cīcitlāltin ōmpa catê in ilhuicac	*The stars are (up there) in the sky*

and a locative can be focalized:

Ilhuicac in (ōmpa) catê in cīcitlāltin	*In the sky is where the stars are*
Tepēc in (ōmpa) yauh	*It's to the mountain that he's going*

The other locatives, which we will examine later, have the same syntactic characteristics.

---

[2] Spoken by someone outside. Someone inside would say **calco onquīza** *he's going out of the house* (see 6.1).

13.3 Possessed Locatives

If the noun is possessed, the locative suffix supersedes the morphological modifications for the possessed form. Thus, there is no possessive suffix -**uh** or dropping of the final vowel of the stem (10.7):

Mocalco câ in nochichiuh	*My dog is in your house*
Àmo tle tētōpco, tēcōmic, tēcaxic ticcuīz	*You (s.) are not to take anything from (in) someone else's chest, jar or plate*
Nocamac nicmati in chīlli	*I taste the chili pepper (lit., sense it in my mouth)*
Ïitic in īnān câ in conētl	*The child is in its mother's womb*

Nonetheless, one says:

Īmāc (*and not* **īmāic) câ cē cuahuitl	*He has a stick in his hand (lit., in his hand is a stick)*

And with the addition of -**pa**:

In conētl ïiticpa (ïiticcopa) huālquīza in īnān	*The child emerges from its mother's womb*
Īmmācpa ōniquīz in otomî	*I escaped from the Otomi (lit. emerged from their hands)*

13.4 Locative nouns: -*pan*

The other locative phrases are formed with *locative noun suffixes*, which correspond broadly (in sense if not usage) to English prepositions. These do not have the morphological characteristics of -**c(o)**. Instead, they were originally regular nouns that have developed adverbial uses.[3] (Most locative nouns no longer exist as independent words, though some do.) What would be the object of the English preposition appears as the possessor of the Nahuatl locative noun, which takes the possessive prefixes like a regular noun. A locative noun frequently has the same syntactical relationship with the "possessor" that a regular noun has with its possessor, but sometimes the locative noun is appended to the noun as a suffix.

For a concrete illustration of locative nouns, let us first look at the most common such suffix: -**pan**.

---

[3] Note how many English prepositional phrases have their origins in nouns, such as 'in back of', 'on top of', 'along side of'. Transferred to English, the Nahuatl expressions would correspond to something like 'I go top the mountain' instead of 'I go onto the mountain', or 'I stand side of the man' instead of 'I stand beside the man'.

(1) In terms of meaning, the locative noun -**pan** indicates contact without entry, a localization that is conceived of as being adjacent to an object and not within it. Originally, it must have been a noun that signified something like 'the outer surface'. In sense, it is equivalent to the English 'by' and is mostly translated into English with 'on' or 'in' (not meaning 'inside'). It can be added directly to a noun stem, in effect forming a compound noun (for the discussion of regular compound nouns, see Lesson 17): **mīlpan** 'in the field' (**mīlli** 'field'[4]). Contrast **calco** 'in(side) the house' with **calpan** 'by, at the house' (and not necessarily in it).

Tepēpan ca cuahuitl	*There are trees on the mountain*
Āpan huāllàquê in caxtiltēcâ	*The Spaniards arrived by (lit., on) water*
Tlālpan mani in ātl	*Water is spread over (lit., on) the earth*

Sometimes, it is equivalent to the French preposition 'chez'. English has no direct correspondence for this, but the general sense is 'at the place of' the object of the preposition, the nature of this "place" being determined by the context. This meaning is rendered in English with various idiomatic prepositions such as 'before' (e.g., 'appear before the judge'), 'in the presence of', 'among', or quite frequently 'with' (in contexts of residing and the like). Thus:

Teōpan yauh	*He's going to church (lit., before God)*
Tēcpan[5] câ	*He's in the palace (lit., with the lord)*
Yāōpan ōmic	*He died in war (lit., among the enemy)*

(2) In terms of morphology, -**pan** is not only added to nouns as a suffix but also used by itself in the possessed construction with possessive prefixes (which is impossible for -**c(o)**):

Ō topan quiyauh	*It rained on (atop) us (**quiyahui** rain)*
Ca huel cocōc in ō topan mochīuh	*What happened to us (lit., was done upon us) was very harsh*

(Note how forms like **nopan, mopan, īpan** etc., can intervene between the "augment" **ō** and the verb itself; see 8.8.)

Īpan by itself means 'upon him/her/it', but it can also used in the possessive construction with a noun (see 10.6), with the third person possessive prefix referring to the noun and agreeing with it in number. Thus:

Īpan ōnicalac in Pedro	*I entered Peter's place*
Yālhua in ōnàcic nicān īpan amāltepēuh	*Yesterday I arrived (here) at your (pl.) city*

---

[4] **Milpa** is borrowed into Spanish in the sense of 'cultivated field'.
[5] Not ****tēucpan**. It is usual for the labiovelar consonant /kʷ/ to be simplified to /k/ in front of /p/ (so too in front of /k/: **ōquitzacquê** 'they closed it' rather than **ōquitzaucquê**).

In syntax, an expression like **in īpan Pedro** is parallel to **in īcal Pedro, in īcihuāuh Pedro**. Naturally, if the noun possessing the locative noun is plural, then the third person possessive prefix is plural:

Īmpan ōnicalac in cihuâ   *I entered where the women are*

This possessed locative construction may seem to overlap with suffixed forms like **calpan, tepēpan** etc. In fact, the suffixed forms have something of the non-productive character of fixed expressions, and the possessed construction is much more common. The latter is actually obligatory with an animate noun if a specific person is meant. **Tēcpan** does not indicate the location in which a particular lord is found but a "lordly" place, that is, one characteristic of a lord. If you wish to indicate 'where the lord is' with a precise lord in mind, you say **īpan tēuctli** (or **īmpan tētēuctin** for 'where the lords are'). Under these circumstances, it is clear that with a proper name only the expression **īpan Pedro** is acceptable and that ****Pedropan** is not possible.

A phrase with **īpan** often has a temporal or abstract meaning:

Àtle īpan tinēchitta, tinēchmati   *You (s.) do not respect me (you don't see, feel me as anything)*

Zan huēyi ilhuitl īpan nitlāhuāna   *I get drunk only on holidays (big days)*
Ca īpan inon xihuitl ōnitlācat   *In that year I was born*
Īmpan totàhuān àmo mochīhuaya in   *This was not done in the time of our fathers*

(3) Certain locative expressions with **-pan** have corresponding ordinary nouns in **-pan-tli**, which have the syntax of regular nouns and not that of locatives:

Ca huēyi inin tēcpantli   *This palace is large*
Niquitta in teōpantli   *I see the church*

Such forms are not always possible, and the dictionary must be consulted to verify their attestation. For example, it cannot be deduced from **teōpantli** that one can say ****teōpanco**. No such form exists, and the locative of **teōpantli** is **teōpan**.

Let us summarize the characteristics of the locative nouns/suffixes that we have seen in connection with **-pan**:

▶ They are noun stems, and as such they can appear in the possessed form (and at times with an expressed possessor, as in **īpan Pedro**). However, they are generally not found independently in the absolutive form.

▶ When added as a suffix to a noun stem, they form compound (locative) nouns that regularly have an adverbial meaning. Such forms can (rarely) appear with the absolutive suffix, thereby becoming regular nouns.

▶ Locative nouns most frequently appear with an adverbial (locative) sense, but
such forms never take the locative ending -c(o) since the locative noun itself
suffices to indicate that the whole phrase has a locative meaning.

We will encounter the essence of these characteristics with a good dozen other
suffixes (i.e., locative nouns), the most important of which are listed in a later
discussion (we will see the rest in Lesson 24).

13.5 -cpac

This locative noun/suffix signifies '(the area) on top of' something and thus is
used adverbially to signify 'atop, above, over'. Like -**pan**, -**cpac** can appear with
the personal prefixes:

Nocpac câ quetzalli	*There are feathers atop me (i.e., I have feathers on my head)*

Unlike -**pan**, however, this locative noun is not added directly to a noun
stem; that is, the two cannot form a compound noun. Instead, the important
suffix -**ti**- is inserted between the initial noun and the locative suffix. This intervening suffix has no meaning of its own, and as its function is simply to link
the noun with the locative suffix, the term for it in traditional grammars is
"ligature". Thus:

Tepēticpac (*i.e.,* tepē + ti + cpac) câ cē calli	*There's a house atop the mountain*
Tlālticpac nemî in tlācâ	*Humans live on (the) earth*

Note that if we consider the earth as a flat surface, we have **tlālpan**. In Aztec
thought, however, life on earth is compared metaphorically to walking dan-
gerously on a tight rope, and this is why **tlālticpac** is always used to express
human life in this world.

The "ligature" -**ti**- causes the disappearance of a preceding final short -**i**-.
That is, a noun ending in -**itl** loses the short vowel at the end of the stem, unlike
the case when the suffix -**c(o)** is added. Thus:

Cuauhticpac patlāni in tōtōtl	*The bird flies at the top of the tree*

A phrase formed with the locative noun -**cpac** can take the absolute suffix,
and in this way it become a new noun:

Cuix olōltic in tlālticpactli?	*Is the earth (lit. the top of the earth, i.e., its surface) round?*

It can also take certain a derivational suffix such as those that form possessive
nouns (11.7):

In Dios ca ilhuicahuâ, ca tlālticpaquê	*God is master of the heaven and of earth*

13.6 -tlan

The original sense of -**tlan** is '(area) under', but in many cases (especially with nouns signifying human beings), it means 'alongside of, beside' (often, but not always, someone hierarchically superior; cf. the English expresion 'at the foot of'). It appears either with the possessive prefixes or a noun. With a noun, two constructions are possible. The noun can be attached directly to the suffix by means of the ligature -**ti**- (cf. this usage with -**cpac** in 13.5). Alternatively, the noun may appear separately from -**tlan**, which then takes the appropriate third person possessive prefix (cf. this usage with -**pan** in 13.4 sec. 2).

Notlan ximotlāli	*Sit (s.) beside me*
Ītlan ōninotlālî in Pedro	*I sat beside Peter*
Nocaltitlan câ cē mīlli	*There's a field beside my house*

The ligature can be dropped in certain fixed expressions:

Nocxitlan ōmotlāz	*He threw himself at my feet*

Also note the difference between:

Ātlan	*In the water, under the surface of the water*
Ātitlan	*By the water, along a river, a lake or the sea*

13.7 -tech

This locative noun suffix means 'against, on (especially vertical surfaces), touching'. The ligature is normally used but can be dropped, particularly if the phrase is used as a noun with the absolutive suffix (with the noun governed by -**tech** being generic rather than specific). Thus:

Tetitech câ zoquitl	*There's some mud on the rocks*
Caltitech niczaloa āmatl	*I'm gluing paper onto the house*
Iztāc in caltechtli	*The wall of the house is white*

It is frequently used with the derivative meaning 'concerning, with reference to':

Motech pōhui in	*This belongs to you (lit., counts with reference to you)*
Nimitzpanahuia in ītech chicāhuacāyōtl	*I am stronger than you (lit., I surpass you in terms of strength) (Note the use of **in** with the whole phrase dependent upon -**tech**.)*

If **-copa** is added, the form means 'about, on the subject of':

Ītechcopa nitlàtōz in ilhuicatl

I'm going to speak about heaven (note the separation of **in ilhuicatl** from **ītechcopa**)

13.8 *Chān(-tli)*

This is the word for 'dwelling, house, home' in the sense of 'your place' (denoted by the preposition 'chez' in French) rather than the building. 'Your place' can refer more broadly to the town or country from which you come or where you live.

It has the characteristics of locative nouns, that is, it is hardly used except in the adverbial form without -**c(o)**. In addition, it is almost always in the possessed form. Thus:

Nochān xicalaqui   *Enter (s.) my place*
Īchān niyāz in Pedro   *I'll go to Peter's place*

The locative meaning can be seen clearly when its construction is contrasted with that of **calli**:

Cān mochān?   *Where are you (s.) from?* (and not ****Cān câ mochān**, cf. 5.5)
Cān câ mocal?   *Where is your (s.) house?* (and not ****Cān mocal**)

A possessive noun in -**ê** designates an inhabitant:

Cāmpa catê in nicān chānèquê?   *Where are the inhabitants, the people from here?* (those who have their residence here)

13.9 Honorific Locatives

If a noun with the locative suffix -**c(o)** is made honorific, the locative suffix is placed after the honorific suffix -**tzin**:

Momātzinco nictlālia in   *I put this in your (s.) (honored) hands*
Cuix ye mocaltzinco oncalac?   *Has he already entered your (s.) house?*

This compound suffix -**tzin-co** is also if a phrase involving any locative noun is made honorific. As we have seen, the suffixes -**pan**, -**cpan** and -**tech** (and also **chān**-) normally form adverbial phrases that are not followed by the locative suffix -**c(o)**, but when these locatives nouns have -**tzin** added to them, the new honorific form is considered a regular noun to which -c(o) has to be added. Thus:

Teōpantzinco niyauh	*I'm going to the (revered) church*
Īpantzinco ōnicalac	*I entered his (respected) presence*
Īcpactzinco câ xōchitl	*There are flowers on his head*
Motlantzinco ninotlālia	*I'm sitting down beside you (s.)*
Ītechcopatzinco nitlàtōz in Dios	*I'm going to speak about God*
Motechtzinco pōhui in	*This belongs to you (s.)*

13.10 Locatives and "Adjectives"

If the noun in a locative phrase is modified by an adjective, only the noun takes the locative marker:

cualli calco	*in the pretty house*
huēyi tepēpan	*on the big mountain*
tlīltic zoquic	*in the black mud*

Note that the locative suffix -c(o) is never found after the participial suffix -c/-qui/-cā/-ø.

VOCABULARY

Impersonal verb[6]
quiyahui *to rain*

Intransitive verbs

calaqui	*to enter*	pōhui	*to be counted, to be assigned*
mani	*to extend, to be spread*	tlāhuāna	*to get drunk (tlāhuānqui*
patlāni	*to fly*		*drunk, drunkard)*

Transitive verbs

panahuia	*to surpass, to exceed*	zaloa	*to glue*

Nouns

ācatl	*reed*	mīlli	*(cultivated) field*
camatl	*mouth[7]*	nòpalli	*nopal, prickly pear plant*

---

[6] As in English, impersonal verbs are always in the third person singular, with 'it' as the subject (see 15.10).

[7] With the mouth conceived of as a "place" rather than a "thing," lists of anatomical terms normally give **tocamac** (lit., 'in our mouth') for 'mouth' instead of **tocan.**

caxtiltēcatl	(pl. /–'/) Spaniard	oztōtl	cave
chapōlin	(pl. /–tin/) grasshopper	tlāchtli	game of pelota[8]
chāntli	residence[9]	tlālli	earth
cuāuhtli	(pl. /–tin/) eagle[10]	tletl	fire
ilhuicatl	sky, heaven	tōptli	box, chest
mācēhualli	(pl. /–tin/) commoner, subject	zoquitl	mud

Adjective
ololtic   round

EXERCISES

(a) Put the following nouns into the locative (in -c, -co).
   1. āltepētl
   2. tāltepēuh
   3. cōzcatl
   4. mocōzqui
   5. cuahuitl
   6. iztatl
   7. nòti
   8. nīx
   9. nacaztli
   10. omitl
   11. nomiuh
   12. oztōtl
   13. ītēn
   14. moyac
(b) Translate into English.
   1. Ilhuicacopa patlāni in tōtōtl
   2. Ca àtle īpan nicmati inon tlācapōl.
   3. Nocalticpac câ miyac tōtōtl
   4. Ōmpa oztōc ommotlātìquê in cōcoyô.
   5. Tlaxcallāmpa motlaloâ in yāô.
   6. Cuix mēxìcacopa antlàtoâ?
   7. Mācamo xiyauh ōmpa: ca mopan quiyahuiz.
   8. Cān īchān Pedro? – Ca nicān.

---

[8] The game pelota is found in many of archaeological sites in Central America. It consisted of shooting a ball through a ring attached to a wall.
[9] Always in the possessed locative form, cf. 13.7.
[10] Not to be confused with **cuahuitl** 'tree, stick, wood'.

    9. Cuix amochāntzinco nicochiz?

   10. Yāōpan zan yèhuāntin miquiyâ in mācēhualtin.

   11. Ācatitlan câ in nocal.

   12. Nòpalticpac mocāhua in cuāuhtli.

(c) Translate into Nahuatl.

    1. I govern ("I am on a mat, on a seat")

    2. There's meat on my plate.

    3. The small child has taken a grasshopper in his hand.

    4. Has nothing good happened to you (s.)?

    5. Today, Peter is in the (honorable) palace.

    6. I will go to ("enter") bed.

    7. It was in that year that Peter's wife died.

    8. In the time of our (respected) fathers, the city was beautiful. Today in our time it has become very dirty.

    9. Your (s.) place is nice.

   10. Where are these people from ("where is their place")? – They aren't from here.

   11. Will you (s.) live with the lords?

   12. What opinion do you (s.) do you have about me ("upon what do you see me")?

   13. Eight people live at Peter's home.

   14. Our town is by the water. – As for us, we live by the mountain.

Coordination, Phrases of Time and Manner

14.1 'And'

Nahuatl has three means for expressing coordination with 'and': **īhuān**, **auh** and simple juxtaposition.

14.1.1 *Īhuān*

The exact meaning of this is 'with it' (see 24.3):

Ye ōniccōuh etl īhuān tlaōlli	*I already bought beans and corn*
Nōhuiyān yauh, īhuān nōhuiyān tlachiya	*He goes everywhere and looks everywhere*
Mōztla huāllāz (*or* huāllāzquê) in Pedro īhuān in Malintzin	*Peter and Mary will come tomorrow*

When there are two animate nouns connected with **īhuān**, the verbal agreement can be either singular or plural. When the connected nouns are inanimate, the verbal agreement is always singular.

14.1.2 *Auh*

While **īhuān** marks a combination of things that naturally go together, **auh** signifies a transition to a new range of ideas. This shift can be strong enough for **auh** to take on an adversative sense, and it is not uncommon for **auh** to be translated as 'but'.

Auh most commonly connects two sentences or clauses, and only rarely does it connect two nouns. In the development of a narrative, it is commonly the case that almost every sentence begins with **auh**. In this usage, it is the preeminent marker of a succession of events, whereas **īhuān** marks simultaneity.

Ca nicān ōnitlacuâ, auh cāmpa nicochiz?	*I've eaten here, but where will I sleep?*
Cualli, auh yancuīc in mocuē	*Your (s.) skirt is pretty, and new too*

Xiccui inon āmoxtli, auh oncān xictlāli	*Take that book and put it there*
Miyac in ōtiquìiyōhuìquê, auh oc miyac in tiquìiyōhuīzquê	*We've endured a lot and we'll endure a lot more*

14.1.3 Juxtaposition

When items are closely connected in sense, they are often juxtaposed without any marker of coordination, with a simple pause sometimes indicated in writing with a comma:

Tictlazòtlaz in monān, in motâ	*You are to love your mother and father*

▶ **Note.** In this case, agreement in the object marker is in the singular.

Tīxèquê, tinacacèquê	*We are sensible, shrewd (lit., we have eyes, we have ears)*
Ca īntlacual yez in tzopilōmê, in cōcoyô	*He'll be the food of vultures and coyotes*

One of the most characteristic methods in literary texts is to pile up virtually synonymous nouns or verbs (sometimes as many as four or five in a row).

Àmo nimīlê, àmo nitlālê	*I have no fields, I have no land*
Àmo ticcuīz in tēāxcā, in tētlatqui	*You are not to take other people's property or possessions*
Zan ēhuac, onyâ, cholô	*He departed, went away, fled*

It is a basic stylistic feature of Nahuatl to refer to a thing or concept indirectly by juxtaposing two items that are characteristic of that thing/concept. This technique is a form of metaphor or metonymy, and it is often designated with the Spanish word 'difrasismo'. Thus:

In cuēitl in huīpilli	*The skirt and blouse (a woman/women)*
In mītl in chīmalli	*The arrow and shield (war)*
In tetl in cuahuitl	*Stone and wood (punishment)*
In xōchitl in cuīcatl	*Flower and song (poetry)*
In petlatl in icpalli	*Mat and seat (authority)*[1]
In cōzcatl in quetzalli	*Jewel and feather (ornament, itself used metaphorically to refer to one's 'child')*

We have already seen **in ātl in tepētl** ('water and mountain', generally in the contracted form **in āltepētl**) for 'town'.

---

[1] These are symbols of a ruler.

14.2 *Nō, Àzo, Ànozo*

Nō means 'also'. It is placed in front of the word to which it refers.

Nō nèhuātl nicchīhuaz	*I too will do it*

The word that follows **nō** has a predicative sense (i.e., the meaning is 'I too am one who will do it'). In Nahuatl, we are compelled to repeat the whole phrase in a case where English is satisfied with coordinating two nouns with 'and also':

Nicnequi chīlli, nō nicnequi etl	*I want chili peppers, and (I want) beans too*

(and not ****nicnequi chīlli nō etl**; one could of course say **nicnequi chīlli īhuān etl**)

Àmo nō is equivalent to 'nor':

Àmo ōnicoch, àmo nō ōnitlacuâ	*I've neither slept nor eaten*

Zan ye nō means 'the same', 'likewise':

Zan ye nō yèhuātl in ōniquìtô	*It's the same as (what) I said*
Ca nicān ōnitlacuâ, auh cāmpa nicochiz? – Zan ye nō nicān.	*I've eaten here, where am I going to sleep? – Here as well.*

Nō can be compounded with the particle **zo**, whose original sense must have been something like 'again', but it only appears attached to other particles (note that the vowel of **nō** is short in compounds). The simple compound **nozo** means 'or':

Cuix ōmpa catê pitzōmê, nozo ichcamê?	*Are there pigs or sheep there?*

More frequently, we have **ànozo**:

Mōztla huāllāz in nonāntzin ànozo in notàtzin	*My mother or my father will come tomorrow*

In **ànozo** we have **à-**, a particle that regularly has a negative sense (cf. **àmō**) but originally indicated doubt.

The compound **àzo** has the sense 'perhaps':

Àzo ye ōhuāllâ	*Perhaps he has already arrived*
Àzo quichīhuaz, ànozo àmo	*Maybe he'll do it, maybe not*

In such phrases, the relationship in sense and formation between **àzo** and **ànozo** is clear.

14.3 -(ti)ca

-**Ca** is a suffix that is combined with both possessive prefixes and inanimate noun stems. With a noun, two constructions are possible (cf. the similar behavior of -**tlan** in 13.7). -**Ca** can be added to the noun, in which case the noun takes the ligature -**ti**-. Alternatively, the noun appears separately from -**ca**, which then appears with the appropriate third person possessive prefix referring to the noun.

When associated with an animate noun (always in the possessive construction), -**ca** indicates that the person in question is the cause of something:

Noca tihuetzca	*You're (s.) laughing at (*lit., *because of) me*
Àmo toca ōmochīuh	*This didn't happen through our action*
Moca ninochīhua	*I'm busy (*lit., *make myself) on your (s.) behalf*

When used with an inanimate noun, the suffix can indicate a cause or instrument (means). The compound **tleīca** means 'why?' Thus:

Nimitztlazòtla in īca mochi noyōllô	*I love you (s.) with all my heart*
Tleīca ōticchīuh in?	*Why did you (s.) do this?*

On a noun stem with the "ligature," it most often has an instrumental sense, being partly synonymous with the expression with **ic** (14.4):[2]

Mītica chīmaltica micquê	*They died in war (by the arrow, by the shield)*
Ācaltica ōnēchhuīcac	*He took me by boat*
Tetica ōnicmōtlac	*I threw stones at him (*lit., *I stoned him with rocks)*

The sense is sometimes locative or temporal:

Caxtica[3] mani in ātl	*The water is spread in (by) the plate*
Yohualtica	*At night, during the night*
Òtlica	*On the way (note the irregular formation, which is the only one of this type; we would expect **òtica; however, one does say īpan òtli 'on the road')*
Ēyilhuitica	*At the end of three days, on the third day*
Huècauhtica	*For a long time (for example, Huecauhtica in chōcac 'He cried for a long time'; Huècauh means 'it's been a long time': ca ye huècauh in nicmati 'it's been a long time that I've known this'; huèca means 'far off/away': huèca nochān my place is far away.)*

---

[2] A noun with the suffix -**tica** is rarely preceded by **in**: instead of, for example, **micquê in mītica**, **ic** would be used: **ic micquê in mītl** (see 14.4).

[3] Remember that a final short -**i** is dropped in front of the ligature (13.5).

Like the locative suffix, the instrumental suffix -**ti-ca** is added only to the noun when the noun is modified by an adjective:

Cualli tlàtōltica ōnicnōtz	*I addressed him with fine words*

14.4 *Ic*

Ic is one of the most common words in Nahuatl. It is probably a reduced form of **ī-ca** 'by it', 'thereby', but it has become an independent word both phonologically and semantically. In terms of phonology, it almost always appears with a short /i/ (though in Carochi's grammar it sometimes occurs with a long one). As for semantics, the basic sense (clearly derived from the original **ī-ca**) is 'so, thus, under these circumstances', and with this meaning, it can be found at the head of a clause:

Àmo ōnicnāmic: ic ōninocuep	*I didn't find him, so I returned*

After a noun or pronoun, **ic** indicates the *complement of manner* or *instrument* for the verb. Here "manner" signifies *how* the action of the verb is carried out, and the "instrument" is the thing *with which* it is carried out. In English, manner can be indicated with the preposition 'with' ('he did it with care') or an adverb ('he did it carefully'), and means is also usually indicated with the preposition 'with' ('he cut it with a knife'). The order is generally NOUN + **ic** + VERB or (more rarely) **ic** + VERB + **in** + NOUN:

Cualli ic xinemi	*Live (s.) well*
Cuahuitl ic ōnēchcocô	*He injured me with a stick*
Ic ōnēchcocô in cuahuitl	*He injured me with the stick*

A literal translation of these sentences would be something like: 'a good thing is what you should live by', 'a/the stick is what you injured me with'.

With **in ic** the manner or the instrument is focalized:

Cualli in ic titlàtoa	*It's a nice manner that you're (s.) talking in, your (s.) manner of talking is nice*
Cuahuitl in ic ōnēchcocô	*It's with a stick that he hurt me*

Ic can optionally be found after a locative to indicate a place that the subject of the verb is passing by:

Nicān ic ōquīz	*He passed by here*

When it is found *in front* of a number, **ic** makes it the ordinal form (i.e., 'first, second, third …', as opposed to the cardinal forms 'one, two, three …'):

In ic ēyi calli ca nocal	*The third house (lit., the one by which it is three) is mine*

14.5 *Iuh(qui)*

Iuh or **iuhqui**, pl. **iuhquê**, is a predicate meaning 'to be so, such':

Ca mochtin iuhquê	*They're all like that*
Ca tiuhqui!	*That's how you (s.) are! – That's nice of you!*

▶ **Note.** Here we recognize the participial suffix. What we have is actually the preterite (used adjectivally; see 12.4) of the verb **ihui**, which is virtually unused except in fixed expressions like **mā ihui** 'may it be so'.

Iuhqui or **iuhquin** (a contraction of **iuhqui in**) can mean 'to be like, to be similar to …'. In this usage, the form is invariable, and the term of comparison takes the personal markers. Rather than the English translation 'X is like Y', the Nahuatl phrase is comparable to the English idiom '(it's) as if (**iuhqui**) X were Y'. Thus:

Iuhquin tichichi (not ****tiuhqui(n) chichi**)	*You're like a dog (it's as if you (s.) were a dog)*
Iuhquin titōchtli ticìhui	*You're (s.) rushing like a rabbit (as if you were a rabbit)*

14.6 *Quēn*

'How?' translates as **quēn**. As with the majority of the interrogatives seen so far, there is a long form, **quēnin**, whose sense is slightly "stronger" ('how is it possible that …?', 'how is it the case that …?').

Quēn ticâ?	*How are you (s.)?*
Quēn (*or* quēnin) mochīhuaz in?	*How will this be done/happen?*
Quēnin àmo ticmati?	*How can it be that you (s.) don't know it?*

Quēn generally appears in front of a verb. It is also possible to say:

Quēn in? *or* Quēnin in?	*How so?*

There is a corresponding negative form **àquēn** (cf. **ayāc, àtle, àcān**):

Àquēn nicmati	*I don't feel this at all (i.e., it makes no difference to me)*

In quēn in 'in the manner in which' appears in expressions of indirect questions or comparison:

Àmo nicmati in quēn in ōquichīuh	*I don't know how he did it*
In quēn in miqui in mācēhualli, zan nō iuh miqui in tlàtoāni	*As the commoner dies, so too does the ruler die*

14.7 'When?': Īc

For interrogative 'when?' Nahuatl has two words: **īc** and **quēmman**. **Īc**[4] has a long form of the same meaning, **īquin** (cf. **āquin**, **tlein** etc.):

Īc (= īquin) huāllāz? – Zan mōztla.	*When will he come? – Tomorrow.*
Īc (= īquin) ōtihuāllâ? – Ca yālhua.	*When did you (s.) come? – Yesterday.*

There is a negative form **aīc** 'never' as well as the compounds **aoc īc** 'never again', **ayaīc** or **ayamo īc** 'never yet', **mācaīc** 'may/let…never' (with the optative):

Aīc ōniquittac	*I've never seen it*
Ayaīc ninococoa	*I've never been sick yet* (note the present tense, 8.9)
Aoc āc īc quittaz	*No one will ever see it again* (note that when there are a number of compound negatives, only the first one appears with the negative; see 4.9)
Mācaīc xicchīhuacān in	*Never do (pl.) this!*

In īquin means 'when(ever)', 'at the time when (whenever that may be)'[5] in temporal subordinate clauses and indirect questions:

Mozōma in īquin nicnōtza	*He gets angry when(ever) I speak to him*
Nimitzcelīz in īquin tihuāllāz	*I'll receive you (s.) when you (will) come*
Àmo nicmati in īquin huāllāz	*I don't know when he'll come*

14.8 'When?': Quēmman

Quēmman has no long form.[6] It is not a mere synonym of **īc**. **Quēmman** implies a specific time within a particular day ('at what moment in the day?', 'at what time?').

Quēmman huālquīza in tōnatiuh? – Ca yohuatzinco. – Auh quēmman oncalaqui? – Ca teōtlac	*What time does the sun rise (come out toward here)? – In the morning. – And what time does it set (enter going away)? – In the evening.*
Quēmman ticochi? – Àmo tlàcâ, zan yohuac.	*When do you (s.) sleep? – Not during the day, just at night.*
Quēmman tàcizquê? – Āxcān teōtlac.	*When will we arrive? – This evening.*

[4] Not to be confused with **ic** (14.4).
[5] Cf. the distinction between German 'wenn', meaning 'whenever, if' and 'als', meaning 'at the specific moment when' (as in 14.9).
[6] This is the case with all the compound interrogatives (cf. **cāmpa**), **quēmman** being composed of **quēn** and a locative-temporal suffix **-man**.

There is a negative form, **àquēmman**. Paired with **aīc**, it intensifies a negation (cf. English 'never, ever').

Zan tinēchtequipachoa, àquēmman tinēchcāhua	*You just bother me, you never leave me alone*
Aoc īc, aoc quēmman yez in mēxìcayōtl	*Mexica civilization is done for forever (it will never again exist)*

We can also have **in quēmman** 'at the time when':

Niccelīz in quēmman àciz	*I'll receive him when he arrives (knowing that he will do so today)*

▶ *Note.* Nouns for times of day are locative forms with a temporal meaning: **yohuatzinco** 'in the morning', **nepantlâ tōnatiuh** 'at noon',[7] **tlàcâ** 'in the daytime, late',[8] **teōtlac** 'in the evening', **yohuac** 'at night, during the night'.

14.9 Subordinate Temporal Clauses

In English, we have the non-interrogative 'when' that acts as a subordinating conjunction. We have seen (14.7, 8) that the Nahuatl equivalent can be **in īquin** or **in quēmman**; however, these expressions have an indefinite sense. Other expressions are possible. In particular, **in** can be used by itself:

Ayamo oncalaqui in tōnatiuh in ōninotēcac	*The sun hadn't set yet when I went to bed*

Frequently, **in** by itself introduces a subordinate clause whose verb is in the preterite with the augment, which marks prior action. When the main clause follows, it often starts with **niman**, which means 'then, right after'. In this sense, the subordinating conjunction is often translated with 'after' in English:

In ōquicuâ in, niman mic	*After he ate this, he died*
In ōticchīuh in, niman timocuepaz mochān	*After you've (s.) done this, you are to return (to your) home*

As in English, the prior action may appear in the main clause:

Ye ōnitlacuâ in tihuāllāz	*I'll have already eaten when you (s.) will arrive*

▶ Note that while in English prior action in the future is indicated with the distinctive future perfect tense, Nahuatl simply uses the preterite to

---

[7] For **nepantlâ**, see 24.2.

[8] In the meaning 'late', the opposite of **tlàcâ** is **cualcān**, which in a temporal sense means 'soon, in good time'.

indicate relative rather than absolute temporal priority. That is, here the preterite represents future time that is prior to the **in-** clause and not a past tense in reference to the present time of the speaker.

In is often associated with other particles like **oc** and **ye** (7.9):

In ye cochi in calê, niman īchān calacquê in ichtecquê	*Once the householder was (already) sleeping, the thieves entered his house*
Nēchhuālitta in oc ninococoa	*He comes to see me as long as (when … still) I'm ill*

But the particle most commonly associated with **in** in a temporal sense is **ìcuāc**, which otherwise means 'at that time', most often followed by a demonstrative:

Ca ìcuāc on ōnitlācat	*It was at that time that I was born*

In ìcuāc indicates simultaneous action, whether at a specific moment (punctual) or over a longer period of time (durative):

In ìcuāc ommi in Caxtillān tlaīlli, ca yamānqui, tzopēlic	*When wine (the Spanish drink) is drunk, he is sweet, pleasant* (Note that *ommi* is the reflexive used in a passive sense; see 6.6 sec 6.)
In ìcuāc ninococoa, àmo nitlacua	*When I'm sick, I don't eat*

In instances where English uses the past progressive ('was VERBing') in the main clause followed by a subordinate temporal clause with the simple past, Nahuatl uses the present in the main clause:

Quiyahui in ìcuāc ōninēuh	*It was raining when I got up* (rather than **quiyahuiya**)

14.10 *Quin*

Quin means 'just now', 'momentarily'. With the preterite, it indicates an action in the recent past:

Quin ōnihuāllâ	*I just arrived*

With the future, it is translated 'in a minute, later, not until':

Quin ticmatiz	*You're about to know it*
Àhuel niyāz mōztla, quin huīptla niyāz	*I won't be able to go tomorrow, (I'll go) only the day after tomorrow*

Quin is sometimes reinforced with **iuh**, with the verb generally in the present:

Quin iuh ninēhua	*I've only gotten up just now*

In quin or **in quin iuh** (sometimes just **in iuh**) means 'at the moment when':

> In quin iuh huālàcî caxtiltēcâ, cān   *When the Spaniards had just arrived, where*
> catca cahuayo?   *was a horse (i.e., were horses)?*

VOCABULARY

Intransitive verb

choloa	*to flee*

Transitive verbs

celia	*to receive*	nāmiqui	*to come upon, to find,*
huīca	*to bring, to lead*		*to meet*
ìiyōhuia	*to suffer, to endure,*	tequipachoa	*to bother,*
	to tolerate		*to torment*

Nouns

ācalli	*boat, ship*	mītl	*arrow*
āmoxtli	*book*	tlacualli	*food*
cahuayo	*(pl. /-mê/) horse*	tlaīlli	*drink*
chīmalli	*shield*	tlàtoāni	*(pl. tlàtòquê) ruler, king*[9]
huīpilli	*blouse, huipil*[10]	tlàtōlli	*word, speech, language*
ichcatl	*(pl. /-mê/) sheep*	tōnatiuh	*sun*[11]
Malintzin	*Mary*	tzopilōtl	*(pl. /-mê/) vulture*
mazātl	*(pl. /R–'/) deer*		

Adjectives[12]

ichtecqui	*thief*	yamānqui	*sweet, pleasant*
iuh(qui)	*such, similar*	yancuīc	*new*

Locatives

huèca	*far (away)*	teōtlac	*in the evening*
huècauh	*for a long time*	tlàcâ[13]	*during the day, later*
huīptla	*the day after*	yohuac	*at night*
	tomorrow[14]	yohualnepantlâ	*at midnight (n. tōnatiuh*
nepantlâ	*in the middle*		*at noon)*
nōhuiyān	*everywhere*	yohuatzinco	*in the morning*

---

[9] This is not a true noun but a verbal form (see 16.5).

[10] This sort of blouse is worn today by women everywhere in indigenous Mexico.

[11] This word is likewise a verbal form (see 27.1.6).

[12] All these "adjectives" have the participial suffix -c/-qui and so a plural in -quê.

[13] Not to be confused with **tlàcâ** 'humans'.

[14] **Huīptla** signifies not just the day directly after tomorrow but also any subsequent day as appropriate.

Interrogatives

īc	*when?*	quēn	*how?*
quēmman	*when? what time?*		

Particles

(à)nozo	*or*	īhuān	*and*
àzo	*perhaps*	niman	*then*
auh	*and, but*	nō	*also*
ic	*so, by* (used to form ordinals)	quin	*just now, soon*

EXERCISES

(a) Translate into English.
1. Nēchcocoa in nocxi, nō huel nēchcocoa in notlan.
2. Àmo huel cuauhtic, àmo nō tepitōn.
3. Zan ye nō oncān in ōniquinnāmic.
4. Ōmpa câ Xōchimīlco, ànozo Mēxìco.
5. Niquēhua in xōchitl, in cuīcatl.
6. Cuix nō tèhuātl ye ōtitlacuâ?
7. Āquin on? – Àmo nicmati: àzo mēxìcatl, ànozo caxtiltēcatl.
8. Xiquitta inon tlācatl: ca zan ye nō yèhuātl in yālhua nicān tlacuāya.
9. Ca ye caxtolxilhuitl in ōtiyōl, in ōtitlācat.
10. Ye ōtihuāllâ, Pedrotzé! Auh tlein ticnequi?
11. Quēmman ōtihuāllâ? – Ca āxcān yohuatzinco.
12. Aīc noconitta in Pedro, ca zan yèhuātl nicān nēchhuālitta.
13. Ye yohuac, xommotēcacān. – Ca ayamō, zan oc teōtlac, ayamo oncalaqui in tōnatiuh.
14. In ìcuāc ōmic, huel ōtichōcaquê.
15. Quin tiquittaz in Malintzin yancuīc īhuīpil.
16. Octica ōtlāhuān.
17. Itztli ic ōninoxin.
18. Iuhquin ampitzōmê ancatzāhuaquê.
19. Mācamo iuhquin nichichi xinēchnōtza.

(b) Translate into Nahuatl
1. He has found the path of the rabbit (and) of the deer (*i.e., he leads a dissolute life*).
2. I don't know what that is. Maybe a rabbit, perhaps a dog.
3. Are there still women or children there?
4. I'll go to Xochimilco the day after tomorrow, and I will also go to Tlaxcala.
5. I'm going to Cuernavaca. – That's exactly where I'm going.

6. I've injured Peter. – And what did he say?
7. They all died by fire.
8. When I get drunk, I'm happy.
9. What time will you (s.) go to see Peter? – This evening.
10. When will you (s.) go to Cuernavaca? – The day after tomorrow.
11. How did you (s.) do that?
12. Don't (s.) come at midnight. At night, I sleep.
13. When I've read this book, I'll know many things.
14. After he shouted, I came out ("emerged").
15. He hasn't helped me, and I won't help him either.
16. Whenever I've gotten dirty, I bathe ("wash myself").
17. Is Mexico still far off?
18. I've written it in ink.
19. I've made myself dirty with mud.
20. You (s.) speak like a Mexica.
21. You (s.) are talking to me as if I were a commoner, as if you were my lord.

Impersonal and Passive Verb Forms

15.1 Impersonal Forms of Intransitive Verbs with Animate Subjects

Recall that the prefixes **tē-** and **tla-** (3.6) indicate that the object is indefinite. But what happens if the *subject* is indefinite? You might want to say, for example, 'someone is sleeping', 'there are people sleeping' or 'someone has shouted', 'there was shouting'. In such a case, it is impossible to say ****tēcochi** or ****ōtētzàtzic**. Instead, we have to express it by making use of the *impersonal voice* of the verb. This concept is conveyed in English with various indefinite subjects ('someone is shouting', 'people think', 'one enters') or some sort of verbal abstraction in place of a regular verb ('there is shouting', 'entry is prohibited').

Let us look first at the simplest case of impersonal forms, that of intransitive verbs. This form is usually made in Nahuatl by adding **-hua** to base 1, with lengthening of the final vowel of the stem (there are often phonological changes in this, see 15.2). Thus:

Cochīhua	*Someone's sleeping, everyone's sleeping*
Ōtzàtzīhuac	*Someone shouted, there was shouting*
Tlācatīhuac	*There were births*
Temōhuaz	*People will descend*

As can be seen, this form can take all the tense and mood suffixes. Because the form is not transitive, the verb fits into the category of "verbs with vowel-retaining preterites," so base 2 of the new form ends in **-hua** and the preterite in **-huac** (see 8.7).

It is naturally impossible to have a regular subject prefix; therefore, a form like ****nicochīhua** is ruled out. For the same reason, there is no plural.

15.2 Morphology of the Impersonal Voice

If the last consonant of the stem is /k/ (verbs ending in -ca or -**qui**) or /m/, the following vowel always changes to -ō- in front of the impersonal marker -**hua**:

chōcōhua	*someone's crying, there's crying, everyone's crying* (chōca)
micōhua	*there are deaths, someone's dying* (miqui)
pācōhua	*there's rejoicing* (pāqui)
tlālticpac nemōhua	*there's life on earth* (nemi)

There is the same shift to -ō- if the last consonant is /w/ (verbs in -**hui**, -**hua**), but as we have seen (7.1), /w/ disappears in front of /o/. Thus we have:

ēōhua	*one is leaving* (ēhua)
teòciōhua	*there is hunger* (teòcihui)

and not ****ēhuōhua**, ****teòcihuōhua**.

We find the same phenomenon after /s/ and /c/ (verbs ending in -**ci**, -**za**, -**tzi**, -**tza**), but in addition, /s/ shifts to /š/ (**x**) and /c/ to /č/ (**ch**):

nēxōhua	*people appear* (nēci)
quīxōhua	*there's departing* (quīza)
huechōhua	*someone falls* (huetzi)

However, the vowel **ī** is retained if there is a consonant in front of the /s/ or /c/. In this case, /c/ (**tz**) is retained, as we saw earlier (**tzàtzīhua** 'there is shouting'), but /s/ still shifts to /š/ (**x**):

Mexìco àxīhuac	*people arrived at Mexico* (and not ****àcīhuac** or ****àxōhuac**)

As can be seen, the morphology of the impersonal is a bit complicated, and there are exceptions (in particular, see 15.6 for impersonal constructions built according to a quite different method). There are also some doublets, like **huetzīhua** 'someone falls' alongside **huechōhua**.

We will call *base 4* the form taken by the verb stem (**cochī**-, **chōcō**-, **ēō**-, **quīxō**-, **àxī**- etc.) before the impersonal suffix –**hua**.

15.3 Inanimate Impersonal in *tla*-

We have seen that ****tēcochi** is impossible and that instead we have **cochīhua**. If, however, you wish to speak of indefinite *things* (for instance, 'everything turns green' or 'things dry up'), all you do is add the prefix **tla-** to the regular intransitive form:

Celiya in cuahuitl	*The tree turns green*
Tlaceliya	*Everything turns green*
Huāqui in xihuitl	*The grass dries up*
Tlahuāqui	*Everything dries up, there's a drought*
Polihui in mēxìcayōtl	*Mexican civilization is disappearing*
Tlapolihui	*Things are disappearing*
Popōca in tepētl	*The mountain is smoking*
Tlapopōca	*There's smoke*

In other words, use of the suffix **-hua** is possible only if the indefinite subject is a human being. Hence, there can be two impersonal forms on the same verb, for example, the animate **poliōhua** (for ****polihuōhua**, see 15.2) 'people get lost' and the inanimate **tlapolihui** 'things get lost'; and alongside **nēxōhua** there is also **tlanēci** 'things appear', that is, 'day is dawning'. Similarly:

Tlālpan manīhua	*People spread over the earth*
Quēn tlamani? – Cualli ic tlamani.	*How are things? (lit., how do they lie?) – Well.*
Àmo onacōhuaz	*One is not to enter* (aqui 'enter')
Ca tlaaqui ītech inin cuahuitl	*This tree is fruitful (lit., things emerge onto it)*

Note the use of **tla-** (and not **tē-**!) in verbs that pertain to a human subject but indicate that this subject is undergoing an external influence, reacting to an event independent of him and not acting of his own will. There are fewer than ten verbs of this type. The most common is:

Nicuecuechca	*I'm trembling*
Tlacuecuechca	*There's trembling*

15.4 Passive Voice

Now let us look at what happens with indefinite subjects of transitive verbs. If you want to say, for example, 'Someone loves me' without specifying who is doing the loving, you use the *passive voice*, which looks pretty much like English *I am loved*, that is: the object, which in a transitive verb usually refers to a patient, switches grammatical function and is raised to subject position.

The most frequent passive marker is **–lo** (for more details, see 15.5):

Nitlazòtlalo	*I'm loved*
Tinōtzalo	*You're (s.) addressed, someone is calling you, speaking to you*
Piyalo in malli	*The prisoner is being guarded*

Because the patient acquires the grammatical properties of subject, the verb *agrees with* this subject, and so it can be in the plural:

Titlazòtlalô	*We are loved*
Annōtzalô	*You (pl.) are being addressed*
Piyalô in māmaltin	*The prisoners are being guarded*

The other tenses are formed like all verbs in -o (the three bases are identical and the vowel is long in front of the suffixes other than'; see 8.7 and 9.3):

Nitlazòtlalōz	*I will be loved*
Ōannōtzalōquê	*You've (pl.) been addressed*
Piyalōyâ in māmaltin	*The prisoners were being guarded*

In English, the human agent of a passive verb can be expressed with a prepositional phrase starting with 'by...'. In Nahuatl, however, you cannot mark the agent of the passive directly. Thus, 'I'm loved' can be translated with **nitlazòtlalo**, but to translate 'I'm loved by my father', it is necessary to resort to the active form: **nēchtlazòtla in notàtzin**. It is not uncommon to have both transitive and intransitive verbs appear side by side:

Nitlazòtlalo, nēchtlazòtla in notàtzin	*I'm loved, my father loves me* (this can be translated with *I'm loved by my father*)

15.5 Morphology of the Passive

In reality, the passive marker -**lo** consists of two suffixes. One is -**l**-, which builds base 4 (see 15.2) of most transitive verbs and which also appears in causatives (see Lesson 19) and some derivative nouns (30.2). The second one, -**o**, is actually a variant of the impersonal suffix, which has its basic form -**hua** after a vowel but appears as -**o** after a consonant. Let's now look into the details.

15.5.1 Regular Formation

The most common method is to add the element -**l**- (and therefore the double suffix -**l**-**o**) to *base 3* of the verb. This means that with most verbs the -**l**- is added to the stem (base 1), but verbs in -**ia**, -**oa** lose their final -**a** and the remaining vowel is lengthened in non-final position:

Nipalēhuīlo	*I'm being helped* (**palēhuia**)
Nìtōlo	*I'm mentioned, I'm being spoken of* (**ìtoa**)
Nitolīnīlo	*I'm made unfortunate* (**tolīnia**)
Nicocōlo	*I'm being injured* (**cocōa**)

15.5.2 Other Formations

The second method of forming base 4 consists of adding the suffix -**hua**/-**o** to a special stem of the verb that does not include the element -**l**-. This stem is in principle identical to base 2 (the preterite), but there are some exceptions, as we will see. Because this form of base 4 most often ends in a consonant, -**hua** generally becomes -**o**, but it sometimes does appear in its original form.

This method is obligatory in certain cases and optional in others:

A) OBLIGATORY

▶ with monosyllables in -**i** (which is lengthened):

Īhua   *It is drunk*[1]   Cuīhua   *It is taken*

▶ with certain verbs in -**mi**, the most common of which is **quēmi** 'dress'; the final -**i** is retained and lengthened:

Quēmīhua   *He is dressed*

▶ with verbs ending in -**ca**, -**qui**, base 4 is formed by dropping the final vowel in both instances (whereas base 2 of verbs in -**ca** ends in -**ca**, 8.7):

Teco	*It is cut* (**tequi**)	Tēco	*It is laid down* (**tēca**)
Caco	*He is heard* (**caqui**)	Tōco	*He is buried* (**tōca**)
Ilnāmico	*He is remembered*	Pāco	*He is washed* (**pāca**)
(ilnāmiqui)			

▶ with **mati**, for which base 4 is **mach**-:

Macho   *He is known*

B) OPTIONAL

▶ with verbs in -**ni**, -**na**:

Ānalo *or* āno   *He is taken prisoner*

▶ with verbs in -**ci**, -**za**, with /s/ shifting into /š/ (**x**):

Tlāzalo *or* tlāxo   *It is thrown* (**tlāza**)

▶ with **itta**, whose base 4 is **itt**- in the non-regular formation:

Ittalo *or* itto   *He is seen*

---

[1] In fact, such a form is quite unlikely because the reflexive is used to translate 'it is drunk' (15.9). However, the impersonal **tlaīhua** (15.6) and the -**ni** passive **īhuani** 'drinkable' (16.6) certainly are regular forms.

15.6 Impersonal Forms of Intransitive Verbs Based on the Passive Stem

Certain intransitive verbs build their impersonal form (i.e., one with an indefinite subject) in the same way as the passive of transitive verbs (unlike the forms discussed in 15.1–2, which have the same meaning but are built with base 1). This intransitive use of the passive is not particularly common, and the most frequently met forms are:

mayānalo	*one is hungry, there is famine* (**mayāna**)
cuīco	*people are singing, there is singing* (**cuīca**)[2]
huetzco	*someone's laughing, there is laughter* (**huetzca**)
tlaōcoyalo	*there's sadness* (**tlaōcoya**)

Irregular verbs have the following impersonal forms:

for **câ**: yelōhua	*people are (in some place)*
for **yauh**: huīlōhua	*one goes*
for **huītz**: huīlōhuatz	*one comes*

> ▶ *Note.* These are irregular formations with a double suffix (i.e., the regular impersonal ending -**hua** is added to form ending in -**lo**, which is derived from *-**l-hua**). **Huītz** is formed from **huī** 'go' by adding the directional suffix -**tz** (see 5.3).

15.7 Impersonal Form of Transitive Verbs

In 15.4, we saw that the passive construction is used when transitive verbs have an indefinite agent but a definite patient. Now, we will look at the case in which both agent and patient are indefinite (e.g., 'people eat things', 'people love others'). One simply adds the regular indefinite object prefix **tē**- or **tla**- (depending on whether the indefinite patient is human or non-human) to the passive form. The tenses are formed in exactly the same way as with the passive (except that the form here is exclusively in the third person singular). Thus:

tētlazòtlalo	*there is love, people love others*
tlacuālōz, tlaīhuaz	*there will be eating and drinking*
ōtlacōhualōc, ōtlanamacōc	*there was buying* (**cōhua**) *and selling* (**namaca**)
tēnōtzalo	*people are called, there is a summoning*
tēānalōc *or* tēānōc	*people were taken prisoner, there was a taking of prisoners*

---

[2] The regular impersonal would actually be **cuīcōhua** (15.2).

15.8 Reflexive Impersonal

A subcategory of the impersonal transitive verb is the impersonal reflexive (an indefinite animate agent acts upon itself or there is a reciprocal action among unspecified people: 'people love themselves/each other'; 'people mutually aid each other' etc.). To make this form, the prefix **ne-** is added to the passive stem (i.e., this is basically the same formation as the one described in 15.7, except that here we have a special prefix for a reflexive indefinite object). Thus:

Netlātīlo	*Everyone hides (himself)*
Nepalēhuīlōz, netlazòtlalōz	*People will help and love each other*
Nepācōc, neximalōc	*People washed and shaved (themselves)*

The same form is also used with reflexive verbs that indicate movement, emotion or physical state (6.6):

Netlālīlo	*People sit*	Necocōlo	*People are sick, there's illness*
Necuepalo	*There's a return of people*	Netlalōlo	*There's running*
Nezōmālo	*There's anger*	Netolīnīlo	*There's misfortune*

Ne- does not usually cause elision of an **i-** in front of two consonants:

Neittalo	*People see each other*	Neilnāmico	*People remember each other*
Neilcāhualo	*People forget each other*	Neilpīlo	*People bind themselves*

One can, however, find forms like **nettalo**, a doublet of **neittalo**. If the first consonant is a glottal stop, the elision of **i-** is more frequent than its retention:

Nètōtīlo (**m(o)-ìtōtia** *he dances*)	*There's dancing* (rather than **neitōtīlo**)

If the verb stem begins with **e-** or **ē-**, there may be elision:

Nēhualo *or* neēhualo	*People get up (pick themselves up)* (**ēhua**)

With the addition of this impersonal reflexive prefix to the catalog of reflexives, the list of prefixes (table in section 6.5) is complete; there are no other prefixes.

15.9 Reflexive and Passive

The use of passive verb forms is mostly restricted to situations with an indefinite human agent and definite human patient. In other words, a passive expression is used when one or more people who are not specified do something to one or more specific people. If what we are dealing with is an action carried out by people who are not specified on *things* that are specified, we do not normally have an impersonal or passive construction but an active one in the *reflexive*:

Mochīhua (*and not* chīhualo) in calli	*The house is being built, People are building the house*
Motequi (*and not* teco) in xōchitl	*The flowers are picked*
Mi in ātl	*The water is drunk*
Mocua in nacatl	*The meat is eaten*

The English reflexive does not have this sort of passive meaning, but it is common in the Romance languages. There, however, the usage regularly has a sort of theoretical meaning, so that in French 'l'eau se boit' (lit., 'the water drinks itself') means that the water *can* be drunk, that is, that it is drinkable, rather than signifying the fact that someone specific is actually drinking it. The corresponding Nahuatl phrase **mi in ātl** can have this sense of possibility, but it can also signify that there are (presently) unspecified people drinking the water.

Hence, in Nahuatl one says of a person that he 'is seen' or 'is loved' but of a thing that it 'sees itself' or 'loves itself':

Ōittalōc (*or* ōittōc) in Pedro	*Peter has been seen*
Ōmottac in calli	*The house has been seen*
Titōlōz	*You'll (s.) be spoken of*
Mìtoa in	*This is said, People say this*
Tlazòtlalô in pīpiltin	*The children are loved*
Motlazòtla in teōcuitlatl	*People love gold, Gold is held in esteem*

This principle must be qualified in certain regards. First, the stars, forces of nature and the like are more or less personified, which has grammatical consequences. One of these is pluralization (2.6), and another is the possibility of such nouns appearing as the subject of a passive. Hence, it is possible to say:

Ittalo in mētztli, centetl xīhuitl, centetl citlālin	*The moon, one comet and one star are seen*

as well as **motta in mētztli** etc. Similarly, the phrase meaning 'there is an eclipse of the sun' is:

Cuālo (*and not* mocua) in tōnatiuh	*There is an eclipse of the sun (lit., the sun is eaten)*

Sometimes, we can also find inanimate subjects of passive verbs in more formal texts. It seems that this can be generally viewed as an effect of stylistic solemnity:

Ōìtōlōc inin tlàtōlli   *These words have been said*

The second qualification of the principle has to do with the impersonal forms laid out in 15.7, 8. The impersonal of transitive verbs with an indefinite patient is formed by adding **tla-** to the passive stem, whereas the indefinite reflexive **ne-** is restricted to situations where an indefinite agent acts upon itself. We therefore have to watch out against equating a sentence like **mochīhua in calli** 'the house is built', where the house does not in fact act upon itself, with the "real" reflexive **moxima in Pedro** 'Peter shaves (himself)'. The impersonal version of the latter is **neximalo** 'people shave (themselves), there is shaving', while the corresponding expression for the former is **tlachīhualo** 'things are built, there is building'.

There is also a third qualification involving a derivative formation, which we will see in 16.6.

We have to be careful with reflexive forms of verbs of emotion or state (15.8). If we consider forms like **ninotolīnia, ninococoa** or **ninozōma**, we see that they do not mean 'I oppress myself, I harm myself, I annoy myself' but something like 'there are unspecified things or circumstances that oppress, harm, annoy me', that is, the *sense* is not really reflexive.[3] As we have seen, however, the corresponding impersonal forms are construed as formal reflexives: **netolīnia, necocōlo, nezōmalo** (and not **tētolīnilo, tēcocōlo, tēzōmalo**; such forms exist but mean 'people oppress, harm, annoy other people'; see 15.7).

15.10 Inherently Impersonal Verbs

In English, there are verbs referring to natural phenomena that have no real subject and for this reason are called "impersonal," for example, 'it's raining'. (Such forms have a "dummy" subject 'it', but this refers to nothing in particular and is used merely because an English verb needs an overt subject.) Nahuatl has similar impersonal verbs, such as **tōna** 'to be hot', **quiyahui** 'to rain', **èeca** 'to be windy', and (as one would expect) these do not take the indefinite subject markers **-hua** or **tla-**.

---

[3] That is, the forms are reflexive in construction but not meaning (cf. the English 'I enjoy myself', which simply means 'I have a good time' and is not the reflexive equivalent of a phrase like 'I enjoy the performance').

15.11 The Third Person Plural Substituting for the Impersonal

An active form with the third person plural subject is sometimes found in instances where we might expect the impersonal or the passive. This is the case when it is supposed that the subject represents a group of people whose identity is not so clear or not so important. At times, this must be interpreted as 'the public authorities' (this usage appears in a number of languages, including English):

Xitemo: ca mitznōtzâ	*Come down, they're calling you*
Tiyānquizco ōnēchilpìquê	*I was arrested (they bound me) in the market-place*

15.12 Alternation between Impersonal and Personal Forms

A very common stylistic figure in Nahuatl consists of repeating a verb, first with an impersonal form and then a second time with a personal one. This figure is used with both the subject and the object. Thus, with the object one can have an indefinite prefix followed by a definite one:

Tlàtoa in tīcitl, quìtoa ...	*The midwife speaks, saying ...*[4]
Ontēnāmicquê, quimonnāmicquê in caxtiltēcâ	*They went for a meeting and they had one with the Spaniards (lit., they went to meet people, they met the Spaniards)*

When this figure is used with the subject, we can have a passive followed by an active form:

Tlàpalōlōquê in caxtiltēcâ, yèhuāntin quintlàpalòquê in mēxicâ tētēuctin	*The Spaniards were greeted, it's the Mexica lords who greeted them*

The literal translation is often not very natural in English (in the second example, what we have is close to a passive phrase with an indication of the agent: 'the Spaniards were greeted by the Mexica lords'). What the Nahuatl is trying to do is to emphasize both the verb and the subject or object at the same time, with the two pieces of information 'what happened?' and 'who did it?' (or 'who did this happen to?') appearing one after the other rather than turning up together. Another way of looking at it is that because the passive in Nahuatl cannot indicate the agent (unlike the case with English), the second (active) clause provides the agent for the first (passive) clause.

---

[4] With **quìtoa**, the prefix **qui-** refers to the following quotation of the doctor's words.

VOCABULARY

Inherently impersonal verb

èeca	*to be windy*

Intransitive verbs

aqui	*to enter*	mayāna	*to be hungry*
celiya	*to become green*	popōca	*to smoke*
cuecuechca	*to tremble*	teòcihui	*to be hungry*
huāqui	*to dry up*	tlaōcoya	*to be sad*

Transitive verbs

ilcāhua	*to forget*	quēmi	*to clothe, to put on*
ilnāmiqui	*to remember*	tlàpaloa	*to greet*
ìtōtia	(m-: *to dance*)	tōca	*to bury, to plant,*
namaca	*to sell*		*to sow*

Nouns

mōlli	*sauce*[5]	tiyānquiztli	*market*
tamalli	*tamale*	tōcāitl	*name*
tilmàtli	*cape, sarape*[6]	xīhuitl	*comet*

EXERCISES

(a) Translate the following sentences into English, then rewrite the Nahuatl sentence with the appropriate verb form for an unspecified agent (passive, impersonal or reflexive).

1. Niquilnāmiqui inon tlācatl ītōcā.
2. Àmo nicmati tlein ītōcā.
3. Cualāni in Pedro.
4. In ōtlacuàquê, niman ēhuaquê, onyàquê.
5. Tēcpan calaquî in mācēhualtin.
6. Yāōpan tiquimānazquê in otomî.
7. Petlapan motlāliâ in cihuâ.
8. Mochtin poliuhquê.
9. Àmo huel nicpōhuaz in tetl.
10. Àmo huel niquimpōhuaz in tlācâ.
11. Yālhua ōnamēchittac.

[5] In Mexico, the word 'mole' is given to various sorts of stew or thick sauces, generally prepared with spices and accompanied with poultry or meat.

[6] The Mexican 'sarape' is like a poncho.

      12. Cencâ pāquî in pīpiltin.

      13. Mēxìco ōmocuepquê.

      14. Ilhuicacopa titlachiyâ.

      15. Ācaltica ōnēchhuīcac.

(b) Translate into English.

      1. Inin tlācatl àmo huel panahuīlōz in ītech chicāhuacāyōtl.

      2. Tlein mochīhua in nicān? – Ca tlàcuilōlo, tlapōhualo.

      3. Àmo ōtēcelīlōc: ayāc ōhuāllâ.

      4. Àmo cualli catca in tlacualli: ic necocōlōc.

      5. Ca ye ōnxihuitl in nicān īpan āltepētl àmo tlācatīhua: zan micōhua, nō ōmpa huīlōhua Mexìco.

      6. Ca yohuac, àmo tlattalo, àmo nō huel tlachīhualo: mōztla tlanēciz.

      7. In īpan huēyi ilhuitl, moquēmi in cualli tilmàtli.

      8. Àmo momati in àzo ōmic, ànozo àmō.

      9. Ca àtle ōmocuīc, àmo nō āc ōcocōlōc.

     10. Mōztla ōmpa Xōchimīlco nenāmicōz.

(c) Translate into Nahuatl.

      1. Has the pulque already been drunk?

      2. This has never yet been seen (8.9).

      3. Over there in the market there is buying and selling.

      4. People have gone into the cave and hidden there.

      5. People are listening to Mary's song. – No, it's not Mary that they're listening to.

      6. Tomorrow flowers will be sold in the market.

      7. It won't be possible for you to be helped (s.) ("You won't be able…").

      8. Over there people don't speak Nahuatl (think carefully about the construction of tlàtoa: tlàtoa "say things").

      9. Those little children weren't good, so (**ic**) people got mad.

     10. Did people come here?

     11. Tomorrow there will singing, laughing, eating, drinking.

     12. Yes, mole and tamales will be eaten, pulque will be drunk.

     13. The lord is greeted when he passes by here.

     14. There were deaths here in the city.

     15. You (s.) aren't known here.

     16. People love flowers.

REVIEW EXERCISES FOR PART ONE

(a) Vocabulary text

Here is a list of 100 very common words. Make sure that you can recognize at least 70 of them.

(i) Nouns

1. ācatl	17. icxitl	32. nōchtli	47. tlaōlli
2. āltepētl	18. ilhuitl	33. octli	48. tlaxcalli
3. āmatl	19. iztatl	34. oquichtli	49. tlàtoāni
4. ātl	20. ìtitl	35. òtli	50. tlācatl
5. āxcāitl	21. īxtli	36. petlatl	51. tlālli
6. calli	22. mācēhualli	37. pilli	52. tletl
7. camatl	23. māitl	38. quetzalli	53. tōtolin
8. chāntli	24. metl	39. tàtli	54. tōcāitl
9. chīlli	25. metlatl	40. teōtl	55. tōchtli
10. cihuātl	26. mētztli	41. tepētl	56. tōnatiuh
11. citlālin	27. michin	42. tetl	57. tōtōtl
12. cōhuātl	28. mīlli	43. tēntli	58. xihuitl
13. cuahuitl	29. nacaztli	44. tēuctli	59. xōchitl
14. cualli	30. nāntli	45. tiyānquiztli	60. yacatl
15. cuāuhtli	31. nòpalli	46. tlamantli	61. yōllòtli
16. etl			

(ii) Verbs

62. àci	67. chiya	72. cua	77. ēhua
63. calaqui	68. chīhua	73. cuepa	78. huīca
64. caqui	69. chōca	74. cui	79. huītz
65. câ	70. cochi	75. cuīca	80. i
66. cāhua	71. cocoa	76. èeca	81. itta

82. ìcuiloa	87. nemi	92. pōhua	97. tlazòtla
83. ìtoa	88. nequi	93. quiyahui	98. tlālia
84. mani	89. pāqui	94. quīza	99. tōna
85. mati	90. piya	95. tequi	100. yauh
86. miqui	91. polihui	96. tlami	

(b) Grammatical words

Also, be sure that you can recognize at least 40 of the following words, which have appeared in the text in various contexts.

1. achi	11. cencâ	21. īc	31. nō	41. quin
2. amèhuāntin	12. cē	22. īhuān	32. oc	42. tèhuāntin
3. ayāc	13. cuix	23. mā	33. on	43. tèhuātl
4. àmō	14. ēyi	24. miyac	34. oncān	44. tlā
5. àtle	15. huel	25. moch	35. ōme	45. tlein
6. àzo	16. huèca	26. mōztla	36. quēmâ	46. yālhua
7. āquin	17. huēyi	27. nāhui	37. ōmpa	47. ye
8. āxcān	18. ic	28. nèhuātl	38. quēmman	48. yèhuantin
9. ca	19. in	29. nicān	39. quēn	49. yèhuātl
10. cān	20. iuhqui(n)	30. niman	40. quēzqui	50. zan

(c) Forms of the absolute suffix (Lesson 2) and the possessive suffix (Lessons 10 and 11)

Give the absolute and possessed forms (the latter with a third person singular possessor) for the following nouns, whose stem is given:

1. cuitla- 'excrement'
2. ayò- 'pumpkin'
3. chālchihui- 'jade'
4. tzacual- 'pyramid'
5. totōlte- 'egg'
6. huèxōlo- 'turkey'
7. pōchtēca- 'merchant'
8. cuezcoma- 'cuezcomate' (a sort of large jar for corn storage)
9. mātla- 'net'
10. māxtla- 'loincloth'

(d) Plural of nouns

Without being totally predictable, the plural of nouns tends to conform to certain principles. To what was said in Lesson 2, let us add the following details:

/-'/ and /R-'/ are used only for stems ending with a vowel (absolute form in -**tl**). Nouns ending in -**catl** (in general connected with locatives, as we will see in Lesson 30) have /-'/ (**tlācatl, mēxìcatl, caxtiltēcatl**). Nouns that have a disyllabic stem in the form /CVCV-/ most often have the plural /R-'/ (**mazātl, coyōtl, cōhuātl, tepētl, tīcitl, conētl**; however, **cihuātl** has no reduplication, **teōtl** does have it, and **pitzōtl** and **totōtl** take the plural /-me'/).

/-tin/ and /R-tin/ form the plural of the majority of nouns whose stem ends in a consonant (absolutive form in -**tli** or -**li**). Reduplication generally appears with monosyllabic roots of the type /CVC-/ (**tēuctli, pilli, tōchtli**; however, **cualli** has no reduplication, while **citlālin** does).

/-me'/ has increasingly tended, in the centuries since the Classical period, to form the plural of nouns whose stem ends in a vowel, going so far as to supplant /-'/ and /R-'/ in many modern dialects. In the Classical period, there were already doublets (**cihuāmê, tepēmê** beside **cihuâ, tētepê**). This was normally the plural of nouns without a suffix (the **chichi** type) and with the suffix -**in** (**michin**, which, however, has a plural **mīmichtin** as a doublet of **michmê**). Nevertheless, nouns in -**in** whose stem ends in -**l** normally have a plural in -**tin** (**citlālin, chapōlin, totōlin**, though **totōlmê**, which is undoubtedly the oldest form, is also attested).

/-ke'/ must actually be resolved as /k-e'/, with /k/ (written **k**) being the participial suffix and /-e'/ a variant of /-'/. In the singular, the participial suffix can take the form /-ki/ (**miqui**), /-k/ ("adjectives" in -**c**, -**tic**, -**huac**, see Lesson 12) or /ø/ (possessive nouns in -**huâ**, -**ê**, -**yô**; see Lesson 11).

/-wān/ must undoubtedly be resolved /-wā-n/, /-wā-/ being a variant of the possessive suffix. This is the plural of possessed forms; it is always used without reduplication (10.4).

In the plural, the suffixes -**tzin**, -**pōl**, -**tōn**, -**pil** themselves have reduplication with a short vowel, which is compatible with reduplication of the stem, see Lesson 12.

EXERCISE

Put the following nouns, which conform to the tendencies laid out in the previous discussion, in the plural of the absolute form and then of the possessed form (with a third person singular possessor).

1. cìtli 'hare'
2. mōyōtl 'mosquito'

 3. tōltēcatl 'Toltec' (also 'artisan')
 4. cuānaca 'chicken, rooster'
 5. tītlantli 'messenger'
 6. cueyātl 'frog'
 7. malli 'prisoner'
 8. nāmictli 'spouse'
 9. yōlqui 'living'
10. quimichin 'mouse'

(e) Emphatic, demonstrative, interrogative and negative pronouns (Lesson 4)

Translate into Nahuatl:

 1. Who are you (pl.)? – As for us, we're your (pl.) sons.
 2. Who are those people? – Those are lords.
 3. Who are those people? – Those are the lords.
 4. What do you (s.) see? – Peter's house.
 5. It is we who know it (use **ca** and **in**).
 6. As for us, we know it (use **ca** and **in**).
 7. I haven't seen anyone anywhere.
 8. I've never taken anything.
 9. I have no father, I have no house.
10. Whoever has done that will die.

(f) Suffixes of place names (Lesson 13)

 (i) Turn the following words into locative/possessive expressions (e.g., **calpan** > **īpan in calli**):
        1. īmāpan 2. nocuauhtitlan 3. chīmaltica 4. īitzpan 5. īāmatitech
(ii) Make the opposite change with the following locative/possessive expressions:
        1. īpan in āmoxtli 2. īicpac (*or* icpac) in tetl 3. īca in tlīlli 4. ītech in xihuitl 5. īpan in nopetl

(g) Verbal prefixes (Lessons 1, 3, 6)

 (i) Replace the third person object prefix with **-tla-**:
        1. quitta 2. quilcāhua 3. quìtoa 4. quìcuiloa 5. qui
(ii) With the same forms, replace the object prefixes with the reflexive.
(iii) Add **-on-** to the following forms.
        1. ancochî 2. xictēmo 3. anquicuepâ 4. xiquimpalēhui 5. nitlapōhua

(iv) Add -**huāl**- to the following forms:

     1. xictēmo 2. ammocuepâ 3. cāna 4. xitēpalēhui 5. xitlatēmo

(v) Replace the definite object prefix with an indefinite object (-**tē**- or -**tla**- depending on the sense):

     1. noconcōhua 2. nichuālcuepa 3. xicpalēhui 4. xocompalēhui
5. nichuāllātia

(h) Tenses (Lessons 8 and 9)

Put the following forms in (a) the preterite, (b) the imperative/optative, (c) the future, (d) the imperfect:

1. nihuetzca 'I laugh'
2. titēhuītequi 'you (s.) strike people'
3. xelihui 'it divides'
4. ticpoloâ 'we are losing, destroying it'
5. antecî 'you (pl.) are making flour'
6. tlècô 'they rise up'
7. ticpatla 'you (s.) melt it'
8. tlaināya 'he hides things'
9. tlama 'he hunts (animals)
10. ninìza 'I wake myself up'
11. ammāhuiltiâ 'you (pl.) are having a good time'
12. tiquìtzoma 'you (s.) are sewing it'
13. nicpi 'I pluck it'
14. chamāhua 'he grows fat'
15. nicchamāhua 'I fatten it'

(i) Passive and impersonal (Lesson 15)

In the following phrases, convert the verb (with third person plural subject) to the appropriate form for an indefinite agent (impersonal, passive, reflexive).

1. Amēchcelīzquê, amēchtlàpalōzquê.
2. Tlaīquê, quīquê in ātl.
3. Àmo ōnēchilcāuhquê: ca ye nēchnōtzâ.
4. Huel mococoâ, ca miquizquê.
5. Quipalēhuīzquê in nopil.
6. Quitemoāyâ teōcuitlatl.
7. Quicōuhquê petlatl, quinamacaquê caxitl.
8. Ōnēchmōtlaquê, huel ōnēchcocòquê.
9. Nicān ōmocāuhquê, àmo ōquīzquê.
10. Ca mitzmatî, quimatî in motōcā.

(j) Analytical exercises with quasi-homonyms

Here are pairs of homonyms or of words that are very similar in form. Try to find the meaning for each of them (it is a good idea to break them down into stem, prefixes and suffixes):

1. quīz (two words) 2. ōmic/ōmīc 3. ōman/ōmān 4. meuh/mēuh 5. teco/tēco 6. onēhuac/ōnēhuac 7. tehuâ/tēhuâ 8. ōnipāc/ōnicpāc 9. nitemōz/nictēmōz 10. nicuīca/nichuīca

PART
TWO

Agent Nouns, the -*ni* Form

16.1 The Preterite as Agent Noun

We have spoken (12.5) of deverbal "adjectives" (those derived from verbs), which in reality are forms of the preterite with **-qui**, the post-consonantal variant of the participial suffix (such as **micqui** 'dead', **cualānqui** 'angry', **tlāhuānqui** 'drunk'). These words, which indicate a state, are most frequently translated into English with an adjective, but in certain cases, it is possible to translate them with a noun: **in micqui** can be translated as 'the dead man' or sometimes 'the corpse'. With certain verbs, the translation with a noun is more natural; for instance, **ichtecqui** (from **ichtequi** 'to steal') signifies 'thief'.

When such forms are derived from transitive verbs, the tendency to translate them into English with nouns ("agent nouns" if the verb refers to an action) is very strong without being systematic. (An agent noun indicates the person who carries out the action; in English such nouns generally end in '-er' as in 'giver' or 'doer', but we often have Latinate forms like 'instructor'.) The Nahuatl form must take an indefinite or reflexive object prefix (see the following):

tēpixqui	*guard* (of persons, such as prisoners)
tēyacānqui	*leader, chief* (**yacāna** 'guide, lead')
tlachixqui	*sentinel* (someone assigned to keep watch on things)
mopōuhqui	*conceited, vain person* (lit., 'one who counts himself')
tlanamacac	*seller* (here we have **-c** because base 2 of the verb is **namaca**: 8.7)

If the verb stem ends in **-ia** or **-oa**, there is a clear tendency to use the **-ø** variant of the participial suffix (i.e., no actual ending) rather than the **-qui** variant:

tlàcuilô (*rather than* tlàcuilòqui)	*painter, scribe*

All plurals end in **-què**:

tēyacānquê	*leaders*
tlanamacaquê	*sellers*
tlàcuilòquê	*scribes* etc.

It can be seen that all the plurals and some of the singulars are morphologically identical to the unaugmented preterite used verbally, and depending on the circumstances, such forms can be translated as either nouns or verbs:

| tlàcuilòquê | *(they are) scribes* or *they wrote* |
| tlanamacac | *(it's/he's) a seller* or *he sold* |

Nevertheless, the following forms can be distinguished:

| tēyacān | *he led (people)* |
| tēyacānqui | *(he's a) leader* |

but if such forms are made plural (**tēyacānquê**), the same ambiguity returns.

Several important characteristics illustrate that in this use of the preterite as the equivalent of an adjective or an agent noun, the form really is a noun rather than a verb:

(1) Noun suffixes can be added to it, such as the vocative **-é** (with the final **-i** dropped):

tēyacānqué!	*leader!*
tlanamacaqué!	*seller!*
tēyacānquèé!	*leaders!*

and so can the honorific, diminutive etc. suffixes (in which case the participial suffix takes the form **-cā-**):

| tēyacāncātzintli | *honored leader* |
| mopōuhcāpōl | *arrogant fool* |

(2) In particular, it can appear in a possessed form (with the possessive suffix **-uh** after -cā-):

| notlachixcāuh | *my sentinel (pl.* **notlachixcāhuān***)* |

(3) Like all nouns, these words can be conjugated by subject (**nitlachixqui** 'I'm a watchman', **titēyacānqui** 'you're (s.) a leader' etc.), but never by object (this can never be definite). Let us imagine that you want to say, for example, 'you (s.) are my guard'. It would be impossible to say ****tinēchpixqui** because only the indefinite and reflexive object prefixes are permissible. Hence, you would put **tēpixqui** in the possessed form and say:

| Tinotēpixcāuh | *You're (s.) my guard* |
| Ca totēyacāncāuh (*and not* **Ca tēchyacānqui) | *It's/he's our leader* |

(4) Like nouns, these words are without tense, and to use them in tenses other than the present, the corresponding tenses of **câ** are employed (with both the noun and the verb taking the subject prefixes, as is usual in this construction; see 8.10, 9.8):

Titlàcuilô tiyez *You (s.) will be a scribe*
Nitēyacānqui nicatca *I was leader*

16.2 Inanimate "Agent Nouns"

This sort of agent noun can be used to describe inanimate entities or abstract notions. In this case, however, the participial suffix always has the form -ø after a consonant, and it is to be noted that the English translation generally uses adjectives:

Ca tēcocô, tētolīnî *It's grievous, painful*
Ca huel tēchichinatz *it's really distressing (**chichinatza** 'to torment')*

Note that in this case we always have the same formal identity between the "adjective" and the preterite with an indefinite object prefix. Only the context can resolve this ambiguity.

16.3 The -*ni* Form

An important verb form is built by adding the suffix -**ni** to *base 1*. The final vowel of the stem is lengthened in monosyllables and in verbs ending in -**o** or in -**ia**, -**oa**. In other words, this suffix has exactly the same effect on the verb stem as the imperfect suffix (9.10) does.

The only irregularity involves **câ** and **yauh**, which both have this formed on base 3: respectively, **yeni** and **yāni**.

The fundamental role of the −**ni** form is to indicate not the present, past or future realization of a process but rather the general and unspecified tendency or capacity of the subject to carry it out. In this way, the signification of the form relates not to tense but to *modality*. ("Tense" gives an absolute indication of the time of the action of the verb in relation to the moment of speaking or writing. "Modality," however, gives an indication of the speaker's sense of the likelihood or "usualness" of the action.) In effect, the form signifies that the subject is a "doer" of the action of the verb in general terms without saying anything about a particular realization of this action. A variety of translations are possible, such as 'to have the propensity to VERB', 'to like to VERB', 'to be prone to VERB'. Such translations are often heavy handed, however, as English frequently uses the simple present tense in such contexts. The –**ni** form can often be translated with a noun or adjective:

Nimiquini, nipolihuini	*I'm mortal, perishable*
Ticochini	*You're (s.) fond of sleeping*
Cencâ cuīcani inin tōtōtl	*This bird sings a lot, beautifully* (cf. Spanish 'es muy cantador')

The -**ni** form can indicate a regular behavior (habit):

Yohualnepantlâ nicochini	*At midnight I'm (regularly) asleep*

Naturally, you can also say **yohualnepantlâ nicochi** with a nuance of habit, but the -**ni** form lets it be understood that this habit is not being respected or may be at risk of this ('I'm normally asleep at midnight' could be followed by something like 'but it so happens that tonight I'm not going to sleep' or 'so don't bother me').

With transitive verbs, only the indefinite object or reflexive prefixes are usual:

Nitlàtlacoāni	*I sin, am a sinner* (**itlacoa** 'to harm, to offend, to sin against')
Huel titlamatini	*You're (s.) very intelligent, wise*
Cencâ tlacuāni	*He's a big eater*
Huel mopōhuani	*He's very vain*

However, it is possible to express the object with a noun (in which case the verb takes the definite object prefix). For example, it can be said of a dog that it is **omitl quicuāni** 'a bone eater, fond of eating bones'. Note that in this case the object is "generic"; that is, it refers to 'bones' in general and not to some specific bones.

It is also possible to have the definite prefix without an overtly expressed noun in forms like **quimatini**, which means '(he's) cunning, crafty', literally, something like 'he always knows it (namely, what's required at the moment)'. Contrast the more general **tlamatini** 'wise'.

For other possible uses of definite object with the -**ni** form, see 16.9 and 34.1.

16.4 Plural of the -*ni* Form

There are two possible plurals for the -**ni** form: -' (glottal stop) or -**mê**. The first gives the feeling of a verbal ending, the second of a nominal one. The line separating these two conceptions is rather fluid. With the ending -', the point is that the subject has this characteristic or habit: for example, **tim-iquinî** 'we are mortal' or **yohualpantlâ ticochinî** 'we have the habit of being asleep at midnight'. With the plural in -**mê**, however, the point is that the people in question belong to a group or category of people who have this characteristic: for instance, **titlàtlacoānimê** 'we are sinners' or 'we are categorized as sinners'. The distinction can perhaps be illustrated with the following:

| Ca tlamatinî | *They're wise* |
| Ca tlamatinimê | *They're wise men* |

16.5 *-ni* Form and Preterite

It can be seen that the -**ni** form is often like a noun or an agent noun/adjective in -**c**, -**qui**. Let us next examine both these points.

(1) The English translation of the −**ni** form often makes use of nouns, as the preceding examples have shown, and this form sometimes serves to designate groups of animals or social classes. Thus:

| tēcuāni | *wild beast (people eater)* |
| tlàtoāni | *king, ruler* (lit., *speaker, one who speaks*) |

Like nouns in the strict sense and "agent nouns" in -**c**, -**qui**, the −**ni** form can appear with **câ**:

| Tlàtoāni catca | *He was king* |

and take certain noun endings like the vocative and the diminutive, augmentative etc. suffixes:

| tlàtoānié![1] | *oh, ruler!* |
| nitlàtlacoānipōl | *I'm a wretched sinner* |

In certain texts (above all poetical ones), it is possible to find -**ni** forms with the absolute suffix (e.g., **nicuīcanitl**[2] 'I'm a singer') or possessed ones (e.g., **totlamatiniuh** 'our wise man'). (With the latter, the usual practice is to proceed via the form in -**cā**-; see the later discussion.)

(2) Basically, the -**ni** form does not have the same sense as the forms in -**c**, -**qui**, although sometimes it comes close to overlapping with them. The differences can be formulated as follows:

---

[1] Here, the ending -**i** is not the helping vowel and so is retained in front of -**é**.

[2] In archaizing texts and the peripheral dialects, it happens that there are forms like **micquetl** 'dead' (- **micqui**) consisting of the participial suffix plus the absolute suffix. Such forms are absent from Classical Nahuatl properly speaking apart from a few rare exceptions such as **yōlcātl** 'animal' (alongside **yōlqui** 'living', from **yōli**), whose plural is normally **yōlcāmê**.

-c, -qui indicates a state, -ni a characteristic. Compare:

micqui	*dead*	miquini	*mortal*
cualānqui	*annoyed*	cualānini	*irritable*
xeliuhqui	*divided, split*	xelihuini	*divisible*

Whereas the forms in -c, -qui (or -ø) can indicate a specific social role, trade or function, the ones in -ni suggest a general capacity or tendency. The vast majority of nouns for a trade or social function are of the type **tlanamacac, tēpixqui, tlàcuilô** (most are formed from compound verbs; see Lesson 17). Previously, we have seen **tlàtoāni** for 'ruler', and 'singer' is **cuīcani** and not **cuīcac**. It is also possible to find the –ni form used to make nouns for trades from verbs in -ia, -oa (**tlàcuiloāni** is synonymous with **tlàcuilô**).

Finally, with some verbs (especially transitive ones that do not properly speaking indicate an action) both forms can exist, being close to synonyms. Thus, it seems that there is no difference in meaning between **mopōhuani** and **mopōuhqui**.

In any event, the two formations are connected in at least one regard: *only the preterite formation normally allows the possessed form.* Hence, a possessed –ni form is converted to the corresponding preterite form:

cuīcani *singer*	but tocuīcacāuh *our singer*	
tlàtoāni *ruler*	but totlàtòcāuh *our ruler*	

The same procedure is sometimes found with plurals. Hence, the plural of **tlàtoāni** is **tlàtòquê** rather than ****tlàtoānimê**, and while you can say **tlàcuiloāni** for 'scribe', the plural is always **tlàcuilòquê**. With the honorific, diminutive etc. suffixes (12.1), both formations can be found. That is, these endings can be attached to the -ni form, but sometimes the agent noun in -c, -qui is used instead.

Any abstract nouns in -yōtl are likewise formed with -cā-: **tlàtòcāyōtl** 'position as ruler'.

16.6 *-ni* Form of the Passive

By putting the passive (15.4) of a transitive verb in the -ni form, we have a form that signifies 'which should be' or 'can be' + PAST PARTICIPLE. Hence, it can most often be translated with forms in English ending in '-ible' or '-able', although 'is to be' + PAST PARTICIPLE is also a possible translation:

Ca ēhualōni, ìtōlōni inin cualli tlàtōlli	*These good words should be uttered (raised up) and spoken*
Àmo cuālōni inin nacatl	*This meat is inedible*
Cuix īhuani inin ātl?	*Is this water drinkable?*
Àmo cacōni in tlein tiquìtoa	*Whatever you're (s.) saying is inaudible*

▶ *Important Note*. The -**ni** form is the only passive form that can be regularly used not only of animate beings but also of things (contrary to what was said in 15.9). Thus, for 'it's feasible, it can be done' you say **chīhualōni** and not **mochīhuani**. We have seen that **mochīhua** has both the intransitive meaning 'it happens' and the transitive one 'it is done, it is built' (by someone unspecified). Thus, the form **mochīhuani** does exist, but it has the intransitive meaning 'what happens regularly'.

16.7 -*ni* Form of the Impersonal: Instrument Nouns

By putting the impersonal form of a verb in the -**ni** form (see 15.1–2, 6 for the intransitive impersonal and 15.7–8 for transitive forms with indefinite objects), we have an "instrument noun", which designates something that allows the action of the verb to be carried out:

Ca cochīhuani inin pàtli	*this medicine is sleep-inducing (a thing because of which one sleeps)*
Ca micōhuani in	*this is poison (thing by which one dies)*
Xiccui inon tlatecōni	*take that knife (**tlateco** 'things are cut', from **tequi**)*

Remember that the impersonal forms of transitive verbs always take an indefinite object marker, and if the verb is reflexive, the corresponding noun takes **ne-** (it is the presence of an indefinite prefix that distinguishes these instrument nouns from the passive-based forms discussed in 16.6).

This instrumental relationship is sometimes reinforced with a locative expression, especially if the instrument noun signifies a person:

in īmāc tlācatīhuani	*the midwife (the one in whose hands people are born)*

16.8 Possessed Form of the Instrument Noun

Instrument nouns have a possessed form that is the same as the corresponding *active imperfect*. That is, the suffix -**ya** (without -**uh**) is added (along with the regular possessive prefixes) to the active *base 1* (and *not* the impersonal form used in building the non-possessed version):

Conīc in īmiquiya	*He drank up his poison*
Xiccui in notlatequiya	*Take (s.) my knife*

▶ *Note*. **Tocochiya** signifies 'eyelid' (lit., 'what we sleep with, our means of sleeping').

16.9 Use of the -*ni* Form in Wishes

The -**ni** form also serves to express regret or (if one prefers) a contrafactual hope that relates to the present or past and hence contradicts the real situation, such as 'if only Peter were here!' (which he is not). (We have seen that realizable hopes, i.e., those relating to the future, are expressed in the optative; see 9.5.) In such expressions referring to the present:

▶ the particle **mā** (or **mācamo** in the negative; see 9.5) appears in front
▶ the prefix for the second person (s. and pl.) is **x(i)-**, just as in the optative
▶ the plural suffix is always -'
▶ there is no restriction on the use of definite object prefixes (cf. 16.3)

Thus:

Mā xiccaquini in tlein niquìtoa!	*If only you (s.) would listen to what I'm saying!*
Mā xinēchcaquinî!	*If only you (pl.) would listen to me!*
Mā nicān yeni in Pedro!	*If only Peter were here!*

The contrafactual of the past, that is, a regret relating to the past, is formed by simply adding the augment **ō-** as a prefix:

Mācaīc ōnitlàtlacoāni!	*Would that I had never sinned, I wish I had never sinned!*
Mā ōquìtoāni in nelli!	*If only he had said the truth!*
Mā nicān ōxiyenî!	*If only you (pl.) had been here!*

VOCABULARY

Intransitive verbs

ichtequi[3]	*to steal*	xelihui	*to split, to divide*

Transitive verbs

chichinatza	*to torment, to distress*	māuhtia	*to scare, to frighten*
huītequi	*to hit, to lash, to whip*	poloa	*to lose, to ruin, to destroy*
ìtlacoa	*to harm, to damage, to sin against*	yacāna	*to lead, to guide*

Nouns

malli	*(pl. /R–tin/) prisoner*	tlàtlacōlli	*sin, fault*
nelli	*true, truth*	yēctli	*good, just*[4]

---

[3] This verb can also be transitive (18.7).

[4] **Cualli** indicates a positive external evaluation ('goodness' in terms of niceness if it refers to a person, favorable or agreeable impression in terms of the senses or the mind if it is a thing), and **yēctli** indicates the internal characteristic of moral probity or religious righteousness.

EXERCISES

(a) Give the meaning of the following words:
   1. celīlōni 2. ittalōni (ittōni) 3. pācōni 4. pōhualōni 5. tlazòtlalōni
   6. tlātīlōni 7. tzacualōni 8. zalōlōni

(b) Translate the following words and expressions into Nahuatl, then put them
   into the possessed form of the third person singular (consult 16.7, 8).
   1. glue
   2. instrument for writing
   3. razor, instrument for shaving
   4. love potion
   5. instrument for watching, observing
   6. effect that causes crying, tear-inducing

(c) Translate into English.
   1. Ca cencâ chōcanî in pīpiltotōntin.
   2. Mācamo ōtineminî in īpan tlàtlacōlli! Mā zan ticualtin, tiyēctin tiyenî!
   3. Mā xicmatini tlein ōmochīuh!
   4. Ōquipolô in tlàcuilô in ītlàcuiloāya.
   5. Àmo ittōni in cōhuātl.
   6. Tleīca ticcui in tēhuītecōni? Cuix tinēchhuītequiz?
   7. Ca yèhuātl in totlàtòcāuh yez.
   8. Ōtiquimānquê in tochteccāhuān.
   9. In īpan huēyi ilhuitl teōpan niyāni.
   10. Tiyānquizco ōmocuepquê in notlacōuhcāhuān.
   11. Ca cencâ chicāhuac inin xōchitl: àmo tecōni.
   12. Huel nēchmāuhtiâ in tēcuānimê.

(d) Translate into Nahuatl.
   1. If only you (s.) saw my house!
   2. Knives are very useful ("helping").
   3. You're (s.) just a loudmouth ("miserable shouter").
   4. Mary is very lovable.
   5. Don't (s.) take up ("take") your whip.
   6. I have started (**āna**) the trade of scribe ("scribehood").
   7. The beauty of that woman is unsurpassable.
   8. I should never have stolen ("if only I had never…").
   9. This day is unforgettable.
   10. Peter's very jolly ("is very (much) a laugher").
   11. We greet our wise men.
   12. The guards of the prisoners are sleeping.
   13. You're (s.) here! You don't normally come to our place.

Compound Nouns, Verbal Incorporation

17.1 Compound Nouns

In English, *compound nouns* are created by juxtaposing nouns to form a new word, and this procedure occurs as frequently in Nahuatl as in English. In English, the first noun in the compound generally appears in the singular; sometimes a compound is written as a single word and sometimes the constituent elements are written separately (regardless of the spelling, the compound is treated in speech as a single word, with the accent on the first element). In Nahuatl, a compound noun is written as one word, and the first component appears only in the stem form (the absolutive suffix and -**in** are dropped). For example:

teōcalli	*temple* ('god house')
pitzōnacatl	*pork* ('pig meat')

It can be seen that the word order is the same as in English, that is, determiner-determined. If you prefer, the second noun is the main one and the first one modifies or determines (specifies) it (a **teōcalli** is a sort of **calli** and not a **teōtl**). Sometimes, a Nahuatl compound noun is not translated in English with a compound noun, but instead the determiner appears either as an adjective or as a genitive expression or (idiomatically determined) prepositional phrase after the main noun (e.g., **teōtlàtōlli** 'god word' would be rendered more idiomatically in English as 'divine word' or 'word of God').

We have already encountered the nouns **ācalli** 'boat, ship' (lit., 'water house') and **teōcuitlatl** 'gold' (lit., 'god excretion', **cuitlatl**) as well as the proper name **Quetzalcōhuātl** 'plume(d) serpent', and place names like **Chapōltepēc** 'on grasshopper mountain' or **Xōchimīlco** 'in flower(y) field'. More examples of compound nouns:

oquichtōchtli	*male rabbit*, **cihuātōchtli** *female rabbit*
cōhuāmichin	*fish snake* (a sort of eel)

yāōcalli	*fortress ('war house')*[1]
tecalli	*stone house*
petlacalli	*box, cage ('mat house')*
cuauhcalli	*prison ('wood(en) house')*
chīlmōlli	*chili mole* (a sort of sauce)
mōlcaxitl	*molcajete ('mole vase' or 'vase for mole')*[2]
ācōmitl	*water jar*
nāhuatlàtōlli *or* mexìcatlàtōlli	*Nahuatl language* (**nāhuatl** *clear*)
tōtoltetl	*turkey egg* (lit., *stone*)
īxāyōtl	*tears ('eye water')* (Note –yō, see 11.3.)
cihuāpilli	*noblewoman ('female noble')*
tlācatecolōtl	*demon* ('person' + **tecolōtl** 'owl')
tlenenepilli	*flame* ('fire' + **nenepilli** 'tongue')
tzontecomatl	*skull* (**tzontli** 'hair' + **tecomatl** 'jar')

In the first element, short -i may be dropped; note **cuauhcalli** and also:

mācpalli	*palm* ('seat of the hand', with loss of both the -**i** of **māitl** and of the **i**- of **icpalli**)
cuammāitl	*branch* ('tree arm'; for the assimilation of -**uh** /w/ to the following **m**-, see 7.7 n. 4)

In certain cases that are very difficult to predict, a glottal stop may appear after a vowel at the end of the first stem:

xōchìcualli	*fruit* (lit., *good* (or *edible*; cf. **cua**) part of the flower)[3]
màpilli	*finger* (lit., *child* (or perhaps *appendage*; cf. **piloa** 'to hang') of the hand)
màtlāctli	*ten* (lit., *chest* (**tlāctli**) *of the hands* or rather *chest with the hands*)

but compare the long vowel in **mācuīlli** 'five' (lit. 'grasp (cf. **cui**) of the hand'). "Nouns" and "adjectives" in -**c**, -**qui** can be the first element in compounds, with the -**cā**- variant of the participial suffix:

catzāhuacātlàtōlli	*vile (dirty) words*
cocoxcācalli	*hospital, infirmary (house for sick people)*
yamāncācuīcatl	*sweet song*

As with the possessed form, "nouns" in -**ni** (the habitual, see 16.5) are replaced in compounds with the corresponding form in -**cā**-:

tlàtòcātlàtōlli	*ruler's word, command*

---

[1] Strictly speaking, *yāōtl* is 'foe', but in compounds, it frequently signifies 'war' in general.

[2] A 'molcajete' is a small mortar, generally with three feet, in which vegetables are pounded.

[3] Sometimes, **xōchìtli** can be found for **xōchitl**.

17.2 Meaning of Compounds

As can be seen, the relationship in meaning between the two nouns can be quite varied: membership in two classes (like **cihuā-tōchtli**, which is both a rabbit and a female), comparison (**cōhuā-michin**, which is a fish that resembles a snake), material (**te-calli**), possession (**teō-calli**), purpose (**ā-comitl**), origin (**tōtol-tetl**) etc.

In a general way, the first stem refers not to a particular "thing" but to a class (or material) that characterizes the object or person that the second stem refers to. Hence, Nahuatl normally makes the same contrast that English does between 'the rabbit house' (i.e., a house intended for rabbits in general) and 'the rabbit's house' (i.e., one belonging to a particular rabbit): **tōch-calli/īcal tōchtli**. But note **teōtlàtōlli/ītlàtōl teōtl** ('God word'/'word of God'). The expression 'God word' is obviously impossible in English, but the point in the corresponding Nahuatl construction is that the compound form makes more of a "unit." The same goes for words that are used more or less as adjectives. **Catzāhuacātlàtōlli** simply connects the nouns more tightly than **catzāhuac tlàtōlli** (at the same time, the compound makes it easier to use **catzāhuac** figuratively). Also, **cihuā-tōchtli** 'female rabbit' is more natural than **cihuātl tōchtli**, because **cihuātl** by itself usually refers to human females. However, we find **cihuātl mēxìcatl** or **mēxìcatl cihuātl** because a Mexica woman does possess simultaneously the traits of being a female and a Mexica (****cihuāmēxìcatl** would be somewhat derogatory, like 'female Mexica'). Nonetheless, the word for 'noblewoman' is **cihuā-pilli** and not **cihuātl pilli** because this is a traditional title in which **cihuā-** plays the same role as '-ess' in 'duchess' or 'countess'.

17.3 Verb Incorporation

There is in Nahuatl another very common sort of compounding. This consists of joining a noun stem and a verb to form a compound verb. The procedure is called *incorporation* (i.e., the incorporation of the noun into the verb). There are two kinds of incorporation.

17.3.1 Object Incorporation

In *object incorporation*, the incorporated noun stem represents the direct object of the verb. For example:

Nicacchīhua	*I make shoes* (cactli)
Yālhua ōtinacacuàquê	*Yesterday we ate meat*
Tiyānquizco nitlaxcalnamaca	*I sell tortillas in the market*
Ye ōtlācachīuh in Malintzin	*Mary has already given birth (made a person)*
Nāmapōhua *or* Nāmoxpōhua	*I read (books)*

The noun stem may lose a final -i:

Nicōnchīhua   *I make jars* (cōmitl)

Also note this irregular formation:

Nātli   *I drink water* (and not ****nāi**).[4] (The only reason for this retention of the absolutive suffix in a compound is to "beef up" a compound that is made out of two one-syllable stems. Here we have a manifestation of the "constraint against short words"; see 10.8.)

It can be seen in all these examples that the verb is derived from a transitive one and becomes intransitive. If 'making' involves a maker and the object made, 'shoe making' involves only the maker (the verb no longer takes a regular object prefix because an object is already expressed in the verb).

Incorporation can be carried out only if there is a particularly close relationship between the verb and the object, so that (as already noted) the two of them make a unit. This new unit can be made in two cases:

(1) the object signifies a class of things and not some particular thing (**tlaxcalnamaca, cac-chīhua**)

(2) there is a specific object in mind, but it is such that the verb represents a particular sort of activity that is characteristic of a class of people that the subject belongs to. For instance, in **tlācachīhua**, the woman gives birth to a particular person but in doing so she carries out the sort of "action" characteristic of every mother.

▶ *Note.* Condition 1 alone is not sufficient grounds for using verb incorporation. One can say **nicnamaca tlaxcalli** with an indefinite external object, but while **nicnamaca tlaxcalli** could, for example, be the answer to the question **Tlein ticnamaca?** 'What are you selling?', **nitlaxcalnamaca** would have to answer the general question **Tlein ticchīhua?** 'What do you do?', with the activity 'sell tortillas' appearing as a global answer. Exaggerating the translations a bit, we could have 'tortillas are what I'm selling' on the one hand and 'I'm tortilla selling' on the other. Along the same lines, **niccua nacatl** means 'I eat meat' among other things that I eat, while **ninacacua** signifies something noteworthy because it's not customary, for instance because it happens only on feast days (virtually, 'I'm having a meat day'). Continuing with this reference to Catholic eating practices, one could translate 'I eat fish (regularly)' as **niccua michin**, but if it is a question of fasting on Friday by eating fish instead of meat, one would say **nimichcua**. In short, incorporation of the object is permissible if the grouping together of verb and object signifies a meaningful totality.

---

[4] Because water is the preeminent form of drink, **ātli** could be translated simply as 'drink'. In any case, the form **ātli** (**ātl** + ī) is much more frequent than **tlai** (**tla** + ī). Note the instrument noun (16.8) **tātliya** 'our means of drinking', that is, 'mustache'.

Verbs with object incorporation have a pronounced tendency to form "agent nouns" in **-c**, **-qui** (16.1):

cacchīuhqui	*shoe maker*
petlachīuhqui	*mat maker*
cōnchīuhqui	*potter*
calchīuhqui	*mason*
tlaxcalnamacac	*tortilla seller*
ocnamacac	*pulque seller*
nacanamacac	*butcher*
texinqui	*stonecutter* (from **te-xima** 'stone shave')
calpixqui	*steward (house guard)*
teōpixqui	*priest (God guardian)*

17.3.2 Modifying Incorporation

The second sort of incorporation is called *modifying incorporation*. Here, the noun stem is not the verb's object, which leaves the verb intransitive if the original verb was intransitive and transitive if it was transitive. Let us first look at some examples:

▶ with intransitive verbs

Xōchicuepōni in nocuīc	*My song blosoms (**cuepōni**) like a flower*
Ōtlehuāc in xōchitl	*The flower shriveled up (dried up) from the fire*
Huel nāmiqui	*I'm very thirsty (dying from (lack of) water)*

▶ with transitive verbs

Nictēnēhua in motōcā	*I utter (raise up by lip) your name*
Mācamo xinēchtlàtōlcotōna	*Don't cut off (**cotōna**) my words[5]*
Ōnēchmàpilcotōnquê	*They cut off my finger*
Nicxōchitēmoa cuīcatl	*I seek songs like flowers*
Àmo tiquinyāōnāmiquizquê	*We won't meet them hostilely*
Ōnicmācāuh in nocax	*I dropped my bowl (released it from my hands)*
Ninocxipāca	*I wash my feet*
Ca tēchichicuepa in octli	*Pulque makes people stupid (turns them into dogs)*
Niquicnōitta	*I pity him (look upon him as a poor person)*
Cuix ōninīxcuep?	*Have I made a mistake (turned my eyes back)?*

In compounds, the noun stem 'heart' generally appears **yōl-** and not as **yōllò-**:

Cuix ōnimitzyōlìtlacô?	*Have I offended you (s.) (harmed you in your heart)?*
Ca huel tinēchyōllālia	*You (s.) greatly console me (set me down in my heart)*

---

[5] More exactly: 'don't cut me off in terms of my words', as the object is 'me' (**-nēch-**) and not **tlàtōlli**. So too with the subsequent examples.

The relationship in meaning between the two elements of such a compound can fall under one of four categories:

(1) circumstantial relationship
   That is, the noun indicates some specification of the operation of the verb that would be expressed with a prepositional phrase in English (and naturally with the various corresponding phrases in Nahuatl). Here, an instrumental relationship (**tle-huāqui**) is particularly common, but the relationship can also be a locatival one (**mā-cāhua**). We have already encountered **calaqui** lit. 'enter (**aqui**) into a house (**cal-li**)'.

(2) relationship of comparison
   Such a comparison can be in terms of either the subject (**xōchi-cuepōni**) or the object (**xōchi-tēmoa**). This comparison is often represented in English with a predicate adjective (**icnō-itta** 'view as a poor person') or prepositional phrase (**chichi-cuepa** 'turn into a dog').

(3) a relationship of the part to the whole
   This sort of comparison occurs frequently, especially with parts of the body. The incorporated noun in the Nahuatl is then generally translated into English as the direct object, which is then modified in English with a possessive form corresponding to the Nahuatl direct object. Hence, **icxi-pāca**, **màpil-cotōna** are translated as 'wash (direct object)'s feet', 'cut off (direct object)'s finger' and so on. What the Nahuatl is actually saying is 'wash (direct object) in terms of his/her feet', 'cut (direct object) in terms of his/her finger'.

(4) incorporation of the agent of a passive
   This case is very uncommon and occurs with very limited number of verbs:

   Ōnicōhuācualōc   *I was bitten (lit., eaten) by a snake*

Sometimes, the meaning can be quite far removed from what we would expect on the basis of the components. Thus, **moteōchīhua** means 'he prays' (and not 'he makes himself into a god'). In compounds, **miqui** produces verbs that express a mere ailment or some physical discomfort (**ā-miqui** 'to be thirsty', so too **cec-miqui** 'to be cold, to catch a cold', **yōl-miqui** 'to faint').

Modifying incorporation is very extensive, and it seems that such verbs can be formed practically at will. Furthermore, " compounded compounds" can be made:

   Nimitzmātēnnāmiqui   *I kiss your hands (lit., I meet you with the lips*
                         *(**tēn-**) in terms of the hands (**mā-**))*

It was considered elegant to form elaborate compounds. This practice could result in very long words and is often found in poetry.

▶ **Note.** The same combination of a given noun and verb can form both an object and an modifying compound:

Nicxōchitēmoa	*I look for it like a flower*
Nixōchitēmoa	*I look for flowers*

17.4 Impersonal and Passive Forms of Compounds

17.4.1 Modifying Incorporation

If the subject is indefinite, the same forms (impersonal, passive, reflexive, see Lesson 15) are used as with the simple verb:

Tlatlehuāqui	*Everything is withering from the fire*
Āmicōhua	*There's thirst*
Calacōhua	*People enter*
Motēnēhua in motōcā	*Your (s.) name is uttered*
Ōniyōllālīlōc	*I was consoled*
Ōnimàpilcōtonalōc	*My finger was cut off*
Tiyāōnāmicōzquê	*We'll be met as enemies*
Tēchichicuepalo	*People are made stupid*
Tlaxōchitēmōlo	*Things are looked for like flowers*
Neīxcuepalo	*People are tricked by their eyesight*

17.4.2 Object Incorporation

Here, the original verb is transitive, and the compound is intransitive. If the agent is indefinite, the verb form is made by adding the usual passive suffix to the stem. In effect, this form is comparable to the impersonal forms of transitive verbs with indefinite object (15.7) except that here the incorporated noun takes the place of the indefinite patient:

Cacchīhualo	*People make shoes*
Xōchiteco	*Flowers are cut*
Nacacuālo	*Meat is eaten*
Ātlīhua	*People drink water*

17.5 Placement of *tla-*

It's most common to find **tla-** placed in front of a transitive compound, as one would expect:

Nitlatēnēhua	*I utter things*
Nitlatēnnāmiqui	*I kiss things*

In certain transitive verbs, however, the indefinite object prefix **tla-** is bound to the stem in such a way that when it comes to incorporation, **tla-** + STEM behaves like an intransitive verb stem, so that the incorporated noun stem is placed *in front* of **tla-**. These formations are not predictable, but this phenomenon tends to appear with **tlàtoa** 'to speak', **tlachiya** 'to watch' and sometimes **tlacua** 'to eat':

Nināhuatlàtoa   *I speak Nahuatl* (and not ****nitlanāhua(i)'toa**)

VOCABULARY[6]

Intransitive verbs

āmiqui	*to be thirsty*	yōlmiqui	*to faint*
cuepōni	*to blossom*		

Transitive verbs

cotōna	*to cut, to slice*	tēnēhua	*to mention,*
īxcuepa	*to deceive* (mo-:		*to pronounce, to utter*
	to be wrong)	tēnnāmiqui	*to kiss*
piloa	*to hang*	yōlìtlacoa	*to offend*
teōchīhua	(mo-: *to pray*)	yōllālia	*to console, to comfort*

Nouns

cactli	*shoe(s)*	tecolōtl	(pl. /R–'/) *owl*
cuauhcalli	*prison*	tecomatl	*jar, pot*
cuitlatl	*excretion, excrement*	tlācatecolōtl	(pl. /R–'/) *demon, devil*
icnōtl	(*pl.* /-me'/) *poor person, orphan*	tlāctli	*chest, upper body*
		tōtoltetl	*egg*
nāhuatl	*clear (sounding)*	tzontecomatl	*skull*
nenepilli	*tongue*	tzontli	*hair*
petlacalli	*wicker basket, box*	xōchìcualli	*fruit*

EXERCISES

(a) Form compound nouns of the following meaning.
   1. drunkard's words
   2. sow
   3. water snake
   4. shore, river bank ("water's lip")

[6] As usual, compound nouns and verbs are listed in the chapter vocabularies only if their meaning is not self-evident on the basis of their components.

    5. edge ("lip") of the woods
    6. flower war (i.e., a stylized form of warfare)
    7. monastery, seminary ("house of priests")
    8. snot ("nose excrement")
    9. prickly pear flower
   10. ossuary ("bone house")
   11. clump ("stone") of earth

(b) Translate with incorporating compound verbs and then convert to the appropriate impersonal or passive construction and translate.
    1. He hurries like a rabbit (i.e., behaves crazily).
    2. He emits ("leaves from his mouth") sweet words.
    3. He washes his (own) mouth.
    4. He cuts chili peppers.
    5. He neglects ("leaves from his eyes") his little children.
    6. He washes the inside ("stomach") of the vase.
    7. He's sick in the ears.
    8. He prepares ("makes") food.
    9. He is overcome by heat ("dies of fire").
   10. He leads a pure life ("lives in purity").

(c) Translate into English.
    1. In īpan huēyi ilhuitl mōlchīhualo, tamalchīhualo.
    2. Huel toquichyōllô.
    3. Mācamo xiccua in michomitl.
    4. Ca aīc ōniccuâ tlācanacatl.
    5. Àmo nāmanamaca.
    6. Ōmocaltzauc in Malintzin.
    7. Huel niquimīxpiya in māmaltin.
    8. Quin ōninotzompāc.
    9. Nicān àmo petlachīhualo.
   10. Ca icnōcāhualōquê inìquê in pīpiltotōntin.
   11. Ye nitzoniztāc.
   12. Tiyānquizco àmo câ iztanamacac.
   13. Pitzōpixqué, cān tiquinhuīca in mopitzōhuān?

(d) Translate into Nahuatl.
    1. These are snake eggs ("stones").
    2. It's poor man's food.
    3. It's fish mole.
    4. Do you (s.) know the Otomi language?
    5. I'm going to the pigsty ("pig house").
    6. There's mobilization ("people are war-called").
    7. Peter's in the common fields ("city field").

8. I make wood chips ("wood shave").
9. He winked at me ("called me by eye").
10. You (s.) will abstain from meat ("meat-leave").
11. You (s.) don't yet have mustache ("lip hair").
12. Tomorrow we'll eat meat tamales.
13. As for the prickly pear, it's is the fruit of the prickly pear plant.
14. We're going to the shore ("water lip").

Bitransitive Verbs, Ambitransitive Verbs

18.1 Introduction to Bitransitive Verbs

In English, there are verbs that take two objects, a direct and an indirect object: 'I gave the waiter a tip', 'I cooked him dinner'. The direct object is the thing (seldom a person) that the verb directly acts upon. The indirect object is usually an animate being for or to whom the action is done. The indirect object can be expressed in two ways. Both the direct and indirect objects sometimes appear a simple nouns or pronouns, and in this case, the indirect object precedes the direct one (as in the examples given). The indirect object can also be indicated with the prepositions 'for' or 'to', in which case it follows the direct object: 'I gave a tip to the waiter' or 'I cooked dinner for him'. In terms of Nahuatl grammar, we might term the indirect object the *beneficiary* (this term is to be understood broadly, as the indirect object may be harmed rather than benefited by the action). In these instances, the Nahuatl verb can take two objects, one representing the regular direct object and the other the beneficiary. Such verbs are called *bitransitive*. Unlike the case with English, where word order clearly distinguishes which is which when the beneficiary appears without the preposition, the bitransitive verbs in Nahuatl make no such formal distinction. In the natural order of things, the direct object will be inanimate and the beneficiary animate, but this is by no means always the case.

A clear example of a bitransitive verb is **maca** 'give'. The verb **itoa** 'say' is a regular transitive verb and so cannot express a beneficiary. If you wish to express one, you have to use a different verb, the bitransitive **ilhuia** 'tell'. Let us now look at how the prefixes of these verbs behave.

If both objects are indefinite, the prefixes appear in the order -**tē**, -**tla**:

nitētlamaca	*I give (things to people)*
nitētlalhuia	*I speak (to people)*

If there is a definite and an indefinite object, the former precedes the latter in accordance with the fixed order of prefixes (see 6.4):

nictlamaca in nocnīuh	*I'm giving my friend something*
nimitztlalhuīz	*I'm going to tell you (s.) something*
xinēchtlalhui	*speak (s.) to me*
ōnictēmacac in xōchitl	*I've given the flower (to someone)*
nictēilhuiz in	*I'll tell this (to someone, people)*

18.2 Reduction of Definite Object Prefixes

Things become complicated if there are two definite objects. *There cannot be two definite object prefixes.* The third person prefix gives way to those of the first and second person, and two third person prefixes are reduced to one.

Nimitzmaca	*I give it to you (s.)* (and not **Nicmitzmaca** or **Nimitzquimaca**)
Xinēchilhui	*Tell (s.) me* (and not **Xicnēchilhui** or **Xinēchquilhui**)
Nicmaca	*I give it to him* (and not **Nicquimaca**)

It can be seen that this amounts to expressing only the beneficiary (the indirect object in English).

The absence of the third person prefix does not mean that the object that is "given" or "told" cannot appear in the form of a noun:

Nimitzmaca in xōchitl	*I'm giving you the flower*
Xinēchilhui in nelli	*Tell (s.) me the truth*

The word order is just as free as with transitive verbs (3.8), and we can say:

Nicmaca in xōchitl in cihuātl	*I'm giving the woman the flower*
Nicmaca in cihuātl in xōchitl	*I'm giving the woman the flower*

As usual, if one of the nouns is indefinite (marked with 'a', 'some' or ø in English), it is placed directly after the verb:

Nicmaca xōchitl in cihuātl	*I give the woman flowers* (and not **Nicmaca in cihuātl xōchitl**)

If both the subject and the objects are all expressed with nouns, the preferred placement for the subject is in front of the verb:

In Pedro quimaca in xōchitl in cihuātl	*Peter is giving the flower to the girl*

(Putting all three nouns after the verb, in whatever order, would probably be a source of ambiguity and, in any event, would represent a very clumsy mode of expression.)

Any of the complements of a transitive verb can be focalized (see 2.8), even if it is not represented by a prefix:

Ca yèhuātl in nictlamaca	*He's the one that I'm giving a gift to*
Ca yèhuātl in nēchtlamaca	*He's the one who is giving me a gift*
Ca yèhuātl in nimitzmaca	*It's this that I'm giving to you (s.)*
Ca xōchitl in namēchmaca	*It's a flower that I'm giving to you (pl.)*
Ca nelli in titēchilhuia	*It's the truth that you're (s.) telling us*[1]

18.3 Retention of the Third Person Plural *-im-*

The rule for reducing the number of third person definite prefixes admits an exception when the prefix is in the plural. The element **-im-** in the third plural prefix **-quim-** is retained in all circumstances, and in this case, it is placed after the regularly retained object prefix:

Nimitzimmaca in huēhuèxōlô	*I'm giving you the tom turkeys*
Xinēchimmaca huēhuèxōlô	*Give me tom turkeys*

This is due to the fact that in **-quim-** there are actually two prefixes: **-qu-** marks the third person and disappears in accordance with the general rule, while **-im-** marks the plural.

The form **niquimmaca** is ambiguous. It can mean 'I'm giving them to him', 'I'm giving it to them' or 'I'm giving them to them':

Niquimmaca cē huèxōlotl in nocnīhuān	*I'm giving my friends a tom turkey*
Niquimmaca huēhuèxōlô in nocnīuh	*I'm giving my friend tom turkeys*
Niquimmaca huēhuèxōlô in nocnīhuān	*I'm giving my friends tom turkeys*

---

[1] There is the possibility of ambiguity when two entities in the third person are involved, for example:

Ca yèhuātl in nēchilhuia	*He's the one that's telling it to me/it's this that he tells me*
Ca yèhuātl in niquilhuia	*It's this that I'm telling him/ he's the one that I tell it to*

and even more so if there are three entities in the third person:

Ca yèhuātl in quilhuia	*He's the one that's telling it to him/it's this that he's telling to him/he's the one that he's telling it to*

As usual, these possible ambiguities are mostly theoretical. Although they can be found, they're generally resolved by the context.

18.4 The Reflexive with Bitransitive Verbs

A bitransitive verb can take a reflexive prefix, which appear after the definite but before the indefinite prefixes (6.4):

Tictomacâ xōchitl	*We give each other flowers*
Titotlamacâ	*We give each other presents*
Motlamacâ	*They give each other presents*
Quimomacâ xōchitl	*They give each other flowers*

Certain bitransitive verbs necessarily take the reflexive, for instance **cuitlahuia**, which is reminiscent of the English 'concern oneself with':

Nicnocuitlahuia in nopil	*I concern myself with my son, I take care of my son*
Niquinnocuitlahuia in nopilhuān	*I take care of my children*
Ninotēcuitlahuia	*I care for others*

18.5 Passive/Impersonal Forms of Bitransitive Verbs

A bitransitive verb can be put in the passive (15.4) if the agent of the verb is indefinite. However, only the object represented by a prefix in the active form (i.e., the beneficiary, as we have seen) can become the subject of the passive. For a better understanding of this principle, let us take a few examples in which the agent is first definite (and hence the subject) and then indefinite, and observe the changes:

Nimitzmaca in xōchitl	*I'm giving you the flowers*
Timaco[2] in xōchitl	*You're (s.) given the flowers*
Niquilhuia in Pedro in nelli	*I'm telling Peter the truth*
Ilhuīlo in Pedro in nelli	*Peter is told the truth*
Ōnēchilhuî in	*He told me this*
Ōnilhuīlo in	*I was told this*
Nimitztlamacaz	*I'll give you (s.) something*
Titlamacōz	*You'll (s.) be given something*
Nitētlamaca	*I give people things, I give presents*
Tētlamaco	*People are given presents*

It can be seen that it is impossible to say 'the flowers were given to Peter' or 'flowers were given to you', but the expression 'Peter was given the flowers' is possible, with the beneficiary (the indirect object from the point of view of

---

[2] **Maco** is the regular passive (for verbs ending in **-ca**, **-qui**, see 15.5).

English) becoming the subject of the passive verb.[3] Apart from this, we see the features that were discussed in Lesson 15: the definite animate object (patient) becomes the subject of the passive verb, and any indefinite object prefix is retained. In other words, if the active form takes an animate object, then the verb can be converted into a passive form (15.4), with the indefinite object prefixes retained. To make an impersonal form (as in the last example), it is necessary for all three elements (the subject, the object given and the beneficiary) to be indefinite, and in this case, we have both indefinite prefixes (-tē-tla).

Another point. In **timaco in xōchitl**, if the agent is indefinite, two elements remain: the beneficiary, which becomes the subject, and the object given. It can thus be considered that to some extent this form is transitive, which is also shown by the presence of the object **in xōchitl**. Yet there is no object prefix, because it is impossible to say ****ticmaco**. The passive form is directly modeled on the active form (according to the rules laid out earlier). Because the prefix representing the object given does not appear in the active form **nimitzmaca**, it likewise does not appear in the passive **timaco**. That is, the absence of the direct object marker in these passive forms despite the presence of an overt object is a reflex of the rule for reducing the number of definite object prefixes (18.2).[4]

However, because it is possible to say, for example, **nictēmaca in xōchitl** 'I give (people) flowers', it should also be possible to say **tēmaco in xōchitl**. Such a sentence is in fact possible, but (as we know) in situations with an indefinite agent and a definite inanimate patient, Nahuatl prefers to use a reflexive construction with the patient as subject (15.9). Hence, instead of **tēmaco in xōchitl**, the more likely expression would be:

Motēmaca in xōchitl   *Flowers are given (to people)*

Note that for the object given to become the subject, the agent and beneficiary must both be indefinite. If only the agent is indefinite, the beneficiary necessarily becomes the subject (as we saw earlier).

Let us return to general principle that prohibits the passive (and mandates the reflexive) if the patient is inanimate. We have seen (16.6) that this principle does not apply to the –ni form because a passive –ni form can have an

---

[3] Among western European languages, English is unusual in allowing either the direct or the indirect object of an active verb to act as the subject of the corresponding passive. In languages like Spanish or German, only the direct object can become the subject of the passive verb. Nahuatl takes the opposite course in that only the animate beneficiary and not the inanimate direct object can become the subject of the passive verb.

[4] By the same principle, because the form **nimitztlamaca** takes an overt object marker for the thing given, this marker is retained in the passive form **titlamaco**.

inanimate subject. Take, for example, the bitransitive verb **pòpolhuia** 'to pardon, to forgive'. In the active form, we can say:

Nictlapòpolhuia in Pedro	*I forgive Peter (for something)*
Nictēpòpolhuia in tlàtlacōlli	*I forgive (people) the(ir) sins*

and then with an indefinite agent:

Tlapòpolhuīlo in Pedro	*Peter is forgiven (for things)*
Motēpòpolhuia in tlàtlacōlli	*People's sins are forgiven*

Of these two sentences, the first has a passive verb (15.4) and the second a reflexive used in a passive sense (15.8), both with retained indefinite object prefix.

In the **–ni** form, however, we can have the passive in both instances:

Tlapòpolhuīlōni in Pedro	*Peter is pardonable, forgivable*
Tēpòpolhuīlōni in tlàtlacōlli	*The sin is forgivable*

If the active form includes a reflexive, **ne-** can replace this reflexive in the various constructions involving an indefinite agent. The construction used is determined by the nature of the non-reflexive object of the active verb. If this object is definite and animate, then a true passive construction is used (i.e., the patient becomes the subject), with **ne-** retained:

Nicnocuitlahuia in Pedro	*I care for Peter*
Necuitlahuīlo in Pedro	*Peter is cared for, People care for Peter*
Nimitznocuitlahuia	*I care for you (s.)*
Tinecuitlahuīlo	*You (s.) are cared for*

If, conversely, the definite object is inanimate, then the impersonal reflexive form (15.7) is used, with the patient noun left unmarked in the verb:

Tictomacâ in xōchitl	*We give each other the flowers*
Nemaco in xōchitl	*There's a mutual exchange of flowers*

Here, the verb form refers to the reflexive action of the animate agent, and the inanimate patient is left out of account in the verb. In effect, this form is a reflexive variant of the construction illustrated with the sentence **tēmaco in xōchitl** (i.e., an impersonal verb with both an animate and an inanimate patient marks only the former).

Finally, if the non-reflexive object is indefinite, then a combination of the impersonal form with indefinite object (15.7) and the impersonal reflexive (15.8) is used:

Ninotēcuitlahuia	*I care for others*
Netēcuitlahuīlo	*People are cared for*
Titotlamacâ	*We give ourselves gifts*
Netlamaco	*Gifts are given*

18.6 Incorporation with Bitransitive Verbs

A bitransitive verb can allow the procedure of incorporation (17.3). Thus, if 'giving flowers' is considered a more or less ritual act in which the action and the object jointly form a cohesive "unit," the verb **xōchimaca** can be used. Because this object incorporation removes one of the two objects of the original bitransitive verb, **xōchimaca** behaves like a regular transitive verb.

Tinēchxōchimaca	*You make me a gift of flowers*
Nixōchimaco	*I'm given flowers*
Nitēxōchimaca	*I give people flowers*
Tēxōchimaco	*People are given flowers*
Titoxōchimacâ	*We give each other flowers*
Nexōchimaco	*There's mutual giving of flowers, People give each other flowers*

18.7 Ambitransitive Verbs

A certain number of verbs can be either transitive or intransitive. We will call these verbs *ambitransitive*. Among the most common such verbs are:

tōca	*to sow, to plant, to bury*
teci	*to grind, to crush*
ichtequi	*to steal*
elimiqui	*to work, to till the soil*
tēmiqui	*to dream*

These verbs can take a definite object, but if the object is indefinite, then they do not take the prefix **tla-** but instead only the subject prefix appears as if they were intransitive. In English, such use of a transitive verb without an object is called *absolute* (e.g., the intransitive 'I eat', as opposed to the transitive 'I'm eating steak'). Thus:

Ōmēntin huēhuèxōlô ōniquimichtec	*I've stolen two tom turkeys*
Aîc ōnichtec	*I've never stolen (committed theft)*
Àmo nitēmiqui, àmo ōnictēmic	*I don't dream, I haven't dreamt it*
Yālhua nomīlpan ōnitōcac	*Yesterday I sowed in my field*
Auh tlein ōtictōcac?	*And what did you (s.) sow?*
Āxcān teōtlac motōcaz in miccātzintli	*The revered dead man will be buried this evening*

Metlapan teci in cihuātl	*The woman is grinding on the metate*
Ca tlaōlli in quiteci	*It's corn that she's grinding*

This explains why the "agent nouns" derived from these verbs do not have **tla-**, such as **ichtecqui** 'thief', **elimicqui** 'worker' (but **quelimic in tlālli** 'he worked the land'). Clearly, such forms are based on the intransitive variant.

The (transitive) verb **toloa** means 'to swallow':

Noztlac nictoloa	*I swallow my spit*

Used absolutely, it means 'to bow the head (like someone swallowing)', sometimes as a sign of submission.[5]

> ▶ *Note.* The intransitive **teci** has an impersonal form **texōhua** 'there's grinding, flour making', but in the transitive usage it has a passive form **texo**, for example, **texōni** 'what is ground, crushed'.

18.8 *Àci* and *Mati*

We have a slightly different case from the preceding one in the verb **àci** 'to reach'. You can reach a place, in which case **àci** is intransitive, being construed with a locative and normally translated with 'to arrive at'. You can also 'to reach', that is, 'to catch up with' a person or thing, in which case **àci** is construed transitively:

Àmo huel nimitzàciz	*I won't be able to catch up with you (s.)*

Mati can also be construed intransitively with a locative in the sense of 'to know where something is', 'to know how to get to …'. In the latter case, the directional prefix **-om-** is always required:

Mēxìco tiyāzquê, cuix ōmpa tommati?	*We're about to go to Mexico City, do you (s.) know the way there?*
À mīxco mocpac tommati	*You're (s.) an idiot (lit., you don't know where your face or the top of your head is)*

18.9 *Āyi*

A completely exceptional case is that of **āyi** 'to do', which has exactly the opposite behavior compared to that of the verbs discussed in 18.7 in that it takes the indefinite prefixes but not the definite ones:

Cuix titlaāyi?	*Are you (s.) doing something?*
Huel titlaāyini	*You're (s.) very busy*

---

[5] F. Karttunen, *An Analytical Dictionary of Nahuatl* (Austin: University of Texas Press, 1983) claims that these two verbs can be distinguished according to the vowel length of the first syllable (it being long in 'to nod' and short in 'to swallow').

The only possible objects are indefinite words like **tlê** (not **tlein**), **àtle**, **moch**, and with these no object prefix appears:

Nèhuātl moch nāyi   *It's me who does everything*

Āyi does not mean 'to make something' the way **chīhua** does. Instead, it has the vaguer sense 'to do':

Tlê tāyi?   *How (lit., what) are you (s.) doing? How are you? What's going on with you?*

VOCABULARY

Ambitransitive verbs

āyi	*to do* (18.9)	tēmiqui	*to dream*
elimiqui	*to plow, to till*	toloa	*to swallow, to bow the head*
teci	*to grind, to crush*	tōca	*to sow, to plant, to bury*

Bitransitive verbs

cuitlahuia	(mo-: *to care for*)	maca	*to give*
ilhuia	*to tell*	pòpolhuia	*to forgive, to pardon*

Nouns

huèxōlotl	(*pl. /R–'/*) *tom turkey*
icnīuhtli	(*always in the possessed form* -(i)cnīuh, *pl.* -(i)cnīhuān) *friend*
iztlactli	*spit*

EXERCISES

(a) Translate into Nahuatl.
1. You (s.) give it to him.
2. You (s.) give him to them.
3. You (s.) give them to him.
4. You (pl.) give it to them.
5. You (pl.) give them to us.
6. You (pl.) give them to me.
7. He gives them to me.
8. He gives it to me.
9. He says it to me.
10. I'm told it.
11. You (pl.) are told it.
12. He is told it.

13. They are told it.
14. They are forgiven it.
15. People are forgiven for it.
16. You (s.) forgive people for it.
17. You (s.) forgive me for it.
18. You (s.) forgive me for things.
19. You (s.) forgive us for things.
20. You (s.) forgive them for things.
21. You (s.) forgive them for it.
22. You (pl.) forgive them for it.
23. You forgive each other for it.
24. You (pl.) care of it.
25. You (pl.) take care of us.
26. We are cared for.

(b) Translate into English.
1. Ca àmo tocnīhuān: àmo tiquinxōchimacazquê.
2. Mā nicān ximocāhua, oc miyac tlamantli nimitzilhuīz.
3. Mā zan xinēchtlalhui, in nèhuātl ca nimitzcaquiz.
4. Tiyānquizco niyauh, cuix oc anquimmocuitlahuīzquê in nochi-chihuān?
5. Ca ye cualli, mā zan xitēchimmaca, huel tiquimpiyazquê.
6. Tlê ōtāx yālhua? Ca àmo ōtimitzittaquê.
7. Ye ōtamēchilhuìquê: ca àmo ticnequî nōchtli.
8. In Pedro ca miyac in ōquimacac cōzcatl inon cihuātl.
9. Ōtiquintomacaquê tōtoltin.
10. Zan amichteccāpopōl.
11. Nochān texōhua, tlaxcalchīhualo.
12. Ca àmo cualli in ōnictēmic.

(c) Translate into Nahuatl.
1. It's paper that I've given you (s.).
2. This book's good. – Today, I'm still reading it, I will give it to you (pl.) tomorrow.
3. Mary is sick. – I know, her parents ("fathers") told me, (and) for my part, I've told our friends.
4. Mary is taking care of the small children, she won't make mole.
5. How are you (s.) doing? – I don't know, I can't eat, perhaps I'm sick.
6. Sit (pl.) down here, I'm going to tell you what happened to me ("how I did") yesterday.
7. It's me who will take care of this. As for you (s.), you'll watch.
8. Don't (pl.) give pulque to small children. It will make them sick.

9. It's turkey hens that you're (pl.) giving us, not tom turkeys.
10. The peasants ("those with fields") are plowing.
11. You've (s.) stolen again! You're unforgivable. You won't be forgiven for this sin.
12. The corn has not yet been ground (see 8.9).
13. God is very forgiving ("prone to forgiving").

Causative Verbs

19.1 Introduction to Causative Verbs

The causative construction in English involves an auxiliary verb of causation taking as its direct object the person being made to act plus an infinitive of that action: 'I make/have/let him eat, I cause/compel/force/induce him to eat'. Instead of a construction with an auxiliary verb, Nahuatl creates a derivative version of the original verb with the suffixes -**tia, -ltia** (see details in a later discussion), and the new verb means 'to cause (the object) to VERB': **tzàtzītia** 'make shout', **yōlītia** 'make/let live', **cualtia** 'make eat, feed', **chīhualtia** 'have build'. Verbs formed in this way can be put in any tense.

Causative verbs have a predictable relationship with the verbs from which they are derived. If the verb 'shout' speaks only of the person shouting, to 'make someone shout' speaks of the person shouting and of the "causer" who makes that person shout, and if 'eat' speaks only of the eater and the thing eaten, to 'make someone eat' speaks in addition of a causer who makes someone eat. In other words, when the verb is changed from its *simple* form (i.e., the regular dictionary listing) to the causative, we have the following effects, which are similar in both English and Nahuatl:

▶ intransitive verbs become transitive and transitive verbs become bitransitive.
▶ the subject of the causative verb signifies the "causer", and the term that would be the subject (and agent) of the simple verb becomes the direct object of the causative.

Thus:

Nitzàtzi	*I shout*
Tinēchtzàtzītia	*You (s.) make me shout*
Titlacua	*You (s.) eat*
Nimitztlacualtia	*I make you (s.) eat, I feed you*
Ticcua in nacatl	*You (s.) eat the meat*

Nimitzcualtia in nacatl   *I make you eat the meat* (for the dropping of the
                                     -c- representing the direct object, see 18.2).

19.2 Morphology of Causative Verbs

The general principles for forming the causative are the following (with certain exceptions that we will look at):

▶ intransitive verbs have a causative in **-tia**
▶ transitive verbs form the causative by adding **-tia** to base 4 (the passive stem minus **-o** or **-hua**).

Let us now look at the specifics:

(1) The causatives for intransitive verbs are frequently built on base 1, to which **-tia** is added. This formation is subject to a number of modifications.

   ▶ If base 1 ends in **-i**, this vowel is lengthened:

yōlītia	*make live*
nemītia	*make live*
tzàtzītia	*make shout*
huetzītia	*let fall*
cochītia	*put to sleep*
ìcihuītia	*make hasten, urge on*

   ▶ Final **-i** or **-a** is dropped if the preceding consonant is /k/ (i.e., in verbs ending in **-ca**, **-qui**):

mictia	*kill (make die)*
chōctia	*make cry*
pāctia	*make happy, please*

   However, note the form **huetzquitia** 'make laugh' from **huetzca**; this follows the preceding pattern, presumably because ****huetzctia** would be phonologically impossible.

   ▶ The vowel is also dropped if the preceding consonant is /w/ (verbs in **-hui**, **-hua**), /m/ or /n/, provided that the vowel preceding this consonant is long. Thus:

māuhtia	*make fear, scare* (**māhui** 'be afraid', cf. ìcihuītia)
tlāhuāntia	*make drunk, intoxicate*

   The vowel is also dropped if the preceding consonant is /s/ (verbs in **-za**, **-ci**) or /t/ (verbs in **-ti**), but /s/ then shifts to /š/ (**x**) and /t/ to /č/ (**ch**):[1]

nēxtia	*make appear, recover (something lost)*

---

[1] Note that verbs in **-ti** derived from nouns (e.g., **tlācati**) have a special causative in **-lia** (29.3). Because the majority of verbs in **-ti** are such derivatives, the change **-ti** > **-chtia** that is described here actually applies to a very small number of verbs.

quīxtia	*make pass, withdraw*
ilōchtia	*make return, diminis* (**ilōti** 'return', 'abate', 'wane')

(2) In transitive verbs, most of the time -**tia** is added as a suffix to base 4 (see 15.4), whether this is built with the element -**l**-:

cāhualtia	*cause to abandon, make to release*
chīhualtia	*make do*
chiyaltia	*make watch*
cualtia	*make eat*
ìtōltia	*make speak of*

or by the methods not involving -**l**-:

ītia	*make drink*
cuītia	*make take*
tectia	*make cut*
machtia[2]	*make know, teach*

Because the method of forming the passive stem without -**l**- is sometimes optional, doublets of the causative are possible:

ānaltia *or* āntia	*make catch*
quēntia *or* quēmiltia	*make put on* (the only common passive of **quēmi** is **quēmīhua**)

(3) Certain intransitive verbs have a causative in –**ltia** (most of them also have an impersonal form in -**lo**,15.5):

mayānaltia	'starve'
cholōltia	'put to flight' (from **choloa**, but **choltia** is also found)

There is a tendency to add -**ltia** to all verbs ending in -**a**, intransitive ones as well as the expected transitive ones. Here again, doublets are numerous:

tlāhuānaltia	*beside* tlāhuāntia *make drunk*
chōcaltia	*beside* chōctia *make cry*
pāquiltia	*beside* pāctia *make happy*

The addition of -**ltia** can lead to variation in the stem:

With verbs ending in /ka/, the final vowel of base 1 may become /i/ (i.e., -**ca** becomes -**qui**-):

chōquiltia	*make cry*
huetzquiltia	*make laugh*

Finally, transitive verbs made intransitive through object incorporation (17.3) maintain the causative formation in -**ltia** that is regular for transitives:

nēchcacchīhualtia	*he makes me make shoes*

[2] This verb has peculiarities of its own (see 19.5).

19.3 Notes on the Meaning of the Causative

As can be seen, the rules for forming the causative are not entirely fixed, and for this reason dictionaries generally give the causative verbs their own listing separate from the verbs from which they are derived. Also, not all verbs have a causative attested. In particular, this is the case with **yauh** and **câ**. However, the verb **huīca** 'lead, bring' can be used to make up for the lack of a causative with **yauh**, and the predicative construction with **cuepa** (see 32.4) is to some extent comparable to a causative of **câ**.

The English translation can make use of not only an auxiliary verb like 'make' but also expressions related to the verb from which the causative is formed ('put to flight', 'put to sleep', 'bring to an end') or an entirely different verb ('learn'/'teach', 'appear'/'show', 'die'/'kill'). That is, while Nahuatl has a very transparent system of derivation that is frequently used, there is no regularly used causative system in English, so that the idiomatic way to translate a causative into English often involves some other sort of construction. In particular, you should also be careful about **pāctia** 'please', which can translate the English verb 'like', but with the roles *reversed*. That is, the object of the English verb is the subject of the Nahuatl causative, which has as its object the subject of the English verb:

Nēchpāctia in mēxìcatlàtōlli	*I like the Mexica language (lit., it makes me happy)*
Nēchpāctia in nōchtli	*I like prickly pears*

With certain intransitive verbs that indicate a feeling, physical state or motion, there can be two forms that at first sight seem synonymous: the intransitive verb and its causative used reflexively. Thus, **niquīza** and **ninoquīxtia** could both be translated with 'I go out', but the reflexive causative emphasizes either a voluntary or inchoative aspect to the process ("inchoative" signifies that the process is commencing). Hence, **ninoquīxtia** (lit., 'I make myself leave') means 'I undertake to leave, I withdraw'. Similarly, **nimāhui** 'I fear' but **ninomāuhtia** 'I take fright'; **nihuetzi** 'I fall', but **ninohuetzītia** 'I let myself fall'.

19.4 Causatives of *Itta*

Itta 'see' has two causatives: **ittitia** and **ittaltia**. Both signify 'make see, show' but there's a difference. **Ittitia** (the more common) indicates that the "causer" shows something to someone by acting upon the *thing* being shown (by presenting it, bringing it, revealing it etc.). **Ittaltia**, on the other hand, signifies that the causer acts upon the *person* to whom he wishes to show the thing (e.g., by leading the person to it). Thus, if I intend to look for some books or to take them out of some place in order to show them to someone, I would say:

Mā nimitzittiti in nāmox   *Let me show you (s.) my books*

Here, the sense is something like 'let me arrange things to allow you to see my books'. If, on the other hand, I want to show you my house and in order to do so I have to bring you to either the house itself or a place from which the house can be seen, I would say:

Mā nimitzittalti in nocal   *Let me show you (s.) my house*

Here, the sense is more literally causal: 'let me make you see my house'.

The same distinction applies to the two causatives of **caqui**, which are **caquītia** 'make someone hear a sound (that you produce)' and **caquiltia** 'make someone hear a sound (e.g., by bringing the person to the sound)'. The expected form ****cactia** (modeled after **tequi/tectia**) is not found.

19.5 Causatives of *Mati*

The causative of **mati** is **machtia**, but this verb has a very peculiar behavior. We can find the form

Motlamachtia   *He's rich, prosperous*

which is connected to **mati**'s meaning 'feel' (hence, 'feel well off'). But just as **mati** most frequently has the meaning 'know', the causative **machtia** generally has the meaning 'teach' ('make know'). This sense is theoretically bitransitive, but in practice **machtia** excludes the use of -**tla**-. In effect, the causative marks what the person is 'made to know' only if this is *definite*. Hence, contrast the regular expression:

Namēchmachtia in teōtlàtōlli   *I teach you (pl.) the word of God* (with suppressed **-c-**)

with

Namēchmachtia   *I instruct you (pl.), I teach you things* (whereas we would expect ****Namēchtlamachtia**)

In the same way, contrast:

Nictēmachtia in teōtlàtōlli   *I teach (people) the word of God*

with

Nitēmachtia (*rather than* ****Nitētlamachtia**)   *I teach*

Note the meaning and construction of the reflexive:

Nicnomachtia in mexìcatlàtōlli	*I study Nahuatl*[3]
Ninomachtia (*rather than*	*I study, learn*
**Ninotlamachtia)	

Two "agent nouns" are derived from the singular of the **-ni** form (more rarely the preterite) of this verb:

tēmachtiāni (*more rarely* tēmachtî)	*teacher*
momachtiāni (*more rarely* momachtî)	*student*

The plural is generally derived from the preterite (16.5): **tēmachtìquê, momachtìquê** (more rarely: **tēmachtiānimê, momachtiānimê**). The derived forms are clearly based on the preterite:

Tinotēmachtìcāuh	*you (s.) are my teacher*
Nimonemachtìcāuh[4]	*I'm your student*
tēmachtìcātzintli	*revered teacher*

Another causative of **mati** is **machitia**, which has the slightly different meaning 'bring to someone's attention, inform':

Ye huītzê in Caxtīltēcâ: ōnicmachitî	*Look, here come the Spaniards, I've informed*
in tlàtoāni	*the ruler about this (*lit., *let him know*
	about it)

19.6 Causative of the Reflexive

The causative can be applied to a reflexive form. Take for example:

Motlazòtlâ	*They love each other*

Here, the underlying verb to which the causative ending is added is reflexive. In such cases, where the reflexive does not refer to the subject of the causative verb, the indefinite reflexive -ne- is used. With a causer in the first person, we get the causative form of the previous Nahuatl sentence:

Niquinnetlazòtlaltia	*I reconcile them (make them love each other)*

---

[3] For 'I study Nahuatl', it is also possible to say **ninomachtia mexìcacopa** lit., 'I teach myself about Nahuatl'. **Mexìcacopa** is a locative form (13.1) and therefore is not represented by a definite object prefix. One might have expected -**tla**- (5.5), but as we have just seen, this prefix is excluded with **machtia**.

[4] Note that when this form is possessed, it takes the indefinite reflexive prefix -**ne**-.

If the object of the causation is indefinite, the order is **-tē-ne-** (and not **-ne-tē-** as you would expect from the table of prefixes in section 6.5):[5]

> Nitēnetlazòtlaltia   *I reconcile people*

But there can also be a reflexive that reflects a situation in which the causer is also the subject or object of the underlying form. That is, the subject of the causative is either causing itself to act or causing someone else to act upon it. In this case, the reflexive is *definite*. For example, starting with:

> Nēchitta   *He sees me*

we have:

> Nicnottitia[6]   *I show myself to him* (lit., *I make him see me*)

and with an indefinite:

> Ninotēittitia   *I show myself (to people, others)* (lit., *make them see me*)

As can be seen, the reflexive here is not internal to the simple form that takes the causative.

In other words:

> X makes Y VERB Y > **ne**
> X makes Y VERB X > **mo (no, to)**
> X makes X VERB Y[7] > **mo (no, to)**

▶ *Note.* We have seen that certain verbs in the reflexive form refer to movement, emotion or physical state (6.6), and in this case, causation is expressed with a simple active verb and not with a causative form in **ne-**. For example:

mocuepa	*he returns*
mēhua	*he gets up*
mococoa	*he is sick*
mozōma	*he's angry*

For 'I make him return, get up, (be) sick, grow angry', one would say:

> niccuepa, niquēhua, niccocoa, niczōma (*and not* **nicnecuepaltia** *etc.*)

---

[5] Presumably, the feeling was that the reflexive was an inherent element of the underlying verb from which the causative was formed and therefore was "fixed" to it, which necessitated the placement of the indefinite marker in front of it, contrary to regular practice (cf. the "fusion" of **tla-** in 17.5).

[6] On the basis of 19.4, we have **ittitia** and not **ittaltia**.

[7] This last formulation is rare, but it is what we saw in **nicnomachtia** (19.5), and we will see it later with the honorifics (Lesson 21).

In other words, with such verbs, the transitive sense is primary, and the use of the reflexive to make these verbs intransitive is secondary. Hence, it is redundant to use the causative with the reflexive meaning in place of the primary transitive form.

19.7 Passive and Impersonal of the Causative

The "causer" can be indefinite, and so there are passive and impersonal forms of the causative. These constructions indicate that the agent of the underlying verb doesn't "act" of its own accord:

Niquīxtīlo	*I'm made to leave*
Mictīlo	*He's killed (made to die)*
Nicualtīlo tlaxcalli[8]	*I'm made to eat tortillas*
Nitlacualtīlo	*I'm fed (made to eat)*
Tētlacualtīlo	*People are fed*

We find the expected order -**ne-tē-** if appropriate:

Netētlazòtlaltīlo	*People are reconciled, There's a reconciliation*
	(lit. one makes people love each other)

Note that -**ne-** does not revert to the definite reflexive in the passive:

Tinetlazòtlaltīlô (*and not* **tito-** ...)	*We are reconciled (lit., are made to love one another)*

19.8 Semi-Causatives

Alongside "true" causatives in -**tia, -ltia**, there are verbs that have some affinity to causatives in their relationship to other verbs but are formed differently. We will call such verbs *semi-causatives*. Semi-causatives are verbs to which there exist corresponding intransitive verbs whose subject is most commonly inanimate. This pairing resembles a similar procedure in English whereby a verb can be used intransitive simply to indicate that a process (a change of state) happens to an object, and the same verb can also be used transitively with some external agent as its subject to indicate that someone/something causes the process or event to happen to the object: 'the ice cube melts' vs. 'the sun melts the ice cube' or 'the window broke' vs. 'the boy broke the window'. In Nahuatl, the intransitive verb signifies a state or a change in state, and the corresponding transitive

---

[8] And not **niccualtīlo**; see 18.5 for the explanation for the omission of the definite third person object (the corresponding active form would be **tinēchcualtia tlaxcalli**).

signifies the act of putting the object into the relevant state or causing it to undertake or undergo the relevant change in state.

Although these intransitive/transitive pairs often make perfectly good sense from the point of view of English, frequently the Nahuatl intransitive does not correspond to a verb in English but to an adjectival phrase. For instance, we simply have the transitive verb 'to write', and from this we derive the notion of 'standing/being written' (in the sense of 'appear in written form'). Nahuatl, in contrast, represents the latter idea with the intransitive verb **ìcuilihui** 'be written', to which there is a corresponding transitive verb **ìcuiloa** signifying 'put into written form'. Neither verb takes priority over the other, unlike the case with English, where the transitive verb clearly is the primary form. As can be seen from this pair, the corresponding transitive and intransitive verbs generally (though not always) have different endings (unlike the case with English, where the same verb can be used either transitively or intransitively).

In the most frequent case, the intransitive ends in **-i**, and the transitive semi-causative is obtained by replacing **-i** with **-a**:

tlapāni	*break, split*	tlapāna	*(cause to) break*
cotōni	*snap (be cut off)*	cotōna	*cut (off)*
pōhui	*be counted/assigned, count as*	pōhua	*count, read*

The change of **-i** to **-a** can affect the preceding consonant:

tlazòti	*be precious, valued*	tlazòtla[9]	*esteem, value, love*
pāti	*melt*	pātla	*dissolve*
huāqui	*dry up*	huātza	*(cause to) dry up*

Itta (which in certain modern dialects appears in the form **ithua**) is the semi-causative of a verb **ithui** 'be visible', which is used in the Classical period only in the impersonal form **tlathui** 'day breaks' (lit., 'things become visible').

We also find **-i** for the intransitive and **-ia** for the semi-causative:

olini	*move, be in motion*	olinia	*move, set in motion*
calaqui	*enter*	calaquia	*make enter, insert*
pàti	*get better*	pàtia	*cure, heal*
tlami	*come to an end*	tlamia	*bring to an end*

or **-a** for the intransitive and **-ia** for the semi-causative:

tlatla	*be on fire*	tlatia[10]	*set on fire*

[9] By a regular phonological process, /ta/ shifts to /λa/.
[10] Not to be confused with **tlātia** 'hide'.

or also **-ihui** or **-ahui** for the intransitive and **-oa** for the semi-causative:[11]

polihui	*becomes lost, disappear*	poloa	*lose, destroy, make disappear*
ìtahui	*be said, mentioned*	ìtoa	*say, mention*
ìtlacahui	*be damaged, harmed*	ìtlacoa	*harm, damage*
ìcuilihui	*stand written, drawn*	ìcuiloa	*write, draw*
zalihui	*be glued*	zaloa	*glue*

or **-hua** in both forms (e.g., **tomāhua**, **chipāhua**; see 12.5).

▶ *Notes*

(1) Quite often, the transitive form does not represent an "action" in the proper sense. **Nictlazòtla** and **niquitta** do not mean 'I act in such a way that a certain thing is esteemed (**tlàzotli**) or seen (**ithui**)' but 'I am the person by or for whom the thing is esteemed (valuable) or seen (visible)'.

(2) Paired verbs in **-i** and **-a** have the same base 2 form, but it can be determined from the prefixes whether a preterite is from the intransitive or the semi-causative. For example, **ōtlapān** 'it broke' comes from the intransitive **tlapāni**, and the presence of the object marker shows that **ōquitlapān** 'he broke it' comes from the semi-causative **tlapāna**.

(3) Verbs in **-i** and **-ia** have the same form in the optative singular. Here again, the prefixes show that **xicalaqui** comes from the intransitive **calaqui** 'enter', and **xiccalaqui** comes from the semi-causative **calaquia** 'make enter'. In the plural of the optative and in the future, base 3 of verbs in **-ia** is distinctive in having a long **-ī**: **xicalaquicān** 'enter (pl.)' but **xiccalaquīcān** 'make (pl.) him enter', and **nicalaquiz** 'I will enter' but **niccalaquīz** 'I'll make him enter'.

19.9 Semi-Causatives of Verbs in *-o*

Intransitive verbs in **-o** (there are four of these) have a causative in **-ohuia** or **-ahuia**:

èco	*arrive*	ècahuia	*make arrive*
pano	*pass*	panahuia	*pass, make pass*[12]
temo	*come down, descend*	temohuia	*make come down, bring down*
tlèco	*rise up, ascend*	tlècahuia	*make rise up, raise*

---

[11] It appears that historically the endings /*-iwa/ and /*-awa/ developed into /-owa/ and then into /-oa/. Hence, the seemingly odd correspondence of verbs in **-ihui** and **-ahui** to semi-causatives in **-oa** does in fact fit into the general pattern pairing intransitives in **-i** with transitives in **-a**.

[12] **Panahuia** also has, as will be seen, the applicative sense (see Lesson 20) 'surpass, overtake, cross'.

19.10 Restrictions on the Formation of Causatives

In certain instances, the causative is not allowed. In particular, causation cannot be made in the following circumstances:

(1) when the object of the underlying verb is in the first or second person and its agent (subject) is in the third person or indefinite.[13] Thus:

Nimitznōtzaltia *can only mean*   *I make you call him* (and not *I make him call you*)
Nimitztēnōtzaltia   *I make you call people* (and not *I make people call you*)

That is, the expressed object has to represent the subject of the underlying form. In the opposite situation, it is possible to another construction involving the use of a sort of auxiliary (see 28.10).

(2) when the form that we start from is a true causative. It is not possible to have the suffix -**tia** twice. The construction just cited can be used (28.10) but so can the directional prefix -**on**-, which indicates in some way that the action is carried out through an intermediary:

Ōniquimommictî in māmaltin   *I've had them killed (made them die through the agency of someone else)*

On the other hand, a semi-causative can be used in the causative form in -**(l)tia**; we have seen **tlazòtlaltia**, **ìtōltia** etc.

VOCABULARY

Intransitive verbs

cotōni	*break (in two), snap*	pàti	*get better*
èco	*arrive*	pāti	*melt*
huāqui	*dry up*	polihui	*become ruined, disappear*
ilōti	*return, abate*	tlapāni	*break*
ithui	*(tlathui day breaks)*	tlatla	*burn, be on fire*
ìcuilihui	*stand written*	tlazòti	*be valuable*
ìtahui	*be said*	tlèco	*rise up*
māhui	*be scared*	zalihui	*be glued*
olini	*move*		

---

[13] Unless there is no possibility of ambiguity, as in, for example, **nictēcualtia in tlaxcalli** 'I have people eat tortillas', which is acceptable because the tortillas clearly can't eat people. However, it seems to be impossible to say in Nahuatl something like 'he makes me call you' or 'he makes you call me' with a first or second person form referring to the underlying verb from which the causative is derived.

Transitive verbs

calaquia	*make enter, insert*	pātla	*melt*
huātza	*dry up*	tlamia	*bring to an end*
olinia	*make move*	tlapāna	*break*
pàtia	*cure, heal*	tlatia	*burn*

EXERCISES

(a) Convert the following forms into causatives with a third person singular causer, then translate (ex. **tihuetzi** > **mitzhuetzītia** 'he makes you fall').
1. Ōtichōcaquê
2. Cochizquê
3. Ōtzàtzic
4. Ōnicchīuh calli
5. Tictēmoâ xōchitl
6. Tixōchitēmoâ
7. Ōanquilcāuhquê in ītōcā
8. Quicua nacatl
9. Quīquê octli
10. Ātlīc
11. Titlapōhua
12. Ōnictlāz in tetl
13. Titētlàpaloāyâ
14. Antēnōtzazquê
15. Titottâ
16. Ninopāca
17. Ninotolīnia
18. Ammotēcaquê

(b) In the same sentences, replace the third person causer with an indefinite one.

(c) Translate into English.
1. Mācamo xicchōcti, xictzàtzīti in piltōntli.
2. Xoconquīxtīcān. – Ye ōmoquīxtî.
3. Cuix timāhui? Auh tlein mitzmāuhtia? Mācamo ximomāuhti.
4. Nicchīhualtia tlaxcalli in Malintzin.
5. Ōtlapān in tecomatl, ca nèhuātl in ōnictlapān.
6. Tlazòti in teōcuitlatl: huel quitlazòtlâ in caxtīltecâ.
7. Huāqui in mochi xōchitl: quihuātza in tōnatiuh.
8. Tletica pāti in cetl. – Quēmâ: quipātla in tletl.
9. Ōtlatlac in nocal. – Āquin ōquitlatî?
10. Xictlècahui in tetl. – Àmō, zan nictemohuīz.

11. Ca huel nēchmāuhtiâ inìquê on tlācâ, àmo ninonēxtīz.
12. Īpan inin āmatl ìcuilihui xōchitl.
13. Xinēchilnāmicti āc yèhuātl.
14. Calaquiz in Pedro: tèhuātl xiccalaqui.
15. Ye ōcotōn in ichtli.
16. Ye ōquicotōn in ichtli.
17. Cuix ōchīhualtīlōc?

(d) Translate into Nahuatl.

1. I was made to leave the stone.
2. This water will cure you (s.).
3. This person will get better.
4. The earth was trembling (moving).
5. He was able to move his ears (this refers to a general ability rather than a single action).
6. The sick person has been put to sleep.
7. It won't be possible for him to be made to speak (He won't be able to be made…).
8. I won't make you (s.) guard my gold.
9. You've (pl.) really made us laugh.
10. Yesterday, we got your (pl.) friends drunk. – We made them drink pulque.
11. One of the lords was killed in war.
12. Mexica civilization has been lost, the Spaniards destroyed it.
13. Peter has (already) gotten better. – He was cured by the doctor.
14. Do you (pl.) like pork (pig meat)? – We killed our pig yesterday.
15. We've been made to hear (been informed of), we've been made to understand (been instructed in), the word of God.

Applicative Verbs

20.1 Introduction to Applicative Verbs

In English, we can say 'I built a house', which indicates simply the subject (agent) and object (patient) of the act of building. We can expand this phrase to say 'I built him a house', which indicates the person for whom the action is performed. This concept is basically the same as the indirect object used in verbs of giving and the like ('gave him a book'). We have already seen that bitransitive verbs (see 18.1) indicate not only the direct object but also the indirect object, which is called the "beneficiary." With most verbs, however, the beneficiary is considered to be outside the immediate operation of the verb. For instance, you can build a house 'for someone', but the action could be described perfectly well without any mention of such a beneficiary. With verbs of this variety, Nahuatl uses a special form known as the *applicative* to indicate the involvement of someone or something affected only indirectly by the action of the verb. We will call this indirectly involved element the *beneficiary* noun (or pronoun). Thus, to use the previous examples:

Nicchīhua cē calli	*I build a house*
Nicchīhuilia cē calli	*I build him a house*
Niccui in tomin	*I take the money*
Nimitzcuīlia in tomin	*I take the money from you (s.)*

The applicative has a feature that we have already encountered in the causative (19.1):

▶ Intransitive verbs become transitive, and transitive verbs bitransitive.

But unlike the case with causative forms:

▶ The subject of the applicative form is the same as that of the underlying simple verb. The new element (the "beneficiary") appears as an object (alongside the original object if the underlying verb is transitive).

20.2 The Suffix -*lia*

The mark of the applicative in most instances is the suffix -**lia**, on intransitive as well as transitive verbs:

Nimitztzàtzilia	*I shout after you (s.), I call you by shouting*
Nitētlacuīlia	*I take things from people*

Like -**lo** and -**ltia**, -**lia** appears in principle on base 3, which means that in verbs in -**ia** and -**oa** the -**a** is dropped:

Xinēchtēmōlia xōchitl	*Look (s.) for flowers for me*
Nictlātīlia in ītomin	*I hide his money from (or: for) him*

With verbs ending in an -**a** preceded by a consonant, however, the -**a** turns into -**i**:

Nictēchīhuilia tlaxcalli	*I make tortillas for other people*
Ōniccōhuilî nacatl	*I bought him meat*
Xinēchcuepili in notlaxcal	*Turn (s.) my tortilla over for me*
Xinēchānili inon huèxōlotl	*Catch (s.) that tom turkey for me*

The change of -**a** to -**i** can lead to modifications in a preceding consonant: /c/ and /t/ turn into /č/, /s/ into /š/, and /λ/ into /t/ or /č/. This means that:

▶ verbs in -**tza**, -**tzi**, -**ti** have an applicative in -**chilia**:
nōchilia	*call someone for someone* (**nōtza**)
machilia	*know something about someone* (**mati**)[1]

▶ verbs in -**za**, -**ci** have an applicative in -**xilia**:
tlāxilia	*throw something at someone* (**tlāza**)

▶ verbs in -**tla** have an applicative in -**tilia** or –**chilia**:[2]
tlazòtilia	*love something about someone* (**tlazòtla**)
mōchilia	*stone someone's something* (**mōtla**)

However, final -**a** is maintained in monosyllables, becoming long:

cuālia	*eat something for someone* (**cua**)

and also in verbs ending in -**iya** (Nahuatl avoids the sequence -**iyi**):

piyalia	*guard something for someone* (**piya**)

---

[1] For the problems in meaning posed by such forms, see 20.5.

[2] It seems that the form is -**tilia** when -**tla** is a suffix. This is the case with **tlazòtla** (for the verb suffixes -**ti** and -**tla**, see 29.2, 9). **Mōtla**, however, is unanalyzable in terms of the stem.

20.3 Applicatives in -*ia*, -*(l)huia*

A second (less common) way to form the applicative is to replace a final -**a** with -**ia**. This happens in particular with verbs ending in -**ca** or -**hua**. However, this form appears only if the direct object is indefinite (-**tla**-) or incorporated, and the usual form in -**lia** is always possible.

Nitlaxca	*I'm frying things*
Nimitztlaxquia (or nimitztlaxquilia)	*I'm frying things for you*
Niquixca tōtoltetl	*I'm frying eggs* (**ixca** *to fry*)
Nimitzixquilia tōtoltetl	*I'm frying (s.) eggs for you*
Nitlaxtlāhua	*I pay* (**ixtlāhua** *to pay*)
Nimitztlaxtlāhuia	*I pay you (s.)*
Nimitzixtlāhuilia in motequiuh	*I pay you for your job*

Sometimes, there is a differentiation in meaning. Thus, **pōhua** has the two expected applicatives, and although **pōhuilia** has the ordinary meaning 'count or read something to someone', **nictlapōhuia** has the specialized meaning 'I read his fortune (through divination with kernels of corn)'. Similarly, although **chīhuilia** has the regular applicative meaning 'do something for someone', **nictlachīhuia** means to 'bewitch, enchant him (lit., 'do things to him', with the agent noun **tētlachīhuî** 'enchanter, sorcerer').

The intransitive/semicausative pairs in -**ihui** (-**ahui**)/-**oa** always have a corresponding applicative in -**ilhuia** (-**alhuia**):

ìtalhuia	*say (something) about someone* (**ìtahui, ìtoa**)
ìtlacalhuia	*harm, commit a wrong against someone, damage someone's something* (**ìtlacahui, ìtlacoa**)
malacachilhuia	*spin something for someone* (**malacachihui, malacachoa**)

As can be seen, it is necessary to know the form of the intransitive member of the pair to determine the form of the applicative corresponding to the semicausative.[3]

When the element before the ending -**ihua**/-**ahua** ends in -**l**, however, there's simplification, so we have just -**huia**:

polhuia (*and not* **polilhuia)	*lose, destroy something for someone* (**polihui, poloa**)
ìcuilhuia (*and not* **ìcuililhuia)	*write, draw something for someone* (**icuilihui, ìcuiloa**)

---

[3] The historical explanation of these seemingly odd forms is as follows. The stem-final vowel was dropped before the applicative suffix, and the resulting endings /-iwlia/ and /-awlia/ then underwent metathesis (the reversal in order of two phonological items), yielding the attested /-ilwia/ and /-alwia/.

▶ *Note.* **Cocoa** has no intransitive equivalent ****coquihui**. There is, however, an applicative **cocolhuia** (note the short vowel; this form is *not* derived form base 3).

Ōtinēchcocolhuî in nomā   *You (s.) injured my hand (for me)*

20.4 Applicative in the Form of a Causative

As an exception, the ending -**tia** can have an applicative meaning. The two most common such verbs are **cuīcatia**[4] 'sing for someone' and **namactia** 'sell something to someone'.

Cuix titēchcuīcatīz?   *Will you (s.) sing for us?*
Xinēchnamacti inin huīpilli   *Sell (s.) me this blouse*

20.5 Notes on the Meaning of the Applicative

Let us return to the notion of the "beneficiary," that is, the new object governed by the applicative ending. As noted before, the beneficiary signifies someone or something in relation to which the action of the verb takes place. Most commonly, this signifies the person for whom the action is carried out, as in **nicchīhuilia cē calli** 'I'm building him a house' or 'I'm building a house for him'.

Sometimes the translation 'for' is not possible, as one can have an "interest" in an activity in a number of ways. The beneficiary can receive harm rather than benefit from the action, and if this concerns the taking of something from a person, that person is indicated in Nahuatl by the applicative construction, but in English this person is indicated with the preposition 'from', as in **nimitzcuīlia in tomin** 'I take the money from you'.

In some cases the meaning is ambiguous, as in

Nimitzcōhuilīz nacatl   *I'll buy meat for you/from you*

The new element that is introduced is not necessarily someone who derives advantage or harm from the activity. In particular, Nahuatl always prefers the applicative construction when there is an object in the possessed form. In that case, the possessor of the object appears as the beneficiary. Whereas English says 'I wash your head' and French says 'I wash the head for you' ('je te lave la tête'), Nahuatl uses a combination of both these idioms:

Nimitzpāquilia in mocuā[5]   *I wash your (s.) head (for you)*

---

[4] And not ****cuīctia**, as would be expected. Rather than the applicative of **cuīca**, this verb should perhaps be considered a derivative of **cuīcatl** (29.5).
[5] The most common expression in this instance is **nimitzcuāpāca** (see 17.4 and 20.10).

This expression is not restricted to parts of the body (as it is in French):

Nimitzintlazòtilia in mopilhuān	*I love your (s.) children ('for you')* (note the **-in-** retained from the otherwise omitted third person plural object; see 18.3)
Nimitzmachilia in motlàtlacōl	*I know your (s.) sins (regarding you)*
Mācamo xinēchìtalhui in notlàtlacōl	*don't (s.) tell my sins (regarding me)*
Cuix ōtinēchittilî in nocihuāuh?	*have you seen my wife (for me)?*

rather than **niquintlazòtla in mopilhuān, nicmati in motlàtlacōl, mācamo xiquìto in notlàtlacōl, cuix ōtiquittac in nocihuāuh.**

The applicative construction cannot be used, however, if the possessor is also the subject of the verb. Thus:

Nictlazòtla in nopiltzin (*and not* nicnotlazòtilia in nopiltzin[6])	*I love my child*

▶ *Note.* The verb **ìtalhuia** (applicative of **ìtoa**) means 'to say something *about* someone'. As we've already learned, 'to say something *to* someone' is expressed with a verb from a different root, **ilhuia.**[7]

In some cases, the applicative verb has a *comitative* meaning, that is, it expresses *with whom* the action is carried out:

Ōnicxelô in nacatl – Āquin ōticxelhuî?	*I shared out the meat. – Who did you share it out with?*
Ōnichuetzquilî cē cihuātl	*I laughed with a woman*

So far, the constructions that we have discussed concern animate applicatives (and mostly correspond to the dative case of Western European languages), but the applicative construction can also govern inanimate nouns. This is only natural, because the signification of the Nahuatl beneficiary broadly indicates an element that "relates" to the action of the underlying verb.

With **tlālia**, the applicative indicates where the thing that is "placed" is put, that is, the location of the "putting" is described as the thing with reference to which the object of the verb is acted upon:

Iztatl ōnictlālīlî in ātl	*I've put salt in the water*

An inanimate beneficiary often appears with verbs of motion. If you wish to say, 'I'm passing over the water', you can say **nipano īpan ātl**, where **īpan ātl** is

---

[6] This expression is possible, but it has an honorific sense (see 21.5).

[7] This is the applicative of a series whose first two members, the intransitive **ilihui** and corresponding semi-causative **iloa**, are practically unused, respectively signifying something like 'return' and 'make return'.

a locative phrase (see 13.4). The same meaning can also be conveyed in a transitive form by means of the applicative construction, with **ātl** as the beneficiary object:

Nicpanahuia in ātl	*I'm crossing the water (lit., I'm crossing with reference to the water)*

This construction is used with a number of verbs of motion:

Mēxìco tàcî	*We arrive at Mexico City*
Ticàxiliâ[8] in āltepētl	*We reach the city (lit., arrive with reference to the city)*
Mēxìcopa choloâ	*They're fleeing in the direction of Mexico*
Ōniccholhuî[9] in ātōyātl	*I fled to the other side of the river*

Also note the following usages:

Nitlanemilia	*I ponder*[10]
Nicchōquilia in notlàtlacōl	*I cry for (with reference to) my sins*

20.6 Applicative of the Reflexive

With the reflexive, we have a phenomenon that has already been encountered with the causative (19.6). If the applicative is built on a verb in the reflexive form, then we have **ne-**. If, however, the reflexive signifies the beneficiary element, it is definite. In other words:

X VERBS X for Y (X VERBS himself for Y) > **ne-**
X VERBS Y for X (X VERBS Y for himself) > **mo-**

That is, if an applicative verb takes the indefinite reflexive prefix **ne-**, this prefix represents the direct object of the underlying verb, and if the beneficiary verb takes the direct reflexive **mo-**, this is governed by the applicative ending. Thus:

Nicnetlātīlia in yāōtl	*I hide (myself) from the enemy*
Mācamo xinēchnezōmāli[11]	*Don't (s.) get mad (make yourself annoyed) at me*

---

[8] We could also say **ticàcî** (18.8).

[9] **Choloa** is intransitive (and so there is no form ****cholihui**), but the (transitive) applicative takes **-huia** (for the formation, see 20.4).

[10] This meaning is probably connected with the meaning 'to move' that **nemi** originally had.

[11] As we know, **zōma** follows the morphology of monosyllables (8.6), so the applicative is **zōmālia** (like **cuālia**) and not ****zōmilia**.

but

| Tilmàtli quimolpiliâ | *They tie on capes on themselves* |

▶ **Note**. This time, we have the regular order **ne-tē-** (cf. the opposite order in 19.6):

| Ninetētlātilia | *I hide (myself) from other people* |

20.7 Passive of the Applicative

An applicative can be put into the passive. In Nahuatl, the animate beneficiary becomes the subject of the passive, but the English translation can take two forms. Either the indirect object (or person in a similar construction) becomes the subject (e.g., 'I'm laughed at', 'I have something taken from me'), or it is the patient of the underlying verb that becomes the subject of the passive while the indirect object (or corresponding element) remains in the appropriate construction ('something is taken from me'). Everything that was said about the interplay of prefixes in bitransitive verbs (18.2–3) applies here too. In particular, an object prefix that was dropped in the active in front of another object prefix does not reappear in the passive:

Titzàtzilīlo	*You (s.) are being shouted for*
Tētlacuīlīlo	*People have things taken from them, Things are taken from people*
Cuix ōtitlacuīlīlōc?	*Have you (s.) had things taken from you? Have things been taken from you?*
Quēmâ, ōnicuīlīlōc in nomīl, in notlāl	*Yes, I've had my fields, my land taken from me, My fields and my lands have been taken from me*
In pīpiltotōntin ōcuālīlōquê in īntlaxcal	*The little children had their tortillas eaten*

20.8 Applicative of the Causative

Though such forms are rare, it is possible to put a causative verb in the applicative. If the verb stem is transitive, then we have one subject and three complements (the patient and agent of the underlying simple verb plus the beneficiary). Thus, on the basis of

| Tlacuâ in pīpiltotōntin | *The small children eat* |

we add a second person "causer" and get:

| Tiquintlacualtia in pīpiltotōntin | *You (s.) make the small children eat, You feed them* |

If, then, the children are in the possessed form, then the possessor becomes a beneficiary (20.5) too, and then we have:

Tinēchintlacualtīlia in nopilhuāntotōn   *You (s.) feed my small children (for me)*[12]

with **ti-** representing the causer, **-nēch-** the beneficiary (possessor of the children), **-in-** (vestige of **-quin-**, see 18.3) the children and **-tla-** the indefinite thing(s) that they eat. If you wish to say, for example, 'you're making my children eat meat', **-tla-** simply disappears (it should be replaced with **-qui-**, but the slot for the definite object is already taken, so **-qui-** is dropped): **tinēchincualtīlia nacatl in nopihuāntotōn**. As can be seen, the prefixes follow the order given in section 6.5, and the suffixes appear in the order causative-applicative.

20.9 Semi-Applicative Verbs

There is a small class of verbs that could be called *semi-applicative*. These have the following characteristics:

▶ They are always transitive.
▶ If the direct object is definite, this can only represent a human being whose role in the action is equivalent to that of an beneficiary noun.
▶ If there is no explicit beneficiary element, the prefix **tla-** is added (which leads to an absolute, i.e., intransitive, translation of the verb).

To this class belong **tlāni** 'to gain', **tlācamati** 'to obey', **tequipanoa** 'to work', **huahualoa** or **huahualtza** 'to bark', **nanaloa** or **nanaltza** 'to snarl', **mōtla** 'to throw things (particularly stones)'. Thus:

Ōnitlatlān	*I've made a gain*
Ōnēchtlānquê	*They've defeated (gained) me*
Àmo tlatlācamati	*He doesn't obey*
Àmo tēchtlācamati	*He doesn't obey us*
Nitlatequipanoa	*I work*
Nictequipanoa in tēuctli	*I work for the lord*
Tlahuahualtza in chichi	*The dog is barking*
Tēchhuahualtza in chichi	*The dog is barking at us*

▶ *Note.* We have seen that **mōtla** is construed like the English 'to stone' and not like 'to throw' (i.e., with the person, or sometimes thing, at which

---

[12] Note that 'for me' is simply a redundant (from the English point of view) recapitulation of the possess of **nopihuāntotōn** and should not be confused with the English sense 'in place of me' (i.e., in a situation where you're feeding my children when for some reason I can't).

the things are being thrown as the direct object). If you want to say 'throw something', it is proper to use **tlāza**, but you can also say **nitlamōtla**. To say 'I hurl something specific', this pretty much has to be expressed with 'I stone (**mōtla**) things (**tla**) with (instrumental: 14.3–4) this'. For example:

Īca ōnitlamōtlac in ōnēchmacac	*I've thrown what he gave me (I've stoned things with (**īca**) what he gave me)*

20.10 Applicative and Incorporation

Let us return to the expression **nimitzpāquilia in mocuā** 'I wash you head for you'. We have seen (17.4) that the names for parts of the body have a certain tendency to undergo incorporation into the verb. Hence, we can say (preferably):

Nimitzcuāpāca	*I 'headwash' you*

Be careful. What we have here is modifying incorporation, not the applicative form of the verb. While **pāquilia** means 'wash something for someone', **cuāpāca** means 'wash someone's head' (and thus takes as its object only the person whose head is washed). If you prefer, **nimitzcuāpāca** means 'I wash you in terms of the head'. The form **nimitzcuāpāquilia** isn't impossible, but it would mean (if one were bold enough to use it) 'I wash his head for you', being used as the applicative of the preceding form (with an object possessed by the second person):

Nimitzcuāpāquilia in mopiltzin	*I headwash your son (for you)*

VOCABULARY

Transitive verbs

elēhuia	*to desire*	nanaloa/nanaltza	*to snarl*
huahualoa/huahualtza	*to bark*	tequipanoa	*to work*
ixca	*to fry*	tlācamati	*to obey*
ixtlāhua	*to pay*	tlani	*to gain, to win*
malacachoa	*to roll up*	xeloa	*to divide, to split*

Nouns

ātōyātl	*river*	tomin[13]	*money*
pōchtēcatl (*pl. /–'/*)	*merchant*		

---

[13] A borrowing from Spanish (**tomin** is the name for an old coin denomination). Hence, **tomin** is the stem, and the final **-in** isn't a suffix.

EXERCISES

(a) Add a second person beneficiary (possessor of the object, if appropriate)
to the following phrases and translate.
1. Ōcualān in Pedro.
2. Nicchipāhuaz in petlatl.
3. Ōniquīxcocô in pilli.
4. Niquilcāhua in tōcāitl.
5. Ōquināmic in cihuātl.
6. Ōticpōuhquê in tomin.
7. Ninopiya.
8. Ticpiya.
9. Ōichtecquê.
10. Quipoloa in caxitl.
11. Quinyōllālia in cōconê.
12. Ōniquixtlāuh in etl.

(b) Translate into English.
1. Xinēchinnōchili in nopilhuān.
2. Àmo nèhuātl ōnamēchcuālî in amotlaxcal.
3. Cuix tinēchmalacachilhuīz in ichtli?
4. In tīcitl ōnēchpàtīlî in nocihuāuh.
5. Huel ōantēchinyōlìtlacalhuìquê in totàhuān.
6. Yālhua nicān ōcuīcōc, ōcuīcatīlōc in tēuctli.
7. Chōquilīlô in miccātzitzintin.
8. In otomî ōnēchmictīlìquê in notàtzin.
9. Tēchnanaltza in chichi.
10. Mā nicān xinēchtlālīli in.
11. Xinēchquēmili in notilmâ.
12. Xichuīquili in tēuctli in īpiltzin.
13. Àmo ōtinēchtequipanô: ca àmo nimitztlaxtlāhuīz.
14. Mācamo xinēchtēittitili in notomin.

(c) Translate into Nahuatl.
1. Put chili in ("to/for") the mole.
2. They'll cut off our nose (and) ears (two possible translations).
3. You've (s.) taken the property of your friends, you've wronged them
   greatly.
4. What did the merchant sell to you (s.)?
5. Why have you (s.) hidden my papers?
6. Glue (s.) this paper for me.
7. He's helped my father a lot (very).
8. Receive (s.) my children please (**mā**).

9. That man desired your (s.) wife.
10. I want (the) good for you (s.).
11. We've cast our sins in each other's faces ("at ourselves").
12. I was written to.
13. Have (s.) Peter guard my turkeys (for me).
14. I've already paid you (pl.) your corn.

Honorific and Deprecatory Verbs

21.1 Introduction to Honorific Verbs

Nahuatl, like a number of other languages, has *honorific* verb forms (also called *reverential*), which are used to show respect in speech. These are more complicated than those of Western European languages (e.g., French, Spanish, Italian, German), which shift from the second person singular to the plural or from the second to the third person as a means of showing respect to the addressee; English does not have this feature.

The construction in Nahuatl broadly corresponds to this practice in Western European languages, showing respect to the person being spoken of with a special form. Nahuatl does this by "doubling" the subject, that is, by giving it two slots in the verb, with the person being treated with respect appearing not only as the subject but also as an object. Therefore, the object form used to convey respect in this way is marked with a reflexive prefix.

Because it is being given an additional object, the verb must be placed in a form that will accommodate this added object, and the only way to do this is for the verb to assume either a causative or an applicative form (see Lessons 19–20). This is exactly what happens (see 21.2–4):

Timocochītia	*You're (s.) sleeping (honorific),* lit., *You're making yourself sleep*
Tlein ticmochīhuilia?	*What are you (s.) doing (hon.)?*

Because this construction does not affect plurality, both singular and plural forms can be made honorific (unlike the European usage):

Ammocochītiâ	*You're (pl.) sleeping (hon.)*
Tlein anquimochīhuiliâ?	*What are you (pl.) doing (hon.)?*

Finally, while the European mode of respect relates only to the addressee, the Nahuatl construction can also cover the third person:

Mocochītia	*He's sleeping (hon.)*
Mocochītiâ	*They're sleeping (hon.)*
Tlein quimochīhuilia?	*What's he doing (hon.)?*
Tlein quimochīhuiliâ?	*What are they doing (hon.)?*

This procedure is never used with the first person, however exalted the person speaking may be. The ruler Motēuczōma himself would say **nicochi** and not ****ninocochītia**.

21.2 General Principle for Forming the Honorific

The general rule is as follows:

▶ Intransitive verbs use the causative as their honorific.
▶ Transitive verbs use the applicative as their honorific.

This general ruled must be qualified:

▶ There are some exceptions.
▶ Some verbs have a special honorific that does not correspond to the regular causative or applicative.
▶ In general, the formation of the honorific is less fixed than that of other forms, so that there are doublets, triplets or even quadruplets.

Let us now look at the details.

21.3 Honorific of Intransitives

Intransitive verbs use the causative as their honorific.

Mocochītia	*He's sleeping*
Monemītia	*He lives*
Moyōlītia	*He's alive*
Motzàtzītia	*He shouts* etc.

Sometimes, a causative in **-tia** that is otherwise unattested turns up as an honorific:

| Mopolihuītia | *He disappears, is lost* |

We know that the real "causative" of **polihui** appears in the form of a semi-causative in **-oa** (**poloa**, see 19.8), and in this instance, the regularly formed causative is used solely as an honorific. Sometimes, however, a semi-causative form actually serves as the honorific:

| Mocalaquia | *He enters*[1] |

---

[1] Be careful with **ximocalaqui** 'to enter (s.) (hon.)'. This form is not simply **calaqui** with the reflexive prefix but the regular imperative (9.1) of **calaquia**. The present corresponding to **xicalaqui** is **ticalaqui**, and the one corresponding to **ximocalaqui** is **timocalaquia**.

In a number of verbs, an irregular causative in **-ltia** is used along with the one in **-tia** to form the honorific:

Mohuetzītia *or* Mohuetziltia	*He falls*
Màxītia *or* Màxiltia	*He arrives*
Mochōctia *or* Mochōquiltia	*He cries*
(*also* Mochōquitia)	
Mēhuitia *or* Mēhualtia	*He departs*
Mopanōltia	*He passes* (while **panahuia** serves as both the causative and applicative of **pano**)

Certain intransitive verbs use an applicative form in **-lia** as their honorific. The most common such verbs are **miqui** and **āyi**:

Momiquilia[2]	*He dies*
Tlein timāyilia?	(*And not* ** ticmāyilia, see 18.9) *what are you (s.) doing? how are you?* Alongside the forms cited, **mochōquilia** is also found.

Yauh does not have an honorific. The verb **huīca** 'take (someone somewhere)', 'go with', 'accompany', which serves as its causative, is also used as the honorific:

Cāmpa timohuīca? – Mēxìco niyauh	*Where are you (s.) going? – I'm going to*
(*and not* **ninohuīca)	*Mexico.*

On the basis of **mohuīca**, we can naturally have **huālmohuīca** corresponding to **huāllauh** and **ommohuīca** corresponding to **onyauh**. There is also **mohuīcatz** corresponding to **huītz** (5.3).

Câ does not have either a causative or an applicative. The honorific is **moyetzticâ**, a compound form in which the last element, **câ**, is conjugated in the same way as when it appears by itself:

Mexìco moyetzticâ in Motēuczōma	*Moctezuma is in Mexico*
Cān timoyetzticatca?	*Where were you (s.)?*
Nicān moyetztiyez	*He will be here*

(We will see more examples of this form later, see 27.1.1.)

21.4 Honorific of Transitives

Transitive verbs use the applicative as their honorific. The suffix **-(i)lia** is used except with verbs in **-oa**, which have an honorific, as well as an applicative, in **-huia** (or **-ilhuia**, **-alhuia**, see 20.3):

Quimocāhuilia	*He leaves it*
Quimochīhuilia	*He makes it*

---

[2] Probably because **momictia** means 'to commit suicide'.

Quimēhuilia	*He raises it up*
Quimocelīlia	*He receives it*
Quimopiyalia	*He guards it*
Quimìtalhuia	*He says it*
Quimotequipachilhuia	*He bothers him*
Quimotlàpalhuia	*He greets him*

The reflexive is naturally definite (**mo-**) because the beneficiary object refers to the same person as the subject (see 20.6).

Itta usually has a special honorific: **itztilia**.

Certain transitive verbs have an honorific in the form of the causative. These are:

(1) verbs in which the prefix **tla-** is felt to be strongly connected to the stem, so that **tla-** + STEM is more or less considered to be a new intransitive verb.[3] This is the case with:

Motlàtōltia	*He speaks* (compare **quimìtalhuia** *he says it*, with the definite prefix)
Motlacualtia	*He eats*
Motlachiyaltia	*He looks*

(2) monosyllables in **-i**:

Quimītia	*He drinks it*
Quimocuītia	*He takes it*

(3) verbs in **-qui** and **-ti**, which in addition have a special form. We know that the causative of these verbs is in **-tia**, with the stem-final **-i** dropped (because the causative is based on base 4, which in these instances is base 1 minus the final vowel; see 19.2 and 15.5), but the honorific forms are in **-ltia** or **-tia**, without any loss of the final vowel:

Quimonequiltia	*He wants it*
Quimomachītia *or* quimomachiltia	*He knows it*
Quimocaquītia *or* quimocaquiltia[4]	*He hears it*

Nāmiqui 'meet', however, has the regular form **nāmiquilia** as its honorific.

21.5 Honorific of the Object

With a transitive verb, the respect can apply not only to the subject but also to the object. In this case, we have the same doubling of the *subject*:

---

[3] We have also seen that with incorporation the prefix **tla-** can be treated as if it is "fused" with the stem (17.6).

[4] As it happens, here we have the causatives of **caqui**, but we know that this verb is exceptional in this regard (19.4).

| Nicnotlazòtilia in Totēucyo Dios | *I love our lord God* |
| Timitztopalēhuīlīzquê | *We'll help you (s.) (hon.)* |

It can be seen that in this case, and unlike the case with intransitive verbs (21.1), there can be a reflexive of the first person because this is not the person being shown respect.

21.6 Honorific of Bitransitives

With **maca** (which has no applicative because it inherently includes the beneficiary) and with all the derived bitransitive verbs (and, in general, all the verbs ending in -**tia**, -**lia**, -**huia**), the honorific formation is always in -**lia** (with **maca** undergoing the regular shift of -**ca** to -**qui**, see 20.2). The reflexive prefix is added in the appropriate slot (see section 6.5), and there can be as many as four prefixes (though, as usual, if there are two definite objects, these are reduced to a single prefix). All the examples below are in the honorific form, with the regular form indicated in parentheses:

Nicnomaquilīz	*I'll give it to him* (**nicmacaz**)
Ticmotlamaquilīz	*You'll (s.) give him a gift* (**tictlamacaz**)
Xitēchmotlalhuīli	*Speak (s.) to us* (**xitēchtlalhui**)
Timotētlamaquilia	*You (s.) make gifts* (**titētlamaca**)
Cuix tinēchmocualtīlīz nanacatl?	*Will you (s.) feed me mushrooms?*
	(**tinēchcualtīz**)
Nimitznochīhuilīlia tlaxcalli	*I'm making you (s.) tortillas* (**nimitzchīhuilia**)
Nimitznocelīlīlia in motlàtōltzin	*I accept your venerable words* (**nimitzcelīlia**)
Xinēchmotlapòpolhuīli,	*Forgive (s.) me, forgive me my sins*
Xinēchmopòpolhuīli in notlàtlacōl	(**xinēchtlapòpolhui, xinēchpòpolhui**)

Let's examine the constructions. **Celia, chīhua** are transitive verbs; their (bitransitive) applicatives are **celī-lia, chīhui-lia**; their ("tritransitive") honorifics are **celī-lī-lia, chīhui-lī-lia**. As can be seen, it is possible to repeat the suffix -**lia**, once with a proper applicative meaning and a second time with an honorific meaning.[5] It should even be possible to put a causative-applicative (see 20.8) in the honorific. To illustrate how complicated such forms may be, let us start with the following causative sentence (with the prefixes and suffixes separated for ease of analysis):

| Ti-nēch-in-tla-cua-ltī-lia in | *You're (s.) feeding my children (causing them* |
| nopilhuāntotōn | *to eat).* |

Put in the honorific, this becomes:

Ti-nēch-im-mo-tla-cua-ltī-lī-lia in nopilhuāntotōn

[5] In this, the honorific differs from the causative, whose suffix -**tia** cannot be repeated (18.10).

Here we have a verb with five prefixes:

▶ **ti-**, subject
▶ **nēch-**, definite object governed by the applicative ending generated by the possessive prefix on the noun
▶ **-im-**, vestige of the plural object of the causative that has otherwise been superseded by the definite object of the applicative
▶ **mo-**, reflexive object governed by the honorific applicative
▶ **tla-**, object of the simple verb underlying the causative

and three suffixes:

▶ causative **-ltia**
▶ first applicative generated by the possessive on the noun
▶ second, honorific applicative

21.7 Honorific of Reflexives

When the verb is already in the reflexive form, the usual procedure of doubling the subject cannot be carried out. To form the honorific, the suffix **-tzinoa** is resorted to. This is added to base 2 (the short base) of the verb, which remains straightforwardly transitive and reflexive:

Mocāuhtzinoa	*He remains*
Motlalòtzinoa	*He runs*
Motlālìtzinoa	*He sits down*
Mottatzinoa	*He sees himself*
Mozōmàtzinoa	*He gets angry* etc.

We can also have an intensified honorific, which is made by adding **-tzinoa** to a form that is already honorific:

Nicnotlazòtilìtzinoa in Dios	*I love God*
Mexìco monemītìtzinoa in tlàtoāni	*The king lives in Mexico*

The suffix **-tzinoa** can only be used if there is already a reflexive. The forms for 'he remains', 'it can be seen' are **mocāuhtzinoa, mottatzinoa**, but for 'he leaves it', 'he sees it', the only possible forms are **quimocāhuilia, quimottilia** (and not ****quicāuhtzinoa, **quittatzinoa**).

21.8 Double Reflexive

A verb form which already takes a reflexive **-ne-** (e.g., in an applicative built on a reflexive form; see 20.6) can be made into a regular honorific through the addition of an applicative ending taking the definite reflexive. Such forms are naturally rare. To understand them better, let us follow the derivation process step by step, isolating the suffixes and prefixes:

▶ **mo-tlātia** 'he hides (himself)', **m-ināya** 'he conceals (himself)': both are simple reflexives

▶ **mitz-ne-tlātī-lia** 'he hides (himself) from you (s.)', **mitz-ne-ināyi-lia** 'he conceals himself from you (s.), evades you': applicatives of the preceding

▶ **mitz-mo-ne-tlātī-lī-lia, mitz-mo-ne-ināyi-lī-lia**: honorific applicatives, with the same meaning as the preceding

21.9 Restrictions on the Honorific

A few final remarks about the honorific.

(1) An honorific form cannot be put in the passive or the impersonal because the respect can only apply to specific people. Thus, a form like ****ne-cochī-tī-lo** 'people (hon.) are sleeping' is out of the question. One simply says **cochīhua**.

(2) The honorific forms seen in this chapter are restricted to verbs. They do not appear in nouns derived from verbs or in the more or less nominalized forms in **-qui** and **-ni** (i.e., verbal forms that function as nouns; see 16.1, 4–5). It can be said of God, for example, that he is:

tēmāquīxtiāni,[6] tētlapòpolhuiāni   *savior, merciful (pardoner)*

but not ****motēmāquīxtīliāni, **motētlapòpolhuiliāni**. The only possible honorific form for nouns is the one in **-tzin**:

totēmāquīxtìcātzin   *our savior*

Similarly, a respected leader (**tēyacānqui**) could be called **tēyacāncā-tzin(tli)** but never ****motēyacānilì(qui)**.

(3) The honorific form of certain verbs is not used or, at any rate, it is unattested in the texts. If the dictionary does not give a verb's honorific form, it is no use trying to make one up. In addition, it turns out in the texts that in speaking of a single person, and sometimes even in the same sentence, the honorific and the regular forms are mixed together. Similarly, there is not necessarily a correspondence between the honorific suffix (**-tzin**) on the noun and the honorific form of the verb. An honorific noun can be found as the subject or object of a regular verb, and an regular noun as the subject or object of an honorific verb.

21.10 Deprecatory Verbs

The suffix **-tzinoa** that we just saw in 21.7 is clearly derived from the honorific nominal suffix **-tzin**. As we have seen (12.1), for this suffix there is a corresponding one of opposite meaning, the deprecatory suffix **-pōl**. Parallel

---

[6] **Māquīxtia** 'save', lit. 'make escape, make come out of the hands', causative of **māquīza**.

to -**tzinoa**, there likewise exists a deprecatory verbal suffix -**pōloa**, which is also added to base 2. Unlike -**tzinoa**, however, this suffix is not restricted to reflexives, and it can appear after any sort of verb. Also, it can be used in any person:

Mā xiyàpōlo	*Go (s.) away (deprec.)*
Nèhuātl ōniccuàpōlô	*It's (wretched) me who has eaten it*
Huēyi tlàtlacōlli ōnicchīuhpōlô	*(Wretch that I am) I've committed great sins*
Ōquitlazòtlapōlô in àcualli in àyēctli	*He's (disgracefully) loved (what's) evil and immoral*

VOCABULARY

Transitive verb

ināya[7] *to hide*

Nouns

mecatl	*string*	quechtli	*neck*
nanacatl	*mushroom*	tezcatl	*mirror*

Locative

mictlān *(in) hell* (lit., *in the land of the dead*)[8]

EXERCISES

(a) Put the following in the honorific form and translate.
1. Ōquiquechcotōnquê.
2. Ōquicotōnilìquê in īquech.
3. Ye ōmic in notàtzin.
4. Tlā xoconcāhua in.
5. Cuix àmo ticmati?
6. Mōztla huāllāz.
7. Mōztla xihuālhuiyān.
8. Tlein ōticcōuh?
9. Ōmpa catê.
10. Nimitznōchilia in mopiltzin.
11. Nicān ōmotēcaquê.
12. Huel motolīnia.

[7] Quasi-synonym of **tlātia** and often used redundantly in combination with that verb. It seems that originally **tlātia** indicated the act of hiding an item by burying it, and **ināya** indicated the act of doing so by covering it with something.

[8] The term dates back to pre-Conquest conceptions of the world but was borrowed to designate the Christian hell.

13. Tiqui octli.
14. Tiquimītî octli.
15. Nimitztēnnāmiqui.
16. Quinyacānaya in mēxìcâ.
17. Huel tinēchyōllālia.
18. Mā ximoyōllāli.

(b) Translate into English.
1. Xocommīti inin pàtli.
2. Mācamo xiquimmomāuhtili in pīpiltotōntin.
3. Quēmman ōmpa timàxītīz?
4. Auh quēmman nicān timocueptzinōz?
5. Ca tlàtlacōlli īpan ōninempōlô.
6. Cuix ticmonequiltia tomin?
7. Nimitznottaltīlīz in nohuèxōlohuān.
8. Cuix ticmocuitlahuìtzinōz in nopil?
9. Cuix ōtiquimmotlachīhualtīlî?
10. Zan xinēchimmomaquili in motōtolhuān.
11. Ye mohuīcatz in tlàtoāni.
12. Ca oc yohuac, auh ye titēchmēhuilia?
13. Tezcac mottatzinoa in cihuāpilli.
14. Huel ōtitlàtlacòpōlô, ca mictlān mitzmotlāxilīz in totēucyo.

(c) Translate into Nahuatl (use an honorific every time except 15–16).
1. Shave (yourself).
2. Tomorrow go (pl.) to Cuernavaca.
3. Mary has cut flowers for me.
4. Why are you (s.) getting angry?
5. Why are you (s.) getting angry at me?
6. The king is sick.
7. Mary has rolled up the thread.
8. Don't (s.) tell Peter.
9. Have you (s.) spoken to Peter?
10. I've already given you things.
11. Pass (pl.), enter, sit.
12. Tie (s.) it with a string.
13. I'm having my mother make tortillas.
14. You're (s.) done for ("you've already become lost").
15. I (wretch) have killed my father.
16. I (wretch) have stolen from people's homes.

Pluperfect, Counterfactual, Vetitive, Directional Conjugations

22.1 The Pluperfect

The pluperfect is formed by adding -**ca** to base 2 (the short base) of the verb. The plural marker is -' (glottal stop). Like the preterite, this tense is generally preceded by the augment **ō**- in conversation, much less frequently in narrative.

ōniquīzca	*I had left*
ōnicchīuhca	*I had done it*
ōnicpolòca	*I had lost, destroyed it*
ōninotēcaca	*I had lain down* etc.

Its usages most commonly cover those of the English pluperfect (i.e., 'had' + PAST PARTICIPLE). However, the sense of the Nahuatl tense is different. The English pluperfect indicates an action in the past that took place further back in time (from the point of view of the time of speaking) than some subsequent event in the past. In Nahuatl, the pluperfect is a *transitory preterite*: it signifies an event in the past, but it has an implication that is absent in the regular preterite. When the regular preterite is used, the aim is to say simply that a process has been brought to its conclusion and that at the moment of speaking (or writing) it is complete (i.e., that it was completed previously). On the other hand, when the pluperfect is used, the aim is to say that a process has been brought to its conclusion but that this was true only at a certain moment in the past. In effect, this tense marks a *provisional result*. That is, it designates an event in the past whose consequences have already been undone by a later event. Thus:

Nicān huītz in nochichiuh: ca ōnicpolòca	*Look, here comes my dog! I'd lost him.*
Ōniquilcāuhca, yēcê ōnilnāmictīlōc	*I'd forgotten, but I've been reminded*

In other words, there was a moment when I could have said **ōnicpolô**, **ōniquilcāuh** (i.e., the preterite tense could have been used), but circumstances have changed. At the present time, the action indicated by these verbs is no longer true, and hence I cannot express the thought in the simple preterite anymore. This is precisely the situation for which the pluperfect is intended. Note in particular that in the first example the subsequent event that "undoes" or "cancels" the event in the past is actually the present arrival of the dog. Hence, the canceling event does not have to be one in the past (though it mostly is). Thus, the sense of the Nahuatl pluperfect is quite different from that of the English pluperfect, which is necessarily correlated with another event *in the past*.

In historical or mythological narrative, the facts are not generally correlated with the present, and the issue of their current consequences is not treated in the same way. Nonetheless, the pluperfect is still used to indicate a provisional or reversible fact. Thus, if two facts are being set in relation to each other and the second cancels the effects of the first, the first is put in the pluperfect, unlike the case with English, where the same tense (the simple past) is most often used for both verbs:

Cāncâ in yāô in tlàtoāni, auh quimāquīxtìquê in īmācēhualhuān	*The enemies took the ruler prisoner, but his subjects freed him*

It is practically obligatory for the canceling event to be stated in the clause following the one in which the canceled event is found (in the pluperfect).

> ▶ *Note.* Certain verbs indicating motion or state almost always make use of the pluperfect (and very rarely the preterite or imperfect) to indicate the past nature of the motion or state. In particular, this is the case with **mani** 'be spread (out)', **nemi** 'live, move' and certain defective verbs (23.7). Also recall **catca** (8.10).

22.2 The Counterfactual

This form is built on base 3 (the middle base), with the suffix **-zquia**.[1] The plural is in -' (glottal stop).

The way the counterfactual relates to the future is somewhat comparable to the way the pluperfect relates to the preterite, indicating that at a moment in the past an event was foreseen (and so at that moment it could have been spoken of in the future) but as a result of some hindrance, this event did not in

---

[1] This is apparently the future stem with the participial suffix fixed in the singular form, to which the imperfect formative **-ya** is added (i.e., one could transcribe the form as **-zquiya**, but the /y/ is regularly omitted in texts). If this is so, the counterfactual is a future form transferred to the past, which is a common of building modal forms in numerous languages (e.g., 'would' is simply the past of 'will', and the conditional forms of the Romance languages have a similar derivation).

fact take place. Possible English translations are: 'I was going to VERB', 'I should have VERBed', 'I would have VERBed', 'I almost VERBed', 'I was trying to VERB':

Ca yèhuātl in niquìtōzquia	*That's what I was going to say*
Yālhua huel nimiquizquia	*Yesterday I came close to dying*
Tlàtoāni yezquia, yēcê ōmic	*He should have been ruler, but he died*
Chālco ilpīlōcâ, ōmpa mictīlōzquiâ,	*They were taken prisoner (*lit. *tied up; NB*
auh zan huālcholòquê	*pluperfect) at Chalco and would have been*
	put to death, but they escaped (to here)

The counterfactual is relatively rare in independent statements, but we will see that it is common in conditional constructions (see Ch. 34).

▶ **Note.** It can be seen that in Nahuatl there are two sets of three tenses, grouped according to both their meaning and their morphology:

	Base 2	Base 1	Base 3
Not transferred to the past	Preterite	Present	Future
Transferred to the past	Pluperfect	Imperfect	Counterfactual

Present	says that currently a process	is *taking place* or *takes place* on a regular or repetitive basis
Preterite	says that currently a process	is *complete*
Future	says that currently a process	is foreseen

With the transfer to the past, we get:

Imperfect	says that in the past	a process *was taking place* or would *regularly* take place (and is no longer doing so)
Pluperfect	says that in the past	a process *was complete* (and was undone)
Counterfactual	says that in the past	a process *was foreseen* (not speaking of it in the preterite indicates that in the end it did not take place)

22.3 The Vetitive

The vetitive, which can generally be translated into English with a negative imperative (details following), is built on base 2 (the short base) of the verb. If base 2 ends with a vowel (verbs with -c in the preterite singular, 8.7), the singular takes suffix -'. That is, if the preterite singular ends in -c, this final consonant is replaced with the glottal stop in the vetetive. The plural is always in **-tin** or **-tî**, which takes the place of the ending **-quê** of the preterite (and follows the glottal stop in verbs with preterites in **-c**).

The vetitive is always preceded with **mā** or **mā nēn**, never with **tlā**. **Nēn** is a particle that in its proper meaning signifies 'badly, in vain' (**nēn ōnicchīuh** 'I did it for nothing, with no result', 'I wasted my time in doing it').

In the second person, the vetitive differs from the optative in that we have the regular prefixes **t(i)-**, **am-/an-** instead of the optative prefix **x(i)-**, and the particle **mā** has to be used:

Mā (nēn) ticchīuh in	*Don't (s.) do this*
Mā (nēn) anquichīuhtin in	*Don't (pl.) do this*
Mā chōcâ	*He mustn't cry*
Mā chōcàtin	*They mustn't cry*

There is no vetitive for **câ** or for verbs in **-o** (the passives in particular). Instead, the procedure is to use the optative preceded by the compound negative **mācamo** etc.:

Mācamo nicān xiye mōztla	*Don't (s.) be here tomorrow*
Mācamo xānalōcān (*or* xānōcān)	*Don't (pl.) be taken prisoner*

The meaning of the vetitive is often close to that of the negative optative/ imperative (hence the possibility for substitution that we have just seen), but it works from a very different point of view. With the negated optative, the hope is that something will not take place. With the vetitive, it is stated that *something may happen and this should be avoided*:

Mā tihuetz	*Watch out you (s.) don't fall*
Mā ticcuâ in	*Don't (s.) eat that (because it could make you sick, or it's forbidden to do so)*
Mā namēchonnomāuhtīlî	*Let me not frighten you (pl., hon.) (said by someone who turns up unexpectedly, the vetitive itself forestalling the potential fear)*

It is clear that **mā tihuetz** is a normal expression, while **mācamo xihuetzi** is as incongruous as **xihuetzi** or the English 'fall!' (commands of this kind are generally not given).[2] In a number of instances where the negated optative could be used just as well as vetitive, the vetitive has a more general or more solemn sense. Thus, **mācamo xicchīhua** is an order or invitation applying to

---

[2] Basically, 'falling' is an involuntary action, so it makes sense to tell someone to watch out *against* this (undesirable) eventuality, but because an imperative instructs someone to actively undertake the action in question, you cannot normally tell a person to do something that is not under his or her control.

the present; **mā ticchīuh** is instead an exhortation or warning of more general applicability.

When negated, the vetitive is the equivalent of a strengthened imperative. In this case, the mark of negation is always **mā nēn à-** (and not **mācamo**). This element **â** is a short form of the negative **àmo**, and in this instance is always appended directly to the verb. Thus:

Mā nēn àticchīuh in ōnimitzilhuî   *Don't fail to do what I told you*

In effect, while the affirmative vetitive is an injunction to take care against the possibility that something could or would happen, the negated version indicates the speaker's warning about inadvisability of something *not* happening, which in turn signifies the injunction that it *should* happen. So be sure to take care with the meaning of the vetitive because the negatives seem to be arranged contrary to the sense, with the form indicating the action that is not wanted lacking the regular negative, which then appears with the form indicating the action that is desired.

▶ **Note.** In the singular, outside of the second person, where the prefix clearly shows which form you are dealing with, it is necessary to watch out against confusing the optative and the vetitive. The two forms are never identical in pronunciation (though the frequent failure to mark the glottal stop in the written texts generally obscures the distinction):

(1) With verbs that drop their final vowel to form base 2, the optative maintains this final vowel (base 3 being identical to base 1), while the vetitive loses it.

(2) With verbs in **-ia**, **-oa**, the optative (built on base 3) ends in **-i**, **-o**, while the vetitive (built on base 2) ends in **-î**, **-ô**. Similarly, with monosyllables in **-a**, the optative ends in **-a** and the vetitive in **-â**.

(3) With verbs with "vowel-retaining preterites" (8.7), for which the three bases are identical, the vetitive takes -' after the vowel.

Examples:

	OPTATIVE	VETITIVE
(1)	mā cochi	mā coch
	mā quichīhua	mā quichīuh
(2)	mā quipolo	mā quipolô
	mā motlāli	mā motlālî
	mā tlacua	mā tlacuâ
(3)	mā cuīca	mā cuīcâ
	mā tzàtzi	mā tzàtzî
	mā quicui	mā quicuî

With the vetitive we have completed the inventory of basic tense and mood forms. These number nine: the six grouped into two sets of three above (*present, preterite, future; imperfect, pluperfect, counterfactual*) and somewhat separately the *–ni form* and the two modal forms (*optative* and *vetitive*). In addtion, there are two secondary series of forms comprising the *directional conjugations*, and we will now turn to these.

22.4 The Directional of Motion Toward

This conjugation indicates an approach toward the present situation (the time and place of speaking) in terms of the realization of a process. In its proper meaning, the most common translation is 'come to VERB'.

It is formed on base 3 (the middle base) and consists of:

▶ an imperfective indicated by -**quiuh** (plural -**î**, that is, -**quihuî**)
▶ a perfective indicated by -**co** (plural -**'**)
▶ an optative indicated by -**qui** (plural -**'**)

Imperfective is a linguistic term indicating that an action is incomplete or ongoing, while *perfective* indicates that it has been carried out. In the present context, the imperfective or perfective nature of the form refers to the motion, not the action to be done after the motion. Thus:

Ticchīhuaquiuh	*You'll (s.) come to do it*
(Ō)ticchīhuaco	*You (s.) came to do it*
(Mā) xicchīhuaqui	*Come (s) to do it*
Anquichīhuaquihuî	*You'll (pl.) come to do it*
(Ō)anquichīhuacô	*You (pl.) came to do it*
(Mā) xicchīhuaquî	*Come (s) to do it*
Motlālīquiuh	*He'll come to sit down*
(Ō)motlālīco	*He came to sit down etc.*

The perfective, then, has to refer to motion that has been completed, and so can be translated with the English simple past tense (e.g., 'came') or perfect (e.g., 'has come'). In the latter usage, because the form indicates the situation that results from a goal having been attained, the ō- can be omitted even in conversation. With a past signification, the perfective can be preceded by ō- under the same conditions as the preterite (8.8). The imperfective, on the other hand, has a future meaning. That is, because the "coming" has not been completed yet, the action to be done after arrival remains in the future. The optative of approach has the same usages as the simple optative.

Nicān teōpan ninomāquīxtīco	*I came (or have come) to seek asylum in the church* (see the end of 19.3 for the sense of the reflexive causative)
Quēmman ōtàcico?	*When did you (s.) arrive?*
Nicān Mexìco ōtitotlālīcô	*We've come to take up residence (here) in Mexico*
Tēchānaquiuh in miquiztli	*Death will come to take us*
Mā xiquittaquî in	*Come (pl.) see this*

There are many figurative or metaphorical usages that are often hard to reflect in translation. A sense of arrival at a point of no return (with favorable or unfavorable consequences) is present in expressions indicating a definite achievement.[3] Thus:

Momiquilīco in tlàtoāni	*The ruler has died (reached the point of death)*
Tlamico, cēhuīco yāōyōtl	*The war was completed, extinguished* (cf. the English 'came to an end')

The directional of motion toward may seem to overlap with the prefix **huāl-** (6.1). In fact, it is possible to say:

Ōmpa quīzaquiuh in tōnatiuh	*The sun will rise (emerge) there*

with exactly the same meaning as:

Ōmpa huālquīzaz in tōnatiuh.

Huāl, however, indicates that a process comes into operation through the agent's approach (and **on** that it does so by the agent's departure), while **-co,** **-quiuh** indicates that the intention is to reach a goal in order to put some process into practice. Note that **yauh** can be preceded by **huāl** or **on** but not followed by **-co** or **-quiuh**[4] (motion can involve approach or departure, but if it attains its goal, it ceases to be motion). On the other hand, with the verb **àci,** which indicates the attainment of a goal, the simple preterite is very rare and the **-co** of approach is virtually mandatory (at least when intransitive **àci** is construed with a locative); it seems that **huāl** is excluded.

On the other hand, it is possible to use a combination of a directional prefixes with one of the directional conjugations for a nuanced effect by taking the point of view of the subject or object for the former and that of the moment of

---

[3] One might compare the English idioms 'to wind up' doing something (e.g., 'he wound up finishing on time') and to 'come to' do something ('she came to realize the truth of his words').

[4] Or by any of the suffixes of the directional of motion away (22.5).

speaking for the latter. In a given instance, then, **-on-** and **-co** can be used at the same time without contradiction:

Quēn ōtonnemico?	*How have you (s.) lived till now (how have you gone forward, **-on-**, in your life, **-nemi-**, until the present, **-co**)?*
Ōnoconnāmictīco, ītēch ōnàcico in tēcocô, in tētōnēuh, in tēchichinatz	*I've come before (made myself meet) and made contact with pain, affliction, torment (what causes people illness, afflicts, torments; these are agent nouns, see 16.1)*

22.5 The Directional of Motion Away

This conjugation is a complement of the preceding one, indicating a departure from the situation in terms of the realization of a process. In its proper meaning, it is generally translated with 'go to VERB'. In its figurative (essentially imperfective) meaning, it indicates an indefinite, metaphorical departure, a progression toward a vague goal or some implementation of the process at an imprecise point in the future.

The form is built on base 3 (the middle base) and consists of:

▶ an imperfective in **-tīuh** (note the long ī, while the **i** in **-quiuh** is short); plural in **-î**

▶ a perfective in **-to** (plural **-'**)

▶ an optative in **-ti** or **-'** (plural **-ti'** or **-tin**).

The imperfective can be translated with a future or a present (the goal has not been attained, but the motion may be under way).[5] Note the difference here from the imperfective in the directional of motion toward, which necessarily refers to the future.[6] The perfective cannot be translated with anything but a

---

[5] Note the ambiguity of the comparable English expression to 'be going' to do something, which can indicate either an intention to act that has not yet been implemented ('I'm going to have the car repaired when I get around to it') or actual motion for a given purpose ('Where are you going?' – 'I'm going to see what that noise was').

[6] The explanation for this lack of parallelism between the two forms has to do with the inherently different nature of coming and going. "Going" looks at the motion in terms of the present location of the subject, so it is understandable enough to say from this point of view that he is departing for some purpose. "Coming," on the other hand, necessarily looks at the motion from the point of view of the destination that has not yet been reached (after all, if the subject is already there, he cannot be coming any more). Hence, we cannot speak of someone 'coming' to do something because we cannot know of such motion until it is complete (though we can know of the intention beforehand).

past (because it states that the goal has been attained):

Xitlachiyatî	*Go (pl.) look*
Noconittatīuh in nocniuh	*I'm going to see my friend*
Yālhua ōtictlàpalōtô	*We went to greet him yesterday*
Īpan ōnicalaquito	*I've entered his place*
Cānin tihuīcōtīhuî?	*Where are we being brought to?*
Inin ca oc huècauh in mochīhuatīuh	*This will take place in the distant future*

VOCABULARY

Intransitive verbs

cēhui[7]	*to be extinguished,*	teyīni[8]	*to break*
	to cool off, to be calmed		

Transitive verb

tōnēhua[9]	*to torment, to afflict*

Nouns

ayòtli	*gourd, pumpkin*	tōltēcatl	*(pl. /–'/) craftsman*
miquiztli	*death*		

Locative

Chālco[10]	*Chalco*

Particles

nēn	*in vain*	yēcê	*but, however*

EXERCISES

(a) Put the following forms in (i) the pluperfect, (ii) the counterfactual and (iii) the vetitive.

1. nātli
2. timococoa
3. nēci
4. tìcihuî
5. anquinamacâ
6. moximâ

---

[7] The semi-causative **cēhuia** 'to cool, to relieve, to calm' is often used reflexively (**mocēhuia**) in the sense 'to rest'.

[8] Semi-causative **teyīnia** 'to break'.

[9] Intransitive **tōnēhua** 'to be tormented, to afflicted' (12.5, 19.8).

[10] A town about forty kilometers to the southeast of Mexico City that was long its rival.

(b) Put the following forms into (i) the directional of motion toward and (ii) the directional of motion away.
1. nicochi
2. nitlanamacaz
3. ōtitlacōuh
4. mā quinnōtzacān
5. quiyōllāliâ
6. titlacuâ
7. ōniquimpalēhuî

(c) Translate into English.
1. Ca ōniccuīca in caxitl, auh ōnicmācāuh, tlālpan ōhuetz, zan teyīnizquia.
2. Mā ticmācāuh in, ca tlazòti.
3. Mā titlachix! Mā tiquittâ in tēmāuhtî.
4. Quimictīzquia in Pedro in īcihuāuh, in nèhuātl ōnicmāquīxtīto.
5. Mā nēn anquimoyōlìtlacalhuìtin in amonāntzin.
6. Tocpac moquetzaquiuh in tōnatiuh.
7. Ca ōnichuālzācaca ayòtli, auh aocmo nicān câ, āquin ōquicuīco?
8. Ca cochi in chānê: mā īpan ticalaquitî, mā ticcuīlītî in ītōtol.
9. In yāô ca tēchmictīquihuî.
10. Tlatlazquia in calli, yēcê ōtictlāxilìquê ātl, ic ōcēuh in tletl.

(d) Translate into Nahuatl.
1. I should have gone to Chalco, but I fell sick.
2. Don't (s.) enter! My father is sick.
3. Don't (s.) be afraid, it's me.
4. He had been sick, but the doctor cured him.
5. I wrote to you (s.), but (*auh*) the paper burned (up).
6. Don't fail to pay the craftsman.
7. The Nahuatl language is heading for oblivion ("going to be forgotten").
8. No, it was almost forgotten, but it won't be forgotten any more (8.9).
9. What have you (s.) come to tell us?
10. Our Lord has come to save us.
11. Come (s.) help me! I was going to make tortillas but the fire has gone out.
12. I had bought (some) meat, but my dog has eaten it (i.e., "to my detriment").
13. He was in a big hurry and he almost fell (down).

Morphological Peculiarities of Certain Nouns and Verbs

23.1 Suffixless Nouns

We have seen (2.3) that a set of Nahuatl nouns have neither the absolute suffix nor the suffix -**in**, and for this reason, we will call these *suffixless nouns*. Apart from certain proper names, these nouns are basically encountered in two semantic fields ("semantics" signifies a "classification based on meaning"):

(1) names for plants or animals:

tlatzcan	*cypress*
alo	*macaw*
tecpin	*flea*

(2) "expressive" nouns, which are basically nicknames or terms designating a human failing or defect, the majority of the latter being expressed in the form of synecdoche.[1] This group of nouns can be subdivided into the following categories:

(a) non-compound expressive nouns:

cuetzpal	*glutton*
tzapa	*dwarf*

These often include an initial reduplicated syllable (but with a short vowel):

papal	*gossiper, bigmouth*
coco	*servant*
chichi	*dog* (perhaps analogous to the rhyming English term *bow-wow* the proper Nahuatl word is **itzcuintli** (pl. /-**tin**/) *dog*)

(b) compound nouns consisting of a part of the body plus another noun. Here too there are two groups:

---

[1] Synecdoche is a figure of speech by which a whole is represented by one of its constituent elements or a human being by a physical characteristic. For instance, 'threads' for 'clothing, garment', or 'big mouth' for someone with a tendency to talk excessively.

(i) the second noun designates a "thing" (most commonly a material) and the first noun (the part of the body) contains this thing or something similar. While the full noun (which takes the absolutive suffix) designates the part of the body in question, the suffixless version designates a person of whom this body part is characteristic (e.g., 'fat head' for 'someone with a fat head').

yacacuitlatl	*snot, lit., nose* (**yacatl**) *excretion* (**cuitlatl**)
yacacuitla	*snot nose*
cuānacatl	*crest, comb (as in a rooster's crest)*, lit., *head* (**cuāitl**) *flesh* (**nacatl**)
cuānaca	*chicken*

(ii) the second noun designates a thing to which a part of the body is compared. In this case, only the suffixless form exists:

yacametlapil	*someone with a nose* (**yacatl**) *as long as a* **metlapilli** (*a long stone roller used to spread the corn meal on a* **metlatl**)

The distinction between such suffixless nouns can be seen clearly in doublets, which are not uncommon:

▶ categories 1) and 2a) can have doublets in -**tl(i)** or -**in**:

tecpintli	*flea*
tzapatl	*dwarf*
cuetzpalin	*lizard, iguana* (note difference in meaning)

▶ category 2bi) can have doublets in -**ê** (11.6–7):

yacacuitlê	*snot nose (someone with a snotty nose)*

▶ category 2bii) can have doublets in -**tic** (12.6):

yacametlapiltic	*long nose* (someone with a **metlapilli** in terms of a nose)

In every instance, the dictionary should be consulted for the existence of such doublets (i.e., they cannot be generated at will). Thus, ****cuānaquê** is not found for 'chicken', while a 'cow, ox' is called a **cuācuahuê** (**cuā-cuauh-ê** 'one with wood, i.e., horns, on the head') and not ****cuācauh**.

All suffixless nouns designating an animate being can be put in the plural. They take -**mê** if they end in a vowel, -**tin** if they end in a consonant:

alomê	*macaws*
tecpintin	*fleas*
cuetzpaltin	*gluttons*
tzapamê	*dwarves*
cuānacamê	*chickens, roosters etc.*

They take the usual derivational forms for nouns (e.g., **tecpinyô** 'full of fleas'; **cuetzpalpōl** 'miserable glutton'), in particular the possessive, with -**uh** added to a stem-final vowel if the noun is animate (10.8): **īcuānacauh**[2] 'his chicken', pl. **īcuānacahuān**

Notes

(1) In connection with the suffixes **-tōn, -pōl** (12.1), we have seen the absence of **-tl(i)** in nouns with an expressive sense.
(2) Be careful with nouns ending in **-in**. This ending can be either a suffix added to the stem (**mich-in**, pl. **mī-mich-tin** or **mich-mê**, see 2.3) or an inherent part of the stem itself (**tecpin**, pl. **tecpin-tin**)

23.2 Nouns Borrowed from Spanish

Nouns borrowed from Spanish never take the absolutive suffix and are adapted to Nahuatl phonology to a greater or lesser degree. There is adaptation in a certain number of borrowings that are probably very old (dating back to the immediate aftermath of the conquest). Note that the Spanish **s** is generally interpreted as **x**,[3] and that a Spanish word ending in a vowel can receive a glottal stop after that vowel. Thus (with the Spanish original in parentheses):

xinōla	*lady* (**señora**)
cahuayo (or cahuayô)	*horse* (**caballo**)
ahuax	*beans* (**habas**)
icox	*fig(s)* (**higos**)
Petolo(') (or Pedro)	*Pedro*

Spanish spelling and phonology are maintained in more recent borrowings as well as in the category of religious terms:

llave *or* llavê	*Key*
Dios	*God*
padre[4]	*priest, monk, friar*
diablo	*devil, demon*

As usual, the plural is **-mê** after a vowel, **-tin** after a consonant. The Spanish plural **-(e)s** can be found, as well as a double Spanish-Nahuatl plural in **-smê**:

diablomê	*devils*
padremê, padresmê	*priests*
cahuayomê *or* cahuayòtin	*horses*

---

[2] However, the form **īcuanac** 'his crest' is possible if unusual circumstances allow someone to possess a crest separate from the chicken it came from. The form **īcuanacayo** is naturally used in speaking of the crest if we are dealing with a part of the chicken (11.4).

[3] Mexican Spanish generally renders Nahuatl **x** as **j**: **mulcajete** = **mōlcaxitl**, **guajolote** = **huèxōlotl** etc.

[4] The Nahuatl **teōpixqui** is also used of Christian priests.

The usual derived nouns are possible: **mollavètzin** 'your (s. hon.) key'; **llavechīuhqui** 'keymaker'. In general, the possessed form does not have -**uh** in the singular, but -**huān** is found in the plural: **īndiablo** 'their demon'; **īndiablohuān** 'their demons'.

23.3 *Tēlpōchtli* and *Ichpōchtli*

Tēlpōchtli 'young man' and **ichpōchtli** 'young woman' are old compound nouns. They have a plural of the type /R–tin/, with the reduplication applying to the *second* element (-**pōchtli**):

Ca tēlpōpōchtin īhuān ichpōpōchtin   *They're young men and young women*

23.4 *Huēhuê* and *Ilamâ*

Huēhuê 'old man' and **ilamâ** 'old woman' have a plural in -**quê**. The final glottal stop in the singular is an ancient /t/, which reverts to its original form in front of a suffix (see 5.1 Note):

Ca huēhuetquê īhuān ilamatquê   *They're old men and old women*

Derivational endings are added to either the -**cā**- variant of the participial suffix (which appears in the form -**qu**- in the plural) or the bases **huēhue**-, **ilama**-. The latter procedure implies ancient nouns in the forms **huēhuetl*, **ilamatl*, though these are not attested in the Classical period. Thus:

tohuēhuetcāhuān   *our old men*
ilamatcātzintli or ilamatzintli   *revered old woman*
huēhuetcāyōtl or huēhueyōtl   *old age*

▶ *Note.* With the diminutive ending -**tōn**, **huēhuetōn** is found but so is **huēhuentōn**.

23.5 *Āchcāuh* and *Iccāuh*

The old nouns -**āchcāuh** 'elder brother' and -**iccāuh** 'younger brother' normally appears possessed forms like **nāchcāuh** 'my elder brother', **niccāuh** 'my younger brother', **tēāchcāuh** '(someone's) elder brother', **tēiccāuh** '(someone's) younger brother'. By the Classical period, this **tē**- prefix becomes more or less fused with the stem, and new possessed forms were constructed as if the absolutive forms were **tēāchcāuhtli, tēiccāuhtli**:

notēāchcāuh   *my elder brother*
notēiccāuh   *my younger brother*

The /w/ is not doubled in the plural:

notēāchcāhuān   *my elder brothers*
notēiccāhuān   *my younger brothers*

It was probably a phonological development that resulted in **tiāchcāuh**, which is basically used in the sense of 'warrior, brave, military leader' (**ācalco tiāchcāuh** '(ship) captain', *lit.*, 'shipboard leader'), which behaves like an ordinary noun but becomes **tiāchcāhuān** in the plural; also **tāchcāuh** 'the principal, more important one' (sometimes used adverbially). Perhaps **ti(y)àcāuh**, pl. **ti(y)àcāhuān** 'soldier, brave soldier' should also be ascribed to this form.

23.6 Peculiarities of Certain Preterites

The verbs **ihua** 'to send' and **māma** 'to carry (on the back)' have the morphology of monosyllables in **-a** (cf. **zōma**):

ōniquihuâ	*I've sent it*
ōnitlamāmâ	*I've carried things on my back*

Like **tōna**, the verb **tolīna** 'to be hungry' has a "vowel-retaining" preterite (8.7), and its base 2 is **tolīna**:[5]

ōnitolīnac	*I felt like eating*

The verb **àcocui** 'to raise up' is composed of **cui** 'to take' and the adverb **àco** 'upward' (e.g., **àco yauh** 'it's going up into the air'), but it behaves like a simple verb and not a compound one, so that the preterite is **ōnicàcouc** or **ōnicàcoc**[6] 'I've raised it up' and not, as might be expected, ****ōnicàcocuīc**.

23.7 Verbs of State

Three verbs describing a physical state – **icac** 'to be upright', **onoc** 'to be lying (down)' and **pilcac** 'to be hanging' – are defective, lacking a present form. Instead, the preterite forms in **-c**, **-quê** have a *present meaning*, and as with **câ** (and also **mani**, **nemi**, see 22.1 Note), the pluperfect in **-ca** is used with the meaning of the preterite or imperfect (an imperfect in **-ya** is also found, though much less commonly):

Tlapechco onoc in notàtzin	*My father is lying in bed*
Cuix oc onoquê in pīpiltotōntin?	*Are the small children still lying down?*
Yālhua tlapechco (ō)nonoca	*Yesterday I was (remained) lying in bed*
Tepēticpac ìcac cruz	*A cross stands on the mountain top*
In tiyàcāhuān ītlantzinco ìcaquê in tlàtoāni	*The captains stand beside the ruler*

[5] Seemingly, **tolīnia** is the semi-causative paired with this intransitive (cf. **tlatla** : **tlatia**, 19.8). The paired meanings would have been 'be tormented'/'torment', with the former shifting via 'be afflicted (with hunger)' to simply 'feel hunger'.

[6] We already know that /kʷ/ (**cu-**) is reduced to /k/ (**c-**) in front of /o/ (7.1); this can also happen when it follows /o/ in the same syllable.

| Tiyānquizco ōnìcaca | *I stood in the market* |
| Nicān pilcac in tilmàtli | *The cape is hanging here* |

The other forms (future, counterfactual, -**ni** form) exist and are regular (apart from the vetitive, which is lacking).

Mōztla àmo ninēhuaz, zan tlapechco nonoz	*Tomorrow I won't get up, I'll just stay in bed*
Mā xono/xonocān	*Stay (s.)/(pl.) (lying) in bed*
Mā xìca	*Stay (s.) upright*
Huel nìcazquia	*I almost stayed upright, I nearly remained standing*
Oncān ìcani in pōchtēcatl	*The merchant (regularly) stands there*
In tilmàtli pilcaz īquechtlan	*The cape will hang from his neck (throat)*

Onoc and **ìcac** have impersonals in -**ōhua**, and there are honorifics **m(o-)onoltia** for **onoc**, **m(o-)ìquiltia** for **ìcac** and **mo-pilquitia** for **pilcac**. As can be seen, these forms are real presents and can be conjugated for tense like regular verbs.

Onōhua	*Everyone's lying (down)*
Nicān ìcōhua	*People stand upright here*
Ìcōhuac	*There was standing*
Ximonolti	*Lie (s.) down, stay lying (hon.)*
Mìquiltia in tlàtoāni	*The king is standing (hon.)*

The honorifics are also causatives that can be used literally to mean 'make lie down', 'make stand up', but most of the time other verbs are used in this situation: **tēca** 'to lay down' (**ninotēca** 'I lay (myself) down'), **quetza** 'to pick up' or **ēhua** 'to raise up' (**ninoquetza** 'I get up', **ninēhua** 'I rise up'), **piloa** 'to hang':

Ximotēca	*Lie (s.) down*
Ōmoquetz	*He got up*
Oncān nicpilōz in notilmâ	*I'll hang my cape there*

▶ *Note.* In **onoc**, the real root is -**o**-, but apart from uses of this verb as an auxiliary (Lesson 27), the **o**- is always preceded by the directional **on**- (which "beefs up" this very short stem, see the "constraint against short words" in 10.8–9).

23.8 Suffix -*tz*

We have already met the suffix -**tz** in **huītz** 'to come' (5.3). This suffix, which has the same sense as the prefix **huāl**-, can be placed on two other verbs, **itqui** 'to carry, to bring' and **huīca** 'to take, to carry'. These formations **itquitz** and **huīcatz** conjugate like **huītz** (5.3 and 8.10):

Niquitqui tetl	*I'm carrying stones*
Niquitquitz tetl	*I('ll) bring stones*
Tichuīcâ in Pedro	*We're taking Peter*
Tichuīcatzê in Pedro	*We('ll) bring Peter*
Tichuīcatzâ in Pedro	*We brought Peter*

(We've already encountered the use of **mohuīcatz** as the honorific of **huītz**, 21.3.)

VOCABULARY

Nouns

ahuax	*beans*	metlapilli	*metlapil* (see
alo (*pl.* /–me'*)	*macaw*		23.1)
cahuayo (*pl.* /-me'/)/	*horse*	padre (*pl.* /-me'/,	*priest, monk*
cahuayô (*pl.* /-tin/)		/-sme'/)	
coco (*pl.* /-me'/)	*servant*	papal (*pl.* /-tin/)	*gossiper*
cruz	*cross*	tāchcāuh	*main, important*
cuācuahuê (*pl.*	*cow, ox*	tecpin (*pl.* /-tin/)	*flea*
cuācuahuèquê)		tēāchcāuh (*pl.*	*elder brother*
cuānaca (*pl.* /-me'/)	*chicken, rooster*	tēāchcāhuān)	
cuetzpal (*pl.* /-tin/)	*glutton*	tēiccāuh (*pl.*	
diablo (*pl.* /-me'/)	*devil, demon*	tēiccāhuān)	*younger brother*
huēhuê (*pl.*	*old man*	tēlpōchtli (*pl.*	*young man*
huēhuetquê)		tēlpōpōchtin)	
ichpōchtli (*pl.*	*young woman*	tiachcāuh (*pl.*	*captain, chief,*
ichpōpōchtin)		tiachcāhuān)	*warrior*
icox	*fig*	tiyàcāuh (*pl.*	*warrior, soldier*
ilamâ (*pl.* ilamatquê)	*old woman*	tiyàcāhuān)	
itzcuintli (*pl.* /–tin/)	*dog*	tzapa(tl) (*pl.*	*dwarf*
		/-me'/)	
llave(')	*key*	xinōla (*pl.* /-me'/)	*lady*

Intransitive verbs

| ìcac | *to be upright, to stand* | pilcac | *to hang, to be hanging* |
| onoc | *to be lying* | tolīna | *to have the desire to eat, to be hungry* |

àcocui	*to raise up*	itqui	*to carry, to bring*
ihua	*to send*	māma	*to carry (on the back)*
ohuî (*pl.* ohuìquê)	*difficult, painful*		

Transitive verbs
Adjective
Adverb

àco   *into the air, upward*

EXERCISES

(a) Translate into English.
1. Ca huel ohuî in huēhueyotl (= huēhuetcāyōtl).
2. In coco quichīhua tlaxcalli in īpan metlatl.
3. Ximonacazpācati, ca tinacazcuitla.
4. Yāōpan ōmomiquilīto inon huēyi tiyàcāuh.
5. Tlapechco ōnitecpincuālōc.
6. Iuhquin titzcuintli ticuetzpal.
7. Tlein anquitquizê?
8. Tlā zan ximìquiltīcān, tētēuctzitziné.
9. In nèhuātl huel nonozquia, yēcê ōninōtzalōc, auh tlapechco ōnino-quetz.
10. Zan titzapa, àhuel ticquēmiz inon huēyi tilmàtli.

(b) Translate into Nahuatl.
1. My old woman, what are you (s.) doing?
2. You (s.) are bleary-eyed ("you are excretion-eye(d)").
3. Young men love young girls.
4. Being a younger brother ("younger brotherhood") is very difficult.
5. Let the commoners remain ("be") standing.
6. He's a pumpkin head.
7. The wood (i.e., horns) of the deer are big.
8. You (pl.) are talkative like macaws.
9. At night I usually sleep and am lying down.
10. It's the Spaniards who brought the horses and oxen.
11. We've sent our young women.

More on Locatives

24.1 Review of Locatives

Let us recall the main characteristics of locative constructions:

(1) It is the verb and not the locative itself that indicates whether or not there is motion, and in the case of motion, which direction it is going in (away, toward…).

(2) The suffix -c(o) is placed directly onto the noun stem (but never appears with an animate being).

(3) The other locatives (locative nouns) have two possible constructions:

▶ appended as suffixes to a noun stem. This construction implies a "general" character for the noun onto which such suffixes are added (**calpan** 'at home' does not signify something in a particular house but is being distinguished from some other general location, such as **mīlpan** 'in the fields', **tēopan** 'at church' etc.).

▶ a possessive construction (of the type **īpan in calli** 'in the house'). This is obligatory for nouns representing animate entities (apart from -**pan** in certain instances, 13.4). With nouns for inanimate beings, this construction is preferred if the noun is definite.

(4) Thus, it appears that a suffix like -**pan**, -**cpac**, -**tech**, -**tlan** is actually a somewhat peculiar sort of noun that can either be put in the possessed construction or form a compound noun by being added as a suffix to a regular noun stem (17.1–2). The main characteristic of these compound nouns is that they are most often used in a locative capacity, but:

▶ in certain instances these compound nouns can be used in a nominal capacity (i.e., as subject or object of a verb or in a possessed noun construction), and then they have the suffix -**tli** (as in **teōpantli**).

▶ they never take the locative suffix -**c(o)**, in some way having an inherently locative sense.

▶ on the other hand, their honorific form is **-tzinco**, because the addition of **-tzin** makes them lose their locative character.

(5) When added as a suffix to a noun stem, **-cpac**, **-tech**, and **-tlan** are preceded by the "ligature" **-ti-**.

Let us now look at the other suffixes of this sort.

24.2 Other Locative Noun Suffixes

24.2.1 *-tlōc* and *-nāhuac*

These mean 'with, beside'. They are often used together redundantly:

Monāhuac câ	*He's beside you (s.)*
Notlōc xinemi	*Live (s.) with me*
Ītlōctzinco, īnāhuactzinco ninemi in tēuctli	*I live with the lord*

These two suffixes appear above all in the possessive construction. When **-nāhuac** appears on a noun stem, this is most often the case with proper names for places, like **Cuauhnāhuac** 'Cuernavaca' (lit., 'beside the trees'), **Ānāhuac**, the name for the Valley of Mexico ('beside the water').

▶ *Note*. **Tlōquê nāhuaquê**, lit., 'who has closeness', was one of the names for the pre-Conquest god Tezcatlipoca (and was later applied to the Christian God).

24.2.2 *-tzālan* and *-nepantlâ*

Meaning 'among, in the midst/middle of', these suffixes appear in the possessive construction or attached to noun stems:

Totzālan nemi	*He lives among us*
Cuix amotzālantzinco, amonepantlàtzinco ninotlālīz?	*Am I to sit down among, amidst you (pl.)?*
Tepētzālan câ in īcal	*His house is located in a/the mountain pass (lit., among the mountains)*

-Tzālan readily forms "real" nouns: **tepētzālantli** 'mountain pass', **caltzālantli** 'road, passage between houses'.

-Nepantlâ can be used adverbially by itself (**nepantlâ tōnatiuh** vs. **yohualnepantlâ**).

24.2.3 -huīc

Meaning 'toward, in the direction of' this suffix is most often put in the possessive construction, often followed by -**pa** or -**copa** (5.8, 13.1):

Ca īnhuīc ōtēhuaquê in toyāōhuān	We've risen up against our enemies
Nohuīc ēhua inin tlacualli	This food disgusts me (lit., rises up against me)
Nohuīcpa xihuāllachiya	Look (s.) in my direction
Īhuīctzinco (or īhuīcpatzinco, īhuīccopatzinco) ximocuepa in Dios	Turn (s.) toward God

Sometimes -**huīc** is found after -**copa**:

| ilhuicacopahuīc | in the direction of the sky |

24.2.4 -īcampa

Meaning 'behind', this suffix is used only in the possessive construction:

| Cuix nīcampa tinēchchicoìtoa? | Are you (s.) slandering me behind my back? |
| Īcampa in tepētl nemî | They live behind the mountain |

24.3 Locative Suffixes with Non-Spatial Meaning

Many suffixes in Nahuatl that have locatival characteristics are not translated with a spatial meaning. These are the following:

24.3.1 -huān

This suffix means 'with' (only in the sense of accompaniment, and not in that of instrument/means, which is -**(ti)ca**: 14.3), and is found only in the possessive construction:

Amohuān niyāz	I'll go with you (pl.)
Mā īhuān xihuāllauh in Malintzin	Come (s.) with Mary
Ca īnhuān ninemi in nopilhuān	I live with my children

This is of course the same **īhuān** that we have already seen as a fixed phrase[1] with the meaning 'and'. The honorific of -**huān** is in -**tzinco**:

| Amohuāntzinco niyāz | I'll go with you (pl.) |

---

[1] "Fixed" because one can, for example, say with no plural agreement: **oquichtin īhuān cihuâ** 'men and women' (**oquichtin īnhuān cihuâ** would mean 'men with women') or **tèhuātl īhuān nèhuātl** 'you (s.) and me' (**tèhuātl nohuān** would mean 'you with me').

▶ *Note.* You generally find the expression **nohuānyōlqui** 'my relative, person belonging to my family', **mohuānyōlqui** 'your (s.) relative', **nohuānyōlquê** 'my relatives' etc. written as a single word. These forms must be analyzed as **nohuān yōlqui**, lit., 'someone who lives (in the sense 'be alive' rather than 'inhabit') with me, i.e., 'blood relation'. The possessive prefix modifies only the initial -**huān** and not the phrase -**huānyōlqui** as a whole, because otherwise, we would have ****nohuānyōlcāuh**, ****nohuānyōlcāhuān**.

24.3.2 -pal

Meaning 'thanks to, through the intervention of', this suffix always appears in the possessive construction:

Mopal nitlacua	*I eat thanks to you (s.)*
Īpaltzinco tinemî in Dios	*We live by the grace of God*
Mopaltzinco	*If you (s.) please, by your leave*

▶ *Note.* **in īpal nemōhuani** 'the one thanks to whom people live' (with the -**ni** form of the impersonal, see 16.7) is one of the terms for god/God (again, a pre-Conquest term that was later applied to the Christian God).

24.3.3 -pampa

Meaning 'for, on account of', this suffix always appears in the possessive construction:

Mopampa nicchīhuaz in	*I'll do it on your (s.) behalf*
Mā īpampatzinco in Dios xinēchmaca	*Give (s.) it to me for God's sake*

Tle īpampa, like **tle īca** (14.4), means 'why?'. The answer is given with **īpampa (in)**:

Tle īpampa titzàtzi? – Zan īpampa in tinēchcocoa	*Why are you (s.) shouting, What are you shouting for? – Because you're (s.) harming me.*

24.3.4 -teuh

Meaning 'like, in the manner of', this suffix always appears attached to noun stems (exclusively inanimate ones). It is sometimes reinforced with **iuhqui**:

Chālchiuhteuh teyīnico	*It came to break like jade (**chālchihuitl**)*
Mā iuhqui cōnteuh, caxteuh tiquinchalānî	*Don't cause (s.) disputes among them (lit., don't make them crash together like jars and plates)*

(Note the dropping of the final -**i** in the nouns; see 13.5.)

24.4 -tlâ

The suffix **-tlâ** is a sort of "collective locative." It is attached to noun stems (the possessive construction is never used) to designate a 'place characterized by an abundance of ...':

Cuauhtlâ nonyauh	*I'm going off to the woods (place with lots of trees)*
Tetlâ nemî in cōcōhuâ	*Snakes live in the rocky place, amidst the rocks*

After **-l**, we naturally have **-lâ**:

callâ	*built-up area*
mīllâ	*cultivated region*

There can also be "real" nouns in **-tlàtli**:

Huēyi inon cuauhtlàtli	*That forest is big*

Unlike the majority of locative suffixes, **-tlâ** can be attached to an animate noun:

Ca huel oc tlācatlâ catca	*There was still a crowd (lit., it was still very much a place filled with people)*

24.5 Compound Locatives

Certain nouns, particularly ones designating parts of the body, are used in locative constructions (especially possessed locative ones) in a figurative sense. That is, the part of the body (or other noun) takes a possessive prefix (which may refer in the third person to another noun) and has one of the regular locative suffixes added to it. This construction is then equivalent to a prepositional phrase in English, with the possessor in Nahuatl equivalent to the object of the English preposition. Nouns used in this construction are:

-īxtli *eyes, face*	-īxco *facing*, -īxpan *in front of*, -īxpampa *from in front of*
-ìtitl *stomach*	-ìtic *within, inside of*
-tzintli *lower body*[2]	-tzintlan *at the foot of*
-cuitlatl *excrement*	-cuitlapan *in back of, behind*
-tepotztli *shoulder*	-tepotzco *behind*
-tēntli *lips*	-tēnco *at the edge of*

---

[2] The Aztecs conceived of the human body as being divided into three basic components: the head (**cuāitl**), the torso (**tlāctli**) and the lower body below the waist (**tzintli**).

Examples:

Mīxco nitlachiya	*I'm looking at you (s.) (lit., I'm looking upon your face)*
Amīxpantzinco ōnihuāllâ	*I've come before you (pl.) (to your eyes)*
Ca tīxpan ōmochīuh in	*This took place before our (s.) eyes (in our presence)*
Tleīca nīxpampa tēhua, ticholoa?	*Why are you (s.) leaving, fleeing from me?*
Mòtic³ câ in tlācatecolōtl	*The demon is inside of you (s.)*
Calìtic ōcholô	*He fled inside the house*
Ātlìtic⁴ nemî in mīmichtin	*Fish live in water*
Xitlàcuilo in ītzintlan inin āmatl	*Write (s.) at the bottom of this paper*
Āquin câ in mocuitlapan, in motepotzco?	*Who's behind you (s.)?*
Tēcuitlapan nitēìtoa	*I speak of people behind their back*
Ātēnco nemî in cuēcueyâ	*Frogs live along the water*
Ītēnco in cuahuitl (or cuauhtēnco) tihuî	*We're going along the woods*

▶ *Note.* **Mīxpantzinco**, pl. **amīxpantzinco**, lit., 'in front of your face' is a formula of apology used when you cross in front of someone or have to leave (cf. 'by your leave').

24.6 *Tla-* as Possessive Prefix of Locative

Locatives (locative suffixes and compound locatives) that allow the possessive construction can appear with **tla-** in its function as a possessive prefix. This construction indicates that the object to which the localization relates is not specific. In effect, these forms amount to adverbial indicators of direction without reference to any particular frame of reference. Thus:

Nitemo tlatzintlan	*I'm descending downward*
Cuix tlàtic câ in Pedro?	*Is Peter inside?*
Tlacpac ōtlècōc	*He went up(ward)*
Tlatepotzco niyauh	*I'm going behind/in back*

For 'in the middle', however, the expression is **nepantlâ** rather than **tlanepantlâ**. Also, there are the simple adverbs **pani** 'upward, **tlani** 'downward', which are synonymous with **tlapan, tlatzintlan**:

Àmo pani câ in māmox, zan tlani câ	*Your (s.) book isn't above but below*

---

³ **Nòtic, mòtic, ìtic (ìitic)** etc. is the only way to express 'in' with reference to an animate being.

⁴ It is impossible to say ****āc(o)** or ****āìtic**: instead, **ātl ìtic** or (as a single word) **ātlìtic** is used (here we have another instance of "beefing up" a short stem). It should be noted, however, that the sense 'in the water' is more commonly rendered with the expression **ātlan**, lit., 'under the water, underwater'.

24.7 *Cecni*

In front of a locative we do not have **cē** but **cecni**:

Cecni āmoxpan ōnicpōuh in   *I read this in a book*
Amàcizquê cecni cuauhtlâ   *You'll (pl.) arrive at a forest*

Used by itself, **cecni** means 'in one place':

Cecni yauh in Pedro, auh nō cecni   *Peter is going to one place, Mary to another*
   yauh in Malintzin   *(lit., also to one place)*

Oc cecni (cf. **occē**, 7.9) means 'elsewhere, another place':

Oc cecni niquìcuilōz   *I'll write it someplace else*

24.8 *-cān*

We have already seen (5.5) the possibility of adding the suffix **-cān** to a noun stem (the type **cualcān** 'good place', also 'soon' in a temporal sense). Truth be told, this possibility is seldom taken advantage of, and then only at the end of nouns more or less corresponding to adjectives (12.2). But it can be used with quantifiers:

ceccān (= cemcān *with assimilation*) *in one place*, mācuīlcān *in five places* etc.
Quēzquicān ōtitōcac? – Àmo miyaccān,   *In how many places did you sow? – Not in*
   zan quēzquicān, àzo ōccān, ēxcān   *many, in only a few, maybe two or three*
Nāuhcān xelihui   *it divides into four*

If one of these forms in **-cān** has the suffix **-pa** added to it, the new form is used to indicate motion (either to or from):

Ōccāmpa huāllāzquê   *They'll come from two locations*

On the other hand, **-cān** is frequently connected with the participial suffix (it is actually the locative form of the participial suffix) and so is found associated with "adjectives" in **-c**, **-qui** (12.4–7), possessive nouns in **-huâ**, **-ê**, **-yô** (11.6–8), and "agent nouns" derived from the preterite (16.1–2):

Ōmpa zan ye nō iuhcān in nicān,   *That place is just like this one, it's a terrible*
   ca zan nō ohuìcān   *(hard) place (note how **iuhqui** here*
                              *betrays its origin as an "adjective" in **-qui**,*
                              assuming the "locative" form of the words
                              ***ōmpa** and **nicān** that it's comparing)*

Yancuīcān ōnicnāmic	I met him recently
Michhuàcān nemî in michhuàquê	In Michoacan live the Michuas (people with fish)
Niyauh cōnchīuhcān	I go to the potter's (place) (**cōn-** from **cōmitl**)

When the form is derived from a verb, this is usually an active transitive one, taking the indefinite object prefix or an incorporated object (17.3): **cōnchīuhcān** is the place where the **cōnchīuhqui** can be found. There's at least one noteworthy exception to this principle: **Teōtīhuacān**, which certainly seems to be derived from the impersonal form of the verb **teōti** 'become a god' (see 29.2) and so means 'the place where gods come into existence'.

24.9 -yān

Another way to form locatives from verbs is with the suffix **-yān**. Three separate uses much be distinguished:

(1) Possessed form with human possessor

Such forms mean 'the place or time when/where I ..., you ...' etc. In other words, the possessor is the person(s) that would be the subject of the verb in a conjugated form. The verb is in base 1 (apart from **câ**, which uses the base **ye-**). Transitive verbs must have an indefinite object prefix (including the indefinite reflexive) or an incorporated object:

Cuix nicān mocochiyāntzinco? – Àmo, zan notlacuāyan. Oncān nonepācayān, ōmpa nocochiyān, nonemachtiāyān	Is here where you sleep? – No, this is where I eat. That's where I bathe, and over there's where I sleep and study.

(2) Possessed form with inanimate possessor

Such forms mean 'place or time where/when a certain thing ...'. The base is base 1 or base 2 (seemingly with no distinction, but always **ye-** for **câ**). If the verb is in the reflexive with the passive meaning (15.9), **mo-** remains (while the "real" reflexive becomes **ne-**, see sec. 1):

Cān câ in xoctli? – Zan īyeyān	Where is the pot? – In its place (the place where it's meant to be).
Imman in īmochīhuayān (or īmochīuhyān) in xocotl	Now (**imman**) is the time for the ripening of the fruit (when they are produced)
Īmotēcayān in quiyahuitl ātl ìtic ōhuetz	he fell into the water in the place where rainwater is collected (lays itself down)

(3) Without possessor

These forms have to be derived from the impersonal base of a transitive or intransitive verb (15.1, 7–8) and mean 'place or time where/when people/things VERB/are VERBed. Transitive forms naturally take the appropriate indefinite object prefix (or incorporated noun). Thus:

Nicān cochīhuayān, ōmpa tlacualchīhualōyān	*This is a place for lying down (or bedroom, lit. where people sleep), over there is a kitchen (place people make food)*
Tēilpīlōyān ōhuīcōc in ichtecqui	*The thief was taken to prison (place where people are bound)*
Ocnamacōyān tlāhuāna	*He gets drunk in the tavern (place where pulque is sold)*

It can be seen that a form like **tlacualchīhualōyān** can be equivalent in meaning to **tlacualchīuhcān**, with the former built on the passive (impersonal) stem and the latter on the regular active one.

▶ *Note.* The locative in **-yān** often introduces a nuance of necessity, permission or convenience. Thus, **ītlàtoāyān** generally means 'his turn to speak', and **quīxōhuayān** is often 'time (when it is necessary) to exit'.

24.10 'Himself' etc.

There are also locatives which quite unexpectedly mean 'myself' 'yourself', 'himself' etc. The most common is **nòmâ**, though **nèhuiyān** and **īxcòyān** are found in the same sense.

These are in the possessed form but without any suffix if the possessive prefix is in the plural. There's an honorific in **-tzinco**. Thus:

Zan īnòmâ tlatlac in teōcalli, ayāc ōquitlatî	*The temple burned by itself, nobody set it on fire*
Tonòmâ ticchīhuazquê in	*We'll do it (by) ourselves*
Īnòmàtzinco ōhuāllâ in tlàtoāni	*The ruler came in person*
Zan īnèhuiyān in ōmocalaquî in cuauhtlâ in zacatlâ	*It was of his own accord that he placed himself in a difficult situation (lit., that he inserted himself into the woods, the straw (zacatl) field)*
Nīxcòyān nocontlàpalōz	*I'll go greet him myself*
Ca mīxcòyāntzinco (*or* monèhuiyāntzinco) motlàtlacōl	*It's your own fault*

Nòmâ can also be used without a prefix in the expression **oc nòmâ** 'still, even now':

Oc nòmâ ancochî? Cuix oc nòmâ cochīhua?	*Are you (pl.) still asleep? Do people still sleep at this time?*

▶ *Note*. **Nòmatcà(tzinco)** can be found for **Nòmà(tzinco)**, and **īxcòtiyān** for **īxcòyān**.

24.11 Words for Position

Certain words that indicate a physical state, a form or a position are locatives: **nōncuâ** 'separate(ly)', **necoc** (or **necoccāmpa**) 'on both sides', **patlach** 'crouching', **chico** 'askance, amiss', **īxtlapal** 'askew', **nacacic** 'on the side', **nepapan** 'various, different' (this last word is used almost exclusively to modify a noun in the manner of an adjective).

Nōncuâ tochān, nōncuâ tinemî	*Our dwellings are separate, we each live apart*
Patlach catê in cihuâ	*The women are crouching*
Àmo īxtlapal, nacacic tinēchittaz	*You (s.) are not to look at me askance*
Īxtlapal ōticquetz	*You've (s.) raised it up sideways*
Necoc tinemi, necoc titlàtoa	*You (s.) lead a double life, you speak double talk*
Necoccāmpa ōmicōhuac	*There were deaths on both sides*
Chico ìcac	*He isn't right (lit., stands cockeyed)*
Quinyacāna in nepapan tēteô	*He leads the various gods*
Quichichīna in nepapan xōchitl	*It sucks flowers of every sort*

24.12 Demonstrative Locatives

Alongside the locative adverbs **nicān**, **oncān**, **ōmpa** (5.4), there is another series with a related meaning, but these have a strengthened demonstrative sense (they are generally used in pointing to things).

(1) **Iz** 'here' is often used with no difference from **nicān**:

Quin iz onquīz	*He just passed by here*
Àmo iz tlālticpac tochān	*Our home is not here on earth*

Many times, however, **iz** indicates that an accompanying gesture to point out of the location. In particular, **iz câ** is the equivalent of '(look,) here's/there's X':

Iz câ xōchitl	*There are flowers here*

If the object being pointed out is determined, **câ** is generally replaced with the fuller form **catqui** (in the singular, at any rate, because in the plural only **catê** is found and not ****catquê**):

Iz catqui in pàtli	*Here's the medicine*
Iz catqui in ticchīhuaz	*Here's what you'll (s.) do*

(2) **Nechca** 'there, over there' is used to point out something visible:

| Nechca câ | *There it is* |
| Nechca tepēīxco huālnēci in nocal | *My house can be seen over there on the slope of the mountain* |

(3) **Nēpa** 'over there' is used when you point to a place where something is located without it being possible to see the thing itself:

| Nēpa câ calìtic in nāmauh | *My papers are over there in the house* |
| Nēn ōnictlàpalô, zan nēpa ōmocuep | *I welcomed him to no purpose, he went back to the other side (over there)* |

(4) **Nipa** is different from the previous words in that it designates a vague place: 'away, elsewhere'. It is used most often with verbs conveying a sense of loss or destruction:

| Nipa īca ōnitlamōtlac in ōnēchmacac | *I threw away what he'd given me* (for the construction with **mōtla**, see 20.9) |
| Nipa ōquitlāz in tomin | *He threw the money away* |

VOCABULARY

Nouns

chālchihuitl	*jade*	tzintli	*buttocks, lower body*[5]
cueyātl (*pl.* /R–'/)	*frog*	xocotl	*fruit*[6]
quiyahuitl	*rain*	xoctli	*kettle, pot*
tepotztli	*shoulder*	zacatl	*straw*

Transitive verbs

chalānia[7]	*to knock together*	chichīna	*to suck*

Locatives

cecni	*(at, in) one place*	-huīc	*toward, in direction of*
chico[8]	*crooked, cockeyed*	iz	*here*
-huān	*with*	-īcampa	*behind*

[5] See note 2.
[6] Generic noun for fruit with peel and seeds.
[7] Semi-causative of **chalāni** 'to crash, to knock'.
[8] In compounds, it means to do something in an 'inappropriate, disfavorable' way: **chicotlālia** 'set sideways', **chicoìtoa** 'speak ill of' etc. Cf. the English verbal prefix 'ill' as in 'ill-mannered' or 'ill-conceived', in both of which the prefix signifies that the simple adjective applies in a way that is contrary to the way it ought to.

-īxcòyān	-self/-selves	-nòmâ	-self/-selves
īxtlapal	askew	nōncuâ	separately
nacacic	on the side	-pal	thanks to
-nāhuac	with, beside	-pampa	for, because of
nechca	over there	pani	upward
necoc(cāmpa)	on both sides	patlach	crouching
nepapan	various, different	-teuh	like, in the manner of
-nèhuiyan	-self/-selves	tlani	downward
nēpa	over there (of something not visible)	-tlâ	place with an abundance of...
nipa	away, elsewhere, somewhere	-tlōc	with, beside
		-tzālan	among

EXERCISES

(a) Translate into English.
1. Mohuāntzinco ninocuepaz.
2. Ōmpa niyauh in xōchitlâ.
3. Cuix tepētlâ, oztōtlâ nemî in cōcoyô?
4. Tle īpampa àmo ōtihuāllâ? – Ca zan īpampa in àmo ōnicnec.
5. Mācamo xonyauh ōmpa cuauhtlâ, mā zan tētlōc, tēnāhuac ximocāhua.
6. Cuix cuauhtlâ câ cuauhtzālantli? – Quēmâ, mā ōmpa tihuiyān in cuauhnepantlâ.
7. Nōncuâ tocochiyān.
8. Calacōhuayān ōnicnāmic.
9. Āmanamacacān ōniccōuh in.
10. Ayamo nēci in tōnatiuh, oc nòmâ quiyahui.
11. Àmo īnòmàtzinco in ōmomiquilî, ca mictīlōc.
12. Amīxpantzinco. – Ximopanōlti.
13. Mā nipa xonyàpōlo.
14. Iz catqui in ō nopan mochīuh.
15. Ōmpa mochīhua in nepapan xōchitl.

(b) Translate into Nahuatl.
1. Help (pl., hon.) me if you please.
2. Why are you (s.) crying? – Because my father is dead.
3. I've lived ("had lived") among the Otomi.
4. I've searched above and also below. I've found ("made visible/appear") nothing.
5. Look (s.) behind you.

6. The dog has entered a ("one") house.
7. There are stones in the water.
8. I went to Mexico with the women.
9. Do (the) deer live in areas full of water? – No, only in forests.
10. You're (s.) knowledgeable about military affairs (translate: "war is in your eyes").
11. He didn't go out by the exit.
12. It's not your (s.) turn to speak.
13. He lives in the west ("place where the sun enters").
14. They're going in the direction of the east ("place where the sun emerges").
15. Those people aren't our relatives.
16. We have ears on both sides.
17. Here are (some) beans: eat (s.).

More on Quantifiers

25.1 *Quēxquich*

In English, we distinguish *countable* (also called *aggregate*) nouns like 'dogs' or 'bottles' from *non-countable* nouns like 'milk' or 'help' in terms of how we speak of counting such entities. Sometimes we use different quantifier for the two categories. For instance, 'many' and 'fewer' are used of countable nouns, whereas the same notions are given for non-countable nouns in the form 'much' and 'less'. When we inquire about the quantity of nouns, we use *interrogative quantifiers*, and here again there are different expressions for the two categories. For countable nouns, we say, 'How many?', even if the answer is not expected to take the form of a specific number (i.e., we expect the answer 'a few' or 'not many' rather than 'five'). With non-countable nouns, we ask, 'How much?', and generally the answer has to be given in a non-numeric form (e.g., 'a lot', 'not much').

Nahuatl also has two different interrogative quantifiers, but the distinction between the two words is made on a different basis than in English. Whereas English concentrates on the nature of the *noun* (whether or not it can be counted), the two Nahuatl interrogatives are distinguished by the nature of the *answer* expected. We have already encountered **quēzqui** (7.1), which expects a specific answer in the form of a number. In addition, there's the interrogative **quēxquich**, which expects a non-specific answer like **miyac** 'much/many' or **huēyi** 'big'. This interrogative is used for substances that are inherently uncountable (e.g., nouns designating materials, like 'water', 'earth', 'meat') or for nouns of measurements like distance, duration of time, or value. if no exact answer is expected.

Quēxquich ātl ōtiquīc? – Zan tepitzin.	*How much water did you drink? – Just a little.*
Quēxquich īpatiuh in?	*What does it cost? (how much is its worth?)*

With countable nouns, on the other hand, both sorts of counting are possible, so either interrogative can be used with them, depending, of course, on the expected answer. Thus, you can say **quēxquichtin tlacâ?** 'how many people?' if the answer you expect is not a precise number but something like 'a lot' or 'a few', whereas **quēzquintin tlacâ?** expects a specific number in response.

When preceded by **zan**, **quēxquich** (just like **quēzqui**) loses its interrogative nature, so that **zan quēxquich** 'some amount, a little, just a bit' is virtually equivalent to **zan tepitzin**. **Achi** 'rather, quite' has the same effect on these quantifiers:

> Achi quēxquich cāhuitl, achi quēzqui   *He was in Mexico for a certain amount of*
> xihuitl Mexìco ōcatca   *time, some number of years*

Note that **quēxquich cāhuitl** 'how much time/how long' often appears in the shortened form **quēxquichcāuh**:

> Quēxquichcāuh timocāhuaz?   *How long will you (s.) stay?*

25.2 *Īzqui* and *Īxquich*

Corresponding to the interrogatives **quēzqui** and **quēxquich** are the definite quantifiers **īzqui** and **īxquich**. These terms both mean 'so many/much, that many/much' and are used to indicate that the quantity in question is equal to some other quantity that is already known in the discourse, **īzqui** being used if the other quantity is a specific number and **īxquich** if it is a vaguer amount. Sometimes, they are used in the sense 'as much/many as there is/are', in which case the meaning is close to that of **mochi** 'all'. Thus:

> Ēyintin tlācâ ye ōmicquê, auh oc nō   *Three people have already died, and an equal*
> īzquintin mococoâ   *number are sick*
> Xinēchittiti in īzqui māmox   *Show me all your books (as many as you've*
>   *got)*
> Ye ōniquīc miyac octli. – Mā oc nō   *I've already drunk a lot of pulque. – Drink*
> īxquich xicmīti   *(s., hon.) as much again.*
> Ayaīc ninococoa, in ye īxquich cāhuitl   *I've never yet been sick (for) as long as I've*
> ninemi   *been alive*
> Niquìtōz in īntōcā in īzquintin Mexìco   *I'll say the names of all (or each of) the rulers*
> tlàtòquê   *of Tinochtitlan*
> In īxquichtin ye ōyàquê   *They've all gone already (as many as there are)*

As can be seen, **īzqui(ntin)** 'all individually (taken one at a time)' can be contrasted with **īxquichtin** 'all together (taken as a group)'.

As indefinite relatives (see 4.10), we can have **in īxquich in quēxquich** and **in īzqui in quēzqui** 'however much/many, as much/many as':

Xinēchilhui in īxquich in quēxquich ōtiquittac	*Tell me everything (lit., as much as) you (s.) saw*

Note the expressions **ca ye īxquich** 'that's everything, that's all, that's it' and **zan huel īxquich** 'at the most' (lit., 'only that much really'):

Ca ye īxquich, ye nonyauh	*That's everything, now I'm leaving*
Nicān niyez nāhuilhuitl zan huel īxquich	*I'll be here for four years at the most*

Īxquich cāhuitl (like **quēxquich cāhuitl**) is often shortened to **īxquichcāuh**:

In nèhuātl zan nō īxquichcāuh (= īxquich cāhuitl) ninocāhuaz	*As for me, I'm going to stay that long too*

25.3 *Cequi*

The quantifier **cequi**, pl. **cequin(tin)**, means either 'one (among many)' or 'some, certain (ones) (in an indeterminate number)'. It is often found repeated, with the meaning 'some ... (the) other(s)/the rest ...':

Cequi polihui	*One of them's missing*
Cequin(tin) ayamo nicān catê	*Some aren't yet there*
Cequin(tin) caxtiltēcâ quimatî in mēxìcatlàtōlli	*Some Spaniards know Nahuatl*
Quinamaca tecomatl: cequi huēyi, cequi zan tepitōn	*He sells pots, some big, some small*
Miyactin tlācâ niquimitta: cequin mēxìcâ, cequin caxtiltēcâ	*I see many people, some Mexica, the rest Spaniards*

Occequi, occequintin (= **oc cequi** etc., but traditionally written as one word) are used to express 'other(s)' when the number is not known:

Zan yèhuātl ōxitīn in nocal, in occequi calli àmo ōxitīn	*Only my house collapsed, the other ones didn't*[1]
Tiquimpanahuia in occequintin	*You (s.) surpass the others*

---

[1] Note that in English the contrast relates to the possessors of the houses ('*my* house ... *other people's* ...'), but the use of **yèhuātl** shows that the contrast in Nahuatl relates to the houses themselves.

25.4 'Very Big' and 'Very Small'

The quantifier **ixachi**, pl. **ixachin(tin)** conveys a sort of heightened sense for both **miyac** and **huēyi** ('very much/many' or 'very big'), signifying "largeness" in either number or size:

Ca ixachi inin tōtōtl īquetzallo	*The plumage (note the use of the -yo of inalienable possession; see 11.5) of this bird is very big*
Ixachin(tin) huālquīzâ in azcamê	*Many ants are coming out*

To express a very small number or amount, use is made of either **tziqui-** or the suffix **-tzoco**, which is added to **tepi-** or (**zan**) **quēxquich-**. To these forms **-tzin** or **-tōn** is added (as with **tepi-**, see 12.3), the former generally indicating a quantity and the latter a group (this distinction is not absolute):

Zan tziquitōn (*or* tepitzocotōn) inon chichi	*That dog is very small*
Zan tepitzocotzin (*or* quēxquichtzocotzin, tziquitzin[2]) ātl ōniquīc	*I've drunk (only) a very small amount of water*

25.5 *Aquì-*

Aquìtōn or **aquìtzin** (the element **aquì-** always appears with a diminutive suffix) is the equivalent of 'a little' (while **zan quēzqui**, **zan quēxquich** is 'some, a few'):

Aquìtōn epazōtl ōnictlālīlî in ātl	*I've put a bit of wormseed in the water* (not the use of the applicative to indicate the "location" of the putting; see 20.5)

25.6 Numbers from 20 to 399

Counting above 20 is carried out according to the vigesimal system. You count in multiples of 20 by prefixing to **pōhualli** the form of the multiple that is used for compound nouns (7.8):

cempōhualli	*20 (1 × 20)*	mācuīlpōhualli	*100 (5 × 20)*
ōmpōhualli	*40 (2 × 20)*	chichuacempōhualli	*120 (6 × 20)*
ēpōhualli	*60 (3 × 20)*	màtlācpōhualli	*200 (10 × 20)*
nāuhpōhualli[3]	*80 (4 × 20)*	caxtōlpōhualli	*300 (15 × 20)*

[2] **Tepizcantzin** is also found.
[3] Or **nāppōhualli** (with assimilation of /w/ to /p/).

As we know, the numbers 11–14 and 16–19 are compounds. The compound can be left intact with **pōhualli** added to it as a suffix:

| màtlāctli oncempōhualli | *220* |
| caxtōlli omōmpōhualli | *340* (17 × 20) |

or **pōhualli** is added to each of the components, which are no longer connected with -**om**- but with **īpan** or (more rarely) **īhuān**:

| màtlācpōhualli īpan (*or* īhuān) cempōhualli | *220* |
| caxtōlpōhualli īpan (*or* īhuān) ōmpōhualli | *340* |

This second construction with **pōhualli** repeated, which is less common, is generally avoided if there are unit nouns at the end. In this case, two consecutive compound numbers with -**om**- are avoided, and the preferred arrangement uses -**om**- and **īpan** in alternation:

cempōhualli oncē	*21*
cempōhualli ommācuīlli	*25*
cempōhualli onchicuacē	*26*
cempōhualli ommàtlāctli	*30*
cempōhualli ommàtlāctli īpan cē	*31*
cempōhualli oncaxtōlli īpan ēyi	*38*
caxtōlli oncempōhualli īpan màtlāctli	*330*
caxtōlli oncempōhualli īpan màtlāctli omēyi	*333*

We can also have: **cempōhualli īpan màtlāctli oncē** '31', **cempōhualli īpan caxtolli omēyi** '38'.

Naturally, to convert English numbers to Nahuatl, it is necessary to reanalyze the base 10 numbers of English in terms of base 20 with the remainder distributed among the sub-bases 5, 10, 15 plus any leftover units. Thus, to say '333', we first have to divide by 20 (16 × 20 = 320) and state the remainder (13) as appropriate. In mathematical terms, the Nahuatl equivalent is expressed as $(15 + 1) \times 20 + (10 + 3)$.

25.7 Counting above 400

The next counting units above **pōhualli** are powers of 20: **tzontli** '400 (20 × 20)' and **xiquipilli** '8000 (20 × 400)'.[4] These are then multiplied by the compound forms of the numbers less than 20 in the same way as **pōhualli**:

---

[4] **Tzontli** is properly a '(clump of) hair' and **xiquipilli** a 'sack of (cocoa) beans'.

centzontli	*400*	màtlāctzontli omōntzontli	*4800*
ōntzontli	*800*	màtlāctzontli īpan omōntzontli	*4800*
ētzontli	*1200*	màtlāctzontli īhuān omōntzontli	*4800*
màtlāctzontli	*4000*	cēxiquipilli *or* cenxiquipilli	*8000*
		ōnxiquipilli	*16000*

If multiples of 4000 and 400 or of 400 and 20 are added, this is done with **īpan** and not with **-om-**. Another way is to alternate **īpan** and **-om-** (it is easiest to have two instances of **īpan** in a row rather than two of **-om-**):

ētzontli īpan màtlāctli onnāuhpōhualli īpan ōme	*1482*, lit. $(3 \times 400) + ((10 + 4) \times 20) + 2)$
caxtōlli omōnxiquipilli īpan màtlāctli onnāuhtzontli īpan caxtōlli oncempōhualli īpan chicōme	*141,927*, lit. $((15 + 2) \times 8000) + ((10 + 4) \times 400) + ((15 + 1) \times 20) + 7$

All these numbers can naturally be put in the plural:

xiquipiltin mēxìcâ	*8000 Mexica*
centzontin īpan nāuhpōhualtin ōmēyin mēxìcâ	*482 Mexica*
centzontin mēxìcâ īpan nāuhpōhualtin ōmēyin	*482 Mexica*

25.8 *-pa* Added to Quantifiers

If **-pa** (5.8) is added to a quantifier, we have a word meaning 'so many times'. Note in particular **miyacpa** 'often', lit., 'many times', **mochipa** 'all the time, always', lit., 'every time', and also **tlapōhualpa** 'a countable number of times' (from **tlapōhualli** 'count, computation'; see 30.2 for the construction):

Quēzquipa ōtiyâ Mēxìco? – Zan ceppa (ōppa, ēxpa, nāuhpa, mācuīlpa).	*How many times have you been to Mexico? – (just) once (twice, three times, four times, five times).*
Mōztla occeppa niyāz	*Tomorrow I'll go again (one more time)*
Quin ic ceppa niyauh	*This is the first time that I'm going*
Miyacpa ōnitlāhuān	*I often got drunk*
Mochipa mococoa	*He's always sick*
Àmo zan tlapōhualpa iztlacati	*He lies an uncountable number of times (i.e., he tells countless lies)*

25.9 *-ca* Added to Quantifiers

The suffix **-ca** (14.4) is used with quantifiers in two ways:

(1) **īxquichca** 'that/so far, from there, at that distance', and **quēxquichca** 'how far away, at what distance':

Quēxquichca in Mēxìco?	*How far away is Mexico?*
Tepēticpac ìcaquê auh īxquichca	*They're standing on the mountain and looking*
tlatzintlan tlachiyâ	*down from there (lit., at that distance)*

(2) Added to number nouns (with the final vowel of the noun stem retained) followed by the "ligature" -**ti**-, they indicate a price:

Cētica (ōmetica, ēyitica, nāhuitica,	*I bought it for one real (two, three, four, five reals)*[5]
mācuīltica …) ōniccōuh	

25.10 -(i)xtin

To express 'all NUMBER of us/you/them', the suffix -**(i)xtin** (-**xtin** after vowels) can be added to numbers above 1, which are preceded by the appropriate possessive prefix:

In tōmextin titococoâ	*Both (i.e., the two) of us are sick*
In īmēyixtin nopilhuān yāōpan ōmicquê	*All three of my sons died in war*
In yèhuāntin in immācuīlixtin ca nopilhuān	*All five of them are my children*[6]

If a counting noun (7.8) like **te(tl)** or **tlaman(tli)** is used in this construction, it loses its absolute ending and -**ixtin** is added to it (note the retention of the initial -**i**- in this ending even in the case of **te**-):

In īōnteixtin in ayòtli ye ōpalān	*Both pumpkins are already rotten*
In īmōntlamanixtin on ca mexìcatlàtoâ	*Those two sorts of people speak Nahuatl*

It can be added to forms in –**cān**:

In īōccānixtin ōmicōhuac	*There were deaths on both sides*

25.11 *Cēl* and *El*

These words are always in the possessed form.

---

[5] A 'real' is a Spanish coin.

[6] This is perhaps represented more exactly with the British idiom 'they are all five of them my children'.

25.11.1 *Cēl* 'Alone'

It has a plural in -**tin** like the quantifiers (where we would, of course, expect -**huān**).

Zan nocēl ōnihuāllâ	*I came all by myself*
Cuix amocēltin nicān ancatê?	*Are you here by yourselves?*
Zan īcēltzin moyetzticatca in Dios	*God alone existed*
Zan īcēl in ītlan otztli mocāhua tīcitl	*The midwife remains alone with the pregnant woman*

This word does not take the subject prefixes. 'I'm alone' is **nocēl nicâ** and not ****ninocēl**. (For more on its usage, see 26.10.)

25.11.2 *El* 'By Himself'

This one has no plural suffix. Used by itself, this means 'I am hardworking, eager':

Ca mel; ca àtel	*You're (s.) hard-working; we're not hard-working*

Used with a verb, it means 'willingly, by his (etc.) agreement':

Īel quichīhua	*He does it voluntarily*
Â īmel huālhuî	*They're coming against their will*

25.12 Counting Nouns (cont'd)

The only regular counting nouns are the ones that we saw in 7.8, namely **tetl**, **tlamantli** and the nouns for periods of time. However, there are also nouns for traditional measurements like **matl** (which the Spanish translated with **vara** 'yard', but its exact length is not certain):

Màtlācmatl in ic huēyi	*Ten varas is how high it is*

and also measurements used for counting specific items, for example:

-**camatl** ('mouth') or -**tēntli** ('lips') for 'word':

Cencamatl ic niccuepa in motlàtōltzin	*I answer ('return') your speech with one word*

-**ōlōtl** lit. 'cob' (after the corn has been shelled) is used for counting corncobs up to nineteen (**cemōlōtl** 'one cob', **ōmōlōtl** 'two cobs', **caxtōlōlōtl onnāhui** 'nineteen cobs'). After that, **tlamic**, which means 'twenty cobs', is used, then **tlamic oncē** 'twenty-one cobs', **tlamic omōme** 'twenty-two cobs' and so on, until forty, when the regular method of counting resumes (**ōmpōhualli** etc.).

-pantli designates a 'row' (of people or things):

ōmpantli cuahuitl *two rows of trees*

-tecpantli often replaces **-pōhualli** in the counting of humans or animals:

màtlāctli, caxtōlli, centecpantli āyōtl *ten, fifteen, twenty turtles*
ōntecpantli ommàtlāctli tōtolin *fifty turkeys*

-ipilli is used in counting groups of twenty flat things (mats, pieces of paper or cloth):

màtlāquipilli *two hundred (sheets, mats ...)*

-quimilli 'pack' is used exclusively for groups of twenty pieces of cloth:

ōnquimilli *forty (blankets)*

VOCABULARY

Intransitive verbs

iztlacati	*to lie, to tell falsehood*	xitīni	*to collapse*
palāni	*to rot*		

Nouns

azcatl (*pl.* /-me'/)	*ant*	otztli (*pl.* /-tin/)	*pregnant woman*
āyōtl (*pl.* /-me'/)	*turtle*	ōlōtl	*corncob*
cāhuitl	*time*	quimilli	*pack, bundle*
epazōtl	*wormseed, epazote (aromatic herb)*	tlapōhualli	*count(ing)*
		xiquipilli	*sack of grain*

Quantifiers

aquì-	*few, little*	-ōlōtl	*cob*
cequi	*one (of)*	-pantli	*row*
-cēl	*alone*	quēxquich	*how many*
-el	*diligent, with X's consent*	-quimilli	*twenty (pieces of cloth)*
-ipilli	*twenty (flat things)*	-tecpantli	*twenty (people or animals)*
ixachi	*very many/big*		
īxquich	*all, that many*	tlamic	*twenty (cobs)*
-(i)xti(n)	*all the (number)*	tziqui-	*very small*
īzqui	*all, that much*	-tzoco-	*very small*
-matl	*vara, yard*	-tzontli	*400*
		-xiquipilli	*8000*

EXERCISES

(a) Translate into Nahuatl.
1. 50
2. 75
3. 125
4. 500
5. 1000
6. 2000
7. 5000
8. 10,000
9. 736
10. 1519

(b) Translate into English.
1. Ēxiquipilli īpan màtlāctzontli.
2. Nāuhtzontli īpan caxtōlli omōmpōhualli īpan màtlāctli omōme.
3. Màtlācpōhualli oncaxtōlli.
4. Caxtōlli onnāuhpōhualli īpan mācuīlli.
5. Mācuīltzontli īpan màtlāctli omēpōhualli īpan chicuēyi.

(c) Translate into English.
1. Ōnimitzhuīquilî cequi nōchtli.
2. Anquilhuīzquê in teōpixquê in īzqui amotlàtlacōl.
3. Ca nāhuintin in īpilhuān Pedro, auh nō īzquintin in nopilhuān.
4. Mācamo xiquintolīni in occequintin pīpiltotōntin.
5. Ca ixachi in nicān metl: nochān ca occentlamantli, zan tziquitōn.
6. In Xōchimīlco tlàtōlli, in Cuauhnāhuac tlàtōlli īōntlamanixtin ca mexìcatlàtōlli; in otomî īntlàtōl occentlamantli.
7. À nel ōnicchīuh, ca zan ōnicchīhualtīlōc.
8. Īēxcānixtin ōquīz ātl.
9. Àmo màtlāctica, zan mācuīltica nimitzixtlāhuilīz in.
10. Zan nocēl niyāz cuauhtlâ.
11. Quin ic ōppa niqui octli.

(d) Translate into Nahuatl.
1. I've cut flowers for you (s.), some red, some white.
2. I've got only a little land and a few pigs.
3. All the prisoners were killed.
4. The other peasants ("people with fields") are going to eat. Peter's staying in the fields by himself.
5. On the mountain there are huge trees.
6. These two necklaces please me, I'll buy the two of them.

7. I've already told you a thousand ("four hundred," *used of an indefinite large number*) times.
8. Peter's in Mexico and he's written to me from there.
9. All my property has been lost (**polihui**).
10. Is this the first time that you are coming ("are you coming for the first time") to our city?

Details about Number and Person, Indefinite Pronouns and Adverbs

26.1 Coordination of Noun and Pronoun

In English, when a noun and a first or second person pronoun appear in coordination as subject, the verb is put in the plural (e.g., 'Peter and I are ...'). In such circumstances, Nahuatl uses a rather different procedure. Only the noun is stated expressly, and the other subject (the pronoun in English) is merely implied in the person used for plural verb (lit., 'Peter we are ...):

Ōtitotlàpalòquê in Pedro	*Peter and I greeted each other (lit., Peter we greeted ...)*
Mōtzla huāllāzquê in īnâmic	*His spouse and he will arrive tomorrow (lit., his spouse they ...)*
Cuix ye ōantlacuàquê in monāmic?	*Have your spouse and you already eaten?*

26.2 Nouns in the First and Second Person

We have seen that a noun as subject or object is represented in the verb by a third person prefix. There are also expressions in which the noun is used in conjunction with a subject or object in the first or second person, with the noun taking the appropriate *subject* prefix for that person. The literal translation is 'me/I who (am) X', 'you (who are) X'.

Tlein ticcuāzquê in ticnōtlācâ?	*What are we (who are) poor wretches supposed to eat?*
In niMotēuczōma ca Mēxìco nitlàtoāni	*I, Moctezuma, am ruler of Mexico*
Mācamo xitzàtzicān in ampīpiltin	*Don't you (pl.) shout (you who are) children*
Yālhua àmo ōnimitzittac in tiPedro	*Yesterday I didn't see you (you who are) Pedro*

As can be seen, in English this usage is represented in the first and third person with a noun that is in *apposition* to the pronoun (i.e., the noun is placed along side the pronoun to which it is equivalent), and in the second person, it corresponds to a vocative (i.e., the form used to address the person being spoken to).

> ▶ *Note*. Regular nouns without subject prefixes can be considered as having the zero marker of the third person subject. Hence, they simply represent a particular instance (by far the most frequent) of this phenomenon, and the real sense of, for example, **niquitta in cihuātl** would be 'I see her, her who is a woman' or 'I see the one who is a woman' (which confirms our analysis of emphasis in 2.8).

26.3 Number Agreement with Juxtaposed Nouns

With coordination through simple juxtaposition (see 14.1), the same subject prefix has to be used with all elements. In the first and second person plural, to say 'we/you (pl.) are X and Y' (where one person is X and a different person is Y), two expressions are available, both seemingly paradoxical:

▶ 'I'm X, I'm Y' (or 'you're (s.) X, you're Y'), even if X and Y are represent two different people
▶ 'We're X, we're Y' (or 'you're (pl.) X, you're Y')

In the second construction, both nouns must be in the plural as a consequence of the plural subject prefixes, even if each noun applies to only one of the people represented in the subject prefix.

Thus:

Ca nimonān, ca nimotâ	*We're your mother and father (lit., I'm your mother, I'm your father)*
Ca timonānhuān, ca timotàhuān	*We're your mother and father (lit., we're your mothers, your fathers)*
Xinēchcaqui in nimonān in nimotâ	*Listen to us, your mother and father (lit., me who am your mother, who am your father)*
Xitēchcaqui in timonānhuān in timotàhuān	*Listen to us, your mother and father (lit., who are your mothers, who are your fathers)*

26.4 *Titèhuān*

Titèhuān 'like us, one of us, one of ours' has the peculiarity of being able to function as a first or second person singular or plural, being generally preceded by **zan nō**:

Zan nō titèhuān: cuix àmo titlàtoa mācēhualcopa?	*You're (s.) one of us. – Don't you speak Nahuatl?*
Inìquê on tlācâ zan nō titèhuān	*Those people are like us*

▶ **Note.** Carochi overtly confirms that this form is what is looks to be, namely the independent first person pronoun **tèhuān(tin)** plus the corresponding subject prefix, so it literally means 'we are us'. Carochi cites an example that may suggest the origin of the seemingly strange use of this form in connection with the second and third person. When the Mexica arrived in the Valley of Mexico, the ruler of Azcapotzalco said to his advisers:

Ca zan nō titèhuān in Mēxìtin[1],	*The Mexica are like us. – We understand*
ca tiquintlàtōlcaquî	*them (lit., hear them in speech).*

If we consider this phrase in light of 26.1, we can take the first clause to mean 'the Mexica and we are us'; that is, the two groups 'we' (left unexpressed except in the subject prefix) and the Mexica together constitute the group 'us' (i.e., the speaker and the others he is associated with). Where the sense seems to dictate 'you are like us', presumably the second person is included in the inclusive first person plural subject prefix. That is, when the phrase is used in a context that would be translated as 'you are like us', the 'we' in **ti-** signifies 'we plus you'.

26.5 -pô

The prefix **-pô** is added to noun stems (like diminutive and augmentative endings, see 12.1, except that the honorific **-tzin** can also be added to it). The noun to which this suffix is added is always in the possessed form, and the new form indicates that the person to whom it refers (i.e., the subject prefix) resembles the possessor in that both the possessor and the subject belong to the category designated by the noun (cf. the English prefix 'co-' in 'co-owner', 'co-defendant' or 'joint' in 'joint authors'):

Inin tlācatl ca nocnōpô	*This person is poor, just like me (lit., is my co-poor person)*
Inin tlācatl ca toteōpixcāpô	*This person is a priest just like us (is our co-priest)*
Inìquê on tlācâ ca nomīlècāpòhuān	*Those people are peasants like me (are my fellow peasants)*

The prefix **-pô** can be added directly to a possessive prefix, with the meaning 'similar to, like':

Āquin huel īpòtzin in teōtl?	*Who can be the equal of God?*

[1] This form is sometimes used instead of **Mēxìcâ**.

26.6 'A Man', 'a Woman'

Men did not say 'a man' but 'one of us men', and if they were addressing a woman, they would not say 'a woman' but 'one of you women'. This turn of phrase is the same partitive expression that we saw in 7.4, except that **cē toquichtin** is said rather than **cēmê toquichtin**:

Ōmpa ticnāmiquiz cē toquichtin	*You'll meet a man there* (spoken by a man)
Ōmpa ticnāmiquiz (*or* tiquinnāmiquiz) cēmê ancihuâ	*You'll meet a woman there* (spoken by a man to a woman)

Women, on the other hand, would simply say **cē oquichtli, cē cihuātl**. It is also possible of course to say **cē nocihuāpô, cē tocihuāpô** (26.5).

26.7 'Together', 'Each Other'

To express 'together', use is made of **nehuān** (if it is a question of two) or **cēpan** (if it is more than two). These forms can be used absolutely (i.e., by themselves) as adverbs:

Nehuān nemî	*They live together (both of them)*
Cēpan nemî	*They live together (all of them)*

These words are most often used with the possessive prefixes, however, and they have an honorific in **-tzitzin**.

Mā tonehuān tihuiyān	*Let's both of us go*
Mā tocēpan tihuiyān	*Let's all go together*
Īnnehuāntzitzin ōhuālmohuīcaquê	*Both of them came together (hon.)*

A related concept in Nahuatl involves "reciprocity." This term means that the individuals making up a plural subject act upon other members of that group rather than each acting upon himself. In English, 'they love themselves' would normally mean that each loves himself, while 'they love each other' gives the reciprocal sense of each one loving the others. The Nahuatl reflexive covers both situations and for this reason is potentially ambiguous.[2] Hence, the need at times to distinguish the two uses.

---

[2] **Cēpan** is not absolutely necessary. In the following example, **titàhuâ** alone would mean 'we argue with each other', but **cēpan** reinforces the reciprocal nature of the action and precludes any purely reflexive interpretation. This comment also applies to **nepan** (see section 26.7).

Cēpan can be incorporated into a verb that takes the reflexive object prefixes to give it a reciprocal sense.

Titocēpananàhuâ	*We're all arguing (with each other)*
Necēpanàhualo	*There's a general argument*

Nehuān cannot be incorporated into a verb, but **nepan** can be incorporated with the same meaning as **cēpan**. It is also possible to use **nepanōtl** adverbially as an independent word:

Titonepantlàpaloâ	*We greet each other*
Nepanōtl titotlàpaloâ	*We greet each other*

26.8 Indefinite Pronouns and Adverbs

A simple interrogative is converted into the corresponding indefinite word through the addition of the suffix **-â**:

icâ	*once, ever* corresponds to **īc**
canâ	*somewhere* corresponds to **cān**
acâ	*someone* corresponds to **āc**
itlâ	*something* corresponds to **tlê**[3]

The indefinites are seldom used in regular affirmative statements. They normally appear in the following contexts:

▶ in questions:

Cuix itlâ ōtiquittac?	*Did you (s.) see anything?*
Cuix canâ ōtiquittac in nopiltzin?	*Have you (s.) seen my child anywhere?*

▶ in statements containing
  either a negative (**àmo acâ** then has the same meaning as **ayāc**, and **àmo itlâ** the same one as **àtle** etc.):

Àmo icâ ōnitlāhuān (= aīc ōnitlāhuān)	*I've never gotten drunk* (lit., *not at any time*)
Àmo acâ quimati (= ayāc quimati)	*No one knows it*

or **àzo** 'perhaps':

Àzo acâ ye ōmpa câ	*Perhaps someone's already there*

---

[3] It is probable that **quēmâ** is the indefinite form corresponding to **quēn** and so originally meant 'in some way'. Note the short vowels in the other indefinites as opposed to the long ones in the interrogatives. The relationship between **tlê** and **itlâ** is the only one that is morphologically irregular.

▶ with the optative or the vetitive (and also in conditional expressions, as we will see in Lesson 34):

Mā canâ (*or* canàpa) xonyauh	*Go (s.) somewhere (i.e., elsewhere)*
Mā acâ tiquilhuî	*Don't (s.) tell anyone (watch out about telling …)*

Acâ and **itlâ** can also have a plural in -**mê**

Àzo acàmê itlâ quìtōzquê	*Perhaps some people will say something*
Cuix titlàmê? – Àmo, àtitleìquê	*Are we something? – No, we're nothing.*

Acâ and **itlâ** do not overlap with **tē-** and **tla-**. The indefinite prefixes (which are not subject to the same restrictions as the pronouns in terms of the sorts of statements in which they can appear) neither give nor expect any information about the object, while in principle **acâ** and **itlâ** represent a specific person(s) or thing(s) that the speaker is unwilling or unable to identify or about whom/which information is being sought. Compare:

Cuix ōtitlacuâ?	*Have you (s.) eaten?*
Cuix itlâ ōticcuâ?	*Have you (s.) eaten something?*

In the first question, it makes no difference what has been eaten as the thrust of the question is whether or not you are hungry. The second question might refer, for example, to the items of food available, the expected response being something like 'Yes, I've eaten such-and-such' or 'No, I haven't eaten any of them'. A closer translation of the Nahuatl in the second question would be 'Is there something that you have eaten?' or (even less idiomatically) 'is what you have eaten something?'. To a certain extent, the difference might be expressed with the single-word quasi-pronoun 'something' representing -**tla**- and the two word phrase 'some thing' (i.e., 'a certain specific but unknown/unnamed thing') for **itlâ**.

The basic sense of **acâ** and **itlâ** is respectively 'to be someone' and 'to be something', and for this reason, they are found in expressions indicating existence. When these forms are used with a possessed noun, a possible translation is the English verb 'to have' (the subject being the possessor in the Nahuatl):

Cuix itlâ motomin? – Àmo, ca àtle notomin.	*Do you (s.) have money?– No, I have no money. (lit., Is you money something? – No, my money is nothing.)*

Acâ and **itlâ** can be put in front of a noun, with a meaning close to that of **cē** ('any …', 'a certain …', 'some …'):

Cuix itlâ àmo cualli ō mopan mochīuh?	*Has something bad happened to you (s.) (done itself on you)?*
Àzo acâ tīcitl mitzpàtīz	*Perhaps some doctor will cure you (s.)*

26.9 *Quēmmanyān*

Quēxquich and **quēzqui** have no corresponding indefinite of the type **icâ**, **canâ**, but they can themselves be used with an indefinite meaning in certain instances:

| Ōniccuâ quēzqui nōchtli | *I've eaten some prickly pear* |

The indefinite corresponding to **quēmman** is usually **quēmmanyān** 'sometimes, at certain moments' (though sometimes **quēmman** is used in the sense of **quēmmanyān**). **Quēmmanyān** (like indefinite **quēzqui** and **quēxquich**) can appear in any sort of statement, without the restrictions imposed on the indefinites in 26.8. In particular, **in quēmmanyān** can appear at the head of the sentence, as can **zan quēmmanyān** 'rarely':

| In quēmmanyān huel tinēchtequipachoa | *There are times when you (s.) really bother me* |
| Zan quēmmanyān in nēchhuālitta | *Only rarely does he come to see me* |

26.10 *Iyô*

Iyô means 'only', and it is distinguished from **cēl** (25.11) by the following characteristics:

▶ It is not a quantifier, its plural being **-quê**.
▶ It has no possessive prefix, but instead takes the subject prefixes and can be used as a predicate (e.g., **zan niyô** 'I'm alone').

When used with a verb, it does not have exactly the same meaning as **cēl**. While **cēl** indicates that the person (or thing) in question does (or undergoes) something by himself without others, **iyô** indicates that he does (or undergoes) something that the others do not. The phrase with **cēl** could be rendered as 'he VERBs all by himself', and the phase with **iyô** as 'he's/it's the only one to VERB'. Contrast the following:

| Zan nocēl ōnihuāllâ | *I've come all alone (and nobody accompanied me)* |
| Zan niyô ōnihuāllâ | *I'm the only one to have come (with the possible implication that the others were unable to come)* |

Other examples:

| Zan iyô in nimitzilhuia | *This is the only thing that I'm telling you (s.)* |
| Zan tiyô in ticmati | *You (s.) are the only one who knows it, You alone know it* |

Cēl could hardly be used in these two cases. The distinction is sometimes very slight, however, and it happens that one or the other could be used without any difference. Hence, in one author (Chimalpahin, *Seventh Relation*) the following sentence can be found:

(In īpan xōchiyāōyōtl ...) zan iyòquê in mācēhualtin in miquiyâ	*In the flower war ... the only ones to die were the commoners*

and just a few pages later the same statement is found with **incēltin** in place of **iyòquê**.

Note the phrase **iyòpa** 'a single time, it's the only time':

Zan iyòpa in ōnictlàpalōto	*It's the only time that I went to greet him*

26.11 *Amî*

Amî 'such' appears only in the interrogative **quēnamî** 'like what, of what nature?'. It is generally written as one word if it refers to someone in the third person, but in other persons, split forms like **quēn tamî** 'what are you (s.)?', 'what is your nature?' can be found. The plural is **quēnamìquê**, the honorific is **quēnamìcātzintli**, and there is also a locative **quēnamìcān**:

Quēnamìquê inìquê on tlācâ?	*What sort of people are those?*
Quēnamìcātzintli in Dios?	*What is the nature of God?(what's he like?)*
Quēnamìcān in mochān?	*What's it like at your (s.) place/among you?*

26.12 *Tìquê, Amìquê*

In place of **āc tèhuāntin, āc amèhuāntin** (4.4), the following forms can be found:

Āc tìquê?	*Who are we?*
Āc amìquê?	*Who are you (pl.)?*

In the third person plural, the expected form **āc ìquê** appears in fixed form (written in one word as **āquìquê**) as the plural of **āc** (4.4). The question 'who are they?' generally has the forms **āquìquê?, āquìquê on?** or **āc yèhuāntin?**

There are no singular forms corresponding to **āc tìquê, āc amìquê**.

26.13 *Cātlèhuātl, Cātlia, Cātlî*

These are quite rare interrogative forms of closely related meaning. **Cātlèhuātl** (which is morphologically related to the emphatic pronouns of the type **yèhuātl**) means 'which one?' (in relation to the other ones), while **cātlia/cātlî** seek an answer in which something is pointed out. Hence, the possible translations into English are quite varied: 'which one is…?', 'what is …?', 'where is…?'

Cātlìquê is the only regular plural for all three forms.

Nicān câ miyac calli: cātlèhuātl in mocal?	*There are many houses here. Which one's yours (s.)?*
Cātlia in motlāl?	*Which are your (s.) lands?*
Ticātlî?	*Where are you (s.)?*
Cātlìquê mocnīhuān?	*Which are your (s.) friends? Where are your (s.) friends?*

VOCABULARY

Transitive verbs

àhua	*to argue with, to dispute with, to scold*
zahua	(mo: *fast*)

Nouns

Motēuczōma	*Moctezuma* (proper name)	-pòtli (26.5)	*like*
nāmictli (*pl. /–tin/*)	*spouse*		

Adjectives and pronouns[4]

acâ (*pl. /–me'/*)	*someone*	itlâ (*pl. –me'*)	*something*
(quēn) amî (*pl. /–ke'/*)	*like what?*	iyô (*pl. /–ke'/*)	*the only one*
cātlèhuātl, cātlia, cātlî, (*pl.* cātlìquê)	*which one?*	nehuān	*together (of two)*
cēpan	*(all) together*	nepan	*together, mutually*
		titèhuān	*like us*

Locatives

canâ	*somewhere*	icâ	*ever, once*
Caxtillān	*Spain*	quēmmanyān	*sometimes*

EXERCISES

(a) Translate into English.

1. Ca cencâ titotolīniâ in timācēhualtin.
2. Àmo zan iyòquê in cualtin in yēctin quimmotlazòtilia in Dios.

---

[4] There are all listed together, but clearly they can be divided into sub-categories.

3. Quēnamî mochān in tlaōlli?
4. Ayaīc nonyauh in ōmpa Mēxìco, cuix tèhuātl ye icâ ōmpa ōticatca?
5. Cequintin toquichtin yāōpan ōmictīlōquê.
6. In titlācâ ca titlàtlacoānimê.
7. In īzquintin mācēhualtin zan nocnōpòhuān.
8. In Motēuczōma zan ītlàtòcāpòtzin in Caxtillān tlàtoāni.
9. Huel motlazòtlâ in īnāmic.
10. In mochintin pīpiltotōntin cēpan cuīcayâ.
11. Ōtitonepampalēhuìquê.
12. Ca àtle tomin ōniccuīc, ca zan iyô quēzquitetl nōchtli.

(b) Translate into Nahuatl.

1. I love you (two), my elder brother and my younger brother.
2. We Mexica and Otomi are from here ("have our home here"), you Spaniards aren't like us.
3. Forgive (s.) me for having done wrong ("who did a not good thing").
4. I and my two fellow prisoners like me have escaped.
5. Aren't the Spaniards people like us, made of flesh like us, sinners like us?
6. Have you (s.) seen someone yet? – No, I haven't seen anyone yet.
7. Do you (s.) still want something? – No ("not more"), so give this to someone else.
8. Where are you (pl.)? – Show yourselves.
9. I'm the only one who knows Spanish ("the language of Spain") in our town.
10. The two enemies killed each other.
11. What's tom turkey meat like? – Very good.
12. Was any one ever able to do that? – For my part, I've done it, but rarely.

Compound Verbs

27.1 Auxiliary Verbs

A certain number of verbs indicating a state or a sort of movement can be used as *auxiliaries* of other verbs. The construction is as follows:

(1) Main verb in base 2
(2) "Ligature" in -**ti**- (just -**t**- in front of a vowel)
(3) An "auxiliary" conjugated for tense and person

Thus, with **câ**:

Nicchīuhticâ	*I'm in the process of doing it*
Ticchīuhticatê	*We're in the process of doing it*
Ticchīuhtiyezquê	*We'll be in the process of doing it*

The auxiliary does not affect the transitive or intransitive character of the main verb. Even though **câ** is itself intransitive, we say **nicchīuhticâ**, just like **nicchīhua**. If the form is put into the honorific, this construction affects only the main verb and not the auxiliary:

Ticmochīhuilìticâ	*You're (s.) doing it (hon.)*

The most common auxiliaries are intransitive, and we will now look at them individually.

27.1.1 *Câ*

Câ is the most frequently used auxiliary. It indicates a situation in which a process is ongoing. This usage often corresponds to the English present progressive tense ('be VERBing'), as can be seen in the examples:

Tlein ticchīuhticâ? – Zan nitlacuàticâ.	*What are you doing? – I'm eating.*
Cuīcaticatê in pīpiltotōntin	*The small children are singing*

Àtle tiquilnāmictiyezquê, zan   *We won't remember anything, we'll be happy*
tipāctiyezquê

▶ *Notes*

(1) It is true that sometimes the simple present in Nahuatl is also best
translated with the progressive present, but this apparent overlap is a
matter of English idiom and should not result in any confusion about
the meaning of the Nahuatl. The point of the form with the auxiliary
câ is to emphasize the ongoing nature of the process.

(2) Nahuatl often uses the form in **câ** with the certain varieties of verbs
that do not normally take the progressive construction in English.
This is particularly noticeable with verbs of state and of thinking, perception or emotion, which in English normally appear only in the simple present because they inherently signify ongoing processes and so
the progressive tense is mostly redundant (e.g., 'I want' rather than
'I'm wanting').

Let us recall **moyetzticâ**, the honorific form of **câ** (21.3):

Ilhuicac moyetzticâ totēucyo Dios   *Our Lord God is in heaven*

27.1.2 *Ìcac*

This auxiliary, which means 'be doing something standing', is quite rare:

Cuīcatìcacâ in pīpiltotōntin   *The small children were standing singing*

Ìcac can serve as the auxiliary for itself as the main verb in the honorific:

Mìquiltìtìcac in tlàtoāni   *The ruler is standing (hon.)*
(m-ìqui-ltì-t(i)-ìcac)

27.1.3 *Oc*

This auxiliary is nothing but the verb **onoc** 'be spread out, lying down', but its
prefix **on-** is lost in compounds (23.7). It can have its proper meaning 'be doing
something while lying down':

Cochtoc in chānê   *The householder is lying down sleeping*

Most commonly, however, it indicates a state resulting from an accomplished
process. In this sense, it appears only with intransitive verbs, with the subject
lying down (literally or metaphorically) *after* something has happened to it and
not *while* that action is going on:

Oc nòmâ huetztoc	*He's still lying on the ground (lies fallen)*
Tlapāntoc in xoctli	*The pot is (lies) broken*
Quēchcotōntoquê[1] in māmaltin	*The prisoners are lying with their throats cut*
Cecni āmoxpan ìcuiliuhtoc inin tlàtōlli	*This statement is (stands, to use a different image in English) written in a book*

As with **ìcac**, **(on)oc** is used as the auxiliary of itself in the honorific (23.7):

Mā zan ximonoltìto	*Just stay (s.) lying (hon.)*
(xi-m(o-)on-o-ltì-t(i-)-o)	

27.1.4 *Mani*

Mani 'spread (out), be spread' indicates the spread or extension of a process over a broad spatial expanse ('everywhere, all over'):

Tlanēztimanca	*Day was dawning (things were becoming visible) all over*

Note the following use of this verb as itself own auxiliary (this time not in an honorific usage):

Nōhuiyān mantimani in miquiztli	*Death is spreading out everywhere*

As shown in the first example, the regular past tense in the auxiliary usage is the pluperfect (22.1).

27.1.5 *Nemi*

Nemi 'move' indicates the continuation or constant repetition of the process ('do nothing but VERB', 'keep (on) VERBing'). As with **mani**, the only regular past is the pluperfect **nenca**.

Tlein ticchīuhtinemi?	*What do you (s.) keep doing?*
Oc nòmā ninococòtinemi	*I'm still sick all the time*
Yālhua zan nēchtolīnìtinencâ	*Yesterday all they did was torment me*

27.1.6 *Yauh*

Yauh is the most common auxiliary after **câ**. A noteworthy detail about it is that in the present singular the stem is reduced to just the **-uh** element (e.g.,

---

[1] This form should not be taken as coming from the transitive **quēchcotōna** 'cut someone's throat' but from **quēchcotōni** 'have one's throat cut (be cut in terms of the throat)', with **cotōna** the semi-causative version of **cotōni** (19.8).

this gives **nicchīuhtiuh**). All the other forms are identical to the corresponding forms of the independent verb (e.g., **ticchīuhtihuî** 'we're going along doing it', **nicchīuhtiyāz** 'I'll go along doing it').

The regular meaning is 'to go along doing something'. This motion can be metaphorical, and then the auxiliary indicates that the process is prolonged or continuing:

Nitlàtòtiuh	*I'm going along talking* or *I continue talking, I talk and talk*
Ticmāmàtihuî cuahuitl	*We're walking along carrying a load of wood*

It frequently forms compounds with verbs of motion, including **yauh** itself:

Ximohuīcatihuiyān	*Go (pl.) (hon.)*
Cencâ tlamach in yàtiyàquê	*They were going very slowly*

In certain uses (with the auxiliary in any form but the present), the main verb must be understood as perfective, with the meaning 'to do something and leave', 'to go after doing (having done) something':

Nicān ticcāuhtiyāz	*You (s.) are to go after leaving it here*

▶ Notes

(1) The auxiliary -**(ti)uh** in the present should not be confused with the imperfective of the directional of motion away (22.5), because the directional conjugation has a long vowel (-**tīuh**) and is built on base 3 and not base 2. Note the following contrasts:

nicchīhuatīuh	*I'm going to do it* and
nicchīuhtiuh	*I'm going (along) doing it*
nictēmōtīuh	*I'm going (in order) to look for it* and
nictēmòtiuh	*I'm going along looking for it*

With verbs with "vowel-retaining" preterites (8.7), for which the three bases are identical, it is only the length of the **i** (a feature unmarked in most texts) that makes it possible to distinguish the two forms:

nicuīcatīuh	*I'm going (off) to sing* but
nicuīcatiuh	*I'm going (along) singing*

(2) From the Classical period on, the contracted forms -**tâ**, -**tāz** can be found in place of -**tiyâ**, -**tiyāz**:

Àmo tlayacac timoquetztāz	*You (s.) aren't to put yourself in first place* (lit., *you won't go raise yourself up to the nose, i.e., front, of things, i.e., take charge*)

(3) **Tōnatiuh** 'sun' is just **tōna** compounded with this auxiliary. The proper meaning is 'the one that goes along making heat'.

27.1.7 *Huītz*

This auxiliary (5.3) means 'to come doing something':

Pāctihuītz	*He comes being happy*

27.1.8 *Calaqui*

This means 'to enter doing something':

Motlalòticalaqui	*He comes in running*

27.1.9 *Huetzi*

Literally 'to fall', this auxiliary is used to indicate speed or suddenness in performing the main verb:

Nitlàcuilòtihuetzi	*I'm writing quickly*
Xihuālmocueptihuetzicān	*Come (pl.) back fast*
Tēchhuilāntihuetztiquiuh in miquiztli	*Death is going to come and drag us off without warning*

27.1.10 *Ēhua*

'To leave doing something' or 'to leave after doing something':

Nicān ōquīztēhuac	*He passed by here (and rapidly went on his way)*
Quēn niquincāuhtēhuaz in nopilhuān?	*How could I go off and abandon my children?*

27.1.11 *Quīza*

'To go out after doing something' or 'to do something very fast':

Ōquichīuhtiquīz	*He did it at top speed*

27.1.12 *Àci*

'To arrive and do something right away, to do it immediately upon arrival':

Ōnitlacuàtàcic	*I ate as soon as I arrived*

27.2 Transitive Reflexive Auxiliaries

There are five transitive verbs that can be used as auxiliaries. They are used in the reflexive form, with the reflexive prefix appended to the auxiliary and thus appearing between the -ti- ligature and the auxiliary. Note that the reflexive always appear as **mo-**, even in the *first* person.[2]

These five verbs are:

(1) **(mo)cāhua** 'stay' indicates duration ('remain in a certain state' or 'keep doing something'):

    Tlapouhtimocāhua in puerta   *The door stays open* (**tlapohui** 'be open')

(2) **(mo)tēca** 'lie down' and **(mo)tlālia** 'sit down' indicate a beginning:[3]

    Nitolòtimotlālia   *I let my head nod*
    Ticyahualòtimotēcaquê in āltepētl   *We started besieging the town*

(3) **(mo)quetza** 'get up' and **(mo)mana**[4] 'spread out' indicate a transition or development:

    Tlanēztimoquetza   *Dawn is about to break*
    Tlayohuatimomana   *Night is falling (speeding)*
    In mochintin tēteô quiyahualòtimomanquê *All the gods circled around the hearth*
       in tlecuīlli   *(gathered around it by spreading out)*

27.3 Non-Reflexive Transitive Auxiliaries

The five auxiliaries in the preceding section plus **quīxtia** 'make come out', 'take out' can act as auxiliaries in the *non-reflexive* form. In this usage, the main verb is also transitive, and the object can be considered as being governed by both the main verb and the auxiliary. The auxiliary retains its proper meaning and the compound means 'to bring out/move/raise etc. someone or something by verbing that him/it' or 'to do so after verbing that person/thing':

    Ōtictlapouhticāuh[5] in puerta   *You've (s.) left the door open*
    Nichuilāntiquīxtia   *I'm bringing him out by dragging him*

---

[2] Originally, the **mo-** form of the reflexive was used for all persons, and **no-** and **to-** are central Nahuatl innovations. Some modern dialects still have **mo-** everywhere.

[3] The forms can be considered as inchoatives (i.e., verbs indicating the start of a state) of the auxiliary **oc**, just as **motēca** 'he lies down' is correlated with **onoc** 'he is lying down'.

[4] **Mana** is the semi-causative of **mani**. Used as an independent verb, it means 'to spread out, display' and hence 'to offer, give as an offering, present'.

[5] Here (unlike the case in 27.2) we have the verb **tlapohua** 'open', semi-causative of **tlapohui**. These two verbs must not be confused with **pōhui/pōhua** 'count as/count'.

Niquēhuatitlālia in cocoxqui	*After picking the sick person up I set him down*
Niquēhuatiquetza	*After picking him up I stand him upright*

In this type of construction, the honorific is formed on the auxiliary, but the reflexive prefix is placed in front of the main verb:

Ōticmotlapouhticāhuilî in puerta	*You've (s.) left (hon.) the door open*
Nicnēhuatitlālīlia in cocoxcātzintli	*Having picked up the sick person (hon.), I set him down*
Nicnēhuatiquechilia	*Having picked him (hon.) up, I stand him upright*

27.4 Auxiliaries Added to Auxiliaries

It is possible to find compounds with auxiliaries serving as the main verb in a new compound, with the first auxiliary having the new one added to it:

Iuhquin āyahuitl tlālpan àcitimotēcatoc (àci-ti-mo-tēca-t(i-)-oc) in miquiztli	*Death lay spread out like a fog over the earth*

27.5 Auxiliaries Added to Possessive Nouns

Possessive nouns in **-huâ, -ê, -yô** can themselves be followed by **-ti-** and an auxiliary:[6]

Ìtètinemi	*He's fat, he walks around with a big belly*
Cuauhtenānyòtoc, cuauhtenāmètoc in ithualli	*The courtyard was (lay) equipped with a wooden fence (**tenāmitl**)*

27.6 Stems Appearing Only with Auxiliaries

Some verb stems appear only as the first element in a compound. The two most common examples are:

(1) **cac-**, which means 'to be vacant, abandoned, forsaken'. This appears most frequently with **-oc**, sometimes with **-huetzi, -mani** or **-mo-tēca**:

Cactoc in āltepētl	*The town lies deserted*
Cactimani in āltepētl	*The town lies deserted*
Cactihuetz in calli	*The houses were immediately abandoned*

---

[6] This phenomenon betrays the origin of these forms as the agent nouns (16.1) of no longer attested derivative verbs; the appearance of the participial ending **-cā** when such nouns take various endings points in the same direction.

▶ *Note.* The etymology of this form is obscure. Some evidence suggests a relationship with **cāhua**. If so, one might posit an intransitive ****cāhui** as the basis of the isolated compound form, but the final **-c** is hard to explain (perhaps a dialectal variant?). The slim evidence for the vowel suggests that it is short, but this is hardly conclusive. If the form is related to **cāhua**, the vowel ought to be long.

(2) **itz-**, which means 'to go/head toward', almost always appearing in the form **itztiuh**, sometimes **itztēhua**. The locative associated with it is almost always followed by **-pa**, which means that the verb signifies a general direction rather than a specific goal (5.8, 1):

Àmo etic in ìhuitl, zan àcopa itztiuh	*The feather isn't heavy, it's going up*
Tlacōpampa itztiyàquê	*They left in the direction of Tacuba*
Mā canàpa nitztēhua	*Let me go off somewhere else*

This formation in **itztiuh** even has an impersonal in **itztiōhua** and a causative in **itztiltia** (**itztiltìtiuh**). This is completely abnormal, because the regular procedure would be for these elements to affect the main verb:

Ōmpa itztiōhua in teōithualco	*People are heading for the temple court yard (god court yard)*
In tlācatecolōtl mictlampahuīc quimitztiltìtiuh in tlàtlacoānimê	*The demon sends sinners off to hell*

▶ *Note.* This form must not be confused with the form **itz-** assumed by the stem **itta** in front of the ligature **-ti-** (**itta** is irregular in this regard; also note the honorific **itztilia**, 21.4):

Nicān motzticatca in teōcalli	*The temple could be seen here*
Quimitztimancâ in mìtōtiâ	*They stood (spread out) watching the ones who were dancing*

The problem is complicated by the fact that while the **itz-** associated with **itta** is transitive (as can be instantly recognized because of the presence of an object prefix), there is also an **itz-** associated with the corresponding intransitive **ithui** 'to be visible':

Ōmpa itztimani miyac calli	*Many houses are visible over there*

Finally, there is another intransitive **itz-**, which appears in the reduplicated with the glottal stop (see 28.4) and is always construed with the auxiliary **oc**, the form **ìitztoc** meaning 'to be awake':[7]

Ye nìitztoc	*I'm already awake*

---

[7] In this instance, **itz-** may be the modified stem of the intransitive verb **ìza** 'to wake up'.

27.7 Verbal Compounds with -cā-

In addition to the procedure involving auxiliaries, there is a second way to make compound verbs.[8] The first verb is likewise in base 2, but it is bound to the second one by -cā- instead of -ti-. The first verb can generally be translated with the present participle ('VERBing') or a comparable adverbial expression, for example:

Nimitzpāccācelīz　　　　　　　　　*I'll receive you (s.) with pleasure (rejoicing)*

This method of making compounds is distinct in every regard from the one with -ti-:

▶ The main verb is the *second* one (while this is the first one in compounds with -ti-), with the first merely modifying it.

▶ In these instances, it is the second verb that determines whether the compound is transitive or intransitive (**pāccācelia** is transitive like **celia**), and it is also this verb that takes (any) honorific markers (e.g., **nimitznopāccācelīlīz** 'I'll receive you with pleasure (hon.)')

▶ While only a fixed group of verbs can act as an auxiliary after -ti-, a similar list cannot be drawn up of which ones can appear before or after -cā-. In fact, making compounds with -cā- is merely a particular variety of modifying incorporation (17.3.2). As we know, -cā- is actually the form taken by the participial suffix in compounds. In a compound like **pāccācelia**, all that is going on is that rather than a regular noun stem, it is the "adjective" (12.4) **pācqui** 'be happy' that has been incorporated.

The "noun" or "adjective" in -cā- that has been incorporated generally modifies the subject of the main verb:

Mācamo xinēchcualāncāitta　　　　　*Don't (s.) look at me with anger*
Ōmāuhcāmic　　　　　　　　　　　*He was scared to death (died of fear)*
Miccācochi　　　　　　　　　　　　*He sleeps with his eyes open (like a dead man)*

but sometimes the object instead:

Nicxeliuhcācua in notlaxcal　　　　　*I eat my tortillas in pieces (divided up)*
Ōquitlàtòcātlālìquê　　　　　　　　　*They installed him as ruler (**tlàtòcā-** from **tlàtoāni**, a verbal form functioning as a noun; see 16.4–5)*

---

[8] There is actually a third way, which we will look at in the next lesson (28.9–11).

The verb stem preceding -cā- is most often intransitive. If it is transitive, it must have an indefinite object prefix or a reflexive prefix:

Nimitztlamelāuhcācaqui   *I hear/understand you properly* (transitive
                                          melāhua 'make go to straight'[9])

If the prefix is reflexive, it takes the definite form if the main verb is intransitive:

Ninozcalìcānemi   *I live in a civilized fashion* (**mozcalia** 'be
                                          sensible, well-bred')

but it is indefinite if the main verb is transitive:

Nicneizcalìcāchīhua   *I do it sensibly*

VOCABULARY

Intransitive verbs

cactoc[10]	*to be vacant, to be abandoned*	tlapohui	*to be open*
ìitztoc	*to be awake*	tzacui[11]	*to be closed*
itztiuh	*to be headed (for), to go*	yohua[12]	*to become night*

Transitive verbs

huilāna	*to drag, to take away*	mana	*to spread (out), to offer,*
izcalia	*to revive, to restore, to educate*		*to present*
	(mo-: *be restored,*	tlapohua	*to open*
	be sensible, well-bred)	yahualoa	*to surround, to encircle*

Nouns

āyahuitl	*fog, mist*	tenāmitl[13]	*wall, fence, barrier, enclosure*
ithualli	*courtyard*	tlecuīlli	*hearth* (both indoors
puerta	*door (Sp. borrowing)*		and outdoors)

---

[9] Cf. **nimitzmelāhuacācaqui**, which as usual includes the form **melāhua** from base 2 of the intransitive (with retain vowel in the preterite, see 8.7) as opposed to **melāuh** from base 2 of the transitive.

[10] Of the verbs treated in 27.6 only the ones used most commonly as auxiliaries are listed here.

[11] **Tzacua** is the semi-causative of this verb.

[12] This verb can take the construction of either the inanimate impersonal **tlayohua** (15.3) or the inherently impersonal **yohua** (15.10).

[13] In place of the expected locative **tenāmic**, we find the form **tenānco**, which frequently appears in modern place names in the form '-tenango'.

Adjective

etic　　　　(*pl.* etiquê) *heavy*

Adverb

tlamach　　*slowly*

Locative

Tlacōpan　　*Tacuba*[14]

EXERCISES

(a) Translate into English.
  1. Mā oc nicān ximocēhuìtiyecān.
  2. Palāntoc in xōchitl.
  3. Tzauctoc in calli.
  4. Cuauhtitech zaliuhtìcac in āmatl.
  5. Ōquinamacatiyâ in īxquich ītlatqui.
  6. Tiyānquizco ōquitztiyâ in petlatl.
  7. Tleīca timotlalòtinemi?
  8. Xiccuītihuetzi inin cōmitl.
  9. Ōnictlàpalòtēhuac in nocnīuh.
  10. Ōmāuhcātzàtziquê.
  11. Ōtlāhuāncāhuetz īpan in ītlapech.
(b) Translate into Nahuatl.
  1. God looks ("is looking", hon.) everywhere.
  2. Peter is totally drunk ("lies drunk").
  3. The buyers gathered around ("spread out") to see the merchant.
  4. Leave (s.) the door closed.
  5. I cut (pret.) flowers on my way ("I went cutting flowers").
  6. Yesterday I spent all my time making tortillas.
  7. Hide (s.) (yourself) quick!
  8. I met him all of a sudden.
  9. We'll sleep at my place as soon as we arrive.
  10. That woman goes everywhere covered in necklaces ("with necklaces").
  11. They run in fear.
  12. All the flowers died ("withered") of drought.

---

[14] Today one of the western suburbs of Mexico City.

Reduplication outside of the Plural, More on Verbs

28.1 Verbal Reduplication in /CV:/

Reduplication of the type /CV:/ (i.e., a consonant followed by a long vowel), which is one of the methods of forming the plural in nouns (2.4), is also used in verbs. This formation makes "intensive" verbs, which indicate a quantitative or qualitative heightening of the action ('to do something forcefully or frequently or with devotion or with a particular intensity...').

Huel tzātzàtzi	*He shouts very loudly*
Mācamo xinēchnānānquili	*Don't (s.) answer back to me (don't respond vigorously)*
Àmo, zan nimitznōnōtza	*No, I'm just speaking to you earnestly*
Nonīichtequi in cuezcomac	*I often go to commit theft in the corn-bin*

28.2 /CV:/ Reduplication with Numbers

As well as with verbs and nouns, long-vowel reduplication is found with numbers, giving a distributive sense ('one apiece, two apiece...'). Note that for **quēzqui** 'how many?' there is a corresponding form **quēcīzqui** 'how many each?'.

Quēcīzqui tlaxcalli ōanquicuàquê? – Nānāhui.	*How many tortillas did you (pl.) each eat? – Four apiece.*
Quēcīzqui cintli anquipiyâ? – Cācaxtōlli omēēyi. – Àmo, zan cācaxtolli oncēcē	*How many ears of corn do you each have? – Eighteen. No, only sixteen.*
Ca ōōmentin in topilhuān Pedro	*Peter and I (26.1) have two children each*

Cēcem- followed by a temporal noun means 'every year, every month, every day':

Cēcemilhuitl niyauh tiyānquizco	*I go to the market every day*
Cēcenyohual huālchōchōca in tecolōtl	*Every night the owl comes to screech (cry loudly)*

Contrast:

Cenyohual[1] cemilhuitl ōnicoch	*I slept all day and all night*

where the unreduplicated numeral prefix indicates the totality of a single instance of the period of time in question rather than its regular repetition (see 12.9 sec. 4).

28.3 /CV:/ Reduplication with Locatives

With certain locatives, long-vowel reduplication indicates a spatial interval between each of the items in question ('…among them, …to each other'):

Huèca câ in nocal	*My house is far away*
Huēhuèca câ in tocal	*Our houses are far apart from each other*
Netech câ in nomīl	*My field is distant*
Nēnetech câ in tomīl	*Our fields are widely separated*
Nōncuâ xictlāli in	*Set (s.) it aside*
Nōnōncuâ tochān	*We're from separate homes (our houses are separate from each other)*

28.4 /CV'/ Reduplication

There is a different method of reduplication, in the form /CV'/ (i.e., with a short vowel followed by the glottal stop in place of a long vowel). This is used above all with verbs, where it is much more common than /CV:/ reduplication.

Whereas /CV:/ reduplication indicates an intensification of the process, /CV'/ indicates its apportionment, with the effects of the process being distributed among various objects or in various places. Note the following contrasts:

Nitlazāzaca	*I transport many things*
Nitlazàzaca	*I transport things to various places*
Nicxēxeloa in nacatl	*I carve the meat (in large amounts)*

---

[1] The forms **cenyohual, cēcenyohual** without the absolute suffix are used instead of **cenyohualli, cēcenyohualli** (but **cenxihuitl, cemilhuitl, cemmētztli, cēcenxihuitl** etc.).

Nicxèxeloa in nacatl	*I carve the meat (into sections for distribution to various people)*
Motlātlaloâ	*They run (hard)*
Motlàtlaloâ	*They run apart, run in different directions*
Nonìichtequi	*I'm going to commit thefts all over the place (cf. **nonīichtequi** in 28.1)*
Titonònōtzazquê	*We'll have a discussion (cf. **nimitznōnōtza** in 28.1; here the /CV'/ reduplication indicates 'we'll address each other, each in his own turn')*

In certain cases, reduplication can act as a real substitute for the plural (understood here as indicating a plurality of the inanimate things), with reference to either the subject:

Motlātlapohua in puerta	*The door opens all the time*
Motlàtlapohua in puerta	*All the doors open*

or the object:

Mā xiquimmìmictīcān	*Kill (pl.) them all (individually)*

With some verbs (especially those indicating a feeling), the /CV'/ reduplication has an expressive sense, indicating a feeling (or sometimes an action) that is somehow more subtle, delicate or toned down:

Nipàpāqui	*I'm very happy, I rejoice*
Huel tēchòchōctî in	*This is really sad, regrettable (makes people cry; see 16.2)*
Àmo tlàtoa, zan huèhuetzca	*He doesn't speak, he just smiles*
Moyàyāōtlâ	*They play at war (or they make war on each other)*

The /CV'/ reduplication can even change the sense of the verb quite significantly, so that the new meaning is not immediately predictable:

Tlacuàcuâ in ichcamê	*The sheep are grazing (eating here and there)*
Mitzcuàcuāz in chichi	*The dog is going to bite you*
Ìciuhca nènemi	*He's walking quickly*
Mochìchīhua	*He's preparing himself or he's decking himself out*

Here we should recall **pòpoloa** 'to forgive' alongside **poloa** 'make disappear, get rid of'.

28.5 Morphology of the /CV'/ Reduplication

There are three specific points relating to the /CV'/ reduplication:

(1) A reduplicated syllable can itself be duplicated:

Màààhuiltìtinemi   *He spends his time looking for fun everywhere*
                                    (**m(o-)āhuiltia** 'he amuses himself, takes
                                    pleasure'; **āhuiltia** 'to amuse, to give pleasure')
Nènènemi   *He paces back and forth*

(2) It can be applied to the prefix **tla-**:

Tiyānquizco tlàtlatta, tlàtlacōhua   *In the market, he checks things out, buys
                                    various items*

(3) If we have a reflexive form and the **-o** of the prefix elides the initial **i-** of
the verb stem (6.7), the verb is treated as if the **-o** belonged to the stem, so
that this is what gets reduplicated:

Mòottâ   *They look at each other* (as if the word were
                                    divided **m-ottâ** instead of **mo-ttâ**)

28.6 /CV'/ outside of Verbs

The /CV'/ reduplication can be found (sporadically) on nouns and locatives.
In the possessed form and with a plural possessor, it indicates plurality in the
possessed, virtually giving the meaning 'respective' or 'each of them':

Īnchān ōyàquê   *They went (to their single) home*
Īnchàchān ōyàquê   *They went home (each to his own)*

It is also found with certain "adjectives" (particularly **huēyi**) to indicate the
(factual rather than linguistic) plurality of the noun to which it applies:

Huèhuēyi in cuahuitl[2]   *The trees are (all) big*

It is found in an expressive sense with certain nouns for feelings:

Ca huēyi ààhuilli catca   *It was a great pleasure*

as well as with place names in **-tlâ** (24.4), without any perceptible change:

Yauh in īxòxōchitlâ   *He's going to his flower garden*

---

[2] It is of course still possible to say **huēyi in cuahuitl**.

28.7 /CV/ Reduplication

The third kind of reduplication has the form /CV/ (with a short vowel). Unlike the /CV:/ and above all the /CV'/ form, this one cannot be made freely with just any verb, but is restricted to certain types of formations. These involve expressive verbs that most often indicate physical phenomena (especially ones of light and sound). We have already met this sort of reduplication in "adjectives" like **totōnqui** 'hot', **cecēc** 'cold' and **chichīltic** 'red'. It is generally found with intransitive verbs ending in -**ca**, which have a corresponding transitive form ending in -**tza**, such as **popōca** 'emit smoke' (referring to a thing) and **popōtza** 'make something smoke' (referring to a person):

Popōca in tepētl	*The mountain's giving off smoke*
Mochān tlapopōca	*There is smoke at your (s.) place*
Nochān nitlapopōtza	*I'm making smoke at my place*

Most frequently, these pairs in -**ca**/-**tza** are quadrisyllabic and constitute expressive forms that correspond to an intransitive form without reduplication (and so trisyllabic) ending in -**ni** (see next section): **momoloca** 'bubble', **momolotza** 'make bubbly', **molōni** 'to be effervescent'. In front of this -**ni**, there is always a long vowel, which is shortened in the reduplicated forms. There are several dozen pairs of this sort, with a slight difference in meaning between the form in -**ni** and the reduplicated ones:

Cualāni	*It crackles, boils/he is angry, loses his temper*
Tlacuacualaca	*There's thunder, crackling, boiling*
Petlāni in teōcuitlatl	*Gold is shiny*
Pepetlaca in teōcuitlatl	*The gold is glittering*
Molōni in ātl	*The water is flowing*
Momoloca in ātl	*The water is bubbling, frothing*
Nitlamomolotza	*I make eddies (in the water)*
Calāni in tepoztli	*The iron clatters*
Tlacacalaca	*There's a tinkling noise*
Āquin tlacacalatza?	*Who's making this clattering noise?*
Chipīni in ātl	*The water is dripping*
Chichipica in ātl	*The water is dripping (in quantity)*
Xitlachichipitza	*Pour (s.) it in drops*

With a few nouns, this sort of reduplication refers to a "fake" thing, that is, the copy of a real one, for example, **coconētl** 'doll' (from **conētl** 'child').

Inin cihuāpiltōntli huel quipiya in īcoconēuh	*That little girl takes good care of her doll*

28.8 Verbs in -*ni*

Verbs in -**ni** are quite numerous, and the great majority (though not all of them) belong to the triplets seen in the preceding section (this -**ni** should not be confused with the marker of the -**ni** form; there are actually forms with both endings like **cualānini** 'irritable'). These forms also have a morphological peculiarity of their own in that the semi-causative is not predictable and can be in -**na** or –**nia**, and there is also the possibility of a regular causative in -**naltia** (the dictionary has to be checked). Thus:

Cotōni in mecatl	*The string snaps in two*
Niccotōna in ichtli	*I snap the thread in two*
Coyōni in āmatl	*The paper has a hole in it*
Ticcoyōniâ in tenāmitl	*We're making a hole in the wall*
Xitīni in calli	*The house collapses*
Ticxitīniâ in calli	*We pull the house down*
Pozōni in ātl	*The water's boiling*
Nicpozōnaltia in ātl	*I'm boiling the water (making it boil)*
Cuepōni in xōchitl	*The flowers are blossoming*
Nimitzcuepōnaltia	*I sing your praises (make you bloom)*

28.9 *Nequi* as Auxiliary

To say 'I want to VERB' (i.e., when the subject of 'want' and the infinitive are the same), a frequent expression involves adding **nequi** as an auxiliary to the *future* form (without the participial suffix):

Nimiquiznequi	*I want to die*
Nitlacuāznequi	*I want to eat*
Ticcuāznequî in nacatl	*We want to eat the meat*

The auxiliary can be put in any tense:

Ōnitlacuāznec	*I wanted to eat*

In the honorific, only the first verb is affected:

Cuix timotlacualtīznequi?	*Do you (s.) want to eat (hon.)?*

In place of this expression with the auxiliary, it is also possible to use a noun clause in the same sense (see Lesson 30).

▶ *Note*. When used as an auxiliary, **nequi** often has a meaning that is not exactly the same as that of 'want' and instead has the sense of an "immediate" future, 'to be about to VERB, to be on the point of VERBing':

Ye patlāniznequi in tōtōtl	*The bird is getting ready to fly*
Chōcaznequi in piltōntli	*The small child is about to cry*

28.10 *Mati, Toca, (Nè)nequi*

The verbs **mati, toca** and **nequi** (or **nènequi**) have common characteristics in terms of certain types of compounds that we are about to look at. In these compounds, **mati** means 'consider/take to be …', **toca** 'to (wrongly) consider to be …, to claim to be …'[3] and **(nè)nequi** 'to pretend to be …'. The element that appears in front of the auxiliary is a quality of the object, so the reflexive prefix is used if the sense is 'I believe myself to be …', 'you believe that you …' or 'I claim to …'. The methods of making the compound are:

(1) with a noun

This is simple object incorporation (17.3.1):

Nicteōmati in totēucyo	*I consider our Lord to be God*
Cuix timoteōtoca?	*Do you take yourself for a god?*
Inìquê on tlācâ ca tlateōtocanimê	*Those people are idolaters (people who take things to be God)*

(2) with an intransitive verb

This involves incorporation of the -cā- form (27.7), with the same meaning as the preceding:

Nimitzcualāncāmati	*I believe, feel you to be angry*
Ōnicmiccātocaca	*I had thought him dead*
Ninomiccānequi *or* ninomiccānènequi	*I'm pretending to be dead*

(3) with a transitive verb

The incorporated verb is in base 4. There are two usages:

(a) 'I believe that X is VERBed'. Here we have the object prefix corresponding to X (**nimitz-, nic-, nino-** etc.):

Nictelchīhualmati in Pedro	*I consider Peter to be despised, that he is despised*
Ninotelchīhualmati	*I think that I'm despised*
Motelchīhualtoca	*He imagines himself to be despised*
Ninonōtzalnequi	*I pretend to be called*

(b) 'I believe that I (active) VERB'. The compound is bitransitive (17.1) and has to take a reflexive (the subject of the verb of 'belief' and the other verb being the same):

---

[3] As an independent word, **toca** means 'follow', with the meaning 'believe, assert' found only in compounds. The compound **neltoca** (**nelli** 'true thing') means 'believe' (rightly or wrongly): **nicneltoca in motlàtōltzin** 'I believe what you say'. This verb must not be confused with **tōca** 'bury, sow'.

| Àmo nicnochīhualtoca | *I don't imagine that I'm doing it* |
| Àmo nicnomachitoca[4] | *I don't imagine that I know it* |

With (**nè**)**nequi**, we can have the derivational form in -**cā**- in this pattern:

Àmo nicnocaccānènequi in ītlàtōl   *I pretend not to hear his words*[5]

In other words, if the verb put in this compound construction is transitive, its agent must either be indefinite ('I believe that X is VERBed, that people VERB X', which is 3a) or identical with the subject of the auxiliary ('I believe that I VERB X', which is 3b). In both instances, the object X is represented by a prefix. In 3b there is also a reflexive, which represents the subject of the compounded transitive (because it is necessarily identical with the subject of the auxiliary); in 3a the single object may also be reflexive if the subject of the compounded verb is the same as that of the auxiliary ('I consider myself to be VERBed').

The verb put in the compound may be bitransitive. In this instance, its subject must be either indefinite or identical with the subject of the auxiliary ('I believe that I'm given...', 'I claim to be given...'). For example:

Cuix ticmomactoca in tlàtòcāyōtl?   *Do you (s.) want to be given the kingdom ?*

In the case where the subject of the main verb is neither indefinite nor identical with the subject of the auxiliary, use of this sort of compound is precluded, and a noun clause (Lesson 31) must be used.

28.11 -tlani

The auxiliary -**tlani** poses problems that resemble the ones treated in the previous section. This verb exists independently in the form **ìtlani** 'ask for':

| Cuix itlâ tiquìtlani? | *Do you (s.) want something? do you have a request to make?* |
| Miyac in tēchìtlaniliâ in caxtiltēcâ | *The Spaniards ask us for many things* |

In compounds, -**tlani** (-**lani** after **l**) means 'want' and often appears as a somewhat "stronger" variant of the causative. As we will see, there is some uncertainty in the construction of this compound. Two cases must be considered:

(1) use with an intransitive verb
     This usage is rather restricted. The most frequent forms are **miqui-tlani** 'want someone to die' and **nen-tlani** 'want s.o. to live'. If the subject of the

---

[4] The form -**machi**- is irregular (we would expect -**mach**- from the passive **macho**).
[5] And not 'I don't pretend to hear'. It is not the auxiliary but the main verb that the negation pertains to.

first verb is different from that of -**tlani**, its subject appears in the form of an *object* prefix:

| Quimiquitlani | *He wants him to die* |
| Nicnentlani | *I want him to live* |

If the subject is the same as that of -**tlani**, the preceding construction is used with the appropriate reflexive prefix:

| Àmo momiquitlaniya | *He didn't want to die (want himself to die)* |
| Ninonentlani | *I want to live* |

A passive version of this construction can be formed:

| Miquitlano | *Some people want him to die* |

(2) use with a transitive verb
In this usage, the agent of the first verb is always indefinite ('I want X VERBed', 'I want someone to VERB X'), and there is a great diversity in contructions. The first verb generally appears in base 4 (the passive stem minus -**hua** or -**o**), but base 2 is at times used.

Sometimes, the only object marked is the patient of the first verb, with the agent going unmarked. The most common use of this construction is when the patient of the first verb is identical to the subject of the auxiliary ('I want to be VERBed'):

Ninopalēhuīllani	*I want to be helped*
Mottallani, melēhuīllani inon cihuātl (and not ****motēittallani**, etc.)	*That woman wants to be seen and desired*
Ayāc mocotōntlani (*or* mocotōnallani)	*No one wants to be cut* (i.e., *no one wants a part of himself cut off*, said by a man asked to give up his son)

It is also possible for the single object (the patient of the first verb) to be different from the subject of -**tlani**:

| Nicchīhuallani (*or* nicchīuhtlani) in teōcalli | *I want (someone) to build the church, I want the church built* |

This is the regular construction when the first verb has an inanimate patient, and it is noteworthy that the agent of the first verb is left unexpressed.

In another construction, the agent of the first verb is marked. Thus, the compound verb is bitransitive, with a definite object prefix for the patient of the first verb and an indefinite prefix for its agent. The only form attested in the texts for this indefinite agent is **ne-** (Carochi, the generally reliable grammarian of the seventeenth century, gives examples with **tē-**).

> Nicnenōtzallani (*or* nictēnōtzallani)   *I ask someone to call Peter*
>   in Pedro

The texts attest this construction only with an animate patient for the first verb, but Carochi cites an example with an inanimate object for the first verb:

> Nictēchīhuallani in tlaxcalli   *I want people to make tortillas*

(As noted earlier, the regular construction leaves the agent unmarked if the patient is inanimate.)

> ▶ *Note.* This construction with an indefinite agent and definite patient for the first verb can be used to remedy a problem with the causative system. As you may recall, with a causative verb, an indefinite object marker can only be governed by the underlying verb and not by the causative. That is, **nictēnōtzaltia in Pedro** can only mean 'I have Peter call someone' and not 'I have someone call Peter'. The construction with **-tlani** is not subject to such a restriction and thus can act as a way to express this sort of indefinite causation:

> Quinnōtzâ, quinnenōtzallanî in tlàtòquê   *They summon the rulers, They have someone*
>   *summon the rulers*

This thought could not have been expressed with the causative **nōtzaltia** (i.e., **quintēnōtzaltiâ in tlàtòquê** could only mean 'they have the rulers summon people').

VOCABULARY

Nouns

(à)āhuilli	*pleasure, fun, joy*	cuezcomatl	*cuezcomate*[6]
		tepoztli	*workable metal*
cintli	*ear of corn*		*(copper or iron)*[7]

---

[6] A large jar used for storing corn.
[7] Not to be confused with **tepotztli** 'shoulder'.

Intransitive verbs

calāni (/R–ka/, s-c **ia**)[8] *to make a sound*

chipīni (/R–ka/, s-c **ia**) *to drip, to trickle*

coyōni (/R–ka/, s-c **ia**) *to be pierced, to have holes*

molōni (/R–ka/, s-c **ia**) *to flow, to bubble*

petlāni (/R–ka/, s-c **ia**) *to shine*

pozōni (/R–ka/, s-c **ia**) *to boil*[9]

Transitive verbs

āhuiltia *to amuse, to please (m(o)-: to be pleased, to have fun)*

ìtlani *to ask for (-tlani in comps.)*

nānquilia *to answer*[10]

telchīhua *to despise*

toca *to follow (to believe in comps.)*

yāōtla *to make war on*

Locative

netech *near*

EXERCISES

(a) Translate into English.
1. Àmo huēhuèca in Mēxìco īhuān in Xōchimīlco.
2. Nōhuiyān càcalaquî.
3. Huel ōtinēchmàmāuhtî.
4. Àmo nēciznequi: zan motlàtlātìtinemi.
5. Nitlāhuāna in huèhuēyi ilhuitl īpan.
6. Quihuīcâ in tiyàcāhuān in īnchìchīmal.
7. Nictètēmòtiuh in Pedro.
8. Xìxitīni in calli.
9. Ōniquincuīlî in īntlàtlaxcal.
10. Cēcenxihuitl huālmocuepa.
11. Ōnictzauccātocaca in puerta.
12. Àmo nimitzyāōmati.
13. Tlapechco onoca, zan mococoxcānènequiya.

---

[8] /R–ka/ means that for this verb there is a corresponding expressive verb with reduplication and -**ca** (28.7), and hence a corresponding quasi-causative in -**tza**; "s-c -**ia**" means that the semi-causative ends in -**ia** (28.8).

[9] Though both verbs are translated as 'to boil', **pozōni** designates the action itself, while **cualāni** refers to the accompanying sound of bubbling.

[10] This verb behaves like a semi-applicative, see 20.9 and 31.7.

14. Nicmictlani in noyāōuh.
15. Tlein ticchīhuaznequi? Cuix tiquīznequi octli?

(b) Translate into Nahuatl.
1. Prepare yourselves, warriors!
2. I've cut various flowers.
3. There was a round-up ("people were taken here and there").
4. We live close to each other.
5. He's dozing ("he's sleeping off and on").
6. The one (25.3) is smiling, the other is whimpering.
7. The rocks are falling on all sides.
8. They're putting on their belts ("are each binding themselves"; 28.5).
9. Bring this water to the boil.
10. They recognized him as king.
11. He had the prisoners killed (28.10).
12. He doesn't want to answer.
13. Does Peter want to come?
14. He wants to be loved.
15. He imagines that he's being abandoned ("believes himself to be abandoned").
16. He's pretending to cry.

Derivative Verbs

29.1 Verbs from Non-Verbal "Adjectives" in -c

"Adjectives" in -c that are not derived from verbs (12.6–7) produce two types of derived verbs.

29.1.1 Intransitive Derived Verbs in -ya

These verbs have a stative or inchoative meaning ('to be …', 'to become …'):

Iztāya in tepētl	*The mountain is/becomes white*
Ye xocōya in mōlli	*The mole is becoming sour*
Nocamac tlachichiya	*I've got a bitter taste in my mouth*
Celiya in cuahuitl	*The tree is turning green (**celic** 'fresh, green')*

This final -ya (which must not be confused with the imperfect, as the verbs under discussion here can be put into any tense) is generally treated as a verb with a vowel-retaining preterite (8.7) and so usually has a preterite in -yac:

Huel ōiztāyac in tepētl	*The mountain has become all white*
Ōcoztiyac in xihuitl	*The plant has become yellow*

However, these forms in -ya can also found treated as vowel-dropping preterites (8.3) with the now final -y turning into -x or –z (8.4): ōiztāz (rather than ōiztāx), ōcoztix (cf. cocoxqui 'sick' from cocoya).

29.1.2 Transitive Derived Verbs in -lia

These are the corresponding semi-causatives ('to make …'):

Ōquimiztālî in cepayahuitl in tētepê	*The snow has made the mountains white*
Inin quixocōlīz, quichichilīz in mōlli	*This is going to make the mole sour, bitter*
In nèhuātl ca aīc ōnimitzcocōlî, tleīca tinēchcocōlia?	*For my part, I've never hated you (made you sorrowful), why do you hate me?*

These two suffixes -**ya** and -**lia** (used reflexively) are also added to **huēyi** with the same sense:

Ye ōhuēyiyaquê (*or* ōhuēyixquê) in mopilhuān	*Your (s.) children have already gotten big*
Mohuēyiliâ	*They boast (lit., make themselves big)*

29.2 *-ti*

All nouns stems can take the suffix -**ti**. This is used to form intransitive verbs meaning 'to act the…', 'to be temporarily…', 'to behave/act like/as…', 'to become…':

Nipōchtēcati	*I engage in commerce, act as a merchant*
Ca ōneltic	*It turned out to be true*
Otztiticâ in nocihuāuh	*My wife is pregnant (acting in the capacity of pregnant woman)*
Àmo cualtizquê, àmo yēctizquê	*They won't reform (become good and virtuous)*
Cuetzpalti	*He acts like a glutton*
Yāōpan ōnimaltic	*I became a prisoner in war*

The verbs **tlācati** 'to be born (become a person)' and **tlazòti** 'to be valuable, esteemed, loved' (**tlazòtli** 'valuable thing, dear person') clearly belong to this class.

"Agent nouns" derived from the preterite or the -**ni** form regularly have the -**cā**- variant of the participial suffix in front of -**ti**:

Niteōpixcāti	*I carry out the functions of a priest*
Mexìco tlàtòcāt in Motēuczōma	*Moctezuma ruled in Mexico*

In certain cases, the sense of such derivatives is not 'to act in the manner of…' but 'to accomplish…'. Thus:

Nitequiti	*I work (accomplish **tequitl**)*

The suffix -**ti** can be added to numbers, adverbs and locatives (except those in -**c(o)**):

Ca ye teōtlacti	*He's now late*
Cuix timōztlatizquê, tihuīptlatizquê?	*Will we arrive by tomorrow or later?*
Ōnēntic in notequiuh	*My work was fruitless, was performed in vain*
Cētî	*They unite (become as one)*

29.3 *-tic, -tiya, -tilia*

We have already spoken (12.6) of "adjectives" in -**tic** of the type **cuauhtic** 'tall, high' (like a tree, **cuahuitl**), **tlīltic** 'black' (like ink, **tlīlli**). Strictly speaking, these forms are the preterites of verbs in -**ti** derived from nouns. Nonetheless, the suffix -**tic** is retained as such even after a vowel:

Tetic (*pl.* tetiquê)   *(He is) petrified, hard as a rock (we would*
                                        expect ****tetqui**, *pl.* ****tetquê)**

but

(Ō)tet   *He became petrified (pl.* **(ō)tetquê)**

That is, if a noun stem to which -**ti** is added ends in a consonant, it has a vowel-retaining preterite (8.7) and an identical adjectival form, but if the stem ends in vowel, it has a regular vowel-dropping preterite (as we would expect, 8.3), but the corresponding adjectival form has the same ending -**tic** as the forms based on consonant stem (i.e., it retains the full form of the ending). Thus, alongside the regular preterite (ō)**tlācat** 'he was born', we also have the adjectival **tlācatic** '(he is) human'.

These "adjectives" in -**tic** can take the suffixes -**ya** and -**lia** (29.1.1–2). Verbs in -**tiya** are basically no different from those in -**ti**, but perhaps they are more clearly inchoative ('start to …'):

Tetiya inin tlaxcalli   *These tortillas are in the process of hardening*
Ātiya in cetl   *The ice is melting (**ātic** 'be like water', i.e.,*
                                        liquid or transparent)

Verbs in -**tilia** function simply as causatives to those in -**ti**. It is not possible to have -**ti** followed by -**tia** (just as it is impossible to have -**tia** twice in a row; see 19.10):

Quitetilia in cihuātl in nextamalli   *The woman is making the corn meal harden*
                                        (become like stone)
Cātilia in tōltēcatl in tepoztli   *The craftsman makes the iron melt (turns it*
                                        into liquid: **c-ā-tilia**)
Tētōchtilia, tēmazātilia in octli   *Pulque makes people stupid (lit., makes them*
                                        become rabbits and deer)
Ca ōnimitztlācatilî in nimonān   *I, your mother, have given birth to you*
Niquincētilīz   *I'll unite them, reconcile them (make them*
                                        one)

29.4 Verbs with Possessive Prefixes

Certain verbs in -**ti** are built on possessed forms in various persons. These are:

(1) **nopanti, mopanti, īpanti** etc. 'it happens to me, you (s.), him' etc. (lit. 'it takes place on me, you ...') from **nopan, mopan, īpan** etc.:

Tlein nopantiz?	*What will become of me?*
Tlein topantiz?	*What will become of us?*

(2) three almost synonymous verbs: **nolhuilti, nomàcēhualti, nocnōpilti** (**molhuilti, momàcēhualti** etc.). The first two are derived from **ilhuilli, màcēhualli** 'payment, favor, merit'; the third comes from **icnōpilli** 'orphan' but also 'favor'. These forms basically mean 'such a thing becomes my (your, his) reward'. This can be rendered in English as 'I'm worthy of ...', 'I deserve ...', which may give the misleading impression that we're dealing with irregular verbs in which the subject is indicated with a possessive prefix.

In the present, the nominal form is generally used rather than the derived verb:

Àmo nolhuil, àmo nomàcēhual in monāhuac nitlacua	*I'm not worthy of eating beside you (s.), I don't deserve to eat ...*
Àmo tocnōpil in ōmpa tiyāzquê in ilhuicac	*We don't deserve to go to heaven*

For the other tenses, it is necessary to use the verbal version:

Àzo itlâ momàcēhualtiz	*Perhaps you'll (s.) have some reward (lit., there will be some reward of yours)*
Cuix nocnōpiltiz, nomàcēhualtiz in motētlazòtlaliztzin?	*Will I have the happiness, the favor of your (s.) love? (lit., will your love become my merit?)*
Mā nocnōpilti, nomàcēhualti in motētlazòtlaliztzin	*Deign (s.) to grant me your love (may your love be my favor, my recompense)*

(3) the verb **ōnotlahueliltic** (**ōmotlahueliltic** etc.), which is derived from an otherwise unattested noun that must have meant something like 'misfortune'. The exact sense of the verb (always in the preterite) is 'this is my misfortune', which is translated with 'poor me', 'how miserable I am' etc.:

Īyoyahue ōnotlahueliltic!	*Alas, woe is me!*
Ōtotlahueliltic in timēxìcâ!	*How wretched we Mexica are!*

▶ *Notes*

(1) With possessive prefixes in the plural, the verb remains in the singular (since the real subject of the verb is a noun signifying merit, misfortune etc.).

(2) Also note the exceptional formation of **nopani, mopani** etc. 'it suits me, you ...' (said, e.g., of a piece of clothing).

29.5 -tia

Derived verbs in -**tia** can be built on noun stems. Such verbs can be:

(1) transitive

These mean 'to equip, to furnish, to supply someone with ...':

Ōnēchcaltî in notàtzin	*My father provided me with a house*
Cuix timocaltīznequi?	*Do you want to get yourself a house?*
Ninonāmictia	*I get married (provide myself with a spouse,* nāmictli*)*
In Dios tēchmāxcātīlia, tēchmotlatquitīlia	*God endows us with property and possessions* (honorific forms for **tēchāxcātia, tēchtlatquitia**)

A few nouns (especially **pilli, oquichtli** and **cihuātl**) can take a form of the possessive suffix (-**huā** after a consonant, -**uh** after a vowel) in this construction, and in this case, the object has to be reflexive:

Tlāllan in mopilhuātia	*She bears her young (gives herself her children) underground*
Huèca moquichhuātia	*She takes her husband from afar*
Huèca mocihuāuhtia	*He takes his wife from afar*

(2) bitransitive

These most often take a reflexive prefix and mean 'to take something/ someone as ...', 'to appropriate something/someone as one's own':

Xicmocalti in nocal	*Consider (s.) my house yours*
Nimitznochīmaltia	*I take you (s.) as my shield*
Quimāxcātia, quimotlatquitia in tēāxcā, in tētlatqui	*He appropriates other people's property, wealth (makes it his own)*
Nicnoteōtìtzinoa in Totēucyo	*I make Our Lord my God*

Such a form can be made passive (with the reflexive represented by -**ne**; see 18.5):

Miyaquintin tēteô neteōtīlōquê	*Many gods were venerated (considered as gods)*

Here too, certain noun stems take a version of the possessive suffix:

Ōmitzmotlācahuātî in ātl in tepētl	*The city has adopted you (take you to itself) as (its) servant* (**tlācatl**)
Ca achi ohuî in tinēchtequiuhtia	*The assignment you're (s.) giving me (what you give me as my task) is rather difficult*

(3) intransitive
This case is restricted to nouns indicating a length of time. Such verbs are
composed of a number and a noun like **xihuitl**, **mētztli** or **ilhuitl** (7.8) and
mean either 'to be so many years etc. old' or 'to spend such a period of time
somewhere':

Ye ēxiuhtia inin piltōntli	*This little child is already three years old*
Ōmpa cēxiuhtìquê	*They spent a year there*
Amochāntzinco nōmilhuitīz	*I'll be at your (pl.) place for two days*

▶ *Note.* The form **cuīcatia** (20.4) serves as the applicative of the verb **cuīca**
but is actually the transitive in **-tia** of the noun **cuīcatl**, meaning 'provide
someone with a song', that is, 'sing for them'.

29.6 Verbs Based on Nouns in *-yō*

The intransitive suffix **-hua** can be added to nouns that end in the abstract
suffix **-yō** (11.3). Verbs formed in this way mean 'to be full of...', 'to possess a
lot of...':

Āyōhua in tlālli	*The land abounds in water*
Azcayōhua in òtli	*The path is swarming with ants*
Ōtēnyōhuac, ōtōcāyōhuac	*He's attained (become full of) great fame,*
	great renown (name)

The corresponding semi-causative ('make to be full of...') is formed by adding
-tia to **-yō-**:

Ticāyōtia in mōlli	*You're (s.) making the mole watery*
Inon tlācatl motōcāyōtia Pedro[1]	*That person's name is Peter (gives himself the*
	name ...)

29.7 *-oa*

As we have seen, the suffix **-oa** regularly forms transitive verbs (semi-
causatives) corresponding to intransitives in **-ihui** or **-ahui** (19.8). It can also
be used to form *intransitive* verbs derived from nouns. This formation is much
rarer and is used only with stems ending in a consonant. These verbs mean
'make use of...', 'engage in an activity that puts... into operation':

Niteponāzoa	*I drum, play the **teponāztli** (a sort of drum)*
Nitlaxcaloa	*I make tortillas (**nitlaxcalchīhua** is much*
	more common)
Mōztla nitiyānquizōz	*I'll do the shopping tomorrow*

---

[1] For this construction, see 32.4, 2.

29.8 -huia

This suffix is frequently used to form verbs from noun stems. The general meaning of these verbs is to 'apply ... to someone/something'. From this starting point, numerous developments in meaning are possible, such as 'put ... on/in something', 'make use of ... to deal with something/someone', 'to strike with blows of ...', 'to transport/convey by means of ...'. Frequently, English will convert the noun into a verb (sometimes adding a suffix). Thus:

Cāmahuiâ in tetl	*They wrap the stones in paper (paper the stones)*
Ōniquezhuî in notilmâ	*I've gotten blood on my cape (bloodied my cape)*
Quimīxhuia in cīcitlāltin	*He observes (eyes) the stars*
Ticmātlahuiâ in tōtōtl	*We catch birds with nets (**mātlatl**) (net the birds)*
Tictlacomolhuiâ in miztli	*We trap the puma (by making a **tlacomolli** hole for the puma to fall into)*
Xictlālhui in cōhuātl micqui	*Throw (s.) dirt on the dead snake*
Nicchīlhuīz in mōlli	*I'll put chili powder in the mole*
Cācalhuiâ in quilitl, in tomātl	*They transport the quelite (an edible grass) and tomatoes by boat (cf. the English verbs 'to ship', 'to truck')*
Tictlapechhuīzquê in cocoxqui	*We'll convey the sick man by litter (bed)*

The meaning can be close to that of verbs in **-yō-tia** (29.6), so that **nicchīlhuia** 'I put chili powder in it' could also be expressed as **nicchīllōtia**. However, the "application" indicated by a verb in **-huia** generally signifies an effect on the outside of the object: **tlālhuia** 'put earth on', **tlāllōtia** 'fill with earth'.

29.9 -tla

A final type of transitive verb derived from a noun is in **-tla**. This type is relatively rare and means 'to consider as ...'.[2] **Tlazòtla** 'to love' is a very common member of this series, and so are:

Niquicnīuhtla	*I consider him my friend (note the possessive suffix on the noun; cf. 29.5)*
Nicyāōtla	*I consider him a foe, make war on him*

---

[2] Formally, this ending appears to be the semi-causative corresponding to **-ti** (/ta/ regularly shifts to /λa/, but the sense is somewhat different from that of a semi-causative.

VOCABULARY

Intransitive verbs

nopani, mopani, etc.	*suits me, you…*	tiyānquizoa	*to go shopping*

Transitive verb

cocolia   *to hate*

Nouns

cepayahuitl	*snow*	quilitl	*quelite* (edible green)
icnōpilli	*orphan (pl. /tin/), merit, favor*	teponāztli (sort of drum)	
ilhuilli	*favor, payment*	tētlazòtlaliztli	*love*
màcēhualli[3]	*merit, dignity*	tlacomolli	*ditch, hole*
mātlatl	*net*	tlahuēlilli (only in the derived	
miztli (*pl.* /-tin/, /R–tin/)	*cougar, mountain lion, puma*	**ōnotlahuēliltic** etc., 'poor me…')	
nextamalli	*nixtamal, corn meal*		

Adjective

celic   *fresh, green*

Interjection

iyoyahue   *alas!*

EXERCISES

(a) Translate into English.
1. Xiquimmocnīuhti in caxtiltēcâ.
2. Mā ticēticān.
3. Quixōchihuia, quiquetzalhuia in ītilmâ.
4. Ōninozoquihuî in īpan òtli.
5. In Malintzin huel īpani in īcuē.
6. Ca huel tecpinyōhua in notlapech.
7. Quēn nicān tlatōcāyōtīlo? – Titlatōcāyōtiâ Chapōltepēc.
8. Īpaltzinco in Dios ōtitlàtòcātīlōquê.
9. Ca huel tēcocô tētolīnî, in yālhua ōnopantic!
10. Ōninotlehuî, ōninomàpillatî.

(b) Translate into Nahuatl.
1. How miserable we sinners are!
2. This lake (water) is full of fish.

---

[3] Not to be confused with **mācēhualli** 'macehual, commoner'.

3. The craftsman plates the necklace with gold.
4. He strikes the iron with (blows of) a stone.
5. If only I had deserved the love of God ("if it had been my due ...")!
6. Everything's turning green all over the place, the earth is abounding in flowers.
7. Here in the town I act as teacher.
8. He has been ennobled (made to become a noble).
9. We walk on foot ("we apply feet to things").
10. You (s.) are my protector ("I take you as my father and as my mother").

Derivative Nouns

30.1 Action Nouns

Every verb can have a corresponding "action noun" that designates the process or action signified by that verb. In English, this concept can be expressed with the infinitive ('to VERB') or the "gerund" (i.e., 'VERBing', a nominal form which should not be confused with the formally identical present participle), though some verbs borrowed from Latin have a form ending in "-ion" (e.g., from 'to form', 'to act', we have 'formation' and 'action' as well as 'forming' and 'acting'); sometimes the concept is expressed simply with a related noun ('hate/hatred' for 'to hate', 'murder' for 'to kill'). The Nahuatl version ends in -z-tli or -li-z-tli.

It seems that in the distant past -ztli was added to intransitive verbs and -liztli to transitives. By the Classical period, however, the -liztli variant had been generalized, with only a few verbs in -i retainin the noun in -ztli (e.g., **miquiztli** 'death', **māhuiztli** 'fear, respect', **ciyahuiztli** 'fatigue') and forms like **miquiliztli** already attested.

If the verb is transitive, the action noun in -liztli has to take an indefinite object prefix (**tē-**, **tla-**, **ne-**) or an incorporated noun (17.3):

Ōnēntic in nociyahuiz, in notlatequipanōliz	*My exhaustion (**ciyahui,** 'get tired'), my toil have proved to be in vain*
Nicmati in āmapōhualiztli, in tlàcuilōliztli	*I know reading (book-reading) and writing*
Mā nomàcēhualti in motēpalēhuīliztzin	*May I deserve your assistance!*
Īc mochīhuaz in Pedro īnenāmictīliz?	*When will Peter's marriage (from **mo-nāmictia** 'get married') take place?*

As can be seen, the ending -liztli is in principle added to base 3, but there can be a few modifications. A final -ci in the verb shifts to -xi (e.g., **tlaàxiliztli** 'achieving something' from **àci**). With verbs ending in /ka/ (-ca) and /wa/ (**hua**), the final vowel of the stem may shift to /i/ (e.g., **chōquiliztli** or **chōquiztli** 'crying', neàhuiliztli 'quarrel(ing)' from **mo-àhua** 'quarrel'). As for **câ**, its action noun is regularly **yeliztli** 'nature, essence, situation.'

Nouns in **-liztli** can be derived from the stem of "adjectives" in **-c** (12.8, 29.1). Thus, **cocoliztli** 'illness, disease' is derived from the stem **coco-** (which gives **cocoya, cocoxqui** etc.) and not from the verb **cocoa** (which can, for its part, give **tēcocōliztli** 'doing harm').

Action nouns can be put into the same sorts of compounds and derivations as regular nouns:

Àmo cualnemilicê	*He doesn't have a good character* (i.e., *good way of living;* for the ending, see 11.6–7)
Cuix ōtimonemilizcuep?	*Have you changed your way of life?* (see 17.3.2)
Ye tlacualizpan	*It's already time to eat* (for the sense of **-pan**, see 13.5)
Ca māhuiztic tlācatl	*He's a respectable person* (see 12.6)
Nō nèhuātl nicmāhuiztla	*I too revere him* (see 29.9)
Ōpoliuh in tomāhuizzo	*Our honor has been lost* (see 11.3–4)

▶ *Note.* In the distant past, there must have been a formation in **(li)ztli** for transitive verbs without object prefixes. This had the meaning of the passive **-ni** form (16.6), but there were only a few isolated remnants of the formation in the Classical period: e.g., **chīhualiztli** 'doable (thing)', **ittaliztli** 'visible (thing)' and **caquiztli** 'audible (thing)', with the last noun giving the very common derivative verb **caquizti** 'make oneself heard', lit., 'become audible'.

30.2 Object Nouns: Regular Formation

An object noun can be formed from any *transitive* verb, and such a noun indicates either the result of an action or the thing or person directly affected by it. Object nouns derived from any transitive verb always have the prefix **tla-**, even if they refer to a human being (but see 30.3). They are morphologically clearly related to the impersonal form (15.7). The absolute form of object nouns is then built by adding the ending **-tli/-li** to base 4 but also sometimes to base 2.

This means that most commonly, they end in **–l-li**, and we've already encountered such nouns in **tlacualli** 'food', **tlaīlli** 'drink, beverage',[1] **tlaxcalli** 'tortilla' (from **ixca** 'to bake'), **tlàtlacōlli** 'fault, sin' (**ìtlacoa** 'harm'), **tlàtōlli** 'word, speech, language', **tlapōhualli** 'countable, thing to be counted', **tlaōlli** 'corn' (which comes from the ancient verb **oa** 'shuck' preserved in the Classical

---

[1] Even though the impersonal of **i** is **tlaīhua** and not ****tlaīlo**.

period in the form **oya**[2]). Similarly, **tlàcuilōlli** 'writing,'[3] **tlachīhualli** 'work, creation', **tlatlazòtlalli** 'person/thing loved', **tlacāhualli** 'legacy, deposit' (what is left behind), **tlaināyalli** 'hidden thing'.

Object nouns can also be derived from base 4 stems that do not use the suffix **-l** (15.4 sec. 2). Thus:

tlatectli	*something cut, scar* (from **tequi** *to cut*)
tlatquitl	*good(s), possession* (from **itqui** *to carry*)
tlàmachtli	*embroidered item* (from **ìmati** *to do something deftly*)

Because some verbs have doublets in the passive/impersonal form (15.5), doublets are possible in the object noun:

tlapèpenalli/tlapèpentli	*chosen one* (**pèpena** *choose*)
tlatlāzalli/tlatlāxtli	*thing thrown* (from **tlāza**)

Such doublets exist in object nouns derived from verbs that end in **–hua** or **–ya** (although these only have **–lo** to form the passive/impersonal):

tlachīhualli/tlachīuhtli	*work, thing made*
tlacāhualli/tlacāuhtli	*deposit*
tlaināyalli/tlaināxtli	*thing hidden*
tlapōhualli/tlapōuhtli	*thing counted*

In these doublets, the **–l-li** form is usually more frequent. However, from **mana** 'spread out, present', the most common object noun is **tlamantli** 'thing, object'. From **quēmi** 'put on (clothes)', come both **tlaquēmitl** and a somewhat anomalous **tlaquēntli** 'clothes, garment'.

The meaning of these object nouns can potentially reflect all the various tenses and voices that the original verb can take. Thus, **tlapōhualli** can be interpreted as 'what has been counted' (the most frequent interpretation) on the basis of the verbal form **pōhualōc** (or perhaps **mopōuh**, cf. 15.9), as 'what can be counted' from **pōhualōni**, as 'what is counted' from **pōhualo** (**mopōhua**), or as 'what is going/has to be counted' **pōhualōz** (**mopōhuaz**).

English does not have a direct equivalent for this formation. Sometimes, the gerund or other sorts of verbal noun used to translate the action noun of 30.1 have also developed a sense equivalent to the object noun. For instance, 'stuffing' can designate both the act of stuffing (sticking one thing into another) and the food produced by being stuffed into a turkey before cooking. The

---

[2] In the Classical period, **tlaōlli** is used only of shucked corn (the emerging corn plant is called **tōctli**, green cobs are called **elōtl** and dry corn that is to be kept and shucked is **centli/cintli**).

[3] Not the act of writing, which is **tlàcuilōliztli**, but the thing written (e.g., 'the writing on the page is hard to read').

Nahuatl noun can be used in an attributive construction in which it is best rendered with the past participle in English:

Ōztōc câ tlaināyalli (*or* tlaināxtli) teōcuitlatl   *There's gold hidden in the cave*
Inin notech tlacāhualli   *This was deposited with me*

▶ *Note.* In the possessed form, the "possessor" of action nouns and object nouns is generally to be interpreted as the subject of the verb from which the noun is derived. Thus, **notlachīhual** is 'my work, my creation' (what I made). This interpretation is not obligatory, however, particularly with object nouns. **Notlaxcal** does not imply that I made the tortilla in question myself, and I can perfectly well own a **tlàcuilōlli** (drawing or piece of writing) that I would call **notlàcuilōl** without being the person who draw or wrote it.

30.3 Other Ways to Form Object Nouns

In addition to the regular (productive) method described in the preceding section, there are various other formations, some with the same suffixes but without **tla-** and others with some prefix other than **tla-**. These forms cannot be made from just any verb, and their existence has to be verified in the dictionary.

(1) with **tē-**
These object nouns are derived from verbs that govern both a person affected by the action and the item conveyed to the human object through the action, such as **machtia** ('teach someone something'; see 19.5 for the peculiarities of this verbs construction). The noun with **tla-** indicates the *animate* object (beneficiary of the action), the noun with **tē-** indicates the the *inanimate* object (the thing conveyed). Thus, **tēmachtīlli** means 'assignment, lesson', and **tlamachtīlli** 'student' ('person taught'):

Xiccaqui in tēmachtīlli   *Listen (s.) to the lesson*
Timotlamachtīlhuān   *We're your (s.) students*

We have the same phenomenon with **nāhuatia** (for its construction, see 31.7), which means 'give someone an order': **tēnāhuatīlli** is an 'order', and **tlanāhuatīlli** designates the person to whom the order is given.

▶ *Note.* The explanation of this seemingly paradoxical procedure is that in form and meaning the object nouns are closely connected to the impersonal verb forms. For example, **tēmachtīlli** is what makes it possible to say **tēmachtīlo** 'people are educated', and hence is the 'thing taught', while **tlamachtīlli** is what makes it possible to say **tlamachtīlo** 'there's instruction', and hence is 'the person instructed'.

(2) with **ne-**

These nouns generally have more or less the meaning of an instrument noun (i.e., the thing with which the action is done) and are connected with the reflexive forms of the verb:

nechìchīhualli   *adornment* (what people **mochìchīhuâ** *adorn themselves* with; also note the alternative form **nechìchīuhtli** based on stem 2)

necuiltonōlli   *riches* (what people **mocuiltonoâ** *prosper* with)

nenōnōtzalli   *story* (what people **monōnōtzâ** *speak to each other* with)

nemachtīlli   *study, learning* (what happens when people **momachtiâ**)

With a bitransitive noun like **maca**, **nemactli** means 'gift' (the form **tētlamactli** is also found).[4]

(3) without prefix, from intransitive and naturally impersonal verbs

It can be said that these nouns represent the process itself. It is noteworthy that the verbs from which these nouns are formed generally do not have action nouns in -**(li)ztli**. Thus:

cuīcatl   *song*

èecatl   *wind*

quiyahuitl   *rain*

cepayahuitl   *snow* (cepayahui *it snows*)

yohualli   *night* (yohua *night falls*)

tōnalli   *daylight, heat* (also *day* in the divinatory **tōnalpōhualli** calendar)

tēmictli   *dream*

textli   *flour* (from **teci**)

(4) without prefix, from transitive verbs

This formation is totally unpredictable. Where it does exist, this is as a lexically fixed doublet of the noun in **tla-** (30.2), often with a specialized meaning, so that on the whole it is better to consider these formations separately from the verbs. Thus:

nahuatīlli   *instruction, order* (nahuatia *command*; see sec. 1)

piyalli   *deposit* (piya *guard*)

nāmictli   *spouse* (nāmiqui *meet*)

malli   *prisoner* (ma *take by hunting or fishing*)

màcēhualli   *deserts* (màcēhua *get what one deserves, do penance*)

pōhualli   *twenty* (lit., *count*; cf. tlapōhualli)

Cualli is most likely to be connected with **cua** (the original meaning would have been 'something edible'), and **quetzalli** 'feather, plumage' with **quetza** (etymologically, this would be 'something raised up', alongside **tlaquetzalli**,

---

[4] **Ītētlamac** is 'his gift' from the point of view of the giver ('what he gives'), and **īnemac** is the same thing from the point of view of the recipient ('what he is given').

which designates 'something set upright', such as a column). So too **tzacualli** 'pyramid' (**tzacua** 'close').

30.4 Nouns of State

We have already seen (12.8) that there are nouns in **-cā-yō-tl** that indicate a state or an abstract quality. Because **-cā-** is a variant of the participial suffix, it is possible to derive such nouns from verbs in base 2 (these nouns designate the state or quality associated with the "adjectives" or "agent nouns" based on the preterite, 12.5 and 16.1). Note in particular:

(1) With intransitive verbs, there are no problems. Such nouns indicate a state or what produces the state (cf. English 'living' as in 'make a living' = 'earn one's livelihood'). They are most commonly in the possessed form, which ends in **-ca** rather than **-cāyo** (12.8) if it is considered to be a state of the subject of the verb:

Ìciuhcā huītz in topoliuhca   *Our disappearance is coming quickly*
Nictēmòtinemi in noyōlca, in nonenca *I'm constantly looking for my subsistence*
                                      (what makes me live)

-cāyo can be used if, through an extension of meaning, the noun designates some physical manifestation. Thus, **tōnacāyōtl** means 'crop' (this sense is to be connected with the primary meaning of **tōna**, which is 'prosper, bear fruit'), and the possessed form 'our crop' is **totōnacāyo** (**totōnaca** would perhaps be 'our own prosperity').

(2) With transitive verbs, it is very uncommon to have this formation in the active, for instance **notlapixca** 'my position as guardian', **nonēuhca** (or **noneēuhca**) 'my ability to pick myself up' (often associated with **noyōlca**, **nonenca, nocochca** in the meaning 'my subsistence', see earlier discussion), **notlàtòcāyo** 'my kingdom'.

On the other hand, this formation is very common with the passive. These "nouns of state" in **-(l)ōca** are generally translated into English in the same way as action nouns, but in English there is an ambiguity about the relationship between the possessor and the noun that is not possible in Nahuatl. A phrase like 'the man's love' could be taken as meaning 'love that the man feels for someone else' or 'love felt for the man (by someone else)'. In Nahuatl, the action noun can only be used to signify the action of the *agent* of the underlying verb, while the noun of state is used to represent action that affects the *patient* of the underlying verb. Hence, **in oquichtli ītētlazòtlaliz** is 'the man's love (toward others)', and **in oquichtli ītlazòtlalōca** is '(someone else's) love of the man'. Another way to understand the passive nouns of state in terms of English is to think of them as corresponding to the idiom 'being VERBed', so that the Nahuatl phrase just cited would be interpreted as 'the man's being loved' (though such a turn of phrase is usually not a suitable translation). Thus:

Àmo ticcaqui in notēnōnōtzaliz	*You (s.) don't listen to my words of advice (to you)*
Àmo niccaqui in nonōnōtzalōca	*I don't listen to the words of advice given to me*
Àmo ōquittac in notētlàpalōliz	*He hasn't seen my greeting*
Niquìtōz in ītlàpalōlōcātzin tlàtòcācihuāpilli	*I'll say the Hail Mary (greeting of the Noble Queen)*

▶ *Notes*

(1) The locative **-tech** can be used to indicate the patient of an action noun, with the agent appearing as the possessor of the noun. Thus, **in notech ītētlazòtlaliz** is 'his love for me', and **in ītech notētlazòtlaliz** is 'my love for him'. (The straightforward way to express the latter would be **in ītlàzòtlalōca**, though of course this form lacks any indication of the agent.)

(2) All the nouns derived from verbs can be put in the honorific form, but the honorific applies to the *noun* (with the -tzin suffix). As we have learned (21.9), the honorific forms of the verb are never used in the formation of nouns.

(3) The **-cā** form derived from intransitive verbs can be used adverbially without possessor. Only certain verbs take this construction, however. Apart from **ìciuhcā** 'quickly, rapidly', which we saw earlier (from **ìcihui** 'hurry'), the most common such form is **pāccā** 'happily' (from **pāqui**). Note the retention of the final long vowel.

30.5 Thematic Nouns

There is a final sort of nouns derived from verbs. Based on verbs in **-hua** (12.5) or **-ni** (28.7–8), such nouns are obtained by removing these verbal suffixes and replacing them with the "thematic" suffix. In principle, this suffix takes the form /-k/, to which the absolutive suffix is added. The vowel in front of the suffix is short (whereas it's long in front of **-hua** and **-ni**).

Nouns formed in this way are close in meaning to both object nouns (30.2) and "adjectives" in the form of preterites. They designate an object (or part of an object) characterized by the notion contained in the verb. Thus, **patlactli** 'large, broad (thing)' (**patlāhua** 'broaden'), **tlapactli**[5] 'fragmented (thing)' (**tlapāni** 'break').

---

[5] Not to be confused with **tlapāctli** 'bathed (thing)', the regular object noun of **pāca**.

These nouns are quite uncommon in the independent form. They mostly appear either as the second element in a compound noun:

| tepatlactli | *large stone (broad instance of a stone)* |
| òpitzactli | *narrow path (narrow stretch of road)* |

or especially in the form of derivatives in **-tic** (12.6, 29.3). In the second case, an "adjective" in **-ctic** formed in this way is fully synonymous with those in **-huac** or **-nqui** (i.e., **-n(i)** + **-qui**):

pitzactic	*narrow* (= **pitzāhuac**)
chipactic	*clean, pure* (= **chipāhuac**)
patlactic	*broad* (= **patlāhuac**)
melactic	*right, just* (= **melāhuac**)
coyoctic	*pierced* (= **coyōnqui**)
yamactic	*soft* (= **yamānqui**)
tlapactic	*broken* (= **tlapānqui**)

It can happen that instead of /k/ (**c**), the suffix takes the form /c/ (**tz**), /č/ (**ch**), /s/ (**z**), /š/ (**x**). Such forms are quite rare and unpredictable, almost always having a doublet in which the suffix is /k/:

patlachtic	*broad* (= **patlactic**)
yamaztic	*soft* (= **yamānqui**)
melaztic	*right, just* (= **melactic**)

Also note **cualaxtli** 'rage, madness' (also **cualāntli**) and **popochtli** 'incense, perfume' (alongside **pōctli** 'smoke').

30.6 Delocative Nouns (Names for Inhabitants)

On the basis of place names are formed the names for the inhabitants of those places. The suffix is **-catl** (always pluralized in /-'/), which replaces **-co** and is added to **-tlâ**. Thus:

mēxìcatl	*Mexica, from Mexico*
xōchimīlcatl	*from Xochimilco*
chālcatl	*from Chalco*
cuauhtlàcatl	*savage (resident of the forest)*
ātlàcatl	*coastal dweller (someone who lives beside the water)*

With other suffixes, **-catl** combines with a variant form of each suffix. Place names in **-tlān**,[6] **-mān** (we have not seen these suffixes before because they only

---

[6] Don't confuse **-tlān** (with long ā and no ligature) with **-(ti-)tlan** (13.7).

form proper names for places) have inhabitant names in -**tēcatl** and -**mēcatl**:

Tepoztēcatl	*from* **Tepoztlān**
Tlaxcaltēcatl	*from* **Tlaxcala, Tlaxcallān**
Aztēcatl	*Aztec, from* **Aztlān** *(mythical place of origin of the Mexica)*
Caxtiltēcatl	*Spaniard* (**Caxtillān** is the Nahuatl modification of the Spanish **Castilla**).[7] The nouns **tōltēcatl** *craftsman* and **pōchtēcatl** *merchant* originally designated the inhabitants of **Tōllān** (Tula) and **Pōchtlān**
Ācōlmēcatl	*from* **Ācōlmān**

Nouns in -**pan** have a name for inhabitants in -**panēcatl**:

Tlacōpanēcatl	*from* **Tlacōpan** *(Tacuba)*

Nouns in -**cān** can have an inhabitant name in -**camēcatl**, e.g., **xāltocamēcatl** 'inhabitant of **Xāltocān**'. Because the majority of proper place names in -**cān** are derived from nouns designating people (possessive nouns in -**huâ, -ê, -yô**, see 11.6–8, or "agent nouns" in -**c, -qui**, see 16.1), it is these nouns that are used as the names for the inhabitants (i.e., the place name is derived from the common noun describing the inhabitants rather than the other way around). Thus, the inhabitants of Michoacan (**Michhuàcān**) are simply called **michhuàquê** (sing. **michhuâ**) 'fish people'.

The other locatives (-**ti-tlan, -nāhuac** etc.) do not have their own formations. The common nouns **tlācatl** 'person of...', **calcatl** 'who has a house in...' or **chanê** 'resident of...' are simply used in conjunction with the locative:

in Cuauhtitlan tlācâ	*people of Cuauhtitlan*
(*or* chānèquê *or* calcâ)	

In the first and second person, **tlācatl** can form a compound with the locative (and the subject prefix is placed in front of the compound): **ticuauhtitlantlācâ** 'we're from Cuauhtitlan'.

> ▶ *Note.* The nouns **tlālticpacayōtl** 'things on earth, earthly goods' and **ilhuicacayōtl** 'things in heaven' are remarkable formations. These are abstract nouns in -**yō** (11.3), and even though there are no "inhabitant nouns" ****tlālticpacatl** 'resident of the earth' (from the locative **tlālticpac** 'on earth') or ****ilhuicacatl** 'resident of heaven' (from **ilhuicac** 'in heaven'), the abstracts look as if they are built on such forms in the same way that **mēxìcayōtl** 'Mexica civilization' is based on **mexìcatl** ('resident of **Mexìco**').

---

[7] The Spanish forms 'español' and 'españoles' are also possible.

VOCABULARY

Intransitive verbs

caquizti	*to make oneself heard*	ciyahui	*to get tired*

Transitive verbs

cuiltōnoa	*to enrich, to gladden* (mo-: *to be rich, to be happy*)	màcēhua	*to deserve, to obtain* (mo-: *to do penance*)
ma	*to catch, to capture* (by hunting, fishing or in war)	nāhuatia	*to order, to command*[8]
		oya	*to shuck*

Nouns

comālli	*comal*[9]	popochtli	*incense, perfume*
cualaxtli	*rage, anger*	pōchtli	*smoke*
cualāntli	*ditto*	tōctli	*corn (plant)*
elōtl	*ear of corn*	tōnacāyōtl	*crop*
èecatl	*wind*	tzacualli	*pyramid*
māhuiztli	*fear, awe*	yohualli	*night*
nāhuatīlli	*order, command*		

Place names[10]

Ācōlmān	Tepoztlān	
Aztlān	Tōllān	*Tula*
Cuauhtitlān	Xāltōcān	

Adverbs

ìciuhcā	*quickly*	pāccā	*happily*

EXERCISES

(a) Translate into English.
1. Ca nēchmāuhtia in amìcihuiliz.
2. Cuix tiyānquizco tlacōhualli (= tlacōuhtli) tlaxcalli inin?
3. In yèhuāntin in ca otomî, tochān tlacelīltin.
4. Ca cualli tlācatl, huel quipāctia in netēcuitlahuīliztli.
5. In teōcuitlatl ca yèhuātl in īntlaelēhuīl in caxtiltēcâ.
6. Tlālpan ōhuetz in tlatlāzalli cuahuitl.

[8] For the construction of this verb, see 31.7.
[9] A sort of heated plate on which food is cooked or baked (**ixca**), especially tortillas.
[10] No translation is given unless a Spanish derivative is commonly used.

    7. Ca àtle ōniquichtec: huel nēchtolīnia in notzacualōca.

    8. Quimomaca in āhuilpāquiliztli.

    9. Miyac in quicāhua ītēnahuatīl tīcitl.

   10. In Dios mitzmomaquilīz in ītētlamactzin.

   11. Īpal in motlazòtlalōca nicchīhuaz.

   12. Ōnictlāz in cotoctic ichtli.

   13. Comālpan xictlāli in textli.

(b) Translate into Nahuatl.

    1. The day is divided into twenty-four (*use the locative of the number*).

    2. It's not good to get drunk.

    3. Your (s.) love of yourself ("self-love"), your arrogance ("action of counting yourself"), will destroy you.

    4. His knowledge ("knowing things") is great.

    5. I like only mole that's been made at my place ("only made at my place the mole pleases me").

    6. In front of my place there are many transported stones.

    7. I demand that he be guarded ("his being guarded").

    8. The fact of being despised ("being known as nothing") has made him cry.

    9. Remember (s.) the scourging ("whipping") of our Lord.

   10. We are the creations of God.

   11. You're (s.) my beloved.

   12. I'll drink only clear water ("water purity," *a thematic noun*).

   13. At Teotihuacan there are two large pyramids: the pyramid of the sun and the pyramid of the moon.

Noun Clauses

31.1 Clauses as Subject or Object: Indirect Questions

As in English, a clause in Nahuatl can serve as the subject or object of a verb, in one of two ways.

The first is when it is used as an *indirect questions*. We have already seen examples several times (4.10, 5.4, 14.6–7 etc.). The term *indirect question* signifies that a question is being reported (i.e., it is dependent upon a verb of saying or thinking), and in English, this change in the status of the question is indicated by a change in word order. In the direct question, the order of the subject is inverted, so that the verb precedes the verb, but in an indirect question, the regular order SUBJECT–VERB is retained. Also, the person of the verb in the question is changed as appropriate. Thus, you would report the direct question 'What do you want?' by saying 'He asks what I want'. In Nahuatl, an indirect question changes the person of its verb if necessary, but the tense and word order are otherwise unaffected. If the corresponding direct question would be introduced by an interrogative word, the indirect question likewise begins with this interrogative, which may or may not be preceded by **in**. An indirect question of the type 'if/whether' in English, which goes back to a direct question expecting simple yes/no answer, can be introduced in Nahuatl with **(in) cuix** but also with **(in) àzo**. Thus:

Àmo nicmati in àzo (*or* in cuix) huāllāz	*I don't know if he'll come*
Xinēchilhui (in) tlein ticnequi	*Tell me what you (s.) want*
Cuix ticmati in quēzquintin tlācâ ōmpa catê?	*Do you (s.) know how many people are there?*
Àmo nicmati in quēnin huel mochīhuaz	*I don't know how it can be done*
Ōnēchtēmōlìquê in āc nèhuātl	*They asked me (sought from me) who I was*

31.2 Object Noun Clauses

The second use of a clause as subject or object consists of *noun clauses*. These correspond broadly to clauses introduced in English with 'that' or sometimes 'the fact that' (e.g., 'I said that he was coming' or 'the fact that he is coming pleases me'), though in some instances they can be represented with an infinitive (see 31.3–4). Such noun clauses are regularly represented in the verb on which they depend by a third person singular object prefix and are generally introduced by **in**.

If someone's words are being reported, two independent clauses can be used. For example:

Quìtoa in Pedro: ca nihuāllāz	*Peter says: "I'll come"* (note that in this case, the introductory verb is still marked with the third person object prefix)

The reported speech can also be turned into a noun clause. In this case, the person of the reported verbs is changed just as in English ('he says, "I'll come"' > 'he says that he'll come', 'he tells me, "you're a fool"' > 'he tells me that I'm a fool'). Thus:

Quìtoa in Pedro in (ca) huāllāz	*Peter says that he'll come*

On the other hand, there is no "sequence of tense." That is, in English, the tenses of the reported speech are regularly changed if the introductory verb is in a past tense (e.g., 'Peter says, "I'll come"' > 'Peter said that he would come' and 'Peters says, "I've seen it"' > 'Peter said that he had seen it'). In Nahuatl, the original tenses of the reported verbs are retained (with just the person changed as necessary):

Ōquìtô in ca huāllāz	*He said that he would come* (lit., *will come*)
Ōnēchilhuî in ca quimati	*He told me that he knew it* (lit., *knows it*)

In addition to **ìtoa**, the same sort of construction is found with declarative verbs like **ilhuia** 'tell someone', **tēnēhua** 'mention', **mocuìtia** (bitransitive) 'admit, confess', with verbs of intellectual activity like **mati** 'know', **ilcāhua** 'forget', **ilnāmiqui** 'remember', and with verbs of perception like **itta** 'see', **caqui** 'hear'.

Ye ōnimitzilhuî in àmo nicnequi	*I already told you (s.) that I don't want it*
Nicmati in ōmic	*I know that he's dead*
Quimâ in aocmo huèca huītzê	*He realized (knew) that they were coming quite close (no longer from far off)*
Nicnocuìtia in ca nèhuātl ōnicchīuh	*I admit that I did it*

Ōquilcāuh in ca ye ōmitzilhuî	*He forgot that he'd already told you (s.)*
Ōniccac in ca huāllaz	*I heard (it said) that it would come*

The predicate in the noun clause is not necessarily a verb. It can be a noun or locative or even an adverb like **quēmâ** or **àmo**:

Nicmati in ca otomitl	*I know that he's an Otomi*[1]
Ōnēchilhuî in ca àmo	*He said no to me*

In an instance where it is not stated who it is that "says" or "knows," we know (Lesson 15) that two constructions are possible. A bitransitive verb is put in the passive, with the person who is being told appearing as the subject (18.5):

Ōnilhuīlōc in ca nelli	*I was told that it's true*

If, on the other hand, the verb is transitive, then, because the object is not animate (being a clause), the verb is put in the quasi-passive reflexive (15.9), with the clause as the subject. In the corresponding English passive expression, the clause normally retains its regular position after the verb, whose subject is an anticipatory ("dummy") 'it'. Thus:

Mìtoa in ōmic	*It is said that he's dead*
Àmo momatiz in ōmic	*It won't be known that he's dead*
Ōmolcāuh in ca yèhuātl ōquichīuh	*It's been forgotten that he's the one who did it*
Ōmottac in ca chicāhuac	*It was seen that he's strong*

Note that this construction is also possible with indirect questions:

Cuix momati in àzo huāllāz?	*Is it known if he'll come?*
Àmo momati āc yèhuātl	*It's not known who he is*

31.3 Noun Clauses with the Future

The future in Nahuatl has a number of usages that correspond not to the future in English but to the infinitive. This is the rule with noun clauses that do not express a simple fact but an eventuality or an event that is envisioned or hoped for. This is the case especially in the following circumstances:

(1) After **mati,** the noun clause is equivalent to the English expression 'how to VERB' (the subject of **mati** etc. and of the verb in the noun clause must be identical). Such clauses are not normally introduced with **in.** Thus:

Nicmati nitlàcuilōz	*I know how to write*
In ichpōpōchtin quimatî tlàtzomazquê	*The young women know how to sew*

---

[1] If this was phrased as **nicmati in otomitl, otomitl** would probably be taken as a noun ('I know the Otomi'), whereas in **nicmati in ca otomitl, otomitl** is taken as a clause.

We can also have an action noun (30.1) with the same meaning:

Nicmati in tlàcuilōliztli	*I know (the act of) writing (how to write)*
Quimatî in tlàtzomaliztli	*They know sewing (how to sew)*

(2) After **ilcāhua** and **ilnāmiqui**: 'forget to VERB', 'remember to VERB':

Ōquilcāuh quichīhuaz	*He's forgotten to do it*
Mā xiquilnāmiqui ticchīhuaz	*Remember (s.) to do it*

(3) In certain constructions in English, the subject of the Nahuatl noun clause becomes the object of a verb of ordering, and the finite verb of the noun clause becomes the English infinitive. This construction arises in two situations:

(a) in indirect commands

After declarative verbs (e.g., **ìtoa, ilhuia**), the noun clause represents the substance of a command or the like: 'tell him to VERB'. In this case, there is an alternative construction with a clause in English, which is closer to the use in Nahuatl of a noun clause: 'say that he should VERB'. Thus:

Ōmitzilhuî in ticchīhuaz	*He told you (s.) to do it (that you should do it)*
Ōnilhuīlōc in nicchīhuaz	*I was told to do it*

In Nahuatl, the future in these indirect commands may be preceded with **mā** (see 9.5 for future imperatives with **mā** + FUTURE; for more details, see 31.4):

Ōnilhuīlōc in mā nicchīhuaz	*I was told to do it*

(b) with **nequi**

The verb **nequi** takes a noun clause in the future if the subject of the clause is *different* from that of the introductory verb. Here again, the normal equivalent in English involves an infinitive: 'to want him to VERB'. Generally, **in** is not used in this case:

Cuix ticnequi nicchīhuaz?	*Do you (s.) want me to do it?*
Nicnequi ammomāpòpōhuazquê	*I want you (pl.) to wash (**pòpōhua**) your hands*

Recall that if the subject of the two verbs is the same (a circumstance in which English has to use an infinitive), Nahuatl can incorporate the future of the dependent verb into the appropriate form of **nequi** (28.9):

Nicchīhuaznequi	*I want to do it*

In this case, Nahuatl may also (unlike English) use the noun clause:

Nicnequi nicchīhuaz	*I want to do it (lit., that I should do it)*

This construction sometimes has the meaning 'like to VERB' and is frequently used in expressions of a more or less exclamatory nature:

Anquinequî antlàtōzquê!	*You (pl.) do like to talk!*
Ticnequi in timāhuiltīz!	*You sure like to play around! (i.e., aren't you) tired of playing around?)*

The reflexive form **monequi** (lit., 'it is wanted') can be used to express an obligation, in which case it is always followed by a future noun clause. This is equivalent to the English 'I must/have to VERB', with the noun clause turned into an infinitive and **monequi** expressed as the auxiliary 'must' or 'have to' with the subject of Nahuatl noun clause appearing as its subject. Thus:

Monequi achtopa titlacuāzquê	*We have to eat first*
Cuix monequi ōmpa niyāz?	*Do I have to go there?*

Àmo monequi means 'don't have to' and **monequi àmo** 'musn't'. That is, in the first instance, the obligation is negated, but in the second, it is a negated concept that is obligatory (lit., 'that you should not do this is necessary'):

Àmo monequi in āxcān tinēchtlaxtlāhuīz	*It's not necessary for you (s.) to pay me right now*
Monequi àmo tiquilhuīz in	*You (s.) mustn't tell him this*

▶ *Note.* Both **nicnequi nitlàcuilōz** 'I want to write' and **nicmati nitlàcuilōz** 'I know how to write' are legitimate expressions, but while **nicmati in tlàcuilōliztli** 'I know writing' is possible, ****nicnequi in tlàcuilōliztli** is not a valid construction for 'I want to write'. Conversely, **nitlàcuilōznequi** is possible, but ****nitlàcuilōzmati** is not.

31.4 Noun Clauses with the *-ni* Form and Optative

Nequi and verbs of kindred meaning like **elēhuia** 'desire' or **ìtlani** 'request' also have the option of using the optative (always preceded with **mā**) in a noun clause. **Nequi** with the optative more or less indicates a longing or inclination:

Nicnequi, mā canàpa nitztēhua	*I yearn to head off (for the verb, see 27.6 sec. 2) somewhere*
Niquelēhuia in mā nipàti	*I'd like to get better*

The -ni form preceded by **mā** (16.9) can also be used to express a present contrafactual wish:

Nicnequi in mā nicān yeni	*I wish he were here (which he is not)*

or a past contrafactual one (to indicate unhappiness that something did not happen). In this case, the **-ni** form is preceded with the augment **ō-**:

| Nicnequi in mā ōtiquittani | I wish you had seen it |

31.5 Noun Clauses Introduced by *in ic*

The **in** that introduces a noun clause is often reinforced with **ic** (14.4). This can be written as a single word (**inic**) or as two (**in ic**) without any difference. The addition of **ic** often has no perceptible effect on the meaning:

| Mācamo quimonequilti in totēucyo in ic tictoyōlìtlacalhuīzquê | May our Lord not wish us to offend him/that we offend him (hon.) |
| Ōnicmâ in ic ye ōmàxitīco | I learned (knew) that he had already arrived (hon.) |

but it often has a nuance that can be rendered with 'how' or 'the way that':

| Ca ye ōmottac in ic chicāhuaquê, in ic tiyàcāhuān | It has already been seen how strong, how valiant they are |
| Xicnēxti inic titiyàcāuh, inic toquichtli | Show (make it be visible) how courageous, how (much of) a man you (s.) are |

Quichīhua inic is also used in a sense close to that of the causative: 'to bring it about that...':

| In totōlpixqui àmo quichīhua inic mochòchopīniâ totōltin | The turkey watcher doesn't bring it about that the turkeys peck at each other (cause them to peck...) |

(Here the sense is very close to that of result clauses, see 33.4.)

31.6 Noun Clauses as Subject

A noun clause acts most often as the equivalent of the object of a verb. It can also be the subject in the following circumstances (once more, in English such noun clauses are sometimes anticipated with 'it' as the stand-in subject of the verb):

(1) with reflexive forms like **momati, mìtoa, monequi** (see 31.2, 3)
(2) with certain intransitive verbs like **nēci** 'it seems that...', **nelti** 'it turns out (proves true) that...':

| Nēciz in (ic) titlahuēlīlōc | It will appear that you're (s.) a villain |
| Ca ōneltic ōmic | It turned out that he died (or was dead) |

(3) with verbs indicating the cause of a feeling:

Ca nēchpāctia in nicān ticâ	*It pleases me (makes me happy) that you're (s.) here*
Ca nēchtequipachoa in ōmic	*It grieves me that he's dead*

(4) in copulative sentences with nouns or "adjectives" as the predicate:

Cualli yez in timocnōmatiz	*It will be good for you to humble yourself (lit., that you consider, **mati**, yourself wretched, **icnōtl**; see 17.3.2)*
Àmo cualli in ōtinēchàhuac	*It's bad that you (s.) argued with me*
Tēchòchōctî in ōmic	*It's sad (what makes people cry; see 16.2) that he is dead*
Ca nelli ōquichīuh	*It's true that he did it*
Ca huel nelli nimiquiz	*It's quite true that I'm going to die*

In ic (or, as a single word, **inic**) frequently appears in such sentences either to express 'the way that, how' (14.4):

Cencâ melāhuac, māhuiztic in ic ōtlàtô	*Very just(ly) and nobl(y) is how he spoke (i.e., he spoke very justly and nobly)*
Tēmàmāuhtî inic ōnimitzizcaltî, inic ōnimitzhuapāuh	*It was daunting how I raised and hardened you*

or to elaborate on a noun:

Ca totequiuh in tèhuāntin titeōpizquê in ic īpan titlàtōzquê in īteōyōtzin in totēucyo	*It's the task of us priests to speak of the divinity of our Lord (lit., our task is that we speak ...)*
Huel tonahuatīl inic tictotlayecoltilīzquê in totēucyo	*It's our mandate to serve our Lord (lit., our order is that we serve ...)*

Also note the expression consisting of **zā tepitōn inic** or **zā achìtōn in ic** + FUTURE or COUNTERFACTUAL, which means 'it is/was virtually/all but the case that I/you/he etc. VERB/VERBed'. **Zā** means 'no more than', and in certain cases 'in the end'. (This word is not to be confused with **zan** 'only', which is very close to it in form and sense: **zan cē** 'there's only one', **zā cē** is 'there's no more than one'.) Hence, the phrase means something like 'there is/was no more than a little (needed) for me etc. to VERB'.

Zā huel tepitōn inic nicmācāhuazquia in nāpilōl	*I nearly (lit., it was virtually the case that I) dropped my water jar*
Zā achìtōn inic huālquīzaz in tōnatiuh	*The sun is on the point of rising*

Note. We have a slightly different situation with sentences like:

Inin cocōliztli in īpàyo nèzōtlalōz	*The cure for this illness is to vomit (**nèzōtlalōz** is the reflexive impersonal form of **ninìzōtla** 'I vomit')*

Here, the appearance of the "article" **in** in front of **īpàyo**[2] shows that it must be the subject of the copulative sentence, while the verb form **nèzōtlalōz** functions, in its capacity as a clause, not as the subject of the sentence but as the predicate of **īpàyo** (see 4.2 sec. 3).

(5) with **tlein on** 'what is that?' This is basically found in riddles, in which there are very free constructions that suggest the answer in a very allusive manner:

Zā zan[3] tlein on, ye huālquīza, xiccui moteuh? – Cuitlatl.	*What exactly is that? Here it comes, take (s.) your stone. – A turd.*
Zā zan tlein on, ēxcāmpa ticalaquî, zan cecni tiquīzâ? – Ca tocamisa.	*What exactly is that? We enter in three places, but come out from just one. – Our shirt.*
Zā zan tlein on, xoncholo, noncholōz? – Yèhuātl in ōlmāitl.	*What exactly is that? Run away, I'll run away. – That's the stick (lit., hand) of rubber.*

31.7 Noun Clause Not Represented with a Prefix

It can happen that a noun clause or indirect question is not directly represented by a prefix. This is naturally the case when it is dependent upon a bitransitive verb like **ilhuia** (18.2):

Ōnimitzilhuî in ōmic	*I told you that he died*

In this case, however, making the person being spoken about indefinite is enough to allow the prefix -**c**- to reappear:

Ōnictēilhuî in ōmic	*I told people that he died*

On the other hand, certain verbs cannot ever represent the noun clause with a definite object prefix, even though these verbs are often associated with clauses that resemble noun clauses. This is particularly the case with:

(1) certain transitive verbs like **nānquilia** 'answer', **nāhuatia** 'order', and (most frequently) **tlàtlauhtia** 'request, ask'. Given their meaning, we might

---

[2] Note the use here of **īpàyo**. **Īpâ** is 'his cure' in reference to someone, while **īpàyo** is 'its cure' in reference to a disease (the relationship being considered one of inalienable possession, see 11.5).

[3] A standard expression in riddles (see earlier for **zā**), and for this reason, riddles are called **zāzanilli**.

expect that these verbs would be bitransitive like **ilhuia**, but they only take an object prefix representing the person spoken to. Two constructions are possible:

▶ representation of the person being spoken to:

Quinānquilia in ca quimati	*He replies to him that he knows it*
Quināhuatia in àmo quichīhuaz	*He commands him not to do it*
Tināhuatīlōz in ic titēyacānaz	*You'll (s.) be ordered to lead (others)*
Nimitztlàtlauhtia in mā xicchīhua	*I'm asking you (s.) to do it*

▶ no representation of the person being spoken to. In this case, these verbs can only take the prefix **-tla-** (and not **-c-/-qu-**). This is reminiscent the behavior of semi-applicatives (20.9):

Tlanānquilia in àmo quimati	*He answers that he doesn't know (it)*
Tlanāhuatia in tīcitl, àmo tlaōcoltīlōz, àmo tequipachōlōz in otztli	*The midwife orders that the pregnant woman should not be saddened or bothered*
Quìtoa, tlanāhuatia àmo quittaz in tlapalli	*She (the midwife) says, she orders (that) she (the pregnant woman) shouldn't see the color red*

(2) verbs in the reflexive form indicating a mental operation, like **ninomati** 'I believe, I have the impression that …', **ninotlàpaloa** 'I dare':

Ninomatiya àzayāc (= àzo ayāc) nēchpalēhuīz	*I felt that maybe no one would help me*
Cequintin momatquê ca mictlampa in quīzaquiuh	*Some people thought that it was to the north (lit., from the land of the dead) that he would come out*
Ayāc motlàpaloāya in occē ommīxquetzaz	*No one dared to offer himself as a second (lit., raise himself up to the eyes as another)*

▶ *Note.* In the first person, just **nomati** is sometimes found in place of **ninomati**.

(3) certain expressions like **iuh câ in noyōllô** 'I know well' (lit., 'my heart is thus'):

Luh câ in noyōllô in ca nimiquiz	*I'm certain that I'm going to die*

(4) sporadically when the noun clause consists of an impersonal form of the verb:

Tlacacticatca in nenònōtzalo	*He was listening to the deliberations (that words were being spoken in turn)*

Āquin tlatquiz, āquin tlamāmāz in tōnaz, in tlathuiz?	*Who will undertake and take it upon himself (to cause) that there should be sunshine, that there should be light?*

In such cases, however, it is often possible to wonder whether this is a situation involving result or purpose clauses (33.4–5) rather than noun clauses. In this way, one could interpret the last sentence as 'who will undertake things (necessary) so that there should be sunshine?'

Along similar lines:

Xommotta in mīcampa in motepotzco, quēn ōtonnemico?	*Go look (s.) (lit., let it be seen) behind you, in back of you, how you have lived until now (this could be interpreted as consisting of two sentences, the second being a direct question: How have you …?)*
Nōhuiyāmpa ōtlayèyecô, mā nēchceyalti	*He tried in every way (from every direction) to make me consent (here the relationship is very close to that of purpose clauses: he put everything into operation so that …)*

VOCABULARY

Intransitive verb
ceya   *to consent, to be in agreement*

Transitive and intransitive verbs
huapāhua	*to stiffen, to harden*	huècāhua	*to linger, to be late; to delay, to postpone*

Transitive verbs
chopīnia	*to peck*	pòpōhua	*to wash*
izcaltia	*to rear, to nourish (mo-: to grow up)*	tlaōcoltia	*to take pity on*
		tlayecoltia	*to serve, to beseech*
ìtzoma	*to sew*	tlàtlauhtia	*to request*
ìzotla (m-: *to vomit*)		(yè)yecoa	*to try, to test*

Bitransitive verb
cuītia, mo-: *to admit, to confess*

Nouns
āpilōlli	*water jar*	tlahuēlīlōc	*fool, madman*
camisa	*shirt (Spanish borrowing)*	tlapalli	*color red*
ōlli	*rubber (ball)*	zāzanilli	*riddle, story*

Particles
achto(pa)	*first (of all)*	zā	*no more than, finally*

EXERCISES

(a) Translate into English.

  1. Cuix àmo ticmati in ca ye huècauh in ōnimitzittac?

  2. Iuh ōninomâ in ca àmo ōnihuècāhuac.

  3. Nicnequi in mācaīc ōniquilhuiāni in.

  4. Occeppa ōniquilcāuh in niccōhuaz iztatl.

  5. Nicnocuītia ca ōppa ōnichtec.

  6. Àmo nicmati in àzo huāllāz, ànōzo àmo.

  7. Àmo momati in quēzquintin īpilhuān.

  8. Cualli ic quimatî mēxìcatlàtōzquê.

  9. Ōquìtlanquê in caxtiltēcâ in mā tiquintequipanōcān.

 10. Ca huel ìtōlōni, tēnēhualōni in ic titiyàcāuh.

 11. Xitlanāhuati, mā calaquicān.

(b) Translate into Nahuatl.

  1. You (s.) needn't get angry, I've already told you (s.) that I would do it tomorrow.

  2. It became clear that you (s.) are brave.

  3. They questioned me ("sought things from me"), and I responded to them that I didn't know.

  4. Tell (pl.) me if you'd like to eat.

  5. He said that he didn't know if it was true that Peter was dead.

  6. I admit that I've gotten drunk many times.

  7. I know that it's you (s.) who took the old man's money from him (his money from the old man).

  8. It isn't known if he is dead or not.

  9. You (s.) know how to read well ("good is how ..."; *translate* "read books *with an incorporated object*").

 10. I think that we can't ("won't be able to") arrive at Mexico City this evening.

Attributives, Relative Clauses, Copula Verbs, Semi-Auxiliaries

32.1 Attributives

We have already had occasion to see (Lesson 12) that in Nahuatl there are not any adjectives properly speaking, just nouns derived from verb forms that tend to be translated by adjectives in languages such as English. Conversely, the capacity to modify nouns does not constitute a specific category of words in Nahuatl, because a noun can be modified by an "adjective," another noun, a locative, or (as we will see later) any verbal form. In English, an adjective that directly modifies a noun is placed in front of it (e.g., 'the big dog...'). We will call any Nahuatl form that modifies a noun in this way an *attributive*. Here we will deal with nouns with an adjectival sense in English (12.2), quasi-adjectives derived from verbs (12.4–6), possessive nouns (11.7), and locatives used adjectivally.

The attributive can precede or follow its noun. The order is (DETERMINER)-ATTRIBUTIVE-NOUN or (DETERMINER)-NOUN-ATTRIBUTIVE ("determiner" means a form like in or inin, inon, or cē, ōme, miyac etc.). This order is obviously much freer than in English; it is difficult to give general principles for the placement of attributives, and the most that can be said is that the following forms always appear before their noun:

▶ cualli, yēctli 'good': cualli tlācatl 'good person'
▶ quantifiers, including huēyi
▶ huēhuê 'old': in huēhuê Motēuczōma 'Moctezuma the Elder'
▶ locatives: in Caxtillān tlaīlli 'wine (drink from Castile)', in huècapan tlālli 'the high country, uplands'; in nechca tetl 'the stone (located) there'; in ilhuicac āhuiyacāyōtl 'the fragrance in heaven, heavenly fragrance'

Otherwise, the order is virtually free, and in all the following examples, the word order could probably be reversed:

Tlanānquiliâ in pilhuàquê cihuâ	*The women with children answer*
Ōquelēhuî cē cihuātl nāmiquê	*He lusted after a married woman (a woman with a spouse)*
Ōquichīuh in tēmictiāni tlàtlacōlli	*He committed a mortal (killer) sin*
Quitlampachoa totōnqui chīlli	*He smears (**pachoa**) hot chili on his teeth (**tlantli**)*
Ō topan quimochīhuilî in totēucyo in ātl itztic, in ātl cecēc	*Our Lord poured (lit., made) cold water, icy water over us (i.e., brought calamity upon us)*
Metl tlàchictli ommotlālia	*Grated maguey (or maguey scrapings) is (are) set down (**ìchiqui** 'scrape maguey cores to collect liquid')*

If the noun being modified is in a locative form, the attributive retains its basic form (13.11, 14.3):

Huēyi āpan onotiuh	*He sails (goes lying down) on the sea (big water)*
Cualli tlàtōltica ōnicnōnōtz	*I preached with fine words*

Similarly, only the main noun assumes the possessed form (if appropriate):

Nēchpāctia in cualli notlaxcal	*My good tortilla pleases me*

On the other hand, any subject prefix has to appear on *both* words:

Ticualli titlàtoāni	*You're (s.) a good ruler*

In such cases, Nahuatl most frequently prefers to form a compound noun rather than keep the attributive separate:

Ticnōtlācâ	*We're poor people* (rather than **ticnōmê titlācâ**)
Tihuēyitlācatl	*You're (s.) a great man* (rather than **tihuēyi titlācatl**)

Also: **in titlālticpactlācâ** 'we people on earth'.

32.2 Relative Clauses

With an adjective, a noun is modified by a single word that tells us something about that noun. Nouns (and locatives) can also be modified in a similar way by an entire clause, and such clauses are called *relative clauses*. A relative clause in English can be fairly complicated. A noun that is modified by such a clause is called the *antecedent* or *head noun*, and whatever role that the head noun would take in the relative clause is indicated by the relative pronoun, which is placed at the front of the clause. Thus, if you want to indicate that a man that you are talking about has helped you in the past, you speak of him as 'the person who helped me'. Here 'who helped me' is the relative clause equivalent of the independent statement 'he helped me' with the relative pronoun 'who' taking the place of the subject 'he'. If you wish to indicate that it was you who saw him, you say, 'the man whom I saw' with 'whom' taking the place of 'him'. Any syntactical role in the relative clause can be replaced with a relative pronoun, and there are a number of different relative pronouns in English, some of which indicate a specific function in the relative clause ('whom', 'whose'), but most of which do not ('who', 'that', 'which'). Nahuatl likewise has clauses that serve to modify antecedents, but the principles here are formally simpler than those of English and less overt in indicating the relationship between the relative clause and the antecedent. Basically, these are verbal clauses that act as attributives in that they modify a noun (the antecedent), and such clauses follow the principles of attributives in terms of function, placement, and the use of **in**.

A relative clause can be overtly marked by the determiner **in** at the start of the relative clause. Whereas the relative pronoun of English generally *replaces* some element in its own clause, in Nahuatl the role of the antecedent in the relative clause almost always continues to be represented by some sort of prefix (subject, object, possessive) or in certain instances by an adverb. That is, in such clauses, **in** simply indicates that the clause modifies an antecedent, and the modifying clause then appears in the same form that it would otherwise appear in as an independent sentence. Thus, the element being modified by the relative clause continues to appear overtly in the relative clause *in its regular form*, unlike the case in English where it is entirely displaced by the relative pronoun. If the verb of the relative clause is in a different person or number from the antecedent, there is not much room for confusion:

in tlācatl in ōniquittac	*The person that I saw (lit., the person that I saw him)*
in tlācâ in ōnēchittaquê	*The people who saw me (lit., the people that they saw me)*

Here, the determiner **in** marks the clause as relative, and in the first example, the third person object prefix is the only one available to agree with the antecdent noun **tlācatl**, while in the second, it is the subject of the third person plural verb **ōnēchittaquê**, which agrees with the plural noun **tlācâ**.

But there is the possibility for confusion if there is more than one possibility for agreement with the markers of the verb in the relative clause. Thus, the relative clause

in tēuctli in ōquimictî in tlàtoāni

could equally mean 'the lord who killed the king' (with the antecedent acting as the subject of the third person singular verb and third person definite object of the verb referring to **tlàtoāni**) or 'the lord whom the king killed' (with third person definite object referring to the antecedent and **tlàtoāni** acting as the subject of the verb). In such instances of ambiguity, only the context can resolve which nouns refer to which prefixes.

In English, it is possible to omit the relative pronoun when this serves as the object of the verb in the relative clause ('the man I saw' instead of 'the man that I saw'). In Nahuatl, it is likewise possible to omit the determiner **in** at the start of a relative clause. The only restriction is that **in** can be omitted only if the relative clause is short (in this case, it often consists of only a verb, and if the verb has any modifiers, these must be few in number, such as **àmo** and/or a locative expression). Thus:

in cihuātl ōniquittac   *The woman (that) I saw*

Because relative clauses are basically the equivalent of an adjective, it is not surprising that they share with attributives the ability to be placed either before or after the antecedent (unlike the case with English, where the relative clause has to follow the antecedent):

Niquēhuatitlālia in huetztoc cocoxqui	*I pick up the sick man who's lying down*
In nechca câ tlahuānqui àhuīc yāyàtiuh	*The drunk man who's over there wanders from one side to the other*
Àmo cualli yez in tlācatiz piltōntli	*The small child who's going to be born will be ugly*
Nictētequi in tlaxcalli mocuāz	*I'm dividing up the tortilla that's going to be eaten*
Niquilnāmiqui cē cihuātl ōniquelēhuî	*I recall a woman that I lusted after*
In pàtli quimacac, yèhuātl in iztāc octli	*The medicine that he gave him is white pulque (note the use of **yèhuātl** because the predicate is definite; see 4.2)*

Note carefully the word order in the example **in tlācatiz piltōntli** 'the child (who is) about to be born', with the verb placed between the determiner **in** and the noun that it modifies. Such word order may seem counterintuitive to an English-speaker, but it makes perfectly good sense if one conceives of the verb as performing the same function (modifying the noun) as does an adjective, which could take that position.

The order **in** NOUN **in** CLAUSE is obligatory if the relative clause is quite long, and it always remains a possibility even if there is only a verb or an "adjective" in the clause:

Ōquīc in ātl in àmo cualli	*He drank water that was bad (bad water)*
Ōtlāhuāntīlōquê in cuauhcalpixquê in ōquipiyayâ[1]	*The prison guards who were guarding him were made drunk*
Cāmpa onyâ in tītlantli in quin iz ōcatca?	*Where did the messenger go who was here just now?*
Xicmotlazòcāmachilti in tlàtoāni, in ōmitzmochìchīhuīlî,[2] moquechtlan ōquimopilhuî inon tilmàtli in oc nòmā āxcān tictlālìtinemi	*Thank (s.) (**tlazòcāmati**, here honorific) the king, who decorated you, who hung (**piloa**, hon.) around your neck that cape which you still wear (here we have one relative clause inserted into another)*

This order is likewise obligatory if the relative clause modifies a demonstrative (**in**, **on**) or an emphatic pronoun:

Āquìquê in, in mochipa nicān tonāhuac māhuiltiâ?	*Who are these people who are always playing with us here?*
Aocmo quihuelcaqui in cualli tlàtōlli in yèhuātl in ēhualōni, in ìtōlōni	*I no longer hear in good will (well) the good words that (were the ones that) had to be brought forth and said*[3]

As in many languages, the relative clauses in Nahuatl often convey various nuances (being tantamount, for instance, to causal, result, purpose clauses etc.). It is sometimes difficult to render such clauses into English with mere relative clauses:

Huel huēyi cuācuahuê in, in àcān iuhqui ōniquittac	*That's so big a cow that I've never seen its like (lit., that's a very big cow, which I've never seen the like of)*
Quitēmoāya tìcitl in quipàtīz	*He was looking for a doctor to cure him (lit., who would/was to cure him)*

32.3 Relatives for Relationships Other Than Subject/Object

In English, the relative pronoun can not only represent the subject or object of its clause ('who/whom' or 'that/which'), but it can also indicate the possessor of a noun in the relative clause ('whose', 'of whom/which') or the object of

---

[1] It happens here that the imperfect is preceded by the augment **ō-**. This has practically become the rule in many modern dialects.

[2] Honorific of **chìchīhua** 'to prepare, to adorn' (28.4).

[3] Here the final relative clause takes the form of focalization (4.2 sec. 2) in which the "real" focalized form (**in cualli tlàtōlli**) cannot be expressed directly because it is definite and hence is represented by the pronoun **yèhuātl**, which is then "elaborated" by the definite form. This would be reasonably straightforward if the sentence were **in cualli tlàtōlli (ca) yèhuātl in ēhualōni**, but the syntax is made less obvious because **in cualli tlàtōlli** is the antecedent of this relative construction and so stands outside it.

a proposition (e.g., 'to whom', 'about which' etc.). There can also be adverbial relatives, like 'where', 'when'. In Nahuatl, the relative form is not so explicit. Instead, it is enough to introduce a relative clause with **in**, which is then followed (not necessarily directly) by an appropriate word within the clause to indicate the sense of the relative. Thus:

(1) instrument ('with/by which')
Here the relative clause must include **ic** (14.3), generally placed in front of the verb:

Nicān câ in tetl in ic ōnechmōtlac	*Here is the stone that he hit me with (or with which he …)*
Nicān tlami in nenōnōtzalli zāzanilli in ye huècauh ic tlàtlanōnōtzayâ huēhuetquê	*Here ends the story, the account that the ancients would tell tales with (with which …) long ago*

(2) 'where'
In oncān or **in ōmpa** (5.4 sec. 2):

Quiyahualòtimomanquê in tlecuīlli in oncān nāhuilhuitl ōtlatlac tletl	*They gathered around the hearth where (lit., that there) fire had been burning for four days*

(3) 'of whom/which, whose'
Here, a possessive phrase is needed. Where English says 'the person whose child I know', Nahuatl says **in tlācatl in niquīxmati īpiltzin** lit., 'the person that I know his child':

Mā yèhuātl īòhui (10.9), īxopech tictocâ in aoc huel câ in īīx in īyòllô	*Don't (s.) follow (**toca**, here in the vetitive) the path, the trail of him whose eyes and heart are no longer well (i.e., who can't reason properly) (note how **yèhuātl** at the start of the sentence anticipates the relative clause dependent upon it at the end of the sentence)*
Quināmictihuî, quìcaltihuî in tēlpōpōchtin, in īntequiuh yāōyōtl	*The young men whose occupation (**intequiuh**) is war go meeting (**nāmiqui**) him, go attacking (**ìcali**) him*
Conītia in xihuitl in ītōca cihuāpàtli	*He has her drink the plant whose name is **cihuāpàtli** (woman's medicine)*

This turn of phrase is perhaps most common with **ītōcā**. Here, **in** is not obligatory:

Cē tlācatl ītōcā Pedro	*A man named (whose name is) Peter*

The locative-possessive construction (13.4) is likewise possible:

In tepētl in īicpac câ cē calli ...	*The mountain on which there's a house*
In tlācâ in īnnāhuac ninemi ...	*The people with whom I live*
Quēn mach huel tèhuāntin in tīxpan in tomatiyān (24.9) pòpolihuiz in mēxìcayōtl!	*How wretched (see 35.5) are we under whose eyes and with whose knowledge Mexica civilization will perish!*

32.4 Copula Verbs

Let us recall a detail about noun predicates in Nahuatl: a noun can be used as a predicate only in the present. Otherwise, it is necessary to use a form of the verb **câ** in the same person (8.10, 9.8). This principle applies both to nouns properly called and also to certain more or less tenseless verb forms like the "agent nouns" or "adjectives" derived from the preterite (12.4, 16.1–2) and the -**ni** form in its function as a noun (16.3, 5):

Tipōchtēcatl tiyez	*You'll (s.) be a merchant*
Nitlàtoāni nicatca	*I was ruler*

Traditionally, **câ**, as well as English 'to be', is called a *copula*. The same sort of construction (NOUN PREDICATE + VERB in the same person) is found, *in all tenses*, with other verbs, which we will call *copula* (or: *copular*) *verbs* because they correspond to verbs that introduce what is called a predicate noun or adjective in languages like English. These are basically:

(1) **nēci** 'to seem, to appear'. The predicate form is generally placed after the verb and can be preceded by **in**:

Tinēciz (in) titlahuēlīlōc	*You'll seem a villain, You'll be taken for a criminal*

We have already seen (31.6) that **nēci** can also take a noun clause as its subject:

Nēci (in) titlahuēlīlōc	*It seems that you're a criminal*

(2) Reflexive verbs like **mocuepa** 'to be turned', i.e., 'to turn into', **mochīhua** 'to be made', i.e., 'to become'; **monōtza**, **motōcāyōtia**, **motēnēhua** 'to be named/called':

Tixolopìtli timocuepa	*You're (s.) turning into an idiot*
Anchichimê ammocuepâ	*You're (pl.) turning into dogs*
Tohuāmpòtzin ōmochīuhtzinô in Totēucyô Dios	*Our Lord God became like us*[4]

---

[4] In this usage, -**pô** (26.4) is appended to -**huām**- (related to the plural marker for possessed nouns), the whole phrase taking the possessive prefix and meaning 'my/your/his etc. like', i.e., 'like me/you/him etc.'

Tipiltōntli timochīhuaz	*You'll (s.) turn into a little child*
Inìquê on motēnēhuâ otomî	*Those people are called Otomi*
Timēxìcâ titotōcayōtiâ	*We're called (call ourselves) Mexica*
Cuix tiPedro timonōtza?	*Are you named Peter?*

This construction can also appear in the passive:

Ca Pedro tōcāyōtīlōc	*He was called Peter*

(3) In English, the predicative notion can apply to the object of a verb: 'I think him a criminal', where 'criminal' agrees with the object 'him' (contrast the sentence 'he seems a criminal', where 'criminal' agrees with the subject 'he'). The same construction can be used to signify the creation of a state ('they made him ruler). In Nahuatl, the corresponding construction appears with the same verbs as in the previous section, in their usual transitive use: **chīhua**, **cuepa** 'make/turn X (into) Y', **nōtza, tōcāyōtia, tēnēhua** 'call, name':

Quitōcāyōtìquê Pedro	*They named him Peter*
Epazōyô xicchīhua in mōlli	*Make (s.) the mole (into) one containing wormseed (**epazōyô** signifies something that contains **epazōtl** 'wormseed')*

With **cuepa** and **chīhua** it seems difficult to have a predicate in the first or second person unless it is accompanied by **iuhquin** 'like':

Iuhquin tichichimê tēchcuepa in octli	*Pulque makes us like dogs*

A related construction is found with **mati** in the meaning 'consider as', but in this case the predicative notion describing the object is governed by the locative **īpan**:

Àtle īpan nimitzmati	*I consider you as (lit., upon) nothing (i.e., I have a poor opinion of you)*

Here too we can have **iuhquin**:

Zan iuhquin tēmictli īpan ticmatizquê in iz tlālticpac ic pācōhua	*We'll consider the joys on earth (the thing(s) by which people feel happy here on earth) as (being) merely like a dream (note that the relative clause **in … ic pācōhua** has no overt antecedent and is reflected in the main clause only with the definite object marker of **ticmatizquê**)*

(4) As in English, predicative expressions can be quite free, being used with virtually any verb to indicate that the subject or object participates in the process in some particular capacity or that the process puts the subject or object into that capacity. **In** often appears between such a predicate and the verb that it is dependent on:

Cocoxqui in tlālticpac quīzaz	*He'll come (emerge) on earth sick (lit., it's (as) a sick person that he'll come ...)*
Cecēc in mīz in pàtli	*The medicine is to be taken (drunk) cold*
Totōnqui in xiccua in motlaxcal	*Eat (s.) your tortilla hot (lit., hot is how you should eat ...)*
Tlàtoāni ōquitlālìquê	*They installed him as king*

Also see the comparable expressions with a quantifier as predicate (7.2).

32.5 Semi-Auxiliaries

In English, certain verbs are used to indicate the way in which the action of another verb is carried out. The introductory "modal" verb conjugates normally, and the second (dependent) verb appears as an infinitive or gerund (e.g., 'I start to flee', 'they stopped crying', 'he'll finish eating soon'). Nahuatl has a similar construction, but here *both* verbs are inflected, sharing a common subject. We will call such modal verbs *semi-auxiliaries*. These can be divided into to groups:

(1) Verbs indicating a phase in the development of a process, such as **pēhua** 'to start, to begin', **tzinti** 'to start, to begin', **tlami** 'to end', **ìcihui** 'to hasten, to hurry', **pachihui** 'to have enough of', and in a similar meaning with the same features, reflexive forms like **mocāhua** 'to stop'. In these constructions, the semi-auxiliary can appear in any tense, but the other verb can only be in the *present*. Most often, there is not any sort of conjunction between the two verbs, though sometimes we have **in** or **inic**:

Nipēhua in ninococoa	*I'm beginning to be ill*
Yālhua ōnipēuh in ninococoa	*Yesterday I started getting sick*
Pēuh tlàtlahuēlīlōcāti	*He began being an evildoer*
Mā oc nitlami ninoteōchīhua	*Let me first finish praying*
Ayamo tlami inic tlatla citlālin	*The star hasn't yet finished shining*
In ōpachiuhquê ātlî, niman ōyàquê	*After they had their fill of drinking, they left*
Mā xìcihui in ticchīhua	*Hurry up (s.) and do it!*

However, if **yecahui** 'to finish' is in the preterite, the dependent verb has to be in the preterite too:

Ōyecauh inic tlàtô	*He finished speaking*

Tlami 'to end' can also take a noun clause as its subject:

In ōtlan titlachpāna, titēnìzaz	*After you've (s.) finished sweeping (lit., when the fact that you're sweeping has finished), you'll have breakfast (lit., wake up,* **iza***, by the lips)*

For 'to begin', the causative **pēhualtia** can be used in place of **pēhua**, and in this case the dependent verb is treated like a noun clause in that it is represented by an object prefix added to **pēhualtia**:

Compēhualtìquê in ye tlamàcēhuâ	*They began to do penance*

Pēhualtia + inic means 'begin by VERBing', and here too the dependent verb can appear in the preterite:

Quipēhualtî inic ātlīc	*He started by drinking*

▶ *Note.* The preterite of **pēhua** is **pēuh** and not ****pēhuac**, even though it is intransitive (8.7.5). A verb ending in -**hua** is treated as having a vowel-retaining preterite only when -**hua** is a denominal derivational suffix (29.6) or the intransitive mate of a transitive verb in -**hua** (12.5). **Pēhua** is one of the very few intransitive verbs ending in -**hua** that do not belong to any of these categories. Also note that there is a transitive homonym **pēhua**, which means 'to defeat'.

(2) **Yauh** 'to go'. This turn of phrase somewhat overlaps with the directional of motion away in -**tīuh** (22.5), except that **yauh** + VERB can only be taken in its literal meaning of 'to go', while the directional of motion away lends itself to figurative usages. Also, the tense system for the directional is, as we know, restricted, while **yauh** can be put in any form.

In principle, the dependent verb is in the future or the imperfective form of the directional of motion away (-**tīuh**). **In** can be put between the two verbs, but this is relatively rare:

Nonyauh teōpan ninoteōchīhuaz	*I'm going to pray in church*
Niyauh (in) nitequitiz	*I'm going to work*
Oc niyauh (in) nitlàchiquitīuh	*Now I'm going to scrap (the core of the maguey)*

It is possible, however, to have the perfective form of the directional of motion away (-**to**) if **yauh** is in the preterite and the action in mind has been carried out:

Ōniyâ ōnictlàpalōto	*I went and greeted him*

(3) **Cāhua** 'to let, to allow': its object is the same as the subject of the second verb, which is usually in the future:

Àquēmman nēchcāhua in ninocēhuīz	*He never lets me rest*

However, if **cāhua** is in some form other than the present tense, the second verb can appear in the same form:

Mā nēn ticcāuh ilhuicacopa tlachix	*Don't (s.) let him look toward the sky* (two vetitives)

VOCABULARY

Nouns

tītlantli (*pl.* /–tin/)	*messenger*	xopechtli	*track*
xolopìtli (*pl.* /–tin/)	*madman, fool*		

Intransitive verbs

ìza	*to wake up* (tēnìza *to have breakfast*)	pēhua[5]	*to start*
		tlachpāna	*to sweep*
		tzinti	*to start, to begin*
pachihui	*to have one's fill, to be satisfied*		

Transitive verbs

ìcali	*to attack*	pēhua	*to defeat*
ìchiqui	*to scrape (the maguey)*	tlazòcāmati	*to thank*
pachoa	*to press, to bend, to direct*		

Adjectives

āhuiyac	*sweet, pleasant*	itztic	*cold*

Locatives

àhuīc	*over here, over there*	huècapan	*up*

Particle

mach	*as it were, apparently*

---

[5] The preterite loses its final vowel, see 32.5.1 Note.

EXERCISES

(a) Translate into English.
1. Xinēchoncuīli inon āmatl in tlani câ, àmo yèhuātl in pani câ.
2. Ōmpa tlachix Quetzalcōhuatl, ic ōntetl ītōcā Èecatl.
3. Ca ōntlamantli in Caxtillān tōchtli īhuān in nicān tōchtli.
4. Xinēchhuīquili cē cuahuitl canāhuac.
5. Xicmotlazòtili in Dios in yèhuātl in ōmitzmochīhuilî, in īpaltzinco tinemi.
6. Āc inon oquichtli, in huel huēyiyac in ītzon?
7. Ca yèhuātl in tepētl in ītepotzco câ in īcal nocnīuh.
8. Cecēc in mocua in icox.
9. Ca huel cocōc ōticchīuh in mōlli!
10. Ōmpa tihuî Mēxìco titiyānquizōzquê.
11. Cuix ye ōampachiuhquê antlacuâ?
12. Ye ōtlan tlatla in tletl, mā titocāhuacān in titonònōtzâ, mā tihuiyān ticochitīhuî.

(b) Translate into Nahuatl.
1. You (pl.) are great lords.
2. What I've done is only a venial ("pardonable") sin.
3. Look (s.) at ("see") the woman who has a pretty skirt ("whose skirt is pretty").
4. I see the house where I was born.
5. We'll cut (down) the tree on top of which there's an eagle.
6. Give (s.) me the razor with which you shaved (yourself).
7. The man who did that has become my friend.
8. Don't turn (yourself) into a rabbit, a deer.
9. He was installed (as) ruler.
10. Let ("allow") (s.) the child cry, he'll soon (go to) sleep.
11. I haven't begun to shuck yet.
12. I hurried to put on my cape.

Comparisons, Clauses of Result, Purpose and Cause

33.1 Comparative

Many languages (particularly Indo-European ones) have special markers to indicate the comparative (forms meaning, e.g., 'bigger', 'more exciting'). In English, the comparative is usually formed by either placing 'more' in front of the adjective ('more interesting') or adding '-er' to the word in the case of monosyllabic adjectives ('hotter'). This comparatively straightforward procedure does not apply to Nahuatl, which has several phrases available to say 'X is more ADJECTIVE than Y'. In English, the phrase indicating the person/thing against which the comparison is made is introduced with 'than' and follows the comparative. For the sake of convenience, we will use the express "than-phrase" to refer to the corresponding part of the Nahuatl comparison (even though there is no simple word for 'than').

A major type of comparative phrase consists of saying (with assorted variants), 'X is ADJECTIVE, Y not'. There is often a mark of intensification in front of the "adjective". This can be **oc** 'still', **cencâ** 'very', **achi** 'rather', **yê** 'yet' (see 33.7), or more often with a combination of these: **oc achi** (most frequent), **oc cencâ, oc yê, oc yê achi, oc yê cencâ**:

Oc (yê) achi/cencâ nichicāhuac in àmo tèhuātl	*I'm stronger than you (s.) (lit., I'm rather strong, which you aren't)*

Tāchcāuh 'strongly' or **huālcâ** 'more' can be used in place of **achi** or **cencâ**, but most commonly **oc tāchcāuh** or **oc huālcâ** is followed by **inic**:

Oc tāchcāuh (*or* huālcâ) inic nichicāhuac in àmo tèhuātl	*I'm stronger than you (s.)*

Tlapanahuia 'it is surpassing' can also be used:

Oc tlapanahuia inic nichicāhuac in àmo tèhuātl

Note carefully that in these constructions we do not have ****oc nitāchcāuh/ nihuālcâ** or **nitlapanahuia**; these verbs remain in the third person singular because their subject is the clause **inic nichicāhuac** 'how I'm strong'. Thus, the literal sense is something like 'surpassing/greater is the way I'm strong, which you aren't'.

Tāchcāuh, huālcâ and **tlapanahuia** can be combined with **cencâ** and **oc** to give a strengthened comparative:

Oc cencâ tāchcāuh (*or* oc cencâ tlapanahuia *or* cencâ oc huālcâ) inic nichicāhuac in àmo tèhuātl	*I'm much stronger than you*

Mach 'apparently, seemingly' or **iuhqui** 'like' or both can also appear in the than-phrase:

Oc achi nichicāhuac in àmo mach (*or* iuhqui *or* mach iuhqui) tèhuātl	*I am much stronger than you*

If the than phrase contains a definite noun, this noun must be preceded by **yè(huātl)** on account of the constraint against a definite predicate (4.2):

Oc achi nichicāhuac in àmo yê (in) Pedro	*I'm stronger than Peter*
Oc achi tihuēhuê in àmo yê (in) nocōl, in nocî	*You're (s.) older than my grandfather and grandmother*

A second type of comparative phrase is 'X surpasses Y as being strong' or 'X surpasses Y as regards strength':

Nimitzpanahuia inic nichicāhuac	*I'm stronger than you*
Nimitzpanahuia in ītech chicāhuacāyōtl	*I am stronger than you*

33.2 Equation

If two items under comparison are found to be equal or equivalent, the construction that expresses this relationship is called an *equation*. In English, an equation of adjectives is expressed as 'you're (as) strong as my father'. We have already seen (14.5) that such an equation can be expressed with **iuhqui(n)** in phrases like:

Iuhquin tocēlōtl tichicāhuac	*You're (s.) strong as (like) a jaguar (lit., you're strong as if you were a jaguar)*

This construction is also subject to the restraint against a definite predicate (4.2), so that if, for instance, you want to say 'you're as strong as my father' (or 'as me/as I am' or 'as Peter' or 'as *the* jaguar'), **iuhqui** has to be repeated, appearing by itself (lit., 'in this way') in the main clause, and with **in** at the start of the clause indicating the person/thing against which the equation is made ('as', 'in which way'):

Iuhqui tichicāhuac in iuhqui notàtzin   *You're (s.) as strong as I (Peter, the jaguar)*
(nèhuātl, Pedro, yê in ocēlōtl)   *am (is).*

The same construction can be used to compare something other than "adjectives," in particular verbs. Here, however, **iuh** appears in place of **iuhqui**:

Iuh xicchīhua, in iuh quimonequiltia   *Do (s.) it the way God wants*
in Dios
Àmo iuh nemiznequi, in iuh nenca   *He doesn't want to live as his father did*
ītàtzin

In Nahuatl and in English, the order of the two clauses can be exchanged, with the equated clause preceding the main clause. In English, this inverted construction is not very common, but when it is used, the equated clause is introduced by 'as', and the main clause tends to begin with 'so (too)' (e.g., 'as Maine goes, so goes the nation', 'as ye sow, so shall ye reap'). The Nahuatl version follows pretty much the same pattern, with the equated clause introduced with **in iuh** '(just) as' and the main clause most often starting with **zan nō iuh**, lit., 'just also so':

Auh in iuh onhuetzquê tleco, zan nō iuh   *And just as they fell into the fire, they also*
huālquīzquê   *came out of it* or *They came out of the fire*
                                             just as they had fallen into it

The initial **in iuh** can be replaced with **in quēnin** (14.6):

In quēnin miqui in icnōtzin, zan nō   *The ruler dies the same way that the poor man*
iuh miqui in tlàtoāni   *does*

It is also possible to use the repeated correlation **in ic ... in ic ...**:

In ic ōtitētolīnî, in ic titolīnīlōz   *Just as you've tormented others, you'll be*
                                             tormented (yourself)

To say 'as big as' or 'as many as', the words **īxquich** and **īzqui(ntin)** (25.2) can be used respectively:

Inin tōtōtl ca īxquich in canauhtli   *This bird is the same size as a duck (lit., as*
                                             for this bird, it's the (same) amount that a
                                             duck is)

A negated equation is used to show a comparison of inferiority. Although the Romance languages are fond of the construction 'X is less ADJECTIVE than Y', Nahuatl resembles English in preferring to say 'X is not as ADJECTIVE as Y' to express the inferiority of X compared to Y:

Àmo iuhqui nichicāhuac in iuhqui tèhuātl	*I'm not as strong as you (s.) are (i.e., less strong than you)*

33.3 Superlative

In English, the superlative forms mean that 'X is the most ADJECTIVE'. The superlative is formed by prefixing 'most' in front of most adjective or adding '-est' in the case of monosyllables. Nahuatl has several circumlocutions to express this idea. One way is to add the intensifying prefixes **cem-** or **cenquīzcā-** to the adjectival form (see 12.9; the latter form is an incorporated preterite agent noun, see 16.1).

In ilhuicac cihuāpillàtoāni ca cenchipāhuacātzintli (*or* cenquīzcāchipāhuacātzintli)	*The noble queen of heaven is perfectly pure*

Another way is to use the phrase **màci(ticâ) inic**, that is, 'attains perfection in being…' (lit., 'attains itself being…'; the verb is **àci** used reflexively, and here too **cem-** can be added as a prefix; see 12.9 sec. 4). Thus:

In ilhuicac cihuāpillàtoāni màcitzinòticâ (*or* mocemàcitzinòticâ) inic chipāhuacātzintli	*The noble queen of heaven is perfectly pure*

This is a sort of absolute superlative, in which there is no external frame of reference, and there are several ways to indicate a superlative in relation to other people or things. Generally, the verb form **tlacempanahuia + inic**, lit. 'surpasses everything[1] in being…', is surpassing/superlative in being…' is used:

Yèhuātl tlacempanahuia inic chicāhuac	*He's the strongest one*
In ilhuicac cihuāpillàtoāni motlacempanahuialia inic chipāhuacātzintli	*The noble queen of heaven is the purest*
Tlacempanahuia inic tēmāuhtî in miquiztli	*Death is what's the most terrifying (lit., it's surpassing as something terrifying)*

---

[1] The indefinite inanimate prefix is used even if it is probable that the comparison is being made with people or other animate beings. Of course, it is also possible to say **quimpanahuia in occequintin** 'he's stronger than the others' (see 33.1), which is tantamount to saying 'he's the strongest'.

Another possible expression is **aoc tle (aoc āc) iuhqui inic ...**, lit., 'nothing/no one else is similar in being ...':

Aoc āc iuhqui inic chicāhuac	*No one is stronger than he is*
Aoc tle iuhqui inic tēmāuhtî in miquiztli	*Nothing is more terrifying than death*

It is also possible to say (with a rare construction) **àtle (ayāc) ihuīhuî inic** (**ihuīhuî** means 'with difficulty, barely, hardly'):

Ayāc ihuīhuî inic chicāhuac	*No one's so strong*
Àtle ihuīhuî inic tēmāuhtî in miquiztli	*Nothing's as terrifying as death*

33.4 Result

Similar to the comparative and equative expressions discussed in 33.1, 2 is the English pattern in result clauses of the type 'he is so strong that he carried the stones'. Such sentences are normally introduced with 'so', 'such' or the like in the main clause, and the result is introduced with 'that'. That is, an entity is said to have a quality to such a degree ('so ...') that some action or state results from this. It is also possible to drop 'that': 'he's so strong, he carried those stones'. In colloquial style, we can even invert the two clauses: 'he carried those stones, he's so strong'. The comparable Nahuatl idiom resembles this last mode of expression: an **inic** clause generally corresponds to the 'so + ADJECTIVE' of English, and the result clause usually lacks any special marker. That is, the result clause from the point of view of the formal English expression is phrased as the main clause, and the circumstance that leads to this result appears in the form of a subordinate **inic** clause. In effect, the Nahuatl says, 'as he's strong, he carried the stones'. The **inic** clause can either precede or follow the main clause. Thus:

Inic chicāhuac ōquimāmâ in tetl	*He's so strong he carried the stones*
In huèhuēyi tlàtòcācalli inic cuàcuauhtic, inic huèhuècapan iuhqui ilhuicatl quizòzōtimani	*The great palaces (ruler houses) are so lofty, so high up, it's as if they pierce (zo) the sky* (note the reduplicated verb, see 28.4, and the use of the auxiliary **-mani**, see 27.1.4)

The same turn of phrase can be found with **inic** introducing a verbal (rather than an adjectival) clause:

Inic motēcaya mācēhualli, in nel quēmman àmo onacōhuaya	*The commoners were so crowded (lay themselves down to such an extent) that in truth it was sometimes impossible to get in* (impersonal of **aqui**)

In oc ic cencâ tēchmotlazòtlatilia in Dios, in àmo zan tlapōhualli	*God loves us so much that the indulgences* (**tlaōcolia** 'to be indulgent, helpful toward')
ītētlaōcolīliztzin ō topan quimochīhuilî	*that he has granted us (done upon us) are innumerable* (**àmo zan tlapōhualli** 'not countable' *from object noun of* **pōhua**)

A more common sort of result clause is not introduced with 'so', 'such' or the like in the main clause, and instead simply introduces a circumstance that results from the main clause. In English, such clauses begin with 'so (that)', 'with the result that', and are introduced in Nahuatl with **(in)ic** (14.4):

Ôtlāhuāntīlōquê in cuauhcalpixquê, ic ōmāquīz	*The guards were made drunk, so (that) he escaped*
Amēchchichicuepa in octli, in ic zan tlalhuiz antēcuàcuâ	*Pulque makes you (pl.) stupid (turns you into dogs), so that you bite people without reason*

33.5 Purpose

In English, purpose clauses are used to indicate the intention for which the action in the main clause is carried out. Such clauses are sometimes introduced with the conjunctions 'so that' or 'in order that', and they can also be expressed with an infinitive, which may or may not be preceded with 'in order' (i.e., 'to VERB' or 'in order to VERB'). Purpose (intention, goal) is regularly expressed in Nahuatl with the future tense (9.9). There is an indication of purpose in subordinate clauses with the future tense that depend on a verb of the type **yauh** 'go' (32.5.2), but there the sense of purpose is comparatively vague. Purpose clauses in the narrower sense corresponding to the English constructions are introduced by **inic** + VERB in the *future*:

Nimitzilhuia inic ticmatiz	*I'm telling you so that you'll know (it)*
Piyalô in māmaltin, inic àmo canâ huel huālquīzazquê	*The prisoners are being guarded so that they won't be able to get out anywhere*
Inic tiquittaz, monequi ōmpa tiyāz	*In order for you (s.) to see it, you must go there*

The goal can be focalized if an anticipatory **ic** is placed in the main clause:

Àmo ic ōnihuāllâ inic nimitznotequipachilhuīz	*I didn't come to bother you (s.) (hon.) (lit., I didn't come for this reason, that I should bother you, which means it wasn't to bother you that I came)*

or through use of the constructions **inic ... yèhuātl inic** or **inic ... ca īpampa inic ...** Thus:

Inic nicān ōnihuāllâ, huel yèhuātl inic namēchmachtīz	*The reason why I came here was to instruct you (pl.) (lit., why I came here, this was precisely so that ...)*
Inic ōmonacayōtìtzinô in totēucyo, ca zan īpampa inic tēchmomāquīxtīlīz	*As for the fact that Our Lord was made incarnate, it was simply for this reason, (namely) that he was to help us (hon.)*

An imperfective directional (22.4–5) can replace the future:

Motlaloâ in tītlantin, inic quinōnōtzatīhuî in Motēuczōma	*The messengers are running in order to (go) report to Moctezuma*

The counterfactual tense (22.2) can be used to express a regret that a goal was not attained. Thus:

Mā niccaquini, inic àmo iuhqui nopan mochīhuazquia in āxcān ye nopan mochīhua	*I should listen to him so that the things that are now being done to me (upon me) would not have been done to me in this way*
Mācamo iuh niquìtoāni, inic àmo mīxnāmiquizquiâ	*I shouldn't speak like that (**iuh**), so that they wouldn't have quarreled (met each other with their eyes/ face)*

(In these examples, **mā** + **-ni** form appears in the main clause to indicate the wish that something that did not happen had happened; see 16.9.)

The interrogative relating to purpose is **tle ic** or as a single word **tleic** 'why?' (i.e., 'for what reason?' 'to what end?'):

Tleic ticchīhua in?	*Why are you (s.) doing this?*
Tleic nēn ticnōnōtza?	*Why are you wasting your time talking to him? (i.e., what's the point of advising him when he won't listen?)*

Note the expression **tle ic nonāyiz** (cf. **āyi**, 18.9) 'what's the use of my VERBING', with an object noun clause (31.2) corresponding to the gerund clause in English:

Tle ic nonāyiz in ōmpa niyāz?	*What's the use of my going there? (lit., why should I go on doing (this, namely) that I will go there?)*

33.6 Cause

The most common equivalent in Nahuatl of an English causal clause ('because') is **īpampa** (24.3.3) at the head of a clause that is generally introduced with **in** or **ca**:

Tle īpampa tinēchàhua? – Ca īpampa in tinēchtequipachoa	*What are you (s.) telling me off for? – Because you're bothering me (lit., it's for this reason, namely that …)*
Nitlapòpolhuīlōni, īpampa ca àmo huēyi in notlàtlacōl	*I'm forgivable because my sins aren't big*
Mochōquilia in nonāntzin, īpampa ca ōmomiquilî in notàtzin	*My mother's crying (hon.) because my father has died (hon.)*
Nimitzchicāhuacātlazòtla, īpampa ca tiyēcnemi	*I love you (s.) a lot (strongly) because you lead a virtuous life*
Aocmo nitlāhuānaz, īpampa ca huel ōnēchcocô in octli	*I won't get drunk any more because the pulque really made me sick*

Yê īca (or as a single word **yèīca**) is also found (cf. the interrogative **tleīca**), especially in admonitions of a more or less solemn nature or with the meaning 'since, as (causal)' (in the latter usage, the subordinate clause generally precedes the main one):

Ca yèhuātl Dios huel monāntzin, motàtzin, yèīca ca yèhuātzin ōquìtô, ōquiyōcox inic ōtiyōl, inic ōtitlācat	*God is indeed your mother and father, because it was he who said, who conceived (the idea) that you would be born, that you would come into the world[2]*
In tlein àmo cuālōni, àmo tictēcualtīz, yèīca cencâ māhuiztilīlōni in ītlachīhualtzin in Dios	*You (s.) aren't to feed people what isn't edible because the creations of God are to be respected (**māhuiztilia** 'to respect'; cf. **māhuiztic** 'respectable', 29.2–3)*
Yèīca tinēchnōtza, ic niyāz mochān	*Since you're (s.) calling me, I'll go to your place*
Yèīca in huel huècapan catê in cīcitlāltin, iuhquin tepitotōn ic huālnēcî	*Since the stars are very high up, they appear as if they're very small*

(Note in the last two sentences how the initial causal clause is "picked up" by **ic** in the main clause; see 14.4.)

As in English, the mere juxtaposition of two sentences sometimes introduces an implied causal relationship. In Nahuatl, **ca** is most often included

---

[2] Note the use of the preterite instead of the expected future in the **inic** clauses. These indicate purpose, but because the purpose was realized when the person came into the world, the preterite reflects this realization rather than the contingent intent that the future tense would express.

with the second sentence, which gives an explanation for the preceding one:

Mā xicmotlapòpolhuīli: ca oc piltōntli, ayamo mozcalia	*Excuse (s., hon.) him, (since) he's still a small child and hasn't yet become sensible*
Mā titlacuācān, ca ye nepantlâ tōnatiuh	*Let's eat, it's already noon*
Ca zan nō titèhuān: ca tiquintlàtōlcaquî	*They're our people (**titèhuān**, 26.4), we understand their language (lit., hear them in speech)*
Mācamo xicchīhua in: ca mitzàhuaz motàtzin	*Don't do this, your father will rebuke you (s.)*

This explanatory **ca** ('for ...', 'you see ...') refers to the entire sentence that follows, and not just to its predicate. Hence, it is not necessary for **ca** to be immediately followed by the predicate. In fact, the sentence can begin with the subject, a locative or a subordinate clause. It can even begin with an interrogative word. Thus:

Mìtoa: cuix īxquich quitta in huitziltzin? Ca in huitziltzin cencâ pitzactōn in ītēn.	*It's said, does the hummingbird (huitzilin) see that much?[3] For the hummingbird has a very small beak (lips).*
Quìtoa in tīcitl àmo tlālcuāz, àmo nō tīzacuāz in otztli: ca in tlein quicua nāntli,[4] nō yèhuātl quimonacayōtia in piltzintli.	*The midwife says that the pregnant woman shouldn't eat dirt or **tiza** (a sort of edible chalk). For whatever the mother eats, the child incorporates into his body.*
Àtle ōniccuīc, ca tlein ōniccuīzquia?	*I didn't take anything. What was I going to take? (i.e., there wasn't anything for me to take)*

Ca would not be permissible in this position in any of these examples if the sense were not explanatory.

The causal relationship is often very close to the sense of a purpose clause (e.g., 'he came to do something' = 'he came because he wanted to do something') or a result clause ('he did something so that it happened' = 'something happened because he did it'). For this reason, expressions with **(in)ic** can be found that one might be inclined to translate with a causal clause or that could

---

[3] **Cuix īxquich quitta in huitziltzin?** is what you say in protest when you have been given too little food.

[4] Note the absolutive form **nāntli**. It is permissible for a noun that is normally construed with inalienable possession (11.1) to assume the abolutive form when it is used in a precept or a general truth.

be interpreted in two ways. Thus:

Inic cencâ ìiyô[5] in tlacuātl, mochi quixīx *As the (flesh of) opossum is very strong, this*
 in īcuitlaxcōl inin chichi *dog emptied all its bowels (or the opossum*
  is so strong that …)
Mopāccāhuèhuetzquitia *They smile and sing with joy because they*
 mopāccācuìcuīcatiâ in ic *are happy (hon.) (or so happy are they*
 motlamachtìtzinoâ. *that …)*

33.7 Yê and -ê

We've already seen **yê** in comparisons (33.1). This is perhaps a fixed use of the short form of the pronoun **yèhuātl**, which may be what appears in phrases like:

Àmo cualli on, yê cualli in *That's bad, but this is good*

In any event, **yê** acts as an adverb meaning 'on the other hand, to the contrary':

Īxpampatzinco tēhuatinemi in totēucyo, *You (s.) keep fleeing from our Lord; instead,*
 mā yê īxpampa xēhua in *flee from the demon*
 tlācatecolōtl
Àmo nimitzàhua, yê tèhuātl in *I'm not rebuking you (s.). – On the contrary,*
 tinēchàhua. *it's you that's rebuking me.*

In the form **-ê**, it is added to other particles without any clear change in their meaning. This is particularly the case with **àzo** 'perhaps' and **nozo** 'or', which become **àcê**, **nocê** (with elision of the final **-o**). Perhaps these forms in **-ê** have a vaguer sense:

Cuix àcê ītōcā Pedro? *Is his name Peter by any chance?*
Cuix itlâ àcualli ōtiquittac, nocê ōticcac? *Did you see, or maybe hear, something bad?*
Cuix ōtitlāhuān, cuix nocê *Did you get drunk, or did you make other*
 ōtitētlāhuāntî? *people drunk?*

Mā nocê means 'nor', 'instead' (**mā nozo** is also found):

Mā nocê xiccāhua in *Leave this instead*
Àmo timomachtia, mā nocê *You (s.) don't study, you don't work either*
 titlatequipanoa

---

[5] Lit. 'with breath' (11.9). The flesh of an opossum tail was reputed for its qualities as a purgative.

VOCABULARY

Transitive verbs

tlaōcolia	to be indulgent, to be compassionate toward	yōcoya	to shape, to conceive
xīxa	to eject (of urine or excrement)	zo[6]	to stab, to pierce (for the purpose of blood letting)

Nouns

canauhtli (pl. /–tin/)	duck	ìiyōtl	breath (ìiyô strong)
cìtli (pl. /–tin/)	1) grandmother, 2) hare	ocēlōtl (pl. /–mê/ /R–'/)	jaguar
cōlli[7] (pl. /–tin/)	grandfather	tīzatl	chalk
cuitlaxcōlli	intestines	tlacuātl	opossum
huitzilin	hummingbird		

Particles and adverbs

ihuīhuî	barely, with difficulty	yê	on the other hand, but
nel	truly	yèīca	since, because, for
tlalhuiz	without thought		

EXERCISES

(a) Translate into English.
1. Ōmitzàhuaquê, auh àmo ic ōtimonemilizcuep.
2. Oc huālcâ tāxcāhuâ, titlatquihuâ in àmo nèhuātl.
3. Oc cencâ tāchcāuh inic tlazòtli in teōcuitlatl, in àmo yê tepoztli.
4. In īxquich amāltepēuh, zan nō īxquich tèhuāntin tāltepēuh.
5. In cepayahuitl tlacempanahuia inic iztāc, aoc tle iuhqui inic iztāc.
6. In ic nicān amāltepēuh īpan ōnihuāllâ, ca zan īpampa inic ītech nitlàtōz in teōyōtl.
7. Ayāc quichōquilīz, yèīca ca huel tlahuēlīlōc catca.
8. Àmo niccōhuaz: ca inic niccōhuaz, monequi nicpiyaz tomin.
9. Xictlāti in, inic àmo quittaz notàtzin.
10. Xìxitīn in calli inic tlālolin.

---

[6] The only transitive verb ending in -o.

[7] Cōlli and cìtli 'grandmother' almost always appear in the possessed form (so the plurals are -cōlhuān, -cìhuān; see 11.1).

(b) Translate into Nahuatl.
1. I didn't do it because you (s.) haven't ordered me (to).
2. I have as many children as Pedro ("my children are as many as Peter's children").
3. This small child is wiser than the others.
4. This young woman is the prettiest (one) in our town.
5. They are so unfortunate (*use the reflexive of* tolīnia) that they sob all the time (*use a compound verb with the first verb form reduplicated*).
6. Since you (s.) want me to do the shopping ("that I go to the market"), give me money.
7. Throw stones at the dog so that he'll go somewhere (else).
8. Here is what you must do in order to be loved.
9. My house is smaller than your (pl.) house.
10. The food was so spicy that I couldn't eat it.

Conditions, More Particles

34.1 Conditional Clauses

A *conditional* sentence is one in which a possibility is posited in a subordinate clause and the consequences that would result from the realization of this possibility are laid out in the main clause. The clause that lays out the posited condition is introduced in English with 'if' and in Nahuatl with **in tlā** (which can also be written as one word; this is the same **tlā** that we have already met with the optative, 9.5), and the two elements of such a sentence are called the "if-clause" and the "then-clause". When the subordinate clause contains a negative ('unless' or 'if...not'), **intlācamo** is used in Nahuatl instead of ****in tlā àmo** (cf. **mācamo** for ****mā àmo**). If there is a negative pronoun or adverb, a compound with **tlā** is again used: **intlācayāc** 'if no one...' (or 'if...no one'), **intlàcàtle** 'if nothing...' (or 'if...nothing'), **intlācaīc** 'if...never'), etc.

   In tlā has virtually the same range of meaning as 'if'. It is necessary to distinguish between two broad categories of conditional sentences. Here we will look at true hypotheses. In such sentences, the 'if' of English and the **in tlā** of Nahuatl mean 'under the hypothesis that...', 'in the case where...', 'given that...'. Nahuatl has four basic sub-varieties for these sorts of conditions. English more or less shares the same categories, but has a number of alternative ways to express some. We will look at the four Nahuatl sub-varieties and consider the English correspondences.

34.1.1 Past Contrafactual[1]

Here, the hypothesis posits a circumstance in the past that did not in fact hold true. In Nahuatl, the if-clause has **in tlā** + **-ni** FORM (often preceded by the augment), and the result clause has the COUNTERFACTUAL (again, often

---

[1] Be sure not to confuse the term *contrafactual*, which refers to a condition that is contrary to the factual situation, with the term *counterfactual*, which is a verb form (22.2).

preceded by the augment). In English, this is rendered with 'If X had VERBed, Y would have VERBed'.

In the second person, the **-ni** form preceded by the augment takes the subject prefix **x(i)-** (16.9):

In tlā ōxinēchtequipanoāni, ca ōnimitztlaxtlāhuīzquia	*If you (s.) had worked for me, I would have paid you*

Just as with the preterite (8.8), the augment is not necessary in narrative, and if it is omitted, the past contrafactual is not distinguishable from the present contrafactual (see 34.1.2):

Ca yèhuātl tōnatiuh yezquia in mētztli, in tlā yê achto onhuetzini tleco	*The moon would have become the sun if it had instead been the first to fall into the fire*

(As can be seen, the word order in both English and Nahuatl can be either the if-clause–then-clause or the other way around.)

34.1.2 Present Contrafactual

This is a hypothesis that presupposes a circumstance in the present that does not hold true. In Nahuatl, this is indicated with **in tlā +-ni** FORM (with second person prefix **x(i)-**), and the then-clause has the COUNTERFACTUAL. In English, the if-clause can take several forms: 'if X were Y', 'if X VERBed', 'if X were VERBing' (e.g., 'if I were you', 'if I had the money', 'if I were having fun', none of which is the truth); the result clause is simpler: 'Z would VERB'. Thus:

In tlā xinēchtequipanoāni, ca nimitztlaxtlāhuīzquia	*If you (s.) were working for me, I would pay you*
In tlā nicān yenî, ca niquimilhuīzquia	*If they were here, I would tell them*

There can be a mixture of a past contrafactual if-clause and a present contrafactual then-clause, which indicates the present situation that would result if the hypothesis had held true in the past:

Intlācayāc tlālticpac tlācatl ōtlàtlacoāni, ayāc miquizquia, â nō āc mococōzquia	*If no person on earth had sinned, no one would die and no one would get sick*

34.1.3 Hypothetical

Here, a plausible or implausible condition referring to the future is presented as hypothetical proposition. That is, if we assume that a certain circumstance is the case (without saying anything about our expectations of its proving true), then something else would result. Although some set of future circumstances that we do think likely to happen can be expressed with this sort of condition, it more readily lends itself to the expression of notions that are considered either rather contingent or not so likely to be realized. In Nahuatl, the if-clause takes **in tlā** + OPTATIVE, and the then-clause takes the future. In English, the if-clause takes the form 'if X would VERB', 'if X were to VERB', 'should X VERB' or 'if X VERBed' (note that this last form is the same as one of the ones used for the present contrafactual, and only the context can distinguish the two), and the then-clause has 'X would VERB' (e.g., 'it would be nice if you would stop', 'if I were to win the lottery/should I win the lottery/if I won the lottery, I would pay off my debts'). Thus:

Àzo ic nicnoyōlìtlacalhuīz in tlàtoāni, in tlā cēmê niquimmictīli in īitzcuinhuān	*Perhaps I would offend the ruler if I were to kill one of (7.4) his dogs*
In tlā iuh xicchīhua, ca huel oncān tinēciz in tihuēyitlahuēlīlōc	*If you acted that way, you would then really seem (to be) a criminal*
In tlā xiquimmāhuiztili in ītlachīhualhuān in Dios, zan īhuiyān, zan īcemel timomiquilīz	*If you would respect God's creations, you would die in repose, in peace*

34.1.4 Simple Future

This is a possible and plausible hypothesis that refers to the future and is in some way less hypothetical than the preceding case. The point here is that if the condition does prove true, then some consequence will in fact follow. This sort of condition is generally used to express circumstances whose realization is considered either likely or at least perfectly reasonable to expect. In Nahuatl, the if-clause takes **in tlā** + FUTURE, and the then-clause also takes the future. In English, the if-clause normally takes the present and the then-clause takes the form 'X will VERB' (e.g., 'if you study hard, you'll do well on the test'). Thus:

In tlā huel ticchīhuaz in, ic titlācamachōz, tiyēquìtōlōz (yēc + ìtoa), ticualìtōlōz	*If you do this well, then you'll be respected, spoken well of, commended*
In tlā huālēhuazquê in toyāōhuān, in tlā tēchìcalizquê, ca tiquinyāōnāmiquizquê, ca tiquimìcalizquê	*If our enemies invade, if they attack us, we'll fight them (meet them in a hostile manner), we'll attack them*

With these sorts of expressions, we slide imperceptibly from real hypotheses into the "weak" hypotheses treated in the next section.

Notes

(1) To reinforce the notion that the hypothesis necessarily entails certain consequences, the counterfactual or future tense in the then-clause can be replaced with the -**ni** form:

In tlā ōnimitzcāhuāni, ca ye ōtimiquini	*If I'd abandoned you (s.), you would be dead by now*
Intlācamo nèhuātl nimitzompalēhui, ca ye ōtipòpolōlōni	*If I hadn't gone and helped you (s.), you would already have been finished off*

(2) To reinforce the notion that a certain fact would have inevitably entailed another one (and that the present situation would differ from what it would otherwise be), the then-clause can begin with **in tlā zan āxcān** 'in that case' (lit., 'at the present time'), with its verb in the the appropriate tense to signify the real situation. For its part, the if-clause retains the regular **in tlā** 'if'. Thus:

In tlā ōniyāni yohuatzinco in Tepotzòtlān, in tlā zan āxcān àmo ye ō nopan quiyauh?	*If I'd gone to Tepotzotlan this morning, wouldn't it have rained (lit., didn't it already rain) on me?* (This is said by someone who canceled a planned trip to Tezpotzotlan and is reflecting on the fact that it rained meanwhile, so that he would have been rained on during the journey had he undertaken it.)

(3) If-clauses allow the inclusion of indefinite pronouns and adverbs like **acâ, itlâ, canâ, icâ** (26.8):

In tlā acâ nēchilhui in, ca nicmictīz	*If someone were to say this to me, I'd kill him*
In tlā canâ ōniquittani, ca ōnicnònōtzazquia	*If I'd seen him somewhere, I would have spoken with him*

34.2 Semi-Hypothetical Conditions

Both the Nahuatl **in tlā** and the English 'if' can be used to express "watered down" conditions or semi-hypotheses. The meaning of these can be close to

▷ a causal clause ('if it's true that ...' = 'since it's the case that ...')
▷ a temporal clause ('if ...' = 'when ...', 'whenever ...')

In these instances, the use of the tenses is much freer, and in either clause the predicate can appear in the form of a noun, "adjective" or locative in place of a verb (and naturally the verb 'to be' has to be used in the English translation):

In tlā cē tomiyo chicopetōni, huēyi tēcocô	*If one of our bones becomes dislocated (sticks out of kilter), it's a serious injury*
Tlein nicchīhuaz, intlācamo tlatlācamati?	*What am I to do if (= since) he doesn't obey?*
Intlācamo motlàtoāyan, àmo titlàtōz	*If it's not your (s.) turn (24.9), you're not to speak*
Àmo tlayacac timoquetztāz², intlācamo ōtināhuatīlōc	*You (s.) aren't to put yourself in first place if you haven't been ordered to (for the idiom in the main clause, see 27.1.6 sec. 2.)*
In tlā oncatê in mitzpanahuiâ, yèhuāntin achto quīzazquê	*If there are people who surpass you, it is they who pass by first*
In tlā tipilli, àmo oncān ticcāhuaz in mopillo	*If you're (s.) a nobleman, you won't leave your nobility there*
In tlā ōmic piltōntli, itztli quicalaquia in ītic cihuātzintli in tīcitl	*If the baby's dead, the midwife inserts the knife into the woman's womb*
In tlā ōittōquê nicān Mēxìco, niman quintzītzquiāyâ, īhuān quimmictiāyâ	*If (= whenever) they were seen here in Mexico, they (15.11) would seize and kill them*

The English 'if…then' belongs to this category of semi-hypotheses when it takes the form 'if (= since) X is true now, then how much more will it be the case under some other circumstance!' (i.e., we have here an a fortiori conception expressed in the form of an exclamation). The Nahuatl equivalent of 'how much more!' is in principle **quēn oc yê** or **quēn zan yê**:

In tlā āxcān xōpantlâ ticecmiqui, quēn oc yê (*or* quēn oc yê) ticecmiquiz in cehuetzilizpan!	*If you're (s.) freezing now in the spring, then how much more will you be in the winter (in the time of ice fall)!*
In tlā īxquich netolīniliztli topan mochīhuaz in āxcān, quēn oc yê cencâ hualcâ in mochīhuaz in ìcuāc tlamiz in cemānāhuatl!	*If so much misery is happening to us now, how much more will happen when the world ends!*

---

² For **timoquetztiyāz**, see 27.1.6.

34.3 Concessive Clauses

A *concessive* clause is a subordinate clause that makes a statement that is at variance in someway with the main clause. In English, there are several types of concessive clauses, and these have equivalents in Nahuatl.

(1) '(Al)though, even though' = **(in) mā nel**, **mā zo** or **mācihui** (for **mā zo ihui**). Such clauses take the appropriate tense, with the future signifying 'to be about to' (**mā nel quichīhuaz** 'although he is on the point of doing it'):

In mā nel mochintin tēteô ōmicquê, zan nel àmo ic olin	*Though all the gods were dead, he still wasn't stirred by this*
Mā zo titotlācapô, mā zo titohuāmpô, mā zo titocnīuh, ca aocmo titotlācapô, aocmo timitztlācaittâ	*Even though you're a human like us, you're our companion* (**-huām-pô**, see 26.4), *and you're our friend, you're no longer a human like us and we won't consider you to be a human any more*
Mā zo mìtoa nitīcitl, cuix nomāc nicchīhuaz, niquìmatiz in cōzcatl, in quetzalli?	*Although it is said that I'm a doctor, will I bring the jewel and the feather into being with my hands and create them?* (the phrase 'jewel and feather' refers to a newborn, see 14.1.3, and the statement is made by the midwife before the mother's lying-in.)
Mācihui (*or* in mā nel) nicnōtlacatl, ca nō ninomāhuiztilīllani	*Though I'm a poor person, I also wish to be respected* (for the verb form, see 28.11)

The four particles **mā zo nel ihui** can also be used:

In oquichtin àmo momāxtlatiāyâ, mā zo nel ihui cencâ oncâ cuāchtli	*The men weren't wearing loin cloths,[3] even though there were large cloths in quantity*

▶ *Note.* **Mā nel zan** or **mā nelê** (for the ending, see 33.7) can be used with a noun in the restrictive sense 'so much as', 'even', 'at least':

Mā nel zan canâ tepitzocotzin (*25.4*) ātōlātzintli xinēchmomaquili	*Give (s., hon.) me just a tiny bit of atole[4]*

---

[3] The **māxtlatl** (possessed form -**māxtli**: 10.7) is a sort of loin cloth that goes between the legs and around the waist, and a **cuāchtli** is a large piece of cloth that serves as a covering or cloak.

[4] Atole is a thick drink made from corn pulp.

Aīc mā nel zan cē pīnacatl nomāc miqui	*Not even a single black beetle has ever died at my hands*
Āquin cahuayòpan tlècōya, in mā nelê tlazòpīpiltin?	*Who used to mount a horse, even among the high (precious) nobility?*
Ayāc āquin tiquīxtilia, ticmāhuiztilia, mā teōpixquê, mā tlàtòquê, mā huēhuetquê	*You (s.) don't respect or honor anyone, be it priests or rulers or elders* (note the use of the interrogative **āquin** as an indefinite in non-initial position, so that **ayāc āquin** means something like 'not anyone')

(2) The phrase 'even if' can have two somewhat different senses. In one it grants for the sake of argument a proposition that the speaker does not actually consider to be a definite fact or perhaps would prefer not to be the case: 'even if it is true (which I do not necessarily concede) that …', 'granted that …'. The corresponding Nahuatl is **mā zo tēl** (with the appropriate tense):

Mā zo tēl ōniccuīc, cuix motequiuh?	*Even if (let's say that) I took it, what business is this of yours (is it your business)?*
Mā zo tēl nimiqui, ca ye ōnìixhuic	*Even if I'm dying, I'm content*
Mā zo tēl ōnicchīuh, tlein īpan motta in ōnicchīuh?	*Even if I did it, what view can be held about what I did?(lit., what is the fact that I did it seen as?;* see 13.4 sec. 2)

(3) In its second meaning, 'even if' assumes the validity of the proposition but indicates that regardless of this possibility that it is true, whatever is stated in the main clause negates or undermines the fact in the subordinate clause. Hence, this usage is tantamount to 'despite the fact that …' or 'regardless of the fact that …'. In this sense, one can also say 'even though'.[5] The corresponding Nahuatl is **in tlā nel**:

Auh in tlā nel tiquimpanahuia in occequintin, ayamo niman ìciuhca tiquinyacānaz	*And even if you're (s.) superior to the others, you aren't to lead them right away*
In tlā nel moch ticmocuītīz in motlàtlacōl, intlācamo ticcāhuaznequi, àmo mā nel cē motlàtlacōl mitzmopòpolhuīlīz in totēucyo	*Even if you (will) confess all your sins, if you aren't willing to abandon them, our Lord won't forgive so much as a single one of them*

---

[5] Note that 'even though' is a valid translation for the Nahuatl expressions in both secs. 1 and 3; there is clearly a difference between these two categories in that 'even if' is a valid alternative only for sec. 3 and could not be used for the expressions in sec. 1.

In tlā nel acâ mitzilhuīz in ticnēxtīz, in tiquìtōz, àmo tiquilhuīz, àmo ticnēxtīz	*Even if someone will tell you (s.) what (you are) to disclose and what to say, you won't tell him this or disclose it*

(4) For 'whoever', 'whatever', 'wherever' etc., Nahuatl uses **in zāzo** (or **in zācê**, 33.7) + INTERROGATIVE:[6]

In zāzo tāc[7] tê titlàtlacoāni, in zāzo quēmman īhuicpatzinco timocuepaz in totēucyo, mitzmopòpolhuīlīz in zāzo quēxquich īhuān in zāzo tlein ic ōticmoyōlìtlacalhuî	*Whoever you are, you sinner, whenever you will turn to God, he will forgive you whatever it was that you offended him with, however great that was*
In zāzo cāmpa yāz nocommictīz	*Wherever he goes (will go), I'll go and kill him (there)*

▶ *Note.* In **zāzo**, the **zā** element is the particle meaning 'no more than, in the end' (31.6 sec. 4) and **zo** is the one that we have seen in **àzo** (14.2), **nozo** and **mā zo**.

Now we will look at other particles that are used in concessive clauses (and ones of kindred meaning).

34.4 *Tēl*

This is the particle that appears in the phrase **mā zo tēl** (34.3 sec. 2), and it is also found between two clauses with the meaning 'but', 'nonetheless', 'all the same' (when the second clause is something positive that remains the case despite the negative implications of the first):

Ca icnōtlācatl, tēl cualli tlācatl	*He's a poor man, but he's a good one all the same*

As can be seen, the basic sense of **tēl** is one of contrast, and when it is used by itself, the particle serves to indicate a remark of exculpation or self-justification in the face of a criticism (whether overt or only implicitly) or one of relief that when something bad has been feared, no harm has in fact been suffered. Thus, it corresponds to English expressions like 'anyway', 'after all', 'at any rate',

---

[6] The English expressions 'whoever' 'whatever' etc. are ambiguous. The meaning here is concessive, so that 'whoever you are' means 'regardless of who you are'. This usage has to be distinguished from the indefinite relative 'whoever' etc., which is the equivalent of 'anyone who' and translates the Nahuatl **in** + INTERROGATIVE, i.e., **in āquin** etc. (4.10).

[7] Note the personal prefix added to **āc**, which is a rare usage (4.9 at end). The plural in this case is **āquê: in zāzo tāquê** 'whoever we are'.

appearing after other particles that introduce statements (**ca**), questions (**cuix**) or wish (**mā**):

Ca àtle tēl mà (34.7) ōquìtlacô	*Nothing's harmed it after all* (said after fearing that a field had been ruined but then finding that it was unharmed)
Ca tēl ye cualli, yê tèhuātl ticmati	*Okay, have it your (s.) way (lit., you know it, i.e., you know what you're doing).*
Cuix tēl nèhuātl notlàtlacōl?	*Anyway, is it my fault? (i.e., it isn't really my fault)*
Mā tēl xicchīhua	*Go ahead, then, do it (s.)!* (said after determining that a perceived objection to the action doesn't in fact pose an unsurmountable obstacle.)

34.5 *Nel*

This is the stem of **nelli** 'true, truth' used adverbially, strengthening statements, questions and wishes:

Cāmpa nel niyāz?	*Where am I to go?*
Àmo nel niyāz? Āquin nel yāz?	*Am I not supposed to go then? who will go?*
Mā xiyàpōlo, ca nel àmo tinēchtlācamatiznequi	*Go (s.) away (deprec.), you're completely unwilling to obey me*

In questions, **nel** can be strengthened with **nozo**:

Quēn nel nozo (*or* quēn nozo nel) mochīhuaz?	*How ever can this be done?*

34.6 *Cuēl*

This particle basically suggests that the action of the sentence was carried out with (undue) haste or suddenness. It appears most frequently after **ye** 'already', but here the sense 'already' emphasizes the surprising or disagreeable nature of the event:

Ye ō cuēl nimic in àciquiuh	*I'll already be dead (alas) when he arrives*
Cāmpa ō cuēl onyâ in tītlantli?	*Where has the messenger gone?*

It is also encountered in veiled criticisms:

Quin ōtihuālmohuīcac, auh ye cuēl timohuīcaznequi!	*You (s.) just got here and already you want to leave!*
Quin ōnàcico, auh ye cuēl tinēchmihuālia!	*I've barely arrived and you're (s.) already sending me away!*

So too **ye nō cuēl** 'once again' (of something disagreeable):

Ōmìtô ca ye ōyàquê in caxtiltēcâ, aocmo huāllāzquê, auh in ōquīz ōnxihuitl, ye nō cuēl ceppa ōmìtô inic ye nō cuēl huītzê	*It was said that the Spaniards had gone and that they wouldn't return, but after two years passed, it was said once again that they were returning once more*

Nō cuēl, nō cuēl yê, nō cuēlê (see 33.7) is 'on the other hand' (in argumentation and reasoning):

In quēmmanyān nicnequi, mā canàpa nitztēhua, nō cuēl yê nēchtlaōcoltiâ in nopilhuān: quēn niquincāuhtēhuaz?	*Sometimes I'd like to go someplace else, but on the other hand I feel pity for my children (they make me feel pity). How could I go off and abandon them?*
In quēmmanyān huel nicehuapāhua, auh in nō cuēlê quēmmanyān huel nitlemiqui	*Sometimes I'm really numb with cold, but sometimes, on the other hand, I die of heat (fire)*

Mā (ye) cuēlê is used with the **-ni** form and the optative:

Mā cuēlê xinēchcaquini!	*If only you'd listen to me!*
Mā cuēlê niccēhuito in nonacayo!	*Oh, may I go and set my body at rest!*

Hence, the elliptical expression **mā ye cuēlê** 'let's go, come on!' (indicating impatience) and **tlācuēlê** (i.e., **tlā cuēlê**) 'come one, then', 'cheer up' (more polite encouragement).

   Zan cuēl 'in a short period of time':

Ōmpa Cōlhuacān ōilhuīlōquê in mēxìcâ in àmo ìciuhca, in àmo zan cuēl àciquihuî in oncān tlàtòcātizquê	*At Colhuacan the Mexica were told that it would not be quickly, not soon, that they would arrive at the place where they would rule*

34.7 Mâ

The proper meaning of this particle (which is not to be confused with **mā**)[8] is something like 'being such that …', and it is used to "strengthen" interrogative and negative words:

Āquin mâ quimati?	*Who ever knows that? (is such that he …)*
Cuix mâ ōmomiquilî in motàtzin?	*Has your (s.) father really died? (it is possible that …? are things such that …?)*

---

[8] In the many texts that do not mark vowel lengths or glottal stops, it is easy to distinguish the two forms because **mā** is normally the first word in its clause but **mâ** never appears in this position.

Àcān mâ ōniccac	*I haven't heard that anywhere (there's no place where …)*
Ayāc mâ quimati	*There's no one who knows that*
Aīc mâ ōnimitznotequipachilhuî	*I've never bothered you*

The pronouns **ayāc** and **àtle** are often repeated with an indefinite one in the form **ayāc mâ acâ** or **ayāc mâ cēmê** (with plural agreement)/**àtle mâ itlâ**:

Ayāc mâ cēmê ōmonēxtìquê in āltepēhuàquê	*Not a single one of the inhabitants showed himself*
Àtle mâ itlâ ic ōnicnoyōlìtlacalhuî	*In not one way (in the manner of nothing, 14.3) have I offended him (hon.)*

Mâ can also be found after **àzo**, the combination being used to introduce a question:

Àzo mâ ōticmomachitî?	*Perhaps you've (s.) already learned it (hon.)?*

Mâ can also turn up in comparisons, combining with **iuhqui(n)** in the forms **in mâ iuhqui** or **iuhquin mâ** 'as if it were …':

Cuahuitl īpan huālpatlāni in cōhuātl: iuhquin mâ tlācatl īpan quichīhua	*The snake flings itself onto a tree as if he were doing so onto a person*
Huel ìilac iuhquin mâ zoquipan in īmācpal	*His palm really sank down (**ilaqui**) as if into mud*
Mā īhuicpatzinco tihuiyān in tlàtòcācihuāpilli, in mâ iuhqui pōchōtl, āhuēhuētl	*Let's go to Our Lady (the noble queen) as if she were a silk cotton tree or a cypress[9]*

Mâ has the corresponding negative forms **màca** or **màcamo** (not to be confused with **mācamo**, 9.6):

Āquin màca quimati?	*Who ever doesn't know it?*
Ayāc màca quimati	*There isn't anyone who doesn't know it (= everyone knows it)*

In màca(mo) is also found introducing relative clauses dependent on an interrogative or a negative:

Tlein oc īhuān monequi nicchīhuaz in màcamo ōnicchīuh?	*What else do I still have to do that I haven't done yet? (i.e., there's nothing that I haven't …)*

---

[9] These trees provide much shade and symbolize protection.

Àmo màca 'it's not as if...not...', 'it's not the case that...not...' is the equivalent of a strengthened statement:

Àmo màca nicneltoca in tlein ticmìtalhuia   *It's not as if I don't believe what you (s.) say (hon.)*

VOCABULARY

Intransitive verbs

cecmiqui	*to be cold*	(ì)ixhui	*to have one's fill*
ilaqui	*to sink down*	petōni	*to be out of alignment*

Transitive verbs

ìmati	*to put into practice carefully*	neltoca	*to believe*
		tzītzquia	*to seize, to lay hands on*
m(o)-:	*to be clever, to be shrewd*		

Nouns

āhuēhuētl	*ahuehuete (kind of cypress)*	cuāchtli	*piece of cloth*
		mācpalli	*palm*[10]
ātōlli	*atole (kind of drink, see note 4)*	māxtlatl	*piece of cloth*
		pīnacatl	*black beetle*
		pōchōtl	*silk cotton tree*
cemānāhuatl	*world, universe*		

Locatives

Cōlhuàcān	*Colhuacan*	xōpantlâ	*(in the) spring*
Tepotzòtlān	*Tepotzotlan*		

Adverbs

īcemel/cemellê	*peacefully, happily*	īhuiyān	*mildy, peacefully*

Particles

cuēl	*already (alas)*	tēl	*nonetheless*
mâ	*(being) such that...*	(in) zāzo (INTERROGATIVE)	*ever*

[10] Lit. 'seat' (**icpalli**) of the hand.

EXERCISES

(a) Translate into English.

1. Intlācamo nicān ōniyeni, intlācamo ōnimitzommāquīxtiāni, in tlā zan āxcān àmo ye ōtimictīlōc?
2. Intlācamo melāhuac ōtiquinnānquilî, ca mitzàhuazquê.
3. Àmo nimitzcāhuaz, intlācamo achto tinēchmacaz in.
4. In mā nel cualli in, ca àmo niccōhuaz.
5. Àmo zan cuēl in ōtlan, in ōcēuh yāōyōtl.
6. Ye cuēl ōnxihuitl in àcān niquīza.
7. Ye ō cuēl moch quicuàquê in ōnàcico.
8. In mā nel titlamatini, ca oc tāchcāuh inic nèhuātl nitlamatini.
9. Tōtolin ca ye huel yèhuātl in huèxōlotl, tēl cihuātl.
10. Āquin màca momāuhtīzquia, in tlā quittani in tlācatecolōtl?
11. Iuhquin mâ tichichimê titēchnōtza.
12. In zāzo tlein ticmacaz, ca àmo quipāctīz.

(b) Translate into Nahuatl.

1. If you (s.) were to help me, it can perhaps be done ("it will be able to ...").
2. He's the one who would have been ruler if he hadn't died.
3. Who won't rebuke you (s.) if you do this?
4. Although he's very strong, he was ("just") defeated.
5. It's not yet evening and you already want to go to sleep!
6. Give (s.) that poor man at least one tortilla.
7. Even if they (will) kill me, I won't say anything.
8. Where (ever) am I to take my food?
9. They sit down on the paper as if it were a mat.
10. No one wants to help me, but there's nothing I can't do myself.
11. You (s.) just got up and you're working already!
12. However many they are, they won't be able to defeat us.

Temporal Clauses, Particles, Interjections

35.1 More on Temporal Clauses

(1) The Nahuatl equivalent of the subordinating conjunction 'when' can be **in, (in) ìcuāc** or **in īquin** (there are subtle differences, 14.9). Action simultaneous with the main clause can also be indicated with **inic** (cf. English 'as'):

In Motēuczōma motequipachô inic quimâ in aocmo huèca huītzê in caxtiltēcâ	*Moctezuma was upset when he learned (knew) that the Spaniards were no longer coming from far off (i.e., the approaching Spaniards were no longer far off)*
Inic huetzi in huēyi tomāhuac tlequiquiztli, iuhquin cencâ huēyi tlàtlàtziniliztli	*When the artillery (great big trumpet) goes off (falls = fires), it is like a very big explosion (a bursting, like an egg)*
Inic ōniquīz, pēuh quiyahui	*As I came out, it started raining*

Inic often has to be translated with '(while) VERBing":

Chōca inic moteōchīhua	*He cries while praying*

The **ic** is not obligatory, so the same thought could be expressed:

Chōca in moteōchīhua	*He cries while praying*

The construction **in** + PRESENT TENSE can express an action that generates the one indicated by the main verb. This can be translated with 'by VERBing', 'from VERBing":

Ōniciyammic in nimitznotēmōlia	*I became exhausted (lit., died of fatigue, cf. **ciyahui**) (from) looking for you*

In oc, in oc ic are the equivalent of 'during (the time when), while':

Mācamo xicòcochtiyecān in oc ic   *Don't (pl.) be dozing off while I'm teaching*
  nontēmachtia
Nicān ximocāhua in oc nitlacōhuatīuh   *Stay (s.) here while I go buy some things*

(2) When 'when' means 'after', it can be rendered with **in** followed by the preterite with augment, the main clause often being introduced with **niman** (14.9). **Iuh** can be added to specify the sense 'right after, as soon as'. In this usage, the **iuh** can optionally separate the augment from its verb:

In iuh ōconìtô in, niman quīz   *Having said this (right after saying this), he*
                                            left
In ō iuh quicac in, ilhuiz tlahuēlcuīc   *As soon as he heard this, he became further*
                                            *enraged (**ilhuiz** or **ilhuicê** 'more'; **tlahuēlli***
                                            *'rage'; **tlahuēlcui**, lit., 'take rage')*

Quin iuh or **quin ye iuh** + PRESENT TENSE means 'to have just VERBed, when (**in**)':

Quin ye iuh ontlami in tlacua, in ye ō   *He'd just finished eating when he heard the*
  cuēl quicac in tēcciztli mopītza   *trumpet sound*
Quin iuh ninonāmictia, in ōmomiquilî   *I'd just gotten married when my father died*
  in notàtzin

Quin ìcuāc means 'only then', 'not until'. To say 'X will happen only after Y has happened' or 'X won't happen until Y has happened', two constructions are possible, either 'only then (**quin ìcuāc**) does X happen when (**in**) Y has happened':

Quin ìcuāc timocāhuaz in ōmocāuh   *You (s.) are to stop only when he has stopped*

or 'X won't happen until the time (**quin ìcuāc**) when (**in**) Y has happened':

Àmo nimitzcāhuaz, quin ìcuāc in   *I won't leave you (s.) (alone) until you give*
  ōtinēchmacac in tinēchhuīquilia   *me what you're bringing me*

(3) 'Before' is usually indicated with **in ayamo** (lit., 'when … not yet …') + PRESENT TENSE (but also see next section):

In ayamo tzinti, in ayamo pēhua in   *Before the world started, before it began,*
  cemānāhuatl, zan huel oc īcēltzin   *there existed only Our Lord God*
  ommoyetzticatca in totēucyo Dios

(4) As in English, succession in time can be expressed with two independent clauses ('first …, then …'). Nahuatl indicates 'first' with **achto(pa)** (also **acatto(pa)**, **acachto(pa)**), and 'then' with **quin**, **zātēpan** (or, as two words, **zā tēpan**), **quin tēpan**, **quin zātēpan**:

Mā oc nitlacua, quin nitlapōhuaz	*Let me eat right now, then I'll read*
Achtopa ximopāca, zā tēpan titēnìzaz	*Wash (s.) first, then you'll have breakfast*
Oc niccāhua in, quin zātēpan nictzonquīxtīz in ītlàtōllo	*I'm setting this aside right now, later I'll finish talking of it (its discourse) (note the final -lo, e.g., -yo, of* **ītlàtōllo**; **ītlàtōl** *would mean the speaker's discourse)*

(5) **Yēquenê** means 'finally, in the end':

Àhuel mochīuh, ic yēquenê ōcualān	*It wasn't possible and for that reason (ic) he finally lost his temper*

35.2 Expressions for Various Temporal Relationships

(1) Time at which

To indicate the time at which an event took place, locative expressions are used. These can be:

▶ adverbs

We have already seen **mōztla** 'tomorrow', **huīptla** 'after tomorrow', **yālhua** 'yesterday', **āxcān** 'now, today', **teōtlac** 'in the evening', **tlàcâ** 'during the day', **icuāc** 'then' etc. Let us add yeōhuīptla 'the day before yesterday' and **yectel** 'the other day, some days ago':

Yeōhuīptla ōnipēuh in ninococoa	*I started getting sick the day before yesterday*
Yectel Tlacōpan ōniquittato cē nohuānyōlqui	*I went to see a relative of mine at Tacuba the other day*

▶ locatives derived from nouns or verbs

For example, **tlacuālizpan** 'at the time of eating', **yohualnepantlâ** 'in the middle of the night, at midnight', **cehuetzilizpan** 'with the arrival of cold weather (fall)', **motlàtoāyān** 'when it's your (s.) turn to talk'.

▶ locative-possessive phrases

These most often involve **-pan**. For example, **īpan inon xihuitl** 'in that year', **īpan in tlācaxipēhualiztli** 'in the (month) of flaying people', **īmpan in ye huècauh tlàcâ** 'in the time of the ancients'.

Locatives with a temporal meaning can of course constitute the predicate in a sentence:

Ye tlàcâ	*He's already late*
Oc yohuac	*It's now becoming night*
Àmo motlàtoāyān	*It's not your (s.) turn (24.9) to talk*
Ye tlacuālizpan	*It's time to eat now*

'It's time to ...' can also be expressed with **imman in(ic)** + FUTURE TENSE or with **oncān in(ic)** + FUTURE TENSE:

Ye imman (*or* oncān) in(ic) tlacuālōz	*It's time to eat*
Ayamo imman (*or* oncān) in(ic) titēhuazquê	*It's not yet time for us to get up*

(2) Length of time

The length of time is generally expressed with a combination of a number with a noun for a period of time (7.8), these nouns being in the absolutive and not in a locative form: **cemilhuitl** 'for one day', **ōnxihuitl** 'for two years'. However, **-yohual** is used in place of **-yohualli**: **nāuhyohual** 'for four nights'.

It is also possible to have instrumental forms in **-tica** in this sense (cf. **huècauhtica** 'for a long time'):

Cemilhuitica (= cemilhuitl) ōninocāuh	*I stayed for one day*

Most of the time, however, such instrumental forms have the meaning '(with)in so much time', 'at the end of so much time':

Ōmilhuitica ōnicchīuh	*I did it in two days*
Ōmilhuitica ōniyâ Mēxìco	*At the end of two days, I went to Mexico City*

Achi means 'for a little while', as do its diminutives **achìtōnca** and **achìtzinca** (hence, **zan achìtōnca** 'a little time', as in **ye cuēl achìtonca** 'it's been some while'):

Mā zā oc achìtzinca iz nonye	*Let me rest here a little bit longer*
Àmo huel tāxcā in tlālticpac āxcāitl, ca zan achìtonca, ca zan cuēl achīc tipiyaltīlô	*The goods on earth aren't really ours, we're just allowed to hold them for a little while*

(3) 'It's for so long that X has been going on …'

The phrase for this is **ye** (sometimes **ye iuh**) + length of time. The present indicates how long the process has been going on, and the preterite (or the imperfect, counterfactual or transitory preterite, as appropriate) how long ago it happened:

Ye cemilhuitl, ye cenyohual in àhuellācachīhua[1] in cihuātzintli	*It's been a day and a night that the woman has been unable to give birth*
Ye iuh ōnxihuitl ōniquittac	*I saw him two years ago*

Ye huècauh or **yēppa** means 'for (= since) a long time':

Ca ye huècauh in nicmati	*It's been a long time that I've known it*
Àmo quin āxcān nipēhua in ninococoa, ca yēppa nicocoxqui	*It isn't today that I started getting sick, it's been a long time that I've been sick*

---

[1] Or **àhuel tlācachīhua**. Here, **huel** causes the assimilation of **tl** > l (2.2) in a following verb. In the instance here, it is written as a single word.

The distant past ('of old', 'in the old days', 'long ago') can be expressed with **in (oc) ye huècauh**, or **in (oc) ye nēpa, in (oc) ye nechca** (see 24.12),[2] or **in ye mācuīl, in ye màtlāc** (i.e., 'it's been five or ten'; note the absence of the absolutive suffix):

Quēn ōtonnemico in ye mācuīl, in ye màtlāc?	*How did you (s.) live in the past?* (note the use of the directional of motion toward, which is often used with **nemi**)
In oc ye huècauh, in oc ye nēpa, in oc ye nechca, in oc īmpan huēhuetquê, cualli ic tlamaniya in īpan tāltepēuh	*Long ago in the past, during the time of the ancients, things went (spread out) well in our city*

Yēhua means 'previously, some time ago', and **ye cuēl yēhua** means 'quite long ago':

Yēhua ōniquittac in ōmpa teōpan	*I saw him before in church*
Ye cuēl yēhua in ōnitlacuâ	*It's been a fair while since I've eaten*

Nozan means 'still' (in speaking of an ongoing process):

Àmo ōtimonemilizcuep, nozan āxcān zan ye iuh īpan tinemi in màcualnemiliz	*You (s.) haven't changed your life, you're still living in your evil (way of) life today*

(4) 'In how long ...', 'how long until ...'
   Oc + length of time:

Oc nāuhxihuitl ninocuepaz	*I'll return in three days (i.e., three days later)*
Oc huècauh in àciquiuh	*He'll return in a long time, He'll take a long time to return*

   Quin ōme, quin ēyi etc. express 'in two, three (days)';

Quin chicōme huāllāz	*He'll come in seven days*

Oc iuh or **zā iuh** + length of time and a verb in the future means 'so long before/until':

Oc iuh mācuīlilhuitl àciquihuî in mēxìcâ in mochīuh in	*It was five days before the arrival of the Mexica that this happened (lit., it was five days until the Mexica arrived when ...)*
Zā iuh nāuhxihuitl huālàcizquê in caxtiltēcâ ōmochīuh in	*This happened four years before the Spaniards arrived*
Oc iuh huècauh huāllāzquê in caxtiltēcâ in ye cuēl quimomachitiāya in Nezahualcoyōtl in īnhuāllāliz	*Long before the Spaniards arrived, Nezahual- coyotl was already informed of their arrival*

---

[2] This is the only instance in which it is possible to combine **oc** and **ye**, which are otherwise mutually exclusive.

(In) **īmōztlayōc** means 'the next day' and **oc īmōztlayōc** 'the day before' (a variant of the preceding construction):

In ìcuāc nàcico nipāctihuītz, auh in īmōztlayōc ye cuēl ninococoa	*When I arrived, I was in fine form (arrived happy), but all of a sudden the next day I got sick*
Oc īmōztlayōc tàcizquê in Pascua nicān ōnàcico	*On the eve of Easter (the day before we reached Easter) I arrived here*

Quin achīc is used to express both 'a short time ago, recently' and 'in a short time, soon':

Quin achīc onquīz	*He just left*
Quin achīc nimiquiz	*I'm going to die soon*

This same phenomenon (a form capable of referring to either the past or the future) applies to **in īquin on** or **in īquin in cānin**, which designate a distant time, often mythical:

Quil cānin huèca ōhuāllàquê in īquin on	*It's said that they arrived from a distant place, long ago (note that in non-initial position, the interrogative **cānin** becomes indefinite)*
Inin ca topan mochīhuaz in īquin on	*This will happen to us a long time from now*
Ca tlamiz in cemanāhuatl in īquin in cānin	*The world will end one day (at some future date)*

(5) Repetition

Repetition is generally marked with an instrumental phrase with **-tica**:

Yohualtica	*Every night*
Viernestica	*Every Friday* (a borrowing from Spanish)

If the phrase expressing the period of the repetition contains a number noun ('every three days, every four years' etc.), this is reduplicated with the long vowel (/CV:/, 28.2):

cēcenxiuhtica	*every year*
ōōmilhuitica	*every two days*
nānāhuilhuitica	*every four days*. However, note **èeyilhuitica** (with the /CV'/ form of reduplication) *every three days* and **huēhuècauhtica** *at long intervals*.

Thus:

Huēhuècauhtica in tlāhuāna, àzo cācaxtōltica, àzo cēcempōhualtica	*He seldom gets drunk, maybe every fifteen or twenty days* (**Ilhuitl** is understood, and the forms **cācaxtōlilhuitica, cēcempō-hualilhuitica** could have been used)

'Everyday' is expressed with **cēcemilhuitl** as well as **cēcemilhuitica**. The adverb **mōmōztlaê** can also be used:

Mōmōztlaê (= cēcemilhuitl) in quiyahui   *It rains everyday*

(6) 'For the X-th time'

This is expressed with **(quin) ic** + NUMBER (14.3 at end) + **-pa** (25.8):

Quin ic ōppa in tzàtzi cuānaca	*This is the second time that the cock has crowed (is shouting)*
In ye ic ēxpa motlatlàtlauhtilìtìcaya in totēucyo, yēquenê moquīxtìtihuetzico in ītlachīhualtzin in angel	*When Our Lord stood praying for the third time (hon.), his creation the angel suddenly (-huetzi) appeared (hon.)*

By itself, **iyòpa** means 'for a single time', but it always appears with another particle: **quin iyòpa** means 'for the first time', while **zan iyòpa** means 'for the only time'. Thus:

Quin iyòpa yālhua ōnitlāhuān, auh zan   *Yesterday was the first time that I've gotten*
   iyòpa yez   *drunk, and it will be the only one*

'(For) the first time' can also be expressed as **quin yancuīcān** (lit., 'recently'):

Àmo quin yancuīcān noca timocayāhua   *This isn't the first time that you've scoffed at me*

35.3 Particles for Statement Modulation

These are particles that modulate an affirmation or a non-affirmative statement (a question, wish or hope). We already know **ca** (assertion), **cuix** (question), **mā** (wish) and **tlā** (hypothesis). These are mutually exclusive, but they are all compatible with negation (**àmo** etc.). Let us add some additional items:

(1) *Anca*

Meaning 'well (then), apparently', **anca** indicates that on the basis of new evidence, the speaker has reached a conclusion that contradicts what he had previously thought:

Anca zan tēmictli īpan ticmatizquê in iz tlālticpac ic pācōhua	*Well, then, we've got to consider as (just) a dream the things on earth that people enjoy (lit., by which there is joy)*
Hui anca īpampa in nicnōtlācatl, àtle īpan nitto	*Alas, in that case, I'm despised (viewed as nothing) because I'm a poor man*

(2) *Quil*

Meaning 'as is said, as they say, allegedly', **quil** is used to indicate that the speaker is not vouching for the statement in which it appears because this statement is known from a third party rather than from personal experience:

Quil ye ōmàxitīco in tlàtoāni	*It would seem, the ruler has already arrived (hon.)*
Quil huèca ōhuāllàquê in mēxìcâ	*As is said, the Mexica came from far away*

(3) **At**

At 'perhaps' has the meaning of **àzo**:

Àmo cualli yez in piltōntli: at cocoxqui, at nozo àmo tlācamelāhuac	*The small child will not be healthy (good): maybe sickly, or maybe (cf.* **ànozo***) malformed (not correct in the way of humans)*

▶ *Note.* In fact, this must be a variant of **â** (for instances of the weakening of final -**t** into a glottal stop, see 5.1 Note 1, 8.4 sec. 3, 23.4). While **â** has been specialized with a negative meaning (generally appearing in a compound with -**mo**), **at** has been specialized with a dubitative meaning (as has the **â** variant in the compound **àzo**).

35.4 *Ach*

This particle can be used in two ways.

(1) In front of an interrogative, it indicates a lack of knowledge on the part of the speaker ('I don't know…', 'I wonder…', 'who knows…?'):

Ach cāmpa ōitztēhuac (27.6.2) in nopiltzin	*Where could my son have gone, I wonder?*
Cāmpa ōmohuīcac? – Ach cāmpa.	*Where's he gone (hon.)? – I don't know where.*
Ach tlein ōnāx in ye yohuac, cenyohual ōninocuitlacueptinen	*I wonder what happened to me (18.9) last night. – All I did the whole night was roll over (I kept turning my back)*
Ach quēmman occeppa nitlacuāz	*I have no idea when I'll eat again*
Īquin huāllāz in motàtzin? – Ach īquin, àzo tēl huīptla.	*When will your (s.) father come? – I don't know, anyway maybe the day after tomorrow.*

(2) In front of another particle, **ach** strengthens it: **ach â** 'isn't it the case that…?', **ach ca** 'it's certainly the case that…', **ach zā** 'after all, in the end', **ach zan** 'all the time, always':

Ach àye (= negative prefix **à-** plus **ye**) nitelchitl?	*Doesn't this serve me right?* (**telchitl** 'one who gets what he deserves')
Ach ca nel tlamatini	*For he is truly wise*

Ach zā ye nelli *That's possible by God! that is true*
Ach zan quìtoa inin tlàtōlli *He always says these words*

35.5 *Mach*

This is the most common of the particles looked at in the chapter. It is used:

(1) at the start of a sentence as a particle for statement modulation, with the meaning 'as it would seem', 'it could be said that…':

Tlein ōtimāyilî? Mach huel ōchichīliuh *What happened to you (s.)? – As far as I can*
in mīxtelolo. *tell, your eyes are all red (reddened).*
Āquìquê in? Mach àmo mēxìcâ. *Who are they? Seemingly, not Mexica.*

(2) after an interrogative to strengthen the sense of uncertainty:

Tlein mach tiquìtoa? *What ever are you (s.) saying?*
Tlein mach ic tlatlàtlauhticâ? *God knows what he's asking for (what he's making a request with)*

Note the expressions **quēn mach tamî** (26.11) or **quēn mach huel tèhuātl**, lit., 'what a state you're (s.) in!', which can be taken in a favorable or unfavorable sense (respectively, 'what good luck you have' or 'how unfortunate you are'):

Quēn mach tamî (*or* Quēn mach huel *Lucky you (s.), having been given so much!*
tèhuātl) in īxquich in ōtimacōc!
Quēn mach huel amèhuāntin in ō amopan *You poor people, to whom such grievous and*
mochīuh in tēcocô in tētolīnî! *distressing things have happened!*

(3) after another particle, generally to indicate the feigned weakening of a statement ('it could be said that…'). Here, the speaker appears not to be making a firm declaration, but the actual effect is to give added weight to what is being said:

Tlā ximocāhuacān, zan mach antlàtoâ *Do stop (pl.). – You just talk, one might say.*
Ō mach niciyammic *You might say I'm exhausted*
Ye ō mach teuhyōhuac in īxāyac *It could be said that his face (**xāyacatl**) is covered with dust (**teuhtli**; for -**yōhua**, see 24.6)*

Quil mach mocentlālìquê in tēteô in *As might be said, the gods gathered in*
ōmpa Teōtihuacān *Teotihuacan*
Zan machê tinēchàhua *One could say that you (s.) just criticize me (for -**ê**, see 33.7)*

In machê means 'especially, above all':

Ca huel mochintin quimomacatinemî in mīxītl, in tlāpātl, in machê huel yèhuāntin in tēyacānquzê	*Everyone's addicted to (keeps giving himself to)* **mixitl** *and* **tlapatl** *(plants used as narcotics), especially the leaders*

We have already encountered the us of **mach** in comparisons (33.1).

35.6 Connectives

Readers who know Latin are aware of the pronounced reluctance in that language to have one sentence follow another without a connective (a word that indicates the logical relationship of the new statement to what precedes). This attitude also applies to Nahuatl stories, myths and narratives. We have already met all the connectives, which are basically **auh** 'and', **niman** 'then', **ic** 'under these conditions/circumstances', **ye** 'already, look'. These can appear in combinations, some of which are frequent, such as **niman ic, niman ye ic, auh niman ye ic**, while others are less common, such as **(auh) in ye iuhqui** 'things being so', **auh īhuān** 'and also', **nō** 'also, likewise', **zan ye nō ihui** 'similarly'. A literal translation would often be quite clumsy (**niman ye ic** 'now then under these circumstances'; when a narrator or writer uses such a combination, all that he generally wishes to do is show that one fact follows upon another). Thus:

Auh in ye iuhqui in Quetzalcōhuātl in ye motequipachoa, niman ye ic quilnāmiqui in yāz. Auh in ye iuhqui niman ye ic ompēhua … Niman ic àcico cecni cuauhtitlan.	*So now that Quetzalcoatl is very distressed, he recalls that he must leave. Accordingly, he then sets on his way (begins in that direction) … Then he arrived at a forest*

35.7 Interjections and Exclamations

Ō and **a** are used like 'o' or 'oh' in English:

Ō nopilhuāné ximohuīcatihuiyān	*Oh my children, go off on your way (hon.)*
Ō iuhqui on, nocnīuhtzé (for the vocative of **-tzin**, see 12.1 sec. 1)?	*Oh, is that so, my friend?*

Hui indicates astonishment or fear, **āuh** (not to be confused with **auh**) attracts attention, **iyo** (not to be confused with **iyô** 'alone', see 26.10) or **iyoyahue** is a cry of pair or distress:

O hui, tlê tāxticâ?	*Uh-oh, what's going on with you (s.)?*
Āuh tlein tiquìtoa?	*Hey, what are you saying?*
Iyoyahue ōnotlahuēliltic (29.4.3)!	*Alas, poor me!*

Tlacâ (not to be confused with **tlācâ** 'people' or **tlàcâ** 'during the day') is used to make a recover after a mistake:

Àmo nicmati in ītōcā; tlacâ ye niquilnāmiqui!	*I don't remember his name. Oh, now I remember it!*

Tlacàzo or **tlacàcê** is an exclamation whose meaning is close to that of **anca** (35.3a):

Tlacàzo ca ye nelli in quìtoa nocihuāuh!	*Good lord, what my wife says is true!*
Hui tlacàcê iz timohuīcatz!	*Oh, no, here you (s.) come (hon.)!*

If the exclamation applies to the whole sentence ('how...!'), this is expressed with **inic**:

Inic tetecuica motleuh!	*How your (s.) fire crackles!*

VOCABULARY

Intransitive verbs

chichīlihui	*to grow red*	tlàtzini	*to burst, to explode*
tecuīni (*expr.* tetecuica, 28.2)	*to blaze, to crackle*		

Transitive verbs

cayāhua (tēca mo-)	*to make fun of, to dupe, to cheat*	pītza	*to blow, to play an instrument*
		xipēhua	*to skin, to flay*

Nouns

īxtelolōtl	*eyeball, eye*	teuhtli	*dust*
mīxītl	*mixitl (narcotic plant, datura)*	tēcciztli	*seashell, trumpet*
		tlahuēlli	*anger, rage*
quiquiztli	*trumpet*	tlāpātl	*tlapatl (narcotic plant)*
telchitl (*pl.* /-mê/)	*one who gets his reward*	xāyacatl	*face, countenance*

Locatives and adverbs

achīc	*a little while*	imman	*it's time*
ilhuiz	*more*	mōmōtzlaê	*everyday*

nozan	*still* (of continuing process)	yeōhuīptla	*day before yesterday*
		yēhua	*previously*
yectel	*the other day, some time ago*	yēppa	*a long time ago*
		yēquenê	*finally, in the end*
		(zā) tēpan	*next*

Particles and interjections

ach	*I wonder, really*	hui	*oh, no*
anca	*well, then*	iyo	*alas!*
at	*maybe, perhaps*	quil	*they say*
āuh	*hey*	tlacà(zo)	*Good lord!*

EXERCISES

(a) Translate into English.
1. Achtopa nitlacuāz, quin zātēpan nimitzittaz.
2. In yectel iz moquīxtî in totlàtòcāuh.
3. Quēn namēchcāuhtēhuaz? Cuix àmo yēquenê huel ammotolīnīzquê?
4. Àmo quin yancuīcān in ticchīhua in àcualli, ca yēppa tiuhqui.
5. Ye cuēl yēhua in ōnìzac.
6. Aocmo imman in tiyāz ticnāmiquitīuh: ye cuēl onyâ.
7. Quēn mach huel tèhuātl! Anca àtle māxcā, motlatqui.
8. Cān īchān? – Ach cān, mach àmo titèhuān.
9. Quin chicōme titōcazquê.
10. Ayamo nimitzittaya, quin ìcuāc in mochi tlācatl ōhuetzcac.
11. Quēquēzquilhuitica titlāhuāna?
12. Monònōtzâ in nènemî.

(b) Translate into English.
1. My father died in the evening the day before yesterday.
2. Before the start of the world ("when the world doesn't yet start"), God had already existed ("already exists") for a long time.
3. It is not yet the time to go away.
4. Yesterday, it rained all day, today there's still water on the ground ("the water is spread on the earth").
5. What is he saying? – I dunno, you could say that he doesn't speak Nahuatl.
6. The jaguar is, they say, the ruler of animals (yōlquê).
7. I'll pay you in fifteen days.
8. In the old days, the commoners still obeyed.

9. Three days before my father died, I brought him to the fields.
10. When Spaniards first arrived, the Mexica were very afraid of ("feared very much") guns ("fire trumpets").
11. I go to the forest every month.
12. As soon as he saw the jaguar, he fled.

Traditional Orthography

When you go on to apply your knowledge to reading Classical Nahuatl literature, you will find in both the original documents and the editions that have
been made from them an orthography that is somewhat different from the one
that you have become accustomed to during the use of this book. Recall that the
uniform orthography adopted here (and used by many linguists) substantially
agrees with the traditional manner of spelling but eliminates from it certain
ambiguities and errors.

The traditional orthography is at once less exact, regularly leaves out significant elements and is applied erratically. In this appendix, you will find notes
that will hopefully spare you any astonishment when you first come into contact with texts that follow the old orthograph and put you in a position to recognize the true phonetic structure of words where that orthography is uncertain
or defective[1].

The information is correlated with the presentation of the phonology given
in the Preliminary Lesson. In Table A.1 you will find, from left to right:

▶ the phonological unit (phoneme) between slashes
▶ the spelling used in this book
▶ any relevant discussion of the traditional writing, with examples (the traditional spelling comes first and then the "normalized" spelling used in this book
follows in parentheses)

When there is no discussion, the reason for this is that the traditional spelling
is the same as the normalized one. In the absence of any indication to the contrary, a spelling retained as "normalized" is always used in a number of the
instances (often the majority) in the old texts.

---

[1] For a comprehensive introduction to older written Nahuatl, see James Lockhart's book
Nahuatl as Written (Stanford, CA: Stanford University Press and UCLA Latin American
Studies, 2001).

TABLE A.1 How phonemes are written

Consonants		
/p/	(p)	
/t/	(t)	
/k/	(c, qu)	Sometimes, the verbal prefixes are written separately from the verb stem, and in this case, you can find **nic** 'I ... it', **tic** 'you, we ... it', even in front of **i** or **e**: **nic itta** 'I see it' (**niquitta**).
/c/	(tz)	Sometimes (quite seldom), **tç** in front of a vowel: **itçon** 'his hair(s)' (**ītzon**).
/č/	(ch)	
/λ/	(tl)	
/kʷ/	(cu, uc)	Most often written as **qu** in front of **a**: **qualli** 'good' (**cualli**), **tlaqua** 'he eats' (**tlacua**).
		At the end of a syllable, the writing is quite erratic, taking the form **uc, cu** or **cuh**: **teuctli, tecutli** or **tecuhtli** 'lord' (**tēuctli**). Sometimes, just **c** is used: **oquitzac, oquitzacu** or **oquitzauc** 'he has closed it' (**ōquitzauc**).
/m/, /n/	(m), (n)	We know (Preliminary Lesson Complementary Note 6, 1.3) that in writing (and the phonetic system) the contrast of **m** and **n** is operative only in front of a vowel, where traditional orthography clearly maintains the distinction. In front of a consonant or at the end of a word, things are less clear. We find:

    ▶ **n** (in place of **m**) very often in front of **p** or **m**: **onpehua** 'he is going to start' (**ompēhua**), and likewise if the base form is /m/: **anpehua** 'you (pl.) start' (**ampēhuâ**), **quinmictia** 'he kills them' (**quimmictia**).

    ▶ quite frequent disappearance of **n** at the end of a word: **itlaque** 'his clothing' (**ītlaquēn**), **itzonteco** 'its mane' (**ītzontecon**), **omoma** 'he presented himself' (**ōmoman**), **nica** 'here' (**nicān**), **yehuatl i** 'this one' (**yèhuātl in**), **totoli** 'turkey' (**totōlin**) etc.

    ▶ quite frequent dropping of **n** in front of /y/ and /w/ (**hu**): **tonauan** 'our mothers' (**tonānhuān**) **teyotl** 'fame' (**tēnyōtl**); sometimes also in front of /s/ (**c, z**) and /š/ (**x**): **acihua** 'you (pl.) are women' (**ancihuâ**), **tiquixoxa** 'you (s.) bewitch them' (**tiquinxōxa**). Assimilated forms like **azcihua** and **tiquixxoxa** are also found.

    ▶ sometimes a post-vocalic nasal is represented merely with a tilde drawn over the vowel: **nicã** 'here', **xitlaquacã** 'eat (pl.)' (**xitlacuācān**), **quimõmaca** 'he's going to give it to them' (**quimommaca**), **itetzõ** 'his beard' (**ītentzon**).

| /s/ | (c, z) | In the oldest texts, **ç** is the most common spelling in front of **a, o, u**: **çan** 'only' (**zan**), **aço** 'perhaps' (**àzo**), **quiça** 'he emerges' (**quīza**), **tlaçotli** 'valuable' (**tlazòtli**); in front of a consonant or at the end of a word, only **z** is found. |
| /š/ | (x) | Sometimes **s** in front of **u** (/ō/) or consonant: **suchitl** 'flower (**xōchitl**), **isco** 'before him' (**īxco**). |

/y/	(y)	In addition to **y**, **i** or (less commonly) **j** are also found: **ia** 'he went' (**yâ**), **jaotl** or **iaotl** 'enemy' (**yāōtl**), **oiez** 'he'll be' (**onyez**).

Most of the time, it is omitted between **i** and a vowel: **nicpia** 'I guard him' (**nicpiya**), **tlachia** 'he looks' (**tlachiya**), **niez** 'I'll be' (**niyez**), **xiauh** 'go (s.)' (**xiyauh**), **cochia** 'he was sleeping' (**cochiya**); likewise between a vowel and **i**: **ei** or **ey** 'three' (**ēyi**), **ai** or **ay** 'he does' (**āyi**). Needless to say, this procedure can lead to much confusion (e.g., does written -**ia** indicate a present tense with that ending or a verb in -**i** in the imperfect?).

/w/	(hu, uh)	Only **uh** is used regularly at the end of a word or syllable. At the start of a word or syllable (in front of a vowel), **hu** is rare and there are two regular spellings:

▶ one consists of writing **u**: **uel** 'well' (**huel**), **ueue** 'old man' (**huēhuê**), **xiuitl** 'year' (**xihuitl**), **chicauac** 'strong' (**chicāhuac**), **mocaua** 'he stays' (**mocāhua**).

▶ the other consists of writing **v** in front of **e** and **i**, and **o** (sometimes **u**, more rarely **v**) in front of **a**: **vei** or **vey** 'large' (**huēyi**), **veve** 'old man' (**huēhuê**), **xivitl** 'year' (**xihuitl**), **xivia** 'go (pl.)' (**xihuiyān**), **chicaoac** 'strong' (**chicāhuac**), **mocaoa** 'he stays' (**mocāhua**), **otioalmovicac** 'you (s.) returned' (**ōtihuālmohuīcac**), **ioan** 'and' (**īhuān**), **tonaoan** 'our mothers' (**tonānhuān**) etc.

Between **o** and **a**, the sound is most often ignored in the spelling: **coatl** 'snake' (**cōhuātl**), **tlapoa** 'he counts' (**tlapōhua**), **micoa** 'there's death' (**micōhua**), **yoalli** 'night' (**yohualli**), **totecuioan** 'our lords' (**totēuchyōhuān**). Conversely, less careful scribes add **hu**, **u** or **v** between **o** and **a** when this is not necessary: **tlahtohuani** 'king' (**tlàtoāni**).

/l/	(l)	At the end of a word or syllable, certain texts routinely use the spelling **lh**: **nocalh** 'my house' (**nocal**), **uelh** 'well' (**huel**), **tlalhticpac** 'on earth' (**tlālticpac**). Presumably, this reflects devoicing in this position (Preliminary Lesson, Complementary Note 6).

Sometimes, **ll** is found representing a simple **l**: **callaqui** 'he enters' (**calaqui**), **tlacuilloque** 'writers' (**tlàcuilòquê**), **motlalli** 'he sat down' (**motlālî**).

/'/	(`,^)	Except in the works of certain old grammarians (Carochi and Aldama y Guevara) and the *Bancroft Dialogues*, where the system of accents adopted here is used, the glottal stop is not indicated, or if it is, only sporadically: **oiaque** 'they went' (**ōyàquê**), **vitze** 'they come' (**huītzê**), **aci** 'he arrives' (**àci**).

H is most often found between two vowels: **ehecatl** 'wind' (**èecatl**), **ihiotl** 'breath' (**iiyōtl**), and sometimes in front of a consonant: **tlahtoani** 'king' (**tlàtoāni**), **yehuatl** or **yehoatl** 'he' (**yèhuātl**), **ahci** 'he arrives' (**àci**). A word-final glottal stop is occasionally indicated with **h**: **yeh** (**yê**), **cueleh** (**cuēlê**), **catcah** (**catcâ**). In a word that starts with a vowel + glottal stop, the latter can be represented by an **h** in *front* of the vowel: **hatle** 'nothing' (**àtle**), **hamo** 'not' (**àmo**), **hivitl** or **hiuitl** 'feather' (**ihuitl**). Sometimes, the demonstrative **in** is written **hi**: **tlein hi** 'what's this?' (**tlein in?**).

Vowels

The long vowels are practically never marked as such.

/a/, /ā/	(a, ā)	In the sequence /iya/ (with short i), the spelling **ie** competes with **ia**: sometimes **nicpie** 'I guard him' (**nicpiya**) and **tlachie** 'he watches' (**tlachiya**) are found alongside **nicpia, tlachia**, and **miec** 'much' (**miyac**) is much more common than **miac**. This must reflect a palatalization of the **a** after the /y/.
/e/, /ē/	(e, ē)	Sometimes, an initial **e** turns into a diphthong, with the result written as **ie** or **ye: yehecatl** 'wind' (**èecatl**), **yey** or **yei** 'three' (**ēyi**). This tendency is systematized in some modern dialects, and it is probable that certain Classical words that are always written with initial **y** began originally with **e**, in particular **yèhuātl**.
		In contact with **y**, **e** is sometimes raised to **i**, and confusion can then be heightened if the **y** is omitted: **cia** 'he agrees' (**ceya**), **huiac** or **huiiac** 'long' (**huēyiyac**).
/i/, /ī/	(i, ī)	The spelling fluctuates in a totally anarchic fashion between **i**, **y** and **j**, with some texts preferring **i** and **y**, others **i** and **j**: **jquac** or **yquac** 'when' (**icuāc**), **jpiltzin** or **ypiltzin** 'his son' (**īpiltzin**), **yoan, joan, yoā** 'and' (**īhuān**), **jc** or **yc** 'thus' (**ic**). This procedure goes back to Latin orthography, where **i** is used internally, and **j/y** initially; without there being any fixed rule, it seems that in the Nahuatl texts **j** or **y** are preferred in grammatical morphemes (prefixes, suffixes, particles) and **i** in stems. Note the total confusion in writing of /i/ and /y/, a confusion that is shown by spellings like **yiollo** 'his heart' (**īyōllô**).
/o/, /ō/	(o, ō)	Most frequently, /ō/ and sometimes /o/ (especially in front of **p**, **m**, and a pair of consonants) are written as **u** or even **v** (see earlier discussion on /w/ for the distribution of these forms): **teutl, tevtl** 'god' (**teōtl**), **ume, vme** 'two' (**ōme**), **umpa, vmpa** 'over there' (**ōmpa**), **vncan, vncā**, 'there' (**oncān**), **vtli** 'road' (**òtli**). Presumably, the sound was pronounced with a slightly higher articulation in these positions, which led to it being heard as resembling the Spanish **u** (though confusion about the underlying phonology led to the letter **v** being used for **o**-sounds that were not in fact raised in this way).

Complementary Notes

▶ Word division. Certain combinations of particles are traditionally written together as single words: e.g., **inic, jnjc, injc** etc. 'thus, so that …' (**in ic**), **intla** 'if' (**in tlā**), **maçonelivi** 'although' (**mā zo nel ihui**), **oquiuh** 'again so' (**oc iuh**). Presumably, such spellings reflect an accentual system in which these combinations were pronounced as a single unit. Apart from clusters for which a grammatical or phonetic justification can be given, fusions or divisions are sometimes found that must be considered scribal errors.

▶ Simplification. Basically, this takes place in two cases:

    ▶ Double consonants are often written as a single one: **amiquizque** 'you (pl.) will die' (**ammiquizquê**), **conaoatia** 'he gives this order to him' (**connāhuatia**), **ieço** 'his blood' (**īezzo, īezyo**).

    ▶ "Difficult" consonantal clusters (see Preliminary Lesson, Complementary Note 8) such as **-tzch, -chch-, -tztz-, -chtz-**. Here the first consonant is often omitted, but it may also be assimilated or "simplified": **nimichiaz** 'I'll wait for you (s.)' (**nimitzchiyaz**), **onimixxiccauh** 'I've abandoned you (s.)' (**ōnimitzxiccāuh**), **quexquittzin** 'just a little bit' (**quēxquichtzin**).

▶ Abbreviations. Certain sequences of letters are replaced with an abbreviation borrowed from Latin. The basic ones are:

    ▶ An apostrophe (') after **q** to represent **qui**: **iuhq'n** 'as' (**iuhquin**), **q'nvicac** 'he brought them' (**quinhuīcac**), **qujtozneq'** 'it wants to say it' (**quìtōznequi**).

    ▶ The tilde over **q** to indicate **que, quê**: **oallaq̃** 'they'll come' (**huāllàquê**), **tlatoq̃** 'kings' (**tlàtòquê**); and sometimes (properly in a more jagged form that may resemble a tilde) for **qua**: **tlaq̃lli** 'food' (**tlacualli**).

Supplementary Comments

▶ Elements not reflected in spelling:

    ▶ long vowels (never represented)

    ▶ /w/ (**hu**) between o and a, and /y/ between i and a vowel or a vowel and i (almost never represented)

    ▶ **n** at the end of a word (frequently omitted).

▶ Pay attention to **i, y, j** and **o, u, v**, and in particular to sequences such as **ia**, which can represent /ia/, as in **nictlatlia** 'I place it', or /iya/, as in **nicpia** 'I guard him' (**nictlālia, nicpiya**), and **oa**, which can represent /oa/, as in **tlatoa** 'he speaks' (**tlàtoa**) or /owa/, as in **tlacoa** 'he makes purchases' (**tlacōhua**), or even /wa/, as in **ixoa** 'it sprouts' (**ixhua**).[2] The sequence **ioa** is even more ambiguous, cf. **ioan** or **yoan, ioã** etc., which can represent 'during the night' (**yohuan**), 'and', 'with him' (**īhuān**) or 'with them' (**īnhuān**); also cf. **totzcuioa** 'our dogs' (**totzcuinhuān**) and **totecuioa** 'our lords' (**totēucyōhuān**), **itoalli** 'inner courtyard' (**ithualli**) and **tlatoa** 'he speaks' (**tlàtoa**).

---

[2] With the final vowels of verbs, the varying procedures in certain tenses can help reveal the underlying phonological structure. Hence, in the future, **nictlaliz, tlatoz** (**nictlālīz, tlàtōz**) are distinguishable from **nicpiaz, tlacoaz** (**nicpiyaz, tlacōhua**), and so too in the preterite, **nictlali, tlato** (**nictlālî, tlàtô**) are distinct from **nixpix, tlacouh** (**nicpix, tlacōuh**).

TABLE A.2 How to read letters

ç:	represents /s/ (z) in front of a vowel: **quiça** 'he emerges' (**quīza**).
e:	can represent /a/ after /iy/, with the /y/ unmarked: **miec** 'much' (**miyac**), **tlachie** 'he watches' (**tlachiya**).
h:	can represent /'/ (glottal stop) after a vowel: **ahco** 'upward' (**àco**), **ehecatl** 'wind' (**èecatl**), **tlahtoani** 'king' (**tlàtòāni**). Sometimes, it is placed in front of the vowel: **hatle** 'nothing' (**àtle**), **hivitl** 'feather' (**ìhuitl**), and sometimes it has no value: **hin** 'this' (**in**).
i:	can represent /y/: **ie** 'already' (**ye**), **aiamo** 'not yet' (**āyamo**); /iy/: **nicpia** 'I hold it' (**nicpiya**), **miquia** 'they were dying' (**miquiyâ**), **iacac** 'at its tip' (**īyacac**), **niez** 'I will be' (**niyez**); /yi/: **uei** 'large' (**huēyi**).
j:	can represent /i/: **juh** 'thus' (**iuh**), **oanqujmjctique** 'you (pl.) killed him' (**ōanquimictìquê**), **njman** 'then' (**niman**); (more rarely) /y/: **javtl** 'enemy' (**yāōtl**); /iy/ **mjec** 'much' (**miyac**).
n:	can represent **m** in front of **p, m**: **anmjquizque** 'we'll die' (**ammiquizquê**), **onmehua** 'he gets up' (**ommēhua**).
o:	can represent /w/ (**hu**) in front of **a**: **oallauh** 'he's coming' (**huāllauh**), **chicaoac** 'strong' (**chicāhuac**), **yehoatl** 'he' (**yèhuātl**); /ow/: **micoa** 'there's dying' (**micōhua**), **toteucioan** 'our lords' (**totēucyōhuān**), **coatl** 'snake' (**cōhuātl**).
qu:	can represent /kʷ/ (**cu**) in front of **a**: **qualli** 'good' (**cualli**).
s:	sometimes represents /x/: **suchitl** 'flower' (**xōchitl**), **quiquistia** 'he brings him out' (**quiquīxtia**).
u:	often represents /ō/ and sometimes /o/: **ume** 'two' (**ōme**), **teutl** 'god' (**teōtl**); sometimes /w/ (**hu**): **uel** 'well' (**huel**). **Hu** (and sometimes just **u**) can also represent the "glide" from o to a: **tlahtohuani, tlahtouani** 'king' (**tlàtòāni**).
v:	often represents /w/, especially in front of **e** and **i**, sometimes in front of **a**: **vel** 'well' (**huel**), **ihvitl, ivitl** or **hivitl** 'feather' (**ìhuitl**), **vei** 'large' (**huēyi**), **chicavac** 'strong' (**chicāhuac**); sometimes it represents /ō/ or /o/: **vncan** 'there' (**ōncān**), **tevtl** 'god' (**teōtl**).
y:	sometimes represents /i/: **yn** 'the' (**in**), **yquac** 'when' (**ìcuāc**); /yi/: **vey** 'large' (**huēyi**).
˜/ˆ:	often represents a nasal that follows the vowel over which the stroke is placed: **njmã** 'then' (**niman**), **tlamãtli** 'thing' (**tlamantli**). Over **q**, it represents an abbreviation for **que** or **qua**: **tlatoq̃** 'kings' (**tlàtòquê**).
':	represents an abbreviation for **qui**: **iuhq'n** 'as' (**iuhquin**).

This list is arranged by the written form of the letters and indicates what sound they represent (only spellings that present difficulties are given).

Inflexional Patterns

BY CHRISTOPHER S. MACKAY

Nouns

(1) Absolute form

Absolutive forms in singular take the suffixes

-**tl** after a vowel: **cihuā-tl**
-**li** after /l/: **cal-li**
-**tli** after other consonant: **oquich-tli**

A limited number of nouns take the suffix -**in**:

mich-in

Some emotive nouns take no absolutive ending:

chichi, papal, yacacuitla

Absolutive forms in plural (R: long-vowel reduplication)
Stems ending in vowel:

/-'/: **cihuâ** (< **cihuā-tl**)
/R-'/: **māmazâ** (< **mazā-tl**)
/-me'/: **ichcamê** (< **ichca-tl**)

Stems ending in a consonant:

/-tin/: **oquichtin** (< **oquich-tli**)
/R-'/: **tētēuctin** (< **tēuc-tli**)

Verb-derived forms ending in a glottal stop in the singular have a plural in -**quê**:

tlàcuilòquê (**tlàcuilô**)

(2) Possessed forms

Possessive prefixes

Singular		Plural	
1st person	n(o)-	1st person	t(o)-
2nd person	m(o)-	2nd person	am(o)-
3rd person	ī-	3rd person	īm-
Indefinite:	tē-		

Possessed stem

All possessed forms drop the absolutive ending.
Regular forms in the singular take the endings
/w/ after a vowel: **-cihuāuh**
ø after a consonant: **-oquich**

▶ *NB.* When possessed, nouns ending in **-yo** (abstractions and inalienable nouns) do not take the suffix **-uh** despite ending in a vowel.

Other formations

Nouns of the structure /VC/ take **-hui: -òhui**
Nouns in /VCCV/ optionally take **-hui: -oquichhui**
Most nouns in **-itl, -atl** simply drop the stem final vowel: **-petl** (<**petlatl**), **-nac** (< **nacatl**)
But various subcatetories of nouns in **-itl, -atl** take the regular ending
    Animate nouns: **-tīciuh**
    nouns in **-quitl, -titl, -chitl: -tequiuh, -patiuh, -xōchiuh**
    nouns of the structure /VCV/: **-āmauh**
    optionally nouns in /VCCV/: **-ilhuiuh**
Plural nouns loose any reduplication, add **-huān: -mazāhuān, -oquichhuān**

(3) Possessive nouns

Generally, stems ending in a vowel take **-huâ: cihuāhuâ** (**cihuā-tl**) and stems ending in consonant take **-ê: calê** (< **cal-li**)
    But:
        all animate nouns take **-huâ: pilhuâ** (< **pil-li**)
        exception: **nānê** (< **-nān**), **tàtê** (< **-tâ**)
        all parts of the body take **-ê: yaquê** (< **yaca-tl**)

Suffixes of size
honorific (diminutive): -**tzin**
diminutive: -**tōn**
diminutive (pity): -**pil**
augmentative: -**pōl**
deprecatory: -**zōl**

Pronouns/Demonstratives

(1) Emphatic

Singular	Short forms	Long forms
1st person	**nê**	**tèhuātl**
2nd person	**tê**	**tèhuātl**
3rd person	**yê**	**yèhuātl**
Plural		
1st person	**tèhuān**	**tèhuāntin**
2nd person	**amèhuān**	**amèhuāntin**
3rd person	**yèhuān**	**yèhuāntin**

(2) Demonstratives

'this': **in**, pl. **inìquê**; **yèhuātl in**, pl. **yèhuāntin in**
'that': **on**, pl. **inìquê on**; **yèhuātl on**, pl. **yèhuāntin on**
'that much': **īzqui** (specific amount)/**īzquich** (vague amount)
'at that time': **ìcuāc**

Interrogatives

Who?: **āc/āquin** (pl. **āquìquê**)
What?: **tle/tlein** (pl. **tleìquê**)
Where?: **cān/cānin**
How?: **quēn/quēnin**
Why?: **tle īca, tle īpampa**
When?: **īc/īquin** or **quēmman**
Which?: **cātlèhuātl/cātlia/cātlî**
How much?: **quēzqui** (expecting quantitative answer)/**quēxquich** (expecting
    vague answer)

Construction of Locatival Suffixes/Nouns

-**ca** 'by': ligature or possessed construction
-**chān** 'house of': possessed construction
-**c(o)** 'in': appended to inanimate noun stems
-**cpac** 'on top of': possessed or ligature construction
-**huān** '(together) with': possessed construction
-**huīc** 'in the direction of': possessed construction
-**īcampa** 'behind': possessed construction
-**pal** 'thanks to': possessed construction
-**pampa** 'on account of': possessed construction
-**pan** 'upon': compound or possessed construction
-**tech** 'against (the side of)': compound (rare), ligature or possessed
     construction
-**teuh** 'like': appended to inanimate noun stems
-**tlâ** '(place) full of': compound construction
-**tlan** 'under, beside': compound, ligature or possessed construction
-**tlōc, -nāhuac** 'beside, with': possessed construction
-**tzalān, -nepantlâ** 'among': compound or possessed construction

Numbers

Counting up to twenty involves adding the units **cē** (1), **ōme** (2), **ēyi** (3), **nāhui** (4) to the subbases **chicua-** (5, **mācuīlli** by itself), **màtlāctli** (10), **caxtōlli** (15). With **chicua-**, the unit is appended directly to it, and with the other two subbases, the unit is appended to the intervening element **om-**:

1 cē	6 chicuacē	11 màtlāctli oncē	16 caxtōlli oncē
2 ōme	7 chicōme	12 màtlāctli omōme	17 caxtōlli omōme
3 ēyi	8 chicuēyi	13 màtlāctli omēyi	18 caxtōlli omēyi
4 nāhui	9 chiucnāhui	14 màtlāctli onnāhui	19 caxtōlli onnāhui
5 mācuīlli	10 màtlāctli	15 caxtōlli	20 cempōhualli

The units have special forms for use as compounds: **cem-, ōm-, ē-, nāuh-**, while the subbases are regular nouns that lose the absolutive ending in compounds.

Multiples of 20 up to 400 are produced with the compounding forms appended to -**pōhualli**. For multiples involving **on-**, **pōhualli** can appear with only the unit after **on-** or with both elements of the multiple with **īpan** (or **īhuan**) connecting the two: **màtlāctli oncempōhualli** or **màtlācpōhualli īpan oncempōhualli**.

Tzontli is 400, and **xiquipilli** 8000, with compounding of multiples.

Individual items can be counted by using the compound numbers with **tla-mantli** or **tetl** (or specific counting nouns like **camatl** for 'word'). The compound numbers can also be used with the periods of time **ilhuitl, mētztli, xihuitl**.

The units take the plural ending -(i)n(tin).

A number with the appropriate possessive prefix and the suffix -**ixtin** means 'both of', 'all three of' etc.: **tonāhuixtin** 'all four of us'.

The suffix -**pa** gives the sense 'X times': **nāppa** 'four times' (with assimilation).

Verbs

(1) Prefixes

Subject (with helping vowel -i- added if followed by a consonant)

Singular		Plural	
1st person	n(i)-	1st person	t(i)-
2nd person	t(i)-	2nd person	am-
3rd person	ø-	3rd person	ø-

Definite object (only one permitted)

Singular		Plural	
1st person	-nēch-	1st person	-tēch-
2nd person	-mitz-	2nd person	-amēch-
3rd person	-c-/-qu-	3rd person	-quim-

Directional (only one permitted)

-**on**-: motion away
-**huāl**-: motion toward

Reflexive (only one possible)

Singular		Plural	
1st person	-n(o)-	1st person	-t(o)-
2nd person	-m(o)-	2nd person	-m(o)-
3rd person	-m(o)-	3rd person	-m(o)-
Indefinite:	-ne		

Indefinite external object (both permitted)

-**tē**-: animate
-**tla**-: inanimate or indeterminate animateness

Order

subject + definite external object + directional + reflexive + -**tē**- + -**tla**-

(Note that the indefinite reflexive occasionally appears after -**tē**-.)

(2) Conjugational Categories (Tenses etc.)

Bases

1:   *Present stem*
Dictionary listing (generally equivalent to base 2 plus -**i** or -**a**, occasionally -**ia** with semi-causatives)

2:   *Preterite stem*
(a) If base 1 ends in CV (with exceptions noted in the further discussion), the final vowel of base 1 is dropped: **cāuh**- (< **cāhua**). The final consonant of base 2 may undergo phonetic change: **nen**- (< **nemi**), **āx**- (< **āyi**).
(b) Base 2 = base 1:
for verbs ending in:
-**ca**: **maca**-
-**tla**: **tlatla**-
-**o** (which lengthens): **panō**-,
for intransitives ending in -**hua**: **ēhua**-
except: **pēuh**- < **pēhua**),
for monosyllables ending in -**i** (which lengthens): **cuī**- (< **cui**),
for **tōna**: **tōna**-,
for verbs whose base 1 ends in /-CCV/: -**itta**,
optionally for intransitive verbs ending in -**ya**: **huēyiya**- (< **huēyiya**; but also **huēyix**).
(c) Verbs with base 1 ending in -**ia** or -**oa** drop the -**a** and add a glottal stop: -**ilhuî** (< -**ilhuia**), **cholô** (< **choloa**).
(d) Monosyllables in -**a** add a glottal stop: **cuâ** (**cua**).
Base 2 of **yauh** is **yâ**.

3: *Future/optative stem*

Identical to base 1 (with verbs ending in -o and monosyllables in -i lengthening the final vowel) except with verbs ending in -ia, -oa, which drop the final -a and lengthen the preceding vowel: ilhuī- (< ilhuia), cholō- (< choloa). Câ and yauh have as base 3 ye- and yā.

4: *Passive/impersonal stem*

Most verbs add -l- to base 3: cāhual- (< cāhua), ilhuīl- (< ilhuia), cocōl- (< cocoa)

Other formations are used:

obligatorily with:

(a) verbs ending in -mi and monosyllables in -i, base 1 is used (with lengthening of the -i): quēmī- (< quēmi), ī- (< i),

(b) verbs ending in /-ka/ or /-ki/ drop the final vowel of base 1: tēc- (< tēca), tec- (< tequi) and

(c) the verb mati drops the final vowel of base 1 and the final consonant shifts: mach-; optionally (i.e., in addition to the formation in -l-):

    (a) verbs ending in -na, -ni and itta drop the final vowel of base 1: ān- (< āna), tlapān- (< tlapāni), itt-

    (b) verbs ending in /-sa/, /-si/, drop the final vowel of base 1, with shift of the final consonant to /š/: tlāx- (< tlāza), tex- (< teci)

(3) Tenses, Modal Conjugations etc.

(i) Present

Base 1, plural in /'/: -cāhua, -cāhuâ. A very small number of presents have a present stem ending in a consonant in the singular with a plural in -ê: câ, catê.

(ii) Imperfect

Base 1 (with lengthening of final vowel in verbs ending in -o, -ia and -oa, and monosyllables in -i) + -ya, plural in /'/: -cāhuaya, -cāhuayâ; panōya, panōyâ; -ilpiāya, -ilpiāyâ; choloāya, choloāyâ. Yauh has two imperfects huīya, huīyâ and yāya, yāyâ.

(iii) −ni form

Base 1 (with lengthening of final vowel in verbs ending in -o, -ia and -oa, and in monosyllables) + -ni, plural in /'/: -cāhuani,

-cāhuanî; panōni, panōnî, -ilpiāni, -ilpiānî; choloāni, choloānî, -cuāni,
-cuānî. Câ and yauh have yeni, yenî and yāni, yānî respectively.

(iv) Preterite
Base 2 + -c for verbs with base 2 = base 1, otherwise -ø; plural in
-quê: -macac, -macaquê (< maca), -cāuh, -cāuhquê;-ilpî, -ilpìquê; cholô,
cholòquê; -cuâ, -cuàquê; yâ, yàquê. Certain verbs of state use the pluperfect preterite for the regular preterite: catca, catcâ (< câ).

(v) Pluperfect
Base 2 + -ca, plural in /'/: -macaca, -macacâ (< maca), -cāuhca,
-cāuhcâ (< cāhua); -ilpìca, -ilpìcâ; cholòca, cholòcâ; -cuàca, -cuàcâ; yàca,
yàcâ.

(vi) Vetitive
Same as preterite in the singular except that verbs with base 2
= base 1 take /'/ in place of -c (whether this glottal stop appears
in the plural too isn't clear), plural in -tin or -tî: -macâ, -macatin/-tî
(< -maca), -cāuh, -cāuhtin/-tî; -ilpî, -ilpìtin/-tî; cholô, cholòtin/-tî; -cuâ, -
cuàtin/-tî; yâ, yàtin/-tî.

(vii) Future
Base 3 + z, plural in -quê: -cāhuaz, -cāhuazquê; -ilpīz, -ilpīzquê; cholōz,
cholōzquê; yāz, yāzquê.

(viii) Counterfactual
Singular future + -quia, plural in /'/: -cāhuazquia, -cāhuazquiâ;
-ilpīzquia, -ilpīzquiâ; cholōzquia, cholōzquiâ; yāzquia, yāzquiâ.

(ix) Optative
Base 3 (with long vowels shortened in final position), plural in -cān:
-cāhua, -cāhuacān; -ilpi, -ilpīcān; cholo, cholōcān. The optative of yauh is
yauh, huīyan.

(x) Directionals
Directionals are different from other verbal forms in that they come
in two aspects (imperfective and perfective) plus an optative. All
have a plural in /'/.
Directional of Motion Toward
Base 3 plus:
  -quiuh, plural -quihuî (imperfective): -cāhuaquiuh, -cāhuaquihuî;
    -ilpīquiuh, -ilpīquihuî.
  -co, plural -cô (perfective): -cāhuaco, -cāhuacô; -ilpīco,
    -ilpīcô.
  -qui plural -quî (optative): -cāhuaqui, -cāhuaquî; -ilpīqui,
    -ilpīquî.
Directional of Motion Away

Base 3 plus:

-tīuh, plural -tīhuî (imperfective): -cāhuatīuh, -cāhuatihuî; -ilpītīuh, -ilpītīhuî.

-to, plural -tô (perfective): -cāhuato, -cāhuatô; -ilpīto, -ilpītô.

-ti plural -tî (optative): -cāhuati, -cāhuatî; -ilpīti, -ilpītî.

xi) Ligature verbs

Base 2 + ligature (-ti-) + VERB OF STATE or MOTION

(xii) Impersonal

Impersonal verbs signify that there is no specified subject. The impersonal form is mostly identified with the suffix -hua, which takes the form -o after a consonant. The verb can then be put in any of the forms available to a regular active verb.

Intransitives with animate agent

Usually, -hua is appended to base 1, whose final vowel is lengthened: cochīhua (< cochi), temōhua (< temo). With verbs ending in /CsV/, /s/ shifts to /x/: àxīhua (< àci).

But verbs whose base 1 has in front of its final vowel, the consonants /k/, /m/, /w/ instead drop the final vowel and take the ending -ōhua (with the verbs with /w/ dropping it): micōhua (< miqui), pācōhua (< pāqui), nemōhua (< nemi), ēōhua (< ēhua). The same process takes place with stems ending with /VsV/ and /VcV/, but here the consonant undergoes shifting, respectively to /x/ and /č/: nēxōhua (< nēci), quīxōhua (< quīza), huechōhua (< huetzi). There is some irregularity in the formations as huetzīhua is also used alongside huechōchua.

A limited number of intransitives form the impersonal with base 4 + -hua (always in the form -o) to: mayānalo < mayāna), huetzco (< huetzca). A few common verbs take this construction and add -hua to it a second time: yelōhua (< câ), huīlōhua (< yauh), huīlōhuatz (< huītz).

Intransitives with inanimate unspecified subject take the prefix tla-: tlahuāqui (<huāqui), tlaceliya (< celiya).

Passive

If the agent is indefinite and the patient definite, the verb is passive, the verb takes the form base 4 + -hua, with the patient appearing as the subject and the verb agreeing in number: nitlazòtlalo 'I am loved' (< tlazòtla), tānōzquê 'we will be captured' (< āna). A bitransitive verb that is reflexive takes the indefinite reflexive ne-: annecuitlahuīlô 'you (pl.) will be looked after' (< cuitlahuia).

Transitive impersonal

Verbs with an indefinite agent and an indefinite object use base 4
+ **-hua**, taking the appropriate indefinite object (or incorporated
noun): **tēano** or **tēānalo** (both < **āna**), **tlaīhua** (< **i**), **tlàcuilōlo**
(< **ìcuiloa**), **netlazòtlalo, cacchīhualo** (< **cacchīhua**), **tētlamaco**
(< bitransitive **maca**).

(3) Derivative verbal suffixes

(a) Applicative
Base 3 + **-lia**: **cuīlia** (< **cui**), **tēmōlia** (**tēmoa**), **tlālīlia** (< **tlālia**), **tzàtzilia**
(< **tzàtzi**).
But with verbs ending in /Ca/, the /a/ becomes /i/: **chīhuilia** (< **chīhua**),
cōhuilia (< **cōhua**). This change can cause a shift in the preceding consonant:
/c/ and /t/ shift to /č/: **nōchilia** (< **nōtza**), **machilia** (< **mati**)
/s/ to /x/: **tlāxilia** (< **tlāza**)
/λ/ to /t/ (if **-tla** is a derivational ending) or /č/: **tlazòtilia**
(< **tlazòtla**), **mōchilia** (< **mōtla**).
However, **-a** is maintained in:
monosyllables (becoming long): **cuālia** (< **cua**)
verbs ending in **-iya**: **piyalia** (< **piya**).
Some verbs in **-a** (especially ones ending in **-ca** and **-hua**) form the
applicative by replacing **-a** with **-ia**: **ixquia** (< **ixca**), **ixtlāhuia**
(< **ixtlāhua**).
Intransitive/semi-causative pairs in **-ahuia** or **-ihui/-oa** form the
applicative with **-alhuia** or **-ilhuia** (the first vowel of this ending
determined by the vowel of the intransitive):
ìtalhuia (< **ìtahui/ìtoa**), **malacachilhuia** (< **malacachihui/malacachoa**).
However, if the stem in front of **-oa** ends in **-l**, the abbreviated
ending **-huia** simply replaces **-oa**: **polhuia** (< **polihui/poloa**),
ìcuilhuia (< **ìcuilihui/ìcuiloa**).

(b) Causative
Intransitives allow for many variants. The general patterns are as follows:
(i) Base 1 (with final **-i** lengthened) + **-tia**: **yōlītia** (< **yōli**).
Base 1 loses its final vowel in verbs ending in:
/-ka/ or /-ki/: **-mictia** (< **miqui**) **-chōctia** (< **chōca**)
/-V:mV/, /-V:nV/ or /-V:wV/: **quēntia**
(< **quēmi**), **-tlāhuāntia** (< **tlāhuāna**), **māuhtia** (< **māhui**)

/si/, /sa/ or -ti (with shift of /s/ to /š/ and /t/ to /č/: -quīxtia
(< quīza), tlāxtia (< tlāza), nēxtia (< nēci).

   (ii) Base 1 + -ltia: mayānaltia (< mayāna), chōcaltia (< chōca). With
      verbs in /-ka/, the stem final vowel can shift to /-i/: -chōquiltia
      (< chōca). (NB This formation could be interpreted as base 4 +
      -tia, but for the most part no such base 4 form is attested. This
      construction is common in verbs ending in -a.)

   (iii) Base 3 + -ltia (which again looks like base 4 + -tia) for verbs
      ending in -oa: cholōltia (< choloa).

Transitives:

Base 4 (however formed) + -tia:

Base 4 with -l-: cāhualtia (< cāhua), ìtōltia (< ìtoa)

Base 4 without -l-: -ītia (< i), āntia (< āna), -tectia (< tequi), -machtia
(< mati).

Transitives with alternative formations for base 4 can have alternative
causatives: ānaltia or āntia (< āna).

(c) Intransitive/transitive pairings

   (i) Intransitive/semi-causative:

      -i/-a: tlapāni/tlapāna; pōhui/pōhua; pàti/pàtla (with shift of /ta/ to
      /λa/)

      -ihui/-oa: ìcuilihui/-ìcuiloa; polihui/poloa

      -ahui/-oa: ìtahui/ìtoa; ìtlacahui/ìtlacoa

      -i/-ia: calaqui/calaquia; tlami/tlamia

      -a/-ia (rare): tlatla/tlatia

      -hua/-hua: chipāhua/chipāhua

      -ca/-tza: see next section

   (ii) Reduplicative groups

      There is a large group of triplet verbs formed on disyllabic stems
      ending in a vowel. An intransitive is formed with -ni, the
      preceding vowel being lengthened: tlapāni, coyōni. Such forms
      can take a semi-causative in -na or -nia: tlapāna, coyōnia. They
      can also form regular causatives in -naltia: pozōnaltia (< pozōni).

      Especially with stems signify a sort of sound or emission of
      light, such verbs in -ni can have a related
      intransitive/semi-causative pair in -ca/-tza that has
      short-vowel reduplication and no lengthening in front of the
      ending: cualāni, cuacualaca, cuacualatza; molōni, momoloca,
      momolotza

(d) Denominative suffixes

   -huia 'apply NOUN to': īxhuia (< īxtli)

   -lia causative of "adjectival" verbs in -ya: iztālia, xocōlia

-oa 'use/do/perform NOUN': teponāzoa (< teponāztli)

-ti 'be/become' NOUN: teti (< tetl), tlācati (< tlācatl)

-tia 'equip with NOUN' (trans.): nāmictia (< nāmictli), 'adopt as one's NOUN' (bitrans.): teōtia (< teōtl); 'spend COMPOUND NUMBER + TIME NOUN', 'be that age' (intrans.): cemilhuitia (< cem- + ilhuitl)

-tiya inchoative of verbs in -ti: tetiya

-tla 'consider as NOUN': yāōtla (< yāōtl)

-ya 'be/become ADJECTIVAL NOUN': iztāya (< iztatl), xocōya (< xocōtl)

-yōhua 'be/become full of NOUN', 'abound in NOUN': āyōhua (< ātl)

-yōtia causative of verbs in -yōhua: āyōtia (< ātl)

(e) Deverbal noun forms

(i) Preterite agent nouns: 'VERB-er'

Formed on base 2, with transitive verbs taking indefinite object prefix. Generally, animate agents take the ending -qui in singular: micqui (< miqui), tēyacānqui. But agent nouns from verbs in -ia, -oa tend to take ending -ø: tlàcuilô (< ìcuiloa). All inanimate agents take -ø: tēcocô (< cocoa). All animate agents have a plural in -quê: micquê, tlàcuilòquê. The ending becomes -cā- when it takes a derivative suffix (including the possessive) or is used as a non-final element in a compound.

(ii) Nouns of state

From the preterite agent noun are formed abstract nouns in -yō-tl: tlàtòcāyōtl (< ìtoa). Such forms mostly appear possessed, with -cāyōtl reduced to -ca. With intransitives, this form signifies either a state: -poliuhca 'disappearance' or what causes it -yōlca, -nenca (< yōli, nemi): 'subsistence, livelihood'. The form is uncommon with transitives in the active: tlapixcāyōtl 'position as guard'. Much more common are possessed forms based on the passive: -tlazòtlalōca 'being loved' (< tlazòtla), -nōnōtzalōca 'advice (given to the possessor)' (< nōtza).

(iii) -ni nouns: 'one prone to VERB, with a tendency to VERB'

This is a nominal use of the –ni form. Transitive verbs generally take an indefinite prefix and take –mê (instead of ') in the plural–: tlamatini, tlamatinimê (< mati). Derivative forms tend to substitute the preterite agent noun.

(iv) Passive -ni nouns: 'VERB-able'

Formed on the -ni form of the passive: ēhualōni (< ēhua), ìtōlōni (< ìtoa), cacōni (< caqui).

(v) Instrument nouns in –ni

'that by which one VERBS, person by whom one VERBS'

Formed on both intransitive and transitive verbs (which take an indefinite object prefix): micōhuani (< miqui), tlatecōni (< tequi), tlācatīhuani (< tlācati). When possessed, these take the form base 1 + -ya (with the sound changes associated with the imperfect): -miquiya, -tlatequiya.

(vi) Action nouns: 'to VERB, 'VERBing', 'act of VERBing'

Usually formed on base 3, adding -z-tli if the verb is intransitive, and –li-z-tli if it is transitive: transitive verbs take an indefinite object prefix (or incorporated noun): cochiztli (< cochi), miquiztli (< miqui), māhuiztli (< māhui), ciyahuiztli (< ciyahui).

tētlazòtlaliztli (< tlazòtla), tlàcuilōliztli (< ìcuiloa).

In verbs ending in -ci, /s/ becomes /x/: texiliztli (< teci)

With verbs ending in /ka/ and /wa/, the stem-final vowel can become -i: chōquiztli or chōquiliztli (< chōca), neàhuililiztli (< m-àhua)

(vii) Action nouns: 'VERB-able'

In a very limited number of instances, the formation in -ztli/-liztli is equivalent to the passive -ni Form nouns: chīhualiztli (< chīhua), īxnāmiquiztli (< īxnāmiqui).

(viii) Object nouns: 'what/who is/has been VERBed, will be/is to be VERBed'

The most common formation is base 4 (however formed) plus tla- (even if the noun represents something animate): tlàcuilōlli (< ìcuiloa), tlachīhualli (< chīhua), tlatectli (< tequi), tlaquēmitl (< quēmi), tlatlāzalli (< tlāza).

The same formation can be built on base 2 with verbs that drop their vowel in the preterite and whose stem then ends in /c/, /n/, /s/, /w/ or /x/ and with verbs whose base 2 ends in /CCi/: tlanōtztli (< nōtza), tlaquēntli (< quēmi), tlatlāztli (< tlāza), tlacāuhtli (< cāhua), tlaināxtli (< ināya), tlatquitl (< itqui).

With certain bitransitive verbs, the form with tē- represents the *thing* involved in the action of the verb, and the one with tla- the *person* affected: tēmachtīlli 'lesson', tlamachtīlli 'student' (both < machtia); tēnāhuatīlli 'command', tlanāhuatīlli 'person ordered' (both < nāhuatia).

Other anomalous formations exist as lexical items: **tōnalli**
(< **tōna**), **tēmictli** (< **tēmiqui**), **textli** (< **teci**).

(ix) Object noun as instrument: 'what one VERBS with'
Derived from reflexive verbs, these forms take **ne-**:
nechìchīhualli (< **mo-chìchīhua**), **nenōnōtzalli** (< **mo-nōnōtza**).

VERB PARADIGMS

(a) Bases

Base 1	cochi	pāqui	nōtza	tēca	cocoa	mictia	cua		câ
Base 2	coch	pāc	nōtz	tēca	cocō	micti	cuā		catê
Base 3	cochi	pāqui	nōtza	tēca	cocō	micti	cuā		catca
Base 4	cochi	pācō	nōtzal	tēc	cocōl	mictil	cual		catcâ

(b) Verb Forms

Present	cochi	pāqui	-nōtza	-tēca	-cocoa	-mictia	-cua	yauh	câ
_pl._	cochi	pāquî	-nōtzâ	-tēcâ	-cocoâ	-mictiâ	-cuâ	huî	catê
Imperfect	cochiya	pāquiya	-nōtzaya	-tēcaya	-cocoāya	-mictiāya	-cuāya	huiya/yāya	catca
_pl_	cochiyâ	pāquiyâ	-nōtzayâ	-tēcayâ	-cocoāyâ	-mictiāyâ	-cuāyâ	huiyâ/yāyâ	catcâ
-**ni** form	cochini	pāquini	-nōtzani	-tēcani	-cocoāni	-mictiāni	-cuāni	yāni	yeni
_pl._	cochinî	pāquinî	-nōtzanî	-tēcanî	-cocoānî	-mictiānî	-cuānî	yānî	yeni
Preterite	coch	pāc	-nōtz	-tēcac	-cocō	-micti	-cuâ	yâ	catca
_pl._	cochquê	pāquê	-nōtzquê	-tēcaquê	-cocōquê	-mictiquê	-cuāquê	yàquê	catcâ
Pluperfect	cochca	pācca	-nōtzca	-tēcca	-cocōca	-mictica	-cuāca		
_pl._	cochcâ	pāccâ	-nōtzcâ	-tēccâ	-cocōcâ	-micticâ	-cuācâ		

Vetitive	coch	pāc	-nōtz	-tēac	-cocō	-micti	-cuā		
pl.	cochtin	pāctin	-nōtztin	-tēcatin	-cocōtin	-micttin	-cuātin		
Ligature form	cochti	pācti	-nōtzti	-tēcati	-cocōti	-mictiti	-cuāti		
	cochti-	pācti-	-nōtzti-	-tēcati-	-cocōti-	-mictiti-	-cuāti-	yāti-	yeti-
Future	cochiz	pāquiz	-nōtzaz	-tēcaz	-cocōz	-mictiz	-cuāz	yāz	yez
pl.	cochizquê	pāquizquê	-nōtzazquê	-tēcazquê	-cocōzquê	-mictizquê	-cuāzquê	yāzquê	yezquê
C'factual	cochizquia	pāquizquia	-nōtzazquia	-tēcazquia	-cocōzquia	-mictizquia	-cuāzquia	yāzquia	yezquia
pl.	cochizquiā	pāquizquiā	-nōtzazquiā	-tēcazquiā	-cocōzquiā	-mictizquiā	-cuāzquiā	yāzquiā	yezquiā
Optative	cochi	pāqui	-nōtza	-tēca	-coco	-micti	-cua	yauh	ye
pl.	cochicān	pāquicān	-nōtzacān	-tēcacān	-cocōcān	-micticān	-cuācān	huiyān	yecān
Dir. toward	cochtiuh	pāquitiuh	-nōtzatiuh	-tēcatiuh	-cocōtiuh	-mictitiuh	-cuātiuh		
pl.	cochtihui	pāquitihui	-nōtzatihui	-tēcatihui	-cocōtihui	-mictitihui	-cuātihui		
Dir. away	cochiquiuh	pāquiquiuh	-nōtzaquiuh	-tēcaquiuh	-cocōquiuh	-mictiquiuh	-cuāquiuh		
pl.	cochiquihui	pāquiquihui	-nōtzaquihui	-tēcaquihui	-cocōquihui	-mictiquihui	-cuāquihui		
Impersonal/passive	cochihua	pācōhua	-nōtzalo	-tēco	-cocōlo	-mictilo	-cuālo	huilōhua	yelōhua

The Aztec Calendar

The Aztec calendar includes two separate computations: a solar calendar of 365 days (**xihuitl**) and a divinatory calendar of 260 days (**tōnalpōhualli**).

The **tōnalpōhualli** operates through the interaction of thirteen numbers and the following twenty signs:

cipactli	*alligator*
èecatl	*wind*
calli	*house*
cuetzpalin	*lizard*
cōhuātl	*snake*
miquiztli	*death*
mazātl	*deer*
tōchtli	*rabbit*
ātl	*water*
itzcuintli	*dog*
ozomàtli	*monkey*
malīnalli	*dry plant*
ācatl	*reed*
ōcēlōtl	*jaguar*
cuāuhtli	*eagle*
cōzcacuāuhtli	*vulture (eagle with a collar)*
olin	*movement*
tecpatl	*flint*
quiyahuitl	*rain*
xōchitl	*flower*

Counting of days is carried out with the numbers one to thirteen, and one sign is given to each number according to the order shown in the list. After the number thirteen is assigned to a certain sign in the list, the next count of thirteen signs begins with the sign that follows the one used for thirteen in the previous one. Because the number of signs is not equally divisible into thirteen, the sign associated with a given number changes with every count of thirteen in a year. Thus, the first count begins with **1 cipactli, 2 èecatl, 3 calli** and ends with **13 ācatl**. The next count begins **1 ocēlōtl, 2 cuāuhtli, 3 cōzcacuāuhtli.** With **7 xōchitl**, the end of the list is reached, and the counting continues at the head of the list with **8 cipactli, 9 èecatl**, down to **13 miquiztli**. The third count of thirteen then begins with **1 mazātl, 2 tōchtli** etc. This continues until the twentieth count, which begins with **1 tōchtli** and ends with **13 xōchitl**. This completes the cycle, so that the next year of 260 days once again begins with **1 cipactli**. Each count of thirteen was dedicated to one or more gods, and certain days were considered lucky or unlucky.

The solar year (**xihuitl**) operated independently of the **tōnalpōhualli** and consisted of 365 days divided among eighteen months of 20 days each plus 5 supplementary days that were considered unlucky. The eighteen months were dedicated to various divinities and bore the following names:[1]

1. Cuahuitl ēhua *The trees rear; or* ātl cāhualo *Ceasing of water*
2. Tlācaxipēhualiztli *Flaying of men*
3. Tozoztōntli *Little vigil*
4. Huēyi tozoztli *Great vigil*
5. Toxcatl *Drought (?)*
6. Etzalcuāliztli *Eating of etzalli*[2]
7. Tēcuilhuitōntli *Little feast day of the lords*
8. Huēyi tēcuilhuitl *Great feast day of the lords*
9. Tlaxōchimaco *Offering of flowers*
10. Xocotl huetzi *Fall of Xocotl*
11. Ochpaniztli *Sweeping of the road (?)*
12. Teōtl èco *The God arrives*
13. Tepēilhuitl *Mountain feast day*
14. Quechōlli *Precious feather*
15. Panquetzaliztli *Raising of banners*
16. Ātemōztli *The falling of water*
17. Tititl *Stretching (?)*
18. Izcalli *Growth, Rebirth*
+ 5 *days called* nēmontemi *Barren or useless days*

The days of each month were counted from 1 to 20, which meant that this counting did not correspond to that of the **tōnalpōhualli**. For example, if

---

[1] These translations, some of them uncertain, appear in Frances Berdan *Aztecs of Central Mexico: An Imperial Society* (Belmont, CA: Thomson Learning, 2004).
[2] A dish with beans.

the counting began with **1 calli 1 cuahuitl ēhua**, the next day was **2 cuetz-palin 2 cuahuitl ēhua**, and so on until **13 cuāuhtli 13 cuahuitl ēhua**, then **1 cōzcacuāuhtli 14 cuahuitl ēhua** and so on through **7 èecatl 20 cuahuitl ēhua**, then **8 calli 1 tlācaxipēhualiztli** and so on through **13 tōchtli 6 tlācaxipēhualiztli**, then 1 **ātl 7 tlācaxipēhualiztli**, and so on.

Each solar year was designated by its first day according to the **tōnalpōhualli**. Only four signs could start a year, namely **calli** 'house', **tōchtli** 'rabbit', **ācatl** 'reed' and **tecpatl** 'flint'. If the first day of a year was **tōchtli**, the 361st was also **tōchtli**, so the 365th was **malīnalli** and the first day of the following year was **ācatl**. If the first day was **1 tōchtli**, then the 365th was **1 malīnalli**, and the first day of the following year was **2 ācatl**. Then the following years were **3 tecpatl, 4 calli, 5 tōchtli** and so on, until **13 tōchtli**. At this point, a new count of thirteen began with **1 ācatl, 2 tecpatl, 3 calli** etc. Because there is no common denominator in the numbers four and thirteen, it took fifty-two years (4×13) for a year bearer to return with the same combination of number and name. This period of fifty-two years is known as a "calendar round" in English.

The juncture of two calendar rounds was called **xiuhtlalpīlli** 'binding of years' and was referred to as **toxiuh molpilî** 'our years have been bound'. It occurred at the start of a year **2 ācatl** and was celebrated with the elaborate ritual for lighting a new fire on Huixachtepētl to the southeast of Tenochtitlan. According to legend, the first binding of our years was performed in A.D. 1091 in Aztlān (the mythical area to the north from which the Aztec populations were thought to have migrated). The ninth and last one (and the fourth celebrated in Tenochtitlan) occurred in 1507. Cortés's entry into Mexico, which is called A.D. 1519 according to the Julian calendar, was designated **1 ācatl** in the Aztec system.

Key to the Exercises

Preliminary Lesson

Transcriptions of Exercises 1 and 3

(1) /āmaλ/, /kikaki/, /nokamak/, /eλ/, /teλ/, /tēnλi/, /kalli/, /ōme/, /tōtōλ/, /piltōnλi/, /kipiya/, /kiselia/, /kiλālia/, /kipoloa/, /yāōλ/, /teōλ/, /pāki/, /tēmiktia/, /kiliλ/, /kimaka/, /conλi/, /čapōlin/, /čiči/, /λeλ/, /kʷalli/, /ye'wāλ/, /tēkʷāni/, /ōkicakʷ/, /sokiλ/, /sēsēk/, /siλālin/, /šiwiλ/, /šōčiλ/, /yakaλ/, /mōyōλ/, /mināya/, /wāki/, /wāllāw/, /nokonēw/, /kʷalāni/, /nomīl/, /kale'/, /koči'/, /e'ekaλ/, /tōpλi/, /tōpko/, /kakλi/, /tōčλi/, /λackan/, /tekpaλ/, /icλi/, /icmōlini/, /tēkʷλi/, /nekʷλi/, /senka'/, /tēnyo'/, /ēyi/, /kāmpa/, /teposλi/, /ikšiλ/, /λaškalli/, /āmošλi/, /yēkyōλ/, /totēkʷyo'/, /tewyo'/, /nikkʷa/, /nikλaso'λa/, /λa'toāni/, /mēši'ko/, /tilma'λi/, /a'si/, /a'kʷalli/, /ca'ci/, /a'mo/

(3) /nopilcé, nokōské, nokecalé, ōtiyōl, ōtiλākat, ōtimoλāltikpakkīštīko; in īλāltikpak in totēkʷyo ōmicyōkoš, ōmicpīk, ōmicλākatili' in īpalnemōwani in dios. Aw mīško mokpak ōtiλačiške' in timonānwān, in timota'wān, īwān in māwi'wān, in moλa'wān, in mowānyōlke' ō mīško ō mokpak λačiške', ōčōkake', ōλaōkoške' mopampacinko in ik ōtiyōl, in ik ōtiλākat in λāltikpak/.

Lesson One

(a) nichōca, tichōca, chōca, tichōcâ, anchōcâ, chōcâ
    nicochi, ticochi, cochi, ticochî, ancochî, cochî
    nicuīca, ticuīca, cuīca, ticuīcâ, ancuīcâ, cuīcâ
    nēhua, tēhua, ēhua, tēhuâ, amēhuâ, ēhuâ
    nimiqui, timiqui, miqui, timiquî, ammiquî, miquî

nitzàtzi, titzàtzi, tzàtzi, titzàtzî, antzàtzî, tzàtzî

niyōli, tiyōli, yōli, tiyōlî, anyōlî, yōlî

(b) 1. I'm singing/sing. 2. They're dying/die. 3. We're shouting/shout. 4. You (s.) are sleeping/sleep. 5. The woman is crying/cries. 6. The Mexica are dying/die. 7. The women are leaving/leave. 8. You (pl.) are shouting/shout. 9. They live.

(c) 1. Miqui. 2. Tiyōlî. 3. Cochî in mēxìcâ. 4. Nitzàtzi. 5. Chōcâ in cihuâ. 6. Ancochî. 7. Ticuīca. 8. Ticuīcâ.

Lesson Two

(a) 1. Ca anchichimê. *You (pl. are dogs).* 2. Àmo ticōcōhuâ. *We are not snakes.* 3. Cuix cōcoyô in tzàtzî? *Are coyotes shouting? (Is it coyotes that are shouting?)* 4. Miquî in tōtōchtin. *The rabbits are dying.* 5. Cuix tētepê? *Are they mountains?* 6. Àmo cīcitlāltin. *They aren't stars.* 7. Ca mīmichtin in ēhuâ. *It is fish that are leaving.* 8. Ca oquichtin in cuīcâ. *It's men who are singing.* 9. Àmo antēteô. *You (pl.) are not gods.* 10. Ca tipīpiltin. *We're children* (or *noblemen).* 11. Cuix amotomî? *Are you (pl.) Otomi?*

(b) 1. Ca chichi in cochi. *It's a dog that's sleeping.* 2. Ca cōconê in cuīcâ. *It's children who are singing.* 3. Ca otomî in tzàtzî. *It's Otomi who are shouting.* 4. Ca oquichtli in miqui. *It's a man who's dying.*

(c) 1. The woman is Mexica. 2. Are the children Mexica? 3. No, they're not Mexica. They're Otomi. 4. Aren't you (pl.) sleeping? 5. (The) fish don't sing. 6. The people live (are alive). 7. The Mexicans don't cry. 8. The dogs are sleeping. 9. They're not stones, they're mountains. 10. The gods are crying. 11. It's not children who are crying, it's women. 12. Are they stars? – Yes, they're stars.

(d) 1. Cochî in cōcōhuâ. 2. Ēhuâ in otomî. 3. Cuix cuīca in cihuātl? 4. Cuix cochi in mēxìcatl? – Quēmâ, ca cochi. 5. Ca àmo mēxìcatl in cihuātl. 6. Cuix ammēxìcâ? – Àmo, ca totomî. 7. Cuix yōlî in cīcitlāltin? 8. Cuix àmo miquî in tēteô? 9. Ēhuâ in cōcoyô. 10. Cuīcâ in cōconê. 11. Ca àmo calli. 12. Cuix chichimê? – Ca àmo, ca cōcoyô. 13. In otomî ca àmo chichimê, ca tlācâ.

Lesson Three

(a) 1. Nimitztlazòtla 2. Nictlazòtla 3. Namēchtlazòtlâ 4. Tamēchtlazòtlâ 5. Tamēchcaquî 6. Amēchcaqui 7. Amēchcaquî 8. Tēchcaquî 9. Tēchittâ 10. Nēchittâ 11. Mitzittâ 12. Timitzittâ 13. Timitzānâ 14. Mitzāna 15. Quimāna 16. Quintlazòtla 17. Tēchtlazòtla 18. Antēchtlazòtlâ

19. Titēchtlazòtla 20. Tiquintlazòtla 21. Titētlazòtla 22. Titèìtoa 23. Titēchìtoa 24. Tēchìtoa 25. Mitzìtoa 26. Tlàtoa 27. Tlàcuiloa 28. Tlacaqui 29. Antlacaquî 30. Antlacuâ 31. Anquicuâ 32. Anquichīhuâ 33. Ticchīhua 34. Tiqui 35. Anquî

(b) 1. He loves Peter/Peter loves him. 2. The man hears the woman (*less likely*: the woman hears the man). 3. He's making the house. 4. He drinks the water. 5. Peter drinks it. 6. I see the house. 7. Peter catches people. 8. Peter hears them. 9. The women hears him/her. 10. The dogs see coyotes. 11. He sees the coyotes. 12. The coyote sees them. 13. It's a house (*or* houses) that Peter's making. 14. Are you (s.) writing (*or* painting)?

(c) 1. Tlacua in cihuātl. 2. Tlatta in Pedro. 3. Qui ātl in tōchtli. 4. Ca ātl in qui in tōchtli. 5. Quitlazòtla in cihuātl in mēxìcatl. 6. Quincaqui mēxìcâ in cihuātl. 7. Quicaquî in mēxìcâ in cihuātl. 8. Quimitta in cīcitlāltin. 9. Àmo niccua in tetl. 10. Quichīhua calli in Pedro. 11. Quimìcuiloa tētepê in Pedro. 12. Cuix àmo tiquìtoa in Pedro? 13. Àmo, niquimìtoa in cihuâ. 14. Ca cōcoyô in tiquincaqui. (*In sentences 1, 2, 3, 5, 6, 7, 10, 11, the subject could appear in front of the verb. This constant possibility will not be noted from here on.*)

Lesson Four

(a) 1. Ca tèhuāntin (in) tamēchnōtzâ. *It's we who are calling you (pl.).* Ca amèhuāntin (in) tamēchnōtzâ. *It's you (pl.) that we are calling.* 2. Ca nèhuātl (in) nitzàtzi. *It's me who's shouting (lit. who am shouting).* 3. Ca yèhuātl cochi in Pedro. *It's Peter who's sleeping.* 4. Ca tèhuāntin (in) titlacuâ. *It's we who are eating.* 5. Ca nèhuātl (in) niquimitta in cīcitlāltin. *It's me who sees the stars.* Ca yèhuāntin (in) niquimitta in cīcitlāltin. *It's the stars that I see.* 6. Ca yèhuāntin (in) mitzcaquî in tētēuctin. *It's the lords who hear you (s.).* Ca tèhuātl (in) mitzcaquî in tētēuctin. *It's you that the lords hear.* 7. Ca yèhuātl (in) nēchtlazòtla in Pedro. *It's Pedro who loves me.* Ca nèhuātl (in) nēchtlazòtla in Pedro. *It's me that Pedro loves.* 8. Ca nèhuātl (in) nicmati in. *It's me that knows this.* Ca yèhuātl (in) nicmati. *This is what I know.* 9. Ca amèhuāntin (in) anquicuî in tetl. *It's you (pl.) who are holding the stones.* Ca yèhuātl (in) anquicuî in tetl. *It's stones that you (pl.) are holding.*

(b) 1. What are these? – They're coyotes. 2. What do you (s.) see? – The house. 3. Who do you (s.) see? – The Otomi (pl.). 4. It's not coyotes that I see, it's dogs. 5. It's meat that Peter is eating, *or* Meat is what Peter eats. 6. It's Peter that eats the meat. 7. The meat is what Peter eats. 8. As for me, I'm a Mexica, and you (pl.), you are Otomi. 9. Every (*lit.* whoever is a) human dies. 10. I don't know who you're (s.) calling. 11. I don't hear what you're (s.) talking about.

(c) 1. Tlein ticnequi? – Ca ātl. 2. Tlein anquicuâ? – Ca yèhuātl in nacatl. 3. Āquìquê on? (*or* Āc yèhuāntin on?) – In yèhuāntin on ca àmo mēxìcâ, ca otomî. 4. Āquin cuīca? – Ca pilli in cuīca. – Àmo, ca yèhuātl in Pedro. 5. In tèhuātl ca àmo timexìcatl. 6. Inìquê on tlācâ àmo quicuâ michin. 7. Àmo nicmati in āquin tlacua. 8. Àmo nicmati in tlein quicua. 9. Àmo niquitta in āquin quicua nacatl. 10. In āquin mēxìcatl quimati in.

Lesson Five

(a) 1. Peter's there, isn't he coming? 2. Is Mexico City where you're (pl.) going (to)? – No, Xochimilco. 3. Is Peter in Tlaxcala? – No, here in Mexico City. 4. There are people over there, what are they doing? 5. The Otomi are arriving here. 6. Snakes are coming out of there. 7. Are the women coming? – Yes, don't you (pl.) see them? 8. I'm eating here. – As for us, we (are eating) over there. 9. These lords live (there) in Mexico City. 10. We're leaving a nice place. Where we're going is not a nice place. 11. What is this place? Is it Mexico City? – No, it's Tlaxcala.

(b) 1. Mēxìco tìcihuî. 2. Cuix Xōchimilco tàcî? 3. Ōmpa Tlaxcallān huî in mēxìcâ. 4. Ōmpa Cuauhnāhuac huītzê inìquê on cihuâ. 5. Cuix Mēxìco titlatlazòtla? 6. Cuix tiyauh in ōmpa yauh Pedro? – Àmo, ca yèhuātl in huītz in nicān ticatê. 7. Cualcān in (ōmpa) annemî. 8. Nìcihui in cānin cualcān. 9. Ca Cuauhnāhuac in nemî inìquê on tlācâ. 10. In āquin Tlaxcallāmpa yauh quitta inon tepētl.

Lesson Six

(a) 1. Nonnotlālia, nihuālnotlālia. 2. Nocontlālia, nichuāllālia. 3. Nontētlālia, nihuāltētlālia. 4. Tommopāca, tihuālmopāca. 5. Tontlacāhua, tihuāllacāhua. 6. Titēchoncāhua, titēchhuālcāhua. 7. Tiquimoncāhua, tiquinhuālcāhua. 8. Toconcāhua, tichuālcāhua. 9. Concāhua, quihuālcāhua.

(b) 1. I lie (lay myself) down (over) there. 2. Those people don't love each other. 3. Are you (s.) coming to put those flowers here? 4. The rabbit is coming to hide (himself) here. 5. Are you leaving? –No, we're staying here. 6. Are you shaving (yourself)? – No, I'm washing (myself). 7. Is Peter sick? – That's what they say (*lit.*, this is said). 8. The coyotes are running off (*or* away). 9. Where are you (s.) going? Aren't you happy here? 10. We're going to throw these stones (over) there.

(c) 1. Cāmpa ommotlātiâ in pīpiltin? 2. Ca amonìcihuî. Cuix Tlaxcallān in anhuî? 3. Àmo mochīhua in. 4. Nicān àmo motta in āltepētl. 5. Cuix mocuâ in cōcōhuâ? 6. Àmo mi inin ātl. Ca tēcocoa. 7. Noconcua in nacatl, noconi in ātl. 8. Timēhua, timopāca, Mēxìco timotlaloa (*or* tommotlaloâ). 9. Titēhuâ, titopācâ, Mēxìco titotlaloâ (*or* tontotlaloâ). 10. Tlein toconchīhua? – Noconquetza in tetl.

Lesson Seven

(a) 1. Ēyin(tin) chichimê. 2. Chicuacentin tōtōchtin. 3. Chiucnāhuin(tin) mīmichtin. 4. Caxtōltin cōcōhuâ oncēmê (*or* caxtōltin oncēmê cōcōhuâ). 5. Caxtōltin cōcoyô. 6. Chicuēyin(tin) tēteô. 7. Màtlāctin cihuâ oncēmê (*or* màtlāctin oncēmê cihuâ). 8. Caxtōltin tōtoltin onnāhuin(tin) (*or* caxtōltin onnāhuin(tin) tōtōltin). 9. Chicōmentin tētepê. 10. Màtlāctli nōchtli omōme (*or* màtlāctli omōme nōchtli *or* màtlāctetl omōntetl nōchtli *or* màtlāctli omōntetl nōchtli). 11. Caxtōlli xōchitl omēyi (caxtōlli omēyi xōchitl). 12. Màtlāctli tlaxcalli omēyi (màtlāctli omēyi tlaxcalli). 13. Miyaquintin (*or* miyaquin *or* miyactin) pitzōmê. 14. Mochintin (*or* mochtin) mexìcâ. 15. Quēzquin(tin) cīcitlāltin?

(b) 1. Look, here come three Otomi. 2. Look, here come three Otomi (the nuance being that there are three Otomi coming and they number three). 3. As for the six tortillas, two dogs are eating them. 4. As for the woman, she's going to make the fifteen tortillas. 5. Are you (pl.) calling all of us (us all)? 6. I see few stars. 7. There are two more pigs there. 8. Those pigs are eating all the corn. 9. It's twenty days now that he's been sick. 10. Of the children, four are no longer sick and only one (of them) is sick. 11. Peter's going to Mexico City, while I'm staying here still. 12. The moon hasn't come out (become visible) yet, can't be (isn't) seen yet.

(c) 1. Niquimmati oc miyaquintin tlācâ (*or* nicmati oc miyac tlācatl). 2. Cēmê cochî in otomî. 3. Cēmê tèhuāntin ticnequî michin. 4. Cuix anquinequî tlaxcalli in ammochintin? 5. Ca ye chicuēxihuitl in nicān câ. 6. Inin citlālin ca chicuacemmētztli in nēci. 7. Àmo ancaxtōltin, zan ammàtlāctin amonnāhuin. 8. In ōmentin pīpiltin ayamo cochî. 9. Nicān mochtin catê in tōtoltin. 10. Ca miyactlamantli in tomātl. 11. Ca ye huitzê nāhuintin pīpiltin, cān catê in oc ōmentin? 12. Ōmpa noconcui oc ēyi cuahuitl, ca zan quēzqui in nicān câ.

Lesson Eight

(a) 1. ōniccac, ōticcacquê 2. ōnicchīuh, ōticchīuhquê 3. ōniccuâ, ōticcuàquê, 4. ōnicuīcac, ōticuīcaquê 5. ōnìciuh, ōtìciuhquê 6. ōniquīc, ōtiquīquê 7. ōniquìcuilô, ōtiquìcuilòquê 8. ōniquìtô, ōtiquìtôquê 9. ōninen, ōtinenquê 10. ōnicnec, ōticnecquê 11. ōnictec, ōtictecquê 12. ōnictlazòtlac,

ōtictlazòtlaquê 13. ōnictlātî, ōtictlātìquê 14. ōnictolīnî, ōtictolīnìquê
15. ōnitzàtzic, ōtitzàtziquê 16. ōniyōl, ōtiyōlquê

(b) 1. Ōmpa ōnonnotēcac. 2. In yèhuāntin on àmo ōmotlazòtlaquê. 3. Cuix
nicān ōtichuāllālî in xōchitl on? 4. Nicān ōhuālmotlātî in tōchtli. 5. Cuix
ōamonyàquê? – Àmo, ca nicān otitocāuhquê. 6. Cuix ōtimoxin? Ca àmo,
ca ōninopāc. 7. Cuix ōmococô in Pedro? – Ōmìtô in. 8. Ommotlalòquê (or
ōommotlalòquê) in cōcoyô. 9. Cāmpa ōtonyâ? Cuix nicān àmo ōtimomâ?
10. Ōmpa ōtocontlāzquê in tetl in.

(c) 1. Have you (s.) already been to Tlaxcala? 2. I saw them (there) in Cuernavaca. 3. I haven't looked there yet. 4. I('ve) looked there, but I didn't
see it. 5. What did you (s.) do? – Nothing, I just slept. 6. I just called him.
Here he comes. 7. What did you (pl.) do? – We (just) cut flowers. 8. Peter
is dead. 9. It's only flowers that I've tied. 10. Did you (pl.) enjoy yourselves (6.6.7) in Mexico City? 11. We didn't go there, we (just) stayed here.
12. This woman loved an Otomi.

(d) 1. Ōmpa ōnēzquê in otomî, ōtēchmōtlaquê. 2. Āquin ōtzàtzic?
3. Ōniquimpix in pīpiltin: àmo ōchōcaquê, zan ōcuīcaquê. 4. In oquichtin
ōquitecquê tetl. 5. Ayamo mēhuâ in pīpiltin. 6. Cuix ōanquicacquê in? –
Quēmâ, ōtēchnōtz in Pedro. 7. Ye ōticcuàquê in tlaxcalli, ye ōtiquīquê
in ātl. 8. Mochtin (or mochintin or in mochintin tlācâ) ye ōēhuaquê (or
ye ōyàquê or ye onyàquê) (or even moch tlācatl ye ōēhuac, ye onyâ ...).
Cuauhnāhuac ōtemōquê (or ōtemōc if you said moch tlācatl) 9. Ye
ōmotēcac in Pedro; ninomati, ca ayamo cochi. 10. Zan quēzquintin
tlācâ ōtlàcuilòquê (or quēzqui tlàcatl ōtlàcuilô). 11. Ca ōhuītza in Pedro,
ōtitlàtòquê, Mēxìco onyâ. 12. Ca ōhuāllâ in Pedro, ayamo ēhua. 13. Ca
nicān in ōtitlācatquê, in ōtihuēyiyaquê.

Lesson Nine

(a) 1. xicāna, xicānacān; ticānaz, ancānazquê; ticānaya, ancānayâ 2. xiccaqui, xiccaquicān; ticcaquiz, anquicaquizquê; ticcaquiya, anquicaquiyâ
3. xicchīhua, xicchīhuacān; ticchīhuaz, anquichīhuazquê; ticchīhuaya,
anquichīhuayâ 4. xiccoco, xiccocōcān; ticcocōz, anquicocōzquê; tic-
cocoāya, anquicocoāyâ 5. xiccui, xiccuīcān; ticcuīz, anquicuīzquê;
ticcuīya, anquicuīyâ 6. xicuīca, xicuīcacān; ticuīcaz, ancuīcazquê;
ticuīcaya, ancuīcayâ 7. xìcihui, xìcihuicān; tìcihuiz, amìcihuizquê;
tìcihuiya, amìcihuiyâ 8. xiquilpi, xiquilpīcān; tiquilpīz, anquilpīzquê;
tiquilpiāya, anquilpiāyâ 9. xiquìcuilo, xiquìcuilōcān; tiquìcuiloz,
anquìcuilōzquê; tiquìcuiloāya, anquìcuiloāyâ 10. xicpiya, xicpiyacān;
ticpiyaz, anquipiyazquê; ticpiyaya, anquipiyayâ 11. xitemo, xitemōcān;
titemōz, antemōzquê; titemōya, antemōyâ 12. xictēmo, xictēmōcān,

tictēmōz, anquitēmōzquê; tictēmoāya, anquitēmoāyâ 13. xictlāti, xictlātīcān: tictlātīz, anquitlātīzquê; tictlātiāya, anquitlātiāyâ 14. xitzàtzi, xitzàtzicān; titzàtziz, antzàtzizquê; titzàtziya, antzàtziyâ 15. xiczōma, xiczōmācān; ticzōmāz, anquizōmāzquê; ticzōmāya, anquizōmāyâ

(b) 1. Chichié! 2. Chichimèé! 3. Cihuàé! 4. Oquichtlé! 5. Pīpiltiné! 6. Tōchtlé! 7. Teōtlé! 8. Otomitlé!

(c) 1. Tomorrow we'll go to Xochimilco. There we'll eat tortillas and (we'll) drink pulque. 2. Peter won't count the beans, he'll throw them. 3. There are tomatoes here, do you (s.) want to (will you) buy one? 4. Where will you reach (arrive at) tomorrow? Just Tlaxcala? 5. I'm leaving this meat today. I'll only eat it tomorrow. 6. These children will grow more (become bigger). 7. Don't (s.) bother the children. They'll cry. 8. Don't (s.) go, (just) sit down. We'll talk. 9. Buy (pl.) those prickly pears. They're good. 10. Peter was sick yesterday. As for me, I went and saw him. 11. What were you (s.) doing? – I was just bathing (washing myself). 12. Children, don't throw stones at the pigs. 13. There's meat, beans, tortillas (and) tomatoes here. Let's eat. 14. Look at (see) (pl.) that man. Isn't that Peter? 15. I didn't know who you (pl.) were.

(d) 1. Pedroé (or Pedró), cuix mōztla Mēxìco tiyāz? – Àmō, ca zan nicān ninocāhuaz, nitlapōhuaz. 2. Ōniccōuh tomātl, nacatl: mōztla ticcuāzquê, in cihuâ quichīhuazquê tlaxcalli. 3. Ca oc cōconê, àmo quīzquê octli. 4. Cuix titlàcuilōz? – Yālhua ye ōnitlàcuilô. 5. Inìquê in pīpiltin àmo cuīcazquê, ca zan chōcazquê. 6. Yālhua nicān àmo nicatca, Mēxìco nitlacōhuaya. 7. Oncān ximocāhua, mācamo xihuāllauh, ca mococoa in Pedro. 8. Mācamo xiccuācān inin nacatl, ca àmo cualli. 9. Mā nicān ninotlāli. – Mā zan ximotlāli. 10. Xictlātīcan in, ca ye huītz in Pedro, ca mozōmāz. 11. Inin pilli quimmōtlaya in chichimê. – Ca àmo cualli on. 12. Xitemōcān, mācamo xonhuiyān, tamēchpalēhuīzquê. 13. Tlā xictēmo in Pedro. – Quēmâ, ōmpa ninotlalōz, yālhua ōmpa catca. 14. Aoc nimitznōtzaz, mā ximiqui in cānin tiyāz. 15. Mācamo ximozōma, àmo nicmatiya in tlein ticchīhuaya.

Lesson Ten

(a) 1. īcōhuāuh 2. īcōhuāhuān 3. īpitzōuh 4. īpitzōhuān 5. ītōch 6. ītōchhuān 7. ītīciuh 8. ītīcihuān 9. īcuauh 10. īmeuh 11. īteuh 12. ītlaōl

(b) 1. My rabbits eat a lot. 2. Aren't you (s.) going to eat your beans? 3. Do you (s.) already know our town? 4. You (s.) have many flowers, have you already counted them all? 5. We've eaten your (s.) wife's good tortillas. 6. Here come the lords of Tlaxcala. 7. Your (s.) song is beautiful. 8. He doesn't know his path. 9. The women of Mexico City have beautiful skirts. 10. Don't (s.) take this mat, it belongs to me (it's mine). 11. This corn is all mine, it isn't Peter's.

(c) 1. In Pedro ca mochtin ōmicquê in ītotōlhuān. 2. In Xōchimīlco tīcitl īpil ca cualli in īīx. 3. Cuix ticmati in Tlaxcallān òtli? 4. Quitēmoa in cihuātl in īichhui. 5. Cuix ye moch ōanquicuàquê in amonac? 6. Quēmâ, zan ōticcāuhquê in tomiuh. 7. In nocihuāuh īcōzqui ca nèhuātl ōniccōuh. 8. Ca zan quēzqui in nomeuh. 9. Mōztla nicānaz in notequiuh. 10. Ca tamopilhuān, mācamo xitēchcāhuacān. 11. Tēteòé (or Tēteô'), mā xic-caquicān in tocuīc. 12. Cuix amèhuāntin amopitzōhuān? – Àmō, ca totīciuh īpil īpitzōhuān. 13. Tlein in mocōn īpatiuh?

Lesson Eleven

(a) 1. This path is rocky. 2. We don't have any beans, we don't have any corn. 3. There's a dog here. Who's its (dog) owner? 4. That woman isn't married/has no husband. 5. These children no longer have a father. 6. The birds have talons (claws) (or birds have talons if the sense is a general description). 7. May all our enemies die! 8. We're not yet fathers. 9. We have two hands (and) ten fingers. 10. We're only humans. Our body (bodies) will die, disappear. 11. What you're (s.) doing is merely childishness. 12. May your (s.) heart not cry. Be happy, laugh! 13. Don't (s.) seek fame, just seek goodness (or perhaps just seek this: goodness). 14. Yes, I hear you (s.). Don't I have ears? 15. Wealth is now coming to an end. 16. I won't drink the pig's blood.

(b) 1. Āquin quìtōz in teōyōtl? 2. Notēucyoé, ca nicmati in mocuallo. 3. Āxcān àmo ōniccōuh michin: àmo ōhuāllâ in michhuâ. 4. Ca tlācahuâ in tēuctli. 5. Ca àmo tlanèquê in tōtoltin. 6. Tīxê, tinacacê tiyez. 7. Ca àmo māyèquê in pitzōmê. 8. Tinacayòquê, tomiyòquê, tezzòquê. 9. Àmo ticchīhuazquê yāōyōtl. 10. Àmo miquiz, àmo polihuiz in mēxìcayōtl. 11. Ca cualli in tàyōtl, in nānyōtl. 12. Nēchcocoa in nonacayo. 13. Ca āyô inin tomātl. 14. Ca tēnyòquê inìquê on tētēuctin. 15. Ca tlācayô inin āltepētl. 16. Inin tōtōtl ca cualli in īquetzallo. 17. In tēuctli ca cualli in īquetzal. 18. Cuix tipilhuâ? – Quēmâ, ca ōmentin in nopilhuān.

Lesson Twelve

(a) 1. Has this mat already (become) dirty? – Not yet, it's still clean. 2. This child is already very strong. 3. Those men are very fat. 4. Is the path still narrow? – Not any more, it's already gotten broad. 5. Yesterday I saw two black people. 6. Now you (pl.) are no longer children. You have become strong and big and are men. 7. This is (just) a lousy tortilla. I won't eat it. 8. This rotten dog is no good. 9. I won't be able to transport this stone. 10. They are very numerous ("many"). I won't be able to count them all. 11. Look (s.) at the height (see 12.8) of that man. 12. Peter used to be very fat, now he is very thin. 13. No one will be able to speak of God's purity. 14. What you (s.) say is very true.

(b) 1. Ca huel pitzāhuac inin òtli: inìquê on tlācâ quipatlāhuazquê. 2. Ca huel catzāhuaquê inìquê on pitzōmê: ca ōquicatzāuhquê in calli. 3. In nocihuāuh moch ōquichipāuh in petlatl. 4. Ca tèhuāntin ōtiquintomāuhquê in pitzōmê. – Quēmâ, niquitta, ca cencâ tomāhuaquê. 5. Oc totōnqui in meuh, xiccua. – Àmo, ye cecēc. 6. Ca iztāquê inìquê in tōtōchtotōntin. 7. In nochichiuh àmo oquichtli, ca cihuātl. 8. Zan ancatzāhuacāpopōl. 9. Nicān xiccāhua inin quetzalzolli. 10. Ōquicōuh in Pedro cencâ cualli, patiyô cōzcatl. 11. Yālhua ōhuitzâ in mēxìcatzitzintin. 12. Ca cencâ cualtzitzintin inìquê on otomî pīpiltotōntin. 13. Āquin huel quichīhuaz in? – Ca yèhuātl in Pedro, ca cencâ chicāhuac. 14. Āquin yāz in ōmpa Xōchimīlco? – In nèhuātl huel niyāz. 15. Huel ninococoa: àmo huel ninēhua. 16. In tīcitl quimonitta in cocoxcātzitzintin. 17. Ca ōnēchcocô inin tlaxcalli ītotōnca.

Lesson Thirteen

(a) 1. altepēc 2. taltepēc 3. cōzcac 4. mocōzcac 5. cuahuic 6. iztac 7. nòtic (*from* ìtitl) 8. nīxco 9. nacazco 10. omic 11. nomic 12. oztōc 13. ītēnco 14. moyacac

(b) 1. The bird is flying toward the sky. 2. I despise that wretch(ed person). 3. There are many birds on my house. 4. The coyotes went to hide in the cave. 5. The enemy are running toward Tlaxcala. 6. Do you (pl.) speak Nahuatl (in the manner of Mexica)? 7. Don't (s.) go there. It will rain on you. 8. Where is Peter's home? – It's here. 9. Will I sleep at your (s., hon.) home? 10. In war, only the commoners would die. 11. My house is near the reeds. 12. The eagle is resting on the prickly pear plant.

(c) 1. Petlapan, icpalpan nicâ. 2. Nocaxic câ nacatl. 3. In piltōntli ōcān cē chapōlin īmāc. 4. Cuix àtle cualli ō mopan mochīuh? 5. Āxcān tēcpantzinco câ in Pedro. 6. Tlapechco nicalaquiz. 7. Ca īpan inon xihuitl in ōmic īcihuāuh Pedro. 8. In īmpan totàtzitzinhuān cualli catca in āltepētl: āxcān topan huel ōcatzāhuac. 9. Ca cualcān in mochān (see 5.5.3). 10. Cān īnchān inìquê on tlācâ? – Àmo nicān chānèquê (*or* àmo nicān īnchān). 11. Cuix īmpan tinemiz in tētēuctin? 12. Tlein īpan tinēchitta? 13. In īchān Pedro nemî chicuēyin tlācâ. 14. Ātitlan câ in tāltepēuh. – In tèhuāntin ca tepētitlan tochān (*or* tichānèquê).

Lesson Fourteen

(a) 1. I have a foot ache and also a really bad tooth ache (my foot is ailing me, and so is my tooth very much). 2. He's not very tall, but he also isn't short. 3. It's the same place where I met them. 4. He's at Xochimilco or at Mexico City. 5. I'm reciting poetry (raising up flower and song). 6. Have you (s.) too already eaten? 7. Who's that? – I don't know. Maybe a Mexica or a Spaniard. 8. Look at ("see") (s.) that person. He's the same person who was eating here yesterday. 9. It's been fifteen years since you became alive, were born. 10. So you've arrived, dear Peter! And what do you want? 11. When did you arrive? – This morning. 12. I never go and see Peter. Instead, it's him that comes to see me. 13. It's already night, go (pl.) to bed. – Not yet, it's still evening, the sun hasn't gone down yet. 14. After he/she died, we cried a lot. 15. You (s.) will soon see Mary's new blouse. 16. He got drunk on pulque. 17. I shaved (myself) with a razor (obsidian). 18. You're (pl.) as dirty as pigs. 19. Don't (s.) speak to me as if I were a dog.

(b) 1. Ōquināmic in tōchtli, in mazātl iòhui. 2. Àmo nicmati tlein on: àzo tōchtli, ànozo chichi. 3. Cuix ōmpa oc catê cihuâ nozo pīpiltin? 4. Huīptla niyāz in Xōchimīlco, nō niyāz in Tlaxcallān. 5. Cuauhnāhuac niyauh. – Ca zan ye nō ōmpa in nèhuātl niyauh. 6. Ōniccocô in Pedro. – Auh tlein ōquìtô? 7. Tletica micquê in mochintin. 8. In ìcuāc nitlāhuāna, nipāqui. 9. Quēmman toconittaz in Pedro? – Āxcān teōtlac. 10. Īc tiyāz Cuauhnāhuac? – Ca huīptla. 11. Quēnin ōticchīuh on? 12. Mācamo xihuāllauh yohualnepantlâ: yohuac ca nicochi. 13. In ōnicpōuh inin āmoxtli, ca miyac tlamantli nicmatiz. 14. In ōtzàtzic, (niman) ōniquīz. 15. Àmo ōnēchpalēhuî, nō nèhuātl àmo nicpalēhuīz. 16. In īquin ōninocatzāuh, zan ninopāca. 17. Cuix oc huèca in Mēxìco? 18. Tlīltica ōniquìcuilô. 19. Zoquitl ic ōninocatzāuh. 20. Iuhquin timexìcatl titlàtoa. 21. Iuhquin nimācēhualli, iuhquin tinotēucyo tinēchnōtza.

Lesson Fifteen

(a) 1. *I remember that person's name.* Molnāmiqui inon tlācatl ītōcā. 2. *I don't know what his name is.* Àmo momati tlein ītōcā. 3. *Peter is angry.* Cualānīhua. 4. *After they ate, they got up and left.* In ōtlācuālōc, niman ēōhuac, onhuīlōhuac. 5. *The commoners enter the palace.* Tēcpan calacōhua. 6. *We will take the Otomi captive in war.* Yāōpan ānalōzquê (*or* ānōzquê) in otomî. 7. *The women sit down on mats.* Petlapan netlālīlo. 8. *They all disappeared.* Polīōhuac. 9. *I won't be able to count the stones.*

Àmo huel mopōhuaz in tetl. 10. *I won't be able to count the people.*
Àmo huel pōhualōzquê in tlācâ. 11. *Yesterday I saw you (pl.).* Yālhua
ōamittalōquê (*or* ōamittōquê). 12. *The children are very happy.* Cencâ
pācōhua. 13. *They returned to Mexico.* Mēxìco ōnecuepalōc. 14. *We look
toward the sky.* Ilhuicacopa tlachiyalo. *He brought me by boat.* Ācaltica
ōnihuīcōc.

(b) 1. This person won't be able to be surpassed (it won't be possible for this
person to be surpassed) in strength. 2. What is going on ("being done")
here? – Writing, reading. 3. There was no receiving (of people). No one
came. 4. The food wasn't good. People got sick from it. 5. It's (been) two
years now that there have been no births in the city. There is only dying,
and people going to Mexico City. 6. It's night, nothing can be (is) seen,
nor can anything be done. Tomorrow it will become light. 7. On holidays
the beautiful capes are worn. 8. It's not known whether he's dead or not
(note the use of **in àzo … ànozo àmo** to indicate an indirect question of
the form 'whether or not'). 9. Nothing was taken, nor was anyone harmed.
10. Tomorrow there will be a meeting at Xochimilco.

(c) 1. Cuix ye ōmīc in octli? 2. Ca ayaīc motta in. 3. Ōmpa tiyānquizco
tlacōhualo, tlanamaco. 4. Oztōc ōhuīlōhuac, ōnetlātīlōc. 5. Mocaqui in
Malintzin īcuīc. – Àmo, ca àmo yèhuātl caco in Malintzin. 6. Mōztla
monamacaz xōchitl in tiyānquizco. 7. Àmo huel tipalēhuīlōz. 8. Ōmpa
àmo tlàtōlo mexìcacopa/mācēhualcopa. 9. Inìquê on pīpiltotōntin
àmo cualtin catcâ: ic ōnezōmālōc. 10. Cuix nicān ōhuālhuīlōhuac?
11. Mōztla cuīcōz, huetzcōz, tlacuālōz, tlaīhuaz. 12. Quēmâ. Mocuāz mōlli,
mocuāz tamalli, mīz octli. 13. Tlàpalōlo in tēuctli in ìcuāc nicān quīza.
14. Nicān īpan āltepētl ōmicōhuac. 15. Nicān àmo timacho. 16. Motlazòtla
in xōchitl.

Review

(a) 1. reed(s) 2. city 3. paper 4. water 5. property 6. house 7. mouth 8. home
9. chili 10. woman 11. star 12. snake 13. wood(s) 14. good 15. eagle
16. bean(s) 17. foot 18. day 19. salt 20. stomach, belly 21. eye(s), face
22. commoner, subject 23. hand 24. maguey 25. metate, grinding stone
26. moon, month 27. fish 28. field 29. ear 30. mother 31. nopal, prickly
pear plant 32. prickly pear 33. pulque 34. man, male 35. path, road 36. mat
37. child, nobleman 38. feather 39. father 40. god 41. mountain 42. stone,
rock 43. lip, edge 44. lord 45. market place 46. item, thing 47. (ground)
corn 48. tortilla 49. ruler, king 50. person, human 51. earth, land 52. fire
53. turkey 54. name 55. rabbit 56. sun 57. bird 58. year; plant 59. flower
60. nose, tip 61. heart 62. arrive at, reach 63. enter 64. listen to, hear 65. be
(in a position) 66. leave, abandon (refl.: stop) 67. wait for, watch (**tla**: look)

68. do, make 69. weep, cry 70. sleep 71. harm, injure, make sick 72. eat
73. turn (refl.: come back, return) 74. take 75. sing 76. blow (wind)
77. get up, leave; raise 78. bring, lead 79. come 80. drink 81. see 82. write,
draw, paint 83. say, speak of 84. spread, be spread out 85. know 86. die
87. live 88. want 89. be happy, rejoice 90. guard 91. become lost, disappear
92. count, read 93. rain 94. emerge, pass by 95. cut 96. end 97. love 98. set,
place (refl.: sit) 99. be hot 100. go

(b) 1. rather, quite 2. you (pl.) 3. no one 4. no, not 5. nothing 6. perhaps 7. who?
8. now, today 9. (*particle introducing an assertion*) 10. where? 11. very
12. one 13. (*particle introducing a question*) 14. three 15. very, be able to
16. far off/away 17. big, large 18. with, by, therewith, thereby 19. this, the
20. such, like 21. when? 22. and 23. (*particle introducing a verb in the
optative*) 24. much, many 25. every, all 26. tomorrow 27. four 28. I, me
29. here 30. then 31. also 32. still 33. that 34. there 35. two 36. yes 37. over
there (*more distant than* oncān) 38. at what time? 39. how? 40. how many?
41. just now, soon 42. we, us 43. you (s.) 44. (*particle introducing a suppo-
sition*) 45. what? 46. yesterday 47. already 48. they, them 49. he, him; she,
her; it 50. only, just

(c) 1. cuitlatl, īcuitl 2. ayòtli, īayô 3. chālchihuitl, īchālchiuh 4. tzacualli,
ītzacual 5. totōltetl, ītotōlteuh 6. huèxōlotl, īhuèxōlouh 7. pōchtēcatl,
īpōchtēcauh 8. cuezcomatl, īcuezcon 9. mātlatl, īmātl 10. māxtlatl, īmāxtli

(d) 1. cīcìtin, īcìhuān 2. mōmōyô, īmōyōhuān 3. tōltēcâ, ītōltēcahuān
4. cuānacamê, īcuānacahuān 5. tītlantin, ītītlanhuān 6. cuēcueyâ,
īcueyāhuān 7. māmaltin, īmalhuān 8. nāmictin, īnāmichuān 9. yōlquê,
īyōlcāhuān 10. quimichmê (quīquimichtin *is also attested*), īquimichhuān

(e) 1. Āc amèhuāntin? – (In) tèhuāntin (ca) tamopilhuān. 2. Āc yèhuāntin
on? – Ca tētēuctin. 3. Āc yèhuāntin on? – Ca yèhuāntin in tētēuctin.
4. Tlein tiquitta? – Ca yèhuātl in īcal Pedro. 5. Ca tèhuāntin in ticmatî.
6. In tèhuāntin ca ticmatî 7. Àcān āc ōniquittac. 8. Aīc tle ōniccuīc. 9. Ayāc
notâ, àtle nocal (*or* àmo nitatê, àmo nicalê). 10. In āquin ōquichīuh in (ca)
miquiz.

(f) (i) 1. īpan in īmā 2. ītlan in nocuauh 3. īca in chīmalli 4. īpan in īitzhui
5. ītech in īāmauh

(ii) 1. āmoxpan 2. teticpac 3. tlīltica 4. xiuhtitech 5. nopetlapan

(g) (i) 1. tlatta 2. tlalcāhua 3. tlàtoa 4. tlàcuiloa 5. tlai

(ii) 1. motta 2. molcāhua 3. mìtoa 4. mìcuiloa 5. mi

(iii) 1. amoncochî 2. xocontēmo 3. anconcuepâ 4. xiquimompalēhui
5. nontlapōhua

(iv) 1. xichuāltēmo 2. anhuālmocuepâ 3. quihuālāna 4. xihuāltēpalēhui
5. xihuāllatēmo

(v) 1. nontlacōhua 2. nihuāllacuepa 3. xitēpalēhui 4. xontēpalēhui
5. nihuāllatlātia

(h)

	Preterite	Imper./optative	Future	Imperfect
1.	ōnihuetzcac	mā nihuetzca	nihuetzcaz	nihuetzcaya
2.	ōtitēhuītec	(mā) xitēhuītequi	titēhuītequiz	titēhuītequiya
3.	ōxeliuh	mā xelihui	xelihuiz	xelihuiya
4.	ōticpolòquê	mā ticpolōcān	ticpolōzquê	ticpoloāyâ
5.	ōantezquê	(mā) xitecicān	antecizquê	anteciyâ
6.	ōtlècōquê	mā tlècōcān	tlècōzquê	tlècōyâ
7.	ōticpatlac	(mā) xicpatla	ticpatlaz	ticpatlaya
8.	ōtlaināx	mā tlaināya	tlaināyaz	tlaināyaya
9.	ōtlamâ	mā tlama	tlamāz	tlamāya
10.	ōninìzac	mā ninìza	ninìzaz	ninìzaya
11.	ōammāhuiltìquê	(mā) ximāhuiltlcān	ammāhuiltīzquê	ammāhuiltiāyâ
12.	ōtiquìtzon	(mā) xiquìtzoma	tiquìtzomaz	tiquìtzomaya
13.	ōnicpīc	mā nicpi	nicpīz	nicpīya
14.	ōchamāhuac	mā chamāhua	chamāhuaz	chamāhuaya
15.	ōnicchamāuh	mā nicchamāhua	nicchamāhuaz	nicchamāhuaya

(i) 1. Ancelīlōzquê, antlàpalōlōzquê. 2. Tlaīhuac, mīc in ātl. 3. Àmo ōnilcāhualōc: ca ye ninōtzalo. 4. Huel necocōlo, ca micōhuaz. 5. Palēhuīlōz in nopil. 6. Motēmoāya teōcuitlatl. 7. Mocōuh petlatl, monamacac caxitl. 8. Ōnimōtlaloc, huel ōnicocōlōc. 9. Nicān ōnecāhualōc, àmo ōquixōhuac. 10. Ca timacho, momati in motōcā.

(j) 1. quīz (base 2 of quiza) *he emerged*/qu-ī-z *he will drink it* 2. ō-mic *he died*/ō-m-ī-c (reflexive m-) *it was drunk* 3. ō-man (from mani) *it spread out*/ō-m-ān (reflexive m-, verb āna) *it's been caught* (with a real reflexive sense, māna means *it expands*) 4. m-e-uh (m- 2nd person possessive, -uh poss. suffix) *your beans*/m-ēuh (reflexive m-, verb ēhua) *he raised himself* 5. tec-o (passive of tequi) *he is cut*/tēc-o (passive of tēca) *he is spread out* 6. on-ēhua-c *he left (for over there)*/ō-n-ēhua-c *I've gotten up* 7. t-e-huâ (-huâ possessive suff.) *you've (s.) got beans*/t-ēhua-' *we leave* 8. ō-ni-pāc (from pāqui) *I rejoiced*/ ō-ni-c-pāc (from pāca) *I've washed him* 9. ni-temō-z (from temo) *I'll come down*/ni-c-tēmō-z (from tēmoa) *I'll look for it* 10. ni-cuīca *I sing*/ni-c-huīca *I bring, lead him*

Lesson Sixteen

(a) 1. receivable, to be received 2. visible 3. washable, to be washed 4. countable, readable 5. lovable 6. to be hidden 7. closable, to be closed 8. sticky

(b) 1. tlazalōlōni, ītlazaloāya 2. tlàcuilōlōni, ītlàcuiloāya 3. neximalōni, īneximaya 4. tētlazòtlalōni, ītētlazòtlaya 5. tlachiyalōni, ītlachiyaya 6. chōcōhuani, īchōcaya

(c) 1. Little children cry a lot. 2. If only we hadn't lived in sin! If only we were good and virtuous! 3. If only you (s.) knew what happened! 4. The scribe has broken (*or* lost) his instruments. 5. The snake is invisible. 6. Why are you taking the whip? Are you going to whip me? 7. He's the one who will be our ruler. 8. We've caught our thieves. 9. I go to church on holidays. 10. My clients ("buyers") came back to the market. 11. These flowers are very strong. They can't be picked. 12. Wild beasts scare me a lot.

(d) 1. Mā xiquittani in nocal! 2. Ca huel tēpalēhuî in tlatecōni. 3. Zan titzàtzinipōl. 4. Ca cencâ tlazòtlalōni in Malintzin. 5. Mācamo xiccui in motēhuītequiya. 6. Ōnicān in tlàcuilòcāyōtl. 7. Ca àmo panahuīlōni inon cihuātl īcuallo. 8. Mācaīc ōnichtequini! 9. Àmo ilcāhualōni inin ilhuitl. 10. Ca cencâ huetzcani in Pedro. 11. Tiquintlàpaloâ in totlamatcāhuān. 12. Ca cochî in īntēpixcāhuān in māmaltin. 13. Nicān ticâ! Àmo tochān tihuāllāni.

Lesson Seventeen

(a) 1. tlāhuāncātlàtōlli 2. cihuāpitzōtl 3. ācōhuātl 4. ātēntli 5. cuauhtēntli 6. xōchiyāōyōtl 7. teōpixcācalli 8. yacacuitlatl 9. nòpalxōchitl 10. omicalli 11. tlāltetl

(b) 1. tōchìcihui, tōchìciōhua 2. quicamacāhua yamāncātlàtōlli, mocamacāhua yamāncātlàtōlli 3. mocamapāca, necamapāco 4. chīltequi, chīlteco 5. quimīxcāhua in īpiltotōnhuān, īxcāhualô in īpiltotōnhuān 6. quìtipāca in cōmitl, mìtipāca in cōmitl 7. monacazcocoa, nenacazcocōlo 8. tlacualchīhua, tlacualchīhualo 9. tlemiqui, tlemicōhua 10. chipāhuacānemi, chipāhuacānemōhua

(c) 1. On holidays, mole and tamales are made. 2. You (s.) are very brave ("have a manly heart", 11.9). 3. Don't (s.) eat the fish bones. 4. I've never eaten human flesh. 5. I don't sell paper. 6. Mary has locked herself up in her house. 7. I'm keeping a close eye on the prisoners. 8. I've just washed my hair. 9. Mats aren't made here. 10. These small children were orphaned ("left as orphans"). 11. I'm already white-haired ("white in the hair"). 12. There isn't any salt seller in the market place. 13. Swineherd, where are you driving your pigs?

(d) 1. Ca cōhuātetl. 2. Ca icnōtlacualli. 3. Ca michmōlli. 4. Cuix ticmati in otontlàtōlli? 5. Pitzōcalco niyauh. 6. Tēyāōnōtzalo. 7. Āltepēmīlpan câ in Pedro. 8. Nicuauhxima. 9. Ōnēchīxnōtz. 10. Tinacacāhuaz. 11. Ayamo titēntzonê. 12. Mōztla ticcuāzquê nacatamalli. 13. In nōchtli ca īxōchlcuallo in nòpalli. 14. Ātēnco tihuî.

Lesson Eighteen

(a) 1. ticmaca 2. tiquimmaca 3. tiquimmaca 4. anquimmacâ 5. antēchimmacâ 6. annēchimmacâ 7. nēchimmaca 8. nēchmaca 9. nēchilhuia

10. nilhuīlo 11. amilhuīlô 12. ilhuīlo 13. ilhuīlô 14. pòpolhuīlô 15. motēpòpolhuia (*or* tēpòpolhuīlo) 16. tictēpòpolhuia 17. tinēchpòpolhuia 18. tinēchtlapòpolhuia 19. titēchtlapòpolhuia 20. tiquintlapòpolhuia 21. tiquimpòpolhuia 22. anquimpòpolhuiâ 23. anquimopòpolhuiâ 24. anquimocuitlahuiâ 25. antēchmocuitlahuiâ 26. tinecuitlahuīlô.

(b) 1. These aren't our friends. We won't give them flowers. 2. Stay (s.) here. I'm going to tell you much more. 3. Just tell (s.) me, I'll listen to you. 4. I'm going to the market. Will you (pl.) look after my dogs in the meanwhile (*oc*)? 5. Okay, give (s.) them to us, (and) we'll take good care of them. 6. What happened to you (s.) yesterday? We didn't see you. 7. We've already told you (pl.), we don't want prickly pears. 8. As for Peter, he's has given many jewels (many are the jewels that Peter has given) to that woman. 9. We've presented each other turkeys. 10. You're just stinking lousy thieves. 11. At my place, grinding (of flour) and tortilla making are going on. 12. I've had a bad dream (what I've dreamed is not good).

(c) 1. Ca āmatl in ōnimitzmacac. 2. Ca cualli inin āmoxtli. – Āxcān oc nicpōhua, mōztla namēchmacaz. 3. Ca mococoa in Malintzin. – Ca nicmati, ōnēchilhuìquê in ītàhuān, in nèhuātl ōniquimilhuî in tocnīhuān. 4. In Malintzin quimmocuitlahuia in pīpiltotōntin, àmo quichīhuaz mōlli. 5. Tlê tāyi? – Àmo nicmati, àhuel nitlacua, àzo ninococoa. 6. Mā nicān ximotlālīcān, ca namēchilhuīz in tlein ōnāx yālhua. 7. Ca nèhuātl nicnocuitlahuīz in, in tèhuātl titlachiyaz. 8. Mācamo xiquimmacacān octli in pīpiltotōntin: ca quincocōz. 9. Ca tōtoltin (*or* tōtolmê) in antēchimmacâ, àmo huēhuèxolô. 10. Elimiquî in mīlèquê. 11. Oc ōtitchtec! Àmo titlapòpolhuīlōni. Àmo tipòpolhuīlōz inin tlàtlacōlli. 12. Ayamo moteci in tlaōlli. 13. Ca cencâ tētlapòpolhuiāni in Dios.

Lesson Nineteen

(a) 1. Ōtēchchōctî/Ōtēchchōcaltî/Ōtēchchōquiltî, *he's made us cry* 2. Quincochītīz, *he'll make them sleep* 3. Ōquitzàtzītî, *he's made him shout* 4. Ōnēchchīhualtî calli, *he's made me build houses* 5. Tēchtēmōltia xōchitl, *he's making us look for flowers* 6. Tēchxōchitēmōltia, *he's making us look for flowers* 7. Ōamēchilcāhualtî in ītōcā, *he's made you (pl.) forget his name* 8. Quicualtia nacatl, *he's making him eat meat* 9. Quimītî octli, *he made them drink pulque* 10. Cātlītî, *he made him drink (or drink water)* 11. Mitztlapōhualtia, *he makes you (s.) count* 12. Ōnēchtlāzaltî in tetl, *he's made me throw the stone* 13. Tēchtētlàpalōltiāya, *he would make us greet people* 14. Amēchtēnōtzaltīz, *he'll make you (pl.) call upon people* 15. Tēchneittaltia, *he makes us see each other* 16. Nēchnepācaltia *he makes me wash (myself)* 17. Nēchtolīnia, *he torments me* 18. Amēchtēcac, *he laid you (pl.) down*

(b) 1. Ōtichōctīlōquê. 2. Cochitīlōzquê. 3. Ōtzàtzītīlōc. 4. Ōnichīhualtīlōc calli. 5. Titēmōltīlô xōchitl. 6. Tixōchitēmōltīlô. 7. Ōamilcāhualtīlōquê in ītōcā. 8. Cualtīlo nacatl. 9. Ītīlōquê octli. 10. Ātlītīlōc. 11. Titlapōhualtīlo. 12. Ōnitlāzaltīlōc in tetl. 13. Titētlàpalōltīlōyâ. 14. Antēnōtzaltīlōzquê. 15. Tineittaltīlô. 16. Ninepācaltīlo. 17. Nitolīnīlo. 18. Antēcōquê.

(c) 1. Don't (s.) make the small child cry and shout. 2. Have (s.) him brought out. – He's already come out on his own. 3. Are you (s.) afraid? What's scaring you? Have no fear! 4. I get Mary to make tortillas. 5. The jug broke and I'm the one that broke it. 6. Gold is valuable – the Spaniards value it a great deal. 7. All the flowers are withering, the sun is wilting them. 8. The ice is melting because of the fire. – Yes, fire melts it. 9. My house caught fire. – Who set it on fire? 10. Raise (s.) the stones. – No, I'll just bring them down. 11. Those people really scare me, I won't show myself. 12. There are some flowers drawn on this (piece of) paper. 13. Remind (s.) me who he is. 14. Peter is to enter – (as for) you (s.) make him enter. 15. The thread has broken. 16. He's broken the thread. 17. Was he made to do it?

(d) 1. Ōnicāhualtīlōc in tetl. 2. Ca mitzpàtīz inin ātl. 3. Ca pàtiz inin tlācatl. 4. Oliniya in tlālli. 5. Huel coliniāya in īnacaz. 6. Ōcochītīlōc in cocoxqui. 7. Àmo huel tlàtōltīlōz. 8. Àmo nimitzpiyaltīz in noteōcuitl. 9. Huel ōantēchhuetzquitìquê. 10. Yālhua ōtiquintlāhuāntìquê in amocnīhuān, ōtiquimītìquê octli. 11. Yāōpan mictīlōquê cēmê tētēuctin. 12. Ye ōpoliuh in mēxìcayōtl, ōquipolòquê in caxtiltēcâ. 13. Ye ōpàtic in Pedro: ōquipàtî in tīcitl. 14. Cuix amēchpāctia in pitzōnacatl? Yālhua ōticmictìquê in top-itzōuh. 15. Ōticaquītīlōquê, ōtimachtīlōquê in teōtlàtōlli.

Lesson Twenty

(a) 1. Ōmitzcualanilî in Pedro. *Peter got mad at you (s.).* 2. Nimitzchipāhuilīz in mopetl. *I'll clean your (s.) mat.* 3. Ōniquīxcocolhuî in mopil. *I've injured your (s.) son's eye.* 4. Nimitzilcāhuilia in motōcā. *I forget your (s.) name.* 5. Ōmitznāmiquilî in mocihuāuh. *He's met your (s.) wife.* 6. Ōtimitzpōhuilìquê in motomin. *We've counted your money.* 7. Nimitznepiyalia. *I'm watching out (guarding myself) against you (s.)* 8. Ticmopiyalia. *You're guarding it for yourself (s.).* 9. Ōmitzichtequilìquê. *They've stolen from you (s.).* 10. Mitzpolhuia in mocax. *He loses/breaks your (s.) bowl.* 11. Mitzinyōllālīlia in moconēhuān. *He consoles your (s.) children.* 12. Ōnimitzixtlāhuî in meul. *I've paid you (s.) your beans.*

(b) 1. Call (s.) my children. 2. I didn't eat your (pl.) tortillas (*i.e., it was someone else*). 3. Will you (s.) roll up the thread for me? 4. The doctored cured my wife. 5. You've (pl.) really offended our parents. 6. Yesterday there was singing (15.5) here, (and) there was singing in honor of the lord. 7. There was crying over the revered dead men. 8. The Otomi (pl.) killed my father.

9. The dog is snarling at us. 10. Set (s.) this down for me here. 11. Wear (s.) my cape. 12. Bring (s.) the lord his son. 13. You (s.) didn't work for me, (so) I'm not going to pay you. 14. Don't (s.) show (people) my money.

(c) 1. Xictlālili chīlli in mōlli. 2. Tēchcotōnilīzquê in toyac, in tonacaz *or* Tēchyacacotōnazquê, tēchnacazcotōnazquê. 3. In mocnīhuān ōtiquincuīlî īmāxcā, huel ōtiquintlàtlacolhuî. 4. Tlein ōmitznāmactî in pōchtēcatl? 5. Tleīca ōtinēchtlātīlî in nāmauh? 6. Xinēchzalhui inin āmatl. 7. Huel ōnēchpalēhuīlî in notàtzin. 8. Mā xinēchincelīli in nopilhuān. 9. Inon oquichtli ōmitzelēhuīlî in mocihuāuh. 10. Nimitznequilia in cualli. 11. Ōtitotlāxilìquê in totlàtlacōl. 12. Nitlàcuilhuīlōc. 13. In nototōltin xinēchimpiyaltīli in Pedro. 14. Ca ye ōnamēchixtlāhuî in amotlaōl.

Lesson Twenty-One

(a) 1. Ōquimoquechcotōnilìquê *they cut his throat* 2. Ōquimocotōnilīlìquê in īquech *they cut his throat* 3. Ye ōmomiquilî in notàtzin *my father is dead (has already died)* 4. Tlā xocommocāhuili in *please go leave this* 5. Cuix àmo ticmomachiltia? *don't you (s.) know it?* 6. Mōztla huālmohuīcaz *he'll come tomorrow* 7. Mōztla xihuālmohuīcacān *come (pl.) tomorrow* 8. Tlein ōticmocōhuilî? *what have you (s.) bought?* 9. Ōmpa moyetzticatê *they're over there* 10. Nimitznonōchilīlia in mopiltzin *I'm calling your (s.) child* 11. Nicān ōmotēcatzinòquê *they've lain (laid themselves) down here* 12. Huel motolīnìtzinoa *he is very unfortunate* 13. Ticmītia octli *you (s.) drink pulque* 14. Tiquimmītīlî octli *you (s.) made them drink pulque* 15. Nimitznotēnnāmiquilia *I kiss you (s.)* 16. Quimmoyacāniliāya in mēxìcâ *he led (used to lead) the Mexica* 17. Huel tinēchmoyōllālīlia *you (s.) greatly console me* 18. Mā ximoyōllālìtzino *console yourself*

(b) (Apart from nn. 5 and 14, all the following verbs are in the honorific form.) 1. Drink up (s.) this medicine. 2. Don't (s.) scare the small children. 3. When will you (s.) arrive there? 4. And when will you (s.) return here? 5. I have (disgracefully) lived in sin. 6. Do you (s.) want money? 7. I'll show you (s.) my tom turkeys. 8. Will you (s.) take care of my child? 9. Have you (s.) made them do things? 10. Just give (s.) me your turkeys. 11. Look, here comes the ruler. 12. It's still night, and you're (s.) already making us get up? 13. The noblewoman is looking at herself in the mirror. 14. You (s.) have (disgracefully) sinned greatly, Our Lord will throw (hon.) you into hell.

(c) 1. Ximoxintzino. 2. Mōztla Cuauhnāhuac xommohuīcacān. 3. Ōnēchmotequilīlî xōchitl in Malintzin. 4. Tleīca timozōmàtzinoa? 5. Tleīca tinēchmozōmālīlia? 6. Ca mococòtzinoa in tlàtoāni. 7. Ōquimomalacachilhuî in Malintzin in ichtli. 8. Mācamo xicmolhuīli in Pedro. 9. Cuix ōticmotlalhuīlî in Pedro? 10. Ye ōnimitznotlamaquilî.

11. Ximopanōlt_icān, ximocalaquīcān, ximotlālìtzinōcān. 12. Mecatica xicmolpīli. 13. Nicnochīhualtīlia tlaxcalli in nonāntzin. 14. Ye ōtimopolihuītî. 15. Ōnicmictìpōlô in notàtzin. 16. Tēchān ōnichtecpōlô.

Lesson Twenty-Two

(a)

	(i)	(ii)	(iii)
1.	ōnātlīca	nātlīzquia	mā nātlî
2.	ōtimococòca	timococōzquia	mā timococô
3.	ōnēzca	nēcizquia	mā nēz
4.	ōtìciuhcâ	tìcihuizquiâ	mā tìciuhtin
5.	ōanquinamacacâ	anquinamacazquiâ	mā anquinamacàtin
6.	ōmoxincâ	moximazquiâ	mā moxintin

(b) Note how the present corresponds to the imperfective of the directional of motion away but to the perfective of the directional of motion toward.

	(i)	(ii)
1.	nicochico	nicochitīuh
2.	nitlanamacaquiuh	nitlanamacatīuh
3.	ōtitlacōhuaco	ōtitlacōhuato
4.	mā quinnōtzaquî	mā quinnōtzatî
5.	quiyōllālīcô	quiyōllālītīhuî
6.	titlacuācô	titlacuātīhuî
7.	ōniquimpalēhuīco	ōniquimpalēhuīto

(c) 1. I took the plate and dropped it (left it from the hand). It fell on the ground but failed to break. 2. Don't (s.) drop this, it's valuable. 3. Don't (s.) look! You mustn't see the fearsome (thing). 4. Peter was about to kill his wife, but for my part, I went to save her. 5. Don't (pl.) offend (hon.) your mother. 6. The sun is coming to rise above us. 7. I brought gourds, but they're no longer here. Who came and took them? 8. The homeowner's asleep – Let's go enter his place and steal his turkey. 9. The enemy will come kill us. 10. The house was going to burn, but we threw water on it and so ("with that") the fire went out.

(d) 1. Chālco niyāzquia, yēcê ōninococô. 2. Mā ticalac! Ca mococoa in notàtzin. 3. Mā timomāuhtî, ca nèhuātl. 4. Ōmococòca, auh ōquipàtî in tīcitl. 5. Ōnimitztlàcuilhuìca, auh ōtlatlac in āmatl. 6. Mā nēn àtictlaxtlāhuî in tōltēcatl. 7. Molcāhuatīuh in mexìcatlàtōlli. 8. Àmō, zan molcāhuazquia, yēcê aocmo molcāhuaz. 9. Tlein (ō)titēchilhuīco? 10. Ōtēchmāquīxtīco (*or better in the hon.:* ōtēchmomāquīxtīlīco) in Totēucyo. 11. Mā xinēchpalēhuīqui! Nicchīhuazquia tlaxcalli, auh ōcēuh in tletl. 12. Ōniccōuhca nacatl, zan yèhuātl ōnēchcuālî in nochichiuh. 13. Huel ìcihuiya, auh zan huetzizquia.

Lesson Twenty-Three

(a) 1. Old age is very difficult. 2. The servant is making tortillas on the metate. 3. Go clean (s.; directional of motion away) your ears, you're dirty eared. 4. That great warrior went and died in war. 5. I was eaten by fleas in bed. 6. You're (s.) greedy as (as if you were) a dog. 7. What are you (pl.) bringing? 8. Please remain standing, lords. 9. For my part, I certainly would have remained lying, but I was called and got up from bed. 10. You're just a dwarf, you can't wear that big cape.

(b) 1. Nilamatcāhué, tlein ticchīhua? 2. Ca tīxcuitla. 3. Quintlazòtlâ in tēlpōpōchtin in ichpōpōchtin. 4. Ca huel ohuî in tēiccāuhyōtl. 5. Mā ìcacān in mācēhualtin. 6. Ca cuāayò(tic). 7. Ca huēyi in māzātl īcuācuauhyo (inalienable possession, see 11.2). 8. Iuhqui amalomê ampapaltin. 9. Yohuac nicochini, nononi. 10. Ca yèhuāntin (see 4.2) in caxtiltēcâ in ōquinhuālitquiquê in cahuayomê (or cahuayòtin) īhuān in cuācuahuèquê. 11. Ōtiquimihuàquê in tochpōchhuān.

Lesson Twenty-Four

(a) 1. I'll return with you (s.). 2. I'm going to the field of flowers. 3. Do coyotes in live in areas with mountains and caves? 4. Why didn't you (s.) come? – (Just) because I didn't want to. 5. Don't (s.) go to the forest, just stay with the others. 6. Are there clearings (spaces between the trees) in the forest? – Yes, let's go to the middle of the woods. 7. We have separate bedrooms. 8. I met him at the entrance. 9. I bought this at the stationary store (paper seller's). 10. The sun is not yet visible, it's still raining. 11. It wasn't by himself that he died. He was killed. 12. Excuse me. – Go (s.) ahead (pass). 13. Go (s.) away! 14. Here's what happened to me. 15. All sorts of flowers bloom ("are made") over there.

(b) 1. Mā amopaltzinco xinēchmopalēhuīlīcān (hon. of xinēchpalēhuīcān). 2. Tle īpampa (or tleīca) tichōca? – Īpampa in ōmomiquilî in notàtzin. 3. Ca īnnāhuac ōninenca in otomî. 4. Tlapan (or tlacpac) ōnitlatemô, nō tlatzintlan ōnitlatemô, ca àtle ōnicnēxtî. 5. Mocuitlapan (or motepotzco) xitlachiya. 6. Cecni calco ōcalac in chichi. 7. Ātl ìtic câ tetl. 8. Ōniyâ Mēxìco in īnhuān cihuâ. 9. Cuix ātlâ nemî in māmazâ? – Àmo, ca zan cuauhtlâ. 10. Mīxco câ in yāōyōtl. 11. Àmo quixōhuayān in ōquīz. 12. Àmo tèhuātl motlàtoāyān. 13. Tōnatiuh īcalaquiyān nemi. 14. Tōnatiuh īquīzayāmpa (for -pa see 5.8 sec.2) huî. 15. Inìquê on tlācâ ca àmo tohuānyōlquê. 16. Necoc tinacacèquê. 17. Iz câ etl, xitlacua.

Lesson Twenty-Five

(a) 1. ōmpōhualli ommàctlāctli 2. ēpōhualli oncaxtolli 3. chicuacempōhualli ommācuīlli 4. centzontli īpan mācuīlpōhualli 5. ōntzontli īpan màctlācpōhualli 6. mācuīltzontli 7. màtlāctli omōntzontli īpan màctlācpōhualli 8. cēxiquipilli īpan mācuīltzontli 9. centzontli īpan caxtōlli oncempōhualli īpan caxtōlli oncē 10. ētzontli īpan caxtōlpōhualli īpan caxtōlli onnāhui

(b) 1. 28,000 2. 1,952 3. 215 4. 385 5. 2,268

(c) 1. I've brought you some prickly pears. 2. You (pl.) are to tell the priest all your sins. 3. Peter has four children, and I've also got the same number. 4. Don't (s.) bother the other little children. 5. The maguey here is huge. At my place there's another kind, but it's very small. 6. The language at Xochimilco and the language at Cuernavaca are both Nahuatl (Mexica). The language of the Otomi is different. 7. I didn't do it willingly, I was made to do it. 8. The water came out in all three places. 9. I won't pay you (with) ten reals, just five. 10. I'll go to the woods alone. 11. It's only the second time that I've drunk pulque.

(d) 1. Ōnimitztequilî xōchitl, cequi chichīltic, cequi iztāc. 2. Zan quēxquich in notlāl, zan quēzquintin in nopitzōhuān. 3. Ōmictīlōquê in īzquintin māmaltin. 4. In occequintin mīlèquê tlacuātīhuî: zan īcēl mīlpan mocāhua in Pedro. 5. Tepēpan (or tepēticpac) câ ixachi cuahuitl. 6. Ca nēchpāctia inin ōme (or ōntetl) cōzcatl, in īōmextin niccōhuaz. 7. Ye centzompa ōnimitzilhuî. 8. Mēxìco câ in Pedro, auh īquichca ōnēchtlàcuilhuî. 9. Ōpoliuh in īxquich nāxcā. 10. Cuix ic ceppa tihuītz nicān īpan tāltepēuh?

Lesson Twenty-Six

(a) 1. We commoners are very unfortunate. 2. It's not just the good and the just that God loves. 3. What's the corn like at your (s.) place? 4. I've never gone to Mexico. (What about you), have you (s.) ever been there? 5. Some (of us) men were killed in the war. 6. We mortals are sinners. 7. All the commoners are poor like me. 8. Moctezuma is a king just like the king of Spain. 9. He and his spouse love each other a lot. 10. All the children used to sing together. 11. We helped each other. 12. I didn't take any money, just some prickly pear (and nothing else).

(b) 1. Ca namēchtlazòtla in annotēāchcāhuān in annotēiccāhuān or Ca nim-itztlazòtla in tinotēāchcāuh in tinotēiccāuh. 2. In timēxìcâ in totomî ca nicān tichānèquê, in ancaxtiltēcâ àmo titèhuān. 3. Xinēchpòpolhui in àmo cualli ōnicchīuh. 4. Ōtoncholòquê ōmentin nomalpòhuān. 5. In cax-tiltēcâ cuix àmo totlācapòhuān, tonacayòcāpòhuān, totlàtlacòcāpòhuān? 6. Cuix ye acâ tiquittac? – Àmo, ayamo āc niquittac. 7. Cuix oc itlâ tic-nequi? – Ca aoc, mā zan acâ xicmaca in. 8. Ancātlìquê (or Cān ancatê)? Mā ximotēittitīcān. 9. Ca zan niyô nicmati in Caxtillān tlàtōlli in nicān īpan tāltepēuh. 10. Ōmonepanmictìquê in ōmentin yāô. 11. Quēnamî in huēxōlotl īnacayo? – Ca cencâ cualli. 12. Cuix icâ acâ huel ōquichīuh in? – In nèhuātl ca ōnicchīuh, yēcê zan quēmmanyān.

Lesson Twenty-Seven

(a) 1. Stay (pl.) here and rest some more. 2. The flowers are rotten. 3. The house is closed. 4. The paper is stuck on the tree. 5. He sold all his property right and left. 6. In the market place, he looked at the mats here and there. 7. Why do you (s.) run all the time? 8. Take (s.) this jar quick! 9. I left after greeting my friend. 10. They shouted in fear. 11. He fell drunk on his bed.

(b) 1. Nōhuiyān motlachiyaltìticâ in Dios. 2. Tlāhuāntoc in Pedro. 3. In tlacōuhquê ōquitztimancâ in pōchtēcatl. 4. Xictzacticāhua in puerta. 5. Ōnictectiyâ xōchitl or ōnixōchitectiyâ. 6. Yālhua ōnitlaxacalchīuhtinenca. 7. Ximotlātìtihuetzi! 8. Ōnicnāmictiquīz. 9. Nochān ticochtàcizquê. 10. Cōzquètinemi inon cihuātl. 11. Momāuhcātlàloâ. 12. Huāccāpolihui in īxquich xōchitl.

Lesson Twenty-Eight

(a) 1. Mexico City and Xochimilco aren't far apart. 2. They (each) enter all over the place. 3. You really scared me (on various occasions). 4. He doesn't want to be seen, he just keeps on hiding everywhere. 5. I get drunk on every holiday. 6. The warriors (each) bring their shields. 7. I'm looking for Peter all over. 8. All the houses are collapsing. 9. I took their tortillas (from each one). 10. He comes back every year. 11. I thought the door was shut. 12. I don't consider you (s.) an enemy. 13. He was lying in bed but he was just pretending to be sick. 14. I want my enemy to die. 15. What do you (s.) want to do? Do you want to drink pulque?

(b) 1. Mā ximochìchīhuacān tiyàcāhuāné! 2. Ōnictètec xōchitl. 3. Ōtēàānōc. 4. Nēnetech tinemî (or nēnetech tochān). 5. Còcochtoc. 6. Cequi huèhuetzca, cequi chòchōca. 7. Nōhuiyān huèhuetzi in tetl. 8. Mòolpiâ. 9. Xicpozōnalti inin ātl. 10. Ōquitlàtòcāmatquê. 11. Ōquintēmictīllan in māmaltin. 12. Àmo tlanānquilīznequi. 13. Cuix huāllāznequi in Pedro? 14. Motlazòtlallani. 15. Mocāhualtoca. 16. Mochōcacānènequi.

Lesson Twenty-Nine

(a) 1. Consider (s.) the Spaniards your friends. 2. Let's unite. 3. He decorates his cape with flowers and feathers. 4. I got mud on myself on the road. 5. Mary's skirt really suits her. 6. My bed is really full of fleas. 7. What's this place called? – We call it Chapultepec. 8. By the grace of God we have been given a king. 9. What happened to me yesterday was really painful (the preterite agent nouns (16.2) tēcocô and tētolīnî often appear together with the sense 'painful'). 10. I've touched the fire and burned myself on the finger.

(b) 1. Ōtotlahueliltic in titlàtlacoānimê! 2. Michyōhua inin ātl. 3. Quiteōcuitlahuia in tōltēcatl in cōzcatl. 4. Quitehuia in tepoztli. 5. Mā ōnolhuiltini, ōnomàcēhualtini in ītētlazòtlaliztzin in Dios! 6. Nōhuiyān tlaceliya, xōchiyōhua in tlālli. 7. Nicān īpan āltepētl nitēmachtìcāti. 8. Ōpiltilīlōc. 9. Titlacxihuiâ. 10. Nimitznotàtia, nimitznonāntia.

Lesson Thirty

(a) 1. Your (pl.) haste scares me. 2. Are these tortillas purchased at the market? 3. These people are Otomi (who are) received at our place. 4. He's a fine person, he likes caring for people. 5. Gold is the Spaniards' desire. 6. The thrown wood fell to the ground. 7. I've stolen nothing; I'm very unfortunate to be imprisoned (my imprisonment makes me very unfortunate). 8. He gives himself over to perverse pleasures. 9. There are many orders that the doctor leaves. 10. God will bestow his gifts on you (s.). 11. Out of (my) love for you (s.) (i.e., what I feel for you), I'll do it. 12. I've thrown (away) the broken thread. 13. Place the flour on the comal.

(b) 1. Cempōhualcān onnāuhcān tlaxelōlli (or xeliuhticâ) in ilhuitl. 2. Àmo cualli in tlāhuānaliztli. 3. Ca mitzpolōz in monetlazòtlaliz, in monepōhualiz. 4. Huēyi in ītlamatiliz. 5. Zan nochān tlachīhualli (or tlachīuhtli) nēchpāctia in mōlli. 6. Nocalīxco câ miyac tlazacalli tetl. 7. Niquìtlani in īpiyalōca. 8. Ōquichōctî in àtle īpan īmachōca. 9. Xiquilnāmiqui in Totēucyo īhuītecōca. 10. Tītlachīhualhuān in Dios. 11. Tinotlatlazòtlal. 12. Zan āchipactli niquīz. 13. Teōtihuacān câ ōme huēyi tzacualli: in ītzacual tōnatiuh īhuān in ītzacual mētztli.

Lesson Thirty-One

(a) 1. Don't you (s.) know that it's been a long time now since I've seen you? 2. I felt I wasn't late. 3. I wish I'd never told him this. 4. I've forgotten once again to buy salt. 5. I confess that I've stolen twice. 6. I don't know whether he'll come or not. 7. It isn't known how many children he has. 8. They know how to speak Nahuatl well. 9. The Spaniards asked that we work for them. 10. It is certainly worth saying and mentioning how brave you (s.) are. 11. Order (s.) them to enter.

(b) 1. Àmo monequi timozōmāz, ye ōnimitzilhuî in ca mōztla nicchīhuaz. 2. Ōnēz in ic titiyàcāuh. 3. Ōnēchtlatemōlìquê, auh in nèhuātl ōniquinnānquilî in ca àmo nicmati. 4. Xinēchilhuīcān in àzo antlacuāznequî. 5. Ōquìtô in àmo quimati in àzo nelli ōmic in Pedro. 6. Nicnocuītia in ca miyacpa ōnitlāhuān. 7. Nicmati in ca tèhuātl ōticcuīlî in huēhuê in ītomin. 8. Àmo momati in àzo ōmic ànozo àmo. 9. Cualli in ic ticmati tāmoxpōhuaz. 10. Iuh ninomati, āxcān teōtlac ca àmo huel tàcizquê in ōmpa Mēxìco.

Lesson Thirty-Two

(a) 1. Take for me that piece of paper that's below and not the one that's above. 2. Quetzalcohuatl, whose second name is Ehecatl, looked there. 3. The Spanish rabbit and the local aren't the same (are two different varieties). 4. Bring me a thin stick. 5. Love (s.) God, who is the one who created you and because of whom you live. 6. Who is that man whose hair has grown so long? 7. That's the mountain behind which my friend's house is located. 8. Figs are eaten cold (it's cold that ...). 9. You've (s.) made the mole really spicy! 10. We're going to Mexico City to shop. 11. Have you (pl.) eaten enough (are you full from eating)? 12. The fire has stopped burning. Let's stop chatting and go to sleep.

(b) 1. Ca anhuēyitētēuctin. 2. Ca zan tēpòpolhuīlōni tlàtlacōlli ōnicchīuh. 3. Xiquitta in cihuātl in cualli in īcuē. 4. Niquitta in calli in ōmpa ōnitlācat. 5. Tictequizquê in cuahuitl in īicpac câ cē cuāuhtli. 6. Xinēchmaca in itztli in ic ōtimoxin. 7. In tlācatl in ōquichīuh in ca nocnīuh ōmochīuh. 8. Mā titōchtli, mā timazātl timocuep. 9. Tlàtoāni ōtlālīlōc. 10. Xiccāhua in piltōntli chōca, quin cochiz. 11. Ayamo nipēhua nitlaōya. 12. Ōnìciuh in nicquēmi notilmâ.

Lesson Thirty-Three

(a) 1. They rebuked you (s.), but you haven't changed your way of life because of this. 2. You (s.) are richer and wealthier than I am. 3. Gold is more valuable than iron. 4. Our city is as big as yours (pl.). 5. Snow is whitest. Nothing is as white (whiter). 6. The reason why I've come to your (pl.) town is to speak of divine matters. 7. No one should cry for him, he was really wicked. 8. I won't buy it because in order to buy it I need to have money. 9. Hide (s.) this so my father won't see it. 10. The houses (28.4) collapsed because of an earth quake (as there was an earth shaking).

(b) 1. Ca àmo ōnicchīuh, īpampa ca àmo ōtinēchnāhuatî. 2. In mopilhuān ca īzquintin in Pedro īpilhuān. 3. Inin piltōntli quimpanahuia in occequintin inic tlamatini (*or* in ītech tlamatiliztli). 4. Inin ichpōchtli tlacempanahuia inic cualtzintli in īpan tāltepēuh. 5. Chòchōcatinemî inic motolīniâ. 6. Yèīca ticnequi niyāz nitiyānquizōz (*or* nitiyānquizōtīuh), mā xinēchmaca tomin. 7. Xicmōtla in chichi, inic canàpa ēhuaz. 8. Iz catqui in monequi ticchīhuaz inic titlazòtlalōz. 9. Oc achi tepitōn in nocal, in àmo yê amocal. 10. Inic cocōc in tlacualli, àmo huel ōniccuâ.

Lesson Thirty-Four

(a) 1. If I hadn't been there, if I hadn't helped you (s.), wouldn't you have been killed? 2. If you (s.) haven't answered them correctly, they'll rebuke you (s.). 3. I won't leave you (s.) (alone) unless you give me this first. 4. Even though this is good, I won't buy it. 5. The war didn't end, didn't settle down right away. 6. For two years now I haven't gone anywhere. 7. They'd already eaten everything when I arrived. 8. Although you're (s.) wise, I'm wiser. 9. A turkey is (the same as) a tom turkey (*lit.*, the tom turkey, with the generalizing use of the article, this definite necessitating the use of **yèhuātl**; see 4.2.3), but female. 10. Who wouldn't be scared if he saw the demon? 11. You're (s.) talking to us as if we were dogs. 12. Whatever you (s.) (will) give him, it won't please him.

(b) 1. In tlā xinēchpalēhui, àzo huel mochīhuaz. 2. Ca yèhuātl tlàtoāni yezquia, intlācamo ōmiquini. 3. Āquin màca mitzàhuaz, in tlā ticchīhuaz in? 4. Mācihui in cencâ chicāhuac, ca zan pēhualōc. 5. Ayamo teōtlac, auh ye cuēl ticochiznequi! 6. Mā nel zan centetl tlaxcalli xicmaca inon icnōtlācatl. 7. In tlā nel nēchmictīzquê, ca àtle niquìtōz. 8. Cāmpa nel nicnocuīlīz in notlacual? 9. Iuhquin mâ petlapan motlāliâ in īpan āmatl. 10. Ayāc mâ nēchpalēhuīznequi, yēcê (*or* tēl) àtle màca nocēl huel nicchīhuaz. 11. Quin ōtimēuh, auh ye cuēl titlatequipanoa! 12. In zāzo quēzquintin, àmo huel tēchpēhuazquê.

Lesson Thirty-Five

(a) 1. First I'll eat, then I'll see you (s.). 2. The other day, our ruler passed by here. 3. How could I abandon you (pl.) and go? Wouldn't you be very unhappy in the end? 4. This isn't the first time that you've (s.) done (something) bad. You've been like that for a long time. 5. I've been awake for a good while. 6. It's no longer time for you to meet him. He's already gone. 7. Poor you (s.)! It's true then that you have no goods, no possessions. 8. Where's he from? – I wonder. He's apparently not one of us. 9. We'll sow in seven days. 10. I couldn't see ("was not yet seeing") you (s.)

until everyone laughed. 11. Every how many days do you (s.) get drunk?
12. They chat (while) strolling.

(b) 1. Yeōhuīptla teōtlac omiquilî in notàtzin. 2. In ayamo pēhua in
cemānāhuatl, yēppa ommoyetzticâ in Dios. 3. Ayamo imman in
onhuīlōhuaz. 4. Yālhua cemilhuitl ōquiyauh, nozan āxcān tlālpan mani
in ātl. 5. Tlein quìtoa? – Ach tlein, mach àmo nāhuatlàtoa. 6. In ocēlōtl
quil īntlàtòcāuh in yōlquê. 7. Quin caxtōlli nimitztlaxtlāhuīz. 8. In ye
nēpa, in ye nechca, oc tlatlācamatiyâ in mācēhualtin. 9. Oc iuh ēyilhuitl
momiquilīz (or miquiz) notàtzin mīlpan ōnicnohuīquilî. 10. In ìcuāc
yancuīcān àcicô in caxtiltēcâ, huel quimmāuhtiāya in mēxìcâ in tle-
quiquiztli. 11. Cēcemmētztica nonyauh in cuauhtlâ. 12. In ō iuh quittac
in ocēlōtl, niman ic oncholô.

NAHUATL-TO-ENGLISH VOCABULARY

In the following list, the glottal stop, indicated by a diacritical mark over a vowel, is treated as a consonant that *follows* the vowel, and this glottal stop is listed as the *last* letter of the alphabet. Long vowels are listed after all permutations of the short vowel. In other words, a short vowel is alphabetized in the order dictated by all of the regular letters that following, including the glottal stop at the end of the list, and only after the combinations with the short vowel have been listed does the long vowel appear. This treatment of long and short vowels and the effect of listing the glottal stop as a consonant should always be borne carefully in mind when a word is being looked up, as the logical result of this procedure is the (at first sight) surprising order: **aqui, ayāc, àci** (i.e., **a'ci**), **àtle, āc, ātl**. Otherwise, the letters are alphabetized in their normal order (i.e., there is no special treatment of the digraphs such as **ch, cu, tl, uc** or **uh**).

A

acâ *(pl. /-me'/) someone (pron.)*
ach *I wonder, really (part.)*
achi *rather, very (adv.)*
achīc *a little while (adv.)*
achto(pa) *first (of all) (part.)*
ahuax *beans (n.)*
alo *(pl. /-me'/) macaw (n.)*
amèhuān(tin) *you (pl.) (pron.)*
anca *well, then (part.)*
aoc(mō) *no longer (part.)*
aqui *enter (intrans. v.)*
aquì- *few, little (takes dim. endings)*
    (quant.)
at *maybe, perhaps (part.)*
auh *and, but (part.)*
aya(mo) *not yet (part.)*
ayāc *no one (pron.)*
ayòtli *gourd, pumpkin (n.)*
azcatl *(pl. /-me'/) ant (n.)*
àāhuilli *pleasure, fun, joy (n.)*
àci *arrive (intrans. v.)*
àcān *nowhere (adv.)*
àco *into the air, upward (adv.)*
àcocui *raise up (trans. v.)*
àhua *argue with, dispute with, scold*
    (trans. v.)
àhuīc *over here, over there (loc.)*
àmo *not, no (part.)*
ànozo *or (part.)*
àtle *nothing (pron.)*
àzo *perhaps (part.)*
āc, āquin *(pl. āquìquê) who? (interrog.)*
ācalli *boat, ship (n.)*
ācatl *reed (n.)*
āhuēhuētl *ahuehuete (kind of cypress)*
    (n.)
āhuiyac *sweet, pleasant (adj.)*
āhuilli, *see* àāhuilli
āhuiltia *amuse, please (trans. v.);* m(o)-:
    be pleased, have fun
āltepētl *town (n.)*
āmatl *paper, amate (n.)*
āmiqui *be thirsty (intrans. v.)*
āmoxtli *book (n.)*
āna *take, seize, take prisoner (trans. v.)*
āpilōlli *water jar (n.)*
ātl *water (n.)*
ātōyātl *river (n.)*

ātōlli *atole (kind of drink) (n.)*
āuh *hey (part.)*
āxcāitl *property (n.)*
āxcān *today, now (adv.)*
āyahuitl *fog, mist (n.)*
āyi *do (semi-trans. v.)*
āyōtl *(pl. /-me'/) turtle (n.)*

C

ca (statement marker) *(part.)*
cacalaca *make a vigorous sound*
    (intrans. v.)
cacalatza *cause to make a vigorous sound*
    (quasi-caus. v.)
cactli *shoes (n.)*
cahuayo *(pl. /-mê/)/cahuayô (pl. /-tin/)*
    horse (n.)
calaqui *enter (intrans. v.)*
calaquia *make to enter, insert*
    (trans. v.)
calāni *make a sound (intrans. v.)*
calānia *cause to make a sound*
    (semi-caus. v.)
calli *house (n.)*
camatl *mouth (n.)*
camisa *shirt (n.)*
canauhtli *(pl. /-tin/) duck (n.)*
canâ *somewhere (adv.)*
canāhua *become thin, thin (trans./*
    intrans. v.)
caqui *hear, understand (trans. v.)*
caquizti *make oneself heard (intrans. v.)*
catzāhua *dirty, become dirty*
    (trans./intrans. v.)
caxitl *bowl (n.)*
Caxtillān *Spain (loc.)*
caxtiltēcatl *(pl. /-tin/) Spaniard (n.)*
caxtōlli *fifteen (quant.)*
cayāhua, mo- tēca *make fun of, dupe, cheat*
    (refl. v.)
câ *be (located) (intrans. v.)*
cac- *isolated stem appearing with*
    compounding verbs and signifying 'be
    vacant, abandoned' (see 27.6.1)
cāhua *stop, leave (*mo-: *stay, remain)*
    (trans. v.)
cāhuitl *time (n.)*
cān(in) *where? (interrog.)*

cātlèhuātl, cātlia, cātlî *(pl. cātlìquê) which one? (interrog. pron.)*

cecēc *cold, frigid (adj.)*

cecmiqui *be cold (intrans. v.)*

cecni *(at, in) one place (loc.)*

celia *receive (trans. v.)*

celic *fresh, green (adj.)*

celiya *become green (intrans. v.)*

cemānahuātl *world, universe (n.)*

cemellê *peacefully, happily (adv.)*

cempōhualli *twenty (quant.)*

cencâ *much, very (adv.)*

cepayahuitl *snow (n.)*

cequi *one (of) (quant.)*

cetl *ice (n.)*

ceya *consent, be in agreement (intrans. v.)*

cē *one (quant.)*

cēhui *be extinguished, cool off, be calmed (intrans. v.)*

-cēl *alone (quant.)*

cēpan *(all) together (adv.)*

chalāni *crash together (intrans. v.)*

chalānia *dash together (semi-caus. v.)*

chapōlin *(pl. /-tin/) grasshopper (n.)*

chālchihuitl *jade (n.)*

Chālco *(at) Chalco (loc.)*

chāntli *residence (n.)*

chicāhua *strengthen (trans./intrans. v.)*

chichi *(pl. /-mê/) dog (n.)*

chichic *bitter (adj.)*

chichinatza *torment, distress (trans. v.)*

chichipica *drip, trickle (intrans. v.)*

chichipitza *make to drip (quasi-caus. v.)*

chichīlihui *grow red (intrans. v.)*

chichīltic *red (adj.)*

chichīna *suck (trans. v.)*

chico *out of kilter, cockeyed (loc.)*

chipāhua *clean, become clean (trans./intrans. v.)*

chipīni *drip, trickle (intrans. v.)*

chipīnia *make to drip, trickle (semi-caus. v.)*

chiya *await, watch (trans. v.); tlachiya look (intrans. v.)*

chīhua *make, build (trans. v.)*

chīlli *chili pepper (n.)*

chīmalli *shield (n.)*

choloa *flee (intrans. v.)*

chopīnia *peck (trans. v.)*

chōca *cry, weep (intrans. v.)*

cihuātl *(pl. /-'/) woman (n.)*

cintli *ear of corn (n.)*

citlālin *(pl. /R-tin/) star (n.)*

ciyahui *get tired (intrans. v.)*

cìtli *(pl. /-tin/) (1) grandmother (2) hare*

cochi *sleep (intrans. v.)*

coco *(pl. /-me'/) servant (n.)*

cocoa *make ill (mo-; be sick) (trans. v.)*

cocoxqui *ill, sick (adj.)*

cocōlia *hate (trans. v.)*

cocōc *strong, spicy, harsh, painful (adj.)*

comālli *comal (heated plate for cooking) (n.)*

conētl *(pl. /R-'/) child (n.)*

cotōna *cut, slice (trans. v.)*

cotōni *break (in two) (intrans. v.)*

coyōni *be pierced, have holes (intrans. v.)*

coyōnia *pierce, make (to be) holed (semi-caus. v.)*

coyōtl *(pl. /R-'/) coyote (n.)*

coztic *yellow (adj.)*

cōhua *buy (trans. v.)*

cōhuātl *(pl. /R-'/) snake (n.)*

cōlli *(pl. /-tin/) grandfather (n.)*

cōmitl *jar (n.)*

cōzcatl *necklace, jewel (n.)*

cruz *cross (n.)*

cua *eat (trans. v.)*

cuahuitl *tree, wood, stick (n.)*

cualaxtli *rage, anger (n.)*

cualāni *boil, become angry (intrans. v.)*

cualāntli *rage, anger (n.)*

cualcān *good place (loc.)*

cualli *(pl. -tin) good, beautiful (n.)*

cuauhcalli *prison (n.)*

Cuauhnāhuac *(at) Cuernavaca (loc.)*

cuāchtli *piece of cloth (n.)*

cuācuahuê *(pl. cuācuahuèquê) cow, ox (n.)*

cuāitl *head (n.)*

cuānaca *(pl. /-me'/) chicken, cock, hen (n.)*

cuāuhtli *(pl. /-tin, R-tin/) eagle (n.)*

cuecuechca *tremble (intrans. v.)*

cuepa *turn, return (trans. v.); (mo-: return)*

cuepōni *blossom (intrans. v.)*

cuetzpal *glutton (n.)*
cuetzpalin *lizard (n.)*
cueyātl *(pl. /R-'/) frog (n.)*
cuezcomatl *cuezcomate (large jar for storing corn) (n.)*
cuēitl *skirt (n.)*
cuēl *already (alas) (part.)*
cui *take (trans. v.)*
cuiltōnoa *enrich, gladden (trans. v.);* mo-: *be rich, happy*
cuitlahuia (mo-) *care for (bitrans. v.)*
cuitlatl *excretion, excrement (n.)*
cuitlaxcōlli *intestines (n.)*
cuix *(interrog. marker) (part.)*
cuīca *sing (intrans. v.)*
cuīcatl *song (n.)*
cuītia, mo-: *admit, confess (caus. of* cui*)*

D

diablo *(pl. /-me'/) devil, demon (n.)*

E

-el *diligent, with X's consent (quant.)*
elēhuia *desire (trans. v.)*
elimiqui *till the soil, work (semi-trans. v.)*
elōtl *ear of corn (n.)*
epazōtl *wormseed, epazote (kind of aromatic herb) (n.)*
etic *(pl. etiquê) heavy (adj.)*
etl *beans (n.)*
eztli *blood (n.)*
èco *arrive (intrans. v.)*
èeca *be windy (impers. v.)*
èecatl *wind (n.)*
ēhua 1) *raise, lift (trans. v.);* 2) *depart, leave (intrans. v.)*
ēyi *three (quant.)*

H

huahualoa/huahualtza *bark (trans. v.)*
huapāhua *stiffen, harden (trans., intrans. v.)*
-huān *with (loc. n.)*
huāqui *dry up (intrans. v.)*
huātza *dry up (trans. v.)*
huel *very (also = 'be able to') (adv.)*
huetzca *laugh (intrans. v.)*
huetzi *fall (intrans. v.)*

huèca *far (loc.)*
huècapan *up (loc.)*
huècauh *for a long time (loc.)*
huècāhua *linger, be late; delay, postpone (trans., intrans. v.)*
huèxōlotl *(pl. /R-'/) tom turkey (n.)*
huēhuê *(pl. huēhuetquê) old man (n.)*
huēyi *(pl. /-n/, /-ntin/) large (quant.)*
huēyiya *grow big (intrans. v.)*
hui *oh (part.)*
huilāna *drag, take away (trans. v.)*
huitzilin *hummingbird (n.)*
-huīc *toward, in direction of (loc. n.)*
huīca *bring, take (trans. v.)*
huīpilli *blouse (n.)*
huīptla *the day after tomorrow or later (loc.)*
huītequi *hit, lash, whip (trans. v.)*
huītz *come (intrans. v.)*

I

i *drink (trans. v.)*
ic *so, by; formative of ordinals (part.)*
icâ *ever, once (adv.)*
ichcatl *(pl. /-mê/) sheep (n.)*
ichpōchtli *(pl. ichpōpōchtin) young woman (n.)*
ichtequi *steal (semi-trans. v.)*
ichtecqui *thief (adj.)*
ichtli *thread (n.)*
icnīuhtli *(always in the possessed form -(i)cnīuh, pl. -(i)cnīhuān) friend (n.)*
icnōpilli *orphan (pl. /tin/), merit, favor (n.)*
icnōtl *(pl. /-me'/) poor person, orphan (n.)*
icox *fig (n.)*
icpalli *seat (n.)*
icxitl *foot (n.)*
ihuīhuî *barely, with difficulty (adv.)*
ilamâ *(pl. ilamatquê) old woman (n.)*
ilaqui *sink down (intrans. v.)*
ilcāhua *forget (trans. v.)*
ilhuicatl *sky, heaven (n.)*
ilhuia *tell (bitrans. v.)*
ilhuilli *favor, payment (n.)*
ilhuitl *day (n.)*
ilhuiz *more (adv.)*
ilnāmiqui *remember (trans. v.)*

ilōti *return, decrease (intrans. v.)*
ilpia *bind, tie (trans. v.)*
imman *it's time (adv.)*
in 1) *this (demons.);* 2 (subordinating
  marker) *(part.)*
ināya *hide (trans. v.)*
inin *(pl.* inìquê īn) *this (demons.)*
inon *(pl.* inìquê ōn) *this (demons.)*
-ipilli *twenty (flat things) (quant.)*
ithualli *courtyard (n.)*
ithui (tla-thui *day breaks) (intrans. v.)*
itlâ *(pl.* -me') *something (pron.)*
itqui *carry, bring (trans. v.)*
itta *see (trans. v.)*
itz- *isolated stem appearing with
  compounding verbs and signifying
  'come' (see 27.6 sec. 2)*
itzcuintli *(pl.* /-tin/) *dog (n.)*
itztli *obsidian, razor (n.)*
itztic *cold (adj.)*
iuh(qui) *such, similar (adj.)*
ixachi *very many/big (quant.)*
ixca *fry (trans. v.)*
ixhui *have one's fill (intr. v.)*
-(i)xti(n) *all the (number) (quant.)*
ixtlāhua *pay, fulfill (trans. v.)*
iyo *alas! (part.)*
iyoyahue *alas! (part.)*
iyô *(pl.* /-ke'/) *the only one (pron.)*
iz *here (adv.)*
izcalia *encourage, educate (trans. v.);* mo-:
  be restored; be sensible, well-bred
izcaltia *rear, nourish (caus. v.);* mo-:
  grow up
iztatl *salt (n.)*
iztāc *white (adj.)*
iztitl *fingernail, claw (n.)*
iztlacati *lie, tell falsehood
  (intrans. v.)*
iztlactli *spit (n.)*
ìcac *be upright, stand (intrans. v.)*
ìcali *attack (trans. v.)*
ìchiqui *scrap (trans. v.)*
ìcihui *hurry, hasten (intrans. v.)*
ìciuhcā *quickly (adv.)*
ìcuilihui *stand written (intrans. v.)*
ìcuiloa *paint, draw, write (trans. v.)*
ìhuitl *feather (n.)*

ìitz- *isolated stem appearing with
  compounding verbs and signifying 'be
  awake' (see 27.6 sec. 2)*
ìixhui, *see* ixhui
ìiyô *strong (adj.)*
ìiyōtl *breath (n.)*
ìiyōhuia *suffer, endure, tolerate (trans. v.)*
ìmati *put into practice carefully (trans. v.);*
  m(o)-: *be clever, shrewd*
ìtahui *be mentioned (intrans. v.)*
ìtitl *stomach (n.)*
ìtlacoa *harm, damage, sin against
  (trans. v.)*
ìtlani *ask for (trans. v.)*
ìtoa *say, speak of, mention (trans. v.)*
ìtōtia, m-: *dance (refl. v.)*
ìtzoma *sew (trans. v.)*
ìza *wake up (intrans. v.)*
ìzotla, m-: *vomit (refl. v.)*
īc *when? (interrog.)*
-īcampa *behind (loc. n.)*
īcemel *peacefully, happily (adv.)*
īhuān *and (part.)*
īhuiyān *mildly, peacefully* (adv.)
-īxcòyān -*self/-selves (loc.)*
īxcuepa *deceive (trans. v.);* mo-: *be wrong*
īxquich *all, that many (quant.)*
īxtelolōtl *eye, eyeball (n.)*
īxtlapal *askew (loc.)*
īxtli *eye, face (n.)*
īzqui *all, that much (quant.)*

L

llave(') *key (n.)*

M

ma *catch, capture (trans. v.)*
maca *give (bitrans. v.)*
mach *as it were, apparently (part.)*
malacachoa *roll up (trans. v.)*
Malintzin *Mary (proper name)*
malli *(pl.* /R-tin/) *prisoner (n.)*
mana *spread (out), offer, present
  (semi-caus. v.)*
mani *extend, be spread (intrans. v.)*
mati *perceive, know, understand (trans. v.)*
-matl *'vara' (Sp. measurement), yard
  (quant.)*

mayāna *be hungry (intrans. v.)*

mazātl *(pl. /R-'/) deer (n.)*

mâ *(being) such that … (part.)*

màcēhua *deserve, obtain (trans. v.)*; mo-: *do penance*

màcēhualli *merit, dignity (n.)*

màpilli *finger (n.)*

màtlāctli *ten (quant.)*

mā (optative marker) *(part.)*

mācēhualli *(pl. /-tin/) commoner, subject (n.)*

mācpalli *palm (n.)*

mācuīlli *five (quant.)*

māhui *be scared (intrans. v.)*

māhuiztli *fear, awe (n.)*

māitl *hand (n.)*

māma *carry (on the back) (trans. v.)*

māuhtia *scare, frighten (trans. v.)*

māxtlatl *piece of cloth (n.)*

mecatl *string (n.)*

melāhua *straighten (trans./intrans. v.)*

melāhuac *straight, just, righteous (adj.)*

metl *maguey (n.)*

metlapilli *metlapil (n.)*

metlatl *metate, grinding stone (n.)*

mētztli *moon, month (n.)*

mēxìcatl *Mexica (pl. /-'/) (n.)*

Mēxìco Tinochtitlan, *Mexico City (loc.)*

michin *(pl. /-mê/, /R-tin/) fish (n.)*

mictlān *(in) hell (lit. land of the dead) (loc.)*

miqui *die (intrans. v.)*

miquiztli *death (n.)*

miyac *much, many (quant.)*

miztli *(pl. /-tin/, /R-tin/) puma (n.)*

mīlli *(cultivated) field (n.)*

mītl *arrow (n.)*

mīxītl *mixitl (narcotic plant) (n.)*

moch(i) *all, every (quant.)*

molōni *flow, bubble (intrans. v.)*

molōnia *make to flow, bubble (semi-caus. v.)*

momoloca *bubble, gurgle (intrans. v.)*

momolotza *flow, bubble (quasi-caus. v.)*

Motēuczōma Moctezuma, Montezuma (proper name)

mōlli *mole, sauce (n.)*

mōmōtzlaê *everyday (adv.)*

mōtla *stone (trans. v.)*

mōztla *tomorrow (adv.)*

N

nacacic *on the side (loc.)*

nacatl *meat (n.)*

nacaztli *ear (n.)*

namaca *sell (trans. v.)*

nanacatl *mushroom (n.)*

nanaloa/nanaltza *snarl (trans. v.)*

-nāhuac *with, beside (loc. n.)*

nāhuatia *order, command (trans. v.)*

nāhuatīlli *power (n.)*

nāhuatl *clear (sounding thing) (n.)*

nāhui *four (quant.)*

nāmictli *(pl. /-tin/) spouse (n.)*

nāmiqui *come upon, find (trans. v.)*

nānquilia *answer (trans. v.)*

nāntia *act as mother for (trans. v.)*

nāntli *(pl. /-tin/) mother (n.)*

nechca *over there (adv.)*

necoc(cāmpa) *on both sides (loc.)*

nehuān *together (of two) (adv.)*

nel *truly (part.)*

nelli *true, truth (n.)*

neltoca *believe (trans. v.)*

nemi *live (intrans. v.)*

nenepilli *tongue (part of body) (n.)*

nepan *together, mutually (adv.)*

nepantlâ *in the middle (loc.)*

nepantlâ tōnatiuh *at noon (loc.)*

nepapan *various, different (loc.)*

nequi *want (trans. v.)*

netech *make war on (loc.)*

nextamalli *nixtamal, corn meal (n.)*

nè(huātl) *I (pron.)*

-nèhuiyan *-self/-selves (loc.)*

nēci *appear, be visible (intrans. v.)*

nēn *in vain (part.)*

nēpa *over there (of something not visible) (adv.)*

nicān *here (adv.)*

niman *then (part.)*

nipa *away, elsewhere, somewhere (adv.)*

nohuiyān *everywhere (loc.)*

nozan *still (of continuing process) (n.)*

nozo *or (part.)*

-nòmâ *-self/-selves (loc.)*

nòpalli *nopal, prickly pear cactus (n.)*

nō *also (part.)*
nōchtli *prickly pear (n.)*
nōncuâ *separately (adv.)*
nōtza *call (trans. v.)*

O

oc *still (part.)*
ocēlōtl *(pl. /-me'/ /R-'/) jaguar (n.)*
octli *pulque*
ohuî *(pl.* ohuìquê) *difficult, painful (adj.)*
olini *move (intrans. v.)*
olinia *make move (trans. v.)*
olōltic *round (adj.)*
omitl *bone (n.)*
on *that (demons.)*
oncān *there (adv.)*
onoc *be lying (intrans. v.)*
oquichtli *(pl. /-tin/) man, husband (n.)*
otomitl *(pl. /-'/) Otomi (n.)*
otztli *(pl. /-tin/) pregnant woman (n.)*
oya *shell (trans. v.)*
oztōtl *cave (n.)*
òtli *path (n.)*
ōlli *rubber (ball) (n.)*
ōlōtl *corncob (n.)*
-ōlōtl *cob (quant.)*
ōme *two (quant.)*
ōmpa *over there (adv.)*

P

pachihui *have one's fill, be satisfied (intrans. v.)*
pachoa *press, bend, direct (trans. v.)*
padre *(pl. /-me'/, /-sme'/) priest, monk (n.)*
-pal *thanks to (loc. n.)*
palāni *rot (intrans. v.)*
palēhuia *help (trans. v.)*
-pampa *for, because of (loc. n.)*
panahuia *surpass, exceed (trans. v.)*
pani *upward (adv.)*
-pani *it suits me, you etc. (quasi-verb taking possessive prefixes for "subject")*
pano *pass (intrans. v.)*
-pantli *row (quant.)*
papal *(pl. /-tin/) gossiper (n.)*
patitl *price (n.)*
patlach *crouching (adv.)*

patlāhua *broaden, become wide (trans./intrans. v.)*
patlāni *fly (intrans. v.)*
pàti *get better (intrans. v.)*
pàtli *medicine (n.)*
pāca *wash (trans. v.)*
pāccā *happily (adv.)*
pāqui *rejoice, be happy (intrans. v.)*
pāti *melt (intrans. v.)*
pātla *melt (trans. v.)*
pepetlaca *shine (intrans. v.)*
pepetlatza *make to shine (quasi-caus. v.)*
petlacalli *petaca, box (n.)*
petlāni *shine (intrans. v.)*
petlānia *make to shine (caus. v.)*
petlatl *mat, petate (n.)*
petōni *be out of alignment (intrans. v.)*
pēhua *(pret.* pēuh) *start (intrans. v.); defeat (trans. v.)*
pilcac *hang, be hanging (intrans. v.)*
pilli *(pl. /R-tin/) child, nobleman (n.)*
piloa *hang (trans. v.)*
pitzāhua *narrow, become narrow (trans./intrans. v.)*
pitzōtl *(pl. /-mê/) pig (n.)*
piya *guard, save (trans. v.)*
pīnacatl *black beetle (n.)*
pītza *blow, play an instrument (trans. v.)*
polihui *become ruined, disappear (intrans. v.)*
poloa *lose, ruin, destroy (trans. v.)*
popochtli *incense, perfume (n.)*
popōca *smoke (intrans. v.)*
poyēc *salty (adj.)*
pozōni *boil (intrans. v.)*
pòpōhua *wash (trans. v.)*
-pò(tli) *like, co-, mate (n.)*
pòpolhuia *forgive, pardon (bitrans. v.)*
pōchōtl *silk cotton tree (n.)*
pōchtēcatl *(pl. /-'/) merchant (n.)*
pōctli *smoke (n.)*
pōhua *count, read (trans. v.); (mo-: be arrogant, presumptuous)*
pōhui *count, be registered (intrans. v.)*
puerta *door (n.)*

Q

quechtli *neck (n.)*
quetza *raise (trans. v.)*

Quetzalcōhuātl (divine name)
quetzalli *feather (n.)*
quēmâ *yes (part.)*
quēmi *clothe, put on (trans. v.)*
quēmman *when? (interrog.)*
quēmmanyān *sometimes (loc.)*
quēn *how? (interrog.)*
quēnamî *(pl. -quê) like what? (interrog. pron.)*
quēxquich *how much? (quant.)*
quēzqui *how many? (quant.)*
quil *they say (part.)*
quilitl *quelite (edible green) (n.)*
quimilli *pack, bundle (n.); -quimilli twenty (pieces of cloth) (quant.)*
quin *just (part.)*
quiquiztli *trumpet (n.)*
quiyahui *rain (impers. v.)*
quiyahuitl *rain (n.)*
quīza *emerge, pass by (intrans. v.)*

T
tamalli *tamale (n.)*
tàtli *(pl. /-tin/) father (n.)*
tāchcāuh *main, important (one) (n.)*
teci *grind, crush (semi-trans. v.)*
tecolōtl *(pl. /R-'/) owl (n.)*
tecomatl *jar (n.)*
-tecpantli *twenty (people or animals) (quant.)*
tecpin *(pl. /-tin/) flea (n.)*
tecuīni *blaze, crackle (intrans. v.)*
telchitl *(pl. /-mê/) one who gets his reward (n.)*
telchīhua *despise (trans. v.)*
temo *come down, descend (intrans. v.)*
tenāmitl *wall, fence, barrier, enclosure (n.)*
teòcihui *be hungry (intrans. v.)*
teōchīhua *(mo-) pray (refl. v.)*
teōcuitlatl *precious metal (gold, silver) (n.)*
teōtl *(pl. /R-'/) god (n.)*
teōtlac *the evening (loc.)*
tepētl *(pl. /R-'/) mountain (n.)*
tepitōn *(pl. /-totōn/) small (quant.)*
tepitzin *a little quantity of (quant.)*
teponāztli *sort of drum (n.)*
tepotztli *shoulder (n.)*

tepoztli *copper, iron (n.)*
tequi *cut (trans. v.)*
tequipachoa *bother, torment (trans. v.)*
tequipanoa *work (trans. v.)*
tequitl *job (n.)*
tetecuica *blaze, crackle (intrans. v.)*
tetl *rock, stone (n.)*
-teuh *like, in the manner of (loc. n.)*
teuhtli *dust (n.)*
teyīni *break (intrans. v.)*
teyīnia *break (semi-caus. v.)*
tezcatl *mirror (n.)*
tè(huātl) *you (s.) (pron.)*
tèhuān(tin) *we (pron.)*
tēāchcāuh *(pl. tēāchcāhuān) elder brother (n.)*
tēca *lay down, spread out (trans. v.)*
tēcciztli *seashell, trumpet (n.)*
tēcpantli *palace (n.)*
tēiccāuh *(pl. tēiccāhuān) younger brother (n.)*
tēl *nonetheless (adv.)*
tēlpōchtli *(pl. tēlpōpōchtin) young man (n.)*
tēmiqui *dream (semi-trans. v.)*
tēmoa *look for, search for (trans. v.)*
tēnēhua *cite, mention, pronounce (trans. v.)*
tēnìza *have breakfast (intrans. v.)*
tēnnāmiqui *kiss (trans. v.)*
tēntli *lip (n.)*
tēnyōtl *fame, glory (n.)*
tēpan *afterward, eventually (adv.)*
tētlazòtlaliztli *love (n.)*
tēuctli *(pl. /R-tin/) lord (n.)*
tiāchcāuh *(pl. tiāchcāhuān) captain, chief warrior (n.)*
tilmàtli *cape, sarape (n.)*
titèhuān *like us (adj.)*
tiyàcāuh *(pl. tiyàcāhuān) warrior, soldier (n.)*
tiyānquizoa *go shopping (intrans. v.)*
tiyānquiztli *market (n.)*
tīcitl *(pl. /R-'/) doctor, midwife, healer (n.)*
tītlantli *(pl. /-tin/) messenger (n.)*
tīzatl *chalk (n.)*
tlacà(zo) *Good lord! (part.)*
tlachpāna *sweep (intrans. v.)*

tlacomolli *ditch, hole (n.)*

Tlacōpan *Tacuba (loc.)*

tlacualli *food (n.)*

tlacuātl *opossum (n.)*

tlahuēlilli *(only in the derived*
ōnotlahuēliltic *etc.: poor me...) (n.)*

tlahuēlīlōc *villain, criminal (n.)*

tlahuēlli *anger, rage (n.)*

tlaīlli *drink (n.)*

tlalhuiz *without thought (adv.)*

tlaloa (mo-) *run (trans. v.)*

tlamach *slowly (adv.)*

tlamantli *thing (n.)*

tlami *end, finish (intrans. v.)*

tlamia *bring to an end (trans. v.)*

tlamic *twenty (cobs) (quant.)*

tlani *downward (adv.)*

tlantli *tooth (n.)*

tlaōcolia *be indulgent, compassionate*
toward (applic. v.)

tlaōcoltia *take pity on (caus. v.)*

tlaōcoya *be sad (intrans. v.)*

tlaōlli *corn (n.)*

tlapalli *color red (n.)*

tlapāna *break (trans. v.)*

tlapāni *break (intrans. v.)*

tlapechtli *bed (n.)*

tlapohua *open (semi-caus. v.)*

tlapohui *be open (intrans. v.)*

tlapōhualli *count(ing) (n.)*

tlathui, *see* ithui

tlatia *burn (trans. v.)*

tlatla *burn, be on fire (intrans. v.)*

tlatquitl *property (n.)*

Tlaxcallān *(at) Tlaxcala (loc.)*

tlaxcalli *tortilla (n.)*

tlayecoltia *serve (trans. v.)*

tlazòcāmati *thank (trans. v.)*

tlazòti *be valuable (intrans. v.)*

tlazòtla *love (trans. v.)*

-tlâ *place with an abundance of... (loc.)*

tlàcâ *during the day, later (loc.)*

tlàpaloa *greet (trans. v.)*

tlàtlacōlli *sin, fault (n.)*

tlàtlauhtia *request, beseech (trans. v.)*

tlàtoāni *(pl. tlàtòquê) ruler, king (n.)*

tlàtōlli *word, speech, language (n.)*

tlàtzini *burst, explode (intrans. v.)*

tlā *if (part.)*

tlācamati *obey (trans. v.)*

tlācatecolōtl *(pl. /R-'/) demon, devil (n.)*

tlācati *be born (intrans. v.)*

tlācatl *(pl. /-'/) person (n.)*

tlāchtli *game of pelote (n.)*

tlāctli *chest, upper body (n.)*

tlāhuāna *get drunk (intrans. v.)*

tlāhuānqui *drunk (agent n.)*

tlālia *set, place (trans. v.)*

tlālli *earth (n.)*

tlāni *gain, win (trans. v.)*

tlāpātl *tlapatl (narcotic plant) (n.)*

tlātia *hide (trans. v.)*

tlāza *throw, hurl (trans. v.)*

tlein, *see* tlê

tlecuīlli *hearth (n.)*

tletl *fire (n.)*

tlê, tlein *(pl. tleìquê) what? (interrog.)*

tlèco *rise up (intrans. v.)*

tlīlli *black ink (n.)*

toca *follow (trans. v.)*

tolīna *have the desire to eat, be hungry*
(intrans. v.)

tolīnia *torment (mo-: be wretched,*
unfortunate) (trans. v.)

toloa *swallow, bow the head (semi-trans.*
v.)

tomāhua *fatten, become fat*
(trans./intrans. v.)

tomātl *tomato (n.)*

tomin *money (n.)*

totōnqui *hot (adj.)*

tōca *bury, plant, sow (semi-trans. v.)*

tōcāitl *name (n.)*

tōchtli *(pl. /R-tin/) rabbit (n.)*

tōctli *(young) corn (n.)*

Tōllān *Tula (loc.)*

tōltēcatl *(pl. /-'/) craftsman (n.)*

tōna *prosper (impersonal: it is warm)*
(intrans. v.)

tōnacāyōtl *crop (n.)*

tōnatiuh *sun (n.)*

tōnēhua *torment, afflict (trans. v.); be*
tormented afflicted (intrans. v.)

tōptli *box, chest (n.)*

tōtolin *(pl. /-tin/ or /-mê/) turkey (n.)*

tōtoltetl *egg (n.)*

tōtōtl *(pl. /-mê/) bird (n.)*
tzacua *close (semi-caus. v.)*
tzacualli *pyramid (n.)*
tzacui *be closed (intrans. v.)*
tzapa(tl) *(pl. /-me'/) dwarf (n.)*
tzàtzi *shout (intrans. v.)*
-tzālan *among (loc. n.)*
tzinti *start, begin (intrans. v.)*
tzintli *buttocks, lower body (n.)*
tziqui- *very small (takes dim. endings)*
    (quant.)
tzītzquia *seize, lay hands on (trans. v.)*
-tzoco- *very small (quant.)*
tzontecomatl *skull (n.)*
tzontli *hair (n.); 400 (quant.)*
tzopelīc *sweet, sugary (adj.)*
tzopilōtl *(pl. /-mê/) vulture (n.)*

X

xālli *sand (n.)*
xāyacatl *face, countenance (n.)*
xelihui *split, divide (intrans. v.)*
xeloa *divide, split (trans. v.)*
xihuitl *year; plant (n.)*
xima *shave (trans. v.)*
xinōla *(pl. /-me'/) lady (n.)*
xipēhua *skin, flay (trans. v.)*
xiquipilli *sack of grain (n.); 8000 (quant.)*
xitīni *collapse (intrans. v.)*
xîhuitl *comet (n.)*
xīxa *eject (of urine or excrement)*
    (trans. v.)
xocotl *fruit (n.)*
xocōc *tart (adj.)*
xoctli *kettle, pot (n.)*
xolopìtli *(pl. /-tin/) madman, fool (n.)*
xopechtli *track, mark (n.)*
Xōchimīlco *(at) Xochimilco (loc.)*
xōchitl *flower (n.)*
xōchìcualli *fruit (n.)*
xōpantlâ *(in the) spring (loc.)*

Y

yacatl *nose (n.)*
yacāna *lead, guide (trans. v.)*
yahualoa *surround, encircle (trans. v.)*
yamānqui *sweet, pleasant (adj.)*

yancuīc *new (adj.)*
yauh *go (intrans. v.)*
yālhua *yesterday (adv.)*
yāōtl *(pl. /-'/) enemy (n.)*
yāōtla *make war on (trans. v.)*
yāōyōtl *war (n.)*
ye *already (part.)*
yecoa *try, test (trans. v.)*
yectel *the other day, some time ago (adv.)*
yeōhuīptla *day before yesterday (loc.)*
yê *on the other hand, yet (adv.)*
yèhuān(tin) *they (pron.)*
yè(huātl) *he, she, it (pron.)*
yèica *since, because, for (part.)*
yèyecoa, *see yecoa*
yēcè *but, however (part.)*
yēctli *good, just (n.)*
yēhua *previously (adv.)*
yēppa *a long time ago (adv.)*
yēquenê *finally, in the end (adv.)*
yohua *become night (intrans. or*
    impersonal v.)
yohuac *at night (loc.)*
yohualli *night (n.)*
yohualnepantlâ *at midnight (loc.)*
yohuatzinco *in the morning (loc.)*
yōcoya *shape, conceive (trans. v.)*
yōli *live (intrans. v.)*
yōlìtlacoa *offend (trans. v.)*
yōllālia *comfort, console (trans. v.)*
yōllòtli *heart (n.)*
yōlmiqui *faint (intrans. v.)*

Z

zacatl *straw (n.)*
zahua *(mo: fast) (trans. v.)*
zalihui *be glued (intrans. v.)*
zaloa *glue (trans. v.)*
zan *only (part.)*
zā *no more than, finally (part.)*
zaca *transport (trans. v.)*
(zā)tēpan *next (adv.)*
zāzanilli *riddle, story (n.)*
(in) zāzo *(+ inter.) ever (part.)*
zo *stab (trans. v.)*
zoquitl *mud (n.)*
zōma *irritate, annoy (trans. v.)*

ENGLISH-TO-NAHUATL VOCABULARY

BY C. S. MACKAY

This vocabulary is by no means meant to be exhaustive and is simply meant to assist in composing the English to Nahuatl exercises. In particular, students should bear in mind that specific constructions discussed in a given chapter and turn up in its exercises are not necessarily mentioned. The list is meant to cover lexical items (dictionary items) rather than purely grammatical terms (like the verbal prefixes).

abandon cāhua
able, to be huel
above tlacpac, tlapan
admit mo-cuītia
afraid, be māhui
alive, see live
all moch(i)
allow cāhua
already ye
also nō
and auh, īhuān
angry, become cualāni
answer nānquilia
appear nēci
arrive àci

behind tepotzco, -cuitlapan
below tlatzintlan
better, get pàti
blood eztli
body -nacayo
boil cualāni
bone omitl
born, be tlācati
brave tiyàcāuh
bring huāl-itqui
build chīhua
burn tlatla
but auh
buy cōhua
by oneself -cēl

cape tilmàtli
carry itqui
cast tlāza
cave oztōtl
Chalco Chālco
city āltepētl
close (v.) tzacua
cold cecēc
come huītz, huāllauh
come down temo
commoner mācēhualli
  (pl. /-tin/)
coyote coyōtl *(pl. /R-'/)*
craftsman tōltēcatl *(pl. /-'/)*
cry chōca
Cuernavaca Cuauhnāhuac
cure (v.) pàtia

day ilhuitl
day after tomorrow huīptla
day before yesterday yeōhuīptla
deer mazātl *(pl. /R-'/)*
defeat pēhua
depart m-ēhua
destroy poloa
die miqui
dirty, become dirty catzāhua
disappear polihui
divide xelihui
doctor tīcitl *(pl. /R-'/)*
draw ìcuiloa
drink i
drink (n.) tlaīlli
drunk, become tlāhuāna
due màcēhualli, icnōpilli
dunno mach

ear nacaztli
eat cua
enter calaqui
evening teōtlac
excretion cuitlatl
exit quīxōhuayān
expensive patiyô
eye īxtli

fall huetzi
famous tēnyô
fat, become tomāhua
father tàtli *(pl. /-tin/)*
fatten tomāhua
feather quetzalli
field mīlli
fire tletl
fish michin *(pl. /-mê/, /R-tin/)*
flee choloa
flesh nacatl
flower xōchitl
food tlacualli
forest cuauhtlâ
forget ilcāhua
forgive pòpolhuia
friend icnōtl
frighten māuhtia

give maca
glue (v.) zaloa

go yauh
God/god teōtl *(pl. /R-'/),*
   Dios
gold teōcuitlatl
good cualli *(pl. -tin)*
good place cualcān
greet tlàpaloa
ground tlālli
guard piya
guide yacāna

hand māitl
hear caqui
help palēhuia
here nicān
hide tlātia
home -chān
horse cahuayo *(pl. /-mê/)*
hurry ìcihui

if in tlā
injure cocoa
ink tlīlli
install tlālia
iron tepoztli

jaguar ōcēlōtl *(pl. /-mê/)*
jar cōmitl *(n.)*
jewel cōzcatl

kind tlamantli
king tlàtoāni *(pl. tlàtòquê)*
know mati

laugh huetzca
lie down onoc
listen caqui
live nemi
live yōli
long time, for a huècauh
look for tēmoa
lord tēuctli *(pl. /R-tin/)*
lost, be polihui
love (n.) tētlazòtlaliztli
love (v.) tlazòtla
lust after elēhua

macaw alo
mad, become mo-zōma

maguey metl
man (human being) tlācatl *(pl. /-'/)*
man (male, husband) oquichtli *(pl. /-tin/)*
make chīhua
many miyac
market tiyānquiztli
Mary Malintzin
mat petlatl
meat nacatl
merchant pōchtēcatl
Mexica mēxìcatl *(pl. /-'/)*
Mexico (City) Mēxìco
miserable -tlahuēliltic
mole mōlli
mountain tepētl *(pl. /R-'/)*
mouth camatl
move olini
much (adj.) miyac
much (adv.) cencâ
mud zoquitl

name tōcāitl
Nahuatl nahuatlàtōlli, mexìcatlàtōlli
narrow pitzāhuac
no àmo
no longer aoc(mo)
no one ayāc
noble(man) pilli
not yet aya(mo)
nothing àtle
now āxcān

old man huēhuê *(pl.: huēhuetquê)*
old woman ilamâ *(pl.: ilamatquê)*
only zan
or ànozo
order nāhuatia
Otomi otomitl *(pl. /-'/)*
ox cuācuahuê

paper āmatl
pardon pòpolhuia
pass pano
pass by quīza
path òtli
pay ixtlāhua
people: see person
person tlācatl *(pl. /-'/)*

Peter Pedro
pig pitzōtl *(pl. /-mê/)*
poor man icnōtl
prepare chìchīhua
pretend nènequi
pretty cualli
price patitl
prisoner malli *(pl. /R-tin/)*
property āxcāitl
pulque octli
pure chipāhua
pyramid tzacualli

question (v.) tēmōlia

rabbit tōchtli *(pl. /R-tin/)*
rain (v.) quiyahui
razor itztli
rebuke àhua
relative -huānyōlqui
remain mo-cāhua
remember ilnāmiqui
residence chāntli
return cuepa
return (intrans.) mo-cuepa
rock tetl
roll up malacachoa

save māquīxtia
say ìtoa
say to ilhuià
see itta
search for tēmoa
seat icpalli
see itta
seize āna
sell namaca
send ihua
shake olinia
shave xima
shout tzàtzi
shuck ōya
sick, be mo-cocoa
sick, make cocoa
sin tlàtlacōlli
sin against ìtlacoa
sing cuīca
sit mo-tlālia

skirt cuēitl
sky ilhuicatl
sleep cochi
small tepitōn *(pl. /-totōn/)*
snake cōhuātl *(pl. /R-'/)*
so ic
speak tlàtoa
speak of ìtoa
speak to nōtza
speech tlàtōlli
spicy cocōc
split xelihui
spread mani
star citlālin *(pl. /R-tin/)*
start pēhua, tzinti
stay mo-cāhua
steal ichtequi
stick cuahuitl
still oc
stone (v.) tetl
stone (v.) mōtla
strong cocōc
sun tōnatiuh
surpass panahuia

take āna, cui
take care of mo-cuitlahuia
talkative papal
tamale tamalli
tell ilhuia
then niman
there oncān
there, over ōmpa
there is/are oncâ
this in, inin *(pl.* inìquê in*)*
that on, inon *(pl.* inìquê on*)*
thread ichtli
throw tlāza
tie ilpia
Tlaxcala, Tlaxcallān
today āxcān
tomato tomātl
tomorrow mōztla
tomorrow, the day after huīptla
tooth tlantli
tortilla tlaxcalli
town āltepētl
tree cuahuitl

trumpet quiquiztli
true nelli
turkey tōtolin *(pl. /-tin/ or /-mê/)*
tom turkey huèxōlotl
   (pl. /R-'/)
turn (mo-)cuepa

very cencâ, huel
visible, be m(o-) itta

want nequi
war yāōyōtl *(n.)*
warm, it is tōna
watch tlachiya
water ātl
what? tlê *(pl.* tleìquê*)*
when? īc
when? quēmman
where? cān(in)
whip (v.) huītequi

white iztāc
who? āc, āquin *(pl.* āquìquê*)*
   (interrog.)
wide patlāhuac
wife, see *woman*
with -huān
woman cihuātl *(pl. /-'/)*
wood cuahuitl
word tlàtōlli
work tequipachoa
wrong ìtlacoa
write ìcuiloa

Xochimilco Xōchimīlco

yesterday yālhua
young man tēlpōchtli *(pl.* tēlpōpōchtin*)*
young woman ichpōchtli
   (pl. ichpōpōchtin*)*
yes quēmâ

INDEX

Made in the USA
Middletown, DE
16 October 2023

40871784R00281